Java 5.0

Program Design

James P. Cohoon
University of Virginia

Jack W. Davidson
University of Virginia

McGraw Hill Higher Education

Boston   Burr Ridge, IL   Dubuque, IA   Madison, WI   New York   San Francisco   St. Louis
Bangkok   Bogotá   Caracas   Kuala Lumpur   Lisbon   London   Madrid   Mexico City
Milan   Montreal   New Delhi   Santiago   Seoul   Singapore   Sydney   Taipei   Toronto

Higher Education

JAVA 5.0 PROGRAM DESIGN: AN INTRODUCTION TO PROGRAMMING AND OBJECT-ORIENTED DESIGN

Published by McGraw-Hill, a business unit of The McGraw-Hill Companies, Inc., 1221 Avenue of the Americas, New York, NY 10020.

Some ancillaries, including electronic and print components, may not be available to customers outside the United States.

This book is printed on acid-free paper.

1 2 3 4 5 6 7 8 9 0 VNH/VNH 0 9 8 7 6 5

ISBN 0-07-296113-9

Publisher: Alan R. Apt
Developmental Editor: Melinda D. Bilecki
Executive Marketing Manager: Michael Weitz
Senior Project Manager: Kay J. Brimeyer
Senior Production Supervisor: Laura Fuller
Media Technology Producer: Eric A. Weber
Designer: Rick D. Noel
Cover/Interior Designer: Rokusek Design
Lead Photo Research Coordinator: Carrie K. Burger
Typeface: 10/13 Times Roman
Printer: Von Hoffmann Corporation

Library of Congress Cataloging-in-Publication Data

Cohoon, James P.
    Java 5.0 program design: an introduction to programming and object-oriented design / James P. Cohoon, Jack W. Davidson. - 1st ed. update.
        p. cm.
    Includes index.
    ISBN 0-07-296113-9 (hard copy : alk. paper)
    1. Java (Computer program language). I. Davidson, Jack W. (Jack Winfred). II. Title.

QA76.73.J38C656   2006
005.13'3-dc22

                                    2005009673
                                    CIP

www.mhhe.com

To Joanne McGrath Cohoon and Audrey Irvine

Brief table of contents

Java 5.0 edition foreword

WHAT IS DIFFERENT AND WHY

It is *now* a great time to learn to design and develop programs in Java! The release of Java 5.0 introduced a number of components for easing development efforts. These additions are important especially for beginning programmers because they help make program development a simpler and clearer process.

The following list highlights some of the more important changes in Java and how our textbook makes use of them. Other changes are noted throughout the text.

- *Formatted input*: Class `Scanner` is now available. This straightforward class operates on a variety of input text and stream sources. The class automatically parses an input source into individual elements. The class also offers intuitively named methods for extracting the next input as a primitive type value and for reporting whether any more values are in the input source. No longer do beginning programmers have to go through the mystifying procedure of turning `System.in` into a `BufferedReader` and then manually extracting strings and parsing them into primitive type values. We are happy to report this version of our text is `BufferedReader` free. By using class `Scanner` for extracting input, our code is both more concise and simpler to understand. These are important properties for the beginning programming student.

- *Formatted output*: `System.out` and other print streams now have access to a method `printf()` that provides straightforward output formatting functionality. Although Java already provides a rich collection of formatting classes (e.g., `NumberFormat` and `DateFormat`), the relative ease of `printf()` formatting makes it possible for even beginning programmers to produce nicely formatted output. In addition, a new appendix provides a detailed description of format specifiers.

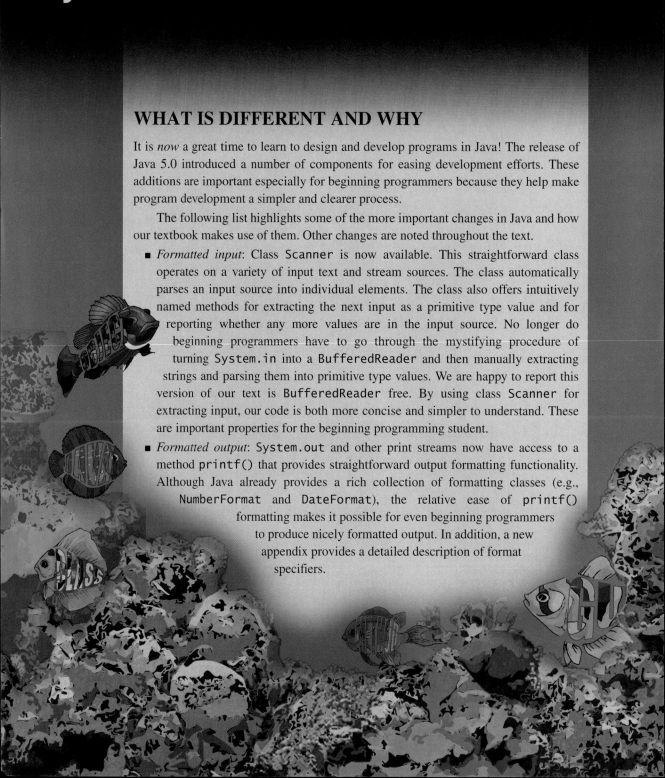

- *Automatic boxing and unboxing*: Java now provides automatic boxing and unboxing conversions between the primitive types and the corresponding class representations (e.g., **int** and **Integer**). Because these automatic conversions make code easier to follow, our examples make full use of them. The accompanying discussions describe the conversion process so that the reader can develop an accurate model of the translation and execution process.

- *Iterator **for** loop*: Java now provides an enhanced **for** loop for arrays and collections. The iterator **for** loop offers a simple syntax for the sequential access of the elements in a list. Because the iterator **for** loop ensures only valid elements are considered, experts believe it will become the preferred looping construct for list manipulation. However, programmers will also deal with existing code bases using the traditional **for** loop for list processing. Therefore, while including several demonstrations of the new loop form, our array discussion makes primary use of the traditional **for** loop. The subsequent discussion of collections uses the **for** loop form appropriate for the task at hand.

- *Generic types*: We introduce the new available generic types and their role in developing common functionality for different types of data. More importantly, the textbook introduces the *Java Collection Framework* with particular emphasis on the list data structure **ArrayList<T>** and the generic algorithms of class **Collections**. Our demonstration programs succinctly show their value to the beginning programmer.

- *Variable arity and varargs*: Print stream formatting method **printf()** makes use of the new Java capability of a method taking a variable number of parameters. Our array discussion has been updated with the development of a print method for displaying a variable number of values.

- *User interface composition*: Graphical user interface-based programming is now the dominant program form. This textbook includes two *interludes*—optional chapter-length sections—that introduce the **swing** library and event-based programming. With this new version of Java, the complexity of dealing with a graphical user interface becomes simpler. For example, the explicit acquisition of the content pane for a window is no longer necessary. The removal of such hurdles makes it easier for beginning programmers to develop their own graphical user interfaces.

Besides introducing Java 5.0, the text has undergone many other changes. Many explanations and figures have been improved and additional ones included. The appendices and index have been reorganized to make them more comprehensive and easier to use.

J. P. C

J. W. D

Preface

Java is now a most appropriate choice for introductory programming courses. The reasons are many. The use of the Internet continues its explosive growth. Web-ready application programs are becoming the dominant software model, and Java is *the* programming language for the Internet. Java also offers maturing software development tools, numerous packages for application programming of all types including multithreaded, advanced graphical user interfaces, and portability with its architecture-neutral design. The importance of security and robustness has taken on new meaning in recent years, and Java's support of these concerns is integral throughout its design. Being object-oriented, Java is a good pedagogical vehicle for modern software engineering and programming concepts.

Most of the important concepts and problems in computer science cannot be appreciated unless one has a good understanding of what a program is and how to write one. Unfortunately, learning to program is difficult. Like writing well, programming well takes years of practice. Teaching programming is very similar in many respects to teaching writing.

Students are taught writing by reading examples of good prose and by repeated writing exercises where they learn how to organize their ideas so they can be presented most effectively. As students develop their skills, they progress from writing and editing a paragraph or two, to creating larger pieces of prose, such as essays, short stories, and reports.

Our approach to teaching program design is similar to teaching writing. Throughout the text, we present and discuss many examples of both good and bad programming. Self-check and programming exercises give students the opportunity to practice designing, organizing, and writing code. In addition, we offer examples that facilitate learning the practical skill of modifying existing code. This introduction is done through the use of code that is specifically designed to be modified by the student.

We have found this approach to be effective because it compels students to be active participants—they must read and understand the provided code. To support this effort, the code used in this text is available electronically at our website.

GOALS OF THE TEXT

This book is targeted for a first programming course, and it has been designed to be appropriate for people from all disciplines. We assume no prior programming skills and use mathematics and science at a level appropriate to first-year college students.

The primary goals of the text are to

- Introduce students to the Java programming language;
- Present and encourage the use of the object-oriented paradigm;
- Demonstrate effective problem-solving techniques;
- Engage the student with real-world examples;
- Teach students software-engineering design concepts;
- Introduce students to Java's core and graphical libraries;
- Give students practice organizing and writing code;
- Teach students the practical skill of modifying existing code;
- Offer instructive examples of good and bad programming;
- Provide effective coverage of testing and debugging.

WHAT IS DIFFERENT AND WHY

The text provides in-depth coverage of all materials that an introductory course would need, introduces much of the remaining material generally covered in follow-on courses, and gives pointers to the rest. The breadth and the arrangement of chapters provides flexibility for the instructor in what and when topics are introduced. The chapter coverage and extensive appendices enable advanced learners to go further, and makes the book valuable as a reference source.

Some of the things that distinguish our book include the following:

- *Gentle introduction to objects*: The book implements what we call the "objects right" approach. Teaching the object-oriented paradigm in introductory courses for the last ten-plus years has shown us that Java can be successfully introduced to beginning programmers. We know that delaying user-defined classes to the end of a course inhibits the ability of students to integrate the central pillar of the object-oriented programming paradigm and forces superficial coverage of other important object-oriented programming principles. Therefore, our presentation introduces objects early— or as we prefer, right. Students begin using objects from standard packages right from the beginning. They quickly develop meaningful programs for interesting problems. Using this solid introduction, we then present the *basics* of class and object-oriented design. After exploring control structures, we present a deeper look at methods, classes, and object-oriented design.

- *Focus on problem solving*: One of the biggest obstacles faced by many beginning students is not knowing basic problem-solving techniques. The text addresses this issue by introducing basic problem-solving skills in Chapter 1 and then applying the new concepts in each chapter to problems selected for their appeal to a variety of audiences. Students are first walked through examples that illustrate effective problem solving, and then they are given a chance to tackle similar problems on their own.

- *Introduction to software-engineering design concepts*: Software-engineering design concepts are introduced via problem studies and software projects. Besides numerous small examples, each chapter considers one or more problems in detail. As appropriate, there are object-oriented analysis and design, and algorithm development to realize the design.

- *Coverage of testing and debugging*: An important skill for programmers is how to test and debug the programs they design and implement. Chapter 13 introduces important software engineering concepts and practices with regard to testing and debugging. The chapter discusses testing techniques such as unit testing, integration testing, and code inspections. The sections on debugging focus on teaching students how to use the scientific method to find errors. The chapter also discusses common errors of beginning programmers and how to recognize them. After control structures have been introduced, this chapter material can be taught whenever an instructor deems it appropriate.

- *Engaging and inclusive examples*: Students learn from interesting situations they might encounter in real life. Diverse case studies and programming projects are drawn from topics as varied as physical fitness, spam, medical diagnosis, statistical analysis, psychological typing, data visualization, graphs, entertainment, and animation. By offering this variety of examples, the text demonstrates how programmers can participate and contribute to our daily lives.

- *Exclusive use of standard Java classes*: The text uses only standard Java classes in introducing Java programming concepts. In particular, there are no author-written classes for acquiring input. Instead standard classes and techniques are presented in a way that makes sense to beginning programmers.

- *Lab manual*: A printed lab manual accompanies the text for schools that use laboratories in their introductory courses. The lab material offers a hands-on experience that reinforces Java programming concepts and skills.

- *Programming and style tips*: Besides explaining Java and object-oriented programming, the text also provides advice on how to be a better and more knowledgeable programmer and designer. There are important tips on such topics as avoiding common programming errors, writing readable code, and following software engineering practices.

- *Self-test, exercises, and software projects*: Every chapter provides a self-test exercise section with answers to enable students to evaluate their skills on important concepts. The text also provides several hundred exercises whose solutions are available to instructors through the publisher. Once the basics of Java are introduced in Chapter 2, that chapter and all successive chapters supply a programming project that exercises chapter concepts.

- *Reference appendices*: Appendices D and E provide nearly two hundred pages of description of the standard Java APIs. The coverage makes the text a handy reference manual well after the course ends.

CHAPTER OVERVIEW AND FEATURES

Introduction

Each chapter begins with a brief introduction designed to focus the student's attention and prepare them for the material to be covered. We emphasize both the immediate significance of the topic and its place in the broader programming context.

Objectives

A list of chapter objectives follows the introduction and provides a set of specific learning goals for the student. This list enables students to measure their progress as they move through chapter material and lets them evaluate their level of comprehension at the end. It also serves as a guide for instructors to use when preparing tests and quizzes.

Icons and aside boxes

Icons and shaded boxes indicate warnings, style tips, advanced material, and information pertaining to the Java language itself.

 Indicates a warning about programming. Often these are tips on how to avoid common programming errors.

 Indicates that the associated material is related to programming style.

 Indicates that the associated material is concerned with the Java programming language itself.

 Indicates programming tips or material that presents a more detailed discussion or a sidebar to the current topic.

Full-color design

An inviting, full-color design highlights related material, indicates section breaks, calls out special features, and makes key information easy to reference.

(a) Chapter text

(b) Case study

(c) End-of-chapter material

(d) Reference appendix

Code formatting

Specially formatted code listings make sections of code easy to find and reference. Each complete listing is numbered according to its place in the chapter, separated from related material by coloring and line numbering. Partial sections of code are clearly set off from surrounding text and are generously annotated with easy-to-spot author comments.

UML diagrams

The use of UML diagrams helps clarify relationships between classes while at the same time familiarizing students with this widely used system of notation.

Case studies

The chapters provide multiple case studies that are designed to teach effective problem-solving skills and to reinforce object-oriented programming and software engineering design concepts. The specific learning objective is highlighted at the beginning of each case study, and problem-solving steps are highlighted with special icons. The case studies are colored to distinguish them from other chapter material. Coverage of the case studies is optional; they apply chapter concepts rather than introducing new concepts.

End-of-chapter reviews

Each chapter ends with a thorough, point-by-point summary of the chapter's major ideas. The end-of-chapter materials are color highlighted for easy access.

Self-tests

Each chapter includes a self-test with answers supplied at the end of the chapter. These self-check sections are designed to help students evaluate whether they have mastered the chapter objectives and to reinforce the key ideas of the chapter.

Programming projects

Except for Chapter 1, which provides background material, each chapter has at least one interesting programming case study presented in a manner that makes it suitable for use as a class assignment. Programming case studies include determining your exercise training zone; harvesting e-mail addresses; medical diagnosis; automobile loan calculator; and an aquarium simulation.

Exercises

An exercise section at the end of each chapter offers a variety of problems requiring a range of effort levels.

CHAPTER SUMMARIES

- *Chapter 1: Background*—computer organization; software; software engineering principles; object-oriented software development; problem solving.
- *Chapter 2: Java basics*—program organization; method `main()`; commenting and whitespace; classes, keywords, identifiers, and naming conventions; methods; program execution; JDK; constants; variables; operations; primitive types; operators; precedence; interactive programs; `Scanner`; primitive variable assignment.
- *Chapter 3: Using objects*—`String`; reference variables; `null`; inserting, extracting, and concatenating strings; reference assignment; `String` methods.
- *Chapter 4: Being classy*—introduces user-defined classes; instance variables; constructors; instance methods; inspectors; mutators; facilitators; simple graphics.
- *Chapter 5: Decisions*—boolean algebra and truth tables; logical expressions; **boolean** type; Boolean equality and ordering operators; testing floating-point values for equality; operator precedence; short-circuit evaluation; **if** statement; **if-else** statement; string and character testing; sorting; **switch** statement.
- *Chapter 6: Iteration*—**while** statement; simple string and character processing; file processing; **for** statement; index variable scope; **do-while** statement.
- *Graphics Interlude: GUI–based programming*—graphical user interfaces; **swing**; **awt**; and event-based programming

- *Chapter 7: Programming with methods and classes*—parameter passing; invocation and flow of control; class variables; scope; local scope; name reuse; overloading; overriding; `equals()`; `toString()`; `clone()`; generics.

- *Chapter 8: Arrays and collections*—one-dimensional arrays; definitions; element access and manipulation; explicit initialization; constant arrays; members; array processing; methods; program parameters; vararg; sorting; searching; multidimensional arrays; matrices; generics; collections framework; `ArrayList<T>`; collections algorithms.

- *Chapter 9: Inheritance and polymorphism*—object-oriented design; reuse; base class; derived class; single inheritance; **super**; is-a, has-a, and uses-a relationships; controlling inheritance; default, **protected**, and **private** members; polymorphism; abstract base class; **interface** hierarchies.

- *Graphics Interlude: GUI-based programming*—case studies in the design and implementation of graphical user interfaces for personality typing and the smiley guessing game.

- *Chapter 10: Exceptions*—abnormal event; exceptions; throwing; trying; catching; exception handlers; **finally**; stream specialization.

- *Chapter 11: Recursive problem solving*—recursive functions, sorting, searching, visualization.

- *Chapter 12: Threads*—multiple independent flows of control; processes; threads; scheduling and repeating threads; `Timer`; `TimerTask`; `Thread`; `Date`; `Calendar`; `JOptionPane`; sleeping; animation; systems software.

- *Chapter 13: Testing and debugging*—software development; code reviews; black-box and white-box testing; inspections; test harness; statement coverage; unit, integration testing, and system testing; regression testing; boundary conditions; path coverage; debugging.

- *Appendix A: Tables and operators*—Unicode character set; reserved words; operators and precedence.

- *Appendix B: Number representation*—binary numbers; decimal numbers; two's compliment; conversions.

- *Appendix C: Formatted I/O*—`Scanner`; `printf()`.

- *Appendix D: Applets*—applet programming.

- *Appendix E: Standard Java packages*—`java.applet`; `java.awt`; `java.io`; `java.lang`; `java.math`; `java.net`; `javax.swing`; `java.text`; and `java.util`.

GRAPHICS INTERLUDES

From personal observations and from conversations and communications with colleagues, we recognize that not all introductory programming courses are able to introduce graphical user interfaces (GUIs). The time may not be available to introduce the `swing`

API and event-driven programming. Therefore, we have coalesced this material into two *Graphical Interludes*, and their coverage is optional. However, for instructors who want to stress this material, the GUI coverage can be introduced after the class concepts of Chapter 4 are presented.

We do distinguish between graphical user interfaces and creating graphical images. The Java standard APIs make it quite simple to display rectangles, lines, circles, ovals, triangles, and polygons. Their display is almost as easy as displaying text to a console window. Examples in other chapters make independent use of these Java features. These examples are also for the most part optional. However, it is our experience that students enjoy creating graphical imagery and that the concepts of object-oriented programming are easier to understand when examples have a visual nature.

USING THIS BOOK

The text continues to have more material than can be covered in a single course. The extra coverage was deliberate—it enables instructors to select their topics on programming and software development. The book has been designed for teaching flexibility. For example, if instructors desire to delay the introduction of classes, they first can cover most of the control structure materials (Sections 5.1–5.9 and Sections 6.1–6.5). Similarly, if an instructor desires to introduce arrays before classes, the fundamental array material (Sections 8.1–8.4 and Section 8.8) can precede the discussion of classes. Also except for the example in Section 9.2, the discussion of inheritance can precede the coverage of arrays.

The testing and debugging material of Chapter 13 can be covered anytime after classes and arrays have been introduced.

We use the following layout for our introductory course.

Week	Topic	Readings
1	Computing and object-oriented design	Chapter 1
2	Programming fundamentals	Chapter 2
3	Object manipulation	Chapter 3 (Sections 3.1–3.5)
4–5	Class basics	Chapter 4
5	Conditional statements	Chapter 5 (Section 5.1–5.7, 5.10)
6–7	Iteration statements	Chapter 6 (Sections 6.1–6.5)
8	Graphical user interfaces	Graphics Interludes: 1 and 2
9–10	Classes	Chapter 7
11-12	Arrays and lists	Chapter 8
13–14	Inheritance and polymorphism	Chapter 9

SUPPLEMENTARY MATERIALS

The publisher website at www.javaprogramdesign.com offers the source code and data files for all listings in the text. Other materials include a complete set of slides, which are available in PowerPoint and PDF formats, and introductions to the various

Java programming IDEs. Other educational supplements are available at our class web site http://www.cs.virginia.edu/javaprogramdesign.

THE AUTHORS

Jim Cohoon is a professor in the computer science department at the University of Virginia and is a former member of the technical staff at AT&T Bell Laboratories. He joined the faculty after receiving his Ph.D. from the University of Minnesota. He has been nominated twice by his department for the university's best-teaching award. In 1994, Professor Cohoon was awarded a Fulbright Fellowship to Germany, where he lectured on object-oriented programming and software engineering. Professor Cohoon's research interests include algorithms, computer-aided design, optimization strategies, and computer science education. He is the author of more than 75 papers and books in these fields. He is a member of the Association of Computing Machinery (ACM), the ACM Special Interest Group on Design Automation (SIGDA), the ACM Special Interest Group on Computer Science Education (SIGCSE), the Institute of Electrical and Electronics Engineers (IEEE), and the IEEE Circuits and Systems Society. He is a member of ACM Council, ACM-SIG Governing Board Executive Committee, former member of ACM Publications Board, and is past chair of SIGDA. He can be reached at cohoon@virginia.edu. His Web home page is http://www.cs.virginia.edu/cohoon.

Jack Davidson is also a professor in the computer science department at the University of Virginia. He joined the faculty after receiving his Ph.D. from the University of Arizona. Professor Davidson has received NCR's Faculty Innovation Award for innovation in teaching. Professor Davidson's research interests include compilers, computer architecture, systems software, and computer science education. He is the author of more than 100 papers in these fields. He is a member of the ACM, the ACM Special Interest Group on Programming Languages (SIGPLAN), the ACM Special Interest Group on Computer Architecture (SIGARCH), SIGCSE, the IEEE, and the IEEE Computer Society. He served as an associate editor of *Transactions on Programming Languages and Systems*, ACM's flagship journal on programming languages and systems, from 1994 to 2000. He was chair of the 1998 Programming Language Design and Implementation Conference (PLDI '98) and program co-chair of the 2000 SIGPLAN Workshop on Languages, Compilers, and Tools for Embedded Systems (LCTES 2000). He can be reached at jwd@virginia.edu. His Web home page is http://www.cs.virginia.edu/~jwd.

DELVING FURTHER

The following texts are primary references on the Java language.

- Ken Arnold, James Gosling, and David Holmes, *The Java Programming Language*, Third Edition, Addison-Wesley; June 2000.

- Bill Joy (Editor), Guy Steele, James Gosling, and Gilad Bracha, *The Java Language Specification,* Second Edition, Addison-Wesley; June 2000.

The following texts are good sources on the standard libraries and more-advanced object-oriented design, and program development.

- David M. Geary, *Graphic Java 1.2, Mastering the JFC: AWT,* Volume 1, Prentice Hall; September 1998.
- David M. Geary, *Graphic Java 2,* Volume 2, *Swing,* Prentice Hall; March 1999.
- Joshua Engel, *Programming for the Java Virtual Machine,* Addison-Wesley; June 1999.
- Cay S. Horstmann and Gary Cornell, *Core Java 2,* Volume I, *Fundamentals,* Prentice Hall; August 2002.
- Cay S. Horstmann and Gary Cornell, *Core Java 2:* Volume II, *Advanced Features,* Prentice Hall; December 2001.
- Matthew Robinson and Pavel A. Vorobiev, *Swing,* Manning Publications Company; February 2003.
- Stephen A. Stelting and Olav Maassen, *Applied Java Patterns,* Prentice Hall; December 2001.
- Sun Microsystems, *Java Look and Feel Design Guidelines: Advanced Topics,* Addison Wesley Professional; March 2001.
- Al Vermeulen (Editor), Scott W. Ambler, Greg Bumgardner, Eldon Metz, Alan Vermeulen, Trevor Misfeldt, Jim Shur, and Patrick Thompson, *The Elements of Java Style,* Cambridge University Press; January 2000.
- John Zukowski, *Java Collections,* APress; April 2001.

ACKNOWLEDGMENTS

We thank the University of Virginia for providing an environment that made this book possible. In particular, we thank Jack Stankovic and Mary Lou Soffa for their tireless efforts in leading the computer science department to national prominence. We also thank Aaron Bloomfield, Jenna Cohoon, Joanne Cohoon, Tom Horton, and John Knight for their comments. We thank Hannah Cohoon for her fish artwork and JJ Cohoon for his icon artwork.

We thank all of the people at McGraw-Hill for their efforts in making this edition a reality. In particular, we thank publisher Alan Apt for his support and encouragement; Kay Brimeyer, Sheila Frank, and Laura Fuller for their behind-the-scenes product-management expertise; Rick Noel for leading the art and cover-design team; Kevin Campbell for copyediting; Mary Cahall for her organizational ability; and Michael Weitz for creative marketing ideas. Special thanks go to Melinda Bilecki, our developmental editor—your efforts are always appreciated.

We thank the following testers, readers, and reviewers for their valuable comments and suggestions on the text and associated materials:

A. Arokiasamy, Multimedia University of Malaysia
David Aspinall, University of Edinburgh
Ivan Bajic, San Diego State University

Dwight Barnett, Virginia Tech

Vivekram Bellur, University of Virginia

David Bethelmy, Embry-Riddle Aeronautical University

Robert Biddle, Victoria University of Wellington

Elizabeth Boese, Colorado State University

Gene Boggess, Mississippi State University

Mike Buckley, University at Buffalo

Robert Burton, Brigham Young University

Judith Challinger, California State University, Chico

Errol Chopping, Charles Sturt University

Ilyas Cicekli, University of Central Florida

Charles Daly, Dublin City University

J. Greggory Dobbins, University of South Carolina

Neveen Elnahal, University of Virginia

Stephen Fickas, University of Oregon

Jeffrey Forbes, Duke University

Gerald Gordon, DePaul University

Heng Aik Koan, National University of Singapore

Michael Huhns, University of South Carolina

Norm Jacobson, University of California, Irvine

Cerian Jones, Montana Tech

Katherine Kane, University of Virginia

Cathy Key, University of Texas, San Antonio

Abigail Knight, Tandem School

Barry Lawson, University of Richmond

Susan Lindsay, University of Virginia

Evelyn Lulis, DePaul University

Lauren Malone, University of Virginia

Stephanie Kim Marvin, University of Virginia

Arne Maus, University of Oslo

Blayne Mayfield, Oklahoma State University

Stanley McCaslin, Longwood University

Jim McElroy, California State University, Chico

Daniel McCracken, City College of New York

Hugh McGuire, University of California, Santa Barbara

Christoph Mlinarchik, University of Virginia

Keitha Murray, Iona College

Faye Navabi, Arizona State University

Richard Pattis, Carnegie Mellon

Hal Perkins, University of Washington

Pete Petersen, Texas A&M University

Roger Priebe, University of Texas

Vera Proulx, Northeastern University

Graham Roberts, Flinders University

Roy Ruhling, University of Virginia

Celia Schahczenski, Montana Tech

Carolyn Schauble, Colorado State University

Carol Scheftic, California Polytechnic State University, San Luis Obispo

Jesse Barrack Schofield, University of Virginia

John Scott, Massachusetts Bay Community College

Eric Schwabe, DePaul University

Mike Scott, University of Texas

Barbara Ann Sherman, University of Buffalo

Barry Soroka, California Polytechnic State University, Pomona

Michael Tashbook, State University of New York, Stony Brook

David Vineyard, Kettering University

We thank our first editor and now friend, Betsy Jones. We wish her well in her new adventures.

We thank our spouses, Audrey and Joanne, and our children for their efforts and cooperation in making this book happen.

Finally, we thank the users of this book. We welcome your comments, suggestions, and ideas for improving this material. Please write in care of the publisher, McGraw-Hill, or send electronic mail to cohoon@virginia.edu or jwd@virginia.edu.

J. P. C
J. W. D

Detailed table of contents

1

BACKGROUND

The Internet and computing revolution will provide excellent career opportunities and interesting challenges for years to come. The opportunities run the gamut from designing hardware and software to entrepreneurial activities such as marketing emerging technologies. The challenges include developing software capable of running on many different types of computers and developing programs with hundreds of thousands of lines of code whose correctness is critical (e.g., radiation therapy and online auction systems). To cope with such challenges—both big and small—most computing practitioners now use object-oriented design techniques.

In this chapter, we introduce basic computing and network terminology and the concepts behind object-oriented design. We also introduce Java, an object-oriented programming language that has played a fundamental role in the growth of the Internet. For example, with Java, you can develop interactive Web-based applications offering dynamic graphics and secure communication. Java provides an extensive collection of portable programming resources that enable the rapid development of many different types of applications (e.g., multimedia, e-commerce, and telecommunication). We end the chapter with a discussion of problem solving to help with your development of software solutions.

OBJECTIVES

- Introduce hardware and software terminology.
- Introduce high-level programming languages.
- Introduce Java programming, compilation, and execution.
- Introduce the basics of object-oriented design.
- Present useful problem-solving strategies.

INTRODUCTION

Traditionally programming texts begin with a program that displays the message "Hello, world." They do so because the features of such a program are simple enough to be explained readily and functional enough to make the discussion worthwhile. Our first Java program is different.

```java
// Authors: J. P. Cohoon and J. W. Davidson
// Purpose: display a quotation in a console window

public class DisplayForecast {

    // main(): application entry point
    public static void main(String[] args) {
        System.out.print("I think there is a world market for");
        System.out.println(" maybe five computers.");
        System.out.println("  Thomas Watson, IBM, 1943.");
    }
}
```

Instead of displaying the functional "Hello, world." our program displays a now humorous forecast by a former chairperson of IBM. The output of the program is

```
I think there is a world market for maybe five computers.
   Thomas Watson, IBM, 1943.
```

The differences between this book and the typical Java text come about because our goal is more ambitious than just introducing you to the Java language. *We want to teach you how to program effectively, and we want do so in an interesting manner.* Learning tends to be easier when the proper motivation is given. Our examples have been designed for their relevance and appeal to a wide variety of people. In fact, a caution raised by one reviewer was that the examples sometimes bordered on being too interesting.

So let's begin.

Programming effectively requires a variety of skills and a general understanding of computing.

- Because a program is a set of instructions for how a computer is to behave, a basic understanding of computer organization is important. By having a mental model of the way a computer carries out its instructions, you'll be able to visualize better both how existing software operates and which resources are needed in the design of new software.

- Web-enabled software is fast becoming the dominant software paradigm. Therefore, a familiarity with networking basics is necessary.

- When developing software, standard engineering principles usually are followed. The primary way that these principles are applied is with the object-oriented programming methodology. This important methodology promotes thinking about software in a manner that models how we think about and interact with the physical world.

- Last, but perhaps most important, you must be able to problem solve. Program design, implementation, and testing is problem solving through the use of a computer system. You cannot make a computer do something if you do not know how to do it yourself.

Thus, to be an effective software designer you need to understand the basics of computer organization, software, networking, engineering practices, and problem solving. Therefore, before we analyze any programs, we use this chapter to introduce each of these concepts. In the following chapters, we will expand on them as we present, demonstrate, and explain program design and development using the Java programming language.

1.2   COMPUTER ORGANIZATION

Most computers have four major parts—a central processing unit, memory, input devices, and output devices. The *central processing unit* (CPU) is the brain of the computer. It is where computations are performed and decisions are made. *Memory* is where the data

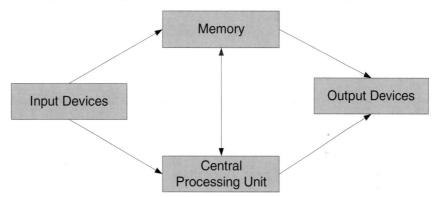

and software are kept while being processed by the CPU. It is essentially a workspace and scratch pad for the CPU. The CPU both *fetches* information from and temporarily *stores* information in the memory. More memory typically means that a computer can run larger software applications and do certain tasks faster. In general, *input devices* and *output devices* communicate information between the computer and its users or between itself and other computers. For example, keyboards and mice are input devices that enable a user to issue requests, while monitors and printers are output devices that enable information to be displayed.

Digital computers use the binary number system, rather than the decimal number system, to represent numbers. The binary number system has only two digits, 0 and 1. A binary digit is referred to as a *bit*. The binary number system is used because the fundamental building block of a computer is a switch, much like the familiar on/off switch for an electric light. The state of the switch indicates whether the value of the associated digit is 0 or 1. In early computers, these switches were built from mechanical relays. The resulting machines were huge. They occupied an entire room, and they required special

Figure 1.1 **Intel Pentium 4 microprocessor.**

power and cooling. In today's machines, the switches are made from ultrasmall transistors. Consequently, an entire computer can fit on a single silicon *chip*. Because the entire computer fits on a chip, these chips are referred to as *microprocessors*. Intel's Pentium 4®️ microprocessor contains about 55 million transistors in an area a little over 1 square inch (see Figure 1.1).

The principles behind the binary number system are the same as those used in the decimal number system. Both the decimal and binary number systems are *positional number systems*; that is, the position of a digit indicates its relative value. For example, in the decimal number 4,506, the 5 is in the 100's place and thus indicates a value of 500. Reading the number from the right, each digit represents an increasing power of 10. Thus, the value of the 4,506 can be expressed as

$$4 \times 10^3 + 5 \times 10^2 + 0 \times 10^1 + 6 \times 10^0$$

The binary number system works the same way except that we use increasing powers of 2. For example, the binary number 1101 represents the decimal 13.

A discussion of the binary number system appears in Appendix B

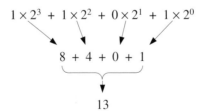

$$1 \times 2^3 + 1 \times 2^2 + 0 \times 2^1 + 1 \times 2^0$$
$$8 + 4 + 0 + 1$$
$$13$$

When talking about computer storage, its size is reported in *bytes*, where a byte is 8 bits.

We now discuss the other terminology scientists use to describe the speed and storage capacity of a computer. Using that terminology, we then continue our introduction to computer organization by analyzing an advertisement for a personal computer (see Figure 1.2 on page 6).

1.2.1 COMPUTING UNITS OF MEASURE

When specifying the speed of a computer, computer manufacturers sometimes report how long it takes the machine to perform a basic operation. In these cases, the units of measure are thousandths, millionths, billionths, and trillionths of a second (see Table 1.1 for the most frequently used measures). Computers currently do most arithmetic operations in picoseconds, but it is expected in the near future that computers will operate in femtoseconds.

Table 1.1 Commonly used powers of 2 and their abbreviations.

Fraction of a Second	Value	Abbreviation
10^{-3}	$\dfrac{1}{1,000}$	millisecond (ms)
10^{-6}	$\dfrac{1}{1,000,000}$	microsecond (μs)
10^{-9}	$\dfrac{1}{1,000,000,000}$	nanosecond (ns)
10^{-12}	$\dfrac{1}{1,000,000,000,000}$	picosecond (ps)
10^{-15}	$\dfrac{1}{1,000,000,000,000,000}$	femtosecond (fs)

Computer manufacturers will also report the speed of a computer using its *clock rate*. Clock rate is an indication of how many operations the computer can perform in a second and typically is expressed as *hertz* (cycles per second). For example, a computer with a clock rate of 2 billion hertz can perform an operation every 500 ps (i.e., $1 \div 2$ billion seconds). When expressing hertz values, scientists use the prefixes in Table 1.2. For our previous example, we would write 2 GHz (spoken as "2 gigahertz") as the computer speed. In general, the higher the clock rate, the faster the computer.

Table 1.2 Commonly used powers of 10 and their abbreviations.

Value	Abbreviation
1,000	kilo (K)
1,000,000	mega (M)
1,000,000,000	giga (G)
1,000,000,000,000	tera (T)

In terms of measures of capacity or size, computer scientists prefer to count things using powers of 2. This system is convenient because digital computers use the binary number system. Table 1.3 shows the powers of 2 that are most often used. As the table

Table 1.3 **Commonly used powers of 2 and their abbreviations.**

Power of 2	Value	Abbreviation
2^{10}	1,024	kilo (K)
2^{20}	1,048,576	mega (M)
2^{30}	1,073,741,824	giga (G)
2^{40}	1,099,511,627,776	tera (T)

shows, the abbreviation for 2^{10} is K, where the K comes from the stem "kilo." The prefix *kilo* is used because 1,024 is closest to 1,000. Similarly, the prefix *mega* is used for 2^{20} because its value (1,048,576) is closest to 1,000,000. When these units are used to specify the storage capacity of a machine, we really do mean the exact power of 2. For example, a machine that has 128 megabytes of memory has 128×2^{20} bytes, or 134,217,728 bytes of memory. The use of these prefixes to mean different things can sometimes be confusing. However, context normally tells us whether the binary or decimal system is being used.

1.2.2 BUYING A PERSONAL COMPUTER

Now we are ready to examine a typical advertisement for a personal computer. Most advertisements will list the specifications of the major components of the computer. Figure 1.2 contains a typical personal computer advertisement specification.

Figure 1.2 **A typical personal computer advertisement.**

- Intel® Pentium 4 Processor at 3.06GHz with 512K cache
- 512MB DDR SDRAM
- 200GB ATA-100 Hard Drive (7200 RPM, 9.0 ms seek time)
- 17" LCD Monitor
- 64MB NVIDIA GeForce4 MX Graphics Card®
- 16x Max DVD-ROM Drive
- 48x/24x/48x CD-RW Drive
- 56K PCI Telephony Modem
- Windows XP Home Edition®
- 10/100 Fast Ethernet Network Card

The first line of the advertisement describes the microprocessor in the computer. The computer comes with an Intel Pentium 4® processor running at 3.06 GHz. The advertisement tells us the processor performs 3.06 billion operations per second (i.e., each operation takes about 327 picoseconds). The microprocessor comes with a 512-kilobyte cache. A cache is a very high speed memory used by a microprocessor to store both recently used and soon to be used information and instructions.

The second line of the ad tells us how much and the type of main memory the machine has. Main memory is where data and software reside when they are being executed by the CPU. This machine has 512 megabytes of main memory, which is a very good amount for running the Windows operating system. More memory is generally better, but having more than 1 GB is not cost effective for the typical user.

This particular machine comes with DDR SDRAM memory. The DDR is an acronym for double data rate. What this characteristic means is that data stored in DDR memory can be supplied to the CPU twice as fast as non-DDR memory. The double data rate is achieved in a manner that is analogous to how the jump rope game "double dutch" is played. Instead of a single clock signal (i.e., one rope), there are two clock signals (i.e., two ropes) that double the rate data can be delivered (i.e., the jumper must jump twice as fast).

The acronym SDRAM stands for synchronous dynamic random access memory. The DRAM portion of SDRAM indicates the type of technology used to store the binary information. In DRAM memory, the 1 or 0 for a bit is stored in a capacitor, where a capacitor is a device that holds an electrical charge. If the device is charged up, then it represents a binary 1; if the device has no charge it represents a 0. The synchronous in SDRAM indicates that the memory is designed to work in lockstep with the clock speed for which the CPU is optimized. Be aware there are many other types of memory—some faster and some slower.

The next line of the advertisement gives the specification of the hard disk drive of the machine (see Figure 1.3 for a photograph of a hard disk drive). The hard disk is where data files and software reside. So the larger your hard disk, the more software you can install and the more data you can store (e.g., pictures and music). The advertisement tells us that the capacity of the disk is 200 GB and that the disk is attached to the system using the UATA-100 interface (ultra-advanced technology attachment). This interface defines how fast data can be moved from the disk to the CPU and vice versa. UATA-100 supports transfer rates of 100 MB/second.

The other parameters of the hard disk give some additional indication of the performance of the disk. The rotational speed (7,200 RPM) tells us how fast the disk platters spin. Because we must wait for the data to pass under a *read/write head* before it can be scanned, the speed of rotation affects how long it takes to read data. A faster rotational speed translates to a smaller delay. Less expensive disk drives spin at 5,400 RPM and more expensive disks spin at 10,000 RPM.

Data is written on the disk by a set of read/write heads that move across the disk. The data is written in concentric rings called *tracks*. Another important disk parameter is the seek time. The seek time is the average time to move the heads to a particular track. The advertisement tells us that it takes 9.0 ms to move the heads to a particular track. The seek time is enormous with respect to the time to read or write main memory. Therefore, we can deduce from this fact that reading or writing to a hard disk is much slower than reading or writing to main memory.

Figure 1.3   The internals of a hard disk drive.

The advertised machine comes with a 17-inch liquid crystal display (LCD). This type of display often is referred to as a flat panel display (see Figure 1.4). These displays show an image using the same technology found in some watches and calculators. The other type of display technology uses a CRT (cathode ray tube). CRT technology is used in most televisions. Compared to CRT displays, LCD panels are very lightweight and take up much less space. LCDs are more expensive currently than CRTs. However, the prices of LCD monitors are dropping as factories convert from production of CRTs to LCDs.

Figure 1.4   Digital LCD monitor (Photo courtesy of Hewlett-Packard).

The two most important characteristics of a monitor are the size of its screen and its resolution. The viewing area of a typical monitor ranges in size from 14 inch to 24 inch. The resolution is how many dots per inch can be displayed across and down the screen. A dot in this context often is referred to as a *pixel,* which stands for "picture element." The higher the resolution, the sharper the image on the screen. Most monitors support a resolution of 1,024 by 768. High-end monitors may support higher resolutions such as 1,280 by 1,024 and 1,920 by 1,200.

The image to display is sent from the computer to the monitor through a device called a *graphics card*. Because displaying high-resolution images requires significant computation resources, graphics cards contain a microprocessor designed specifically for displaying images. These microprocessors often are referred to as GPUs (graphic processing units) to differentiate them from CPUs. Our advertised machine contains a GPU called the GeForce4 from a company called NVIDIA. Some of the other more popular graphics cards are made by ATI Technologies and Matrox. A key characteristic of a graphics card is how much memory it has. The amount of memory on the graphics card determines the resolution of the image that can be displayed, the number of colors that can be displayed, and the speed at which the monitor can be updated. Low-end graphics cards have 16 to 32 MB of memory, while the high-end graphics cards have 128 MB of memory. The listed graphics card has 64 MB of memory, which should perform well for most applications, including graphics-intensive games.

The advertised machine includes both a DVD drive and a CD-RW drive. A DVD drive enables the playing of DVD movies on the computer. This DVD drive does not support creating DVDs, but such drives are commonly available for the consumer market. A key parameter for DVD and CD-RW drives is the speed at which data can be read or written. Speeds for DVD and CD-RW drives are given in multiples of the speed of the first available drives. The specified DVD drive has a speed rating of 16x, which means it can read at 16 times the speed of the first DVD drives.

The RW in CD-RW indicates the drive can both read and write CDs. These drives are very popular because they enable consumers to create their own music CDs. They are also a good way to back up files. A CD can hold 650 MB of data or several hours of music. The specification for a CD-RW is given in sets of three—the listed drive has the specification 48x/24x/48x. This specification indicates that the drive can write to CD-R media at 48 speed, can write to CD-RW media speed at 24 and can read discs at 48 speed. (CD-R media can be written only once and CD-RW media can be rewritten).

The machine comes with a 56K modem. A modem (short for modulator/demodulator) enables the computer to connect to the Internet over the telephone line. The 56K indicates the speed at which the modem can send data. A 56K modem can transmit 56 kilobits per second. However, most 56K modems rarely achieve this maximum rate. First, most telephone networks limit the top speed to 53 kilobits per second. Second, the actual rate depends on several factors including the telephone line conditions (e.g., the presence of static or interference) and the distance to the central telephone company equipment.

The advertisement also gives the operating system that comes installed on the machine. This machine comes with a version of Microsoft Windows—Windows XP. There are a two major variants of Windows XP: the home edition and the professional edition. The professional edition includes additional features: the ability to encrypt the file system to protect valuable data, a remote desktop so that you can access the machine over the Internet, and offline files and folders, which is useful for a mobile machine that sometimes is connected to a file server.

The last detail of the advertisement specifies a high-speed network card. A high-speed network card is useful if you want to create your own local area network in your home, or if you have a broadband connection to the Internet. A *broadband* connection is a

Operating systems

There are other operating systems available for machines. An increasingly popular operating system is Linux. Linux frequently is used by researchers and in computing systems dedicated to high-end applications such as Web servers, network gateways, and file servers. One major reason for Linux's popularity is that the source code for Linux is available freely. By having access to the source code, Linux can be modified to suit the particular needs of the application. There are several different versions of Linux available with Red Hat Linux being the one used most widely. Before downloading a version of Linux over the Internet, make sure you have a fast connection. Linux is quite large and can take several hours to download over a broadband connection.

high-speed connection via either a cable modem or via digital subscriber line (DSL) service from the telephone company. Unlike the slow speed of a telephone modem connection, cable modems and DSL service offer transmission speeds of several megabytes per second.

This particular network card can send and receive data at either 10 MB/second or 100 MB/second. Either speed is more than enough for home networking speeds. The faster transfer rate would be desirable if the machine is to be used to provide services to other machines on the network (e.g., file storage and backup).

Because computer networks and especially the Internet are so important, we now turn our attention to them.

1.3   INTERNET COMPUTING

The birth and growth of the Internet has changed society fundamentally. It is not unreasonable to compare the impact of the Internet to the impact of Gutenburg's printing press.

The printing press made the dissemination of information much more affordable. Consequently, information became available to a much larger group of people. As a result, restricting access to information was harder for those in power. The widespread access to information fomented a fundamental shift in existing social structures.

The Internet is having a similar effect. It has made vast amounts of information available cheaply to a huge and still growing group of people. Similarly, the Internet makes it difficult for those in power to control what information is available and who can access it.

On a societal basis, many experts believe this quantum leap in information availability has again initiated a major shift in our existing social structures.

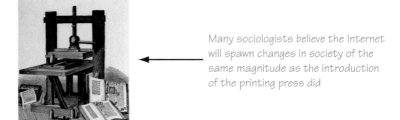

Many sociologists believe the Internet will spawn changes in society of the same magnitude as the introduction of the printing press did

So, what is the Internet and how did it develop? The Internet is a vast infrastructure that supports the rapid transmission of information between computers. The Internet consists of thousands of local, regional, national, and international networks connected together. It is a network of networks. Because the Internet spans national boundaries, no one entity really controls the entire Internet. However, there are organizations responsible for developing technical aspects of the Internet and setting standards.

The beginning of the Internet dates back to the early 1960s and a U.S. government agency called the Advanced Research Projects Agency (ARPA). ARPA's mission was to ensure that the United States kept pace technologically. In the 1960s, ARPA was funding research at both industrial and university laboratories throughout the United States. ARPA decided that research productivity would be improved if the scientists at the laboratories could share computational resources by networking the computers at the various ARPA-supported laboratories. After several years of development, the ARPAnet became operational in 1969. The first network interconnected machines at four universities—three in California and one in Utah.

Over the years, the ARPAnet grew both in number of sites connected and in the number of supported applications. The first ARPAnet e-mail application was developed in 1971. Numerous utilities also were developed for transferring files between machines and for allowing researchers to run software applications remotely at other sites. Realizing the value of networking machines together, the National Science Foundation established NSFNet in 1986. (The National Science Foundation is a U.S. government agency funding basic scientific research.) NSFNet was a high-speed, coast-to-coast transmission line that enabled educational institutions and research laboratories to connect machines together. NSFNet eventually interconnected many existing networks and the term Internet crept into our vocabulary. Then in 1990, Tim Berners-Lee developed the World Wide Web. At this time the size and use of the Internet began to grow exponentially.

1.3.1 NETWORKS

A network consists of a method of connecting machines together, and a set of rules that enable the machines to exchange information. The method of connection can be a stan-

Figure 1.5 **A home network connected to the Internet.**

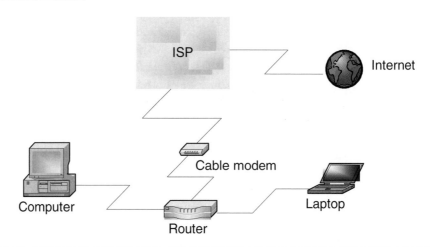

dard telephone line using a 56K modem, a DSL connection, or a connection using a network card. Figure 1.5 shows a home network with two computers.

Because the Internet is a network of networks, there must be some mechanism for connecting networks together. The connections are accomplished by using special computers called *routers* that connect a local or regional network to a high-speed transmission line called a *backbone*. You can think of backbones as a highway system that enables traffic to move speedily from one region to another (up to 10 gigabits per second). Figure 1.6 depicts a backbone map for the United States for a generic Internet service provider.

The job of a router is to direct Internet messages to their proper destinations. Think of a router like a railway yard switch. The switch determines on which track (the particular network) a train (a packet of messages) should be sent to reach its destination. Because of the huge number of messages they must handle, routers usually contain specialized computers designed specifically to handle Internet messages.

In order for machines to communicate over the Internet, there must be a set of rules that govern how data is sent. Without an agreement on the set of rules, the machines cannot communicate efficiently. For example, when people talk over two-way radios, after one person finishes speaking he or she says "Over." The "Over" signals that it is the other person's turn to speak. When a speaker wants to end the conversation, the speaker says "Over and out." The rules that govern communication are called *communication protocols*.

An important part in the growth of the Internet was the development of efficient protocols. The most important Internet protocol is the TCP/IP (Transmission Control Protocol/ Internet Protocol). It governs how packets of information are sent across the Internet. The TCP specifies both how a message is to be split into the packets and how the packets are to be assembled to reproduce the original message. The IP handles the address part of a packet so that it gets to the right destination.

Figure 1.6 **Representative U.S. backbone.**

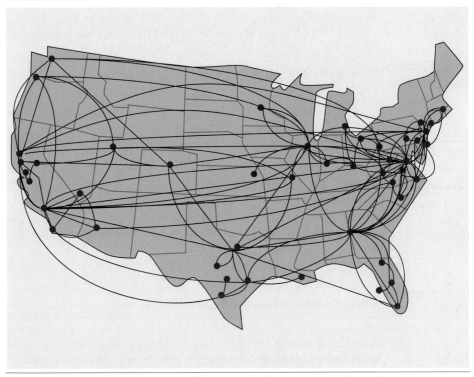

There are other specialized protocols. Most of these protocols are implemented using TCP/IP. Some other common protocols used on the Internet include:

■ The *File Transfer Protocol* (FTP) specifies how to exchange files between computers.

■ The *Simple Mail Transfer Protocol* (SMTP) specifies how e-mail is moved across the Internet.

■ The *Post Office Protocol 3* (POP3) governs how electronic mail (e-mail) is exchanged between your mail reader (e.g., Outlook and Netscape Communicator) and your Internet Service Provider (ISP). Another protocol for communicating e-mail between your local machine and your Internet service provider is IMAP (Internet Message Access Protocol).

■ The *Hypertext Transfer Protocol* (HTTP) is the set of rules for exchanging files (text, graphic images, sound, video, and other multimedia files) over the World Wide Web (WWW). It specifies the actions that are taken when you click on a link within a document.

■ The *Secure Sockets Layer* (SSL) is a protocol that specifies how information is encrypted before being sent over the Internet. It is used widely in electronic commerce. You can tell if a Web page is using SSL by noting whether its WWW address begins with https instead of http.

We now turn our attention to the software components of a computing system and why Java is so important to future software development.

1.4 SOFTWARE AND JAVA

One of the important things to realize about the Internet is that there are many different types of machines connected to it. Personal computers, personal digital assistants, cell phones, workstations, and larger computers referred to as mainframes all are connected to it. This situation creates a very interesting problem. How can we develop software that can run on any machine connected to the Internet regardless of its machine type? Solving this problem was one of the key design goals of the Java programming language. To understand this problem and the importance of Java for Internet computing, this section examines how a Java program is executed on a machine connected to the Internet.

1.4.1 PROGRAMMING LANGUAGES

By itself, a computer will not do anything useful. There must be a program that directs the computer to perform some specific task. A *program* is a sequence of instructions that tells the computer what to do. When the program instructions are carried out by the computer, we say the program is *executed*.

Program instructions are written in a language that is designed specifically for giving commands to a computer. We call these languages *programming languages*.

The most primitive type of programming language is a *machine language*. A machine language program or *object code* is a program to which a computer can respond directly. Each object code instruction corresponds to a fundamental operation of the machine.

The instruction set for a machine is a set of binary codes that are unique to its CPU type. Consequently, different computers use different machine languages. The machine language understood by Intel's Pentium processor is quite different from the machine language understood by IBM's PowerPC® processor.

A major problem with machine language programming is that it is very tedious and error prone to write directly in binary codes. Slightly less tedious is *assembly language* programming. An assembly language is a symbolic language for coding machine language instructions. Like machine language programmers, assembly language programmers must have a complete understanding of basic operations of the machine. Furthermore, because the corresponding machine operations are so primitive, for even very simple tasks, assembly language programs can be quite long and complicated.

Over the years, computer scientists have put much effort into developing programming languages that permit people to write programs in a way that is more natural. Such programming languages are referred to as *high-level programming languages*. The adjective high-level indicates that the programming language is at a higher level than assembly language.

A distinguishing characteristic of a high-level programming language is that detailed knowledge of the machine being programmed is not required. Another characteristic is that a high-level programming language uses a vocabulary and structure that is close to the type of problem being solved. For example, the programming language FORTRAN, which is used to solve scientific and engineering problems, uses a notation that is mathematical. Indeed, the name FORTRAN is derived from the phrase *formula translation*. Because of the close coupling of a programming language to types of problems, there are literally hundreds of high-level programming languages.

The commands in a high-level language program are not executed directly by a computer. A high-level language program has to be translated first. The conversion is accomplished by a specialized program called a *translator*. A translator accepts a program written in a one language and translates it to an equivalent program in another language. The input to the translator is the *source program* and the output of the translator is the *target program*. Most translators convert a high-level language program to a machine language program. For high-level languages, a translator normally is referred to as a *compiler*.

A particular type of translator of interest to Java programmers is an *interpreter*. An interpreter is a translator that both translates and executes the source program.

1.4.2 RUNNING A JAVA PROGRAM

To understand the steps of translating and executing a high-level program, let's discuss how a simple Java program is translated and executed. We will use the forecast program that started this chapter. The program performs the straightforward task of printing a quotation to a *console window* (i.e., a window that allows commands to be entered at a prompt). The program file is named `DisplayForecast.java`. That is, the program is stored in a file whose name is `DisplayForecast.java`. A copy of `DisplayForecast.java` is given in the Listing 1.1.

Listing 1.1   DisplayForecast.java

```
 1.  // Authors: J. P. Cohoon and J. W. Davidson
 2.  // Purpose: display a quotation in a console window
 3.
 4.  public class DisplayForecast {
 5.
 6.      // method main(): application entry point
 7.      public static void main(String[] args) {
 8.          System.out.print("I think there is a world market for");
 9.          System.out.println(" maybe five computers.");
10.          System.out.println("   Thomas Watson, IBM, 1943.");
11.      }
12.  }
```

At this time, we are unconcerned with the details of the program—we leave it to Chapter 2 to explain the various components of this program. For our purposes, the important part of the program is the three *statements* that display the message (lines 8–10). These are the high-level language statements that will be executed when the program is executed.

Normally, there are two steps required to execute a Java program. The first step is to translate the Java source program to a target machine program. The target program produced by a Java compiler is called a *class file*.

There are many different Java software development environments (i.e., Java translation and execution systems) available. For this textbook, we sometimes used the Java translator from Sun Microsystems®. Sun Microsystems is the company that developed the Java programming language and they make available freely the JDK, a software development kit that can be downloaded from www.javasoft.com.

Figure 1.7 contains a screen snapshot showing the compilation of program `DisplayForecast`. The command to invoke the JDK compiler is `javac` and it takes a single argument that is the name of the file that contains the source program. Because there are no error messages from the compiler, the source program was translated successfully to a target program that can now be executed.

Figure 1.7 Compiling DisplayForecast.java.

To execute the target program, we use a Java interpreter. A Java interpreter reads the target program created by a Java compiler and executes it. The JDK Java interpreter is invoked with the command `java` and the name of the program. Figure 1.8 contains a screen snapshot showing the execution of the Java program `DisplayForecast` and the *output* (display) that it produces. When invoking an interpreter to execute a Java program, do not give a file extension, give only the name of the program—`DisplayForecast`.

At the beginning of this section, we mentioned that one of the key features of Java is that a Java program can run on a variety of different types of machines. This feature makes Java ideal for developing Internet applications where there are many different

Figure 1.8   **Executing DisplayForecast.java.**

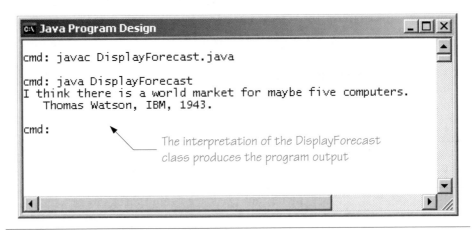

types of machines connected to the network. It is the Java interpreter that makes this happen.

When we compile a Java program, the Java compiler does not produce a machine language program for a particular computer like the compilers for other programming languages such as C, C++, or FORTRAN do. Rather the Java compiler produces a program for an interpreter called the *Java Virtual Machine* (JVM). Essentially, the JVM is a program that mimics the operation of a real machine. The JVM reads the program produced by the Java compiler and executes the Java machine language instructions produced by the Java compiler. The Java machine language instructions are called Java *bytecodes* and can be viewed as architecturally neutral object code. The bytecodes are stored in a file with an extension of `.class`. For program `DisplayForecast.java`, a Java compiler produces a bytecode file named `DisplayForecast.class`.

Now here's the key idea—we can execute a Java `class` file on any machine that has a copy of a JVM on it. Figure 1.9 illustrates this process. Suppose you want to send the program to some friends so that they can run it on their machine, where your machine is a PC, and your friends have an Apple. You first compile `DisplayForecast.java` to produce `DisplayForecast.class`. You then send the file `DisplayForecast.class` to the friends over the Internet (e.g., via e-mail or FTP). Using a JVM that is running on your friends' Apple machine, your friends can interpret the program you sent.

You might wonder what's the big deal. Why not just send the source program and let your friends compile it and run it? There are several potential problems with this approach.

First, application source programs are sometimes quite large. Sending a source program over the network can take significant time—especially if the connection from the Internet to the friends' home computer is a slow modem connection. The Java bytecodes were designed to be small and compact, and thus sending a `class` file is much more efficient than sending a machine-language program or a Java source program.

Second, while you might not care if your friend saw your source program, most companies do not want to send source programs over the Internet as they may contain impor-

Figure 1.9 **Java and the Internet.**

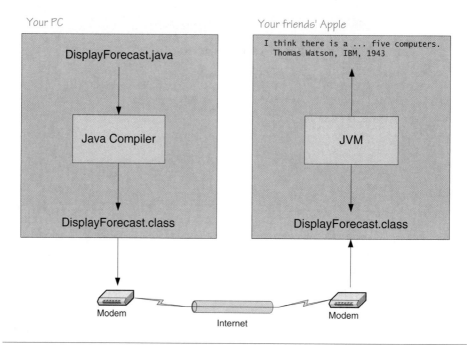

tant information such as formulas that they do not wish to disclose. Sending a `class` file offers some protection for proprietary information.

Third and most important, some devices may not have the necessary computation resources (e.g., memory or CPU speed) to run the Java compiler. For example, many technologists believe that soon household appliances will be connected to the Internet. A refrigerator connected to the Internet might be capable of running a Java application that tracks your food consumption. When you are running low on eggs or milk, the Java application will send an order over the Internet to your grocery store for more eggs and milk. To keep costs reasonable, a refrigerator will contain a low-cost CPU that is unlikely to have the necessary resources to compile a Java application.

We now turn our attention to the practice of designing and developing software.

1.5 ENGINEERING SOFTWARE

As computers have become faster, cheaper, and more powerful, they have become indispensable tools in our everyday lives. They are in appliances such as televisions, DVD players, and microwave ovens. Furthermore, whenever we use a telephone or an automated teller machine, we are accessing a network of computers.

However, faster, cheaper, more powerful computers only are part of the equation. A computer system has *both* hardware and software components. While there have been tremendous advances in hardware technology, the advances in software design have been more modest. Part of the problem is that the expectations for software have grown considerably. Figure 1.10 illustrates the *complexity paradox*—the complexity of a system grows as attempts are made to make it easier to use.

Figure 1.10   Ease of use versus internal complexity.

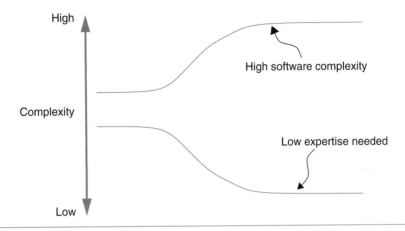

For example, early systems for graphing data required users to specify in detail how the graph should look by supplying information such as the coordinates of the graphical elements, the scale, and how and where the graph should be labeled. Essentially, the user had to do most of the work. However, modern spreadsheet tools contain "wizards," which analyze the data and produce a graph automatically. Such automatic graphing systems are much easier to use, but this ease of use comes at a price—increased software complexity.

Several factors account for the increased complexity. First, to do more, the software is larger. It is not unusual for application programs, such as spreadsheets, word processors, and drawing programs, to consist of millions of lines of code. Another factor that increases complexity is the interaction between components. For example, a word processor may contain one component for spell checking and correction, and another component that provides the services of a thesaurus.

Let's consider the spell-checking component. When a possible spelling error is detected, the spelling checker must report the possible error to the user. Thus the spelling checker must interact with the component of the application that creates a window or a dialog box so that the possible error can be displayed and the user queried about what action, if any, to take. If the user agrees it is a spelling error, the checker can correct the misspelling. To make the correction, the checker must interact with the component of the word processor responsible for replacing text in the document. Obviously, as the number of components grows, the number of interactions between components can grow rapidly.

Software engineering is the area of computer science that is concerned with how to build software systems. The goal of a software engineer is to produce a software system that is *effective, reliable, understandable, cost effective, adaptable,* and *reusable.* Let's examine these properties.

A software application should be effective and reliable. That is, it should work correctly and not fail. Imagine that you have spent several hours writing an important paper with a word processor. Then while doing a pasting operation, the word processor quits unexpectedly and you lose all your work. This ineffective, unreliable action would undoubtedly make you upset, and rightfully so.

One step to making a software system reliable is to make it understandable. The design and operation of the system must be clear to other software professionals. Understandability is important because large software systems are constructed by many people working in teams. The software construction is smoother if everyone working on it understands the overall operation of the system and its components.

Understandability is also important because of the long lifetime of software. A software product usually evolves over time. Software engineers who had nothing to do with its original development often make enhancements and fix *bugs* (errors). This process is called *software maintenance*. As a measure of the difficulty of maintaining software, experts estimate that two-thirds of the cost of developing software is devoted to maintenance. This cost can be reduced when the design and operation of a system are comprehensible.

A software system should be cost effective. That is, the cost to develop and maintain a software system should not exceed the expected profit from selling the system. Many software companies have gone bankrupt because they have underestimated either the cost of developing a system or the time to design, build, and maintain the software.

Because of its potentially long lifetime, software should be adaptable. It often is difficult to predict which features and capabilities eventually will be added to a software product. By designing software so that additional features and capabilities can be added easily, maintenance costs can be reduced.

Because of high development costs, software should be reusable. If many millions of dollars are spent to develop some software, it makes sense to make its components flexible so they can be reused when developing other software. This strategy is common practice in other businesses—the automotive engineer does not design a new car from scratch. Rather, the engineer borrows from the design and components of existing cars.

We now consider some engineering principles whose application encourage the development and maintenance of cost-effective quality software.

I.5.I SOFTWARE ENGINEERING PRINCIPLES

Software engineers have developed a number of design principles that help realize the goals in the previous section by managing the complexity of a large software system. Four of the more important principles are abstraction, encapsulation, modularity, and hierarchy.

Abstraction is the process of determining the relevant properties and features of an object while ignoring nonessential details. The relevant properties are defined by how the object is to be used and manipulated. For example, an auto salesperson views a car from the standpoint of its selling features, while a mechanic views the car from the standpoint of the systems that require maintenance. If you are concerned with developing a help system to assist car owners who do their own repairs, you need to be sure that the mechanic's view is considered.[†]

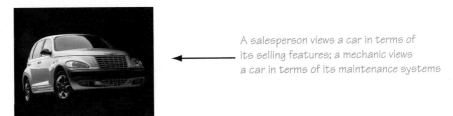

A salesperson views a car in terms of its selling features; a mechanic views a car in terms of its maintenance systems

By focusing programming efforts on the relevant properties and ignoring irrelevant details, the complexity of dealing with an object is reduced. Consider the task of finding a file on a disk and reading its contents. If we had to handle the low-level disk-access details, accomplishing the task would be quite difficult. We would have to understand how data is stored on the disk and the machine language commands that control the operation of the disk drive. Instead, the operating system provides a view that lets us access a file simply by supplying the name of the file. The file system handles the low-level details of reading the data on the disk drive and returning it to the program.

Encapsulation or *information hiding* is the process of separating the component of an object into external and internal aspects. The external aspects of an object need to be visible to other objects in the system. The internal aspects are details that should not affect other parts of the system. Hiding the internal aspects of an object means that they can be changed without requiring changes to other system parts.

Consider a car radio. The external aspects are the controls and the types of connectors needed to hook the radio to the electrical system, the speakers, and the antenna. The internal aspects are the details of how the radio works. To install and use a radio in a car, we do not need to know anything about electrical engineering. The radio can be viewed as a box with buttons and cables. Another big benefit of encapsulation is that it simplifies making changes. The radio in a car can be replaced with one that includes an MP3 player without affecting other components of the car.

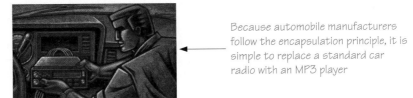

Because automobile manufacturers follow the encapsulation principle, it is simple to replace a standard car radio with an MP3 player

When applied to the design of a software system, encapsulation enables the internal operation of a software component to be changed without affecting other aspects of the system. For example, if an automated voice-mail system has been encapsulated correctly, we should be able to change the component that handles message storing without affect-

---

†   2001 PT Cruiser Photo/Courtesy of DaimlerChrysler Corporation.

Figure 1.11 **A partial organization chart of a company.**

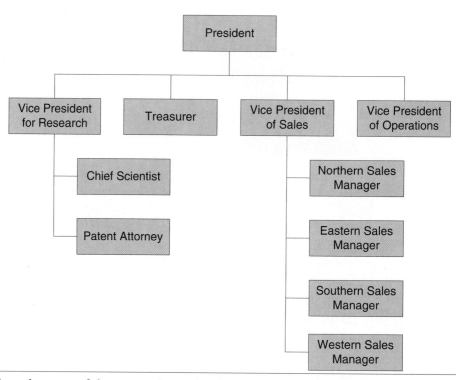

ing other parts of the system. Increasing the number of messages that a user can store should not affect how users access the voice-mail system to retrieve messages.

Most complex systems are *modular*. They are constructed by combining simpler working components or packages. Proper modularization of a complex system also helps manage complexity. Breaking things down into smaller, easier to understand pieces makes the larger system easier to understand. For example, an automobile can be decomposed into subsystems. Automobile subsystems include a cooling system, an ignition system, and an exhaust system. By thinking about an automobile in terms of its subsystems, we can grasp more readily the car's overall structure and operation.

A ranking or ordering of objects based on some relationship between them is a *hierarchy*. Hierarchies can help us understand complex organizations and systems. Figure 1.11 contains a partial organizational chart for the management of a company. The chart shows the management hierarchy based on the relationship of who reports to whom. The hierarchy helps employees understand the structure of their company.

A useful way of ordering abstractions is from most general to least general. A hierarchical ordering based on natural relationships is called a *taxonomy*. Such a hierarchy makes all the abstractions easier to understand because it exposes the relationship of the characteristics and behaviors they have in common. For example, consider a taxonomy of musical instruments that organizes instruments by how they produce their sound.

- Idiophones: Solid instruments that are intrinsically sonorous, e.g., bell and cymbal.

- Membranophones: Instruments with taut membranes, e.g., drum and tambourine.

- Aerophones: Instruments that enclose and free masses of air, e.g., trumpet and saxophone.

- Chordophones: Instruments with stretched strings, e.g., lyre and violin.

- Electrophones: Instruments with oscillating electric circuits, e.g., synthesizer and electric piano.

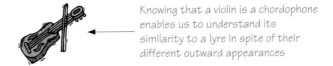

Knowing that a violin is a chordophone enables us to understand its similarity to a lyre in spite of their different outward appearances

We next consider object-oriented design. This methodology provides an approach that supports the software engineering principles of abstraction, encapsulation, modularity, and hierarchy.

1.6 OBJECT-ORIENTED DESIGN

The object-oriented design and programming methodology has been notably successful in helping software developers achieve the goals of reliability, cost-effectiveness, adaptability, understandability, and reusability.

Object-oriented software design promotes thinking about software in a way that closely models the way we think about and interact with the real world. At an early age, we learn about objects and how to manipulate them. Babies learn that if they shake a rattle, it will make noise. Later as we develop our cognitive skills, we realize that objects have properties, and we begin to be able to think about them abstractly. A growing baby soon realizes that noise making is a property of all rattles.

To illustrate how viewing the world as objects with properties helps us manage complexity, consider the following activity. You are getting ready for bed and you remember that you must get up early in the morning. You reach over to your clock radio and set the alarm switch to on and push the hour and minutes alarm buttons to indicate the wake-up time. You go to sleep and the next morning the radio comes on at the desired time.

Now let's analyze this activity. First, you recognized the need for action—having to get up early and deciding that the clock radio could help meet that need. So you go over to the clock radio, which is a physical object. This object has properties like weight and size, and it also can do something. For one it can play music at an indicated time. It's not necessary for you to know entirely how the clock radio works. You need to know only which switches and buttons to use. The switches and buttons are the *interface* to the clock radio. If you understand the interface to an object, you can use it to perform some tasks without understanding how the object works internally. Moving the appropriate switches and pushing the appropriate buttons are signals to the clock radio to modify its behavior.

A clock radio is an object with attributes and behaviors. Its interface provides buttons and switches that signal the clock radio to perform different actions

Such interactions are so routine that it is easy to overlook how amazing this activity is. You were able to make an object perform a complex activity without understanding the internal operation of the object. You were able to do so because you had an appropriate abstraction of the object. Indeed your mental abstraction of a clock radio means that when you travel and stay at a hotel room, you are able to set its clock radio even though it is a different clock radio. Similar objects often exhibit similar behavior.

This way of dealing with the complex world around us also can be applied to software design and programming. A key step in developing a complex system using object-oriented design is to determine the objects that constitute the system. By carefully creating appropriate abstractions of these objects and separating their internal implementation from their external behavior, we can manage the complexity of a large software system.

So what exactly do we mean by an object? Physical things are certainly objects. A ball, a file cabinet, an address book, a tree, and a computer all are objects. What about things like a word, a bank account, or a musical note? These things are not physical objects, but they are objects—in the sense that they have attributes and properties, and we can perform actions on them. A word has a length and meaning, and if we are talking in regard to a word processor, a word can be inserted or deleted from a document. A bank account has a balance to which funds can be deposited or debited. A musical note has pitch, duration, and loudness and can be played. For the most part, something is an object if it has a *name*, *properties associated with it*, and *behaviors such as message handling*.

Typically, when an object receives a message, the message causes the object either to take some action or to change one of its properties. Continuing with our clock radio example, when you push the "music on" button, the current broadcast is played.

If we are going to take an object-oriented approach to developing software, it makes sense to use a programming language such as Java that supports thinking and implementing solutions in terms of objects. A language with features that support thinking about and implementing solutions in terms of objects is an *object-oriented programming language*.

Using an object-oriented programming language to implement an object-oriented design is called *object-oriented programming*. Notice we were very careful to include the phrase "implement an object-oriented design." As you will see later, you can use an object-oriented language, but not think in terms of objects.

Programming languages generally give programmers the ability to specify the *types* of objects to be used in their programs, where a type is a collection of values and the operations that can be performed on those values. An example of a type would be the set of integers and the arithmetic operations that can be performed on them.

Object-oriented languages provide programmers the ability to create a type known as a *class* for representing the properties and message-handling behaviors of a type of object. Classes normally are organized so that the manipulation of a property is handled via a message to the object. Thus, the class encapsulation process is similar in nature to the process of designing a car radio, which has interfaces for both its user and the electrical system. Programmers use a class to create *instances* of it. An instance is an object with a particular value for each property and attribute of the class.

In practical terms, a class can be thought of as a model or template for an object. From the class, objects with specific properties can be created, or *instantiated*. An object is an instance of exactly one class. As another example, consider a star-shaped cookie cutter. When it is pressed into dough, a cookie is formed. The cutter corresponds to a class—it is a cookie mold. An individual cookie is an object—it is constructed using the cookie cutter.

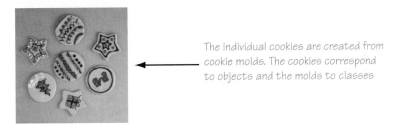

The individual cookies are created from cookie molds. The cookies correspond to objects and the molds to classes

The difference between a class and an object is subtle but important. Whereas a class is a concept, an object is a concrete entity, it is a specific instance of a class. For example, the concept of a car corresponds to a class, but the particular SUVs you may see driving down a street are objects. Similarly, the notion of a bank account corresponds to a class, but your savings account is an object.

We can use a class type to represent playing cards. The properties of a card would be its rank and suit. Card message handling would include *methods* that queried an object regarding its rank value and suit value. The queen of clubs and the nine of diamonds would be playing card instances or objects.

Another important feature of object-oriented languages is that they let programmers exploit the similarity of objects to *derive* new types of objects from existing types of objects. In this situation, we call the old type the *superclass* and the new class a *subclass*. The subclass both *extends* or *specializes* the functionality of the superclass and *inherits* the properties and behaviors of the superclass.

Specialization is something we see all the time. For example, a poem, novel, biography, and office memo are all types of writing with specialized attributes. An example in Java is the graphical superclass for representing the attributes and behaviors expected of any component that can be placed in a window. The superclass is used as the basis for deriving specialized components such as buttons, menus, scroll bars, labels, and text entry areas. As another example, an aquarium simulation is developed in Chapter 12. The superclass for the simulator is a standard Java class rendering (drawing) images. A snapshot of the application is given in Figure 1.12.

We next turn our attention to a more basic aspect of software development—problem solving.

Figure 1.12 **Snapshot of aquarium program of Chapter 12.**

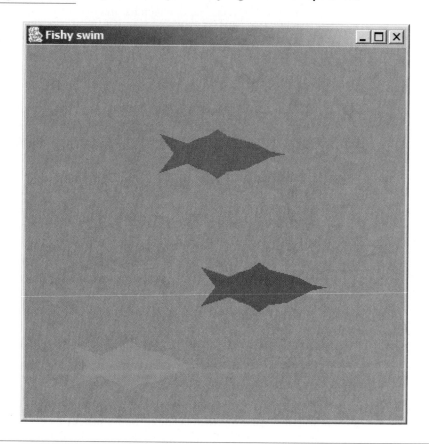

PROBLEM SOLVING

Developing a program with its classes and objects for some particular problem is more than just writing code—it is a creative process. While many programmers liken software creation to the construction of a formal piece of logic, other programmers consider software creation to be an artistic endeavor more like the painting of a large, detailed canvas.

No matter which approach you take, we recommend the following steps when developing a computer program for some problem.

- *Analysis*: Determine the inputs, outputs, and components of the problem. Their description should be sufficiently specific to enable you to solve the problem.

■ *Design*: Describe the required information and methods for solving your problem. If necessary, reanalyze the problem to gain a better understanding so that a relatively straightforward and flexible design can be implemented.

■ *Implementation*: Write the code that implements the various information structures and their associated methods, and write the code that manages the overall process. If necessary, reanalyze and redesign so that clear code can be produced.

■ *Testing*: Test the various code components individually and collectively. If the problem is not solved correctly or satisfactorily, then reanalyze, redesign, reimplement, and retest as appropriate.

These steps provide a framework to help ensure that your problem is solved correctly. You definitely want to make sure that your efforts are geared in the right direction—a clever solution for the wrong problem is not a solution at all.

Each of the steps is important. Analysis emphasizes what needs to be done; design emphasizes how it is to be done; implementation emphasizes the doing; and testing emphasizes whether it was done correctly.

Be aware that the four steps are not performed necessarily just once. Problem solving often is an iterative process. In doing the design, you might realize more analysis is needed. And in doing the implementation, you might find that more design or analysis is needed. Similarly, in doing the testing you might find that more design, analysis, or implementation is needed.

A pictorial representation of the four basic problem-solving steps is given in Figure 1.13. Because of the importance of these steps in producing solid software, this text does not just present code in isolation. For many problems, we trace through the development process.

How you go about the problem-solving process will depend somewhat on your own way of thinking and acting (see Figure 1.14). For example, some people use a *bricolage* approach where the various features and aspects of the problems are tried and manipulated repeatedly according to the programmers' personal ways of organizing information. For these people, a mistake is not an error in calculation, but a correction waiting to be made in the natural course of solving the problem.

In contrast, many other people take a *planned* approach, using logic and formalism coupled with a structured methodology. Our recommendation is to use an approach that is natural for you. However, be aware that the planned approach is by far the dominant method taught. The structure that the planned approach offers often makes it easier to verify that the software meets all problem specifications. Also be aware that some experts believe that object-oriented design encompasses aspects of both the bricolage and planned approaches. A well-designed object requires both concrete and abstract thinking.

To assist your own design and development efforts, in Sections 1.7.1 through 1.7.4 we present basic problem-solving tips. By applying them, you may be inspired on how to solve your own assigned problems.

Figure 1.13 **Problem-solving steps when computer programming.**

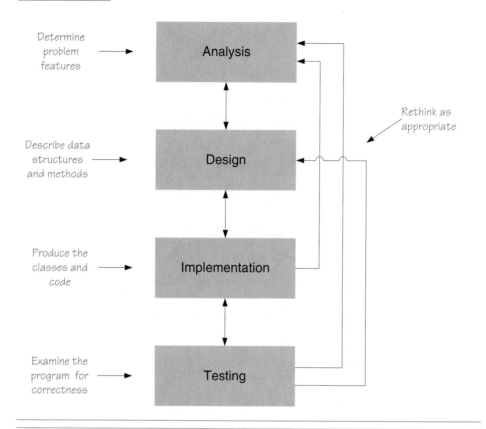

Figure 1.14 **Programming approaches—bricolage versus planned.**

| I.7.I | **ASK QUESTIONS AS NEEDED** |

Suppose some clients ask you to give them a method for performing temperature conversion. If you think briefly about it, you should realize that the request has some ambiguities—there is insufficient information for you to solve the problem (e.g., what type of conversion is needed). Therefore, the best thing for you to do is to ask the clients some clarifying questions—you want as much information as possible about the problem so that you can know what truly is being asked. Some obvious first questions are

- What kind of input temperatures must be dealt with?
- What range of input temperatures must be dealt with?
- What level of precision is required?
- What kind of conversion is wanted?
- Who will use the conversion?
- Under what conditions will the conversion be used?

If the clients then tell you that it will be used by a normal person under normal conditions where the input temperature is always a Celsius temperature and that its Fahrenheit equivalent is what is wanted, you might then ask the clients

- What is meant by normal?

Suppose the answer is temperatures that you might experience in your local area. You might then ask the person

- Are you aware of a formula for this conversion?

Here the answer is most likely no—the clients are asking you because they do not know the formula.

Other obvious questions are

- What type of solution is wanted?
- How should the conversion be expressed?

Suppose the answers indicate that a pen-and-paper procedure is fine. At this point you probably believe that the questions have given you the *inputs*, *outputs*, and *components* of the problem. Together this information forms the *problem requirements* or *problem statement*. Having a problem statement that you understand is an absolute necessity.

A good thing to do when you believe you understand the problem requirements is to write them down in a straightforward manner and to show to them to the person who posed the problem. For your problem, a possible statement could be

> Give a method for converting a requested Celsius temperature to its Fahrenheit equivalent. The requested Celsius temperature comes from the range –50° to 50° and is accurate to one degree.

If you find out that your problem statement is incorrect, then ask additional questions to determine which parts require clarification.

1.7.2 FIND OUT AS MUCH AS YOU CAN

Once you have a problem statement, you typically then attempt to find out what is known about the problem. In general, it is important to know both what attempts have succeeded and what attempts have failed. With respect to the problem at hand, at this point you might excuse yourself to go do a little research. The purpose of the research is to find out what is known about Celsius to Fahrenheit conversion.

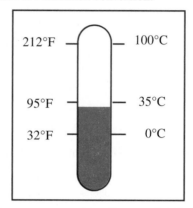

An examination of almost any encyclopedia or major dictionary reveals that the following formula holds always for a Celsius to Fahrenheit conversion.

$$Fahrenheit = \frac{9}{5}Celsius + 32$$

To be sure that you understand the formula, you might try some known Celsius to Fahrenheit correspondents — 0°C and 32°F, 100°C and 212°F, and –40°C and –40°F. Because this formula solves what you believe to be the problem, you can go report back your finding. If the client indicates that the formula is satisfactory, then the problem has been solved and you are done. If the formula is not satisfactory, then additional questions are necessary to modify the problem statement because some miscommunication has occurred.

Your research often can require significant time and also cause you to pose additional questions with the client to *refine* the problem statement. These efforts are worthwhile because the result is a better understanding of the problem. A true understanding of the problem makes it easier to solve and produce a satisfactory solution.

Refinement can also be used in developing a solution. First sketch a solution and then repeatedly refine the components of the solution until the entire process is specified completely. This process is known as *top-down design.*

1.7.3	BREAK COMPLEX PROBLEMS INTO SUBPROBLEMS

Suppose you and your friends have been given a huge collection of postcards and you are asked to determine whether there is a postcard that has a picture of grazing sheep. One way to solve the problem is for you individually to look at the cards one by one. If your scan finds a postcard with the grazing sheep then you can stop and report yes. If you scan all the postcards and do not find such a picture then you report no.

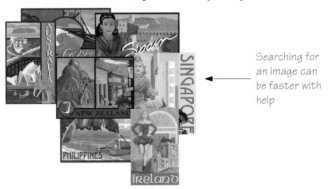

Searching for an image can be faster with help

If your friends will cooperate, a method that generally completes faster than the individual approach is to divide the cards in a roughly even manner among the people present and for each person to scan a separate pile. If someone finds a picture of grazing sheep then you can all stop and report yes. If everyone completes their scan and the desired picture is not found then you report no. Here we have divided the problem into subproblems and defined both how to solve the subproblems and how to combine the solutions to the subproblems into a solution for the overall problem. The name for this method of problem solving is *divide-and-conquer.*

Divide-and-conquer is typically easiest to apply when the subproblems are similar in nature to the original problem. Such similarity occurred in our postcard searching decomposition. The goal of the original problem is to determine whether a postcard collection includes a postcard with grazing sheep and the goal of each of the subproblems is to determine whether a subset of a postcard collection includes a postcard with grazing sheep.

Computer science needs you

Developing software is definitely not just for "geeks." Software projects need individuals with disparate skills. Being an analyst requires communication skills and the ability to perceive and understand a user's needs. Having a strong creative streak is a plus for a designer. An implementer requires detailed knowledge of a program language, clarity of thought and expression, and the ability to pay attention to detail. A tester with good imagination and analytic skills can make sure that software is checked out in all the ways a client might use it.

Divide-and-conquer is also a good technique when you encounter a very complex problem. Such problems may appear overwhelming at first. However, by dividing the problem into its constituent tasks and examining each in turn, you can eventually develop a solution to the entire problem. Be aware that for truly complex problems, it may even be useful to apply the divide-and-conquer technique to the subproblems.

We next turn our attention to some important problem-solving practices—make use of what has come before and prepare now for the future.

1.7.4 REUSE AND EXPECT FUTURE REUSE

If someone were to ask you to build a wooden box, our guess is that you would not first plant an acorn to grow an oak tree for the wood nor would you build a forge to create hammers, nails, and a saw blade.

Starting with an acorn is not the preferred way to begin building a wooden box

Instead you might reuse materials and tools from a previous project or acquire them from an appropriate place such as a lumber or hardware store. You do so because you know there is an available infrastructure that makes this component of the task simple to complete.

Similarly, when developing software for some problem you should also consider *reuse*. Many software libraries have been developed that contain what is called *Application Programmer Interfaces (APIs)*. An API is a collection of programmer resources for developing software for a particular type of application. There are hundreds of APIs available for Java programmers. For example, there are APIs for developing file exchanges, cryptography, telephony, and speech recognition programs. We shall further discuss APIs in the next several chapters. But for now, realize that there might be available software components that can *directly* solve either your entire problem or a component of it. Experienced programmers welcome software reuse because the borrowed software often has been analyzed already and proven to be effective.

For example, suppose a client asked us to produce a program that examines their customer accounts to determine which customer has the largest outstanding balance and which customer has the largest unfilled order. We could make use of an API that contained searching methods. Such methods have been well understood for many years. For both of the client's tasks we can make use of a method that searches a list of numbers for the largest value.

Besides the direct use of previously developed materials, you also should be open to the *indirect* use of the materials. By indirect use we mean that we adapt for the problem at hand some previously developed information structure or method that solved an analo-

Figure 1.15 **Finding the largest value is independent of the measure.**

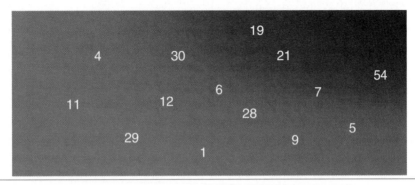

gous problem. For example, suppose you already have developed a process that reported the weight of the largest crystal in a list of crystal weights from some chemical annealing experiment. The procedure that determined the largest weight probably could be used to find the number of copies sold by the most popular book from a list of book sales. Numbers are numbers. When you are finding the largest number in a list all that matters is the size of the number. It does not matter what units the numbers are measuring (see Figure 1.15).

Because you want to reuse previously developed materials, it makes sense that you develop a solution process with as few assumptions as possible. That way, you increase your chances of being able to reuse those materials.

1.7.5 FURTHER READING

There are many ways to problem solve and to program. An interesting sociological examination of different styles can be found in

- Sherry Turkle and Seymour Papert, Epistemological Pluralism: Styles and Voices Within the Computer Culture, *Signs: A Journal of Women in Culture and Society*, pp. 128–157, Autumn, 1990.

This work inspired some of the remarks in this section.

For the interested reader there are many fine books on problem solving with perhaps the most famous one being

- George Polya, *How to Solve It; A New Aspect of Mathematical Method*, Princeton Press, 1988 (reissue edition).

Two others to consider are

- Wayne A. Wickelgren, *How to Solve Mathematical Problems*, Dover Publications, 1995.

- Paul Zeitz, *The Art and Craft of Problem Solving*, John Wiley & Sons, 1999.

1.8 REVIEW

- Information is encoded in a computer using the binary number system. A binary digit is called a bit.
- The basic unit of storage in a computer is a byte or 8 bits.
- The central processing unit, or CPU, is the brain of a computer. It is where computations are performed and decisions are made.
- A microprocessor is a computer on a single chip.
- Performing the action specified by an instruction is known as executing the instruction.
- A program is a sequence of instructions that performs some task.
- A network enables computers to share resources and to transmit data among the computers.
- An operating system is system software that controls and manages the computing resources such as the memory, the input and output devices, and the CPU.
- A programming language is a language for giving commands or instructions to a computer.
- A translator translates a program from one language to another.
- A machine language consists of primitive operations that a computer can perform directly.
- A compiler is a type of translator that typically translates a program written in one language to another language. The typical compiler translates a high-level language program to a low-level language program (e.g., into object codes or bytecodes).
- An interpreter is a translator that both translates and executes the source program.
- A Java compiler translates a Java program into bytecodes. Bytecodes are similar to object codes in that they are low-level instructions. The advantage of a bytecode is that it is machine neutral.
- A Java bytecode interpreter is known as a Java Virtual Machine.
- Abstraction is the process of isolating the essential, inherent aspects of an object while ignoring nonessential or irrelevant details.
- Encapsulation or information hiding is the process of separating the external aspects of an object, which can be viewed or accessed by other objects, from the internal implementation details, which should be hidden from other objects.
- Modularity is the process of dividing an object into smaller pieces so each small object or module can be dealt with individually.
- Object-oriented languages provide a way of forming an abstraction by organizing the properties and messages into a single concept. In particular, abstractions are organized normally so that properties are encapsulated—the accessing and modifying of the properties is done via messages.
- A type is a collection of values and the operations that can be performed on those values.
- A class is a type where the values of the associated objects are viewed as properties and the operations on the objects include message handling.

- In practical terms, a class can be thought of as a model or template for an object. From the class, objects with specific properties can be created, or instantiated.
- When doing problem solving, the recommended steps are
  - *Analysis*: Determine the inputs, outputs, and components of the problem.
  - *Design*: Describe the necessary information and the necessary methods to manipulate that information to solve your problem.
  - *Implementation*: Write the code that implements the various information structures and their associated methods, and write the code that manages the overall process.
  - *Testing*: Test the various code components individually and collectively.

1.9   SELF-TEST

S1.1   What information must the CPU supply to a memory controller to update an attribute of an object?

S1.2   How many of bits of memory are there in a machine with 64 megawords of memory where a *word* is 4 bytes?

S1.3   Give the decimal value of the following numbers:
  a) 01001_2 b) 11111100_2
  c) 0110100_2 d) 1111111110_2
  e) 1010001100101111_2 f) 11111111_2

S1.4   Suppose we have a machine with three words of memory, w_1, w_2, and w_3 with currently w_1 and w_2 in use. Give a sequence of instructions that interchanges the value stored in w_1 and w_2.

S1.5   What kind of program translator is an interpreter?

S1.6   What is a type in the context of a programming language?

S1.7   What is a class?

S1.8   What is a bytecode?

1.10   EXERCISES

1.1   Why is the CPU the brain of the computer?

1.2   How do we measure the power of a CPU?

1.3   How many bytes are there in 10 gigabytes?

1.4   What is the difference in uses between main memory and disk space?

1.5   A computer has 64 megabytes of memory. Exactly how many bits of memory does it have?

1.6   Convert the following numbers to decimal representation.
  a) 111111_2 b) 1001011_2
  c) 1010010011_2 d) 1001111_2
  e) 10000001_2 f) 1010110_2

1.7   What are the differences between assembly and machine language programs?

1.8   What are the differences between assembly and high-level language programs?

1.9   How does Java translation differ from most other high-level program translation?

1.10   What is a Java Virtual Machine?

1.11   Find out all you can about one of the machines in a computer laboratory at your school. At a minimum, you should obtain the following information:

   a) The name of the company that manufactured the microprocessor in the machine.

   b) The clock speed of the processor.

   c) The amount of RAM in the machine.

   d) The size of the hard disk.

   e) The resolution of the graphics display.

   f) The name and version of the operating system.

1.12   Find an advertisement for one of the mail-order companies that sell computers. Find out what the acronyms and terms in the advertisement mean. Some of the terms and acronyms you might see are cache, PnP, SCSI, EIDE, burst mode, EPP, USB, and Firewire.

1.13   The capacity of hard disk drives doubles approximately every 18 months with cost remaining constant. Current hard drives have a capacity of approximately 200 gigabytes and cost about $300. How much can we expect to pay per gigabyte in six years?

1.14   For the operating system you are using, name the commands that manipulate files. In particular, name the command that performs the following actions:

   a) Delete a file.   b) Rename a file.
   c) Copy a file.   d) Move a file.
   e) Create a directory.   f) Delete a directory.

1.15   Interview a computer scientist at your institution. Write a one-page summary of the interview. Here are some questions you might ask the interviewee:

   a) Why did you choose to become a computer scientist?

   b) What are your areas of research expertise?

   c) What are the most important research problems in your research area?

   d) What are the most important research problems in the field of computer science?

   e) Do you work with industry in your research? Which companies are your industrial partners? What are the advantages/disadvantages of working on research with industrial partners?

1.16   What is software engineering? What are its goals? Elaborate.

1.17   Define abstraction, encapsulation, modularity, and hierarchy in your own terms.

1.18   Describe the differences between a class and a object

1.19   Consider an automated teller machine (ATM) at a bank. What are the relevant properties of an ATM for the following people?

   a) ATM user   b) ATM repair person

c) Bank teller   d) Bank president

1.20 Give an example of encapsulation at work in a telephone-answering machine.

1.21 Most organizations have a hierarchical structure. Pick an organization to which you belong and produce a diagram that illustrates its hierarchy.

1.22 Are the following objects? Justify your answer.
a) Beauty   b) Time
c) Jealousy   d) Tree
e) Forest   f) Quantum mechanics

1.23 Most electronic devices are designed using the principle of modularity, which makes the devices easier to manufacture and repair. Name the major components or modules of the following devices:
a) Television   b) VCR
c) Microwave oven   d) Boom box
e) Radio   f) Telephone

1.24 In an object-oriented inheritance hierarchy, the objects at each level are more specialized than the objects at the higher levels. Give three real-world examples of a hierarchy with this property.

1.25 Suppose you have been assigned the job of developing software for the following activities. Formulate a list of relevant questions to ask of your client.

a) Calendar scheduler

b) Spell checker

c) Contacts organizer

1.26 Suppose you have been asked to test software that has been developed for the following applications. Suggest possible test instances and explain their purpose.
a) Rational number calculator (e.g., $\frac{1}{3} + \frac{5}{8}$)
b) Two-dimensional point plotter
c) Loan calculator

1.27 Sketch the object-oriented design of the card game blackjack. What are the key objects? What are the properties and behaviors of these objects? How do the objects interact?

1.28 Sketch the object-oriented design of a system to control a soda-dispensing machine. What are the key objects? What are the properties and behaviors of these objects? How do the objects interact?

1.29 Give an abstraction for rational numbers (e.g, 6/21, 4/30).

1.30 Give an abstraction for a two-dimensional coordinate.

1.31 Give an abstraction for a pixel.

1.32 A traveler with three animals needs to cross the river in a rowboat that can fit at most the traveler and two of the animals at a time. An animal left temporarily by itself is okay. However, if two animals are left alone together even temporarily, they will attack each other. Give a solution for getting the traveler and all three animals safely across the river.

1.33 The Tower of Hanoi puzzle starts with 3 pegs and a stack of 64 rings on the left-most peg. The rings are arranged in order of increasing diameter from top to bottom. The goal of the puzzle is to end up with the stack of 64 rings on the rightmost peg. You are allowed to move only one ring at a time and it must go from one peg directly to another peg. In addition, you can never place a ring of greater diameter on top of a ring of lesser diameter. Give a divide-and-conquer solution for the puzzle.

1.11	SELF-TEST ANSWERS

S1.1 To update the value of an object's attribute the CPU must specify to the memory controller the address of that attribute and the value that is to be stored in that address.

S1.2 A machine with 64 megawords has 64×4 megabytes. Because a byte consists of 8 bits, there are a total of $64 \times 4 \times 8$ megabits = 2048 megabits = 2 gigabits.

S1.3 The decimal conversions are

a) $01001_2 = 9$
b) $11111100_2 = 252$
c) $0110100_2 = = 52$
d) $1111111110_2 = 1,022$
e) $1010001100101111_2 = 41,744$
f) $11111111_2 = 255$

S1.4 To swap w_1 and w_2, we first use w_3 as a temporary holder of w_1's original value. We then update w_1 with w_2's value. We then update w_2 with w_3's value. That is,

w_3 is assigned the value of w_1
w_1 is assigned the value of w_2
w_2 is assigned the value of w_3

S1.5 An interpreter is a translator that both translates and executes the source program.

S1.6 A type is a collection of values and the operations that can be performed on those values.

S1.7 A class is a type where the values of the associated objects are viewed as properties and the operations on the objects include message handling.

S1.8 Bytecodes are machine-neutral, low-level instructions similar in purpose to object codes.

CHAPTER

2 JAVA BASICS

This chapter introduces the basics of Java program design. It presents a series of programs that interact with their users through text-based outputs and inputs. The chapter also introduces the Java primitive types. These types and their associated operators enable programs to create and manipulate integer, floating-point, and character values and variables. The chapter provides detailed coverage of the assignment operator and getting input values. The assignment operator enables variables to be modified. Understanding its behavior is a key concept that all programmers must master. Of equal importance is understanding how to input data values—for most programs to be useful, they must be able to react to user requests.

OBJECTIVES

- Introduce basic program structures using interesting examples.
- Demonstrate how to trace through programs to understand their execution.
- Demonstrate the importance of good programming style.
- Describe how to produce character and numeric output.
- Introduce operators, expressions, and the primitive integer, floating-point, and character types.
- Explain the roles of variables and constants in a program.
- Use Scanner objects as a means of getting input values to a program.
- Introduce method invocation and parameter passing.
- Present the assignment operation and demonstrate its importance in performing computations.

2.1 A FIRST PROGRAM

As part of the computing introduction of Chapter 1, we listed program `DisplayFore-cast.java`. Because the program performs a straightforward task with a minimal amount of language mechanics, we use it to give a sense of basic program structure. The task of program `DisplayForecast.java` is to display an alleged forecast by Thomas Watson. The two-line quotation is *output* (displayed) to a *console window* (i.e., a window that enables commands to be entered at a prompt). The message output by the program is

```
I think there is a world market for maybe five computers.
    Thomas Watson, IBM, 1943.
```

A copy of `DisplayForecast.java` file is given in Listing 2.1. A run of the program is given in Figure 2.1.

Listing 2.1 **DisplayForecast.java**

```
1.  // Authors: J. P. Cohoon and J. W. Davidson
2.  // Purpose: display a quotation in a console window
3.
4.  public class DisplayForecast {
5.
6.      // method main(): application entry point
7.      public static void main(String[] args) {
8.          System.out.print("I think there is a world market for");
9.          System.out.println(" maybe five computers.");
10.         System.out.println("   Thomas Watson, IBM, 1943.");
11.     }
12. }
```

The heart of the program is the three *statements* that display our message (lines 8–10). Each of the statements is an instruction to be executed. Together, they cause the forecast and its attribution to be displayed.

The statements are part of a method named `main()` (lines 7–11). A *method* is the Java term for a *named* unit of code that performs some action or implements some behavior. Some programming languages use the terms *function* or *procedure* or *subroutine* instead of method.

Method `main()` is part of the class `DisplayForecast` (lines 4–12). A *class* defines an object form. (Some programmers use the term declare rather than define.) Think of a class as a model or template for an object. Besides having methods that implement behaviors, objects also can have attributes (*data fields* or *data values*).

The other parts of program `DisplayForecast.java` are *comments* that document the authors, purpose, and parts of the program (lines 1, 2, and 6) and *whitespace*, which is used to make the various elements of the program more distinct (lines 3 and 5).

We now discuss in more detail the form and meaning of the twelve lines of code that make up program `DisplayForecast.java`. The discussion begins with how and why commenting is done. We then discuss the basics of class definitions, statement formation, method definitions, and displaying output.

Figure 2.1   **Executing DisplayForecast.java.**

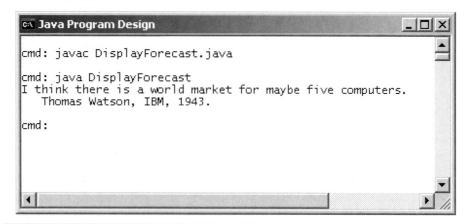

Resources

All programs defined in this text are available at www.javaprogramdesign.com.

2.1.1   ## COMMENTING AND WHITESPACE

A fact that is sometimes difficult for beginning programmers to appreciate fully is that the typical program is read frequently by many other people. A program must be composed of legal Java (i.e., be understandable to the compiler). However, we also want other programmers to understand the program.

Thousands of programmers often work on large commercial software systems. Some programmers might add new features, while others fix *bugs*, the programming term for errors. To accomplish their tasks, programmers must be able to understand how their assigned programs work. Thus, it is important to write and document programs so that other people can understand what they do and if necessary *debug* them (remove errors).

Even when we write programs for our personal use, modification often is necessary. Although we understood how the program worked when we wrote it, as months or years pass, we may forget important details.

Comments are the mechanism that enables us to include notes in a program. These notes are *not* processed by the compiler. Their purpose is to help explain and document how the program works and who its authors are.

Keeping in mind the importance of commenting, program `DisplayForecast.java` begins on lines 1–2 with two *single-line program heading comments*. The double slash delimiter `//` indicates that the rest of the line is a comment to be ignored by the compiler.

Comment that identifies the
authors of the program

```
// Authors: J. P. Cohoon and J. W. Davidson
// Purpose: display a quotation in a console window
```

Consecutive double slashes indicate that the
remainder of the line is a comment

Comment that explains the
purpose of the program

These header comments help readers of the program by indicating both a point of contact for asking questions and the program's purpose.

Line 6 of `DisplayForecast.java` is another single-line comment. The comment describes an important fact about the method that follows—the method is the one where our program starts its execution.

```
method main(): application entry point
```

Observe that the comment on line 6 is indented with respect to line 4. When coding, programmers use *indentation* to indicate that the indented material is a component of the material that preceded it. The comment of line 6 and the method that follows are indented because together they make up the definition of class `DisplayForecast`.

When a program component itself is made up of parts, those parts are indented further. For example, because lines 8–10 make up the actions of method `main()`, they are indented with respect to line 7. Each level of indentation is normally three or four characters wide.

The comment and method are
indented because they are
elements of class DisplayForecast

```
public class DisplayForecast {
   // method main(): application entry point
   public static void main(String[] args) {
      System.out.print("I think there is a world market
for");
      System.out.println(" maybe five computers.");
      System.out.println("   Thomas Watson, IBM, 1943.");
   }
}
```

The statements are indented further
because they are elements of method
main()

Lines 3 and 5 of our program are blank lines. Blank lines can be as important as comments. They enable the various sections of a program to be visually distinct, making the program easier to read and understand. *Whitespace* characters (i.e., blanks, tabs, etc.)

between the various elements of a program are ignored during translation, so they can be inserted as deemed appropriate.

Attention to detail

The single-line comment delimiter // must be typed with no whitespace between the slashes when entering the delimiter into your program file. The presence of whitespace would alter the meaning. For example, whitespace between the slashes would mean that a malformed arithmetic expression was being entered, rather than a comment.

2.1.2   CLASSES, KEYWORDS, AND IDENTIFIERS

The fourth line of program `DisplayForecast.java` begins the definition of the class `DisplayForecast`. All Java programs consist of at least one class definition.

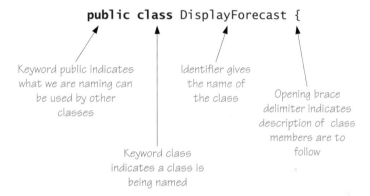

The class definition for program `DisplayForecast.java` begins with the two *keywords* **public** and **class**. Keywords are words that are reserved by the Java language for particular purposes. Because keywords have special meanings, they cannot be changed by the programmer and they cannot be used by the programmer to name things. Keywords are case sensitive and consist of only lowercase letters. Thus the strings

    `PUBLIC`   `Public`

are not keywords. Instead they are valid Java names, or in programming parlance, *identifiers*. Using them as identifiers is not recommended, because readers of your code might not notice the case differences and become confused. A complete list of keywords appears in Appendix A.2. In this text, keywords are displayed in a bold-face monospaced font.

The keyword **class** on line 4 indicates that a class definition is being initiated. Java permits *modifiers* to be placed in front of the keyword **class**. These modifiers can place restrictions on the nature of the class being defined. Modifier **public** indicates that Java classes in other files are permitted to create and use objects of the class in question. A file is allowed to contain at most one **public** class.

The name of the class being defined comes next. Java requires that the name of a public class have the same name as its program file. Therefore, the name of this class is `DisplayForecast`.

Following the name of the class is a left brace {. Java uses braces {} to *delimit* the statements that make up the definition of a class. For class `DisplayForecast`, the right brace on line 12 is the matching brace for the left brace on line 4. Therefore, lines 4–12 contain the definition of `DisplayForecast`.

The rule for forming a valid name is that it must be a valid Java identifier and cannot clash with the keywords. Java's rules for a valid identifier are as follows:

- An identifier must begin with an alphabetic letter, underscore (_), or a dollar sign ($);
- Subsequent characters in an identifier (if any) must be either alphabetic, digits, underscores, or dollar signs;
- Whitespace cannot be embedded among the characters that form an identifier.
- An identifier cannot be composed of more than 65,535 characters.

Examples of valid Java identifiers are

```
height    firstValue    LIGHT_YEAR    $amount    München    π
```

The identifiers München and π might seem surprising. Because Java is an international language, rather than using the customary ASCII character set, it uses the Unicode character set, an international standard. This character set is sufficiently rich to write the major world languages. In particular, the German ü and the Greek π are available with Unicode.

Besides `DisplayForecast`, the other identifier names in `DisplayForecast.java` are `main`, `String`, `args`, `System`, `out`, `print`, and `println`. Identifier `main` is the name of the method where program execution begins; `String` and `System` are the names of Java classes; `args` and `out` are variables that enable us to reference some program resources; and `print` and `println` are the names of methods that enable messages to be sent to the console.

Naming

Besides being a legal identifier, a name should be descriptive of its purpose. For example, use `height` rather than the ambiguous `h` or `ht`. We will discuss naming conventions as we introduce different program elements. The conventions used in this text are based on the standard Java code conventions. Sun Microsystems provides an easy-to-read document that discusses standard code conventions at its website `www.javasoft.com/docs/codeconv`.

2.1.3 METHODS

The *entry point* (starting point) of execution for a Java application program is in a method `main()`. (As indicated previously, a method is a named piece of code.) The style convention for this text when referring to a method is to include a pair of parentheses after its name. The parentheses are a visual cue that we are referring to a method.

In general, a Java method definition may have the following elements in the specified order with the italicized elements being optional.

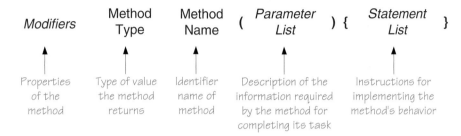

For `DisplayForecast`'s method `main()`, modifiers **public** and **static** are used. Method modifier **public** indicates that the method can be used by other Java classes. These other classes can be defined either in the same file or in other files. Modifier **static** indicates that `main()` is to be a service provided by the class that does not require association with a particular class object. In the object-oriented programming methodology, such methods are known as *class* methods.

Some methods *return* (produce) values that can be used by the part of the program that *invoked* (started up) the methods to be *executed* or *run* (carried out). For example, a square root method returns the square root of its *parameter*, where a parameter is a value given to the method so that it can perform its task. A square root method when invoked with the parameter 64, returns the value 8, and when invoked with the parameter 144, returns the value 12.

Some methods accomplish their task without returning values. Such methods, like method `main()`, are labeled **void** to indicate that no value is returned.

In giving its definition, a pair of left and right parentheses follows the name of a method. The parentheses can contain optionally a *formal parameter list*. The formal parameters describe the types of information that are given to the method when it is invoked. For example, a square root method would expect a number for its parameter.

> Chapters 3 and 4 discuss the basics of parameter passing. Chapter 7 considers parameter passing in detail

In the case of the method `main()` of an application program, Java requires a single parameter of type `String[]`, where type `String[]` is a representation for a list of strings. The meaning behind this particular parameter is deferred to Chapter 8.

Naming

By convention, the parameter to method `main()` has the name `args`. So all of the application programs that we develop have a method `main()` with a formal parameter list `String[] args`.

A pair of matching braces follows the parenthesis that marks the end of the formal parameter list. These braces group the statement list that makes up the method's action.

For method `main()` of `DisplayForecast.java`, the statement list is the statements of lines 8–10.

```
System.out.print("I think there is a world market for");
System.out.println(" maybe five computers.");
System.out.println("   Thomas Watson, IBM, 1943.");
```

In Java, a single statement can span multiple lines so there must be some delimiter that indicates that the statement is finished. The semicolon (`;`) serves this purpose—much as a period serves to end this sentence.

When a Java interpreter starts to run a Java application program, the *flow of control* is given to the application's method `main()`. This action causes the statements of the method `main()` to be executed in order. Therefore, when program `DisplayForecast.java` runs, the statement in line 8 is executed first, then the statements in lines 9 and 10 are executed.

2.1.4   SELECTING METHODS PRINT() AND PRINTLN()

As noted previously, the statement list that specifies the behavior of method `main()` is

```
System.out.print("I think there is a world market for");
System.out.println(" maybe five computers.");
System.out.println("   Thomas Watson, IBM, 1943.");
```

The statements cause our quotation to be displayed in the window in which the program is executed (see Figure 2.1). The quotation is displayed because of the capabilities of the class `System`, which is one of the *standard* (official) Java classes. In particular, `System` is part of a package named `java.lang`, where *package* is the Java term for a software library.

Program `DisplayForecast.java` needs access to a *member* (component) `out` of `System`. To access `System` member `out`, the program *selects* it from `System` using the period (`.`), which is Java's *selector* mechanism.

Member `out` is a *variable*, which means it has a value. With that value, the program has access to an object for displaying text to the console window running the application. This object is known as an *output stream*, where a stream is a programming term for an object representing an output device such as a monitor or an input device such as a keyboard or a file. The methods associated with a stream object enable a programmer to interact with the device without being concerned with low-level details of the device's operation.

Because of its association with the console window, the `System.out` output stream is known as the *standard output stream*. Java uses its standard class `PrintStream` to represent the standard output stream. Figure 2.2 provides a representation of `System.out` and its relation to `PrintStream`.

Figure 2.2   **System.out representation.**

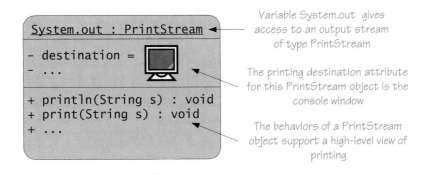

Figure 2.3   **Member selection.**

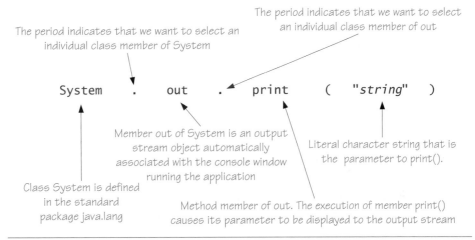

The standard output stream has *member methods* named `print()` and `println()` that the program invokes to print the forecast. Member methods are the means by which objects have behaviors.

The `print()` and `println()` methods are invoked through additional applications of the period selector. Figure 2.3 demonstrates the selection process for the invocation in line 8.

When invoked, the behavior performed by method `print()` is to display the value of its parameter to the associated output stream. In this case, the output stream is the console window running the program and the parameter is the *literal character string* `"I think there is a world market for"`, where a literal character string is a sequence of characters delimited on both sides by the double quote character (`"`).

A literal character string is *not* allowed to span multiple lines in your program. Therefore, the following statement is illegal in Java.

```
System.out.print("I think there is a world
market for ");
```

Illegal a literal character
cannot span multiple lines

When a method is invoked, the action associated with the method is executed. For method `print()`, its action causes its character string argument to be displayed in the console window at the point where the *window cursor* is located currently. A cursor is a special window symbol. It is typically a blinking rectangle or underscore.

After displaying the argument, the cursor is located immediately after the last character that was displayed. In the following depiction of the `print()` output, the ■ is our representation for the cursor.

I think there is a world market ■

After executing the first print()
statement, the cursor is located
immediately after the "t" in market

Method `println()` differs from `print()` in that after displaying its parameter, it moves the cursor to the start of the next line in the window. Therefore, after the execution of the first `println()` statement, program output looks like

I think there is a world market for maybe five computers.
■

After executing the first println()
statement, the cursor is located at
the start of the next line

The execution of the second `println()` statement completes the program output.

I think there is a world market for maybe five computers.
   Thomas Watson, IBM, 1943.

Experiment

The next several programs are similar to `DisplayForecast.java` in that they output textual information. A way to view them is as experiments with the `print()` and `println()` methods. You are encouraged strongly to take the code and make further modifications. Observing how modifications affect program behavior is often an effective way to start making sense of programming constructs.

Suppose instead of displaying a quotation, we wanted to display the following reminders.

   Jan 1: send card to mom.
   May 9: send card to dad.
   May 15: send card to parents.
   Sep 20: send card to in-laws.

With an understanding of `DisplayForecast.java`, such a program should now be easy to write. We call the program displaying the four reminders `CalendarDisplay.java`. The program is presented in Listing 2.2. Notice that we left out the author portion of our header commentary. We continue this policy throughout the remainder of the text. We do so because the authors are obvious within a textbook.

Each of the four `println()` statements in `CalendarDisplay.java`'s method `main()` causes a new output line to be displayed.

```
Jan 1: send card to mom.
May 9: send card to dad.
May 15: send card to parents.
Sep 20: send card to in-laws.
```

Listing 2.2   CalendarDisplay.Java

```
 1.  // Purpose: display a series of four reminders
 2.
 3.  public class CalendarDisplay {
 4.
 5.      // main(): application entry point
 6.      public static void main(String[] args) {
 7.          System.out.println("Jan 1: send card to mom.");
 8.          System.out.println("May 9: send card to dad.");
 9.          System.out.println("May 15: send card to parents.");
10.          System.out.println("Sep 20: send card to in-laws.");
11.      }
12.  }
```

2.1.5   ESCAPE SEQUENCES

Now suppose that we want a program that displays the following quotation of Daniel Hillis from *The Pattern on the Stone* (1999):

> "The difference between the right program and almost the right program is like the difference between lightning and a lightning bug. The difference is just a bug."

The following `print()` and `println()` statements correctly display the text.

```
System.out.print("The difference between the right ");
System.out.println("program and almost the right");
System.out.print("program is like the difference between ");
System.out.println("lightning and a lightning");
System.out.println("bug. The difference is just a bug.");
```

The display produced is the following.

```
The difference between the right program and almost the right
program is like the difference between lightning and a lightning
bug. The difference is just a bug.
```

However, suppose we wanted quotation marks to also be displayed at the start and end of the quotation. A program for this task is given in Listing 2.3. The program is called QuotationDisplay.java.

Listing 2.3 **QuotationDisplay.java**

```
 1. // Purpose: display a quoted quotation
 2.
 3. public class QuotationDisplay {
 4.
 5.     // main(): application entry point
 6.     public static void main(String[] args) {
 7.         System.out.print("\"The difference between the right ");
 8.         System.out.println("program and almost the right");
 9.         System.out.print("program is like the difference between ");
10.         System.out.println("lightning and a lightning ");
11.         System.out.println("bug. The difference is just a bug.\"");
12.     }
13. }
```

The program uses *escape sequences* to produce the quotation marks. An escape sequence is a special two-character sequence representing another character. Without escape sequences it would not be possible to have a literal character string containing a double quote.

Java uses the backslash character \ as the starting character in an escape sequence. The escape sequence for a double quote is \". Thus, to display quotation marks around our quotation, we modify the actions of method main() from QuotationDis-play.java as follows.

```
System.out.print("\"The difference between the right ");
System.out.println("program and almost the right");
System.out.print("program is like the difference between ");
System.out.println("lightning and a lightning");
System.out.println("bug. The difference is just a bug.\"");
```

In the first statement, we added the double quote escape sequence at the start of the literal character string and in the last statement we added the double quote escape sequence at the end of the literal character string. The output of the program is now

```
"The difference between the right program and almost the right
program is like the difference between lightning and a lightning
bug. The difference is just a bug."
```

Java defines several escape sequences. For example, \t is the escape sequence for a tab character, \n is the escape sequence for a newline character, and \\ is the escape sequence for a backslash. The complete list is given in Table 2.1.

The newline escape sequence gives us the ability to move the cursor to the start of the next line in the midst of an output operation. For example, program PetDisplay.java of Listing 2.4 uses the single statement

```
System.out.println("Nilla\nBuffer\nDarby\nGalen");
```

Table 2.1	Java escape sequences.

Escape Sequence	Meaning
\b	backspace
\n	newline
\t	tab
\r	carriage return
\\	backslash
\"	double quote
\'	single quote

Listing 2.4   **PetDisplay.java**

```
1. // Purpose: display pet names
2.
3. public class PetDisplay {
4.
5.     // main(): application entry point
6.     public static void main(String[] args) {
7.         System.out.println("Nilla\nBuffer\nDarby\nGalen");
8.     }
9. }
```

to display four lines to standard output—the names of past and present family pets.

```
Nilla
Buffer
Darby
Galen
```

Program `TabularDisplay.java` of Listing 2.5 uses the tab escape sequence to produce tabular output. The output of the program is

```
Person  Height  Shoe size
=========================
Hannah  5'1"     8
Jenna   5'10"    9
JJ      6'1"     14
Joanne  5'5"     8.5
Jim     6'4"     15
```

Programmers normally use the tab escape sequence rather than a tab character in literal strings because it explicitly tells the reader that a tab is being used rather than what might appear to be an arbitrary number of spaces.

We now turn our attention to programs that make use of some of the numeric types provided by Java. We use these types and their associated operators to create and manipulate values and variables. Understanding how to manipulate values and variables is a crucial programming skill.

Listing 2.5   **TabularDisplay.java**

```
1.  // Purpose: display a quoted quotation
2.
3.  public class TabularDisplay {
4.
5.      // main(): application entry point
6.      public static void main(String[] args) {
7.          System.out.println("Person\tHeight\tShoe size");
8.          System.out.println("=========================");
9.          System.out.println("Hannah\t5'1\"\t8");
10.         System.out.println("Jenna\t5'10\"\t9");
11.         System.out.println("JJ\t6'1\"\t14");
12.         System.out.println("Joanne\t5'5\"\t8.5");
13.         System.out.println("Jim\t6'4\"\t15");
14.     }
15. }
```

Syntax errors

When an invalid Java program is translated, the compiler produces a list of *syntax errors*. A syntax error is a violation of the rules for defining a valid program. For example, suppose the definition of class DisplayForecast had contained incorrectly

public class DisplayForecast (

The Java compiler will display an error message indicating that the left parenthesis was not expected.

When a compiler indicates a syntax error has been found on a particular line, the adjacent lines often need to be examined also. For example, a common mistake in entering a program is to forget a semicolon. This syntax error often is associated with the line after the statement that had the missing semicolon. The mistake is reported there because the error does not occur until that code is considered—it is the starting element of what was intended to be a new statement that is unexpected.

2.2   SIMPLE COMPUTATIONS

Good programmers often write short programs that compute useful things. For example, a value of interest to many people is their *body mass index* (BMI), which is a metric measure of fitness and health. According to the U.S. National Center for Chronic Disease Prevention and Health Promotion Nutrition and Physical Activity at www.cdc.gov, people with scores less than 18.5 may be underweight for their height; people with scores 25 or greater may be overweight for their height; and people with in between scores may be considered normal.

Computing a BMI is a straightforward calculation—it is the ratio of the person's weight in kilograms to the square of the person's height in meters. Thus, in developing a program to compute a particular BMI, two values of interest are the person's metric weight and height. With these two values, the BMI value can be calculated.

Listing 2.6 BMI.java

```java
1.  // Purpose: Compute body mass index for given weight and height
2.
3.  public class BMI {
4.
5.      // main(): application entry point
6.      public static void main(String[] args) {
7.          // define constants
8.          final double KILOGRAMS_PER_POUND = 0.454;
9.          final double METERS_PER_FOOT = 0.3046;
10.
11.         // set up person's characteristics
12.         double weightInPounds = 75.5;   // our person's weight
13.         double heightInFeet = 4.5;      // our person's height
14.
15.         // convert to metric equivalents
16.         double metricWeight = weightInPounds * KILOGRAMS_PER_POUND;
17.         double metricHeight = heightInFeet * METERS_PER_FOOT;
18.
19.         // perform bmi calculation
20.         double bmi = metricWeight / (metricHeight * metricHeight);
21.
22.         // display result
23.         System.out.println("A person with");
24.         System.out.println("  weight " + weightInPounds + " lbs");
25.         System.out.println("  height " + heightInFeet + " feet");
26.         System.out.println("has a BMI of " + Math.round(bmi));
27.     }
28. }
```

The authors live in the United States, and in the United States, weights and heights are expressed normally in the English system of pounds and feet. Therefore, in producing a BMI calculator of general use here, four other values are of interest. Two of these values are the particular person's weight in pounds and height in feet. The other two values are the constants 0.454 and 0.3046, which are respectively the number of kilograms per pound and the number of meters per foot. With these four values, the person's metric weight and height can be calculated, which in turn enables the BMI value to be calculated.

Program BMI.java of Listing 2.6 defines and manipulates these seven values to compute and display the BMI for a person of particular weight and height (75.5 lbs and 4.5 feet tall).

The output of the program is

```
A person with
    weight 75.5 lbs
    height 4.5 feet
has a BMI of 18
```

One difference between this program and our previous programs is the introduction of comments within method `main()`. The internal comments serve to highlight and explain the major activities of the method.

```
// define constants ...
// set up person's characteristics ...
// convert to metric equivalents ...
// perform bmi calculation ...
// display result ...
```

In the following discussion, the other differences between this program and previous programs are highlighted. These differences represent important new program elements.

2.2.1   CONSTANTS

One important difference of `BMI.java` from previous programs is its use of *primitive constants* and *variables* of *type* **double**. A type is essentially a set of values along with the operators that can manipulate and create values from that set.

A Java type is classified as either a *primitive* or *reference type*. The primitive types support the manipulation of numeric, character, and logical values. The type **double** is a numeric primitive type for *floating-point* values; that is, decimal values such as `75.5` and `4.5`. Reference types are used to represent values that are more complex in nature such as an output stream, a bank record, or a graphical user interface. These more complex values are called objects as they have generally both attributes and behaviors.

> The primitive types are discussed in Section 2.3

A *constant* is the symbolic name for a memory location whose value cannot be changed once the program has initialized the location. Its name must be a valid Java identifier.

Before we can use a constant in a calculation, we must first define and initialize the constant. A constant definition normally takes the following form.

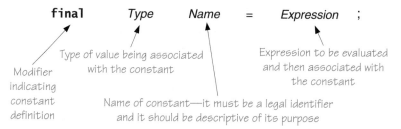

In particular, line 8 of method `main()` statement makes KILOGRAMS_PER_POUND a **double** constant.

```
final double KILOGRAMS_PER_POUND = 0.454;
```

The statement associates `KILOGRAMS_PER_POUND` with a memory location containing the *literal* **double** floating-point value `0.454`, where a literal numeric value is a number. The effect of the definition is depicted in the diagram that follows. (In this and subsequent depictions, a lock indicates that the value cannot be changed.)

KILOGRAMS_PER_FOOT   0.454

The contents of the location are fixed during program execution because of the use of the modifier keyword **final**. The keyword **double** indicates that the constant being defined is associated with a **double** value. The semicolon after the definition indicates that no more **double** constants are being defined in this statement. From this point on in method `main()`, `KILOGRAMS_PER_POUND` is synonymous with the **double** value `0.454`.

Similarly, the statement

final double METERS_PER_FOOT = 0.3046;

makes `METERS_PER_FOOT` synonymous with the **double** value `0.3046`.

METERS_PER_FOOT   0.3046

Java allows several constants to be defined in a single statement by separating the definitions with commas. For example, the following statement defines `DOOR_WIDTH` and `DOOR_HEIGHT` as **double** constants.

final double DOOR_HEIGHT = 2.00, DOOR_WIDTH = 0.75;

Because of concerns of program readability this style of constant definition is discouraged—the definitions do not stand out as much as in individual statements and combining definitions inhibits commenting.

```
final double DOOR_HEIGHT = 2.00;    // meters
final double DOOR_WIDTH = 0.75;     // meters
```

The definitions of constants `DOOR_WIDTH` and `DOOR_HEIGHT` have inline comments. As indicated previously, the `//` indicates the remainder of the line is a comment. There is no requirement that the entire line be a comment.

Constants

Good programmers prefer the systematic use of symbolic names over literal values—so-called "magic" numbers—because the names provide meaning and their use reduces the potential introduction of errant values through incorrect keyboarding.

It is a Java programming convention that the identifier name of a constant be composed of uppercase letters with underscores separating the various words that make up a name. Thus, the use of `KILOGRAMS_PER_POUND` in `BMI.java` rather than `kilogramsPerPound`.

2.2.2   VARIABLES

Besides making use of constants, program `BMI.java` makes use of variables of type **double**. A *variable* is the symbolic name for a memory location whose contents *can* be modified during program execution. A basic variable definition normally takes the following form.

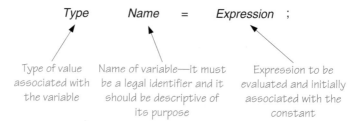

The definition begins with the type of value in which we are interested. The symbolic name comes next, which must be a valid Java identifier. The definition concludes with an equal sign followed by an expression whose value initializes the memory location being associated with the symbolic name.

In our program, `weightInPounds`, `heightInFeet`, `metricWeight`, `metricHeight`, and `bmi` are all local primitive variables of type **double**. They are variables because of the lack of the modifier **final** in their definitions. They are *local* variables because their use is limited to the method that defines them. They are *primitive* variables, because the type **double** is one of Java's primitive types.

> Local versus nonlocal is explored in Chapters 4 and 7

Before we can use a local variable in a calculation, we must first define and initialize the variable. For example, the definition of `weightInPounds` in line 12

```
double weightInPounds = 75.5;   // our person's weight
```

initializes the variable to the **double** value 75.5, where the semicolon indicates that no more **double** variables are being defined in this statement.

The effect of the `weightInPounds` definition is

weightInPounds | 75.5

Because the value of `weightInPounds` is allowed to change, there is no lock used in its depiction.

Similarly, the statement

```
double heightInFeet = 4.5;      // our person's height
```

makes `heightInFeet` a **double** variable whose memory location is initialized to the **double** value 4.5. The effect of the definition is

heightInFeet | 4.5

Together the definitions of `weightInPounds` and `heightInFeet` define the characteristics of the person to be processed.

Java does not require that a variable definition include initialization. For example, consider the following code segment defining local variables `sampleWeight` and `currentTemperature`.

```
double sampleWeight;
double currentTemperature;
```

Local variables are left uninitialized if no initialization value is specified. Our representation of such variables is

sampleWeight	-
currentTemperature	-

where the "-" indicates an uninitialized value.

Although variables can be defined without initialization, Java compilers require that variables be initialized before their values are used.

Multiple variables can be defined in a single statement by separating the definitions by commas. The following statement uses this style to define and initialize **double** variables `currentReading` and `maximumReading`.

```
double currentReading = 6.21, maximumReading = 19.54;
```

As with defining constants, this style of variable definition is discouraged because of program readability. The preferred style has one definition per statement.

```
double currentReading =  6.21;  // meters per second
double maximumReading = 19.54;  // meters per second
```

Naming variables

It is a Java coding style convention that the identifier name of a variable be descriptive of the represented value and that it begin with a lowercase letter. If a variable name is composed of a single word, then the entire name is in lowercase. If a variable name is composed of multiple words, then the words are concatenated together and all letters are lowercase except for the letters that start successive words. Thus, the coding style calls for `bodyTemperature` rather than the nondescriptive `bt` or the underscore using `body_temperature`.

2.2.3   OPERATIONS

The next section of method `main()` from `BMI.java` converts the person's characteristics into their metric equivalents.

```
// convert to metric equivalents
double metricWeight = weightInPounds * KILOGRAMS_PER_POUND;
double metricHeight = heightInFeet * METERS_PER_FOOT;
```

Assignment statement

Section 2.6 discusses the assignment statement, which can assign a value to an uninitialized variable or constant.

The definition of variable `metricWeight` does not initialize the variable with a literal numeric value. Instead, `metricWeight` is initialized with the value of the expression

```
weightInPounds * KILOGRAMS_PER_POUND
```

The expression uses the **double** multiplication operator * to form the product of the current value of variable `weightInPounds` times the constant `KILOGRAMS_PER_POUND`. The product represents the metric equivalent of the weight in pounds. Similarly, the definition

```
double metricHeight = heightInFeet * METERS_PER_FOOT;
```

initializes `metricHeight` with the product of the current value of variable `heightInFeet` times the constant `METERS_PER_FOOT`. Thus, `metricHeight` represents the metric equivalent of the height in feet. The effects of the definition are[†]

| metricWeight | 34.2770 |
| metricHeight | 1.3706 |

Together the two definitions form the conversion section of our program.

At this point, we are ready to compute the BMI of our person. As we stated at the beginning of this section, BMI is the ratio of the person's metric weight to the square of the person's metric height. The program defines a variable `bmi` to store that value.

```
// perform bmi calculation
double bmi = metricWeight / (metricHeight * metricHeight);
```

Variable `bmi` is initialized to the value of the expression

```
metricWeight / (metricHeight * metricHeight)
```

The expression uses the **double** division operator /, **double** multiplication operator *, and the parentheses grouping operators (and). The parentheses cause the subexpression

```
metricHeight * metricHeight
```

to be evaluated as a unit. The value of the subexpression is the square of the current value of variable `metricHeight`. The subexpression value then is divided into `metricWeight`. The result of that division is used to initialize variable `bmi`.

| bmi | 18.2439 |

[†]   When we depict **double** values, the values may be truncated (e.g., the actual value represented by `metricHeight` is 1.3706999999999998).

In general, floating-point division is an approximation of real division. The result is approximate, because Java uses only 8 bytes of memory for each **double** value, which limits the number of digits that can be represented.

The next section of our program displays the BMI information to the user. The section is made up of four `println()` invocations.

```
// display result
System.out.println("A person with");
System.out.println("   weight " + weightInPounds + " lbs");
System.out.println("   height " + heightInFeet + " feet");
System.out.println("has a BMI of " + Math.round(bmi));
```

The first invocation of `println()` is similar to previous `println()` invocations—it gives the method a literal character string for displaying.

```
System.out.println("A person with");
```

After method `println()` completes, the output produced so far is

```
A person with
```

The next invocation of `println()`

```
System.out.println("   weight " + weightInPounds + " lbs");
```

supplies the value of the *expression* `"   weight " + weightInPounds + " lbs"` to `println()`. Our use of the term *expression* is deliberate. `"   weight " + weightInPounds + " lbs"` requires operator evaluation. The expression is composed of two `String` concatenation operations.

A Java compiler can tell by context that the + operators in this expression call for `String` concatenation rather than addition. Operator + performs addition when both of its operands are numeric; the operator performs `String` concatenation when at least one of the operands is a `String`.

> The String class is discussed in detail in Chapter 3

The evaluation of the `String` concatenation expression occurs in the following manner. First, `"   weight "` and `weightInPounds` is evaluated. Because the value of `weightInPounds` is 75.5, the concatenation produces a string with value `"   weight 75.5"`. This string then is concatenated with the literal string `" lbs"`. The resulting string has value `"   weight 75.5 lbs"` and is used as the actual parameter in the `println()` invocation. A pictorial examination of the expression evaluation is given in Figure 2.4.

After executing the statement, the program output to this point is

```
A person with
   weight 75.5 lbs
```

Using similar analysis, after the next `println()` invocation

```
System.out.println("   height " + heightInFeet + " feet");
```

Figure 2.4   **Evaluation of " weight " + weightInPounds + " lbs".**

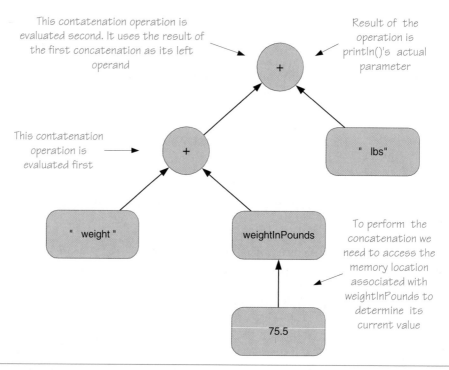

This contatenation operation is evaluated second. It uses the result of the first concatenation as its left operand

Result of the operation is println()'s actual parameter

This contatenation operation is evaluated first

" lbs"

" weight "

weightInPounds

To perform the concatenation we need to access the memory location associated with weightInPounds to determine its current value

75.5

the program output is now

```
A person with
   weight 75.5 lbs
   height 4.5 feet
```

The last `println()` statement requires analysis.

```
System.out.println("has a BMI of " + Math.round(bmi));
```

The program does not display merely the value of variable `bmi`, as in the statement

```
System.out.println("has a BMI of " + bmi);
```

With such a statement the program output would be

```
A person with
   weight 75.5 lbs
   height 4.5 feet
has a BMI of 18.24391242817714
```

The 14 digits displayed after the decimal are distracting and serve no real purpose. Therefore, rather than displaying `bmi`, our statement displays `Math.round(bmi)`.

```
System.out.println("has a BMI of " + Math.round(bmi));
```

Method `Math.round()` is a class method of standard Java class `java.lang.Math`. As it is a class method, the method is a service provided by the class that does not require association with a particular class object. The method takes a **double** floating-point value as its parameter and returns the nearest integer value. Thus, the program outputs

```
A person with
     weight 75.5 lbs
     height 4.5 feet
has a BMI of 18
```

Program `BMI.java` has shown the usefulness of constants, variables, and operators. We now introduce all of the primitive types.

2.3 PRIMITIVE TYPES

Java has seven primitive types besides **double**. There are five primitive integer types **byte**, **short**, **int**, **long**, and **char** (**char** is also the character type); another primitive floating-point type **float**; and a logical type **boolean**, whose values are **true** and **false**. The names of the primitive types are all keywords.

> Chapter 5 examines **boolean** in detail

The different primitive types have different representation capabilities. For example, the **short** uses 2 bytes to represent an integer value and an **int** uses 4 bytes. As a result, a **short** variable can store integer values in the range –32,768 … 32,767, and an **int** variable can store integer values in the range –2,147,483,648 … 2,147,483,647.

As another example of representation capabilities, the **float** type uses 4 bytes to represent a floating-point number and the **double** type uses 8 bytes to represent a floating-point number. As a consequence, a **float** variable has typically 6 places of accuracy and a **double** value has typically 15 places of accuracy.

Java's motivation for having multiple numeric types is to give programmers full access to all the types supported by typical and specialized computer hardware (e.g, PCs, mobile telephones, PDAs). In the applications in this text, we generally use the primary primitive types **int**, **char**, and **double**.

Representation

A complete specification of the values associated with the primitive types is given in Appendix A.3.

2.3.1 INT TYPE

Most programming languages have a basic type for storing and manipulating integer variables and values. In Java this type is **int**.

Java provides the usual integer arithmetic *binary* operators such as addition +, subtraction –, multiplication *, and quotient /, where the term *binary* indicates that the oper-

---

Listing 2.7 **CelsiusToFahrenheit.java**

```java
1.  // Purpose: Convert a Celsius temperature to Fahrenheit
2.
3.  public class CelsiusToFahrenheit {
4.
5.      // main(): application entry point
6.      public static void main(String[] args) {
7.          // set Celsius temperature of interest
8.          int celsius = 28;
9.
10.         // convert to Fahrenheit equivalent
11.         int fahrenheit = 32 + ((9 * celsius) / 5);
12.
13.         // display result
14.         System.out.println("Celsius temperature");
15.         System.out.println("   " + celsius);
16.         System.out.println("equals Fahrenheit temperature");
17.         System.out.println("   " + fahrenheit);
18.     }
19. }
```

---

ator is applied to two operands. The addition, subtraction, and multiplication operators work as expected. For example, 1 + 2 is 3, 18 - 11 is 7, and 3 * 21 is 63.

Integer division sometimes confuses beginning programmers. When given integer operands, the quotient operator produces the integer quotient result (i.e., there is no remainder). For example, 20 / 6 is 3, 19 / 11 is 1, 4 / 5 is 0, and 8 / -3 is -2.

Java also provides a *modulus* operator (%). The modulus operator % produces the remainder associated with an integer division. For example, 18 % 3 is 0, 17 % 2 is 1, 12 % 16 is 12, 7 % –3 is 1 and –7 % 3 is –1. A complete list of integer operators is given in Appendix A.3. Java does not have an exponentiation operator. However, standard class java.lang.Math does provide methods for performing exponentiation.

Listing 2.7 presents a program CelsiusToFahrenheit.java using several **int** operators that converts an integer Celsius temperature of interest to its integer Fahrenheit equivalent. The conversion uses the formula

$$Fahrenheit = 32 + \frac{9}{5}Celcius$$

The output of the program is

```
Celsius temperature
   28
equals Fahrenheit temperature
   82
```

In the program, variable celsius holds the value of our temperature of interest.

```java
int celsius = 28;
```

In writing the definition of **int** variable fahrenheit, we were cognizant of the fact that an **int** initialization expression is being evaluated.

```java
int fahrenheit = 32 + ((9 * celsius) / 5);    // correct
```

For example, we did not express the definition in the manner:

```
int fahrenheit = 32 + ((9 / 5) * celsius);    // incorrect
```

Because of its integer operands, the term 9 / 5 from this errant statement evaluates to 1, which makes the definition equivalent to

```
int fahrenheit = 32 + celsius;                // incorrect
```

The correct implementation reorders and regroups the expression terms 9 and `celsius` so that their product is divided by 5.

2.3.2 CHAR TYPE

Closely related to numeric types is the character type **char**. In Java, characters are encoded in 2 bytes using the Unicode character set encoding.

Normally, programmers do not use a literal numeric representation of a character. Instead they represent the character within single quotes. The compiler will translate automatically the character representation into the Unicode encoding. For example, programmers use `'a'` when they need to refer explicitly to character *a* rather than its Unicode value of 97. Because the underlying representation of **char** is integer, the operators defined on the integer types are defined on **char** variables and values as well.

The Unicode character set encoding guarantees that

```
'0' < '1' < '2' < ... < '9'
'a' < 'b' < 'c' < ... < 'z'
'A' < 'B' < 'C' < ... < 'Z'
```

These relationships are useful, because they enable values that are made up of sequences of characters to be sorted into *lexicographic* (alphabetic) order.

Additionally, with the Unicode character set we know that

```
'2' + 1
```

yields an integer that is the encoding for the character `'3'`. In fact, for any digit *d* except for 9, the expression `'d'` + 1 yields the next sequential character digit. Thus,

- `'0'` + 1 evaluates to `'1'`;
- `'1'` + 1 evaluates to `'2'`;

  ...

- `'8'` + 1 evaluates to `'9'`.

  The following relationship exists with regard to the lowercase Latin letters.

- `'a'` + 1 evaluates to `'b'`;
- `'b'` + 1 evaluates to `'c'`;

  ...

- `'y'` + 1 evaluates to `'z'`.

Listing 2.8 **LowerToUpper.java**

```
1.  // Purpose: Demonstrate char arithmetic
2.
3.  public class LowerToUpper {
4.
5.      // main(): application entry point
6.      public static void main(String[] args) {
7.          // set lowercase character of interest
8.          char lowercaseLetter = 'c';
9.
10.         // convert to uppercase equivalent
11.         int uppercaseLetter = 'A' + (lowercaseLetter - 'a');
12.
13.         // display result
14.         System.out.println("Uppercase equivalent of");
15.         System.out.println("   " + lowercaseLetter);
16.         System.out.println("is");
17.         System.out.println("   " + uppercaseLetter);
18.     }
19. }
```

In addition, the following relationship exists with regard to the uppercase Latin letters.

- 'A' + 1 evaluates to 'B';

- 'B' + 1 evaluates to 'C';

  ...

- 'Y' + 1 evaluates to 'Z'.

These relationships are all useful, as they enable a character to be classified efficiently as to whether it represents a lowercase character, an uppercase character, or a digit.

Listing 2.8 of LowerToUpper.java provides an example of **char** arithmetic. The program converts a lowercase letter to its uppercase equivalent. The character of interest is represented in the program by **char** variable lowercaseLetter.

```
char lowercaseLetter = 'c';
```

The uppercase equivalent is stored in uppercaseLetter.

```
char uppercaseLetter = 'A' + (lowercaseLetter - 'a');
```

The term (lowercaseLetter - 'a') evaluates to the difference in the Unicode encodings of the characters represented by lowercaseLetter and 'a'. In this case, the difference is 99 – 97 or 2, which indicates the character represented by lowercaseLetter has an encoding 2 beyond that of the encoding of 'a' encoding. In general, the difference of any lowercase letter and 'a' represents that character's offset from the encoding of 'a'. Because the uppercase letters also have consecutive encodings, adding such an offset to 'A' produces the uppercase equivalent.

The output of the program is

```
Uppercase equivalent of
    c
is
    C
```

Literal character versus literal character string

A common beginning programmer mistake is to confuse character values and string values. A literal character is an encoding for exactly one character within *single* quotes. Thus, 'a', 'H', '=', and '\n' are all valid literal character values. The expressions "a" and 'abc' are not legal literal characters: "a" is not a literal character because the a is not in single quotes; and 'abc' is not a literal character because abc is not an encoding for a single character.

A literal character string is an encoding for zero or more characters within *double* quotes. Thus, "abc", "", and "a" are all valid literal character strings. Expressions 'a' and 'abc' are not legal literal character strings because of their use of single quotes.

Class Character

Because converting characters from one case to another is a common programming activity, standard Java class `java.lang.Character` provides in part class methods:

char `Character.toLowercase(`**char** `ch)`
> Returns the lowercase equivalent of ch, if it exists; otherwise, the method returns ch.

char `Character.toUppercase(`**char** `ch)`
> Returns the uppercase equivalent of ch, if it exists; otherwise, the method returns ch.

2.3.3   DOUBLE TYPE

The type **double** uses 8 bytes to represent a floating-point value. Java provides the usual arithmetic operators, except for an exponentiation operator. A complete list of floating-point operators is given in Appendix A.3.

Listing 2.9 of `KilometersToMiles.java` converts a **double** distance in kilometers to its mile equivalent. The program makes use of conversion

> *Miles* = 0.621371 × *Kilometers*

The output of the program is

```
3.2 kilometers = 1.9883872 miles
```

As lines 14–15 illustrate, sometimes statements do not fit conveniently on a single line. This situation is not a problem because Java ignores the whitespace between program elements. Therefore, even though the initialization expression for `distanceIn-Miles` is expressed over two lines, its evaluation is unaffected. The standard convention

---

Listing 2.9 **KilometersToMiles.java**

```
 1. // Purpose: Convert kilometers to miles
 2.
 3. public class KilometersToMiles {
 4.
 5.     // main(): application entry point
 6.     public static void main(String[] args) {
 7.         // define constant of interest
 8.         final double MILES_PER_KILOMETER = 0.621371;
 9.
10.         // set mile of interest
11.         double distanceInKilometers = 3.2;
12.
13.         // convert to metric equivalent
14.         double distanceInMiles = distanceInKilometers
15.                                       * MILES_PER_KILOMETER;
16.
17.         // display result
18.         System.out.println(distanceInKilometers + " kilometers = "
19.                                  + distanceInMiles + " miles");
20.     }
21. }
```

Infinity and beyond

Java provides several predefined constants for programming convenience. The constants are members of the classes `Integer`, `Double`, and `Float`. These classes are part of standard package `java.lang`.

`Integer.MAX_VALUE`
> The largest positive value of type **int**.

`Integer.MIN_VALUE`
> The smallest negative value of type **int**.

`Double.MAX_VALUE`
> The largest positive value of type **double**.

`Double.MIN_VALUE`
> The smallest positive value of type **double**.

`Double.POSITIVE_INFINITY`
> The positive infinity value of type **double**. A value bigger than any valid finite **double** value.

`Double.NEGATIVE_INFINITY`
> The negative infinity value of type **double**. A value smaller than any valid finite **double** value.

`Double.NaN`
> The not-a-number value of type **double**. A **double** value that does not correspond to a numeric value. `Double.NaN` is not comparable to any other **double** value including itself. For example, because division by zero is undefined, `1.0 / 0.0` evaluates to `Double.NaN`.

The class `Float` defines an analogous set of constants for the **float** type as `Double` does for the **double** type.

for breaking a long expression into a multiline expression is that the continuation line should begin with an operator and if it is reasonable, the continuation line should be indented to place the trailing part of the expression underneath the leading part of the expression. Both measures signal the reader that the line is a continuation of the expression from the previous line.

Decimal and scientific notation

Java provides two basic ways to write floating-point literals—in *decimal* or *scientific notation*. A number in decimal notation consists of a whole-number part and a fractional part separated by a period. Either the whole-number part or the fractional part can be empty. If present, the whole-number part and fraction part are decimal numerals. For example, `123.456`, `0.0`, `.9`, and `1.` are all in decimal notation.

Java also provides the ability to express floating-point numerals using *scientific notation*. A number in scientific notation consists of a number in decimal notation concatenated with either an e or E followed by an exponent. The exponent is an integer decimal literal. For example, `1.23e10`, `0.23E-4`, `-45.e+23`, and `23.68E12` are all floating-point literals in scientific notation. These numbers are equivalent respectively to 1.23×10^{10}, 0.23×10^{-4}, -45×10^{23}, and 23.68×10^{12}.

2.4 EXPRESSIONS

Our examples have been chosen carefully so that the *expressions* in them would have obvious evaluations. For example, consider the definition of variable `fahrenheit` in program `CelsiusToFahrenheit.java`.

```
int fahrenheit = 32 + ((9 * celsius)/5);
```

Our use of parentheses was deliberate—with the parentheses being present there is clearly one legitimate way to evaluate the expression.

Consider the initialization of variable `expr` in the following code segment

```
int expr = 4 + 2 * 5;
```

It seems that there are two possible values for `expr`. If the addition is performed first, then `expr` is initialized to 30; if instead, the multiplication is performed first, then `expr` is initialized to 14. Now consider the code segment

```
System.out.println(5 / 2.0);
```

What value is displayed? The answer depends on whether integer or floating-point division is performed in evaluating 5 / 2.0.

In fact, the evaluations of 4 + 2 * 5 and 5 / 2.0 are unambiguous in Java. In this section, we discuss Java's rules for evaluating expressions. These rules ensure that the evaluation of *any* Java expression is unambiguous. In particular, the Java rules for evaluating expressions call for `expr` to be initialized to 14 and for 2.5 to be displayed.

2.4.1   UNARY AND BINARY OPERATORS

Expressions are Java's mechanism for applying operations to values and variables. They are the means by which we calculate new values from old ones. The values and variables being operated on are called the *operands*. The process of applying the operation to the operands is referred to as *evaluating the expression*. The evaluation of an expression yields a result that has a value *and* a Java type. The notion that an expression yields *both* a value and type is very important.

The simplest form of a Java expression is a literal or variable with no explicit operation being applied. Suppose `sampleSize` is an **int** variable with definition

```
int sampleSize = 20;
```

Then the result of evaluating the expression

```
sampleSize
```

is the **int** value 20. In a real sense, an operation is being applied to the `sampleSize`. The operation being applied is one that fetches the value in the memory location associated with `sampleSize`.

The – operator in expressions

```
-23
-n
```

is a unary operator, where the term *unary* means that the operator is applied to a single operand. Java has several unary operators. In these expressions, we are using the *unary negation operator* for negating a value. Obviously, the first result is the **int** value –23. Suppose n is a **double** variable with the value 10.5

```
double n = 10.5;
```

Then the expression -n evaluates to the **double** value –10.5.

The *unary plus operator* is included for symmetry with the unary minus operator. The expression

```
+244
```

yields the **int** value 244.

As demonstrated in our introduction to the primitive types, Java has many binary operators. For example, the expressions

```
6 * 21
29 / 11
6.9 + 19.82
1.1 - 2.8
```

yield respectively the values **int** value 126, **int** value 2, **double** value 26.72, and **double** value -1.7.

Although it does not make a difference when doing arithmetic with literal and variable operands, Java specifies for a binary operation that the left operand be evaluated before the right operand.

Multiplication must be explicit

The equation for a line is written normally as $y = mx + b$. In the formula, it is understood implicitly that m and x are being multiplied. In Java, there is no implicit multiplication. The expression mx + b uses the plus operation on variables mx and b.

2.4.2   PRECEDENCE

Like many programming languages, Java allows programmers to write expressions composed of multiple binary and unary operators. For example, consider the statement

```
int result = 3 * 5 / 2;
```

Depending on whether the multiplication is performed first or second, the value of the variable result is either 7 or 6.

To evaluate an expression in general, we need a set of *precedence rules* and *associativity rules* that tell us the order in which to apply the operators.

Let's begin by discussing precedence. Each operator is assigned a precedence level. Operators with higher precedence are applied before operators with lower precedence are applied.

Arithmetic expressions are evaluated just as we learned in grade school. The grouping operators () have the highest precedence. The unary operators – and + have higher precedence than the multiplicative operators of multiplication *, division /, and modulus %. The multiplicative operators have higher precedence than addition and subtraction.

Table 2.2 specifies in part the precedence level of the arithmetic and grouping operators. A complete operator table is given in Appendix A.3.

Table 2.2   Basic operator precedence and associativity

Precedence	Operator	Associativity
17	()	Nonassociative
13	unary + and -	Right associative
12	* / %	Left associative
11	+ -	Left associative

Thus, in the definition

```
int expr = 4 + 2 * 5;
```

variable expr is initialized to 14 rather than 30. It is initialized in this manner because multiplication has higher precedence than addition.

As other examples, consider the following expressions:

```
2 / 3 + 5        // division takes precedence over addition
-8 * 4           // negation takes precedence over multiplication
8 + 7 % 2        // modulus takes precedence over addition
```

In the first expression, because the division operator has higher precedence than the addition operator, the division is performed first. The result is 0, which is added to 5 to yield an overall expression value of **int** value 5. In the second example, the unary minus operator is applied to **8**, and the resulting value -8 is multiplied by 4 to yield an overall expression value of **int** value -32. In the third expression, the modulus operation is performed first and yields the value 1. This value is added to 8 to yield an overall expression value of **int** value 9.

We can use parentheses to override the order of evaluation. Suppose we wanted to compute the average of three **double** variables a, b, and c. The following code segment is *not* correct.

```
double average = a + b + c / 3.0;    // incorrect average
```

Because the division operator has the highest precedence, it is calculated first. The expression is equivalent to a + b + (c / 3.0)

Because of its precedence, the division c / 3.0 is calculated first. The sum of a + b then is calculated. The two intermediary results then are summed. By using parentheses, we can rewrite the definition to achieve the desired result.

```
double average = (a + b + c) / 3.0;  // correct average
```

The parentheses group the terms whose sum is the left operand of the division

Parenthesized expressions can be *nested*. In other words, a parenthesized expression can contain other parenthesized expressions. In such cases, the innermost parenthesized expressions are evaluated first. Consider the following expression:

```
(2 + (3 + 2) * 5) / (4 - 2)
```

Because the parenthesized subexpression (3 + 2) is nested within another parenthesized expression, it is evaluated first. Afterward, the expressions contained in the outer sets of parentheses can be evaluated. The resulting value is the **int** value 13.

In addition to precedence rules, associativity rules are also needed. It is the associativity rules that indicate how to evaluate expressions with operators of the same precedence. Such is the case for the initialization expression in the definition of variable result that started this section.

```
int result = 3 * 5 / 2;
```

As indicated in Table 2.2, multiplication and division are *left associative*. This associativity causes the compiler to evaluate the operands from left to right. Therefore, in the initialization expression for result, operand 5 associates with the operator on its left, and the correct value of the expression is the **int** value 7. (Remember, integer division truncates.)

Use of parentheses

Although it is important to know the rules of precedence, we often use parentheses to make the order of evaluation explicit even in cases where they are not needed. This technique helps readers understand the code more readily—such comprehension is important if they are modifying your code. For example, the expression

```
a * b + c / d - 3.0
```

and the parenthesized expression

```
(a * b) + (c / d) - 3.0
```

both perform the same computation, but the meaning of the latter one is clear.

2.4.3 WIDENING AND NARROWING OPERAND CONVERSION

Up to this point, we have considered numeric expressions where all the operands are of same type. But what if one operand of an addition is of type **int** and the other is of type **char**? Or what if one operand of a multiplication is of type **int** and the other is of type **double**? In total, there are 49 possible operand combinations per numeric binary operator. Rather than having different arithmetic operations for each possible operand combination, Java applies *unary conversion rules* to the operands before any operations are performed. One of these rules governs whether integer or floating-point arithmetic is performed.

- If either of the operands are floating point, then floating-point arithmetic is performed. Otherwise, integer arithmetic is performed.

Other rules ensure that operands are converted to the same type of value. One such rule is

- If either of the operands are of type **double**, then any non-**double** operand is *widened* automatically (i.e., converted) to **double**.

  For example, suppose the following definitions are in effect.

  ```
  int    i = 4;
  int    j = 30;
  double d = 6.21;
  double e = 19.54;
  ```

Then, the following expressions are all integer expressions

```
1 + 2
i * 3
i / j
```

and the following expressions are all floating-point expressions

```
6.9 + 11.28
11.29 * d
e * d
```

Loss of information

While integer widening does not introduce any loss of information about a value, narrowing can introduce a loss of information (e.g., converting an **int** to a **short**). Narrowing is accomplished by discarding the high-order bits. Thus, it is possible a change in a sign can occur with narrowing. For example, the value of expression **(short)** 32768 is −32768.

Floating-point widening from a **float** value to a **double** value does not introduce any loss of information about a value. However, the widening of an integer to a **float** or **double** value can introduce a loss of precision depending on the number. Narrowing a floating-point value also can introduce a loss of information.

In the following floating-point expressions, the integer operands are widened to **double** before expression evaluation.

```
11.29 + 1991
i / d
```

If the result of an integer initialization expression is for a variable of a different type from the value of the expression, then the value is converted to the variable's type by widening or narrowing. For example, in the following code segment, the value of the **int** expression 5 * 5 is widened to **double** in the first definition and narrowed to **char** in the second definition.

```
double a = 5 * 5;
char b = 5 * 5;
```

For detailed information on arithmetic conversion rules, the reader is directed to a Java reference manual such as *The Java Language Specification*, J. Gosling, B. Joy, G. Steele, and, G. Bracha, Addison-Wesley, New York, 2000. An online version of the text is available on the Web at www.javasoft.com.

For operator + there are subtleties besides the unary conversion rules. If at least one of its operands is a String, then concatenation is performed; otherwise addition is performed.

Consider the following code segment. What output does it produce? In determining your answer, use the fact that + is left associative.

```
String s = 1 + 2 + "3";
String t = "1" + 2 + 3;
System.out.println(s);
System.out.println(t);
```

The output is

```
33
123
```

Because + is left associative the additive term 1 + 2 is evaluated first in the initialization expression 1 + 2 + "3". Therefore, s is initialized with the value of the concatenation 3 + "3".

For the same reason, concatenation "1" + 2 is evaluated first in the initialization expression "1" + 2 + 3. Therefore, t is initialized with the value of the concatenation "12" + 3.

<table>
<tr><td>**2.4.4**</td><td>## OVERFLOW, UNDERFLOW, AND EXCEPTIONS</td></tr>
</table>

Arithmetic operators have the potential to produce a value that is larger or smaller than the integer types can handle. These situations are called respectively *overflow* and *underflow*. There is no signal to a program by a Java interpreter that indicates whether an overflow or underflow has occurred. For example, the following code segment

```
int biggestInt = Integer.MAX_VALUE;
int overflowInt = biggestInt * biggestInt;
System.out.println(biggestInt + " * " + biggestInt
                 + " evaluates to " + overflowInt + " in Java");
```

displays as its output

```
2147483647 * 2147483647 evaluates to 1 in Java
```

So take care when dealing with very big and very small numbers.

Java does signal a program automatically when division by 0 is attempted. Consider the following code segment, which attempts a divide by 0. (Because factor is defined to be 1, the expression (factor - 1) evaluates to 0.)

```
int factor = 1;
int result = 2 / (factor - 1);
System.out.println("Divide by zero was completed.");
```

The code segment never executes the println() statement. Attempting a divide by zero is unexpected by Java. As such, it is known as an *exception*. The signaling process is known as *throwing* an exception. If a program does not have code that *catches* (processes) the exception, then the program is terminated.

Chapter 10 examines exception handling

We next turn our attention to developing a program that interacts with its user through the use of statements performing input and output.

<table>
<tr><td>**2.5**</td><td>## INTERACTIVE PROGRAMS</td></tr>
</table>

A major deficiency of BMI.java is that the weight and height of the person is fixed. Unless you know somebody with a weight of 75.5 pounds and a height of 4.5 feet, the program is not that interesting. For the program to be useful, generally it must have interactive input and output (I/O) with its user. What we want is a BMI calculator with the ability to compute the BMI for the weight and height of the user's choosing. We can create such a program by modifying `BMI.java` of Listing 2.6 to make use of an input stream object that is capable of *extracting* (getting) the values a user enters with the keyboard.

```
BMI Calculator

Enter weight (lbs): 130.0
Enter height (feet): 5.75

A person with
     weight 130 lbs
     height 5.75 feet
has a BMI of 19
```

In the preceding sample run of such a program, the bold text was entered by the user in response to the requests for a weight and height. We use this type convention throughout the text. The output was produced by `BMICalculator.java` of Listing 2.10.

Program `BMICalculator.java` begins with an **import** statement.

```
import java.util.*;
```

An **import** statement indicates that the program requires access to other Java resources. In creating and accessing the input stream object for getting input values, the program uses class `Scanner` that is defined in standard Java software library `java.util`.

In Java parlance, a software library is known as a *package* or *application programming interface (API)*. Because only classes defined in package `java.lang` are available implicitly to a program, it is necessary to import class `Scanner` from the `util` API.

There are hundreds of APIs available for Java programmers. For example, there are APIs for developing multimedia, cryptography, telephony, and speech recognition programs. In Java, the resources supplied by an API are primarily classes. The classes and other elements of an API generally are organized in a hierarchical manner to form a package.

> Documentation of the major APIs is included in an appendix. For a reference on all of the standard APIs see www.javasoft.com

The * in the **import** statement is a special character indicating that all resources of `java.util` are to be made available to the program. For this reason, it is sometimes called the *wildcard* character. Rather than using the * shorthand for gaining access to all `util` resources, the program could have imported a particular class resource by *fully specifying* its name.

```
import java.util.Scanner;
```

We chose to use the wildcard form over the fully specified form because wildcard use is the standard programming practice. We defer further discussion of class `Scanner` until we examine the statements that extract the input values.

Method `main()` of `BMICalculator.java` starts in a straightforward manner by defining two conversion constants

```
// defining constants
final double KILOGRAMS_PER_POUND = 0.454;
final double METERS_PER_FOOT = 0.3046;
```

Listing 2.10 BMICalculator.java

```java
1.  // Purpose: Compute BMI for user-specified weight and height
2.
3.  import java.util.*;
4.
5.  public class BMICalculator {
6.
7.      // main(): application entry point
8.      public static void main(String[] args) {
9.          // defining constants
10.         final double KILOGRAMS_PER_POUND = 0.454;
11.         final double METERS_PER_FOOT = 0.3046;
12.
13.         // displaying legend
14.         System.out.println("BMI Calculator\n");
15.
16.         // set up input stream
17.         Scanner stdin = new Scanner(System.in);
18.
19.         // get person's characteristics
20.         System.out.print("Enter weight (lbs): ");
21.         double weight = stdin.nextDouble();
22.
23.         System.out.print("Enter height (feet): ");
24.         double height = stdin.nextDouble();
25.
26.         // convert to metric equivalents
27.         double metricWeight = weight * KILOGRAMS_PER_POUND;
28.         double metricHeight = height * METERS_PER_FOOT;
29.
30.         // perform bmi calculation
31.         double bmi = metricWeight / (metricHeight * metricHeight);
32.
33.         // display result
34.         System.out.println("A person with");
35.         System.out.println("    weight " + weight + " (lbs)");
36.         System.out.println("    height " + height + " (feet)");
37.         System.out.println("has a BMI of " + Math.round(bmi));
38.     }
39. }
```

---

and by displaying a legend.

```java
// displaying legend
System.out.println("BMI Calculator\n");
```

In the next section the program becomes interesting. There, method main() defines and initializes a variable stdin of type Scanner. Its initialization expression uses the **new** operator—operator **new** is the Java mechanism for creating new objects

```java
Scanner stdin = new Scanner(System.in);
```

The **new** expression makes use of variable System.in. System.in is the *standard input stream* counterpart to the output stream variable System.out. By default, System.in is associated with the keyboard.

The program defines the `Scanner` variable because the input methods associated with `System.in` are too low level (e.g., they extract input data on a byte-by-byte basis). With a `Scanner` object, the program has access

Chapters 3 and 4 focus on the general use of objects and reference variables.

to high-level `Scanner` methods for extracting values from an input stream. In particular, a `Scanner` has methods `nextDouble()` and `nextInt()` that extract respectively the next floating-point value and integer value from the input source.

Because `Scanner` is a class, its variables are not primitive type variables—they are *reference type (object) variables*. The initialization of a reference type variable is with a *reference* (pointer) to the memory location that holds an object of the associated type. It is important to understand that the value of an object variable is *not* an object but a *reference* to an object.

The `stdin` initialization expression **new** `Scanner(System.in)` produces a reference to a *new* `Scanner` object that is associated with standard input stream `System.in`. The operand to the **new** operator is a method invocation. In particular, the method invocation is a *constructor* invocation. A constructor configures an object just created by the **new** operator (it is the constructor name that indicates the type of object to be created).

Thus, the definition of variable `stdin` sets aside a memory location for variable `stdin`. The value of this memory location is a reference to a memory location that holds a new `Scanner` object. The new `Scanner` is configured to represent the input stream indicated by `System.in`. The memory depiction for variable `stdin` would be

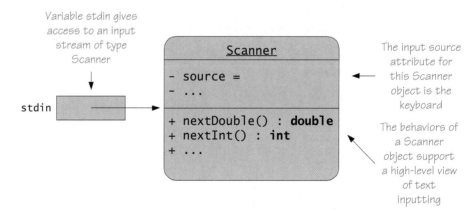

The next section of `main()` first *prompts* the user to supply the weight and then extracts the entered input value. The section then prompts and extracts the height value.

```java
// get person's characteristics
System.out.print("Enter weight (lbs): ");
double weight = stdin.nextDouble();

System.out.print("Enter height (feet): ");
double height = stdin.nextDouble();
```

A prompt is issued by invoking method `System.out.print()`. A prompt cues the user to enter the value that we need. For prompts, `print()` is preferred over `println()`.

Leaving the cursor near the prompt string rather than on the next line makes it more obvious that input is wanted from the user.

To extract the weight of the person, the program needs a place to store the input value. Line 21 defines and initializes the variable `weight` with the associated input value.

```
double weight = stdin.nextDouble();
```

A **double** variable is used because we want to be able to enter the value as a decimal number. The initialization expression for variable `weight` is the result of the invocation

```
stdin.nextDouble()
```

The initialization expression supplies variable `weight` with the input the user supplied in reaction to the prompt.

The extraction of a value from a line of standard input does not proceed until the entire input line has been entered, i.e., until the user provides a terminating newline character (the `Enter` key). Once an input line has been entered, its values can be extracted one-by-one.

For this application, the user should enter a number in reaction to the prompt. Therefore, invocation `stdin.nextDouble()` should successfully return that value in **double** form. If the user instead enters a non-number, then the `nextDouble()` invocation generates an exception that causes the program to terminate.

More to come

The nuances of classes in general and the particulars of `Scanner` are deferred until later chapters. For now only enough background is supplied so that you can make similar uses of the particular classes that `BMICalculator.java` employs.

Interactive input and output

It is important that programs tell the users what is expected of them. For example, `BMICalculator.java` tells the user to input the weight in pounds and the height in feet. These prompts may seem unnecessary: we know that two numbers are needed because we wrote the program. However in general, a user runs a program without seeing the source code, so it is important for a program to tell the user what is expected. That is why the weight prompt of `BMICalculator.java` displays

```
Enter weight (lbs):
```
rather than displaying just
```
Enter weight:
```
The latter is insufficient—the user would not know what type of weight is wanted (e.g., carats, ounces, pounds, grams, kilograms, etc.)

In addition to telling the user what form the input should take, another general principle is to echo the input supplied by the user whenever it is practical. This practice gives the user some assurance that the input was received and interpreted correctly. For example, in `BMICalculator.java`, the weight and height are displayed along with the BMI. Thus, the user can see whether the program correctly interpreted the input.

To extract the height of the person, a process is performed similar to extracting the weight of the person. First, a prompt is issued to tell the user what value we require.

```
System.out.print("Enter height (feet): ");
```

A **double** variable then is defined to store the extracted value.

```
double height = stdin.nextDouble();
```

The remainder of the program performs metric conversions and displays the results in the same way that BMI.java of Listing 2.6 does and warrants no further discussion.

We next turn our attention to the assignment operator. This important operator enables a program to update the value of a variable.

Extracting input values

If in reaction to the first prompt, a user enters two values, then BMICalculator.java may not perform as expected. Consider the following program input/output scenario.

```
BMI Calculator

Enter weight (lbs): 130.0 5.0
Enter height (feet): 5.75

A person with
    weight 130 (lbs)
    height 5 (feet)
has a BMI of 25
```

Because the user entered two values on the first line—130.0 and 5.00—it is these values that are acquired by the two stdin.nextDouble() extractions within the program. Therefore, BMICalculator.java variable weight is assigned 130.0 and variable height is assigned 5.0. In fact, the 5.75 entered in reaction to the second prompt is never even extracted.

Because the program echoes the input values, the user is informed what value was used for the height. As stated previously echoing inputs is an important programming practice. It both provides clarity on how the processing proceeded and serves as a warning when errant input occurs.

2.6   PRIMITIVE VARIABLE ASSIGNMENT

Besides signaling in a variable definition that the variable is to be initialized, the symbol = is also the Java *assignment operator*. The assignment operator takes two operands. The left operand is the *target* variable; the right operand is the *modifying expression*. When evaluated, the assignment operator updates the value in the memory location associated with a *target* variable based on the modifying expression.

$$target \quad = \quad expression \ ;$$

Name of previously
defined object

Expression to be
evaluated

For example, the code segment

```
int j = 6;
j = 1982;
```

first defines an **int** variable j that is initialized to 6. The result of this action is depicted next.

j   6

An assignment statement then updates target j with the **int** value 1982.

```
j = 1982;
```

The result of this action would be

j   1982

The assignment operator works in the following manner. First, the left operand is evaluated to make sure that its value can be modified (e.g., a non-**final** variable). The right operand then is evaluated and its value is used to update the memory location associated with the left operand. For our particular assignment, the memory location associated with variable j is reset to the **int** value 1982. The assignment expression is read as "j gets 1982" or "j is assigned 1982."

Some people find it convenient to think of memory locations as mailboxes. An assignment operator places information in a mailbox. The variable name acts like the address. However, the analogy is not perfect—while a mailbox can hold several pieces of mail at one time, a memory location holds a *single* value. A new value assigned to a memory location *replaces* the existing value.

To better see what the assignment operator does, let's examine the following code segment.

```
int a = 1;
int aSquared = a * a;
a = 5;
aSquared = a * a;
```

The first two lines of the code segment define **int** variables a and aSquared. Each variable has a memory location allocated to it that is initialized to 1. Upon initialization, the memory for the variables has depiction

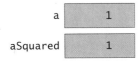

a   1

aSquared   1

When the first assignment statement is evaluated

```
a = 5;
```

variable a is set to 5 and the value of aSquared is unchanged. Memory now has depiction

After the second assignment is evaluated

```
aSquared = a * a;
```

the value of variable aSquared is set to 25 and the value of variable a remains at 5. Memory now has this depiction

Now consider the following code segment

```
int i = 0;
i = i + 1;
```

This code segment first defines an **int** variable i with a value of 0. The memory for the variable has depiction

The assignment may not make sense at first glance.

```
i = i + 1;
```

But you must remember that the = operator is the assignment operator rather than the equality operator. The target of the assignment is the variable i. Variable i is to be reset to the value of the modifying expression i + 1, which equals 0 + 1, which is 1. Thus, i is reset to 1.

The assignment statement is used sometimes to give an initial value to a variable. Although the following example is contrived, it does demonstrates this ability.

```
int asaRating;
asaRating = 400;
```

The first statement in the example defines but does not initialize variable asaRating. Upon its definition, memory for the variable has depiction where character "–" is again our indicator of an uninitialized value. Next, the assignment statement initializes variable asaRating to **int** value 400.

asaRating | 400

SWAPPING

A common programming *pattern* (task) is to *swap* or exchange the values of two variables. For example, let's suppose that variables x and y are defined and initialized and we want to swap their values.

```
double x = 5.12;
double y = 19.28;
```

Thus, the starting memory depiction for the variables is

x | 5.12

y | 19.28

We want to copy the value of x into y and copy the value of y into x. It is tempting to write the following assignment statements to accomplish the task.

```
x = y;   // Copy y into x
y = x;   // Copy x into y
```

However, this code would result in both x and y having the original value of y, which is 19.28. To see this outcome, let's trace through the code.

```
x = y;   // Copy y into x
```

After the first assignment, the value of y, which is 19.28, is copied into the memory location for x. This assignment results in the depiction

x | 19.28

y | 19.28

After the second assignment, the value of x, which is now 19.28, is copied into the memory location for y.

```
y = x;   // Copy x into y
```

Although y is reset, it is reset with the same value. Thus, this assignment also yields the depiction

x | 19.28

y | 19.28

The problem was that the first assignment statement overwrote the value of x that we needed to remember in order to reset y. To perform the task correctly, we use another variable to copy the value of one of the variables it is changed. In the following code segment, **double** variable named `rememberX` serves this purpose.

```
double x = 5.12;
double y = 19.28;
double rememberX = x;   // Make copy of original value of x
x = y;                  // Copy y into x
y = rememberX;          // Copy original value of x into y
```

After the three definitions in the segment are performed, memory has the depiction

```
        x   |   5.12
        y   |  19.28
rememberX   |   5.12
```

The first assignment

```
    x = y;                      // Copy y into x
```

updates x so memory now has depiction

```
        x   |  19.28
        y   |  19.28
rememberX   |   5.12
```

And after the second assignment

```
    y = rememberX;              // Copy original value of x into y
```

memory has depiction

```
        x   |  19.28
        y   |   5.12
rememberX   |   5.12
```

Thus accomplishing our task of swapping variables x and y.

2.6.2   ASSIGNMENT PRECEDENCE AND ASSOCIATIVITY

Like other operators, the assignment operator produces a value. The value of an assignment operation is the new value of the left operand. Assuming j and k have been declared to be **int** variables, the statement

```
    j = 5 * 3;
```

both stores a 15 in the variable j and evaluates to the **int** value 15.

Because assignment produces a value, we can write expressions such as

```
k = j = 5 * 3;
```

So what does the preceding assignment expression mean? The answer lies in knowing the precedence and associativity of the assignment operator. The natural and correct interpretation is that first 5 and 3 are multiplied together. Thus, the precedence of = is lower than that of *. Therefore, the interpretation of the previous expression is

```
k = j = (5 * 3);
```

Continuing with this example, observe that j is surrounded on both sides by the assignment operator =. In this situation, the associativity of = determines whether j binds with the = on the right or the = on the left. Unlike the arithmetic operators, the assignment operator is right associative. Therefore, the correct interpretation of the expression is

```
k = (j = (5 * 3));
```

which says that the result of the assignment of the product of 5 * 3 to j is assigned to k. Again this interpretation is natural because if assignments were left associative, the interpretation would be

```
(k = j) = (5 * 3);
```

which makes no sense.

2.6.3   INCREMENT AND DECREMENT

Java has special operators for incrementing or decrementing a numeric variable. The operator ++ is the increment operator, and the operator -- is the decrement operator. When applied to the primitive variables, these operators respectively add or subtract 1 from the value of the variable. For example, the following code segment

```
int i = 4;
++i;
System.out.println("i is " + i);
```

results in the output

```
i is 5
```

For all intents and purposes, the expression

```
++i
```

is equivalent to assignment

```
i = i + 1;      // also i += 1
```

Interestingly, there are two forms of the increment and decrement operators—*prefix* and *postfix*. The term prefix means the operator appears before the operand; and the term

Compound assignment

Java has several special operators for performing commonly occurring operations. One can think of these operators as language shorthands. For example, a common operation is to apply an operator to a variable and then store the result back into the same variable. As an example, consider adding 5 to a variable i. In many programming languages, this operation might be written as

```
i = i + 5;
```

However, Java has a compound additive assignment operator that accomplishes the same thing. In Java, the above expression is written usually as

```
i += 5;
```

Some of the other compound assignment operators are *=, -=, and /=. They respectively scale, reduce, and divide the target variable. For example,

```
i *= expression; // i's new value is i * (expression)
i -= expression; // i's new value is i - (expression)
i /= expression; // i's new value is i / (expression)
```

Assignment conversions and casting

If the target and modifying expression do not have the same type, it is necessary to convert the modifying expression to the type of the target. If the assignment conversion is a widening conversion, then Java will perform the conversion automatically.

For example, suppose the following definitions are in effect.

```
int i = 1;
double d = 2.0;
```

Then the following assignment is legal.

```
d = 1; // legal: compiler widens int 1 to double 1.0
```

The **int** value 1 is widened automatically to the **double** value 1.0.

Java does not perform automatically narrowing conversions. Therefore, the following statement does not compile.

```
i = d; // illegal: no implicit narrowing of double to int
```

Java does allow a program to request explicitly a narrowing through *casting*. A cast converts a value of one type to a value of another type. The form of a cast is

$$(\text{Type}) \ expression$$

The type to which the
expression is to be converted

Through casting the following statement accomplishes what the preceding illegal assignment could not do.

```
i = (int) d;    // legal: explicitly narrows double to int
```

A cast of a floating-point value to an integer value always truncates. Therefore, the value assigned to i in the following statement is 6.

```
i = (int) 6.9; // truncation of 6.9 to integer 6
```

postfix means the operator appears after the operand. The expressions ++i and i++ are respectively prefix and postfix examples. The earlier code segment could have been

```
int i = 4;
i++;
System.out.println("i is " + i);
```

which would produce exactly the same output. So what is the difference between the prefix and postfix versions of the increment operator? The difference becomes apparent when the operation is used as part of a larger expression. Consider this code fragment:

```
int i = 4;
int j = 4;
System.out.println("i is " + ++i);   // increment is first
System.out.println("j is " + j++);   // concatenation is first
System.out.println("i is " + i);
System.out.println("j is " + j);
```

Are the concatenation operations performed before or after i and j are incremented? In the case of the ++ prefix operator, i is incremented first and then the display is performed. The output is therefore

```
i is 5
j is 4
i is 5
j is 5
```

Be kind to your program readers

Some programmers, in an attempt to be clever, write a single statement that would be better understood if written using several statements. Such coding malpractices often involve the increment and decrement operators. As an example, consider the following statement that defines and initializes a variable k using previously defined **int** variables i and j.

```
int k = 5 + i++ * ++j;
```

The following segment is equivalent and far easier to understand.

```
++j;
int k = 5 + (i * j);
++i;
```

Thus, the prefix increment returns the value of the variable after it has been incremented; whereas, the postfix increment returns the value of the variable before it is incremented.

The decrement operator is similar to the increment operator except that it subtracts 1. Examples are

```
i--;
--i;
```

2.7　CASE STUDY — AVERAGING FIVE NUMBERS

We next develop a program `AverageFive.java` that computes the average of five integer inputs.

> The objective of this case study is to show the use of the assignment statements and input extraction when problem solving

ANALYSIS AND DESIGN

So what constants, variables, and objects are needed to accomplish this task? And how do these data structures interact?

One needed constant is the integer list size, which is 5. Another needed value is an integer variable representing the sum of the input values. With these two values the average can be computed. The average is also an integer value.

The integer sum of input values can be built up in a straightforward manner by extracting the input values one by one and adding the current input value to the running total. Therefore, an integer variable representing the current input value is also appropriate. This summing process also indicates that the variable representing the running total should be initialized to 0—when the program starts, no values have been processed.

To extract the current input value, a `Scanner` object associated with `System.in` is appropriate.

Implementation

Based on the preceding analysis, the following constants and variables should be used by program `AverageFive.java`:

- `LIST_SIZE`: **int** constant representing the number of input values (5);
- `currentInput`: **int** variable representing the current extracted input value;
- `runningTotal`: **int** variable representing the sum of the extracted input values (initially 0);
- `stdin`: references `Scanner` representation of the standard input stream given by `System.in`;
- `average`: **int** variable representing the average of the input values.

Program `AverageFive.java` is given in Listing 2.11. Its method `main()` consists of four sections corresponding to the following steps.

Step 1.　Define necessary data structures.
Step 2.　Process inputs to determine input total.
Step 3.　Compute average.
Step 4.　Display average.

The first section of method `main()` defines the variables that the program needs to compute the average.

```
// define necessary data structures (Step 1)
final int LIST_SIZE = 5;    // list size
int currentInput;           // current input value
int runningTotal = 0;       // running total of processed inputs
Scanner stdin = new Scanner(System.in);    // standard input
```

Listing 2.11 **AverageFive.java**

```
1.  // Purpose: Average five user integer inputs
2.
3.  import java.util.*;
4.
5.  public class AverageFive {
6.
7.      // main(): application entry point
8.      public static void main(String[] args) {
9.          // define necessary data structures (Step 1)
10.         final int LIST_SIZE = 5;    // number of inputs to process
11.         int currentInput;          // current input value
12.         int runningTotal = 0;      // sum of inputs processed so far
13.         Scanner stdin = new Scanner(System.in);    // input stream
14.
15.         // process inputs to determine input total (Step 2)
16.         System.out.print("Enter an integer number: ");
17.         currentInput = stdin.nextInt();
18.         runningTotal += currentInput;
19.
20.         System.out.print("Enter an integer number: ");
21.         currentInput = stdin.nextInt();
22.         runningTotal += currentInput;
23.
24.         System.out.print("Enter an integer number: ");
25.         currentInput = stdin.nextInt();
26.         runningTotal += currentInput;
27.
28.         System.out.print("Enter an integer number: ");
29.         currentInput = stdin.nextInt();
30.         runningTotal += currentInput;
31.
32.         System.out.print("Enter an integer number: ");
33.         currentInput = stdin.nextInt();
34.         runningTotal += currentInput;
35.
36.         // compute average (Step 3)
37.         int average = runningTotal / LIST_SIZE;
38.
39.         // display average (Step 4)
40.         System.out.println("The input average is " + average);
41.     }
42. }
```

The second section individually extracts and processes the five inputs. For each of the inputs, the same tasks are performed: a prompt is issued to supply an input; the input is extracted; and the input is added to the running total of the inputs.

```
System.out.print("Enter an integer number: ");
currentInput = stdin.nextInt();
runningSum += currentInput;
```

The `currentInput` assignment uses `Scanner` method `nextInt()` to extract the next user input as an **int** value. Thus, the method is similar in nature to `Scanner` method nextDouble(). Once the integer has been extracted, its value is used to increment running Sum through the use of the compound assignment operator +=.

The final two program sections compute and display the average in a straightforward manner.

```
// compute average (Step 3)
int average = runningSum / LIST_SIZE;
```

```
// display result (Step 4)
System.out.println("The input average is " + average);
```

Our implementation calculated the average as an integer. An alternative would be to calculate a floating-point average.

```
double average = ((double) runningSum) / LIST_SIZE;
```

For floating-point division to be performed at least one of the operands needs to be floating point. By casting runningSum to a **double** value, floating-point division is performed.

This example completes our introduction to the basics of Java program design and the manipulation of numeric values and variables. Chapter 3 considers the manipulation of objects and their variables.

2.8	**REVIEW**

- Comments enable us to provide notes to readers of a program. Comments are not processed by the compiler. The single-line comment form uses a double slash // to indicate that the rest of the line is a comment.

- Blank lines can be as important as comments. They enable the various sections of program to be distinct visually.

- Keywords are words that are a reserved part of the language with special meanings. Because keywords have special meanings, they cannot be changed by the programmer and they cannot be used by the programmer to name things. Keywords are case sensitive and consist of only lowercase letters.

- An identifier is a name defined by and given meaning by the programmer. Java requires that the names of all program elements be valid identifiers. The rule for forming a valid Java name is that it must be an identifier and cannot clash with the keywords. The rules for a valid identifier are as follows: an identifier must begin with either an alphabetic letter, an underscore, or a dollar sign; subsequent characters in an identifier (if any) must be either alphabetic, numeric, underscores, or dollar signs; no spaces can be embedded among the characters that form an identifier; and an identifier cannot be composed of more than 65,535 characters.

- A class is a description of a type of object. A class description specifies the attributes of an object and the methods for implementing its behaviors.

- A bug is the programming term for an error. To debug a program is to remove its errors.

- The keyword **class** indicates that a class definition is being initiated. Java permits modifiers to be placed in front of the keyword **class**. Modifier **public** indicates that the class in question can be used by Java classes that are defined in other files.

- A method in Java may have the following elements in the order with the italicized elements being optional.

Modifiers | Method Type | Method Name | (| *Parameter List* |) { | *Statement List* | }

- When a method is invoked, the actions associated with the method are executed.

- A class method is a service provided by a class. The method does not require association with a particular class object. The Java method modifier for indicating a class method is **static**.

- Member methods are the means by which objects have behaviors. A member method is invoked in conjunction with an object.

- If a method does not return a value, then the return type of the method is **void**.

- Programmers use indentation to indicate that the indented material is an element of the material that preceded it. Indenting provides visual cues to a reader about the structure of a program. It is normal practice to indent by three to four spaces.

- The entry point of execution for a Java application program is a **void** method named `main()`. Java requires that the parameter list for the method `main()` consist of exactly one formal parameter of type `String[]`.
- Braces {} are used by Java to group statements. The left brace { is the opening delimiter and a right brace } is the closing delimiter.
- A single statement can span multiple lines so there must be some delimiter that indicates that the statement is finished. The semicolon (;) serves this purpose.
- A literal character string is a string of characters delimited on both sides by the double quote character ("). A literal character string is not allowed to span multiple lines.
- `System` is a standard Java class that has a member named `out`. Member `out` gives access to the standard output stream, which is associated automatically with the console window running the application.
- The period is used for selection. We use it when we want to reference a particular member of a class or object.
- An escape sequence is a special two-character sequence representing another character. Java uses the backslash character \ as the starting character in an escape sequence. The complete list is given in Table 2.1.
- A syntax error is a violation of the rules for defining a valid Java program. If the source file is not valid Java, then the compiler produces a list of syntax errors.
- There are five primitive integer types **byte**, **short**, **int**, **long**, and **char** (**char** is also the character type); two primitive floating-point types **float** and **double**; and a logical type **boolean**. The names of the primitive types are keywords.
- A constant is the symbolic name for a memory location whose value cannot be changed during program execution once the program has initialized that memory location. To indicate that the contents of the location are to be fixed use keyword **final**.
- The systematic use of symbolic names is preferred over literal values because the names provide meaning and because their use reduces the potential introduction of errant values through incorrect keyboarding.
- A variable is the symbolic name for a memory location whose contents can be modified by the program during program execution.
- The identifier names of variables and constants should be descriptive of their purposes.
- A variable is a local variable if it is defined within a method.
- By default, local variables are undefined initially. Java requires that an undefined variable be assigned a value before its value is accessed.
- The `String` concatenation operator + concatenates its left and right operands to produce a string.
- For the numeric types, Java provides the usual arithmetic operators: addition +, subtraction -, multiplication *, and division /. Java also provides the modulus operator % that computes remainders.
- Java provides two basic ways to express floating-point literals—in decimal or scientific notation.

- An expression is Java's mechanism for producing new values by applying operations to values and variables. The process of applying the operation to the operands is referred to as evaluating the expression. The evaluation of an expression yields a result that has a value and a type.
- A binary operator requires two operands. The left operand is evaluated first.
- When an expression throws an exception it is signaling that an unexpected behavior has occurred.
- Arithmetic operators have the potential to produce overflow or underflow, i.e., a value that is larger or smaller than the memory location properly can represent. No exception is thrown to indicate that overflow has occurred.
- A unary operator is applied to a single operand.
- Java has unary conversion rules that are applied before any operations are performed. The application of these rules ensures that the operands have the same type.
- For consistent expression evaluation Java uses a set of associativity and precedence rules that specify the order in which to apply operators. The unary operators have higher precedence than the multiplication, division, and remainder operators, which in turn, have higher precedence than addition and subtraction.
- `System.in` references a representation of the standard input stream. The extraction methods of this representation are limited to reading **byte** values.
- The expression **new** `Scanner(System.in)` creates a new `Scanner` object that is associated with standard input.
- Class `Scanner` methods `nextDouble()` and `nextInt()` extract respectively the next floating-point value and integer value from the associated input source.
- The = is the Java assignment operator. The assignment operator updates the value in the memory location associated with a target variable (left operand) with the value of the right operand. The assignment operator, besides storing a value in memory, also produces a result (the new value of the left operand).
- Java allows a program to request explicitly a narrowing through casting. A cast converts a value of one type to a value of another type.
- Java has compound assignment operators for all of the binary arithmetic operators.
- Java has operators ++ and -- for incrementing or decrementing a primitive numeric variable value by 1.

2.9   SELF-TEST

S2.1   What does the following program output?

```java
public class DisplayMotto {
    // main(): application entry point
    public static void main (String[] args) {
        System.out.println("We will not go it\nalone.");
    }
}
```

S2.2   What does the method return type **void** indicate?

S2.3 Provide a single `println()` invocation that displays the following output.

```
JJ
Jenna
Hannah
```

S2.4 Which of the following lines are not valid Java identifiers? Explain.

```
java.awt.Graphics
x-ray
2BeOrNot2Be
Mary'sLostLamb
Spiro Zambini
```

S2.5 What is the length of the literal character string `"1\t2\t3"`?

S2.6 How do methods `System.out.print()` and `System.out.println()` differ?

S2.7 Define a Java constant equal to 2.9979×10^8 that approximates the speed of light in meters per second.

S2.8 Define a **double** variable `area` that is initialized to the area of a circle with radius 3.5. You may find it useful to use the constant `Math.PI`, which is the **double** value closest to π.

S2.9 Evaluate the following Java operations. Your answer should include both the value and its type.

a) `13 % 3`
b) `5 / 4`
c) `5.0 / 4.0`
d) `100  /  2*5`

S2.10 Add parentheses to indicate explicitly how the following expressions are evaluated.

a) `1.5 * 3.0 + 8 + 2 / 8`
b) `8 + 5 * 6 / 4 - 2`

S2.11 Write a Java expression for the following mathematical expression.

$$a^3(a + 1)(a - 7)$$

S2.12 Write a Java expression for the following mathematical expression.

$$\frac{1}{1 + x^2}$$

S2.13 Suppose water costs 0.021 cents per 100 gallons. Write a single statement that defines a floating-point value `total` that is initialized to the cost of buying n gallons of water.

S2.14 What is the output of the following code segment?

```java
int t1 = 17;
int t2 = 3;
int t3 = 7;
System.out.println("value = " + (t1 % t2 * 5 / t3));
System.out.println("value = " + (t3 * (-5 / 2) + t2));
System.out.println("value = " + (t3 + t1 * 4 + t1));
```

S2.15 What is the output of the following code segment?

```java
System.out.println(1 + 1 + "1");
System.out.println("1" + 1 + 1);
```

| 2.10 | **EXERCISES** |

2.1 Why do programmers comment?

2.2 What is the purpose of indentation?

2.3 Separately identify the keywords, variables, classes, methods, and parameters in the following definition.

```java
import java.util.*;

public class Test {
    public static void main(String[] args) {
        Scanner stdin = new Scanner(System.in);
        System.out.print("Number: ");
        double n = stdin.nextDouble();
        System.out.println(n + " * " + n + " = " + n * n);
    }
}
```

2.4 What does the modifier **public** indicate for a class?

2.5 Which of the following are valid Java identifiers?

a) lowScore	j) lifeGuard	s) Not!
b) lowScore_	k) $Cost	t) _123
c) low_Score	l) co$st	u) extends
d) _lowScore	m) Cost$	v) main
e) void	n) x.y.z	w) applet
f) VOID	o) returnValue	x) java
g) Main	p) A	y) Java
h) 2BaseHit	q) C:\Temp	z) JApplet
i) Score2	r) 1	

2.6 Indicate whether the following names conform to the Java naming convention. For those that follow the convention indicate what a reader would expect them to be (e.g, method, class, variable). Explain.

a) issquare	i) Temperature	q) setBoundary
b) IsSquare	j) getToken	r) sendMessage
c) is_square	k) get_Token	s) ThisColor
d) Square	l) _getToken	t) planetType
e) mySquare	m) gettoken	u) PlanetValue
f) BigSquare	n) Token	v) planet
g) fillSquare	o) walking	w) CurrentTime
h) temperature	p) Drawing	x) MyName

2.7 Suppose line 8 of DisplayForecast.java was replaced with the following?
`// System.out.print("I think there is a world market for");`
What would the output of the program then be and why?

2.8 Is System.out.println() necessary? Explain.

2.9 Write a program to display the greeting "Hi-dee-ho daddy-o."

2.10 Write a program to display the family motto "We are even loonier than you think."

2.11 Write a program to produce the following output.

```
Shape                Number of Sides
===================================
Diamond                   4
Rhombus                   4
Square                    4
Triangle                  3
```

2.12 Write a program to produce the following output.

```
Pitter-patter
 .   .   .   .   .
 .  Goes the rain
 .   .   .   .   .   .
 .   .  On the steps
```

2.13 Write a program that displays a tic-tac-toe board. The board should have an "O" preplaced in the center location of the board.

2.14 What is the result of the following expressions? Express your answer as a value and a type.

a) 5 % 3
b) 5 / 3
c) 5.0 / 3.0
d) 7.0 / 0.0
e) 25 / 7
f) 21 / 3

g) 27 / 2.0 / 3
h) 27 / 2 / 3
i) 22.1 + 1.0
j) 31 % 3
k) 30 % 5
l) 7 - 2

m) 28 + 3 * 5
n) (14 / 3) + 4
o) 2
p) -23 + 7 * 2
q) 12 % 5 % 3
r) 12 % 3 % 5

2.15 Assume the following declarations:

```
double d1 = 3.1;
double d2 = 1.0;
int i1 = 5;
int i2 = 10;
int i3 = 7;
char c1 = '0';
```

What is the result of the following expressions? Express your answer as a value and a type.

a) d2 + d1
b) i1 + d1
c) i1 + i2 * i3
d) i2 % i3
e) i3 / i2 + i1 * 5
f) d2 - i3

g) d1 / i2 + d1
h) i2 + i3 + 3.0
i) i2 * d2 + 4
j) i1 / i3
k) c1 + 5
l) 'x' + 2

2.16 Indicate the decimal equivalents of the following values.

a) 3.1234e-5
b) 3.1234e+5
c) 1234.0e-5
d) 0.1234e+5

2.17 Add parentheses to demonstrate explicitly how the following expressions are evaluated.

    a) `9 / 2 * 8 + 5 * 3 - 7 % 4`
    b) `7 * 3 - 5 / 2 * 6 + 12`
    c) `5 % 2 + 3 % 2 - 4 / 3`

2.18 If necessary, add parentheses to the following expressions so that the term $4 + 7$ is multiplied by the term $3 - 8$.

    a) `7 * 4 + 7 * 3 - 8 * 2`
    b) `12 - 4 + 7 * 3 - 8 - 5`
    c) `4 + 7 * (3 - 8) - 12`

2.19 Define constants or variables for the following pieces of information.

    a) The side of a square whose length is 4.5.

    b) One thousand meters.

    c) Avogadro's number.

    d) One-sixtieth of a minute.

    e) The number of wheels on a tricycle.

    f) An exclamation point.

    g) The square root of 2.

    h) The character corresponding to the digit 0.

2.20 Suppose the following definitions are in effect.

```
int a = 10;
int b = 20;
double u = 55.5;
double v = 22.2;
```

Identify which of the following definitions are valid. If the definition is invalid, indicate why. If the definition is valid, your answer should specify its initialization value.

    a) `int i = b + u;`
    b) `double x = b + u;`
    c) `int j = b / 2;`
    d) `double y = a + b;`
    e) `double z = v / 2;`

2.21 Write a Java statement that implements the following equation.

$$q = \left(\frac{T_1 \times T_2}{D - k} \right) + T_2$$

Your assignment statement should use the following variables.

```
double q;                 // result
double k = 1.35;          // constant of irritation
double D = 9.2;           // duration
double T1 = 98.4;         // start time
double T2 = 101.12;       // end time
```

2.22 Write Java expressions that are equivalent to the following mathematical formulas:

a) $a^2 + 5a - 4$

b) $3a + 7 / 4a - 2$

c) $a^3(c + 1)(a + b)$

d) $b^2 + 4ac$

e) $a + \dfrac{b}{c} + d$

f) $\dfrac{4}{3}\pi r^2$

g) $-(a^2 - b^3)$

h) $a\left(\dfrac{b}{c}\right)$

i) $(a + b)(c + d)(e + f)$

2.23 Write a single assignment statement that causes **int** variable n to have the whole number part of **double** variable x. For example, if x had the value 123.45, then n's value should become 123.

2.24 Write a single assignment statement that causes **double** variable y to have the fractional part of **double** object x. Assume that there is an **int** variable n containing the whole number part of x.

2.25 Write a code segment that *circularly shifts* the values of **int** variable a, b, c, and d. For example, if the variable values are initially 10, 20, 30, and 40 respectively, then the final values are 40, 10, 20, and 30 respectively. It may be convenient to introduce a temporary variable to accomplish this task.

2.26 What is the output of the following code segment?

```java
int a = 1;
int b = 2;
int c = 3;
int d = 3;
a = c + (c = 5);
b = (d = 5) + d;
System.out.println("a = " + a);
System.out.println("b = " + b);
```

2.27 Correct the following statements.

```java
int 5 = a;
int b 7;
int c = 9.2;
```

2.28 Suppose x and y are variables of type **double**. Does the following code always successfully swap the values of x and y?

```java
double rmbr = x;
x = y;
y = rmbr;
```

2.29 Write a program that computes the volume of an object. The program should ask the user to input the object mass and density. The mass will be given in grams; the density will be in grams per cubic centimeter. The relationship of mass, density, and volume of a variable is given by

$$Density = \frac{Mass}{Volume}$$

Your program should output the volume in cubic centimeters.

2.30   Redo `LowerToUpper.java` of Listing 2.8 so that it is an interactive program that prompts and extracts the lowercase character of interest.

2.31   Write a program to compute the mass of a block of aluminum. The program should input the dimensions of the block (i.e., length, width, and height) in centimeters. The density of aluminum is 2.7 g/cm^3.

2.32   Write a program that prompts and extracts the distance a train travels in miles and the time it takes to travel that distance. The program should compute and display the average speed of the train for that journey.

2.33   Write a program that prompts for and reads a floating-point number and evaluates the polynomial

$$3x^4 - 10x^3 + 13$$

The program should display both the number read and the result of evaluating the polynomial.

2.34   Write a program that prompts for and reads your age in years and outputs your age in days. Assume that there are 365 days in a year.

2.35   Write a program that computes the number of minutes it takes for light to reach the Earth from the Sun.

2.36   Write a program that prompts for a person's age and heart rate. The program computes and displays the number of heartbeats since the person was born. Assume that there are 365 days in a year.

2.37   Suppose there was a numeric type `longish` that used 6 bytes to represent an integer. What would be the range of integer numbers that could be represented?

2.38   Rewrite `BMICalculator.java` so that the user supplies the height in feet and inches.

2.39   Interest on credit card accounts can be quite high. Most credit card companies compute interest on an average daily balance. Here is an algorithm for computing the average daily balance and the monthly interest charge on a credit card.

Step 1. Multiply the net balance shown on the statement by the number of days in the billing cycle.

Step 2. Multiply the net payment received by the number of days the payment was received before the statement date.

Step 3. Subtract the result of the calculation in step 2 from the result of the calculation in step 1.

Step 4. Divide the result of step 3 by the number of days in the billing cycle. This value is the average daily balance.

Step 5. Compute the interest charge for the billing period by multiplying the average daily balance by the monthly interest rate.

Here is an example to illustrate the algorithm. Suppose a credit card statement showed a previous balance of $850. Eleven days before the end of the billing cycle, a payment of $400 is made. The billing cycle for the month is 31 days, and the monthly interest rate is 1.32%. The calculation of the interest charge is as follows:

Step 1. $850 × 31 = $26,350
Step 2. $400 × 11 = $4,400
Step 3. $26,350 – $4,400 = $21,950
Step 4. $21,950 ÷ 31 = $708.06
Step 5. $708.06 × 0.0132 = $9.34

Write a program that computes the monthly interest charge on a credit card account. Your program should acquire as input the previous balance, the payment amount, the number of days in the billing cycle, the day of the billing cycle the payment was made, and the monthly interest rate.

2.40   Suppose a, b, and c are **int** variables initialized respectively to 1, 2, and 3. What values are assigned to e, f, and g?

a) **int** e = ++a;
b) **int** f = b++;
c) **int** g = ++c + c++;

2.41   Write a code segment that defines a Scanner variable stdin that is associated with System.in. The code segment should then define two **int** variables a and b such that they are initialized with the next two input values from the standard input stream.

2.11   PROGRAMMING PROJECT — YOU

Developing software can be a rewarding experience—it is a chance to be both creative and analytical. People of all sorts report high levels of satisfaction in completing a programming task and demonstrating its capabilities. The goal of this introductory problem-solving case study and our other case studies is for you to experience such satisfaction as you learn to program and problem solve in Java.

> The objective of this case study is to practice the display of information using methods print() and println()

At the end of the main body of each chapter, we present a problem or two for you to consider. The problems have been selected for their relevance to the concepts being discussed, as well as being appropriately complex and interesting to a broad range of people. We provide background and problem-solving guidance on how to go about designing and implementing solutions.

The first case study is a personal one—design and produce a display giving a short autobiography that could be used as part of an application for a club membership. The information you supply and how you present it is your choice. However, at a minimum you must supply contact information such as your name and e-mail address. To get you started, you may consider describing some of your personal favorites (e.g, author, artist, music, activities) and plans (e.g., career, travel).

ANALYSIS AND DESIGN

So what tasks must be accomplished to produce a Java program that creates the desired display? For one, you must determine what personal information is to be displayed. For another, you must determine how the information is to be displayed. After making these decisions, you can create a preliminary design of the information and its layout. You might want to get feedback from friends. They can make suggestions on the information to make sure it is sufficiently interesting.

Snapshots of our own personal efforts are given in Figure 2.5 and Figure 2.6.

Figure 2.5 **A MeDisplay compilation and run.**

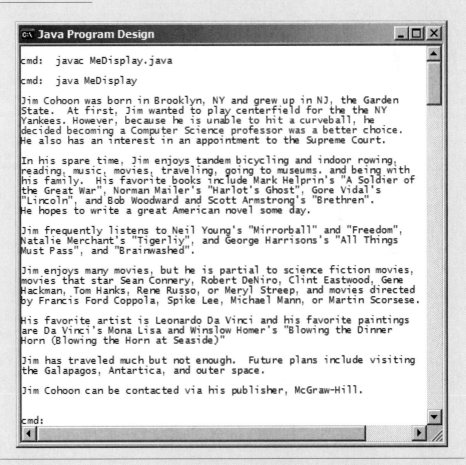

Implementation

Name the program MeDisplay.java. To implement and run the program, you will need access to Java tools. Some versions of this text are bundled with a CDROM supplying a Java IDE for you to use. In addition, our website www.javaprogramdesign.com contains links to some freely available tools such as the JDK.

Figure 2.6   A MeDisplay compilation and run.

For this case study, you will develop a class MeDisplay that consists of a single method main(). The class should be documented and laid out appropriately. For example, the code should make use of program header and method comments, whitespace and a consistent indentation scheme.

For your information, our programs produced each line of text using individual statements.

TESTING

Just as you should seek the comments of others to evaluate your preliminary design, you should also demonstrate your working program to others to get advice on how the presentation might be improved.

| 2.12 | **PROGRAMMING PROJECT — TRAINING ZONE** |

There are two kinds of exercise—aerobic and anaerobic exercise. Normally, sustained activities such as bicycling, running or swimming are aerobic exercises, while activities requiring bursts of action such as weightlifting and tennis are anaerobic exercises. Both types of exercise have their advantages. For example, anaerobic exercise can stimulate muscle growth and aerobic exercise can raise your metabolism by stimulating the production of fat-burning enzymes.

> The objective of this case study is to practice interactive programming in the context of problem solving

For a sustained activity to be an aerobic exercise there needs to be an elevation in the heart rate. However, the elevation cannot be extreme. If the elevation is extreme, then muscles are oxygen deprived and they burn sugars rather than fat. Research indicates that there is a heart beat rate training zone that should be kept in order to get the maximum aerobic effect from an exercise. The actual training zone for a person is based on many factors, such as the individual's normal heart rate, fitness, health, weight, etc. However, there are formulas indicating reasonable training zones for the majority of fit people with normal heart rates. The formula used in this section comes from `HealthCentral.com`. The formula works as follows: subtract the age of interest from 220; 65% of that value is the low end of the training zone range and 80% of that value is the high end of the training zone range.

The goal of this case study is to develop a program that computes a training zone according to the following problem statement.

> *Provide an interactive training zone calculator that prompts a user for her or his age. The calculator program then computes and displays the training zone for that age. The low end of the training zone is 65% of the difference between 220 and the specified age. The high end of the training zone is 80% of the difference between 220 and the specified age.*

ANALYSIS AND DESIGN

Before determining the necessary information structures and algorithm, you should depict a sample input/output behavior. A depiction should help clarify what information is being provided and what information is to be computed. Furthermore, if the software is being developed for a client, then it also aids you in verifying with the client that the proper problem is being solved. An example of a possible input/output behavior for the training zone calculator is given in Figure 2.7.

An analysis of the problem statement indicates one piece of information that must be gotten from the user—the age of interest. From that information and the training zone formula you derive the lower and upper heart beat rates for the training zone associated with that age of interest. An analysis of the problem also indicates that in developing an algorithm three integer variables are appropriate: *ageOfInterest*, *lowBeatRate*, and *highBeatRate*. In addition, three constants are appropriate: *BASE_RATE* with value 220, *LOW_ZONE_MULTIPLIER* with value 65%, and *HIGH_ZONE_MULTIPLIER* with value 80%.

Figure 2.7   **A possible training zone calculator console window display.**

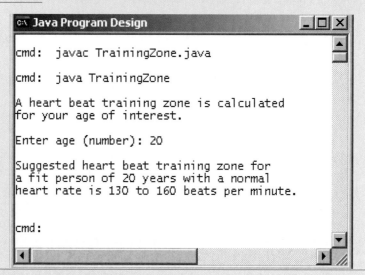

From the preceding discussion, an algorithm for solving the problem is relatively easy.

Step 1.   Provide a suitable legend for the calculator.

Step 2.   Prompt the user for the age for which they desire a suggested training zone.

Step 3.   Extract the user-specified age and assign it to variable *ageOfInterest*.

Step 4.   Compute the low heart beat rate by assigning *lowBeatRate* the value of the expression *LOW_ZONE_MULTIPLIER* × (*BASE_RATE* – *ageOf Interest*).

Step 5.   Compute the high heart beat rate by assigning *highBeatRate* the value of the expression *HIGH_ZONE_MULTIPLIER* × (*BASE_RATE* – *ageOf Interest*).

Step 6.   Display the training zone information as defined by *ageOfInterest*, *low-BeatRate*, and *highBeatRate*.

Implementation

Producing a Java program `TrainingZone.java` from the suggested algorithm can be done nicely with a single class `TrainingZone`. The class should be documented and laid out appropriately. For example, the code should make use of program header and method comments, whitespace, and a consistent indentation scheme.

TESTING

One way to test a program informally is to do a hand-check—compute by hand what the output should be for several different ages. Then run the program using those same ages and compare the results. Determine for any discrepancies whether the program or hand calculation is incorrect. If the program is incorrect, review the formulas already given and your implementation of them. Also consider adding temporarily statements displaying intermediary results in an effort to determine where your program's correctness breaks down. (Such statements are called *debugging statements*.) Testing and debugging is examined in detail in Chapter 13.

| 2.13 | **SELF-TEST ANSWERS** |

S2.1 The program outputs

```
We will not go it
alone.
```

S2.2 The return type **void** indicates that the method does not a produce a return value.

S2.3 The invocation should be

```
System.out.println("JJ\nJenna\nHannah");
```

S2.4 None of the lines are valid identifiers. The first line is composed of three identifiers separated by periods. The second line is not a valid name as a hyphen is not a valid character in composing a name. The third line is not a valid name because it begins with a digit. The fourth line is not a valid name as an apostrophe is not a valid character in composing a name. The fifth line is not a valid name as it contains embedded whitespace.

S2.5 The literal character string "1\t2\t3" has length 5. The three digits each count for 1 and each occurrence of the tab character escape sequence \t counts for 1.

S2.6 System.out.print() differs from System.out.println() in that it allows additional output to be sent to the current line after its invocation. System.out.println() moves the cursor to the start of the next line.

S2.7 **final** double LIGHT_SPEED = 2.9979e8;

S2.8 **double** area = 3.5 * 3.5 * Math.PI;

S2.9

  (a) The **int** value 1.

  (b) The **int** value 1.

  (c) The **double** value 1.25.

  (d) The **int** value 250. The whitespace does not influence the evaluation.

S2.10

  (a) ((1.5 * 3) + 8) + (2 / 8)

  (b) (8 + ((5 * 6) / 4)) - 2

S2.11 Expression: (a * a * a) * (a + 1) * (a - 7)

S2.12 Expression: 1 / (1 + x*x)

S2.13 Statement: **double** total = 0.021 * n / 100;

S2.14 The output is

```
value = 1
value = -11
value = 92
```

S2.15 The output is

```
21
111
```

3 USING OBJECTS

We now explore how to create and manipulate a variety of objects using standard Java classes. Our exploration begins with the String class. The String class is Java's principal mechanism for encapsulating a sequence of zero or more characters. Like the values of all Java class types, a String value is an object. An object is very different from a primitive type value. An object has attributes and behaviors. An attribute is a characteristic. For example, a rectangle object has length and width. An object behavior may be as simple as changing a width attribute or as intricate as drawing its representation on a window screen. Because objects are more complex than primitive values, their variables are treated differently than primitive type variables. The memory location of an object variable stores a reference to a memory location that holds an object rather than holding the object itself.

OBJECTIVES

- Develop a mental model of an object and a reference.
- Describe how to define and use object type constants and variables.
- Explain the roles of constructors, member methods, and class methods.
- Present object assignment.
- Introduce the String class and its methods for creating, examining, searching, evaluating, and manipulating substrings and characters.

3.1 CLASSES

The use of objects in Chapter 2 was limited to input and output operations (e.g., an input stream using variable `stdin` and an output stream using variable `System.out` in `AverageFive.java`). Starting in this chapter and in successive chapters, we create and manipulate objects from many of the other classes that Java provides (e.g, classes `String`, `Rectangle`, `Color`, and `JFrame`).

The Java standard classes are very important in their own right. For example, some provide text processing capabilities and others support the design and development of graphical interfaces. In addition, your exposure to and use of these well-designed classes will give you a firmer foundation in the principles of object-oriented programming and should make it easier for you to design and implement your own classes in a thoughtful manner. In fact, starting with Chapter 4, we show you how to design and develop your own classes!

The first of the standard classes that we consider is the `java.lang` class `String`. The `String` class is ubiquitous in Java programming because it is Java's principal mechanism for encapsulating a sequence of characters into an object with attributes and behaviors. For example, Java internally treats a literal character string as a `String` constant. The `String` class is part of package `java.lang`.

```
public class PersonalComputerForecast {

    // method main(): application entry point
    public static void main(String[] args) {
        System.out.print("There is no reason anyone would want");
        System.out.println(" a computer in their home.");
        System.out.println("  Ken Olson, DEC Chairman, 1977.");
    }
}
```

Literal character strings are represented in Java as String objects

The `String` class provides a variety of methods to implement the behaviors you would expect with strings. For example, there are methods for creating strings; examining, searching, and accessing individual characters; and producing substrings. However, there are *no* methods to modify a `String`—once a `String` object has been created, it is *immutable*. Java provides `java.lang.StringBuffer` for applications requiring the ability to modify an existing sequence of characters.

We begin our examination of Java objects and classes with object variables. We begin here because an object typically is used and manipulated through an object variable.

Figure 3.1   Primitive type and object type variable values.

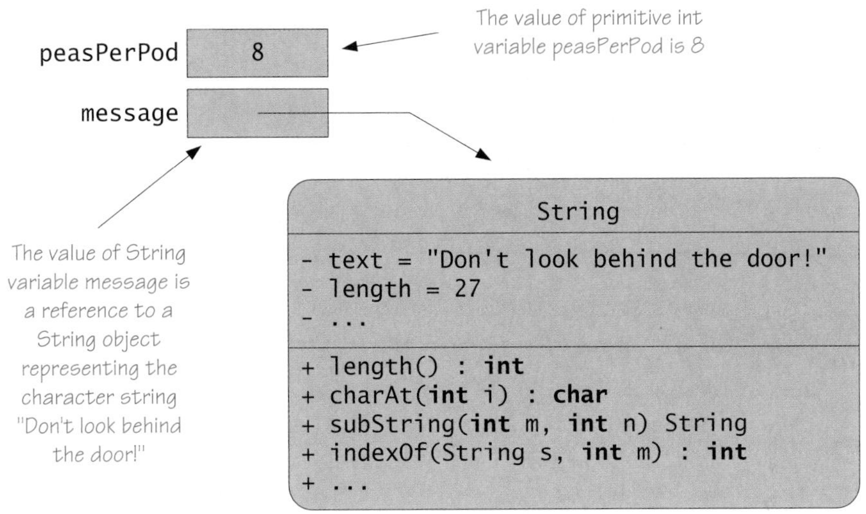

peasPerPod [8] ← *The value of primitive int variable peasPerPod is 8*

message [   ]

The value of String variable message is a reference to a String object representing the character string "Don't look behind the door!"

String
- text = "Don't look behind the door!" - length = 27 - ...
+ length() : **int** + charAt(**int** i) : **char** + subString(**int** m, **int** n) String + indexOf(String s, **int** m) : **int** + ...

3.2   OBJECTS AND VARIABLES

As discussed in Chapter 2, a primitive variable is a symbolic name for a memory location. The type of value stored in that location corresponds to the type of the primitive variable being used; e.g., an **int** variable is associated with a memory location storing an **int** value and a **double** variable is associated with a memory location storing a **double** value.

Java treats object variables differently. Although an object variable is the symbolic name for a memory location being used by the program, the memory location for an object variable does *not* store a value of that object type. Instead the value in the memory location tells the program where to find a value (object) of that type.

We say that an object variable *references* or *points to* an object of the object type. Thus, a String variable references a memory location that holds a value of type String. Similarly, a Scanner variable references a memory location holding a Scanner value.

Figure 3.1 illustrates the difference between a primitive and an object variable. In the figure, peasPerPod is variable of type **int** with value 8 and message is a variable of type String that refers to a String object representing the character string "Don't look behind the door!". As the illustration indicates, the memory location associated with **int** variable peasPerPod contains the 8, but the memory location for String variable message contains a reference to a memory location containing the String representation of "Don't look behind the door". Our subsequent representations of

String variables will be more concise. For example, our shorthand representation of message is

message   "Don't look behind the door!"

In this representation, we are giving only the crucial attribute—the text associated with the String object. We do not list the other attributes as they can be inferred from the text, and we do not list the methods implementing the String behaviors as they are the same for every String object.

3.2.1 ### INITIALIZATION

In principle, the syntax for object variable definitions is similar to that of primitive variable definitions. There are two forms—definitions that do and do not specify initial values.

The following code segment defines three String variables prompt, errorMsg, and fileType. All three definitions specify initial values for the variables.

```
String prompt = "Enter a new number: ";
String errorMsg = "Number must be positive.";
String fileType = "html";
```

The initial values are given through the use of literal character strings, which Java considers to be String constants. In particular, the value associated with a literal character string is a reference to a String representation of the associated character string.

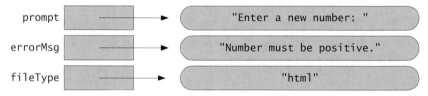

prompt   "Enter a new number: "

errorMsg   "Number must be positive."

fileType   "html"

A String variable cannot be initialized with a **char** variable or a literal **char** value. Therefore, the following definition is illegal.

```
String s = '!';     // illegal
```

The rules of Java require the use double quotes even for strings of length 1.

```
String s = "!";     // legal
```

We can initialize a String variable using another String variable. The following code segment first defines and initializes a String variable a. Variable a is then used to initialize String variable b.

```
String a = "excellence";
String b = a;                    // b references the same object as a
```

The definitions result in both variables being associated with the same value—the memory location associated with the `String` representation of the literal character string `"excellence"`. Thus, the two definitions have representation

The variables in the preceding examples get their values either directly or indirectly from literal values (i.e., quoted strings). However, we also previously have provided examples where variables are initialized with references to newly constructed objects. In particular, Chapter 2 used the class `Scanner` to encapsulate an input stream.

```
Scanner stdin = new Scanner(System.in);
```

In this definition, variable `stdin` references a newly *constructed* (created) `Scanner` *instance* (object), which in turn is built out of the standard input stream.

The use of the **new** operator coupled with a *constructor* method invocation to produce and configure a new object is normal practice. For this reason, `Scanner`, like almost all of the other standard classes provides public constructors so that `Scanner` objects can be instantiated.

For example, the next code segment uses a `Rectangle` constructor in its initialization of a `Rectangle` variable r that references a new `Rectangle` object with width 5 and height 2, which is situated with its top-left corner at coordinate (3, 4). Class `Rectangle` is part of the package `java.awt` and it provides a representation for a rectangular area whose attributes are its top-left corner location, width, and height.

```
int x = 3;
int y = 4;
int width = 5;
int height = 2;
Rectangle r = new Rectangle(x, y, width, height);
```

The initialization expression for `Rectangle` variable r is a **new** expression. The *evaluation* of this expression causes the creation and configuring of a new `Rectangle`.

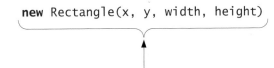

A new operation creates and initializes a new object. The value of the operation is a reference to the new object. This new operation constructs a new Rectangle object

The *value* of the **new** expression is a reference to the memory location that holds the newly constructed `Rectangle` object.

It is the **new** operator that causes memory to be set aside for a new object, which in this case is a `Rectangle`. The new object is given to the `Rectangle` constructor for configuring. The parameters to the constructor indicate how the new object is to configured.

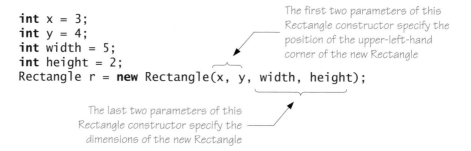

```
int x = 3;
int y = 4;
int width = 5;
int height = 2;
Rectangle r = new Rectangle(x, y, width, height);
```

The first two parameters of this Rectangle constructor specify the position of the upper-left-hand corner of the new Rectangle

The last two parameters of this Rectangle constructor specify the dimensions of the new Rectangle

Thus, the representation of the variables defined in the code segment is

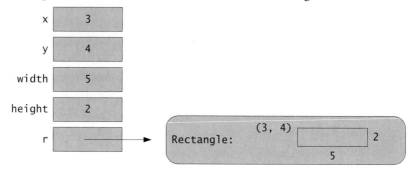

In the next chapter, we shall again make use of the **new** operator. However, starting there the use of the **new** operator will include applications to our own classes and not just to standard classes.

3.2.2 ## NULL AND UNINITIALIZED REFERENCES

The next code segment defines three local variables `dayOfWeek`, `inStream`, and `frame` without specifying initial values for these variables.

```
String dayOfWeek;
Scanner inStream;
Rectangle frame;
```

Like other local variable definitions that do not specify initial values, the values of these variables are undefined. The representation of these variables would be

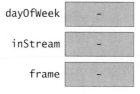

where "−" indicates an uninitialized value. Although Java allows local object type variables to be defined in this manner, it requires that the variables be initialized before their values are used.

Besides assigning object references to an object variable, a program can also assign the **null** reference. Conceptually, a **null** reference corresponds to the empty address. The value indicates that the variable is not referencing an object. In the code segment

```
String fontName = null;
Scanner fileIn = null;
Rectangle boundingBox = null;
```

variables fontName, fileIn, and boundingBox are all initialized to the **null** reference. A pictorial representation of these definitions would be

fontName	**null**
fileIn	**null**
boundingBox	**null**

It is important to realize that a variable with value **null** is different than an uninitialized variable. Although neither of them references an object, a variable with value **null** can be assigned to another variable.

```
String s1 = null;
String s2;
String s3 = s1;        // legal: s1 has the value null
String s4 = s2;        // illegal: s2 does not have a value
```

The **null** value indicates that no information is being represented by the variable.

3.3   ASSIGNMENT

Like primitive variables, one object variable can be assigned to another. The assignment results in both variables referring to the *same* object.

Suppose String values word1 and word2 that have been initialized as follows.

```
String word1 = "luminous";
String word2 = "graceful";
```

Thus, the two variables have representation

If a code segment assigns word2 to word1 as in the following statement

```
word1 = word2;
```

then word1 now references the same object as word2.

Variable word1 is now an *alias* for the object referenced by word2.

Because the String representation of the character string "luminous" is no longer needed, the memory for that String object is reclaimed *automatically* by Java so that it can be reused by other parts of the program. This memory recycling is known as *garbage collection* and is an important feature of Java.

An assignment statement also can be used to give a value to an uninitialized object variable. For example, the following code segment first defines a local Rectangle variable inset and then assigns inset a newly constructed Rectangle value.

```
Rectangle inset;
inset = new Rectangle(1, 1, 6, 2);
```

From its definition, inset has representation

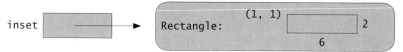

With the assignment, inset references a 6×2 rectangle located at (1, 1).

Now consider the following code segment.

```
String a = "alpha";
String b = a;
a = "beta";
```

The segment begins by defining a String variable a. After that definition, variable a has depiction

The segment then defines a String variable b. The definition causes variables a and b to reference the same String.

The code segment then assigns a new value to variable a—variable a now references a `String` whose value is `"beta"`. Even though a and b were both referencing previously the same `String`, the assignment to variable a does not affect variable b's reference.

Variable b remains a reference to the string `"alpha"`. It does so because variables a and b had their own independent references to the representation of `"alpha"`. Therefore, a change to variable a does not affect variable b and vice-versa.

<table>
<tr><td>3.4</td><td></td></tr>
</table>

FINAL VARIABLES

In Chapter 2 we used modifier **final** to define primitive type constants. We can also use this modifier to define object constants. However, when an object constant is defined—be it `String` or any other object type—we are specifying *only* that the reference cannot be changed. That is, the constant must always refer to the same memory location.

The following code segment defines two `String` constants.

```
final String POEM_TITLE = "The Appearance of Brown";
final String WARNING = "The weather ball is black";
```

We are not allowed to make changes to what these variables reference. Our representation for these definitions is

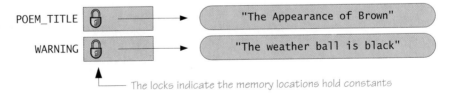

The locks indicate the memory locations hold constants

Thus, the following statement would not compile as it attempts to change what variable WARNING references.

```
WARNING = "The weather ball is green";   // illegal for constant
```

Although an object constant must always refer to the same memory location, it does not mean necessarily that the value stored at that location cannot be modified through its member methods.

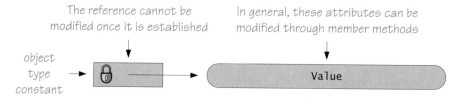

For example, because of its definition `Rectangle` constant BLOCK must reference a particular `Rectangle` memory location throughout its existence. Initially, that memory location references a 4×2 rectangle situated at (6, 9).

```
final Rectangle BLOCK = new Rectangle(6, 9, 4, 2);
```

The depiction of constant BLOCK would be

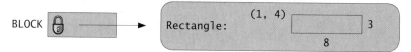

However, we can change the `Rectangle` object that BLOCK references. For example, the following code segment reconfigures the `Rectangle` so that its top-left corner is at (1, 4) and that its dimensions are 8×3.

```
BLOCK.setLocation(1, 4);
BLOCK.resize(8, 3);
```

After the code segment completes, the depiction of memory would be

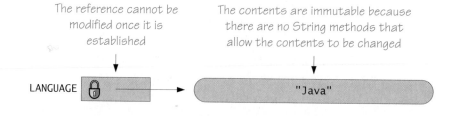

The `String` class does not provide any methods to modify an existing `String`. Therefore, it is always the case that the object to which a `String` constant references is itself unchanging. (i.e., a `String` is immutable). Thus, for `String` constant LANGUAGE defined next

```
final String LANGUAGE = "Java";
```

the following representation occurs.

3.5 STRING OPERATIONS AND METHODS

To display a `String`, a program can make use of the `print()` and `println()` methods of `System.out`. For example, the following code segment displays the value referenced by `String` variable `adage` to standard output.

```
String adage = "Every day can be a good day!";
System.out.println(adage);
```

The first statement defines `adage` to be a `String` variable that is initialized to reference a memory location containing a `String` representation of the character string `"Every day can be a good day!"`.

The second statement invokes `System.out.println()` to display the character sequence associated with `String` variable `greeting`. The invocation produces output

```
Every day can be a good day!
```

The next code segment shows how to use a `Scanner` to extract a user-supplied string from standard input and assign it to a `String` variable.

```
Scanner stdin = new Scanner(System.in);

System.out.print("Enter your account name: ");
String response = stdin.nextLine();
```

First, variable `stdin` is initialized to reference a `Scanner` view of standard input.

As in the interactive console programs of Chapter 2, the code segment uses the `print()` method to display the prompt message. After executing the `print()` statement, standard output looks like

```
Enter your account name:
```

The character string that the user supplies in reaction to the prompt is extracted by `Scanner` method `nextLine()` and a reference to that string is returned by the method. The value of that reference is used to initialize variable `response`. For example, if the user entered *artiste*,

```
Enter your account name: artiste
```

then the variable `response` defined in the last statement of the segment would reference a `String` representation of `"artiste"`.

The next code segment uses our `Scanner` variable `stdin` to extract the first and middle names of a person. The segment also echoes the names back.

```
System.out.print("Enter your first name: ");
```

```
String firstName = stdin.nextLine();

System.out.print("Enter your middle name: ");
String middleName = stdin.nextLine();

System.out.println("Your name is " + firstName + " "
    + middleName + ".");
```

Like the previous code segment, this code segment begins with the definition of a variable `stdin` that is initialized to reference a `Scanner` representation of standard input. A prompt then indicates that the user should enter a first name. Suppose the user's response to the prompt was to enter *Joanne*.

```
Enter your first name: Joanne
```

The next statement in the code segment defines a `String` variable `firstName`. The variable is initialized with the value returned by the invocation of `stdin.nextLine()`. Given the user's response, variable `firstName` has representation

Suppose the user's response to the second prompt has depiction

```
Enter your middle name: Audrey
```

The second `nextLine()` invocation results in `middleName` being assigned a reference to a `String` object representing the character string `"Audrey"`. Therefore, variables `firstName` and `middleName` have representation

The next statement of the code segment

```
System.out.println("Your name is " + firstName + " "
    + middleName + ".");
```

echoes the extracted values back to the user to complete the code segment. The parameter `"Your name is " + firstName + middleName + "."` to `println()` makes multiple uses of the `String` concatenation operator + for combining strings. The result is a `String` object whose value represents the character string `"Your name is Joanne Audrey."` Therefore, the display would now show

```
Enter your first name: Joanne
Enter your middle name: Audrey
Your name is Joanne Audrey.
```

The concatenation operator also can be used to combine numbers or **char** values with literal character strings or `String` objects. The result is a `String` with the natural interpretation. For example, the definitions

```
String s1 = 1000 + " grams to a kilogram.";
String s2 = "Pi is less than " + 3.1416 + '.';
```

result in variables with the following representations.

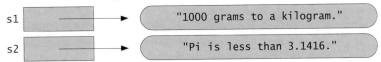

Java also provides the `String` append assignment operator, +=. The append assignment causes its left operand to be assigned a reference to a *new* `String` object representing the concatenation of the left operand's value before the assignment with the value of the right operand. Like concatenation, the append assignment operation's right operand can be a number, character, or string. The following code segment makes multiple uses of the += operator.

```
String s = "Jeepers";
s += '-';
s += "creepers";
s += '!';
System.out.println(s);
```

The segment results in output

```
Jeepers-creepers!
```

Because the right operand of the += operator can be an expression, the following code segment results in the same output.

```
String s = "Jeepers";
s += '-' + "creepers" + '!';
System.out.println(s);
```

The preceding code segments give the illusion it is the `String` object to which s references that undergoes change. However, what really changes in the code segments is the value of variable s. Each append assignment operation causes variable s to reference a different `String`.

Besides working with the concatenation and assignment operators, a `String` can be directed through its member methods to perform a variety of behaviors. At this point, we mention only some of the most useful `String` member methods. In subsequent chapters, we introduce others. As a reminder, member methods are the means by which an object Java implements a behavior, and class methods are services provided by the class.

`String` member method `length()` enables a `String` object to communicate the number of characters that make up the string that *it* represents. When invoked, the method does not take any parameters. The absence of parameters is typical of most member methods that return an attribute of their associated object.

Program `WordLength.java` of Listing 3.1 uses the method to help display the number of characters in a user-specified word. A sample run of the program is demonstrated below.

```
Enter a word: tarantism
Word tarantism has length 9.
```

Like previous console programs, `WordLength.java` consists of a single method named `main()`. Method `main()` begins with the definition of `Scanner` variable `stdin`

Listing 3.1 **WordLength.java**

```
1.  // Purpose: Display the length of a user-specified word
2.
3.  import java.util.*;
4.
5.  public class WordLength {
6.
7.      // main(): application entry point
8.      public static void main(String[] args) {
9.          // set input stream
10.         Scanner stdin = new Scanner(System.in);
11.
12.         // get desired word
13.         System.out.print("Enter a word: ");
14.         String word = stdin.nextLine();
15.
16.         // compute length of word
17.         int wordLength = word.length();
18.
19.         // display result
20.         System.out.println("Word " + word + " has length "
21.             + wordLength + ".");
22.     }
23. }
```

---

that is associated with the standard input stream. A section of code then both prompts the user for a word and extracts the user's response.

```
System.out.print("Enter a word: ");
String word = stdin.nextLine();
```

The program then determines the length of the user-specified word in line 17.

```
int length = word.length();
```

Invocation `word.length()` causes Java to initialize the **int** variable `wordLength` to the length of the word entered by the user.

The program completes its job by displaying the result of its calculation.

```
System.out.println("Word " + word + " has length "
    + wordLength + ".");
```

Another useful `String` member method is `charAt()`. This method expects a single index as its parameter and returns the value of the character at that position in its `String`. While such behavior seems *relatively* natural given the method name and its parameter, what is not natural is that in Java, as in several other programming languages, *the first character of a String is located at index 0.*

Consider the following definition of `String` variable `alphabet`.

```
String alphabet = "abcdefghijklmnopqrstuvwxyz";
```

Our customary representation for this variable while convenient is misleading.

alphabet [ ] ⟶ ("abcdefghijklmnopqrstuvwxyz")

The representation does not show that each character in the string is stored in its own memory location. A representation that captures this important notion is

In this depiction each letter in the string is boxed individually. The letter 'a' is in the first box, which has index 0; the letter 'b' is in the second box, which has index 1; and so on.

Keeping this representation of variable `alphabet` in mind, the values of the **char** variables `c1`, `c2`, and `c3` defined in the following code segment can be determined readily.

```
char c1 = alphabet.charAt(9);
char c2 = alphabet.charAt(15);
char c3 = alphabet.charAt(2);
```

The variables are initialized respectively to the values `'j'`, `'p'`, and `'c'`.

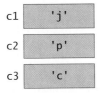

Yet another useful `String` processing capability is being able to obtain a substring of a string. Class `String` provides this capability in part with a member method `substring()` that takes two integer parameters. The first parameter specifies the index of the starting position in the string to be copied and the second parameter specifies the index of the position that is one *beyond* the last character to be copied. Method `substring()` returns a new `String` representing the portion of its string specified by the two indices.

The following code segment initializes variable `month` so that it references a `String` object whose representation is the first six characters referenced by `weddingDate`. The `substring()` invocation is `weddingDate.substring(0,6)`. Observe that the difference $6 - 0$ is 6, which is the length of the substring to be returned.

```
String weddingDate = "August 21, 1976";
String month = weddingDate.substring(0, 6);
System.out.println("Month is " + month + ".");
```

The segment displays

```
Month is August.
```

The class `String` also has a member method `substring()` that takes a single **int** parameter. The method returns a new `String` that is a substring of the `String` being manipulated. The substring starts with the character whose index is specified by the parameter and continues to the end of the string. The next code segment uses the method to determine the last four characters of the `String` referenced by `firstDate`.

```
String firstDate = "January 9, 1974";
int n = firstDate.length();
String year = firstDate.substring(n-4);
System.out.println("Year is " + year + ".");
```

The segment displays

```
Year is 1974.
```

Yet another useful `String` member method is `trim()`. Method `trim()` returns a newly created string that represents the portion of its `String` excluding any leading and trailing whitespace. For example, the code segment

```
String t1 = "    world    is turning   ";
String t2 = t1.trim();
```

produces `String` variables `t1` and `t2` with representation

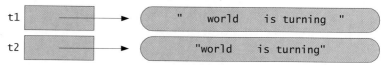

Observe that method `trim()` did not affect the spacing between the words—it removed only the leading and trailing spaces.

The class `String` also includes member methods to search for a substring within a `String`. One of these methods is the method `indexOf()` taking two parameters. The first parameter is the substring to be found and the second parameter is the index from which to start the search of the `String` object. If the substring can be found, then the method returns the starting position of the first such occurrence. Otherwise, the method returns –1.

Consider the following code segment.

```
String fruit = "banana";
String searchString = "an";

System.out.println("Looking for \"" + searchString + "\" in \""
        + fruit + "\"");

int n1 = fruit.indexOf(searchString, 0);
int n2 = fruit.indexOf(searchString, n1 + 1);
int n3 = fruit.indexOf(searchString, n2 + 1);

System.out.println("    First search result: " + n1);
System.out.println("    Second search result: " + n2);
System.out.println("    Third search result: " + n3);
```

It produces the output

```
Looking for "an" in "banana"
    First search result: 1
    Second search result: 3
    Third search result: -1
```

The two `String` variables defined in the segment have the following "boxed" representations

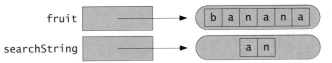

The first search for substring `"an"` in the `String` referenced by variable `fruit` begins at index 0. Because this search first finds the substring at index 1, variable `n1` is initialized to 1.

Last occurrence

The `String` class also provides member methods for searching for the last occurrence of a string. For example, there is a method `lastIndexOf()` that takes two parameters—the substring of interest and a maximal index value to be used in searching for the substring. If the substring can be found in the `String` starting at some index not greater than the index parameter, then the method returns the starting position of the last such occurrence within the `String` object. If the substring cannot be found, `lastIndexOf()` returns –1.

Consider the following code segment that searches for `"iss"` in `"Mississippi"`.

```
String state = "Mississippi";
String searchString = "iss";
System.out.println("Looking for \"" + searchString
        + "\" in \""+ state + "\"");
int n1 = state.indexOf(searchString, 0);
int n2 = state.lastIndexOf(searchString, state.length()-1);
System.out.println("   First search result: " + n1);
System.out.println("   Second search result: " + n2)
```

The segment produces output

```
Looking for "iss" in "Mississippi"
    First search result: 1
    Second search result: 4
```

The second search for `"an"` in the string referenced by variable `fruit` begins at index 2 (i.e., `n1` + 1). This search first finds the substring at index 3. Therefore, variable `n2` is initialized to 3.

The third search for `"an"` in the string referenced by variable `fruit` begins at index 4 (i.e., `n2` + 1). Because this search is unsuccessful, variable `n3` is initialized to –1.

The `String` class also provides a collection of class methods all with the name `valueOf()`. Because they are class methods, they are providing services. In particular, they provide services related to strings.

For each of the primitive types (e.g, **char**, **int**, and **double**) there is a `valueOf()` class method, which takes a single parameter of that type. A `valueOf()` method returns a reference to a newly created `String` representing the value of its parameter in character string form. The `valueOf()` methods

A complete description of the String class is available in Appendix E.

are defined to be class methods rather than member methods because their tasks do not involve accessing or manipulating existing strings.

The next code segment makes use of three of the `valueOf()` methods.

```
int v1 = -12;
double v2 = 3.14;
char v3 = 'a';
String s1 = String.valueof(v1);
String s2 = String.valueof(v2);
String s3 = String.valueof(v3);
```

The segment results in variables with the following representation.

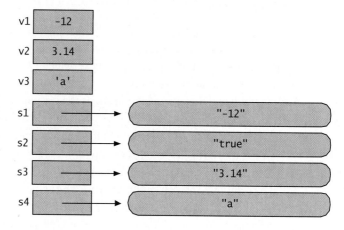

| 3.6 | **CASE STUDY — DATE TRANSLATION** |

To gain additional experience with the `String` library and problem solving, we next develop a program that converts a date from American format to standard format.

> The objective of this case study is to show the use of the String library for manipulating information when problem solving

A date expressed in American format consists of a month followed by whitespace followed by a particular day of that month followed by a comma followed by whitespace followed by a year. For example, April 13, 1743, and January 15, 1929, are both dates in the American format.

A date expressed in international format consists of the year followed by a hyphen followed by month followed by a hyphen followed by the particular day of a month. For example, 1874-November-30 and 1918-July-18 are both dates in the standard format.

PROBLEM STATEMENT

Provide a console-based interactive program that converts a user-specified date in American format (e.g., July 4, 1776) to international format (e.g., 1776-July-4).

SAMPLE OUTPUT

```
Date format translator
   Converts a date from American format (e.g., July 4, 1776)
   to standard format (e.g., 1776-July-4).

Enter date in American format: January 1, 2000

The translation of
   January 1, 2000
to standard format is
   2000-January-1
```

ANALYSIS AND DESIGN

An analysis of the problem indicates an input date must be acquired and manipulated. An appropriate object representation for the date is a `String`. From that `String`, three objects can be created representing the input date's month substring, the day substring, and the year substring. The three substrings can then be concatenated in the proper order to produce a `String` object representing the date in standard format.

Thus, in solving the problem the following variables and their associated objects are created, used, and manipulated:

- `stdin`: `Scanner` representing the standard input stream;
- `buffer`: `String` representing the input date in American format;
- `month`: `String` representing the month;
- `day`: `String` representing the day of the month;
- `year`: `String` representing the year;
- `standardDate`: `String` representing the date in standard format.

In addition, although its availability is taken generally for granted, the standard output stream is also needed.

- System.out: PrintStream representing the standard output stream;

With these variables, *pseudocode* (algorithm) can be written that describes the object interactions and manipulations for solving the problem.

Step 1.   Display a suitable legend describing the program's purpose to the standard output.

Step 2.   Issue a prompt to the standard output that requests the user to enter a date in American format.

Step 3.   Get a String representation of the date of interest from the standard input and assign it to variable buffer.

Step 4.   Echo buffer's date representation to the standard output.

Step 5.   Examine buffer's date representation and extract a String representation of the input month. Assign the representation to variable month.

Step 6.   Examine buffer's date representation and extract a String representation of the input day. Assign the representation to variable day.

Step 7.   Examine buffer's date representation and extract a String representation of the input year. Assign the representation to variable year.

Step 8.   Assign to variable standardDate the String concatenation of year, month, and day with appropriate separating hyphens.

Step 9.   Display standardDate's date representation to the standard output.

We next discuss how to implement the pseudocode in Java.

IMPLEMENTATION

The legend display is implemented easily using method System.out.println().

```
// produce a legend (Step 1)
System.out.println("Date format translator");
System.out.println("   Converts a date from American"
    + " format (e.g., July 4, 1776)");
System.out.println("   to standard format (e.g.,"
    + " 1776-July-4).");
System.out.println();
```

Similarly, displaying a prompt is straightforward with method System.out.print().

```
// prompt the user for a date in American format (Step 2)
System.out.print("Enter a date in American format: ");
```

Using Scanner method nextLine(), the date of interest can be extracted from the standard input stream to initialize the variable buffer.

```
// acquire the input entered by the user (Step 3)
Scanner stdin = new Scanner(System.in);
String buffer = stdin.nextLine();
```

Before manipulating the input string represented by buffer, the string is echoed back to indicate its intended purpose.

```
// echo the input back (Step 4)
System.out.println("The translation of");
System.out.println("   " + buffer);
```

For example, suppose `buffer` represented "   February 29, 1904 " with depiction

buffer ➔ "   February 29,   1904"

The output of this segment would then be

```
The translation of
    February 29, 1904
```

The determination of the month portion of the input string begins by trimming any leading or trailing whitespace that surrounds the input date.

```
// get month entered by the user (Step 5)
buffer = buffer.trim();
int m = buffer.indexOf(" ");
String month = buffer.substring(0, m);
buffer = buffer.substring(m + 1);
```

The trimming results in `Buffer` being assigned a newly created `String` that represents the input string without any leading or trailing whitespace (i.e., two initial blanks and one trailing blank were removed).

buffer ➔ "February 29,   1904"

As a result of the trimming, the month substring consists of the characters preceding the first blank in the string now referenced by `buffer`. To search for the index m of that blank, `String` member method `indexOf()` is used. In particular, the method `indexOf()` that takes a single parameter of type `String` is invoked. The invocation returns the starting index of the first occurrence of the search string.

```
int m = buffer.indexOf(" ");
```

To create the `String` representation of the month, a `String` member method `substring()` is used.

```
String month = buffer.substring(0, m);
```

The method's two parameters are 0 and m, which specify respectively the index of the starting position in the string to be copied and the index of the position that is one beyond the last character to be copied. The method creates and returns a `String` copy of the specified characters.

Once the month substring is created, `buffer` is updated to reference the portion of the user input that follows the month.

```
buffer = buffer.substring(m + 1);
```

The update assigns `buffer` the evaluation of the expression `buffer.substring(m + 1)`. The evaluation of this expression produces a `String` copy of the characters starting at index m + 1 and continuing to the end of the string.

buffer ➔ " 29,   1904"

From that copy, a `String` is then created that represents the trimmed version of the copy. After the trimming, the day portion begins with what is left of the input. In particular, the day portion is the substring preceding the comma.

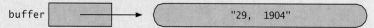

buffer   →   "29,   1904"

Thus, the task of the sixth step is similar to the that of the fifth step. However, instead of searching for a blank, the search in this step is for a comma.

```
// get day entered by the user (Step 6)
buffer = buffer.trim();
int n = buffer.indexOf(",");
String day = buffer.substring(0, n);
buffer = buffer.substring(n + 1);
```

The code reflects the similarity of the tasks. A variable n is assigned the index of the comma. Using that index, a `String` representation of the day is created. Variable `buffer` is then updated so that it references a representation of the portion of the input following the comma.

buffer   →   " 1904"

By trimming `buffer`, the year portion of input can be gotten.

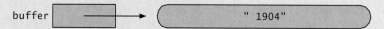

buffer   →   "1904"

Therefore the seventh step is straightforward—variable year is initialized with the trimmed version of `buffer`.

```
// get year entered by the user (Step 7)
String year = buffer.trim();
```

With variables month, day, and year appropriately set, a standard format version of the input date can be created through concatenation and assigned to variable `standardDate`. Doing so completes the eighth step.

```
// create standard format version of input (Step 8)
String standardDate = year + "-" + month + "-" + day;
```

The implementation of the last step is straightforward—display the transformed date.

```
// display the translation (Step 9)
System.out.println("to standard format is");
System.out.printlh("   " + standardDate);
```

To develop a program, the code needs to be assembled in a method `main()` within an appropriately named class. We named the class `DateTranslation` and provide the complete solution for the problem in `DateTranslation.java` of Listing 3.2.

TESTING

Although the preceding analysis demonstrated the correctness of the code, it is possible that the analysis was incomplete or did not take some input cases into account. It is also possible that the implementation of the design introduced errors (e.g., a mistyped index). Therefore, testing of the program is appropriate.

Although testing the program with every possible input date is impossible, it is possible to test the program with each possible input date form. The basic input form has the following elements:

- month whitespace day comma year.

However, whitespace can precede or follow the year. There can also be whitespace preceding the month. Therefore, the other possible input forms are

- month whitespace day comma year whitespace;
- month whitespace day comma whitespace year;
- month whitespace day comma whitespace year whitespace;
- whitespace month whitespace day comma year;
- whitespace month whitespace day comma year whitespace;
- whitespace month whitespace day comma whitespace year whitespace.

The exercises test `DateTranslation.java` using each of the input forms.

Listing 3.2   DateTranslation.java

```java
1.  // Convert user-specified date from American to standard
2.  // format
3.
4.  import java.util.*;
5.
6.  class DateTranslation {
7.
8.      // main(): application entry point
9.      static public void main(String args[]) {
10.         // produce a legend (Step 1)
11.         System.out.println("Date format translator");
12.         System.out.println("   Converts a date from an American"
13.             + " format (e.g., July 4, 1776)");
14.         System.out.println("   to standard format (e.g.,"
15.             + " 1776-July-4).");
16.         System.out.println();
17.
18.         // prompt the user for a date in American format (Step 2)
19.         System.out.print("Enter a date in American format: ");
20.
21.         // acquire the input entered by the user (Step 3)
22.         Scanner stdin = new Scanner(System.in);
23.
24.         String buffer = stdin.nextLine().trim();
25.
26.         // echo the input back (Step 4)
27.         System.out.println("The translation of");
28.         System.out.println("   " + buffer);
29.
30.         // get month entered by the user (Step 5)
31.         buffer = buffer.trim();
32.         int m = buffer.indexOf(" ");
33.         String month = buffer.substring(0, m);
34.         buffer = buffer.substring(m + 1);
35.
36.         // get day entered by the user (Step 6)
37.         buffer = buffer.trim();
38.         int n = buffer.indexOf(",");
39.         String day = buffer.substring(0, n);
40.         buffer = buffer.substring(n + 1);
41.
42.         // get year entered by the user (Step 7)
43.         String year = buffer.trim();
44.
45.         // create standard format version of input (Step 8)
46.         String standardDate = year + "-" + month + "-" + day;
47.
48.         // display the translation (Step 9)
49.         System.out.println("to standard format is");
50.         System.out.println("   " + standardDate);
51.     }
52. }
```

| 3.7 | **REVIEW** |

- The value of an object variable is a reference to a location that holds an object of its object type.

- The **null** reference corresponds to the empty address.

- The memory for unreferenced objects is reclaimed automatically so that it can be reused as needed. This memory recycling is called garbage collection.

- Once initialized, an object type constant cannot change the object to which it refers.

- A String is an encapsulation of a sequence of characters.

- The String method length() returns the number of characters that make up its string.

- The String += operator performs an append assignment.

- The first character of a String object has index 0.

- String provides several substring() member methods that return a new String object representing a portion of the associated string.

- String provides several indexOf() member methods that provide the ability to find the first occurrence of substring subject to some conditions.

- String provides several lastIndexOf() member methods that provide the ability to find the last occurrence of a substring subject to some conditions.

- String member method charAt() expects a single index as its parameter and returns the value of the character at that position in its String.

- String member method trim() returns a newly created string that represents its string except for any leading and trailing whitespace.

- The String class provides a class method named valueOf() for each of the primitive types. A valueOf() method expects a single parameter fundamental type and returns a reference to a newly created String representing the value of its parameter in string form.

- There are no methods to modify a String—once a String object has been created, it is immutable.

- The Java awt API provides the class Rectangle. A Rectangle represents a rectangular area in coordinate space.

- There is a Rectangle constructor that expects as its parameters: the x-coordinate of the top-left corner, the y-coordinate of the top-left corner, the width, and the height.

- Rectangle member method setLocation() uses its parameters to reset the x- and y-coordinates of its rectangle.

- Rectangle member method resize() uses its parameters to resize the width and height of its rectangle.

- The creation of a class type object is accomplished by invoking a member constructor method that creates and initializes the attributes of the object.

| 3.8 | **SELF-TEST** |

S3.1   Give a depiction of memory after the following code segment is executed

```
int i = 1;
String s = "string1";
String t = s;
```

S3.2   Does the following code segment make sense? Explain.

```
String s = "string1";
String t;
s = t;
```

S3.3   What is the output of the following code segment? Explain.

```
String s = "abcdefghij";
System.out.println(s.indexOf("i"));
```

S3.4   True or false: The empty string and **null** are equivalent in concept. Explain.

| 3.9 | **EXERCISES** |

3.1   Define and initialize appropriately named String variables and constants for the following concepts. Justify your choice of variable or constant definition.

a)   The response given by a user when queried for a color.

b)   A message to a user asking for the current temperature.

c)   A response to a user indicating that the input entry was invalid.

d)   The response given by a user when queried for a first name.

e)   The third month of the year.

f)   The English language vowels.

3.2   Give a depiction of memory after the following code segment is executed.

```
int i = 10;
int j = i;
String s = "string1";
String t = s;
s = "string2";
```

3.3   Give a depiction of memory after the following code segment is executed.

```
String s = "string1";
String t = "string2";
String u;
u = s;
s = t;
t = u;
```

3.4   How are primitive and object variables different? Explain.

3.5   What is held constant in an object type constant? Explain.

3.6   What is automatic garbage collection? Why might it be important?

3.7   Why is the String class available to our program without the use of an **import** statement? Explain.

3.8   What is the value of the following expressions?

a) `1 + 2 + " buckle my shoe"`

b) `"one-" + "two"+ " buckle my shoe"`

c) `"" + 1 + 2 + " buckle my shoe"`

d) `'1' + 2 + " buckle my shoe"`

e) `1 + "-2" + " buckle my shoe"`

3.9   Draw a picture of memory after the following code segment completes.

```
String s;
String t = null;
String u = "";
```

3.10 Does the following code segment make sense? Explain.

```
String s = "string1";
String t = null;
s = t;
```

3.11 What is the output of the following code segment? Explain.

```
String s = "abcdefghij";
System.out.println(s.length());
```

3.12 Correct the following code segment. Explain your changes.

```
String s = "1234567890";
int i = s.length;
int j = s.indexOf('5');
int k = s;
```

3.13 What is the output of the following code segment? Explain.

```
String s = "perseverance";
String t = s.substring(4, 6);
String u = s.substring(3, 8);
String v = s.substring(0, 9);
System.out.println(t);
System.out.println(u);
System.out.println(v);
```

3.14 What is the output of the following code segment? Explain.

```
String s = "telephone directory";
String t = s.substring(5, 9);
String u = s.substring(1, 1);
String v = s.substring(12, 16);
System.out.println(t);
System.out.println(u);
System.out.println(v);
```

3.15 What is the output of the following code segment? Explain.

```
String s = "abracadabra";
```

```
int n1 = s.indexOf("ra");
int n2 = s.indexOf("ra", 2);
int n3 = s.indexOf("ra", 5);
int n4 = s.indexOf("ra", 10);
System.out.println(n1);
System.out.println(n2);
System.out.println(n3);
System.out.println(n4);
```

3.16   What is the output of the following code segment? Explain.

```
String s = "deadheaded";
int n1 = s.indexOf("ead");
int n2 = s.indexOf("dh", 2);
int n3 = s.indexOf("d", 5);
int n4 = s.indexOf("d", 10);
System.out.println(n1);
System.out.println(n2);
System.out.println(n3);
System.out.println(n4);
```

3.17   What is the output of the following code segment? Explain.

```
String alphabet = "qwertyuiopasdfghjklzxcvbnm";
char c1 = alphabet.charAt(0);
char c2 = alphabet.charAt(9);
char c3 = alphabet.charAt(25);
System.out.println(c1);
System.out.println(c2);
System.out.println(c3);
```

3.18   What is the output of the following code segment? Explain.

```
String alphabet = "qazwsxedcrfvtgbyhnujmikolp";
char c1 = alphabet.charAt(2);
char c2 = alphabet.charAt(10);
char c3 = alphabet.charAt(24);
System.out.println(c1);
System.out.println(c2);
System.out.println(c3);
```

3.19   What is the output of the following code segment? Explain.

```
int v1 = 3;
double v2 = 1.414;
char v3 = 'c';
String s1 = String.valueof(v1);
String s2 = String.valueof(v2);
String s3 = String.valueof(v3);
```

3.20   What is the output of the following code segment? Explain.

```
char v1 = 'j';
int v2 = 88;
double v3 = 6.21;
String s1 = String.valueof(v1);
String s2 = String.valueof(v2);
String s3 = String.valueof(v3);
```

3.21 What is the output of the following code segment? Explain.

```
String s = "abcd      ";
String t = "    abcd   ";
String u = "  ab   cd  ";
System.out.println(s.trim());
System.out.println(t.trim());
System.out.println(u.trim());
```

3.22 What is the output of the following code segment? Explain.

```
String s = "a b c d e f";
String t = " a   b     ";
String u = "         abc";
System.out.println(s.trim());
System.out.println(t.trim());
System.out.println(u.trim());
```

3.23 After the following code segment is executed, is it safe for Java to reclaim the memory to which s referred upon initialization? Explain.

```
Scanner stdin = new Scanner(System.in);
String s = stdin.nextLine();
String t = s;
s = "aardvark";
t = "weasel";
```

3.24 Define a `String` variable s that represents the concatenation of the values referenced by `String` variables u and v and the character `'!'`.

3.25 Write a program that prompts for and accepts a telephone number in the form *ddd–ddd–dddd*, where *d* is a digit, and prints it out in the following format: (*ddd*) *ddd–dddd*.

3.26 The string @ @ @ is a valid address according to the problem statement for the e-mail address case study of Section 3.10. Why was this allowed? What program abilities are required to handle such cases? What program abilities are required to handle the finding of all e-mail addresses in some text of interest?

3.27 Develop and test an input suite for `DateTranslation.java` of Listing 3.2. The suite should consider the following possibilities.

- month whitespace day comma year whitespace;

- month whitespace day comma whitespace year;

- month whitespace day comma whitespace year whitespace;

- whitespace month whitespace day comma year;

- whitespace month whitespace day comma year whitespace;

- whitespace month whitespace day comma whitespace year whitespace.

3.10	**PROGRAMMING PROJECT — HARVESTER**

Have you ever wondered how unsolicited e-mail or as it commonly is called, *spam*, comes from mass-marketing companies that you have never heard of? Mass-marketers use a variety of techniques, one of which is *e-mail harvesting*. An e-mail harvester is a program that searches the Web for files containing e-mail addresses.

> The objective of this case study is to practice using the String library for manipulating information in the context of problem solving

For example, there are websites such as `http://www.ibiblio.org/` that maintain the archives of postings to electronic news groups such as `comp.lang.java`. Within these archives are tens of thousands of e-mail addresses from the various posters of news group articles. Although we are definitely not encouraging spam, the purpose of this case study is to design and document a program `EmailSearch.java` that searches a user-provided string to see if it contains an e-mail address.

PROBLEM STATEMENT

Provide an interactive program that prompts a user for the text of interest. The program then displays the first e-mail address contained in that text. For our purposes an e-mail address is composed of an "@" and the two maximal-length strings with no embedded whitespace surrounding that "@". If there is no e-mail address in the text, then the program displays an "@".

In developing your solution `EmailAddress.java`, *use only the parts of the Java programming language that we have already introduced. The case study has been designed so that it exercises your use of the material presented in this chapter.*

SAMPLE OUTPUT

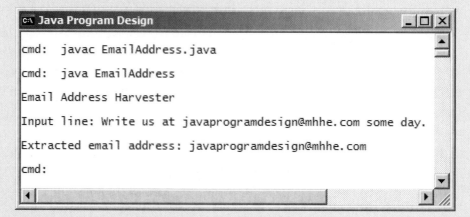

```
Java Program Design                                    _ □ X

cmd:  javac EmailAddress.java

cmd:  java EmailAddress

Email Address Harvester

Input line: Write us at javaprogramdesign@mhhe.com some day.

Extracted email address: javaprogramdesign@mhhe.com

cmd:
```

ANALYSIS AND DESIGN

So how do we search for an e-mail address? According to our definition, an e-mail address is a maximal string of characters that contains an "@" but does not contain whitespace. For example, consider the input text "there is no-one@home.org.moon today, try again tomorrow says nobody@nobody at home."

- "there" is not an e-mail address according to our definition—it does not contain an embedded "@".

- "is no-one@home.org.moon" and "no-one@home.org.moon today" are not e-mail addresses according to our definition—both strings contain whitespace

- "one@home.org" is not an e-mail address according to our definition—the string is not maximally nonwhitespace with respect to the input text; i.e., in the input text there are nonwhitespace characters immediately preceding and following the string "one@home.org"

- "nobody@nobody" is an e-mail address according to our definition—the string is a maximal-length nonblank string containing an "@". However, because "nobody@nobody" is not the first e-mail address within the supplied text, it is not the solution to our problem.

- "no-one@home.org.moon" is a valid e-mail address according to our definition—the string is a maximal-length nonblank string containing an "@". Because it is the first e-mail address in the supplied text, the address is the solution to our problem.

We express one caveat as we design a solution to our problem. At this point in the text we have not yet introduced how to execute actions selectively based on some test for conditions. Our programs have what is known as *straight-line* behavior—they perform the same tasks every time they are run. Because of this restriction, we must be especially thoughtful in how we process the user-supplied text so that we always produce a correct solution to our problem regardless of whether the user's entry contains an e-mail address.

It is clear that knowing the position of the first "@" in the text message is important. Suppose we know that the first "@" in the text is the j-th character there; i.e., its *index* is j. We are then interested in determining indices i and k, where i is the minimal index into the text such that all characters in positions i through j are nonblank and k is the maximal index into the text such that all characters in positions j through k are nonblank. The solution to our problem is then the string composed of the characters from index i to index k of the input text.

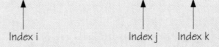

Input line: Write us at javaprogramdesign@mhhe.com some day.

       Index i   Index j Index k

IMPLEMENTATION

Our analysis suggests the following algorithm.

  Step 1. Prompt for an input text message.
  Step 2. Get input text *message*.
  Step 3. Set j to the index of the first "@" in *message*.
  Step 4. Set i to the minimal index in *message* such that all characters in positions i through j are nonblank.
  Step 5. Set k to the maximal index in *message* such that all characters in positions j through k are nonblank.
  Step 6. Set *address* to the substring of *message* with indices i through k.

Step 7.   Display *address*.

So how can we can implement such an algorithm? The first step is not difficult, we already have the ability to acquire `String` input via a console program.

The second statement is straightforward with the `String`. Member method `indexOf()` can be used to determine index *j*. But how do we find the indices *i* and *k* of the next two steps of the algorithm? What we can do is search for the indices of the last blank in *message* that precedes index *j* and the first blank in *message* that follows index *j*. These indices can be found respectively using `String` member methods `lastIndexOf()` and `indexOf()`.

With indices *i* and *k* we can use the `String substring()` method to determine *address*. But what if there are no blanks before or after the e-mail address or what if there is no e-mail address? In these cases, the values of *i* and *k* do not make sense for specifying the answer string.

So how can we ensure success? We can handle the special case of missing blanks by searching

    " " + *message* + " "

rather than searching *message*. The surrounding blanks ensure that if the e-mail address is present, then there are definitely blanks surrounding the message. When problem solving be open to modifying the input. It often can simplify the problem handling. However, be sure the modification does not affect whether the correct solution is calculated.

If a further alteration is made to the string to be searched, all cases can be handled readily. This alteration is left to you.

TESTING

Start the verification of your program with our example string "there is no-one@home.org.moon today, try again tomorrow says nobody@nobody at home". However, this string does not exhaustively test your program. For example, input strings with no blanks should also be considered. As part of your documentation, list your test set and explain how it considers all important cases. (For an example of what is expected, see the date translation test case analysis beginning on page 126.)

<table>
<tr><td>**3.11**</td><td></td></tr>
</table>

SELF-TEST ANSWERS

S3.1   The memory has the following depiction.

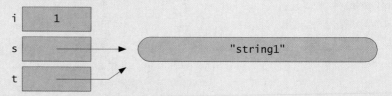

This depiction occurs because `i` is a primitive integer variable with value 1 and because `s` and `t` are `String` variables referencing the same location.

S3.2 The code segment does not make sense. Variable t is uninitialized and therefore it cannot be assigned to s. We can however assign s to t.

S3.3 The output is 8. An 8 is displayed because String positions are numbered starting at 0 and the first position in the character sequence represented by s is in the eighth position.

S3.4 False: The empty string and the **null** address are not equivalent in concept. The empty string corresponds to a character sequence of length 0. The **null** address corresponds to the empty address, which is more like the absence of a string.

4 BEING CLASSY

We now introduce how to create and manipulate simple objects with attributes and behaviors that *you* can specify. We do so through the use of classes. The class is Java's principal mechanism for supporting object-oriented design. A class enables objects to be created with attributes and behaviors. In Java, an attribute is represented using a data field and a behavior is implemented with a method. By using classes to represent the various types of information being examined and manipulated, *each information type is designed and implemented only once and then reused as often as needed without having to reanalyze and rejustify the representation.*

OBJECTIVES

- Introduce Java's primary object-oriented design mechanism—the class.
- Explore the use of instance variables and class constants.
- Consider class construction using default and nondefault constructors.
- Explore the use of member methods for accessing and mutating the attributes of an object.
- Explore the use of member methods for manipulating an object.
- Demonstrate the value of encapsulation and information hiding,
- Introduce the basics of window creation and graphical rendering.

4.1 PREPARATION

After this chapter, your programming skills will be very different. Thus far, our introduction to effective Java programming has given you experience with computing systems and problem solving, variables, types, input and output, expressions, assignments, objects, and standard classes and their methods. That material was background for what Java is really about—*the ability to design and implement your own objects*. With that ability you can model, create, and manipulate the attributes and behaviors of any information item or physical world object.

This chapter *introduces* you to the *basics* of designing and implementing your own objects by using Java's principal mechanism for specifying a new type of object—the class.

In a very real sense, this entire chapter is a case study. It is a case study that focuses on using classes and object-oriented design to problem solve. Chapters 7 and 9 will extend this introduction to consider the intricacies of methods, classes, object-oriented design, and inheritance. The intervening chapters will consider other important Java programming mechanisms.

The importance of classes to object-oriented design cannot be overrated. A class enables an information type to be *designed and implemented only once* and then *reused as often as needed* without having to reanalyze and rejustify the representation.

Before starting our introduction to class creation, we present a short program TwoWindows.java in Listing 4.1 that displays two empty graphical windows. One of the windows is titled "Bigger" and the other window is titled "Smaller."

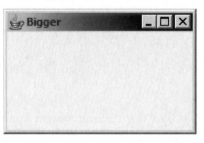 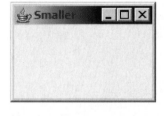

We examine the program TwoWindows.java because our first class will be manipulating a window. By becoming familiar now with the Java window class, its use later on will not be a distraction to our exploration of classes.

Method main() of program TwoWindows.java begins by defining and initializing JFrame variables w1 and w2.

```
JFrame w1 = new JFrame("Bigger");
JFrame w2 = new JFrame("Smaller");
```

A JFrame is the principal way in Java to represent a titled, bordered graphical window. Class JFrame is part of the standard package swing. The swing package is one of several APIs (application programmer interfaces) that comprise the *Java Foundation Classes (JFC)*. Although now part of the Java standard, the Java Foundation Classes are

---

Listing 4.1   **TwoWindows.java**

```
1.  // Purpose: Displays two different windows.
2.
3.  import javax.swing.*;
4.
5.  public class TwoWindows {
6.      // main(): application entry point
7.      public static void main(String[] args) {
8.          JFrame w1 = new JFrame("Bigger");
9.          JFrame w2 = new JFrame("Smaller");
10.
11.         w1.setSize(200, 125);
12.         w2.setSize(150, 100);
13.
14.         w1.setVisible(true);
15.         w2.setVisible(true);
16.     }
17. }
```

extensions of the original Java specification. Because it is an extension, the swing package is found at javax.swing.

The JFrame constructor used in the definitions of w1 and w2 takes a single String parameter that specifies the title of the window.

Method main() then sizes the windows. The resizing is accomplished through JFrame member method setSize(). The parameters of method setSize() specify the desired width and height in pixels. (*Pixel* stands for picture element and it is the size of the smallest dot that can be drawn on the monitor.)

```
w1.setSize(200, 125);
w2.setSize(150, 100);
```

As a result of these invocations, the window referenced by w1 has a width of 200 pixels and a height of 125 pixels and the window referenced by w2 has a width of 150 pixels and a height of 100 pixels.

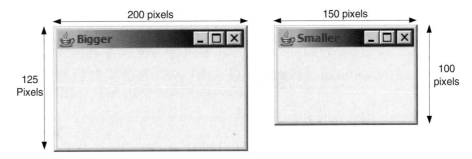

Now that the windows are configured properly, method main() makes them visible using JFrame member method setVisible().

```
w1.setVisible(true);
w2.setVisible(true);
```

The invocations must be made because a JFrame is invisible by default. A parameter with value **true** indicates that the JFrame is to be visible; and a parameter with value **false** indicates that the JFrame is not to be visible.

> Chapter 5 discusses **true**, **false** and the **boolean** type.

Now that you have seen how to represent and display graphical windows, we are ready to start our introduction to creating your own classes.

Because understanding and learning is easier when you are able to visualize what is going on, the introductory class examples in this chapter involve the representation and drawing of colored rectangles. Later chapters will consider many other class representations including ones for clocks, calculators, aquariums, and instant messengers.

4.2 A VERY SIMPLE CLASS

Our class representation of a colored rectangle will be called ColoredRectangle and its initial definition is given in Listing 4.2. This first version is for objects that support the display of a square window containing a blue filled-in rectangle, where the window has a side length of 200 pixels and the rectangle is 40 pixels wide and 20 pixels high. This lack of flexibility is a temporary condition accepted to enable a simpler introduction to the class concept.

Classes exist to be used and the first use of class ColoredRectangle will be by the program BoxFun.java of Listing 4.3. A look at program BoxFun.java should help you understand class ColoredRectangle—the program is an illustration of the capabilities of ColoredRectangle.

The following screen capture depicts the windows produced by program BoxFun.java.

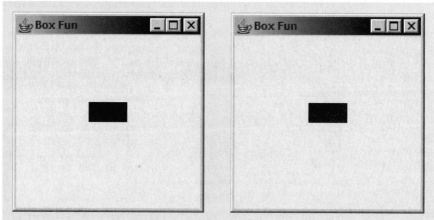

That the two windows are the same is the result of the ColoredRectangle's simplicity—the attributes of the ColoredRectangle objects are fixed (e.g, size, location, and color). In Section 4.3, we consider a second version of class ColoredRectangle that support objects with different attributes and with several behaviors. The result is a more realistic representation of a colored rectangle.

Listing 4.2　　ColoredRectangle.java — version I

```
 1.  // Purpose: Displays a colored rectangle within a window.
 2.
 3.  import javax.swing.*;
 4.  import java.awt.*;
 5.
 6.  public class ColoredRectangle {
 7.      // instance variables to describe object attributes
 8.      private int width;        // rectangle width
 9.      private int height;       // rectangle height
10.      private int x;            // rectangle x-coordinate position
11.      private int y;            // rectangle y-coordinate position
12.      private JFrame window;    // window displaying rectangle
13.      private Color color;      // color of rectangle
14.
15.      // ColoredRectangle(): default constructor
16.      public ColoredRectangle() {
17.          window = new JFrame("Box Fun");
18.          window.setSize(200, 200);
19.
20.          width = 40;
21.          height = 20;
22.          x = 80;
23.          y = 90;
24.
25.          color = Color.BLUE;
26.
27.          window.setVisible(true);
28.      }
29.
30.      // paint(): display the rectangle in its window
31.      public void paint() {
32.          Graphics g = window.getGraphics();
33.          g.setColor(color);
34.          g.fillRect(x, y, width, height);
35.      }
36.  }
```

As the listing of BoxFun.java suggests, with class ColoredRectangle we can make use of the same object-oriented programming features as we do with standard classes. In particular, we can create instances of class ColoredRectangle

```
ColoredRectangle r1 = new ColoredRectangle();
ColoredRectangle r2 = new ColoredRectangle();
```

and initiate behaviors through method invocations.

```
r1.paint();   // draw the window associated with r1
r2.paint();   // draw the window associated with r2
```

As with objects of the standard classes, a ColoredRectangle member method invocation sends a message to the object targeted by its invocation. For example, the Box-

---

Listing 4.3 **BoxFun.java**

```
1.  // Purpose: Create two windows containing colored rectangles.
2.  import java.util.*;
3.
4.  public class BoxFun {
5.     // main(): application entry point
6.     public static void main(String[] args) {
7.        ColoredRectangle r1 = new ColoredRectangle();
8.        ColoredRectangle r2 = new ColoredRectangle();
9.
10.       System.out.println("Enter when ready");
11.       Scanner stdin = new Scanner(System.in);
12.       stdin.nextLine();
13.
14.       r1.paint();  // render rectangle r1
15.       r2.paint();  // render rectangle r2
16.    }
17.  }
```

Fun.java invocation r1.paint() instructs the ColoredRectangle referenced by variable r1 to display itself; and the invocation r2.paint() instructs the Colored-Rectangle referenced by variable r2 to display itself.

We now turn our attention to the definition of ColoredRectangle itself. The class definition has three major sections each of which is introduced with a comment. The first section lists the attributes of a ColoredRectangle object; the second section defines a ColoredRectangle constructor; and the third section defines member method paint().

4.2.1   INSTANCE VARIABLES AND ATTRIBUTES

In Java, an object attribute commonly is referred to as a *data field* with the variable representing a data field known as an *instance variable*. In particular, each ColoredRectangle object has the following instance variables.

    private int width
        Represents the width of the rectangle to be displayed.
    private int height
        Represents the height of the rectangle to be displayed.
    private int x
        Represents the x-coordinate of the upperleft-hand corner of the rectangle to be displayed.

`private int y`

Represents the y-coordinate of the upperleft-hand corner of the rectangle to be displayed.

`private JFrame window`

Represents the window containing the rectangle drawing.

`private Color color`

Represents the color of the rectangle to be drawn. Class `Color` is part of awt API. The awt was Java's original graphical library. It is used now primarily for color and font representation, and drawing.

The definitions of the six `ColoredRectangle` instance variables in Listing 4.2 use the simplest available form,

```
private int width;     // rectangle width
private int height;    // rectangle height
private int x;         // rectangle x-coordinate position
private int y;         // rectangle y-coordinate position
private JFrame window; // window displaying rectangle
private Color color;   // color of rectangle
```

Each instance variable is defined without specifying an initial value. Therefore, whenever a new `ColoredRectangle` object is to be constructed, Java first initializes the new instance variables to default values. By default, numeric instance variables are initialized to 0, **boolean** instance variables are initialized to **false**, and reference-type instance variables are initialized to **null**. (Primitive type **boolean** is discussed in detail in Chapter 5.)

Thus, *every* time a new `ColoredRectangle` object is built, *new* width, height, x, y, window, and color instance variables are created and default initialized for the new object. The numeric attributes width, height, x, and y are initialized to zero and the class-type attributes window and color are initialized to **null**.

The instance variable definitions specify each of the variables to be **private**. This modifier indicates that direct access to the instance variables is limited to the class itself. Thus, class `ColoredRectangle` practices *information hiding* by *encapsulating* its attributes.

> Chapters 7 and 9 discuss the nuances of instance variables. Remember, our intent is to keep this introduction as simple as possible

Defining instance variables to be **private** is a standard practice. When attributes are **private**, other classes are forced to use the class's interface methods to manipulate its attributes. Those interface methods normally are programmed to ensure that the requested manipulations are valid. Because the initial definition of class `ColoredRectangle` does not provide any methods to give access to the attributes, once a `ColoredRectangle` is constructed it is immutable. In Section 4.3, we introduce several `ColoredRectangle` methods for accessing and modifying the attributes of a `ColoredRectangle` object.

4.2.2   A DEFAULT CONSTRUCTOR

The second section of Listing 4.2 defines a default constructor for class `ColoredRect-angle`. A *constructor* is a special type of Java method. When a constructor is used, Java automatically creates a new object with all the attributes of its class. It is the job of the constructor to assign those attributes sensibly. A *default constructor* configures the new instance of the class without any external guidance.

    `public ColoredRectangle()`

> Constructs an object representing a 40 × 20 blue rectangle centered in a new 200 × 200 window.

Unlike other methods (e.g., method `main()` of program `BoxFun.java`), a constructor does not have a return type. A return type for a constructor is considered superfluous—a constructor always returns a reference to the newly built object of its class. Furthermore, the name of a constructor is always the same as the name of the class. Therefore, `ColoredRectangle()` indicates a constructor for class `ColoredRectangle`.

```
public class ColoredRectangle {
// instance variables to describe object attributes
...

// ColoredRectangle(): default constructor
public ColoredRectangle() {
...                     The name of a constructor always matches the
}                       name of its class
...
}                       A constructor does not list its return type. A constructor
                        always returns a reference to a new object of its class
```

The statement list or *body* of the `ColoredRectangle` constructor begins with an assignment to the `window` instance variable for the `ColoredRectangle` object under construction. As a result of the assignment, `window` references a new `JFrame`. The `JFrame` constructor creating that window object titles the window using its `String` parameter `"Box Fun"`.

    `window = new JFrame("Box Fun");`

The `ColoredRectangle` constructor then sizes the window to the desired dimensions. For this purpose, the `ColoredRectangle` constructor signals the window through `JFrame` member method `setSize()`. Method `setSize()` expects two parameters giving the new width and height of the window in pixels.

    `window.setSize(200, 200);`

In this invocation, both parameters have value 200.

The `ColoredRectangle` constructor then initializes the width, height, and coordinate position of the rectangle to be displayed.

    `width = 40;`

```
height = 20;
x = 80;
y = 90;
```

The object under construction then has its instance variable `color` set to `Color.BLUE`.

```
color = Color.BLUE;
```

`Color.BLUE` is a `Color` class constant of awt class `Color` representing the color blue. The other `Color` class constants are listed in Table 4.1.

Table 4.1   Color constants.

Color.BLACK	Color.GREEN	Color.PINK
Color.BLUE	Color.LIGHT_GRAY	Color.RED
Color.CYAN	Color.MAGENTA	Color.WHITE
Color.DARK_GRAY	Color.ORANGE	Color.YELLOW
Color.GRAY		

To complete the construction of the colored rectangle, its window is made visible.

```
window.setVisible(true);
```

By using the `ColoredRectangle` default constructor in a **new** expression, a new `ColoredRectangle` object is created by Java. The attributes of this new object then are configured by executing the statement list that makes up the body of the `ColoredRectangle` constructor.

For example, the following statement defines and initializes a `ColoredRectangle` variable `rectangle`.

```
ColoredRectangle rectangle = new ColoredRectangle();
```

The statement causes variable `rectangle` to be initialized with a reference to a new `ColoredRectangle` object with attributes that represent a `Color.Blue` rectangle that is 40 pixels wide and 20 pixels high. The rectangle is associated with a new `JFrame` window that has a side length of 200 pixels with the `String` title of "Box Fun". A depiction of the memory for variable `rectangle` is given in Figure 4.1.

We now turn our attention to `ColoredRectangle` method `paint()`.

4.2.3   AN INSTANCE METHOD

The third section of Listing 4.2 defines an instance method `paint()` that displays its `ColoredRectangle` object. Method `paint()` is known as a *member method* or *instance method* because it must be invoked in conjunction with an instance of a `ColoredRectangle` (i.e., a `ColoredRectangle` object).

Figure 4.1   Depiction of memory associated with variable rectangle.

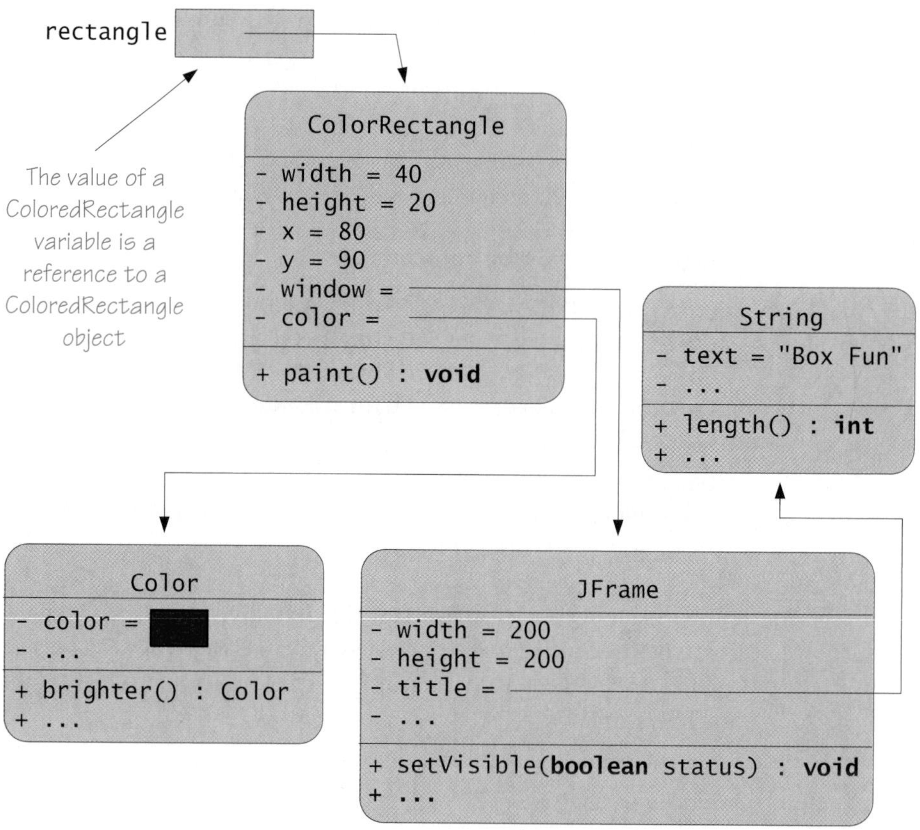

The value of a
ColoredRectangle
variable is a
reference to a
ColoredRectangle
object

rectangle

ColorRectangle
- width = 40
- height = 20
- x = 80
- y = 90
- window =
- color =
+ paint() : **void**

String
- text = "Box Fun"
- ...
+ length() : **int**
+ ...

Color
- color =
- ...
+ brighter() : Color
+ ...

JFrame
- width = 200
- height = 200
- title =
- ...
+ setVisible(**boolean** status) : **void**
+ ...

public void paint()

>   Draws a rectangle of appropriate size and position in the window associated with
>   the rectangle.

Instance methods are similar to constructors in that they are associated with a particular
object when they are invoked. Different invocations can associate an instance method
with different objects. (In BoxFun.java, ColoredRectangle member method
paint() is invoked twice: once for the ColoredRectangle referenced by variable r1
and once for the ColoredRectangle referenced by variable r2.)

A *member method definition* includes both a *header*, which describes its invocation
interface, and a *body*, which comprises the method's actions. The actions are given as a
statement list nested within matching braces. A method header always must supply the

Nondefault initialization

Instead of defining the `ColoredRectangle` attributes to be initialized with default values, we could have defined them to have explicit values.

```
// instance variable alternative definitions
int width = 40;           // rectangle width
int height = 20;          // rectangle height
int x = 80;               // rectangle x-coordinate position
int y = 90;               // rectangle y-coordinate position
JFrame window = new JFrame("Box Fun");// window displaying
                                      // rectangle
Color color = Color.BLUE; // color of rectangle
```

With these definitions, the body of the default constructor could be shorter—it would need only to size the window and make it visible.

```
// ColoredRectangle(): alternative definition
public ColoredRectangle() {
    window.setSize(200, 200);
    window.setVisible(true);
}
```

We chose to implement the default constructor for better reader understanding. The default constructor describes completely what a new `ColoredRectangle` object looks like.

return type, method name, and a specification of its parameters. Supplying an access right is optional (e.g., **public**, **private**)

Optional modifier
indicating access rights

Type of value that
the method returns

Identifier name
of method

Modifier ReturnType MethodName (ParameterList)

A description of the form the parameters are to take. The parameter declarations (if any) are comma separated. A parameter declaration consists of the parameter's type and name

The method name and the types of its parameters form the *signature* of a method. Java requires that all methods of a class have distinct signatures.

From Listing 4.2, we see that `paint()` has the following definition.

```
public static void paint() {
    Graphics g = window.getGraphics();
    g.setColor(color);
    g.fillRect(x, y, width, height);
}
```

The definition shows that `paint()` has a return type of **void** and an empty parameter list. The method signature is therefore `paint()`.

A method header can be preceded with *modifiers* that indicate access rights and other characteristics of the method. The modifier **public** for paint() indicates that other classes are allowed to invoke method paint().

The method body of paint() consists of the statements

```
Graphics g = window.getGraphics();
g.setColor(color);
g.fillRect(x, y, width, height);
```

By using the rectangle and window attributes of the associated object, an appropriate rectangle can be drawn (*rendered* or *painted* in computer graphics parlance).

The rendering is accomplished by first accessing the *graphical context* in which the drawing commands are to be issued. A graphical context is of type java.awt.Graphics.

A Graphics object provides all the necessary information for carrying out a rendering request (e.g., color, component on which the rendering is to occur, font, etc.). Besides encapsulating such information, Graphics objects have a variety of methods for drawing rectangles, lines, polygons, arcs, ovals, and strings.

Access to the graphical context of the window is obtained through JFrame instance method getGraphics(),

```
Graphics g = window.getGraphics();
```

Variable g is a variable whose *scope* of use is *local* to method paint(). Such a limitation is not imposed on instance variables. Their scope of use is the entire class.

Chapter 7 discusses the nuances of scope

The access to the window's graphic context through local variable g enables the rendering color to be set with Graphics method setColor().

```
g.setColor(color);
```

The actual display within the window is accomplished by using the position and size attributes of the associated object as parameters in the invocation of Graphics method fillRect().

```
g.fillRect(x, y, width, height);
```

Method fillRect() renders a filled-in rectangle. The method expects four parameters. The first two parameters specify respectively the locations of the x- and y-coordinates for the upperleft corner of the rectangle to be drawn. The rendering origin is the upperleft-hand corner of the window's container. The next two parameters specify respectively the width and height of the rectangle to be filled. (See Figure 4.2 for a depiction of the Java coordinate system properties.) All four values are given in pixels. The rectangle is rendered using the current color.

If we desired to draw only the perimeter of the rectangle, we would have used method drawRect().

In a rendering request, the location of the rendering is specified relative to the *upper-left-hand* corner of the object on which the drawing commands are performed. The direction of the x-axis is rightward. Therefore, increasing an x-coordinate value means moving

---

Figure 4.2   Java coordinate system properties.

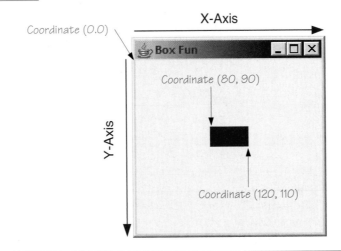

---

rightward. The direction of the y-axis is downward. Therefore, increasing a y-coordinate value means moving downward.

4.2.4   USAGE

Now that we have presented all of class ColoredRectangle, let's revisit program Box-Fun in Listing 4.3.

```java
public class BoxFun {
    // main(): application entry point
    public static void main(String[] args) {
        ColoredRectangle r1 = new ColoredRectangle();
        ColoredRectangle r2 = new ColoredRectangle();

        System.out.println("Enter when ready");
        Scanner stdin = new Scanner(System.in);
        stdin.nextLine();

        r1.paint();   // render rectangle r1
        r2.paint();   // render rectangle r2
    }
}
```

Its method main() begins with the definitions of variables r1 and r2. These definitions are similar in form to object variables definitions in the previous chapters—the variables are initialized with references to newly constructed objects. *Each of these new ColoredRectangle objects has its own instance variables for maintaining its particular attributes.*

Except for the values of their window instance variables, the ColoredRectangle objects referenced by variables r1 and r2 have like instance variables values. The win-

Figure 4.3 **Depiction of the memory associated with variables r1 and r2.**

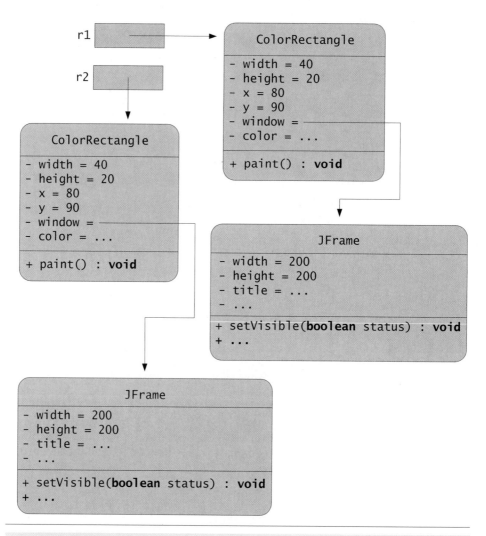

CLASSPATH

Our implementations of ColoredRectangle.java and BoxFun.java have them in the same folder. The compiled versions of those files are also in that same folder. Therefore, when an interpreter executes program BoxFun.java, the interpreter automatically finds the .class file for class ColoredRectangle. If the .class file for Colored-Rectangle was kept in a different folder, then the operating system variable CLASS-PATH would need to have that folder included in its folder list.

dow instance variables are different because the default constructor always assigns the window instance variable a reference to a new JFrame. (See Figure 4.3 for a depiction of r1 and r2.)

The next three lines effectively pause the program so that users can arrange the "Box Fun" windows prior to the rectangle rendering.

```
System.out.print("Enter when ready");
Scanner stdin = new Scanner(System.in);
stdin.nextLine();
```

The prompt tells the user that an input is expected in order for the program to proceed. Until an input is given, the program waits.

If your computing system is like our system, the two windows produced during the ColoredRectangle construction are placed one on the top of other. Before providing some input in reaction to the prompt, we arrange the windows so that they can both be seen. After doing so, the Enter key is typed. Its value is extracted by Scanner method nextLine() and the program continues with the invocations of the paint() method.[†]

Because r1 and r2 reference different ColoredRectangle objects with different window attributes, the paint() invocations modify two windows.

```
r1.paint();  // render rectangle r1
r2.paint();  // render rectangle r2
```

The first invocation renders a rectangle in the window of the ColoredRectangle referenced by r1. The second invocation renders a rectangle in the window of the ColoredRectangle object referenced by r2.

Thus, when an instance method is being executed, the attributes of the object associated with the invocation are accessed and manipulated. This property of instance methods is of paramount importance in the object-oriented programming paradigm. It is what enables objects to have behaviors. Therefore, it is crucial when examining code that you understand what object is being manipulated.

```
public class ColoredRectangle {
    // instance variables to describe object attributes
    ...

    // paint(): display the rectangle in its window
    public void paint() {
        window.setVisible(true);
        Graphics g = window.getGraphics();
        g.setColor(color);
        g.fillRect(x, y, width, height);
    }
    ...

}
```

Instance variable window references the JFrame attribute of the object that caused the invocation. That is, the invocation r1.paint() causes the window attribute of the ColoredRectangle referenced by r1 to be accessed. Similarly, the invocation r2.paint() causes the window attribute of the ColoredRectangle referenced by r2 to be accessed.

The values of these instance variables are also from the ColoredRectangle object that invoked method paint().

[†]   If during the rendering, one window is on top of the other, the bottom window will not show its rectangle after the top window is moved—the reason being the code displays the rectangle only once. Chapter 9 considers how to have an image rerendered automatically on an *exposure* event.

When analyzing code, we encourage you to first diagram each of your objects, and you then use the appropriate diagram to supply the values for the code being analyzed.

This discussion completes our basic introduction to classes. We now develop a more realistic version of class `ColoredRectangle`. This new definition has an additional constructor and several methods for accessing and modifying the attributes of a `Colored-Rectangle` object.

Program termination

The closing of a `JFrame` does not terminate its program automatically. One way to terminate the program is to type the operating system break sequence `Ctrl+c` in the console window.

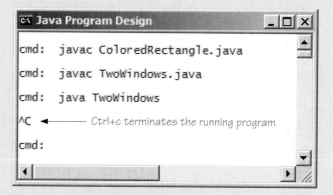

Another way is to configure the `JFrame` to do the termination through its member method `setDefaultCloseOperation()`. If the following code segment is added to `TwoWindows.java` of Listing 4.1 at line 10, the program will terminate automatically when either of its windows is closed.

```
w1.setDefaultCloseOperation(JFrame.EXIT_ON_CLOSE)
w2.setDefaultCloseOperation(JFrame.EXIT_ON_CLOSE)
```

4.3   METHODS WITH PARAMETERS AND RETURN VALUES

When designing a class, always consider its possible uses. The intended usage of an object determines what behaviors are appropriate, and what attributes are needed to implement those behaviors.

Before reading on, list what you would expect of a `ColoredRectangle`. You are encouraged to perform this activity every time our text introduces a new class—to become an effective programmer you should practice design whenever possible.

ANALYSIS AND DESIGN

If you think about it you will agree that a new `ColoredRectangle` object should be able to have any color; be positioned anywhere within its window; be visible or invisible; and have no restrictions on its width and height. Furthermore, the attributes of a Colored-Rectangle object should be accessible and updateable.

This analysis indicates there should be several additions to class ColoredRectangle. One of these additions should be the following construction behavior:

- *Specific construction*: construct a rectangle representation using supplied values for its attributes.

A reasonable class design almost always calls for encapsulating the attributes of its objects (i.e., protecting the attributes from direct modification by nonclass code). By providing both *accessor methods* that supply the values of the attributes and *mutator methods* that manage requests for changing attributes, a class can ensure that its objects always have sensible values. Our new ColoredRectangle design will follow this important software engineering practice. In particular, the following behaviors should be added to ColoredRectangle in support of *information hiding*.

- *Accessors:* provide the width, height, x-coordinate position, y-coordinate position, color, or window of the associated rectangle.

- *Mutators:* set the width, height, x-coordinate position, y-coordinate position, color, or window of the associated rectangle to a given value; set the visibility or invisibility of the window.

We next implement the methods that carry out these behaviors.

IMPLEMENTATION

The definition of the new ColoredRectangle class is given in Listing 4.4. The new accessors, mutators, and constructor start on line 37 after the unchanged definitions of default constructor ColoredRectangle() and method paint(). Methods such as paint() are sometimes referred to as *facilitators* because they support an expected use of the object.

The first of the new definitions is that of mutator setWidth().

```
// setWidth(): width mutator
public void setWidth(int w) {
   width = w;
}
```

By invoking mutator setWidth() of a ColoredRectangle object, the object is signaled to change its width attribute. The mutator requires that the invoking expression *pass* (supply) a single parameter value to it. The passed information is referred to as the *actual parameter* or *actual argument*. The parameter provides information that is otherwise unavailable to setWidth(). In particular, the parameter supplies the desired value for the width attribute of the associated ColoredRectangle. For example, the following code segment first defines a variable s that references a new ColoredRectangle object, which initially has the default width attribute of length 40. The mutator for that object then is invoked to reset the width to 80.

```
ColoredRectangle s = new ColoredRectangle();
s.setWidth(80);
```

A depiction of the memory associated with the code segment is given in Figure 4.4.

Listing 4.4   ColoredRectangle.java — version 2

```java
1.   // Purpose: Support the manipulation of a rectangle in a window.
2.
3.   import javax.swing.*;
4.   import java.awt.*;
5.
6.   public class ColoredRectangle {
7.      // instance variables to describe object attributes
8.      private int width;      // rectangle width
9.      private int height;     // rectangle height
10.     private int x;          // rectangle x-coordinate position
11.     private int y;          // rectangle y-coordinate position
12.     private JFrame window;   // window displaying rectangle
13.     private Color color;    // color of rectangle
14.
15.     // ColoredRectangle(): default constructor
16.     public ColoredRectangle() {
17.        window = new JFrame("Box Fun");
18.        window.setSize(200, 200);
19.
20.        width = 40;
21.        height = 20;
22.        x = 80;
23.        y = 90;
24.
25.        color = Color.BLUE;
26.
27.        window.setVisible(true);
28.     }
29.
30.     // paint(): display the rectangle in its window
31.     public void paint() {
32.        Graphics g = window.getGraphics();
33.        g.setColor(color);
34.        g.fillRect(x, y, width, height);
35.     }
36.
37.     // setWidth(): width mutator
38.     public void setWidth(int w) {
39.        width = w;
40.     }
41.
42.     // setVisible(): visibility mutator
43.     public void setVisible() {
44.        window.setVisible(true);
45.     }
46.
47.     // setInvisible(): invisibility mutator
48.     public void setInvisible() {
49.        window.setVisible(false);
50.     }
51.
52.     // setHeight(): height mutator
53.     public void setHeight(int h) {
54.        height = h;
```

Listing 4.4   **ColoredRectangle.java — version 2 (Continued)**

```
55.      }
56.
57.      // setX(): x mutator
58.      public void setX(int ulx) {
59.         x = ulx;
60.      }
61.
62.      // setY(): y mutator
63.      public void setY(int uly) {
64.         y = uly;
65.      }
66.
67.      // setWindow(): window mutator
68.      public void setWindow(JFrame f) {
69.         window = f;
70.      }
71.
72.      // setColor(): color mutator
73.      public void setColor(Color c) {
74.         color = c;
75.      }
76.
77.      // getWidth(): width accessor
78.      public int getWidth() {
79.            return width;
80.      }
81.
82.      // getHeight(): height accessor
83.      public int getHeight() {
84.         return height;
85.      }
86.
87.      // getX(): x accessor
88.      public int getX() {
89.         return x;
90.      }
91.
92.      // getY(): y accessor
93.      public int getY() {
94.         return y;
95.      }
96.
97.      // getWindow(): window accessor
98.      public JFrame getWindow() {
99.         return window;
100.     }
101.
102.     // getColor(): color accessor
103.     public Color getColor() {
104.        return color;
105.     }
106.
107.     // ColoredRectangle(): specific constructor
108.     public ColoredRectangle(int w, int h, int ulx, int uly,
```

Listing 4.4   **ColoredRectangle.java — version 2 (Continued)**

```
109.                                        JFrame f, Color c) {
110.         setWidth(w);
111.         setHeight(h);
112.         setX(ulx);
113.         setY(uly);
114.         setWindow(f);
115.         setColor(c);
116.         setVisible();
117.     }
118. }
```

Figure 4.4   **Depiction of memory associated with variable s.**

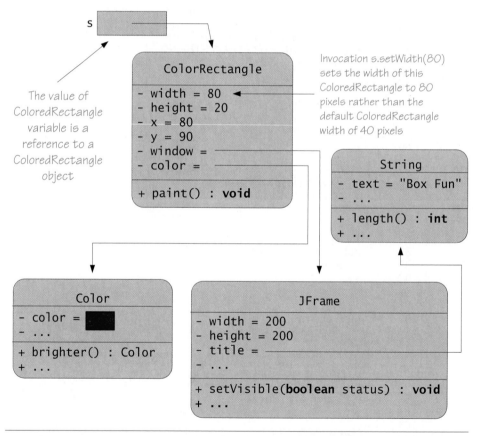

Whenever a method is invoked, Java executes the statement list that makes up the invoked method's definition. In particular, the next statement to be executed is the first statement in the invoked method's statement list. We say that *flow of control* is *transferred* temporarily to that method. The actual parameters in the invocation are used to initialize the *formal parameters* in the method's definition. For *each* method invocation,

Java individually sets aside memory for that *particular* invocation to store the values of the formal parameters. This memory is known commonly as an *activation record*.

Actual Parameters $\xrightarrow{\text{Initialize}}$ Formal parameters

Once the actual parameters have been used to initialize the formal parameters, the actual parameters and the formal parameters are independent of each other. The method then begins executing its statement body. If during its execution, a method updates the value of a formal parameter, the change does not affect the actual parameter. The change is limited to the activation record containing the value of the formal parameter. This type of correspondence between the actual and formal parameters is known as *value parameter passing*. In general, the first actual parameter initializes the first formal parameter, the second actual parameter initializes the second formal parameter, and so on. Thus, to invoke a method, the number of actual parameters and formal parameters must be the same.

Because the definition of mutator `setWidth()` specifies the name of its formal parameter to be w, the invocation `s.setWidth(80)` causes method `setWidth()` to be executed with formal parameter w initialized to 80.

Formal parameters are essentially variables that are *local* to their method. The formal parameters are created with the invocation of their method, their values are accessible only within the method, and they are destroyed when their method completes. The only difference between the formal parameters and the other variables defined by a method is that the formal parameters are initialized using the values of the actual parameters.

Therefore, if `setWidth()` were to update the value of formal parameter w (which it does not), the change would be visible only within `setWidth()`—the actual parameter would remain unchanged.

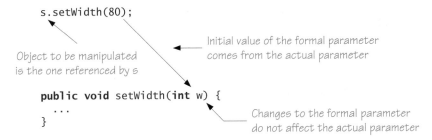

In a transfer of control to method `setWidth()`, its single statement method body is executed. The statement assigns the value of formal parameter w to instance variable `width`. The particular instance variable that is updated is the one belonging to the `ColoredRectangle` object initiating the invocation. After executing the statement body, Java transfers control back to the code segment that invoked the method. A depiction of an invocation process is given in Figure 4.5.

There is a subtlety to recognize about the `ColoredRectangle` mutator `setWidth()`. While the mutator updates the width attribute of its `ColoredRectangle` object, the mutator does not invoke method `paint()` to reflect that change in its window. Therefore, the rendering of a `ColoredRectangle` is unaffected by a `setWidth()` invo-

Figure 4.5 **Evaluation of the invocation s.setWidth(80).**

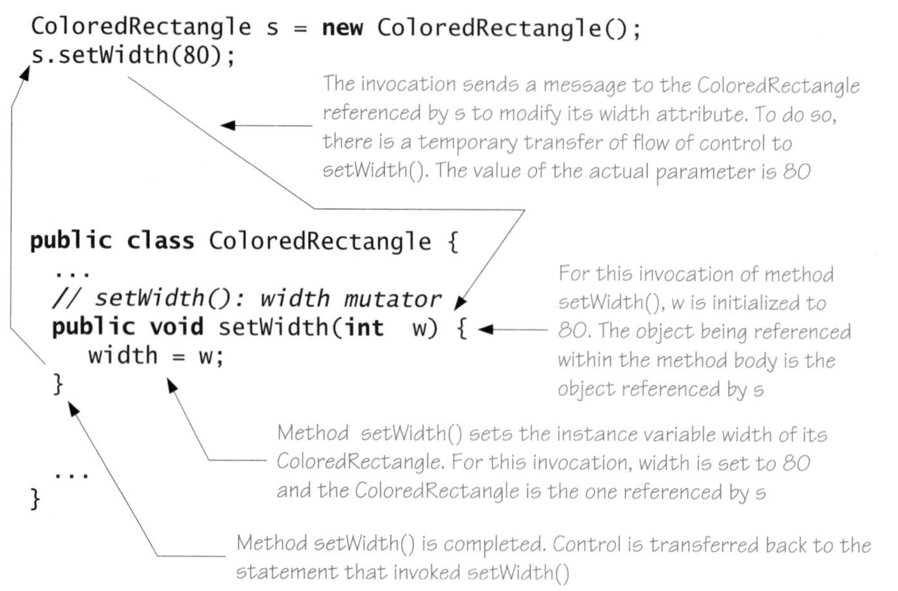

```
ColoredRectangle s = new ColoredRectangle();
s.setWidth(80);
```

The invocation sends a message to the ColoredRectangle referenced by s to modify its width attribute. To do so, there is a temporary transfer of flow of control to setWidth(). The value of the actual parameter is 80

```
public class ColoredRectangle {
  ...
  // setWidth(): width mutator
  public void setWidth(int  w) {
    width = w;
  }

  ...
}
```

For this invocation of method setWidth(), w is initialized to 80. The object being referenced within the method body is the object referenced by s

Method setWidth() sets the instance variable width of its ColoredRectangle. For this invocation, width is set to 80 and the ColoredRectangle is the one referenced by s

Method setWidth() is completed. Control is transferred back to the statement that invoked setWidth()

cation. A `ColoredRectangle` object must be *repainted* for the update to be visible in the window.

```
ColoredRectangle r = new ColoredRectangle();
r.paint();        // a default colored rectangle is rendered
r.setWidth(100); // rectangle has mutated, but not its
rendering
r.paint();        // rendering reflects the rectangle mutation
```

Mutator `setVisible()` is defined next. A `setVisible()` invocation signals its `ColoredRectangle` that the associated window should be made visible.

```
// setVisible(): visibility mutator
public void setVisible() {
  window.setVisible(true);
}
```

The statement to make the window visible passes the **boolean** value **true** to the `JFrame` method controlling visibility.

The complementary mutator `setInvisible()` is then defined. A `setInvisible()` invocation signals its `ColoredRectangle` that the associated window should be made invisible.

```
// setInvisible(): invisibility mutator
public void setVisible() {
  window.setVisible(false);
}
```

The statement to make the window invisible passes the **boolean** value **false** to the `JFrame` method controlling visibility.

The other `ColoredRectangle` mutators perform tasks comparable to `setWidth()` for the other attributes.

```java
// setHeight(): height mutator
public void setHeight(int h) {
    height = h;
}

// setX(): x mutator
public void setX(int ulx) {
    x = ulx;
}

// setY(): y mutator
public void setY(int uly) {
    y = uly;
}

// setWindow(): window mutator
public void setWindow(JFrame f) {
    window = f;
}

// setColor(): color mutator
public void setColor(Color c) {
    color = c;
}
```

The use of these mutators is demonstrated in the following code segment that defines and manipulates two `ColoredRectangle` variables u and v.

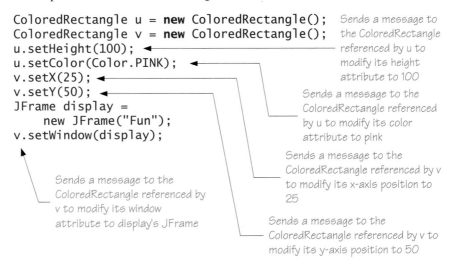

```java
ColoredRectangle u = new ColoredRectangle();
ColoredRectangle v = new ColoredRectangle();
u.setHeight(100);
u.setColor(Color.PINK);
v.setX(25);
v.setY(50);
JFrame display =
    new JFrame("Fun");
v.setWindow(display);
```

Sends a message to the ColoredRectangle referenced by u to modify its height attribute to 100

Sends a message to the ColoredRectangle referenced by u to modify its color attribute to pink

Sends a message to the ColoredRectangle referenced by v to modify its x-axis position to 25

Sends a message to the ColoredRectangle referenced by v to modify its y-axis position to 50

Sends a message to the ColoredRectangle referenced by v to modify its window attribute to display's JFrame

The six `ColoredRectangle` accessor methods do not require parameters. When invoked, these methods each signal the object associated with the invocation to supply the value of a particular attribute.

```java
// getWidth(): width accessor
public int getWidth() {
```

```java
        return width;
    }

    // getHeight(): height accessor
    public int getHeight() {
        return height;
    }

    // getX(): x accessor
    public int getX() {
        return x;
    }

    // getY(): y accessor
    public int getY() {
        return y;
    }

    // getWindow(): window accessor
    public JFrame getWindow() {
        return window;
    }

    // getColor(): color accessor
    public Color getColor() {
        return color;
    }
```

Because the accessors do not take parameters, when they are invoked there is an immediate temporary transfer of the flow of control to their method bodies. For example, in the following code segment, the invocation `t.getWidth()` causes the body of accessor `getWidth()` to be executed.

```java
ColoredRectangle t = new ColoredRectangle();
int w = t.getWidth();
System.out.println(w);
```

Like the bodies of the other accessors, the body of the `getWidth()` accessor consists of a single statement. The statement is a **return** statement. A **return** statement is an explicit indication that the flow of control is transferred back to the invoking statement. For non-**void** methods, the **return** statement supplies the value associated with the invocation. A **return** statement has the form

$$\textbf{return } \textit{ReturnExpression} \text{ ;}$$

For non-void methods, this value is returned to the invoking method; for void methods no value is supplied. Execution continues at the statement that did the method invocation

where *ReturnExpression* evaluates to a value of the method's return type.

Figure 4.6   **Evaluation of the invocation t.getWidth().**

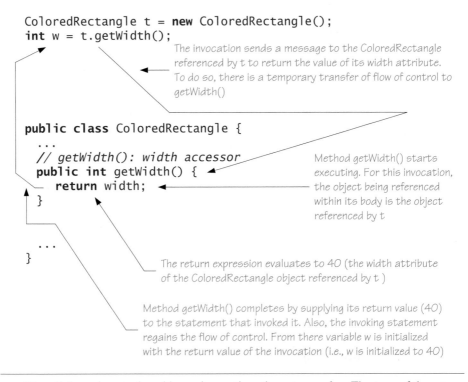

```
ColoredRectangle t = new ColoredRectangle();
int w = t.getWidth();
```

The invocation sends a message to the ColoredRectangle referenced by t to return the value of its width attribute. To do so, there is a temporary transfer of flow of control to getWidth()

```
public class ColoredRectangle {
  ...
  // getWidth(): width accessor
  public int getWidth() {
    return width;
  }
  ...
}
```

Method getWidth() starts executing. For this invocation, the object being referenced within its body is the object referenced by t

The return expression evaluates to 40 (the width attribute of the ColoredRectangle object referenced by t)

Method getWidth() completes by supplying its return value (40) to the statement that invoked it. Also, the invoking statement regains the flow of control. From there variable w is initialized with the return value of the invocation (i.e., w is initialized to 40)

We call the value produced by an invocation, the *return value*. The type of the return value is the method's *return type*. The return type of getWidth() is **int**.

The method return type precedes the name of the method in the method definition

```
public int getWidth() {
  return width;
}
```

For method getWidth(), the return value is the value of the width attribute for the ColoredRectangle associated with the invocation. In invocation t.getWidth(), the return value is the value of the instance variable width for the ColoredRectangle referenced by t

The return value is used as the value of the invocation. Because the ColoredRect-angle object referenced by t was constructed using the default constructor, the value used to initialize **int** variable w is 40.

Figure 4.6 depicts the flow of control process for our t.getWidth() invocation.

The other new method defined in Listing 4.4 is a specific constructor for ColoredRectangle.

```
// ColoredRectangle(): specific constructor
public ColoredRectangle(int w, int h, int ulx, int uly,
                        JFrame f, Color c) {
```

```
        setWidth(w);
        setHeight(h);
        setX(ulx);
        setY(uly);
        setWindow(f);
        setColor(c);
        setVisible();
    }
```

This constructor requires that an invoking expression pass six actual parameter values to it. These values are used by the constructor in setting the attributes for the Colored-Rectangle object under construction. Once the attributes are set, the invocation set-Visible() makes the window visible. For example, the following code segment results in variable w being initialized with reference to a new ColoredRectangle object.

```
JFrame display = new JFrame("Even more fun");
display.setSize(400, 400);
ColoredRectangle w = new ColoredRectangle(60, 80, 20, 20,
                            display, Color.YELLOW);
```

The new ColoredRectangle represents a yellow rectangle with a width of 60 pixels and a height of 80 pixels. In addition, when rendered, the rectangle is to be drawn with its upperleft-hand corner positioned at coordinate (20, 20) in the JFrame represented by variable display.

The definition of ColoredRectangle() specific constructor has the names of its formal parameters being w, h, ulx, uly, f, and c. Therefore, the invocation Colored-Rectangle(60, 80, 20, 20, display, Color.YELLOW) causes ColoredRectan-gle() to be executed with its formal parameters w, h, ulx, uly, f, and c initialized respectively to the values of 60, 80, 20, 20, display, and Color.YELLOW.

Observe that rather than directly setting the instance variables representing the attributes, specific constructor ColoredRectangle() uses the mutators. There are three major benefits to using the mutators. First, the code is more readable. The mutator names indicate explicitly how the formal parameters are being used. Second, errors in represen-tation are less likely with consistent use of mutators and accessors. By limiting direct access of instance variables to mutators and accessors, it is easier to ensure that an object represents a reasonable instance of its class. Third, enhancements and changes to a class are generally simpler to make when direct access to the instance variables is controlled. By limiting the direct access, fewer methods typically need to be considered when ana-lyzing for bugs or improvements.

Using accessors to get attribute values has similar benefits. Therefore, the use of accessors is also encouraged.

Because of the preference for use of the public interface over direct access to attributes, the self-test section considers a reimplementation of the ColoredRectangle default constructor and instance method paint().

We conclude our introduction to programmer-defined classes with one more example using ColoredRectangle. The example is program SeeingDouble.java and a copy of the program is given in Listing 4.5.

Listing 4.5   SeeingDouble.java

```
1.  // Purpose: demonstrate a nuance of graphical programming
2.
3.  import java.util.*;
4.  import java.awt.*;
5.
6.  public class SeeingDouble {
7.      // main(): application entry point
8.      public static void main(String[] args) {
9.          ColoredRectangle r = new ColoredRectangle();
10.
11.         System.out.println("Enter when ready");
12.         Scanner stdin = new Scanner(System.in);
13.         stdin.nextLine();
14.
15.         r.paint();
16.
17.         r.setY(50);
18.         r.setColor(Color.RED);
19.         r.paint();
20.     }
21. }
```

The program first creates a ColoredRectangle object and then pauses for the window to be rendered.

```
ColoredRectangle r = new ColoredRectangle();

System.out.print("Enter when ready");
Scanner stdin = new Scanner(System.in);
stdin.nextLine();
```

The program then renders the colored rectangle for the first time.

```
r.paint();
```

The program then modifies the y-coordinate position and color of the ColoredRectangle object. The modified colored rectangle is then repainted.

```
r.setY(50);
r.setColor(Color.RED);
r.paint();
```

The result is the display given in Figure 4.7.

Observe in the figure that there are two rectangle renderings. It is not a bug that both rectangles are visible—when method paint() is invoked it just displays a rectangle using the current values of its object's instance variables. It has not been designed to erase a previous rendering. If such behavior is wanted, an erase() method should be introduced to the class and invoked prior to the method paint() invocation. (An erase() method is considered in the exercises.)

Figure 4.7 **The display associated with ColoredRectangleDemo.**

4.4   SUMMARY

Although our focus in this chapter has been the design and development of a representation for a colored rectangle, the Java class mechanism enables you to represent any object. Constructors enable you to create new objects and configure them; instance variables enable you represent the attributes of an object; and methods enable you to describe the behaviors of an object.

We encourage you to consider the programming case study of Section 4.8 to try out your new object-oriented programming skills.

4.5	REVIEW

- The value of an object variable is a reference to a location that holds an object of its type.
- The creation of a class type object is accomplished by invoking a member constructor method that creates and initializes the attributes of the object.
- An instance variable is Java's mechanism for defining an object attribute. Every object of a class has its own copy of the instance variables for representing its particular attributes. An instance variable also is known as a data field.
- Object behaviors are implemented using member methods. Member methods can access the instance variables of the associated object. This capability enables a constructor to configure the instance variables of the object being created and it enables a member method to manipulate the attributes of its associated object.
- Information is passed to a method via parameters. The result of a method's computation is brought back as the return value. The type of value brought back by a method is the return type.
- A **return** statement supplies a value from the invoked method to the invoking method.
- A method that does not return a value has a return type of **void**.
- A statement block is a list of statements within braces.
- To define a method, a programmer must specify completely its interface and actions. The actions occur within the method body. The method body is a statement block.
- The parameters in the invocation are called the actual parameters. The actual parameters are represented in the invoked method by its formal parameters.
- Every method invocation creates an activation record. The values of the formal parameters and other objects defined in the method are kept in the activation record.
- When a method is invoked, flow of control is transferred from the invoking method to the invoked method. When the invoked method completes, control is transferred back to the invoking method. If the invoked method returns a value, then that value essentially is substituted for the invocation.
- Java uses the pass-by-value parameter-passing style. When an actual parameter is passed in this style, the formal parameter is called a value parameter because it is initialized to the value of the actual parameter. Subsequent changes to the formal parameter do not affect the actual parameter.
- By practicing information hiding in a data abstraction, client programs are generally immune from changes in the implementation of the abstraction.
- Constructors initialize objects of a class type. It is standard practice to ensure that every class object has all of its data fields sensibly initialized.
- A constructor has the same name as its class.
- A default constructor is a constructor that requires no parameters.
- An accessor method returns the value of an attribute of an object. Accessor names often begin with "get".

- A mutator method provides the means to modify an attribute of an object. Mutator names often begin with "set".

- A facilitator method performs a task that depends in part on the attributes of an object.

- An instance variable is a data field for which each object has its own copy of the data.

- Whenever a new object is to be constructed Java first initializes the new instance variables. By default, numeric instance variables are initialized to 0, **boolean** instance variables are initialized to **false**, and reference-type instance variables are initialized to **null**.

- Instance methods are similar to constructors in that they are associated with a particular object when they are invoked. Different invocations can have the method associated with different objects.

- When designing your own classes, keep in mind that instance variables normally are declared to be **private**. This information hiding helps ensure the integrity of the variables.

- The programmer interface to a class is made up of the **public** members.

- The **private** members of a class can be used only by other members of the class.

- JFrame is the swing class for representing a window. A JFrame is similar in form to the other windows on your desktop and can be manipulated like those other windows.

- A JFrame constructor takes a single string as its parameter, which is displayed as the window title.

- A JFrame can be displayed by invoking its member method setVisible(); it can be resized by invoking its member method setSize().

- Rendering is accomplished by first accessing the graphical context in which the drawing commands are to be issued. The graphical context is of type awt class Graphics. A Graphics object provides all the information necessary for carrying out a rendering request (e.g., color, the component on which the rendering is to occur, font, etc.). Besides encapsulating such information, Graphics objects have a variety of methods for drawing rectangles, lines, polygons, arcs, ovals, and strings.

- Access to the graphical context of a JFrame is obtained through member method getGraphics().

- The current rendering color can be set using Graphics method setColor().

- Graphics method fillRect() renders a filled-in rectangle. The method expects four parameters. The first two parameters specify respectively the locations of the x- and y-coordinates for the upperleft corner of the rectangle to be drawn. The next two parameters specify respectively the width and height of the rectangle to be filled. All four values are given in pixels. The rectangle is rendered using the current color. To draw only the perimeter of a rectangle use Graphics method drawRect().

- In a rendering request, the location of the rendering is specified relative to the upperleft-hand corner of the object on which the drawing commands are performed. The direction of the x-axis is rightward. The direction of the y-axis is downward. Both x- and y-coordinates are given in pixels.

4.6 SELF-TEST

S4.1 Implement **public** methods getArea() and getPerimeter() for class ColoredRectangle. The perimeter of a rectangle is the sum of its side lengths and the area of a rectangle is the product of its width and length.

S4.2 Define an instance method doubleSize() that doubles the size of a ColoredRectangle.

S4.3 Define an instance method rotateClockwise() that rotates the shape of a ColoredRectangle object by 90°.

S4.4 Implement a class Name for representing names. Each Name object should have three attributes—a first, middle, and family name. There should be a default and specific constructor. The class should support encapsulation and information hiding by providing accessors and mutators for the three Name attributes. The class should also provide a method toString() that supplies the entire name.

S4.5 Why might an instance method be defined to be **private**?

S4.6 Reimplement the ColoredRectangle default constructor and facilitator paint() to use mutators and accessors to achieve their purposes.

4.7 EXERCISES

4.1 Describe what happens during a method invocation.

4.2 What is an actual parameter?

4.3 What is a formal parameter?

4.4 Discuss flow of control.

4.5 What are the differences between a data field and a method?

4.6 What are the differences between a mutator and an accessor method?

4.7 Whose purpose is to configure initially the values of instance variables?

4.8 What type of method is responsible generally for setting the value of an instance variable?

4.9 What type of method is responsible generally for providing the value of an instance variable?

4.10 What are the differences in using **public** and **private** access modifiers?

4.11 Why is it unnecessary (inappropriate) for constructors to have return types?

4.12 How many parameters does a default constructor require? Why?

4.13 Why are data fields typically defined in a nonpublic section?

4.14 Does a non-**void** method necessarily contain a **return** statement? Explain.

The definition of the following class C is in effect for Exercises 4.15–4.22.

```
public class C {
    private int counter;
```

```
    public C() {
        counter = 0;
    }

    public C(int n) {
        counter = n;
    }

    public void increment() {
        ++counter;
    }

    public void decrement() {
        --counter;
    }

    public int getCount() {
        return counter;
    }

    public void display() {
        System.out.println(getCount());
    }
}
```

4.15 How many constructors does class C have? List them.

4.16 How many accessors does class C have? List them.

4.17 How many mutators does class C have? List them.

4.18 How many facilitators does class C have? List them.

4.19 What is the output of the following code segment?
```
C c1 = new C();
c1.increment();
C c2 = new C();
c2.increment();
c1.increment();
c2.decrement();
c2.increment();
c1.display();
c2.display();
```

4.20 What is the output of the following code segment?
```
C c1 = new C();
c1.increment();
C c2 = new C();
c2.increment();
c1.increment();
c2.decrement();
c2.increment();
int counter = 0;
c1.display();
c2.display();
```

4.21 What is the output of the following code segment?
```
C c1 = new C();
c1.increment();
```

```
        C c2 = new C();
        c2.increment();
        c1.increment();
        c2.decrement();
        c2.increment();
        int c1_counter = 0;
        int c2_counter = 0;
        c1.display();
        c2.display();
```

4.22 Which statements in the following code segment are legal? Explain.

```
        C c1 = new C();
        C c2 = new C(c1.getCount());
        C c3 = new C(5);
        c1.increment(5);
        c2.decrement() = 5;
        c1.counter = 5;
        c2.counter = 5;
        C c4 = new C(c2.counter);
```

4.23 Implement a method `erase()` for `ColoredRectangle`.

4.24 Develop and implement a class `Account` that represents a savings account. An `Account` object should have three attributes: the name of the account, the owner of the account, and the current balance. The class should provide the following constructor behaviors.

- `Account()`: configures a new account with name `"name"`, owner `"owner"`, and balance 0.
- `Account(String s, String t, double n)`: configures a new account with name s, owner t, and balance n.
- `void deposit(double n)`: adds amount n to the current balance of the associated account.
- `void withdraw(double n)`: subtracts amount n from the current balance of the associated account.
- `void close()`: zeroes out the account balance, sets the owner to `""`.
- `String getAccountName()`: returns the name of the associated account.
- `String getOwner()`: returns the owner of the associated account.
- `double getBalance()`: returns the balance of the associated account.
- `void setName(String s)`: sets the name of the associated account to s.
- `void setOwner(String s)`: sets the owner of the associated account to s.
- `String toString()`: returns a textual representation of the attributes of the associated account.

4.25 Develop and implement a class `Date` to represent a date. A `Date` object should have three attributes: the day of the month, the month, and the year. The class should provide the following constructor behaviors.

- `Date()`: configures a new account to represent the date 1 January 2000.
- `Date(int d, int m, int y)`: configures a new date with day d, month m, and year y.
- `int getDay()`: returns the day of the associated date.

- **int** getMonth(): returns the month of the associated date.
- **int** getYear(): returns the year of the associated date.
- **void** setDay(**int** d): sets the day of the associated date to d.
- **void** setMonth(**int** m): sets the month of the associated date to m.
- **void** setYear(**int** y): sets the year of the associated date to y.
- String toString(): returns a textual representation of the associated date.

4.8   PROGRAMMING PROJECT — RATIONALITY

The purpose of this case study is to design and implement the class Rational as a representation for manipulating rational numbers. To begin, we remind you about rational number basics.

> The objective of this case study is to practice object-oriented design and development when problem solving

A rational number is the ratio of two integers and is represented typically in the manner *a/b*. We call *a* the *numerator* and *b* the *denominator*. The denominator is supposed to be nonzero.[†] The basic operations have the following definitions:

- Addition: $\dfrac{a}{b} + \dfrac{c}{d} = \dfrac{ad + bc}{bd}$

- Subtraction: $\dfrac{a}{b} - \dfrac{c}{d} = \dfrac{ad - bc}{bd}$

- Multiplication: $\dfrac{a}{b} \times \dfrac{c}{d} = \dfrac{ac}{bd}$

- Division: $\dfrac{a}{b} \div \dfrac{c}{d} = \dfrac{ad}{bc}$

ANALYSIS AND DESIGN

To represent a rational number, you need to represent its numerator and denominator. This necessity implies that a class representing rational numbers needs at least two instance variables—one variable to represent the particular numerator and the other variable to represent the particular denominator of the object.

> private int numerator
>   Numerator of the associated rational number.
> private int denominator
>   Denominator of the associated rational number.

Previous experience with rational numbers and other Java APIs tells us that the Rational abstraction should provide methods to initialize and manipulate a rational number object in at least the following ways:

[†]   In Chapter 5, we consider the **if** statement that allows us to determine whether a value is valid.

Figure 4.8 **A possible interaction with RationalDemo.java.**

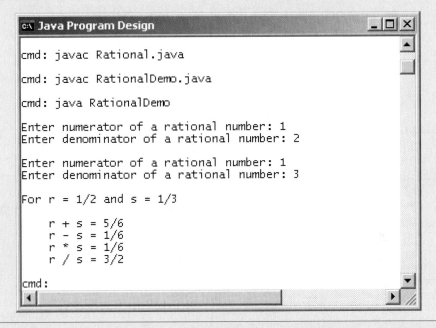

- Construct a rational number by default or from a numerator and denominator specification.

- Compute the rational result of adding, subtracting, multiplying, and dividing two rational numbers.

- Produce a `String` representation of a rational number suitable for displaying to the standard output stream.

To support both these client activities and information hiding, methods implementing the following activities should also be present:

- Access the values of the numerator and denominator.

- Set the values of the numerator and denominator.

You may find it convenient to define other methods. We also leave it to you consider what documentation is necessary for the other methods.

To aid you in your design of the necessary information structures and algorithms, we provide the `Rational` client program `RationalDemo.java` of Listing 4.6. This program illustrates the look and feel that we want in the various components of the class `Rational`. We depict a sample input/output behavior of the program in Figure 4.8.

IMPLEMENTATION

Produce the rational number abstraction `Rational.java` and a client Java program `MyDemo.java` that thoroughly tests your rational implementation.

Listing 4.6 **RationalDemo.java**

```java
1.  // Demonstrate Rational data abstraction
2.
3.  import java.util.*;
4.
5.  public class RationalDemo {
6.      // main(): application entry point
7.      public static void main(String[] args) {
8.          Scanner stdin = new Scanner(System.in);
9.
10.         System.out.println();
11.
12.         // extract values for rationals r and s
13.         Rational r = new Rational();
14.         System.out.print("Enter numerator of a rational number: ");
15.         int a = stdin.nextInt();
16.         System.out.print("Enter denominator of a rational number: ");
17.         int b = stdin.nextInt();
18.         r.setNumerator(a);
19.         r.setDenominator(b);
20.         System.out.println();
21.         System.out.println();
22.
23.         Rational s = new Rational();
24.         System.out.print("Enter numerator of a rational number: ");
25.         int c = stdin.nextInt();
26.         System.out.print("Enter denominator of a rational number: ");
27.         int d = stdin.nextInt();
28.         s.setNumerator(c);
29.         s.setDenominator(d);
30.
31.         // operate on r and s
32.         Rational sum = r.add(s);
33.         Rational difference = r.subtract(s);
34.         Rational product = r.multiply(s);
35.         Rational quotient = r.divide(s);
36.
37.
38.         // display operation results
39.         System.out.println("For r = " + r.toString() + " and s = "
40.             + s.toString());
41.         System.out.println("    r + s = " + sum.toString());
42.         System.out.println("    r - s = " + difference.toString());
43.         System.out.println("    r * s = " + product.toString());
44.         System.out.println("    r / s = " + quotient.toString());
45.         System.out.println();
46.
47.         System.out.println();
48.     }
49. }
```

TESTING AND DOCUMENTATION

While our program RationalDemo.java illustrates and tests much of the behavior, it is not complete. Expand upon this program in MyDemo.java to provide more explicit evidence regarding the correctness of all your methods.

You should document both your design and implementation. In documenting your design, justify the access specification of all members. You should justify your approach and explain the behaviors and nuances of your methods. For example, when discussing the default constructor, you should state what is the default representation and why it was selected.

4.9	**SELF-TEST ANSWERS**

S4.1 Definitions of methods for computing the area and perimeter would be
```java
public int getArea() {
    int w = getWidth();
    int h = getHeight();
    return w * h;
}

public int getPerimeter() {
    int w = getWidth();
    int h = getHeight();
    return 2*w + 2*h;
}
```
S4.2 A definition for method doubleSize() would be
```java
public void doubleSize() {
    int w = getWidth();
    int h = getHeight();
    setWidth(2*w):
    setHeight(2*h);
}
```
S4.3 A definition for method rotateClockwise() would be
```java
public void rotateClockwise() {
    int w = getWidth();
    int h = getHeight();
    setWidth(h):
    setHeight(w);
}
```
S4.4 A class definition would be
```java
public class Name {
    // instance variables
    String firstName;
    String middleName;
    String familyName;

    // Name(): default constructor
    public Name() {
        firstName = middleName = familyName = "";
```

```
        }

        // Name(): specific constructor
        public Name(String first, String middle, String family)
    {
            setFirstName(first);
            setMiddleName(middle);
            setFamilyName(family);
        }

        // getFirstName(): first name accessor
        public String getFirstName() {
            return firstName;
        }

        // getMiddleName(): middle name accessor
        public String getMiddleName() {
            return middleName;
        }

        // getFamilyName(): family name accessor
        public String getFamilyName() {
            return familyName;
        }

        // setFirstName(): first name mutator
        public void setFirstName(String s) {
            firstName = s;
        }

        // setMiddleName(): middle name mutator
        public void setMiddleName(String s) {
            middleName = s;
        }

        // setFamilyName(): family name mutator
        public void setFamilyName(String s) {
            familyName = s;
        }

        // toString(): whole name supplier
        public String toString() {
            return getFirstName() + " " + getMiddleName()
                                  + " " + getFamilyName();
        }
    }
```

S4.5 An instance method might be declared **private** if it was used to assist in implementing some behavior, or if accessing the method would be inappropriate.

S4.6 A reimplementation of the class members would be

```
        // ColoredRectangle(): default constructor
        public ColoredRectangle() {
            JFrame w = new JFrame("Box Fun");
            w.setSize(200, 200);
            setWindow(w);

            setWidth(40);
```

```
            setHeight(20);
            setX(80);
            setY(90);
            setColor(Color.BLUE);
        }

        // paint(): display the rectangle in its window
        public void paint() {
            int w = getWidth();
            int h = getHeight();
            int ulx = getX():
            int uly = getY();
            Color c = getColor();
            JFrame w = getWindow();

            w.setVisible(true);

            Graphics g = w.getGraphics();
            g.setColor(c);
            g.fillRect(ulx, uly, w, h);
        }
```

5 DECISIONS

Up to this point, our programs have had the *straight-line* property that each time they are run, the same sequence of statements is executed. This form of programming is adequate for solving simple problems. However, for general problem solving we need the ability to control which statements are executed and how often. In this chapter, we consider both the **if** and **switch** *conditional constructs* that control whether a statement list is executed. (In Chapter 6, we consider Java's iterative constructs.) Because the **if** constructs use logical expressions to determine their course of action, we begin with logical expressions.

OBJECTIVES

- Present the logical type **boolean** and its associated operators.
- Explain how to construct truth tables.
- Explore the nuances of the **if**, **if-else**, and **if-else-if** statements.
- Introduce the **switch** statement.
- Demonstrate the differences in integral equality testing, floating-point equality testing, reference equality testing, and **equals()** testing.
- Strengthen program design skills.

5.1 BOOLEAN ALGEBRA AND TRUTH TABLES

A *logical expression* is an expression whose value is either the logical value *true* or the logical value *false*. For example, two logical expressions are

- A square is an equilateral rectangle (true).

- The year 2007 is a leap year (false).

The three primary logical operators for combining logic values into logical expressions are *and*, *or*, and *not*. The operators are used in the following examples:

- Jim is smiling *and* Patricia is puzzled.

- Gertrude is going to the musical *or* Jim is going for a walk to buy a newspaper.

- Joanne is *not* watching television.

In normal conversation, there may be some mild confusion over the meaning of a logical operator. For example, if Gertrude is going to the musical or Jim is going for a walk to buy a newspaper, can it be the case that they are both going out? However, unlike normal conversation, there is no mathematical ambiguity—each operator has a well-defined specification for the value of its operation given the values of the operands.

A *truth table* is an easy way of indicating the conditions that make a logical operation true and the conditions that make it false. A truth table lists all possible combinations of operand values and the result of the operation for each combination.

The truth table for the binary logical operator *and* is given in Table 5.1(a). In this and successive truth tables, we use p and q as placeholders to represent the left and right operands of the binary logical operator being discussed. We also use p in the discussion of the unary logical operator *not*.

Binary logical operators have four possible operand value combinations and therefore four entries in their truth tables. Unary logic operators have two table entries.

The logical *and* truth table, Table 5.1(a), shows that the operation is true only if both of its operands are true; otherwise, the operation is false. For example, the second entry of the truth table indicates that when p is false and q is true, the *and* operation evaluates to false. In the fourth entry where both p and q are true, the *and* operation evaluates to true.

Table 5.1(b) gives the truth table for the logical *or* operator. This truth table indicates that the *or* operation evaluates to true if at least one of its operands is true; otherwise, the operation evaluates to false.

Table 5.1(c) gives the truth table for the unary logical *not* operator. The *not* operation evaluates to true if its operand is false, and to false if its operand is true.

Table 5.1   **Truth table for the fundamental logic operators.**

p	*q*	*p and q*
false	false	false
false	true	false
true	false	false
true	true	true

(a) Logical *and*

p	*q*	*p or q*
false	false	false
false	true	true
true	false	true
true	true	true

(b) Logical *or*

p	*not p*
false	true
true	false

(c) Logical *not*

5.1.1   LOGICAL EXPRESSIONS

We can form *compound* expressions by combining logical operations. For example, the following expression is true when both *p* and *q* are false; otherwise, the expression is false.

not (p or q).

When *p* and *q* are both false, subexpression *(p or q)* is false and the negation of subexpression *(p or q)* is true, making the overall expression *not (p or q)* true. Any other combination of values for *p* and *q* makes subexpression *(p or q)* true, and the negation of that subexpression false, making the overall expression *not (p or q)* false.

The truth table in Table 5.2 shows the evaluation of *not (p or q)* in tabular form. To do so, the table has entries for the subexpression *(p or q)* and the expression *not (p or q)*.

Table 5.2   **Truth table for not(p or q).**

p	*q*	*p or q*	*not (p or q)*
false	false	false	true
false	true	true	false
true	false	true	false
true	true	true	false

Table 5.3   **Truth table for (not p) and (not q).**

p	q	not p	not q	(not p) and (not q)
false	false	true	true	true
false	true	true	false	false
true	false	false	true	false
true	true	false	false	false

Another truth table is given in Table 5.3. This truth table shows the evaluation of the expression *(not p) and (not q)*. To do so, the table has entries for subexpression *(not p)*, subexpression *(not q)*, and expression *(not p) and (not q)*.

It is interesting to compare the values of the expressions *not (p or q)* and *(not p) and (not q)* for each operand combination, By doing so, you can see that the two expressions are *equivalent* to each other. That is, when given the same operands, they produce the same values. This equivalence is famous and is known as a DeMorgan's equivalence. There is another DeMorgan equivalence — *not (p and q)* equals *(not p) or (not q)*. The proof of this equivalence is left to the exercises. Together the two equivalences are known as DeMorgan's law. The equivalences are sometimes useful in simplifying logical expressions.

5.2   BOOLEAN TYPE

The Java logical type is named **boolean** after the 19th-century British mathematician George Boole who formalized the study of logical values. The type **boolean** has two symbolic literal constants **true** and **false** that correspond to logical true and false respectively.

Like other local Java primitive variables, **boolean** variables are uninitialized by default. Thus, the following code segment defines two uninitialized variables.

```
boolean isWhitespace;
boolean haveFoundMissingLink;
```

Recalling that we use an "–" to indicate an unknown value, the depiction of these variables would be

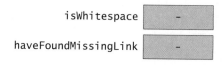

Observe that the variables have names indicating conditions. Such a naming style is a standard Java programming practice for **boolean** variables. The reason for using this naming style is that **boolean** variables normally are used in testing whether some program or data property is true.

The preferred definition of a **boolean** variable includes an explicit initialization value. The following code segment defines two variables with initialization values.

```
boolean canProceed = true;
boolean completedSecretMission = false;
```

Our representation of these variables would be

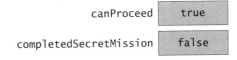

| canProceed | true |

| completedSecretMission | false |

5.2.1 BOOLEAN EQUALITY AND ORDERING OPERATORS

There are three **boolean** logical operators: &&, ||, and !. Operator && performs an *and* operation, operator || performs an *or* operation, and operator ! performs a *not* operation.

In addition, there are other operators such as the *equality* operators == and !=. The == operator, when given **boolean** operands, evaluates to **true** if both operand expressions have the same value, and it evaluates to **false** otherwise. Operator !=, when given **boolean** operands, evaluates to **true** if the two operand expressions have different values, and it evaluates to **false** otherwise.

Suppose the following definitions are in effect.

```
boolean p = true;
boolean q = false;
boolean r = true;
boolean s = false;
```

The following expressions evaluate to **true**.

```
p          // p has value true
p && r     // logical and is true when both operands are true
p || q     // logical or is true when at least one of the operands
           // is true
!s         // logical not is true when its operand is false
p == r     // equality is true when the operands have the same
           // value
q != r     // inequality is true when the operands have different
           // values
```

And the following expressions evaluate to **false**.

```
q          // q has value false
p && s     // logical and is false when at least one of the
           // operands is false
q || s     // logical or is false when both operands are false
!r         // logical not is false when the operand is true
r == s     // equality is false when the operands have different
           // values
q != s     // inequality is false when the operands have the same
           // value
```

The equality operators can also be applied using other primitive type values as operands. The operators work generally as expected. (Later, we discuss the pitfalls of testing floating-point values for equality and the appropriateness of the equality operator with reference variable operands.)

Suppose the following integer and character variables definitions are in effect.

```
int i = 1;
int j = 2;
int k = 2;
char c = '#';
char d = '%';
char e = '#';
```

The following expressions evaluate to **true**.

```
j == k    // equality is true when the operands have the same
          // value
i != k    // inequality is true when the operands have different
          // values
c == e    // equality is true when the operands have the same
          // value
d != e    // inequality is true when the operands have different
          // values
```

And the following expressions evaluate to **false**.

```
i == j    // equality is false when the operands have different
          // values
j != k    // inequality is false when the operands have the same
          // value
c == d    // equality is false when the operands have different
          // values
c != e    // inequality is false when the operands have the same
          // value
```

Java also provides *ordering* operators for the primitive types. They are used to determine the relative size of two values. There are four Java ordering operators, <, >, <=, and >=. These operators correspond respectively to the mathematical operators of $<$, $>$, $\leq$ and $\geq$. Together the equality operators and ordering operators are known as the *relational* operators.

For **boolean** comparison purposes, **false** is less than **true**.

For character comparison purposes, orderings are based on the Unicode character representation. For example, because the Unicode encoding of character 'e' is 101, the Unicode encoding of character 'j' is 106, and the Unicode encoding of character '=' is 51, character 'e' is both less than character 'j' and greater than character '='.

The Unicode character set has the following properties.

■ Character digits '0', '1', ..., '9' are arranged in the expected comparison order. In particular, digit character '0' has the encoding 48, character '1' has the encoding 49, and so on.

> A partial listing of the Unicode character set is given in Appendix A.

Short-circuit evaluation

When evaluating a logical expression, the value of the expression is sometimes known before all the operands have been considered. For example, if an operand of an && operation is known to be **false**, then the value of the && operation must be **false**. Similarly, if an operand of an || operation is known to be **true**, then the value of the || operation must be **true**. Java uses these properties to make the evaluation of logical operations more efficient.

When evaluating a logical operation, Java evaluates the left operand before it evaluates the right operand. If the value of the operation can be determined from the left operand, then the right operand is not evaluated. This kind of evaluation is known as *short-circuit evaluation*.

Short-circuit evaluation is useful when some property must be true for some other expression to be evaluated. For example, suppose you are interested in knowing whether scoreSum divided by nbrScores is greater than the value expectation. This condition can be evaluated only if nbrScores is nonzero. The following expression correctly represents the condition.

```
(nbrScores != 0) && ((scoreSum / nbrScores) > expectation)
```

Because the left operand of the && is evaluated first, we know that if the right operand of the && is evaluated, nbrScores cannot be 0 and therefore dividing by nbrScores makes sense. Without short-circuit evaluation, the right operand of the && could be evaluated with nbrScores being 0, causing an illegal divide-by-zero to occur.

- Uppercase Latin letters 'A', 'B', ..., 'Z' are arranged in the expected comparison order. In particular, character 'A' has the encoding 65, character 'B' has the encoding 66, and so on.

> The comparison of strings and other objects is considered in Section 5.7.

- Lowercase Latin letters 'a', 'b', ..., 'z' are arranged in the expected comparison order. In particular, character 'a' has the encoding 97, character 'b' has the encoding 98, and so on.

Thus, with the Unicode encodings the lowercase character digits are less than the uppercase Latin letters, which are less than the lowercase Latin letters.

We now consider some examples using the ordering operators. Suppose the following definitions are in effect.

```java
int i = 1;
int j = 2;
int k = 2;
char c = '2';
char d = '3';
char e = '4';
char f = 'c';
char g = 'D';
```

The following expressions are then **true**.

```java
i < j    // < is true when the value of the left operand is
         // less than the value of the right operand
```

```
d > e      // > is true when the value of the left operand is
           // greater than the value of the right operand
i <= k     // <= is true when the value of the left operand is
           // less than or equal to the value of the right operand
j >= k     // >= is true when the value of the left operand is
           // greater than or equal to the value of the right
           // operand
g < f      // < is true when the value of the left operand is
           // greater than the value of the right
           // (the Unicode values for uppercase Latin letters are
           // (smaller than values for lowercase Latin letters)
```

And the following expressions are **false**.

```
j < k      // < is false when the value of the left operand is
           // not less than the value of the right operand
c > e      // > is false when the value of the left operand is
           // not greater than the value of the right operand
d <= c     // <= is false when the value of left operand is
           // greater than the value of the right operand
i >= k     // >= is false when the value of the left operand is
           // less than the value of the right operand
```

5.2.2   OPERATOR PRECEDENCE REVISITED

More complicated expressions can be built by using multiple operators in the same expression. To evaluate such expressions, the precedence of the relational and logical operators must be known with respect to the other operators.

The not operator ! has the same high precedence as other unary operators. Among the binary operators, the relational and logical operators have lower precedence than the arithmetic operators and higher precedence than the assignment operators. Relational operators have greater precedence than the logical operators. Among the relational operators, the ordering operators have higher precedence than the equality operators. Among the logical operators, && has higher precedence than ||. Because of operator precedence, the following two expressions are equivalent.

- `depth + delta < prevDepth * 1.1 && isOn || !rising`
- `(((depth + delta) < (prevDepth * 1.1)) && isOn) || (! rising)`

And the next two expressions are also equivalent.

- `prevCheckIsOk != rpm < d || isWarm && isRunning`
- `(prevCheckIsOk != (rpm < d)) || (isWarm && isRunning)`

To ensure understanding, we continue to recommend the use of parentheses.

The precedence and associativity of the arithmetic, relational, ordering, logical, and assignment operators are summarized in Table 5.4. A complete specification of the precedence of Java operators is given in Appendix A.

Given this introduction to logical expressions, we are now ready to use them in control constructs. The first control construct that we consider is the **if** statement.

Table 5.4 **Precedence and associativity of selected operators.**

Operation	Precedence	Associativity
Grouping operator: ()	17	None
Unary operators: +, -, !	13	Right
Multiplicative arithmetic: *, /, %	12	Left
Additive arithmetic: +, -	11	Left
Relational ordering:<, >, <=, >=	10	Left
Relational equality: ==, !=	9	Left
Logical and: &&	4	Left
Logic or: ||	3	Left
Assignment: =, +=, -=, *=, /=, %=	1	Right

5.3 IF STATEMENT

The **if** statement has two forms. The simpler of the two forms has syntax

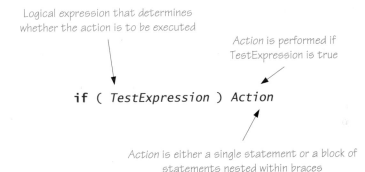

Logical expression that determines
whether the action is to be executed

Action is performed if
TestExpression is true

if (TestExpression) Action

Action is either a single statement or a block of
statements nested within braces

When an **if** statement is reached within a program, the parenthetic expression *TestExpression* is evaluated. If *TestExpression* evaluates to **true**, *Action* is executed; otherwise, *Action* is not executed. Either way, program execution continues with the next statement in the program.

The preceding description of an **if** statement execution process is its *semantic* definition. The semantics are demonstrated in the *flowchart* diagram in Figure 5.1.

Suppose `measure` is a variable that has been defined previously, and we now need to make sure it is positive. The following code segment accomplishes this task.

```
if (measure < 0)          // is measure less than 0?
    measure = - measure;  // it is, so change its sign
```

The segment uses an **if** statement. If the test expression (`measure < 0`) evaluates to **true**, then `measure` is negative and assigning it with its additive inverse changes `measure` to the equivalent positive number. If instead the test expression (`measure < 0`) is

---

Figure 5.1   Representation of basic if statement semantics.

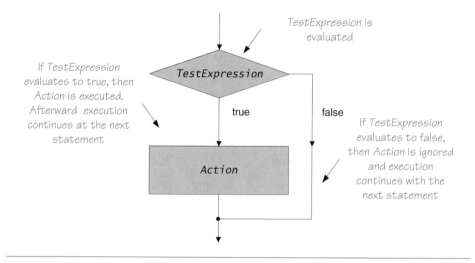

Figure 5.2   Semantics of updating measure if it is negative.

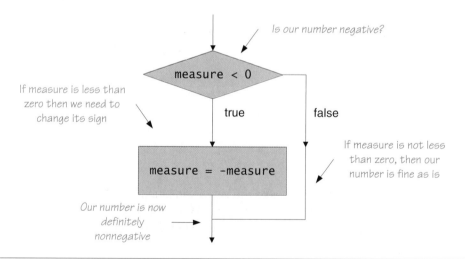

---

false, then measure must be nonnegative and no action needs to be performed. The action associated with the code segment is given pictorially in Figure 5.2.

Often, several statements need to be executed based on the value of an expression. To indicate that a group of statements is to be executed, the statements in the group are surrounded by left and right braces. The various statements in the group are separated by semicolons. The semicolons are necessary so that the individual statements can be distinguished.

Figure 5.3   **Semantics of swapping based on variable values.**

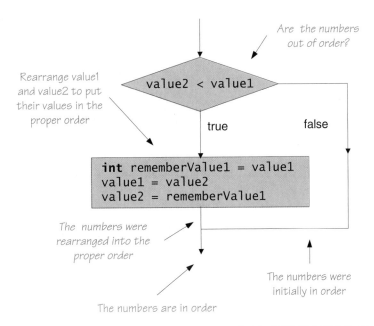

An **if** statement with a statement-list action is demonstrated in the following code segment, which swaps the values of variables `value1` and `value2`, if `value2` is less than `value1`. The action associated with the code segment is depicted in Figure 5.3.

```
if (value2 < value1) {    // values are not in sorted order
    // swapping puts them in order
    int rememberValue1 = value1;
    value1 = value2;
    value2 = rememberValue1;
}
```

In this segment, the expression (`value2 < value1`) tests whether `value2` is less than `value1`. If the expression (`value2 < value1`) evaluates to **true**, then those two variables have their values interchanged in the associated action.

```
int rememberValue1 = value1;
value1 = value2;
value2 = rememberValue1;
```

This interchange swaps the two values so that the value in `value2` is at least as large as the value in `value1`. It is important to note that variable `rememberValue1` exists only within the action associated with the **if** statement. The braces of that action delimit its *scope*. (We consider the notion of scope in detail in Chapter 7.)

If instead the test expression (`value2 < value1`) is **false**, then it is already the case that `value2` is at least as large as `value1`. In this case, nothing needs to be done with the two values.

Listing 5.1 SortTwo.java

```java
1.  // displays two user-specified values in sorted order
2.
3.  import java.util.*;
4.
5.  public class SortTwo {
6.      // main(): application entry point
7.      public static void main(String[] args) {
8.          // set input stream
9.          Scanner stdin = new Scanner(System.in);
10.
11.         // get numbers
12.         System.out.print("Enter an integer number: ");
13.         int value1 = stdin.nextInt();
14.         System.out.print("Enter another integer number: ");
15.         int value2 = stdin.nextInt();
16.
17.         // rearrange numbers if necessary
18.         if (value2 < value1) {     // values are not in sorted order
19.             // swapping puts them in order
20.             int rememberValue1 = value1;
21.             value1 = value2;
22.             value2 = rememberValue1;
23.         }
24.
25.         // display values
26.         System.out.println("The numbers in sorted order are "
27.             + value1 + " and then " + value2);
28.     }
29. }
```

A complete program `SortTwo.java` for sorting two numbers is given in Listing 5.1. One run of the program had the following input/output behavior.

```
Enter an integer number: 21
Enter another integer number: 6
The numbers in sorted order are 6 and then 21
```

And another program run had the following input/output behavior.

```
Enter an integer number: 4
Enter another integer number: 30
The numbers in sorted order are 4 and then 30
```

Because the only interesting code in the program is the **if** statement, we do not discuss the program further.

Before discussing the **if-else** statement, we first turn our attention to two safe programming practices.

5.3.1   AVOIDING GOTCHAS

When developing programs with **if** statements, there are two practices that you should follow generally.

- Use braces to surround the actions;
- Do not compare floating-point values using the equality operators.

We *strongly* recommend the use of braces to surround the action of an **if** statement regardless of whether the action is composed of single or multiple statements. Software often is modified—sometimes to correct errors and other times to extend its functionality. These changes can cause the action of an **if** statement to change from simple to complex. By having the braces already in place, it is easier to avoid introducing logic errors when making changes.

By using braces consistently, errors such as the following can be avoided.

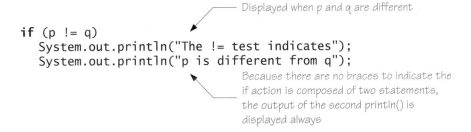

The underlying reason that programs generally should not test floating-point values for equality is the finite precision of the floating-point types. Finite precision coupled with expression evaluation can lead to anomalies. For example, the following expression, while mathematically true, does not evaluate to **true** within a Java program.

$$1 == 0.1 + 0.1 + 0.1 + 0.1 + 0.1 + 0.1 + 0.1 + 0.1 + 0.1 + 0.1$$

It does not evaluate to **true**, because the right operand of the == operator sums to the **double** value 0.9999999999999999.

Rather than directly testing for floating-point equivalence, programs test whether the values of interest are sufficiently close to each other to be considered the same. This testing is done by using a tolerance constant. Two values are considered equivalent if the absolute value of their difference is less than the value of the tolerance constant. For example, suppose the tolerance is specified through a Java constant EPSILON.

```
final double EPSILON = 0.000001;
```

The following expression would then indicate whether variables x and y are sufficiently close to be considered equivalent.

```
Math.abs(x-y) <= EPSILON
```

The expression makes use of the Math class method Math.abs() that returns the absolute value of its floating-point parameter. Thus, the expression evaluates to **true** when x and y are sufficiently close to each other to be considered equivalent and **false** otherwise.

5.4　IF-ELSE STATEMENT

The second form of the **if** statement deals with situations where different actions are to be taken based on the value of a logical expression. This form of the **if** statement has syntax

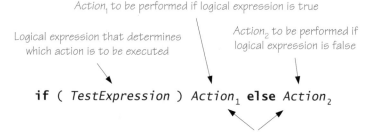

where *Action₁* and *Action₂* can each be either a single statement with a terminating semicolon (;) or a block of statements enclosed in left and right braces. When the **if-else** statement is executed, *TestExpression* is evaluated. If *TestExpression* evaluates to **true**, *Action₁* is executed; otherwise, *Action₂* is executed. Figure 5.4 demonstrates the semantics of the **if-else** statement.

In the following code segment, two input values are extracted, and the maximum of the two values is displayed.

```
Scanner stdin = new Scanner(System.in);

System.out.print("Enter an integer number: ");
int value1 = stdin.nextInt();
System.out.print("Enter another integer number: ");
int value2 = stdin.nextInt();

int maximum;
if (value1 < value2) {   // is value2 larger?
    maximum = value2;    // yes: value2 is larger
}
else { // (value1 >= value2)
    maximum = value1;    // no: value2 is not larger
}
System.out.println("The maximum of " + value1 + " and "
    + value2 + " is " + maximum);
```

| Figure 5.4 | **Semantic representation of an if-else statement.** |

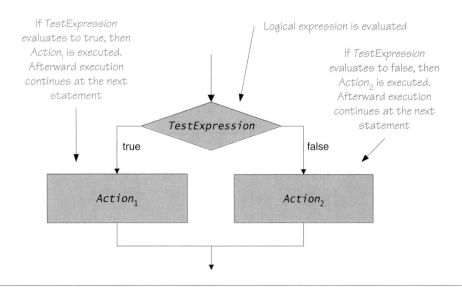

If *TestExpression*
evaluates to true, then
Action₁ is executed.
Afterward execution
continues at the next
statement

Logical expression is evaluated

If *TestExpression*
evaluates to false, then
Action₂ is executed.
Afterward execution
continues at the next
statement

TestExpression

true

false

Action₁

Action₂

After determining the inputs `value1` and `value2`, the code segment evaluates the expression (`value1 < value2`) in the **if-else** statement.

```
if (value1 < value2) {   // is value2 larger?
    maximum = value2;    // yes: value2 is larger
}
else { // (value1 >= value2)
    maximum = value1;    // no: value2 is not larger
}
```

If the test expression evaluates to **true**, `value2` is the maximum of the two inputs and it is used to set variable `maximum`. Observe that the right brace signals the end of the action taken if the test expression evaluates to **true**.

If instead the test expression (`value1 < value2`) evaluates to **false**, `value1` is at least as large as `value2`. Therefore, in the **else** part, `value1` is used to set `maximum`. Figure 5.5 demonstrates the semantics of this statement.

Thus our analysis shows that when this **if-else** statement is completed, `maximum` is appropriately set and can be used as needed.

A complete program `Maximum.java` for finding the larger of two numbers is given in Listing 5.2. One sample run of the program had the following input/output behavior

```
Enter an integer number: 9
Enter another integer number: 23
The maximum of 9 and 23 is 23
```

And another program run had the following input/output behavior

```
Enter an integer number: 16
Enter another integer number: 3
The maximum of 16 and 3 is 16
```

Figure 5.5   Finding the maximum of two values.

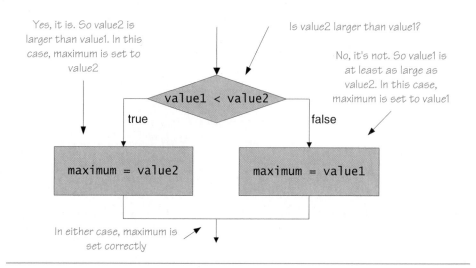

Listing 5.2   Maximum.java

```java
1. // displays two user-specified values in sorted order
2. import java.util.*;
3.
4. public class Maximum {
5.    // main(): application entry point
6.    public static void main(String[] args) {
7.       // set input stream
8.       Scanner stdin = new Scanner(System.in);
9.
10.      // get numbers
11.      System.out.print("Enter an integer number: ");
12.      int value1 = stdin.nextInt();
13.      System.out.print("Enter another integer number: ");
14.      int value2 = stdin.nextInt();
15.
16.      // determine maximum
17.      int maximum;
18.      if (value1 < value2) {    // is value2 larger?
19.         maximum = value2;      // yes: value2 is larger
20.      }
21.      else { // (value1 >= value2)
22.         maximum = value1;      // no: value2 is not larger
23.      }
24.
25.      // display maximum
26.      System.out.println("The maximum of " + value1 + " and "
27.            + value2 + " is " + maximum);
28.   }
29. }
```

Because the only interesting code in program Maximum.java is its **if** statement, we do not discuss the program further.

Consistent indentation and brace location

In the programs for this chapter, we always indent the *Action* statements associated with the **if** statements. The indentation is a clue to the reader that the execution of an *Action* statement depends on the less-indented **if** statement expression. A consistent indentation scheme is necessary for program readability. Most programmers typically use three or four blanks per level of indentation.

The placement of the braces that group the statement list is a matter of personal taste. Our method for brace placement is the following:

- Include the opening left brace on the initial line of the **if** statement to conserve line space.
- Place the closing brace on its own line at the same indentation level as the associated **if** statement as a visual clue that subsequent statements in the program are not associated with this **if** statement.

To get a sense of how hard it can be to understand a poorly indented program, consider the following nonindented, noncommented version of SortTwo.java from Listing 5.1.

```java
import java.util.*;
public class SortTwo {
public static void main(String[] args) {
Scanner stdin = new Scanner(System.in);
System.out.print("Enter an integer number: ");
int value1 = stdin.nextInt();
System.out.print("Enter another integer number: ");
int value2 = stdin.nextInt();
if (value2 < value1) {
int rememberValue1 = value1;
value1 = value2;
value2 = rememberValue1;
}
System.out.println("The numbers in sorted order are "
+ value1 + " and then " + value2);
return;
}
}
```

5.5 NESTED CONSTRUCTS

As stated in the discussion of the **if** and **if-else** statements, the associated actions can be any Java statement or any list of statements with braces. Therefore, the actions can contain other **if** and **if-else** statements!

The following code segment uses a nested **if** statement to control the navigation of a robot when it encounters a door. (In the segment, assume isDoorUnlocked and isLightOff are previously defined **boolean** variables.)

```java
if (isDoorUnlocked) {
   System.out.println("Open the door");
   if (isLightOff) {
      System.out.println("Turn on the light");
   }
   System.out.println("Enter the room");
}
else {
   System.out.println("Turn around and leave");
}
```

The code segment has the robot enter the room if the door is unlocked. However, before entering, the robot ensures that the light is on in the room. If the door is locked, then the code segment has the robot turn and around and leave.

The indentation pattern of the code segment indicates that the described actions are what we intend. But how does the Java compiler—which ignores indentation—know to match the **else** action with the outer **if** statement rather than the nested **if** statement?

The compiler can tell to which **if** statement to match an **else** action based on the Java requirement that only either a single statement or a list of statements enclosed within braces separate an **else** action from its associated **if**. For our code segment, this requirement necessitates that the turn around and leave command be associated with the status of door being locked.

As another example, consider the following code segment that makes use of some previously defined **boolean** variables p and q. The segments differ in what **if** statement is matched with the **else** action,

```java
if (p) {                           // p is true
   if (q) {                        // p is true, q is true
      System.out.println("A");     // p is true, q is true
   }                               // p is true, q is true
   else {                          // p is true, q is false
      System.out.println("B");     // p is true, q is false
   }                               // p is true, q is false
}                                  // p is true
```

In this segment, the **else** and its statement are associated with the **if** statement that evaluates q. For the string "B" to be displayed, expression p must be true and expression q must be **false**. In the next code segment using variables p and q, braces surround the inner **if** statement:

```java
if (p) {                           // p is true
   if (q) {                        // p is true, q is true
      System.out.println("A");     // p is true, q is true
   }                               // p is true, q is true
}                                  // p is true
else {                             // p is false
   System.out.println("B");        // p is false
}                                  // p is false
```

Objects and == and !=

The values of reference variables (e.g., `String` variables) generally are not tested using the == and != operators. The reasons why are discussed in Section 5.7 where we discuss the `equals()` method for objects.

The ? : operator

The operator ? : can sometimes be used in place of a conditional statement. The operator has the following form:

    TestExpression ? *Expression*$_1$: *Expression*$_2$

When executed, *TestExpression* is evaluated first. If *TestExpression* evaluates to **true**, then the value of the operation is *Expression*$_1$; otherwise, the value of the operation is *Expression*$_2$. A colon separates the two expressions.

Suppose `value1` and `value2` are **int** variables that have been initialized already. The following statement uses operator ? : in defining a variable **min** that is the lesser of those two values.

```
int min = (input1 <= input2) ? input1 : input2;
```

Without the use of the operator, the definition and initialization would take several statements.

```
int min;
if (input1 <= input2) {
    min = input1;
}
else {
    min = input2;
}
```

Following convention

Avoid writing expressions such as `(a == `**true**`)` or `((a < b) == `**true**`)`. Instead, write respectively the equivalent expressions, `(a)` and `(a < b)`, which are easier to understand.

Similarly, avoid expressions such as `(a == `**false**`)` or `((a < b) == `**false**`)`. Instead, write respectively the following equivalent expressions, `(!a)` and `(a >= b)`, which are easier to understand.

If you do not follow this advice, realize that explicitly testing whether a **boolean** expression equals a particular **boolean** value is viewed disdainfully by many programmers—they consider it a sign of programming immaturity.

Because of these braces, the **else** is matched to the first **if** statement. Therefore, string `"B"` is displayed whenever p evaluates to **false**, regardless of the value of q.

In the next section, we turn our attention to a specialized form of nested **if-else** statements—the **if-else-if** construct.

5.6 IF-ELSE-IF CONSTRUCT

Consider the following simple task: report whether a user-specified input integer value is zero, positive, or negative. An algorithm for this task is straightforward.

Step 1. Prompt for and extract a user-supplied value.

Step 2. If the value is zero, then report that the value is zero.

Step 3. If instead the value is positive, then report that the value is positive.

Step 4. Otherwise, report that the value is negative.

Now consider the following code segment using a nested **if-else** structure to implement the algorithm.

```
Scanner stdin = new Scanner(System.in);

System.out.print("Enter an integer: ");
int number = stdin.nextInt();

if (number == 0) {
    System.out.println(number + " is zero");
}
else {
    if (number > 0) {
        System.out.println(number + " is positive");
    }
    else {
        System.out.println(number + " is negative");
    }
}
```

We argue that this code segment is correct, but its indentation style does not communicate sufficiently that one of three possible conditions is being determined and reported. We can rewrite this code segment in the following manner to better communicate the situation.

```
Scanner stdin = new Scanner(System.in);

System.out.print("Enter an integer: ");
int number = stdin.nextInt();

if (number == 0) {
    System.out.println(number + " is zero");
}
else if (number > 0) {
    System.out.println(number + " is positive");
}
else {
    System.out.println(number + " is negative");
}
```

In the new code segment, the second **if** statement is placed on the same line as the first **else** and the trailing code is reduced by one level of indentation.

```java
if (number > 0) {
   System.out.println(number + " is positive");
}
else {
   System.out.println(number + " is negative");
}
```

The **if** statement is still the action associated with the first **else**. However, the overall appearance of the code segment indicates that one of three conditions is being determined and reported. This code segment is an example of the **if-else-if** idiom. The **if-else-if** idiom is built by combining multiple **if-else** statements.

Our next example is SortThree.java of Listing 5.3. The program uses the **if-else-if** idiom to assist in the sorting of three numbers. In particular, the program extracts three user-specified values n1, n2, and n3 and displays those values in sorted order, that is, nondecreasing order. We use the term *nondecreasing* rather than "ascending" because the input values may contain duplicates.

For three numbers, there are only six possible number orderings:

- $n1 \le n2 \le n3$
- $n1 \le n3 \le n2$
- $n2 \le n1 \le n3$
- $n2 \le n3 \le n1$
- $n3 \le n1 \le n2$
- $n3 \le n2 \le n1$

The program first defines and extracts the input values using int variables n1, n2, and n3.

```java
Scanner stdin = new Scanner(System.in);

// extract inputs
System.out.print("Enter three integers:");
int n1 = stdin.nextInt();
int n2 = stdin.nextInt();
int n2 = stdin.nextInt();
```

The program next defines variables sorted1, sorted2, and sorted3 for recording the sorted ordering.

```java
// define outputs
int sorted1;
int sorted2;
int sorted3;
```

The program then proceeds to determine what is the sorted ordering of the input. The first of these tests checks whether the inputs n1, n2, and n3 are sorted already.

```java
if ((n1 <= n2) && (n2 <= n3)) {  // n1 <= n2 <= n2
    sorted1 = n1;
    sorted2 = n2;
    sorted3 = n3;
}
```

Listing 5.3   SortThree.java

```java
1.  // Sorts three user-specified numbers
2.
3.  import java.util.*;
4.
5.  public class SortThree {
6.      // main(): application entry point
7.      public static void main(String[] args) {
8.          // set input stream
9.          Scanner stdin = new Scanner(System.in);
10.
11.         // extract inputs
12.         System.out.print("Enter three integers: ");
13.         int n1 = stdin.nextInt();
14.         int n2 = stdin.nextInt();
15.         int n3 = stdin.nextInt();
16.
17.         // define outputs
18.         int sorted1;
19.         int sorted2;
20.         int sorted3;
21.
22.         // determine which of the six orderings is applicable
23.         if ((n1 <= n2) && (n2 <= n3)) {   // n1 <= n2 <= n2
24.             sorted1 = n1;
25.             sorted2 = n2;
26.             sorted3 = n3;
27.         }
28.         else if ((n1 <= n3) && (n3 <= n2)) { // n1 <= n3 <= n2
29.             sorted1 = n1;
30.             sorted2 = n3;
31.             sorted3 = n2;
32.         }
33.         else if ((n2 <= n1) && (n1 <= n3)) { // n2 <= n1 <= n3
34.             sorted1 = n2;
35.             sorted2 = n1;
36.             sorted3 = n3;
37.         }
38.         else if ((n2 <= n3) && (n3 <= n1)) { // n2 <= n3 <= n1
39.             sorted1 = n2;
40.             sorted2 = n3;
41.             sorted3 = n1;
42.         }
43.         else if ((n3 <= n1) && (n1 <= n2)) { // n3 <= n1 <= n2
44.             sorted1 = n3;
45.             sorted2 = n1;
46.             sorted3 = n2;
```

```
            Listing 5.3    SortThree.java  (Continued)
47.           }
48.           else { // n3 <= n2 <= n1
49.               sorted1 = n3;
50.               sorted2 = n2;
51.               sorted3 = n1;
52.           }
53.
54.           // display results
55.           System.out.println("\nSorted order of " + n1 + " " + n2 + " "
56.               + n3 + " is " + sorted1 + " " + sorted2 + " " + sorted3);
57.       }
58. }
```

If the input values are sorted, then they are copied respectively to sorted1, sorted2, and sorted3. Observe that the test expression is

    (n1 <= n2) && (n2 <= n3)

and not

    (n1 <= n2 <= n3)   // illegal

This alternative expression has the right mathematical look but is not a syntactically correct Java expression. Because of operator associativity, the alternative expression is equivalent to

    (n1 <= n2) <= n3

which compares a logical value (the result of comparing n1 to n2) to n3. Such an expression is invalid Java and cannot be used.

If the three input values are not in sorted order, then a test is made to determine whether n1 is the smallest, n3 is the middle value, and n2 is the largest value. If this test evaluates to **true**, then n1 is copied to sorted1, n3 is copied to sorted2, and n2 is copied to sorted3.

```
        else if ((n1 <= n3) && (n3 <= n2)) { // n1 <= n3 <= n2
            sorted1 = n1;
            sorted2 = n3;
            sorted3 = n2;
        }
```

If instead this test evaluates to **false**, another ordering is considered.

The testing process continues until five different orderings have been considered and rejected. At that point, there is only one untried ordering (i.e., n3 ≤ n2 ≤ n1), and it must represent the sorted ordering. For this case, n3 is copied to sorted1, n2 is copied to sorted2, and n1 is copied to sorted3.

```
        else { // n3 <= n2 <= n1
            sorted1 = n3;
            sorted2 = n2;
            sorted3 = n1;
        }
```

We now turn our attention on how to test whether two objects are equivalent.

5.7 TESTING OBJECTS FOR EQUALITY

In the next series of examples, the definition of Scanner variable stdin is in effect.

```
Scanner stdin = new Scanner(System.in);
```

The first example determines whether two user-specified **int** values n1 and n2 are the same.

```
System.out.print("Enter an integer number: ");
int n1 = stdin.nextInt();
System.out.print("Enter another integer number: ");
int n2 = stdin.nextInt();

if (n1 == n2) {
    System.out.println(n1 + " and " + n2 + " are the same");
}
else {
    System.out.println(n1 + " and " + n2 + " differ");
}
```

The code is straightforward. It first defines and initializes two variables n1 and n2 with user-specified values. It then tests whether the values are the same by evaluating the **boolean** expression n1 == n2.

If we wanted a code segment that reports whether two user-specified **boolean** values are the same, we would use comparable code for the testing.

```
System.out.print("Enter a boolean value: ");
boolean b1 = stdin.nextBoolean();
System.out.print("Enter another character: ");
boolean b2 = stdin.nextBoolean();

if (b1 == b2) {
    System.out.println(b1 + " and " + b2 + " are the same");
}
else {
    System.out.println(b1 + " and " + b2 + " differ");
}
```

Similarly, if we wanted a code segment that reports whether two user-supplied character strings are the same, we would be tempted to use comparable code.

```
System.out.print("Enter a string: ");
String s1 = stdin.nextLine();
System.out.println("Enter another string: ");
String s2 = stdin.nextLine();

if (s1 == s2) {                          Tests whether s1 and s2
    System.out.println(s1 + " and " + s2 + " are the same");    reference the same String
}
else {
    System.out.println(s1 + " and " + s2 + " differ");
}
```

However, this code segment does not do what is intended. Yes, String variables s1 and s2 are initialized to be references to the input values. But the **boolean** expression s1 == s2 does not test whether these input values are equivalent; instead this expression tests whether s1 and s2 are referencing the same memory location, which for this code segment is never **true**.

To understand why the code segment behaves so, suppose the user in reaction to both prompts enters the string "pastel".

```
Enter a string: pastel
Enter another string: pastel
```

The definitions of variables s1 and s2 cause them to reference separate String objects. These two String objects both have values that correspond to "pastel".

The expression s1 == s2 tests whether *variables* s1 *and* s2 *have the same value*; that is, it tests whether s1 and s2 both reference the same location. And because they do not, the expression is **false**.

To instead test whether the *strings referenced by* s1 *and* s2 *have the same representation*, we use the String member method equals().

Tests whether s1 and s2 represent
the same character sequence

```
if (s1.equals(s2)) {
    System.out.println(s1 + " and " + s2 + " are the same");
}
else {
    System.out.println(s1 + " and " + s2 + " differ");
}
```

String method equals() returns **true** only when its parameter corresponds to the same character string as the character string represented by the invoking string.

Listing 5.4 uses the code segment in the complete program StringTest.java to report whether two user-specified input strings are the same.

Literal string constants

Consider the following definitions for String variables s and t.

```
String s = "abc";
String t = "abc";
```

It is clear that s.equals(t) evaluates to **true**, but is s == t also **true**? The answer is yes. Java represents a literal character string internally as a String constant. If the same literal character string appears more than once in a class, then all occurrences reference the same String constant. Therefore, the variables s and t from this example are assigned the same String reference. As a result, s == t evaluates to **true**.

Listing 5.4 **String Test.java**

```
1.  // determines whether user-specified strings are the same.
2.
3.  import java.util.*;
4.
5.  public class StringTest {
6.      // main(): application entry point
7.      public static void main(String[] args) {
8.          // set input stream
9.          Scanner stdin = new Scanner(System.in);
10.
11.         // get strings of interest
12.         System.out.print("Enter a string: ");
13.         String s1 = stdin.nextLine();
14.         System.out.print("Enter another string: ");
15.         String s2 = stdin.nextLine();
16.
17.         // are the strings equivalent
18.         if (s1.equals(s2)) {
19.             System.out.println(s1 + " and " + s2 + " are the same");
20.         }
21.         else {
22.             System.out.println(s1 + " and " + s2 + " differ");
23.         }
24.     }
25. }
```

The awt class `Rectangle` also provides a member method `equals()`. Two `Rectangle` objects are equal if and only if they have the same width, height, and top-left corner. Its use is demonstrated in the following code segment.

```
Rectangle r1 = new Rectangle(0, 0, 5, 3);
Rectangle r2 = new Rectangle(0, 0, 5, 3);
Rectangle r3 = r1;

if (r1 == r2) {
    System.out.println("r1 and r2 refer to the same object\n");
}
else if (r1.equals(r2)) {
    System.out.println("r1 and r2 refer to different objects "
        + "representing the same\nrectangle\n");
}
else {
    System.out.println("r1 and r2 refer to different objects "
        + "representing different\nrectangles\n");
}

if (r1 == r3) {
    System.out.println("r1 and r3 refer to the same "
        + "rectangle");
}
else if (r1.equals(r3)) {
    System.out.println("r1 and r3 refer to different objects "
        + "representing the same\nrectangle");
}
```

```
else {
    System.out.println("r1 and r3 refer to different objects "
        + "representing different\nrectangles");
}
```

In the segment, `Rectangle` variables `r1`, `r2`, and `r3` all refer to a 5 × 3 rectangle with a top-left corner situated at the origin (0, 0). The `Rectangle` objects referenced by `r1` and `r2` were constructed individually. The `Rectangle` object referenced by `r3` is the same `Rectangle` object referenced by `r1`. The output of the program reflects this initialization.

```
r1 and r2 refer to different objects representing the same
rectangle

r1 and r3 refer to the same object
```

All objects have a method `equals()`. However, the implementation of the method is type specific. For many classes, its implementation is analogous to the implementations of the `equals()` for `String` and `Rectangle`—the method determines whether the two references have equivalent representations. However, some classes report merely whether the references are the same. You should make it a practice to read the documentation associated with a class so that you understand its various behaviors.

Character processing

Programmers who are doing string processing often are interested in determining whether characters have some particular property. For this purpose, Java provides a collection of class methods as part of the standard package `java.lang.Character`. For example, method `Character.isWhitespace()` tests whether its parameter is a space, tab, formfeed, or newline character; and method `Character.isDigit()` tests whether its parameter is a decimal digit. The following list includes some of the more frequently used `Character` class methods for testing properties of characters.

- `isDigit()`: Tests whether character is numeric.
- `isLetter()`: Tests whether character is alphabetic.
- `isLowerCase()`: Tests whether character is lowercase alphabetic.
- `isWhiteSpace()`: Tests whether character is one of the space, tab, formfeed, or newline characters.
- `isUpperCase()`: Tests whether character is uppercase alphabetic.

Two other `Character` class methods of frequent interest are

- `toLowerCase()`: If the character is alphabetic, then the lowercase equivalent of the character is returned; otherwise, the character is returned.
- `toUpperCase()`: If the character is alphabetic, then the uppercase equivalent of the character is returned; otherwise, the character is returned.

In Section 5.8, we turn our attention to the other Java conditional statement, the **switch** statement.

5.8 SWITCH STATEMENT

Programmers are confronted sometimes with a task where the action to be executed depends on the value of a specific integral expression. The **if-else-if** construct can be used to solve such tasks by separately comparing the desired expression to a particular value and, if the expression and value are equal, then executing the appropriate action.

For example, suppose we are developing a program with a graphical display where the location of a graphical element named `sprite` is to be updated based on the value of **char** variable cmd ('u', 'd', 'l', 'r' for up, down, left, and right, respectively). Using **if** statements, the code might look like the following:

```java
if (cmd == 'u') {
   sprite.moveUp();
}
else if (cmd == 'd') {
   sprite.moveDown();
}
else if (cmd == 'l') {
   sprite.moveLeft();
}
else if (cmd == 'r') {
   sprite.moveRight();
}
else {
   System.out.println("Unexpected request: " + cmd);
}
```

Because such programming tasks occur frequently, Java includes a **switch** statement. The command decoding can be done in a more readable manner using that statement.

```java
switch (cmd) {
   case 'u':
      sprite.moveUp();
      break;
   case 'd':
      sprite.moveDown();
      break;
   case 'l':
      sprite.moveLeft();
      break;
   case 'r':
      sprite.moveRight();
      break;
   default:
      System.out.println("Unexpected request: " + cmd);
}
```

Switch statements and floating-point values

Because of the requirement that both the *SwitchExpression* and the individual *CaseExpressions* be integral, the **switch** statement cannot be used to determine actions based on the value of a floating-point object. Such processing requires **if-else-if** statements.

As our example suggests, a basic **switch** statement has the following syntax:

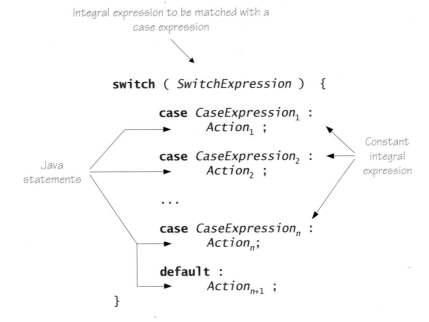

The *Action* associated with a *case* expression is either a single statement or a group of statements. Even if the *Action* is a group of statements, no surrounding braces are required.

When a **switch** statement is executed, its *SwitchExpression* is evaluated; if the value of that expression equals the value of a *CaseExpression* in that **switch** statement, then flow of control is transferred to the $Action_i$ associated with the matching $CaseExpression_i$.

If no *CaseExpression* equals the value of the *SwitchExpression* and if a **default** case is supplied, then the **default** $Action_{n+1}$ code is executed. In the command character example, the **default** case issues an error message.

If no *CaseExpression* equals the value of the *SwitchExpression* and no **default** case is supplied, then none of the *Actions* are executed. In practice, most **switch** statements include a **default** *Action* that handles unexpected conditions.

What happens after the selected *Action* is executed depends on the statements that make up *Action*. Normally, the last statement in an *Action* is a **break** statement. The **break** statement indicates that the **switch** statement has completed its task and that the flow of control should continue with the statement after the **switch** statement. If no **break** statement is supplied, then control continues with the next statement within the **switch** statement itself.

In the next code segment, **break** statements are not used within the **switch** statement.

```java
switch (i) {
    case 3:
        System.out.println("Hello, friend");
    case 2:
```

```
            System.out.println("Hello, friend");
        default:
            System.out.println("Hello, friend");
    }
```

If the value of i is 3, then the segment displays "Hello, friend" three times.

```
Hello, friend
Hello, friend
Hello, friend
```

The message is displayed three times, as the value of i matches the first case. Therefore, each of the three actions in the **switch** statement are executed because there are no **break** statements that stop the *fall-through* behavior.

If the value of i is 2, then the string "Hello, friend" is displayed two times.

```
Hello, friend
Hello, friend
```

The message is displayed two times, as the value of i matches the second case. Therefore, each of the two subsequent actions in the **switch** statement are executed because there are no **break** statements that stop the fall-through behavior.

If the value of i is neither 2 nor 3, then the **default** action is executed and the string is displayed just once.

```
Hello, friend
```

Normally, one should avoid using the fall-through behavior of the **switch** statement to achieve a desired effect. The *Action* of a case should almost always end with a **break** statement. However, there is one situation where using the fall-through behavior makes sense.

What if we would like the same *Action* to be performed for different values of the *SwitchExpression*? For example, suppose we wanted to allow a movement command character to be entered in either lowercase or uppercase. In this situation, we can use the fall-through behavior to write clearer code. For example, to handle lowercase or uppercase 'u', the **case** statements would be:

```
case 'u':
case 'U':
    sprite.moveUp();
    break;
```

The *Action* for the **case 'u'** is empty, and control flows into the **case 'U'** and its *Action* is executed. The following code fragment uses this fall-through technique to allow movement commands to be entered in either lowercase or uppercase. It follows the common practice of placing the cases for identical code on a single line.

```
switch (cmd) {
    case 'u': case 'U':
        sprite.moveUp();
        break;
```

```
            case 'd': case 'D':
                sprite.moveDown();
                break;
            case 'l': case 'L':
                sprite.moveLeft();
                break;
            case 'r': case 'R':
                sprite.moveRight();
                break;
            default:
                System.out.println("Unexpected request: " + cmd);
        }
```

Another use of a **switch** statement is demonstrated in program DaysIn-Month.java of Listing 5.5. The program prompts a user for a year and month and then reports the number of days in that month.

Method main() of DaysInMonth.java begins by defining constants that enable the program to use names rather than numeric literals for the 12 months in a year. Method main() also defines a constant CALENDAR_START with the value 1582, which was the year that the current international calendar system—the Gregorian calendar—was first adopted. The program also defines a Scanner variable stdin for extracting values from standard input.

After extracting the input values, the program first determines whether the input represents a valid request.

```
        if ((year < CALENDAR_START) || (month < 1) || (month > 12)) {
            System.out.println("Bad request: " + year + " "
                + month);
            System.exit(1);
        }
```

A request is valid if both the year and month are sensible. If they are not, the program first displays an error message to standard output and then terminates itself.

The program termination is accomplished through System class method exit(). Whenever method exit() is invoked, it terminates the program that invoked the method. The parameter to exit() is a termination status signal for the operating system. Because of the exit() statement, the statements that follow the **if** statement are executed only if the input request was valid.

The program next determines whether the year of interest is a leap year (i.e., a year in which February 29 occurs). In the Gregorian calendar system, years not evenly divisible by 4 are not leap years. All years evenly divisible by 4 are leap years except for years evenly divisible by 100 that are not also evenly divisible by 400. For example,

- 2000 is a leap year (evenly divisible by 4, 100 and 400);
- 2004 is a leap year (evenly divisible by 4 and not evenly divisible by 100);
- 2007 is not a leap year (not evenly divisible by 4);
- 2100 is not a leap year (evenly divisible by 4 and 100, not evenly divisible by 400).

The leap year rules are captured in the Venn diagram of Figure 5.6.

Thus, to determine whether the year is a leap year, the program determines the status of three conditions: is the year divisible by 4, is the year divisible by 100, and is the year

Listing 5.5   DaysInMonth.java

```java
1.  // Compute the number of days in a user-specified month
2.
3.  import java.util.*;
4.
5.  public class DaysInMonth {
6.      // main(): application entry point
7.      public static void main(String[] args) {
8.          final int JANUARY = 1;      final int JULY = 7;
9.          final int FEBRUARY = 2;     final int AUGUST = 8;
10.         final int MARCH = 3;        final int SEPTEMBER = 9;
11.         final int APRIL = 4;        final int OCTOBER = 10;
12.         final int MAY = 5;          final int NOVEMBER = 11;
13.         final int JUNE = 6;         final int DECEMBER = 12;
14.
15.         final int CALENDAR_START = 1582;
16.
17.         // get an input reader
18.         Scanner stdin = new Scanner(System.in);
19.
20.         // get date information of interest
21.         System.out.println("");
22.         System.out.print("Enter year: ");
23.         int year = stdin.nextInt();
24.         System.out.print("Enter month: ");
25.         int month = stdin.nextInt();
26.
27.         // validate input
28.         if ((year < CALENDAR_START) || (month < 1) || (month > 12)) {
29.             System.out.println("Bad request: " + year + " "
30.                 + month);
31.             System.exit(1);
32.         }
33.
34.         // determine whether year is a leap year
35.         boolean isDivisibleBy4 = (year % 4) == 0;
36.         boolean isDivisibleBy100 = (year % 100) == 0;
37.         boolean isDivisibleBy400 = (year % 400) == 0;
38.
39.         boolean isLeapYear = isDivisibleBy4
40.             && ((! isDivisibleBy100) || isDivisibleBy400);
41.
42.     // use month and year information to determine number of days
43.     int days;
44.     switch (month) {
45.         case JANUARY: case MARCH: case MAY: case JULY: case AUGUST:
46.         case OCTOBER: case DECEMBER:
47.             days = 31;
48.             break;
49.         case APRIL: case JUNE: case SEPTEMBER: case NOVEMBER:
50.             days = 30;
51.             break;
52.         case FEBRUARY:
53.             days = isLeapYear ? 29 : 28;
54.             break;
```

Listing 5.5   DaysInMonth.java (Continued)

```
55.        default:
56.            days = 0;
57.    }
58.
59.    System.out.println("");
60.    System.out.println("Month " + month + " in year " + year
61.                        + " has " + days + " days");
62.    }
63. }
```

Figure 5.6   **Diagram capturing leap year specification.**

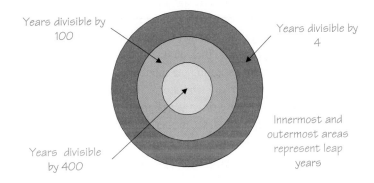

divisible by 400. To determine these conditions, the Java modulus operator % is used to check whether the factors of interest divide the value of variable year evenly.

```
boolean isDivisibleBy4 = (year % 4) == 0;
boolean isDivisibleBy100 = (year % 100) == 0;
boolean isDivisibleBy400 = (year % 400) == 0;
```

For example, the term (year % 4) produces the remainder of year when divided by 4. Therefore, the expression (year % 4) == 0 evaluates to **true** when year is a multiple of 4, and **false** otherwise.

The three conditions are used in the initialization of **boolean** variable isLeapYear that indicates whether the year is a leap year.

```
boolean isLeapYear = isDivisibleBy4
    && ((! isDivisibleBy100) || isDivisibleBy400);
```

The number of days in the input month can then be calculated by determining to which group the input month belongs: months with 31 days, months with 30 days, or February. Although an **if-else-if** construct would work, a **switch** statement yields a more readable code segment.

```
// use month and year information to determine number of days
int days;
switch (month) {
    case JANUARY: case MARCH: case MAY: case JULY: case AUGUST:
    case OCTOBER: case DECEMBER:
```

```
            days = 31;
            break;
        case APRIL: case JUNE: case SEPTEMBER: case NOVEMBER:
            days = 30;
            break;
        case FEBRUARY:
            days = isLeapYear ? 29 : 28;
            break;
        default:
            days = 0;
    }
```

The cases in the **switch** statement use the previously defined constants for representing the months. The named constants contribute to program readability. If the input month is a valid month, the **switch** statement correctly assigns variable days. An invalid month is processed by the **default** case of the **switch** statement, causing variable days to be set to 0. Although this **default** case is not necessary because of the earlier validation of the date, it is prudent to include it.

The action for assigning the number of days in the month of February uses the previously mentioned ternary operator ?. If isLeapYear evaluates to **true**, then days is assigned 29; otherwise days is assigned 28.

With variable days set properly, the program completes its task by displaying the result of its calculation.

```
System.out.println("");
System.out.println("Month " + month + " in year " + year
                + " has " + days + " days");
```

This discussion completes the analysis of DaysInMonth.java. We next turn our attention to two case studies that make use of conditional statements in their implementations. The first application is concerned with recognizing a valid code number; the second application is concerned with developing a representation for triangles.

Using the switch statement effectively

Appropriate use of the **switch** statement makes programs easier to understand and can result in more efficient programs. Here are some guidelines for effective use of the **switch** statement.

- Keep the *Action* code short. This helps make the structure of the **switch** statement clear. A lengthy piece of *Action* code obscures the structure of the code.
- Always provide a **default** case. Failing to provide a **default** case can lead to undetected errors.
- Avoid fall-through cases. They make the code harder to understand and more difficult to maintain. The only time a fall-through case is appropriate is when the cases have identical *Action* statements.
- Order the cases in some meaningful way. Depending on the situation, it may make sense to order the cases alphabetically or according to frequency of occurrence (i.e., put the case that occurs most often at the beginning).

5.9	# CASE STUDY — CHECKSUM VALIDATION

A common requirement for software applications supporting inventory management is to validate the items being manipulated. For example, suppose the manager of a store wants to add a new item to the store's inventory database. To do so, the manager would need to insert a new entry into the database that gives the name and price of the item along with its code number. Correctly entering all three pieces of information is very important; e.g., a wrong price could affect greatly the store's profitability, and an improperly entered code would make it impossible for price scanners to recognize the item.

> The objective of this case study is to practice using the **if-else** statement when problem solving

One way to increase the likelihood of correct data entry is to ask users to verify that the values were entered correctly. With regard to name and price there is not much more that can be done except to follow the standard practice of echoing input values. However, various *checksum* schemes have been created for code numbers so that software can verify whether a number is legal. Checksum software tests whether the digits of a potential code number have some particular property.

For example, there is a verification scheme for the Universal Product Code$^©$ numbers that most manufactured items now have. Figure 5.7 shows a sample UPC number in a form that is scannable by a bar code reader.

Figure 5.7   **A Universal Product Code number in bar code form.**

A valid Universal Product Code (UPC) number is a 12-digit value that meets the following criteria:

- Let m be the sum of the 2nd, 4th, 6th, 8th, and 10th digits. (The numbering of the digits is from left to right.)
- Let n be the sum of the 1st, 3rd, 5th, 7th, 9th, and 11th digits.
- Let $r = 10 - ((m + 3 \cdot n) \bmod 10)$.
- A number meets the UPC encoding criteria if its 12th digit equals r.

Consider 780070121354. For this number,

$$m = 8 + 0 + 0 + 2 + 3 = 13$$
$$n = 7 + 0 + 7 + 1 + 1 + 5 = 21$$
$$r = 10 - ((13 + 3 \cdot 21) \bmod 10) = 10 - (76 \bmod 10) = 10 - 6 = 4$$

Because r equals 4, the number corresponds to a possible UPC code. Now consider the number 123456789011. For this number,

$$m = 2 + 4 + 6 + 8 + 0 = 20$$

$$n = 1 + 3 + 5 + 7 + 9 + 1 = 26$$
$$r = 10 - ((20 + 3 \cdot 26) \bmod 10) = 10 - (98 \bmod 10) = 10 - 8 = 2$$

Because r does not equal 1, the number is not a valid UPC code.

ANALYSIS AND DESIGN

The values to be manipulated by an algorithm for computing a UPC are obvious. Three essential values are m, n, and r. In addition, the input string s is needed and its numeric representation *number*. With *number*, the 12 component digits *d1, d2, …, d12* can be determined for initializing m, n, and r.

We use the UPC encoding criteria and the preceding values in the following algorithm for checking whether a number is a possible UPC code.

```
Prompt user to supply a twelve-digit number.
Extract the input and assign it to s.
Convert s into a numeric representation number.
If number is negative or has more than twelve digits
    Report number is not a UPC code
Else
    Assign the least significant (twelfth) digit of number to
        d12.
    Assign the eleventh digit of number to d11.
    Assign the tenth digit of number to d10.
    Assign the ninth digit of number to d9.
    Assign the eighth digit of number to d8.
    Assign the seventh digit of number to d7.
    Assign the sixth digit of number to d6.
    Assign the fifth digit of number to d5.
    Assign the fourth digit of number to d4.
    Assign the third digit of number to d3.
    Assign the second digit of number to d2.
    Assign the first digit of number to d1.
    Assign m the value of d2 + d4 + d6 + d8 + d10.
    Assign n the value of d1 + d3 + d5 + d7 + d9 + d11.
    Assign r the value of 10 - ((m + 3·n) mod 10).
    If r equals d12 then
        Report number is a feasible UPC code
    Else
        Report number is not a UPC code
```

IMPLEMENTATION

The key insights into translating this algorithm into a valid Java program are knowing how to represent the input, how to organize the program to test for necessary properties, and how to extract the digits from the input number.

Our implementation of the algorithm is UPC.java of Listing 5.6. The program extracts the input number into **long** variable input. It does so because feasible UPC codes are too large to be represented using an **int**—the maximum **int** value is only ten digits long. For the same reason, constant MAX_POSSIBLE_UPC_CODE is defined to be a **long** value.

```
final long MAX_POSSIBLE_UPC_CODE = 999999999999L;
```

In its definition, the "L" in 999999999999L indicates that the numerical literal is a **long** value.

Listing 5.6   UPC.java

```
1.   // Checks whether a user-specified value meets the UPC criteria
2.
3.   import java.util.*;
4.
5.   public class UPC {
6.       // main(): application entry point
7.       public static void main(String[] args) {
8.           final long MAX_POSSIBLE_UPC_CODE = 999999999999L;
9.
10.          // set input stream and get number
11.          Scanner stdin = new Scanner(System.in);
12.
13.          System.out.print("Enter a 12-digit whole number: ");
14.          long input = stdin.nextLong();
15.          long number = input;
16.
17.          // determine whether number is a possible upc code
18.          if ((input < 0) || (input > MAX_POSSIBLE_UPC_CODE)) {
19.              // not a upc code
20.              System.out.println(input + " is an invalid UPC code");
21.          }
22.          else {
23.              // might be a upc code
24.
25.              // determine individual digits
26.              int d12 = (int) (number % 10);
27.              number /= 10;
28.              int d11 = (int) (number % 10);
29.              number /= 10;
30.              int d10 = (int) (number % 10);
31.              number /= 10;
32.              int d9 = (int) (number % 10);
33.              number /= 10;
34.              int d8 = (int) (number % 10);
35.              number /= 10;
36.              int d7 = (int) (number % 10);
37.              number /= 10;
38.              int d6 = (int) (number % 10);
39.              number /= 10;
40.              int d5 = (int) (number % 10);
41.              number /= 10;
42.              int d4 = (int) (number % 10);
43.              number /= 10;
44.              int d3 = (int) (number % 10);
45.              number /= 10;
46.              int d2 = (int) (number % 10);
47.              number /= 10;
48.              int d1 = (int) (number % 10);
49.              number /= 10;
50.
51.              // compute sums of first 5 even digits and the odd digits
52.              int m = d2 + d4 + d6 + d8 + d10;
53.              int n = d1 + d3 + d5 + d7 + d9 + d11;
54.
```

Listing 5.6   **UPC.java (Continued)**

```
55.          // use UPC formula to determine required value for d12
56.          int r = 10 - ((m + 3*n) % 10);
57.
58.          // based on r, can test whether number is a UPC code
59.          if (r == d12) {
60.             // is a upc code
61.             System.out.println(input + " is a feasible UPC code");
62.          }
63.          else {
64.             // not a upc code
65.             System.out.println(input + " is an invalid UPC code");
66.          }
67.       }
68.    }
69. }
```

In doing its manipulations, the program uses a **long** variable number, which is initially a copy of input. The copy is manipulated so that the input value is available after the UPC validation has been performed.

An examination of UPC.java shows that its organization mirrors the organization of the previously supplied algorithm.

```
// set input stream and get number ...

// determine whether number is a possible upc code
if ((number < 0) || (number > MAX_POSSIBLE_UPC_CODE)) {
   // not a upc code ...
}
else {
   // might be a upc code

   // determine individual digits ...

   // compute sums of first 5 even digits and the odd digits ...

   // use UPC formula to determine required value r for d12 ...

   if (r == d12) {
      // is a upc code ...
   }
   else {
      // not a upc code ...
   }
}
```

Once the program extracts the input, it tests whether the number lies outside the legal range for UPC codes. If it does, then the program reports that the number is not a UPC code. Otherwise, the individual digits of the number are determined. A test is then made to see whether the digits form a valid UPC code.

Determining the least significant digit d12 is simple with the Java modulus operator %. The expression `number % 10` evaluates to remainder of `number` divided by 10, which is the value of the least significant digit of `number`.

```
int d12 = (int) (number % 10);
```

The **int** cast is necessary because the expression `number % 10` is a **long** expression.

By updating `number` by dividing it by 10,

```
number /= 10;
```

the next least significant digit can be determined by taking the new value of `number` modulus 10.

```
int d11 = (int) (number % 10);
```

This process can be repeated to determine the other digits of the number.[†]

Once the individual digits have been determined, the variables m, n, and r from the UPC formula can be defined.

```
int m = d2 + d4 + d6 + d8 + d10;
int n = d1 + d3 + d5 + d7 + d9 + d11;
int r = 10 - ((m + 3*n) % 10);
```

Finally, a test comparing the values of r and d12 determines whether the number is a feasible UPC code.

```
if (r == d12) {
    System.out.println(input + " is a feasible UPC code");
}
else {
    System.out.println(input + " is an invalid UPC code");
}
```

We now turn our attention to the development of a representation for triangles.

5.10   CASE STUDY — TRIANGLES

The triangle is an important shape in the world of computer graphics. In particular, when computer animations are created, scenes are decomposed typically into a collection of triangles. Figure 5.8 shows such a decomposition.

> The objective of this case study is to practice using the conditional statements in the context of the design and implementation of a class

Let's suppose that we have been assigned the task of developing and implementing a representation `ColoredTriangle` for a triangle. Clearly, we need to represent the three endpoints that denote the position of the triangle and we also need to know its color. So what constructors and behaviors should be present and what information, if any, must be maintained to implement the behaviors?

---

†   Chapter 6 considers iteration. By using an iteration construct lines 26–53 can be simplified substantially.

Figure 5.8 Preliminary triangular decomposition and rendering.

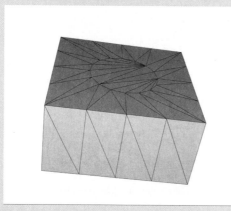

ANALYSIS AND DESIGN

With our experiences from designing and implementing class `ColoredRectangle` of Chapter 4 and using standard classes, we recognize the importance of at least two `ColoredTriangle` constructors—a default constructor and a constructor that enables a specific triangle to be constructed.

- *Default construction*: construct a reasonable triangle representation even though no explicit attribute values are given.

- *Specific construction*: construct a triangle representation from explicitly given attribute values.

We also recognize the importance of accessors and mutators.

- *Accessors*: provide the color or a requested endpoint of the associated triangle.

- *Mutators*: set the color or a specified endpoint of the associated triangle to a given value.

For drawing purposes, we recognize the importance of the following behavior.

- *Render*: draw the associated triangle in a given graphical context.

In designing the rendering behavior, we have a decision to make. Should there be a `ColoredTriangle` attribute that represents the graphical target for the drawing (e.g., a `JFrame` as there was for `ColoredRectangle` of Chapter 4)? Or should the graphical target be specified as a parameter to the rendering method?

If our intention was to add `ColoredTriangle` to a library already containing `ColoredRectangle`, then consistency with `ColoredRectangle` would dictate the form of `ColoredRectangle`.

However, our initial design of `ColoredRectangle` stressed simplicity over functionality—it did not recognize the tension between these two properties. Our `ColoredTriangle` design takes a more balanced view and gives a `ColoredTriangle` object the ability to render itself in different graphical targets (e.g., different windows). This decision is similar to the rendering philosophy of the standard Java graphical packages `awt` and `swing`.

IMPLEMENTATION

To implement our triangle representation, we use an instance variable of type `java.awt.Color` to represent the color of a triangle.

> **private** Color color
>
> > Color of the associated triangle.

To represent the three triangle endpoints we have a choice. We could use six **int** data fields x1, y1, x2, y2, x3, and y3, or we could make three uses of the awt class Point, which provides a representation of a location in integer coordinate space. For our implementation, we chose to use class Point. We did so because Point directly captures the notion of location.

> **private** Point p1
>
> > References the first point of the associated triangle.
>
> **private** Point p2
>
> > References the second point of the associated triangle.
>
> **private** Point p3
>
> > References the third point of the associated triangle.

The following constructors and methods are used to implement the behaviors discussed in the analysis section. (Implementations of some other possible methods are considered in the self-test questions and exercises.)

> **public** ColoredTriangle()
>
> > Constructs a default triangle representation. The default representation is a black triangle with points at coordinates (1, 1), (2, 2), and (3, 3).
>
> **public** ColoredTriangle(Point v1, Point v2, Point v3, Color c)
>
> > Constructs a triangle using color c whose endpoints are equivalent to the points referenced by p1, p2, and p3.
>
> **public** Point getPoint(**int** i)
>
> > Returns the ith point of the associated triangle.
>
> **public void** setPoint(**int** i, Point v)
>
> > Sets the ith point of the associated triangle so that its value is equivalent to the point referenced by v.
>
> **public** Color getColor()
>
> > Returns the color of the associated triangle.
>
> **public void** setColor(Color c)
>
> > Sets the color of the associated triangle to c.
>
> **public void** paint(Graphics g)
>
> > Renders the triangle in graphic context g.

An implementation of the data fields and methods of ColoredTriangle.java is given in Listing 5.7. Because most of the methods have straightforward definitions, we limit our discussion to only some of them.

Listing 5.7   **ColoredTriangle.java**

```
1.  // Representation of a triangle in colored coordinate space
2.
3.  import java.awt.*;
4.
5.  public class ColoredTriangle {
6.      // instance variables
7.      private Point p1;      // first endpoint
8.      private Point p2;      // second endpoint
9.      private Point p3;      // third endpoint
10.     private Color color;  // triangle color
11.
12.     // ColoredTriangle(): default constructor
13.     public ColoredTriangle() {
14.         Point a = new Point(1, 1);
15.         Point b = new Point(2, 2);
16.         Point c = new Point(3, 3);
17.         setPoint(1, a);
18.         setPoint(2, b);
19.         setPoint(3, c);
20.         setColor(Color.BLACK);
21.     }
22.
23.     // ColoredTriangle(): specific constructor
24.     public ColoredTriangle(Point a, Point b, Point c, Color d) {
25.         setPoint(1, a);
26.         setPoint(2, b);
27.         setPoint(3, c);
28.         setColor(d);
29.     }
30.
31.     // getPoint(): endpoint accessor
32.     public Point getPoint(int i) {
33.         switch (i) {
34.             case 1: return p1;
35.             case 2: return p2;
36.             case 3: return p3;
37.             default:
38.                 System.out.println("Unexpected endpoint access: " + i);
39.                 System.exit(i);
40.                 return null;
41.         }
42.     }
43.
44.     // setPoint(): endpoint mutator
45.     public void setPoint(int i, Point v) {
46.         switch (i) {
47.             case 1: p1 = new Point(v.x, v.y); return;
48.             case 2: p2 = new Point(v.x, v.y); return;
49.             case 3: p3 = new Point(v.x, v.y); return;
50.             default:
51.                 System.out.println("Unexpected endpoint access: " + i);
52.                 System.exit(i);
53.         }
54.     }
```

Listing 5.7   **ColoredTriangle.java (Continued)**

```
55.
56.    // getColor(): color accessor
57.    public Color getColor() {
58.       return color;
59.    }
60.
61.    // setColor(): color mutator
62.    public void setColor(Color c) {
63.       color = c;
64.    }
65.
66.    // paint(): render facilitator
67.    public void paint(Graphics g) {
68.       Point v1 = getPoint(1);
69.       Point v2 = getPoint(2);
70.       Point v3 = getPoint(3);
71.       Color c = getColor();
72.
73.       g.setColor(c);
74.
75.       Polygon t = new Polygon();
76.       t.addPoint(v1.x, v1.y);
77.       t.addPoint(v2.x, v2.y);
78.       t.addPoint(v3.x, v3.y);
79.
80.       g.fillPolygon(t);
81.    }
82. }
```

The purpose of the `ColoredTriangle` default constructor is to configure a new `ColoredTriangle` object to represent a black triangle with endpoints at coordinates (1, 1), (2, 2), and (3, 3).

```
// ColoredTriangle(): default constructor
public ColoredTriangle() {
    Point a = new Point(1, 1);    ⎫
    Point b = new Point(2, 2);    ⎬  Create endpoint values
    Point c = new Point(3, 3);    ⎭
    setPoint(1, a);               ⎫
    setPoint(2, b);               ⎬  Copy desired endpoint values to data fields
    setPoint(3, c);               ⎭
    setColor(Color.BLACK);        ⎬ Copy desired color to data fields
}
```

To configure the object, the `ColoredTriangle` constructor first makes use of a `Point` constructor to initialize three `Point` variables a, b, and c so that they reference the desired endpoint values. The `ColoredTriangle` constructor then uses those values to set the endpoints of the new triangle. The endpoints of the new triangle are set using mutator `setPoint()`. The constructor uses the mutator rather than direct assignment to the instance variables. It does so for purposes of encapsulation and information hiding. The resulting code is more readable, less likely to introduce errors in representation, and simpler to manipulate when introducing enhancements.

The endpoint accessor and mutator methods `getPoint()` and `setPoint()` are quite similar in structure. We begin their analysis with method `getPoint()`.

```java
// getPoint(): endpoint accessor
public Point getPoint(int i) {
   switch (i) {
      case 1: return p1;
      case 2: return p2;
      case 3: return p3;
      default:
         System.out.println("Unexpected endpoint access: " + i);
         System.exit(i);
         return null;
   }
}
```

Method `getPoint()` uses case analysis to determine which endpoint is desired. The case analysis uses the **switch** construct. If i has the value of 1, 2, or 3, then the appropriate endpoint is returned. Otherwise, some error handling code is executed.

The error handling code for method `getPoint()` first displays an error message to tell the user what has occurred and then invokes method `System.exit()` to terminate the program. Thus, the **return** statement that follows the `exit()` invocation is never executed. However, most Java compilers (e.g., `javac`) will not successfully compile the class without the **return** statement. The reason most compilers require a **return** statement is because every execution path in this method is supposed to produce a return value of type `Point`. The compilers do not recognize what happens in method `exit()` to make this particular **return** statement unnecessary—to most compilers, the `exit()` invocation is just viewed as another Java statement.

Method `setPoint()` uses similar case analysis to determine which instance variable should be updated based on the value of its parameter v.

```java
// setPoint(): endpoint mutator
public void setPoint(int i, Point v) {
   switch (i) {
      case 1: p1 = new Point(v.x, v.y); return;
      case 2: p2 = new Point(v.x, v.y); return;
      case 3: p3 = new Point(v.x, v.y); return;
      default:
         System.out.println("Unexpected endpoint access: " + i);
         System.exit(i);
   }
}
```

When updating an instance variable, the mutator does not directly assign the value of parameter v. Instead, it assigns the instance variable a reference to a new `Point` object. The new `Point` is a duplicate of the object referenced by v. For example, the following assignment shows the update for instance variable p1.

```java
p1 = new Point(v.x, v.y);
```

The duplicate is assigned so that the `ColoredTriangle` can maintain its representation, regardless of whether the `Point` referenced by v is updated subsequently. Because class

Point allows **public** access to its data fields, accessors are not needed for getting the x- and y-coordinates associated with a Point object.[†]

The last method that we consider is method paint(). This method renders a triangle to the graphics context indicated by its parameter g.

```java
// paint(): render facilitator
public void paint(Graphics g) {
    Point v1 = getPoint(1);
    Point v2 = getPoint(2);
    Point v3 = getPoint(3);
    Color c = getColor();

    g.setColor(c);

    Polygon t = new Polygon();
    t.addPoint(v1.x, v1.y);
    t.addPoint(v2.x, v2.y);
    t.addPoint(v3.x, v3.y);

    g.fillPolygon(t);
}
```

The simplest way to render a triangle is to use Graphics method fillPolygon(). Method fillPolygon() takes a single parameter of type Polygon. Class Polygon is part of the awt package. Its default constructor creates a representation of an empty polygon. A polygon representing our triangle can then be constructed by using Polygon method addPoint(). Method addPoint() takes two **int** parameters specifying the x- and y-coordinates of a new polygon endpoint. Therefore, the following code suffices for adding the three points to the new Polygon,

```java
t.addPoint(v1.x, v1.y);
t.addPoint(v2.x, v2.y);
t.addPoint(v3.x, v3.y);
```

We demonstrate a use of the method in program TriangularCat.java of Listing 5.8. The program creates and draws a collection of triangles to render a picture that vaguely resembles a cat. A depiction of the cat drawing is given in Figure 5.9. When you finish appreciating this postmodern cat drawing, our introduction to the conditional statements of Java is complete.

[†]   Chapter 7 considers the clone() method that returns a duplicate of an object.

Listing 5.8   **TriangularCat.java**

```
1.  // Draw a cat
2.
3.  import java.awt.*;
4.  import javax.swing.*;
5.  import java.util.*;
6.
7.  public class TriangularCat {
8.     public static void main(String[] args) {
9.        ColoredTriangle body = new ColoredTriangle(
10.          new Point(20, 110), new Point(190, 150),
11.          new Point(190, 65), Color.BLACK);
12.
13.       ColoredTriangle head = new ColoredTriangle(
14.          new Point(190, 90), new Point(270, 90),
15.          new Point(230, 30), Color.YELLOW);
16.
17.       ColoredTriangle leftEye = new ColoredTriangle(
18.          new Point(220, 50), new Point(215, 60),
19.          new Point(225, 60), Color.BLUE);
20.
21.       ColoredTriangle rightEye = new ColoredTriangle(
22.          new Point(240, 50), new Point(235, 60),
23.          new Point(245, 60), Color.BLUE);
24.
25.       ColoredTriangle mouth = new ColoredTriangle(
26.          new Point(215, 75), new Point(245, 80),
27.          new Point(245, 70), Color.BLUE);
28.
29.       ColoredTriangle backLegs = new ColoredTriangle(
30.          new Point(20, 110), new Point(25, 160),
31.          new Point(15, 160), Color.GRAY);
32.
33.       ColoredTriangle frontLegs = new ColoredTriangle(
34.          new Point(190, 150), new Point(195, 200),
35.          new Point(185, 200), Color.GRAY);
36.
37.       JFrame window = new JFrame("Triangular cat");
38.       window.setSize(285, 250);
39.       window.setVisible(true);
40.       Graphics g = window.getGraphics();
41.
42.       System.out.print("Enter any key when ready");
43.       Scanner stdin = new Scanner(System.in);
44.       stdin.nextLine();
45.
46.       body.paint(g);
47.       head.paint(g);
48.       mouth.paint(g);
49.       leftEye.paint(g);
50.       rightEye.paint(g);
51.       backLegs.paint(g);
52.       frontLegs.paint(g);
53.    }
54. }
```

Figure 5.9   Triangular cat.

5.11 REVIEW

- A logical expression is an expression whose value is either the logical value true or the logical value false.
- There are three primary logical operators that we use to combine logic values into logical expressions. These logical operators are *and*, *or*, and *not*.
- A truth table is an easy way of indicating the conditions that make a logical operation true and which conditions make it false. A truth table lists all possible combinations of operand values and the result of the operation for each combination.
- The logical *and* operation is true only if both of its operands are true; otherwise, the operation is false.
- The logical *or* operation is true if at least one of its operands is true; otherwise, the operation is false.
- The logical *not* operation is true if its operand is false, and the operation is false if its operand is true.
- The Java logical type **boolean** has two symbolic literal constants **true** and **false** that correspond to logical true and false, respectively. Although technically not keywords, **true** and **false** are reserved identifier literals.
- There are three **boolean** logical operators: &&, ||, and !. Operator && is used to perform an *and* operation, operator || is used to perform an *or* operation, and operator ! is used to perform a *not* operation.
- There are two equality operators == and !=. The == operator evaluates to **true** if both operand expressions have the same value, and it evaluates to **false** otherwise. Operator != evaluates to **true** if the two operand expressions have different values, and it evaluates to **false** otherwise.
- Java provides ordering operators for the primitive types. They are used to determine the relative sizes of two values. There are four ordering operators, <, >, <=, and >=. They correspond to the mathematical operators of $<$, $>$, $\leq$ and $\geq$. Together the equality and ordering operators are known as the relational operators.
- The not operator ! has the same high precedence as other unary operators. Among the binary operators, the relational and logical operators have lower precedence than the arithmetic operators and greater precedence than the assignment operators. Relational operators have greater precedence than the logical operators. Among the relational operators, the ordering operators have greater precedence than the equality operators. Among the logical operators, && has greater precedence than ||.
- When evaluating a logical operation, Java always evaluates the left operand before it evaluates the right operand. If the value of the operation can be determined from the left operand, then the right operand is not evaluated. This kind of evaluation is known as short-circuit evaluation.
- For **boolean** comparison purposes, the value of the constant **false** is less than the value of the constant **true**.
- For character comparison purposes, orderings are based on Unicode character representation.

- Programs generally should not test floating-point values for equality. Instead programs should test whether the values of interest are sufficiently close to each other to be considered the same. The underlying reason for this behavior is the finite precision of the floating-point types.

- The **if** statement has two forms. The simpler of the two forms has syntax

  if (*TestExpression*) *Action*

  When an **if** statement is reached within a program, the parenthetic expression *TestExpression* is evaluated. If *TestExpression* evaluates to **true**, *Action* is executed; otherwise, *Action* is not executed. Either way, program execution continues with the next statement in the program.

- The second form of the **if** statement deals with programming situations where one of two different actions is to be taken based on the value of a logical expression. This form of the **if** statement has syntax

  if (*TestExpression*) *Action$_1$* **else** *Action$_2$*

  where *Action$_1$* and *Action$_2$* can each be either a single statement with a terminating semicolon (;) or a block of statements nested with left and right braces. When the **if-else** statement is executed, *TestExpression* is evaluated. If *TestExpression* evaluates to **true**, *Action$_1$* is executed; otherwise, *Action$_2$* is executed.

- A consistent indentation scheme makes the logic of a program more understandable to a reader, but it does not affect the translation of the program. Language syntax and semantics rules determine precisely how a program is to be translated.

- The == operator when applied to reference variables tests whether the variables refer to the same memory location.

- To test whether two objects have the same representation, use member method **equals()**.

- The **if-else-if** idiom is used to solve tasks requiring one of several actions to be executed depending on which **boolean** condition evaluates to **true**.

- **System** class method **exit()** terminates the program that invoked the method. The parameter to **exit()** serves as a termination status signal for the operating system.

- When a **switch** statement is executed, its *SwitchExpression* is evaluated; if the value of that expression equals the value of a *CaseExpression* in that **switch** statement, then flow of control is transferred to the *Action$_i$* associated with the matching *CaseExpression$_i$*. If no *CaseExpression* equals the value of the *SwitchExpression* and if a **default** case is supplied, then the **default** *Action$_{n+1}$* code is executed. The last statement in an *Action* is normally a **break** statement. The **break** statement indicates that the **switch** statement has completed its task and that the flow of control should continue with the statement after the **switch** statement. If a **break** statement is not supplied, then the flow of control continues with the next statement within the **switch** statement itself.

| 5.12 | **SELF-TEST** |

S5.1 Produce a truth table for the logical operator *nand*. Operator *nand* is true if at least one of its operands is false.

S5.2 Consider the following code segment:

```
if (i == j) {
    System.out.println("A");
}
else if ((i % j) < 3) {
    System.out.println("B");
}
else if (i < (j - 1)) {
    System.out.println("C");
}
else {
    System.out.println("D");
}
```

a) If i is 9 and j is 4, what is the output?

b) If i is 4 and j is 9, what is the output?

c) If i is 5 and j is 6, what is the output?

d) If i is 5 and j is 9, what is the output?

S5.3 What is the output of the following code segment?

```
int i = 5;
int j = 7;
int k = 6;
if ((i < j) || (k < 5)) {
    System.out.println("yes");
}
else {
    System.out.println("no");
}
if ((i < j) && (k < 5)) {
    System.out.println("yes");
}
else {
    System.out.println("no");
}
```

S5.4 Consider the following code fragment whose output is based on the values of **boolean** variables a, b, c, and d.

```
if (a && b) {
    if (!c && !d) {
        System.out.println(1);
    }
    else if (!d) {
        System.out.println(2);
    }
    else {
        System.out.println(3);
    }
```

```
    }
    else if (c == d) {
        System.out.println(4);
    }
    else if (c) {
        System.out.println(5);
    }
    else {
        System.out.println(6);
    }
```

a) Give values for a, b, c, and d that cause the code fragment to display 1 to the standard output stream.

b) Give values for a, b, c, and d that cause the code fragment to display 2 to the standard output stream.

c) Give values for a, b, c, and d that cause the code fragment to display 3 to the standard output stream.

d) Give values for a, b, c, and d that cause the code fragment to display 4 to the standard output stream.

e) Give values for a, b, c, and d that cause the code fragment to display 5 to the standard output stream.

f) Give values for a, b, c, and d that cause the code fragment to display 6 to the standard output stream.

S5.5 Write a code segment that sets integer k to 3 if the integer m is less than 5 and j is less than 0; otherwise, k should be changed to 1 if m is not less than k.

S5.6 Convert the following code into a **switch** statement, where i, k, and n are **int** variables.

```
    if (i == 3) {
        n = 1;
        k = 5;
    }
    else if (i == 4) {
        n = 5;
    }
    else if (i == 6) {
        n = 6;
    }
    else {
        n = 0;
    }
```

S5.7 Implement a code segment that determines the relationship between the intervals b1 ... e1 and b2 ... e2 (i.e., are the intervals the same, do they overlap, does one interval precede the other).

S5.8 Implement a member method getPerimeter() for ColoredRectangle. The method returns the perimeter of the triangle. In your implementation you may find it convenient to use Point method distance(). For Point variables p and q, p.distance(q) returns the Euclidean distance between the Point objects referenced by p and q.

| 5.13 | **EXERCISES** |

5.1   Suppose the following definitions are in effect.

```
boolean p = true;
boolean q = false;
boolean r = false;
String s = "b";
String t = "b";
String u = t;
int i = 10;
int j = 0;
```

Evaluate the following expressions.

a) `!p == q`

b) `s != t`

c) `t != u`

d) `s == u`

e) `t == u`

f) `s.equals(u)`

g) `t.equals(u)`

h) `r == (p && q)`

i) `q && (p || r)`

j) `q || (p && !r)`

k) `p && !q && !r || (p == !q)`

l) `i * j`

5.2   Suppose the following definitions are in effect.

```
boolean p = false;
boolean q = true;
boolean r = true;
int i = 1;
int j = 0;
```

Evaluate the following expressions:

a) `p && q || !p && !q`

b) `p || q && !p || !q`

c) `0 == 1 == true`

d) `p && (q || r)`

e) `! ! p`

f) `false < true`

5.3   Using the operator precedence rules, parenthesize the following expressions.

a) `1 + 2 == 3 * 4`

b) `1 + 2 == 3 * 4 && 5 / 6 == 7`

c) `p == q <= r`

d) `p < q == r`

e) p == q || r

f) p == q && r

g) p || q && r || s

In Exercises 5.4–5.11, i, j, k, m, and n are **int** variables.

5.4 Define an expression that evaluates to **true** when i equals j.

5.5 Define an expression that evaluates to **true** when i lies in the interval 6 ... 9.

5.6 Define an expression that evaluates to **true** only when i is even and j is odd, or when i is odd and j is even.

5.7 Define an expression that evaluates to **true** only if the following conditions are all met: i is greater than 11, j is at most 28, and m and n have different values.

5.8 Define an expression that evaluates to **true** only if none of the following conditions are met: i plus j equals 30, i is less than 4, and i times j is greater than 54.

5.9 Define an expression that evaluates to **true** if any of the following conditions are met: i is twice the value of j, j is smaller than k but larger than n, or m is negative.

5.10 Write code segments that implement the following actions:

a) If i divided by j is 4, then i is set to 100.

b) If i times j is 8, then i is set to 50; otherwise, j is set to 60.

c) If i is less than j, then j is doubled; if instead i is even, then i is doubled; otherwise, both i and j are incremented by 1.

d) If both i and j are 0, then i is set to 1 and j is set to 2; if instead only i is 0, then i is set to 5 and j is set to 10; if instead only j is 0, then i is set to 10 and j is set to 5; otherwise, both i and j are set to 4.

5.11 Consider the following **if** statement:

```
if ((i == 3) || (j == 4)) {
    System.out.println("yes");
}
else {
    System.out.println("no");
}
```

Are there values for i and j that cause the display of both "yes" and "no"? Why?

5.12 Assume the following definitions are in effect:

```
boolean p = false;
boolean q = true;
boolean r = true;
```

Consider the following expressions. Determine whether they have short-circuit evaluations and, if so, where.

a) q && p && r

b) q && p || r

c) !q || (4 != 3)

d) (p || q && r) && (3 <= 4)

e) r || (p || !q || !r && (4 > 3))

5.13 Consider the following code segment using **boolean** objects a, b, c, and d.

```
if (!c || d) {
    if (a && c) {
        System.out.println(1);
    }
    else if (b) {
        System.out.println(2);
    }
    else {
        System.out.println(3);
    }
}
else if (!c == d) {
    System.out.println(4);
}
else if (c) {
}
    System.out.println(5);
else {
    System.out.println(6);
}
```

a) Give values for a, b, c, and d that cause the code segment to display 1 to the standard output stream.

b) Give values for a, b, c, and d that cause the code segment to display 2 to the standard output stream.

c) Give values for a, b, c, and d that cause the code segment to display 3 to the standard output stream.

d) Give values for a, b, c, and d that cause the code segment to display 4 to the standard output stream.

e) Give values for a, b, c, and d that cause the code segment to display 5 to the standard output stream.

f) Give values for a, b, c, and d that cause the code segment to display 6 to the standard output stream.

5.14 Write the truth table that the following code segment computes.

```
if (p) {
    operation = true;
}
else if (q) {
    operation = false;
}
else {
    operation = true;
}
```

5.15 Write the truth table that the following code segment computes.

```
if (p) {
    if (q) {
        operation = true;
    }
    else {
        operation = false;
```

```
      }
   }
   else {
      operation = false;
   }
```

5.16 Write the truth table for the logical binary operation of isomorphism (*iso*). The operation evaluates to true if the operands evaluate to the same value; otherwise, *iso* evaluates to false. Is there a Java operator that computes *iso*? Explain.

5.17 Write the truth table for the logical binary operation of exclusive-or (*xor*). The operation evaluates to true if exactly one of its operands evaluates to true; otherwise, *xor* evaluates to false. Write a code segment that tests whether p *xor* q evaluates to **true**, where p and q are **boolean** variables.

5.18 Prove using truth tables the DeMorgan equivalence *not (p and q)* equals *(not p) or (not q)*

5.19 Provide the truth table for the following logical expressions:

a) *(not p) and q*

b) *p and ((not p) or q)*

5.20 If i is 4, what is the output of the following code segment?

```
switch (i) {
   case 1: case 2: case 3:
      System.out.println("yes");
      break;
   case 5: case 6:
      System.out.println("no");
      break;
   case 10: case 11:
      System.out.println("maybe");
      break;
   default:
      System.out.println("sometimes");
}
```

5.21 If i is 7, what is the output of the following code segment?

```
switch (i) {
   case 1: case 2: case 3:
      System.out.println("yes");
   case 5: case 6:
      System.out.println("no");
   case 10: case 11:
      System.out.println("maybe");
      break;
   default:
      System.out.println("sometimes");
}
```

5.22 Develop a **boolean** expression that evaluates to **true** when a year is a leap year that does not use the unary operator !.

5.23 Search the Web to find the formula for validating a potential ISBN number, where an ISBN number is a book product code. Develop a program that reports when a user-specified value is a potential ISBN number.

5.24 Design and implement a program that extracts a user-specified line slope and intercept. The program should report whether the line is vertical.

5.25 Design and implement a program that extracts two user-specified line slopes and intercepts. The program should report whether the lines are perpendicular to each other.

5.26 Design and implement a program that extracts two user-specified x- and y-coordinates. The program should report the slope and y-intercept of the associated lines.

5.27 Design and implement a program that extracts the coefficients for a quadratic equation. The program should report the number of real and imaginary roots.

5.28 Design and implement a program that extracts two integer values as input. The program should display whether the inputs are both positive, both negative, or one positive and one negative.

5.29 Design and implement a program that extracts two floating-point values as input. The program should determine whether the difference in the two values is at most Epsilon, where Epsilon is a program-defined constant equal to 0.00001.

5.30 Suppose we want to sort four numbers. How many different orderings can there be?

5.31 Design and implement a program that sorts four input values.

5.32 Provide a code segment that prompts a user for an extracted value in the interval 0 ... 99. The segment then displays the value in words. For example, if the input value is 21, then twenty-one is displayed.

5.33 Design and implement a program that displays the absolute value of its input.

5.34 Design and implement a program that accepts a date as input. The program should display the date's position in that year. For example, if the date is 12 29 2006, then the displayed number is 363.

5.35 Design and implement a program `DateValidator.java` that reports whether a user-specified date is a valid date.

5.36 Reimplement the `ColoredRectangle` method `paint()` so that it resembles the `ColoredTriangle` method `paint()`. Your new implementation should make the target a parameter to `paint()` and you should use `fillPolygon()` rather than `fillRect()`.

When solving Exercises 5.37–5.43, you may find it convenient to use `Point` method `distance()`. For `Point` variables p and q, `p.distance(q)` returns the Euclidean distance between the `Point` objects referenced by p and q.

5.37 Implement a **double** member method `getArea()` for `ColoredTriangle`. The method returns the area of its triangle. The area a of a triangle can be computed using Heron's formula: $a = \sqrt{s(s-a)(s-b)(s-c)}$, where s is one-half of the perimeter of the triangle and *a*, *b*, and *c* are the lengths of the three sides of the triangle.

5.38 Implement a **boolean** member method `isEquilateral()` for `ColoredTriangle` that returns whether its triangle is an equilateral triangle. A triangle is an equilateral triangle if all three sides of the triangle have the same length.

5.39 Implement a **boolean** member method `isIsosceles()` for `ColoredTriangle` that returns whether its triangle is an isosceles triangle. A triangle is isosceles if at least two sides of the triangle have the same length.

5.40 Implement a **boolean** member method `isScalene()` for `ColoredTriangle` that returns whether its triangle is a scalene triangle. A triangle is scalene if the sides of the triangle are all of different lengths.

5.41 Implement a **boolean** member method `isRight()` for `ColoredTriangle` that returns whether its triangle is a right triangle. A triangle is a right triangle if there are two side lengths where the sum of their squares is equal to the square of the other side length.

5.42 Implement a **boolean** member method `isObtuse()` for `ColoredTriangle` that returns whether its triangle is an obtuse triangle. A triangle is an obtuse triangle if there are two side lengths where the sum of their squares is less than the square of the other side length.

5.43 Implement a **boolean** member method `isAcute()` for `ColoredTriangle` that returns whether its triangle is an acute triangle. A triangle is an acute triangle if it is neither a right triangle nor an obtuse triangle.

5.14 PROGRAMMING PROJECT — MEDICAL ASSISTANT

In this programming case study you develop a very basic tool for medical diagnosis. Diagnostic tools are examples of *expert systems*. An expert system is a program that behaves like a human expert for a particular application domain. The application domain in this case study contains the likely causes of a fever.

> The objective of this case study is to practice using the **if** and **if-else** statements when problem solving

Expert systems are typically *rule-based*, where a rule has two components. The first component is the conditions under which the rule is applicable; the second component is the recommended action under those conditions.

A rule-based system performs a series of queries to determine the situation at hand so that it can determine which of its rules apply. The queries are done in a manner that uses the responses from previous queries to determine future queries. Such a process enables the program to determine quickly the specifics of the situation.

Because the tool that you are developing is concerned only with suggesting the possible cause of a fever, the first rule to consider is

No fever ⇒*no recommendation* (i.e., no fever implies no recommendation).

where $\Rightarrow$ is the mathematical symbol for implication. If the response to the initial query indicates the user does not have a fever, then the tool should announce no recommendation can be made. If the initial query indicates that the user does have a fever, then a follow-up query is asked. Based on the response to that query, other queries are made.

As a matter of professional ethics before going further, we make the disclaimer that the program you are asked to develop is intended solely for pedagogical purposes. The design and development of a true diagnostic tool requires interaction with medical personnel, testing in controlled environments to determine the validity of the program, and official certification. For information on the professional code for computer scientists, visit the ACM website www.acm.org. The ACM is the major professional society of computer scientists.

PROBLEM STATEMENT

The tool you design and produce should be based on the diagram in Figure 5.10. This diagram is a simplification of the American Medical Association's (AMA) diagram/procedure for dealing with fevers in their reference The American Medical Association Family Medical Guide: Third Edition, C.B. Clayman (medical editor), Random House, ISBN 0-679-41290-5, 1994.

SAMPLE OUTPUT

A sample program run is depicted in Figure 5.11.

IMPLEMENTATION

Your program's name should be FeverDiagnosis.java. The program should start by displaying a legend that provides introductory information on its use and limitations. In particular, your tool should indicate that the program performs no true diagnostic activity, no decisions should be made based on the tool's analysis, and that if the user really has a fever, the user should contact her or his doctor.

After displaying the legend, the tool should then begin a querying process that determines the user's situation. Upon making a determination, the diagnostic analysis should be displayed. As part of this display, list the symptoms that caused that recommendation to be displayed. For example, suppose the user had responded yes to fever, no to coughing, yes to headache, and yes to at least one of the following: pain when bending your head forward, nausea or vomiting, bright light hurting your eyes, drowsiness, or confusion. It is these symptoms that indicate the possibility of meningitis. In this situation, an output similar to the one depicted in Figure 5.11 should occur.

TESTING

Because there is a very limited number of scenarios that your program must handle, you should test your program completely to verify that it correctly implements the process in Figure 5.10. To make sure that your testing is complete, individually list and test the response sequence associated with each possible program outcome. For example, the response sequence (yes, yes, yes,) indicating yes to fever, yes to coughing, and yes to shortness of breath or wheezing or coughing phlegm should cause your program to indicate the possibilities of pneumonia or infection to the airways. And the response sequence (yes, yes, no, yes) indicating yes to fever, yes to coughing, no to shortness of breath or

Figure 5.10 Procedure to diagnose the cause of a fever.

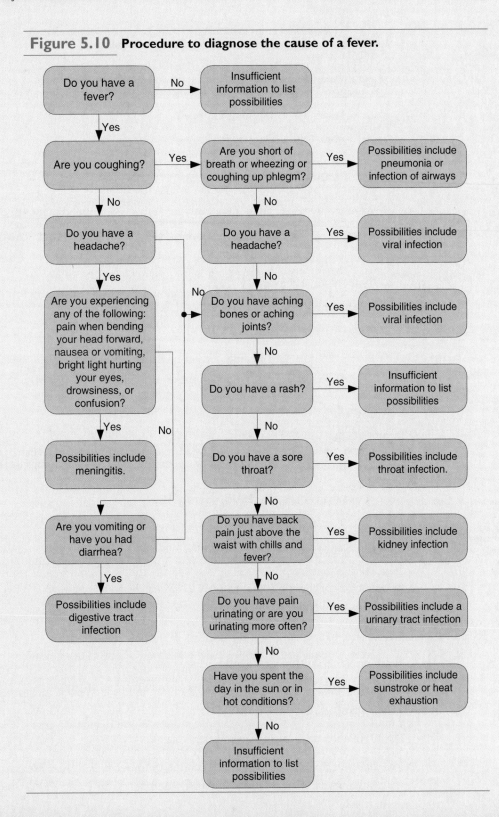

Figure 5.11 **Sample run of FeverDiagnosis.java.**

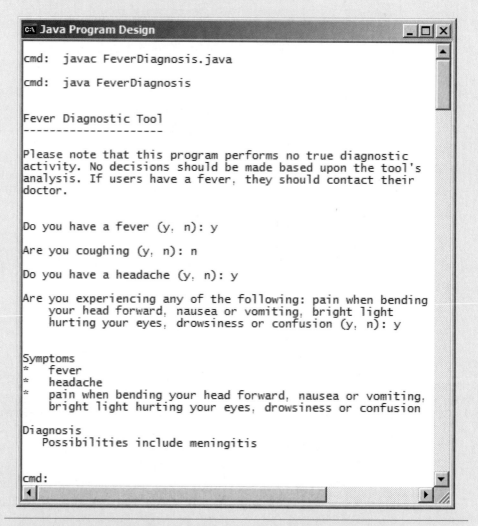

```
Java Program Design                                    _ □ X

cmd:   javac FeverDiagnosis.java

cmd:   java FeverDiagnosis


Fever Diagnostic Tool
---------------------

Please note that this program performs no true diagnostic
activity. No decisions should be made based upon the tool's
analysis. If users have a fever, they should contact their
doctor.


Do you have a fever (y, n): y

Are you coughing (y, n): n

Do you have a headache (y, n): y

Are you experiencing any of the following: pain when bending
     your head forward, nausea or vomiting, bright light
     hurting your eyes, drowsiness or confusion (y, n): y


Symptoms
*    fever
*    headache
*    pain when bending your head forward, nausea or vomiting,
     bright light hurting your eyes, drowsiness or confusion

Diagnosis
     Possibilities include meningitis


cmd:
```

wheezing or coughing phlegm, and yes to headache should cause your program to indicate the possibility of a viral infection.

REFERENCES

For information on expert systems in general see

- *Introduction to Expert Systems*, P. Jackson, Addison-Wesley Longman, ISBN: 0-201-87686-8, 1998.

For information on medical expert systems, see

- *Rationalizing Medical Work: Decision-support Techniques and Medical Practices*, M. Berg, MIT Press, ISBN: 0-262-02417-9, 1997.

5.15   **SELF-TEST ANSWERS**

S5.1   A truth table for the logical operator *nand*.

p	*q*	*p nand q*
false	false	true
false	true	true
true	false	true
true	true	false

S5.2   For the code segment,

   a) If i is 9 and j is 4, the output is B.

   b) If i is 4 and j is 9, the output is C.

   c) If i is 5 and j is 6, the output is D.

   d) If i is 5 and j is 9, the output is C.

S5.3   The output of the code segment is

            yes
            no

S5.4

   a) With a = **true**, b = **true**, c = **false**, and d = **false** the segment outputs 1.

   b) With a = **true**, b = **true**, c = **true**, and d = **false** the segment outputs 2.

   c) With a = **true**, b = **true**, c = **false**, d = **true** the segment outputs 3.
       With a = **true**, b = **true**, c = **true**, d = **true** the segment outputs 3.

   d) With a = **true**, b = **false**, c = **false**, and d = **false** the segment outputs 4.
       With a = **true**, b = **false**, c = **true**, and d = **true** the segment outputs 4.
       With a = **false**, b = **false**, c = **false**, and d = **false** the segment outputs 4.
       With a = **false**, b = **false**, c = **true**, and d = **true** the segment outputs 4.
       With a = **false**, b = **true**, c = **false**, and d = **false** the segment outputs 4.
       With a = **false**, b = **true**, c = **true**, and d = **true** the segment outputs 4.

   e) With a = **true**, b = **false**, c = **true**, and d = **false** the segment outputs 5.
       With a = **false**, b = **false**, c = **true**, and d = **false** the segment outputs 5.
       With a = **false**, b = **true**, c = **true**, and d = **false** the segment outputs 5.

   f) With a = **true**, b = **false**, c = **false**, and d = **true** the segment outputs 6.
       With a = **false**, b = **false**, c = **false**, and d = **true** the segment outputs 6.
       With a = **false**, b = **true**, c = **false**, and d = **true** the segment outputs 6.

S5.5   The code segment could be

```
if ((m < 5) && (j < 0)) {
   k = 3;
}
else if (! (m < k)) {
   k = 1;
}
```

S5.6   An equivalent **switch** statement would be

```
switch (i)
    case 3: {
        n = 1;
        k = 5;
        break;
    case 4:
        n = 5;
        break;
    case 6:
        n = 6;
        break;
    default: {
        n = 0;
}
```

S5.7   A code segment could be

```
String i1 = "Interval " + b1 + " ... " + e1;
String i1 = "Interval " + b2 + " ... " + e2;
if (e1 < b2) {
    System.out.println(i1 + " precedes " + i2);
}
else if (e2 < b1) {
    System.out.println(i2 + " precedes " + i1);
}
else if ((b1 == b2) && (e1 == e2)) {
    System.out.println(i1 + " equals " + i2);
}
else {
    System.out.println(i1 + " intersects " + i2);
}
```

S5.8   An implementation of getPerimeter() could be

```
// getPerimeter(): perimeter facilitator
public double getPerimeter() {
    Point v1 = getPoint(1);
    Point v2 = getPoint(2);
    Point v3 = getPoint(3);

    double a = v1.distance(v2);
    double b = v2.distance(v3);
    double c = v3.distance(v1);

    return a + b + c;
}
```

6 ITERATION

Thus far, our programs have had the property that each statement in the program is executed at most once. In this chapter, we consider the **while**, **for**, and **do-while** *looping constructs* that control how many times a statement list is *iterated* (executed). Loops make programs much more powerful and capable of solving significant problems. Mastering the design and implementation of loops is an important part of a programmer's education.

OBJECTIVES

- Introduce the **while** loop.
  - Introduce the **for** loop.
  - Introduce the **do-while** loop.
  - Demonstrate the importance of looping constructs in problem solving.
  - Encourage a systematic approach to loop design.
- Provide the means for doing simple file processing.

6.1   WHILE STATEMENT

Consider the following problem statement.

> *Prompt a user to supply a list of positive numbers, one per line. The end of the list is to be indicated with a negative number. Report the average of the positive numbers.*

This straightforward task cannot be solved using the Java statements that we have already introduced. The reason is that the list size is unknown.

If we know the size of the list, we can supply sufficient code to extract and sum all of the inputs (e.g., Program `AverageFive.java` of Listing 2.11 determines the average of a list with five values).

However, without knowing the size of the list, we cannot guarantee there would be sufficient code to extract and sum all of the inputs. To process a list of unknown size, we need an iterative construct that enables the execution of statements to occur multiple times.

Java provides several iterative constructs. Our examination begins with the **while** statement.

Program `NumberAverage.java` of Listing 6.1 uses a **while** statement to solve our list processing problem. Its solution form or algorithmic *pattern* is one that you often see in programming.

```
Prepare for processing
Get the first input
While there is an input to process, repeatedly do {
    Process current input
    Get the next input
}
Perform final processing
```

For `NumberAverage.java`, an input is processed both by adding its value to a variable `valueSum` that maintains a running total of the previously processed values and by incrementing a variable `valuesProcessed` that records the number of processed inputs. The iteration ends when a newly extracted input is determined to be a negative number.

A sample run of program `NumberAverage.java` follows.

```
Enter a list of numbers:
4.5 0.5
1.3
-1
Average: 2.1
```

To understand how the **while** statement works, let's trace through the actions of program `NumberAverage.java` as it produced this sample run.

Listing 6.1   *NumberAverage.java*

```
1.  // Compute average of a list of positive numbers
2.
3.  import java.util.*;
4.
5.  public class NumberAverage {
6.     // main(): application entry point
7.     public static void main(String[] args) {
8.        // set up the list processing
9.        Scanner stdin = new Scanner(System.in);
10.
11.       int valuesProcessed = 0;    // no values processed so far
12.       double valueSum = 0;        // running total
13.
14.       // prompt user for values
15.       System.out.println("Enter a list of positive numbers:");
16.
17.       // get the first value
18.       double value = stdin.nextDouble();
19.
20.       // process values one-by-one
21.       while (value >= 0) {
22.          // add value to running total
23.          valueSum += value;
24.          // processed another value
25.          ++valuesProcessed;
26.          // get next value
27.          value = stdin.nextDouble();
28.       }
29.
30.       // display result
31.       if (valuesProcessed > 0) {
32.          // compute and display average
33.          double average = valueSum / valuesProcessed;
34.          System.out.println("Average: " + average);
35.       }
36.       else {
37.          System.out.println("No list to average");
38.       }
39.    }
40. }
```

Method main() begins by defining a Scanner variable stdin to represent the standard input stream.

```
// set up the list processing
Scanner stdin = new Scanner(System.in);
```

It also defines variables valuesProcessed and valueSum that are used in the processing of an input.

```
int valuesProcessed = 0;    // no values processed so far
double valueSum = 0;        // running total
```

The role of valuesProcessed is to indicate how many values have been processed. Because no values have been processed yet, valuesProcessed is initialized to 0. Variable `valueSum` maintains the running total of the input values processed so far. Therefore, it is initialized to 0.

By properly updating variables `valuesProcessed` and `valueSum` whenever an input value is extracted, the average of the inputs can be computed. The average will be equal to `valueSum / valuesProcessed`.

The program next issues a prompt that tells the user both how to supply the values *and* how to indicate that there are no more values to consider.

```
System.out.println("Enter a list of positive numbers:");
```

In particular, the user is told that positive numbers are to be entered. The user is also told that a negative number means that the list is complete. In programming parlance, this end of list value is called a *sentinel*.

The extraction of the values and their processing then can proceed. The first value is extracted before the loop.

```
// get the first value          ← First value acquired before the loop starts
double value = stdin.nextDouble();
```

The value is extracted before the **while** loop because the statements that make up the action of a loop have been designed to process a list value. They are not intended for dealing with the sentinel.

In general, a **while** loop has the following form

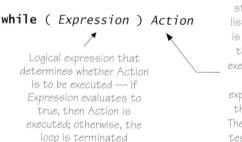

while (*Expression*) *Action*

Logical expression that determines whether Action is to be executed — if Expression evaluates to true, then Action is executed; otherwise, the loop is terminated

Action is either a single statement or a statement list within braces. The action is also known as the body of the loop. After the body is executed, the test expression is reevaluated. If the expression evaluates to true, the body is executed again. The process repeats until the test expression evaluates to false

When a **while** statement is executed, its test expression is evaluated first. If the expression evaluates **true**, its *body* is executed, where the body is the action of the **while** statement. The evaluation process then is repeated. If the expression reevaluates to **true**, the body is executed again. This process is called *looping*, and it continues until the test expression evaluates to **false**. At that point, execution continues with the next statement in the program.

The test expression for the **while** loop of program `NumberAverage.java` is (`value >= 0`). It will be the case for each iteration of the loop that if the test expression is **true**, then there is a value that needs to be included in the average.

```
// process values one-by-one
while (value >= 0) {
    // add value to running total
    valueSum += value;
    // processed another value
    ++valuesProcessed;
    // prepare to iterate -- get the next input
    value = stdin.nextDouble();
}
```

Test expression is evaluated at the start of each iteration of the loop. Its value indicates whether there is a number to process

If test expression is true, these statements are executed. Afterward, the test expression is reevaluated and the process repeats

For this program run, variable `value` is initially 4.5. Therefore, the test expression evaluates to **true** and the body of the loop is executed. Because the processing of a value requires several statements, the **while** loop body is surrounded by braces. However, even if the action is a single statement, our programming style is to use braces *always*.

As the **while** loop body begins its execution, variables `valuesProcessed`, `valueSum`, and `value` have representation

valuesProcessed	0
valueSum	0.0
value	4.5

The first statement in the **while** loop body increments `valueSum` by `value`.

```
// add value to running total
valueSum += value;
```

Because this addition completes the processing of the current input, variable `valuesProcessed` is incremented.

```
// processed another value
++valuesProcessed;
```

Variables `valuesProcessed`, `valueSum`, and `value` now have representation

valuesProcessed	1
valueSum	4.5
value	4.5

Figure 6.1 **Semantic representation of a while statement.**

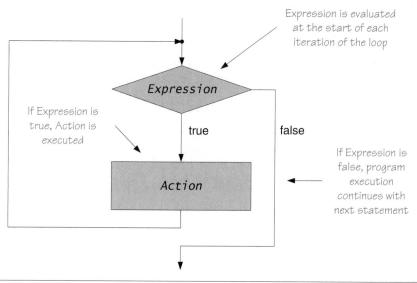

Although the processing of the current list value is completed, the **while** loop needs to perform one more action—it must update `value` with the next input. The update ensures that the **while** loop is ready for another evaluation of its test expression.

```
// prepare for next iteration --- get next value
value = stdin.nextDouble();
```

Update value to prepare for next evaluation of the test expression

For the program run, the input extraction results in variable `value` being assigned 0.5. With the assignment, variables `valuesProcessed`, `valueSum`, and `value` now have representation

valuesProcessed	1
valueSum	4.5
value	0.5

The **while** loop is now ready to repeat, and the repetition causes the **while** loop test expression (`value >= 0`) to be reevaluated. Because the expression evaluates to **true** (0.5 is greater than or equal to 0), the **while** loop body iterates. (See Figure 6.1 for a depiction of the execution of a **while** loop in general.)

The first statement in the body of the loop again increments `valueSum` by `value`.

```
// add value to running total
valueSum += value;
```

Because this addition completes the processing of the current input, variable values-Processed is incremented.

```
// processed another value
++valuesProcessed;
```

Variables valuesProcessed, valueSum, and value now have representation

valuesProcessed	2
valueSum	5.0
value	0.5

Variable value then is updated with the next input value. The update again ensures that the **while** loop is ready for another evaluation of the test expression.

```
// prepare for next iteration --- get next value
value = stdin.nextDouble();
```

For the program run, the input extraction results in variable value being assigned 1.3. With the assignment, variables valuesProcessed, valueSum, and value now have representation

valuesProcessed	2
valueSum	5.0
value	1.3

The **while** loop test expression (value >= 0) then is reevaluated. Because the expression still evaluates to **true** (1.3 is greater than or equal to 0), the **while** loop body iterates.

The first statement in the loop again increments valueSum by value

```
// add value to running total
valueSum += value;
```

and the next statement increments variable valuesProcessed.

```
// processed another value
++valuesProcessed;
```

The assignments cause valuesProcessed, valueSum, and value to have representation

valuesProcessed	3
valueSum	6.3
value	1.3

Variable value then is updated with the next input value. For the program run, the input extraction value results in variable value being assigned –1.

```
// prepare for next iteration --- get next value
value = stdin.nextDouble();
```

Hand-checking

The tracing of the execution of a method by hand is an important program debugging technique. Hand-checking code can give insight into how a method works.

With this assignment, variables `valuesProcessed`, `valueSum`, and `value` now have representation

valuesProcessed	3
valueSum	6.3
value	-1

The **while** loop test expression (`value >= 0`) then is reevaluated. Because –1 is not greater than or equal to 0, the expression evaluates to **false** and the loop is ended.

The list values have now all been processed and the average can be computed and displayed.

```
// display result
if (valuesProcessed > 0) {
   // compute and display average
   double average = valueSum / valuesProcessed;
   System.out.println("Average: " + average);
}
else {
   System.out.println("No list to average");
}
```

Although the sample run processed a list with three values, program `NumberAverage` works for lists of any size. You are encouraged to hand-check the program with other inputs.

We now turn our attention to another task whose solution makes use of a **while** statement. The task is to convert user-supplied text into lowercase.

Our solution to this text conversion problem is program `LowerCaseDisplay.java` of Listing 6.2. The input/output behavior of a sample program run is shown in Figure 6.2.

Program `LowerCaseDisplay.java` follows a similar algorithmic form as `NumberAverage.java`. Besides the different type of processing that is needed—text conversion—the other major difference is that all input is extracted within the loop.

```
Prepare for processing
While there is an input to process, repeatedly do {
   Get the next input
   Process current input
}
Perform final processing
```

To prepare for its input processing, program `LowerCaseDisplay.java` defines a `String` variable `converted`.

```
String converted = "";
```

Listing 6.2 **LowerCaseDisplay.java**

```
1.  // Echo input back in lowercase
2.
3.  import java.util.*;
4.
5.  public class LowerCaseDisplay {
6.     public static void main(String[] args) {
7.        // prepare for conversion
8.        Scanner stdin = new Scanner(System.in);
9.
10.       System.out.println("Enter input to be converted:");
11.
12.       String converted = "";
13.
14.       // process lines one-by-one
15.       while (stdin.hasNext()) {
16.          // get next input line
17.          String currentLine = stdin.nextLine();
18.
19.          // process current line
20.          String currentConversion = currentLine.toLowerCase();
21.          converted += (currentConversion + "\n");
22.       }
23.
24.       // display result
25.       System.out.println("\nThe conversion is:\n" + converted);
26.    }
27. }
```

Figure 6.2 **Sample run of LowerCaseDisplay.java.**

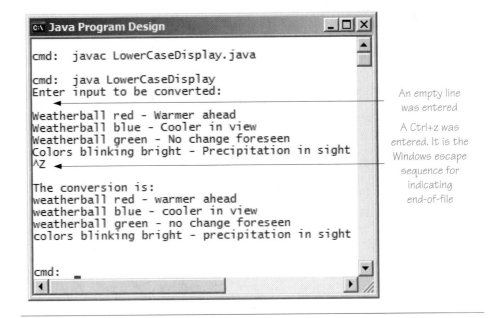

Variable `converted` maintains the input text that has already been converted. Because no text has been converted initially, the variable references initially a string of length 0 (i.e., an *empty string*).

After the initialization of `currentLine`, the **while** loop processing begins. The **while** test expression evaluates whether there is any input to extract.

```
while (stdin.hasNext()) {
```

Scanner method `hasNext()` indicates whether the input stream has any more input. So if the test expression (`stdin.hasNext()`) evaluates to **true**, then there is an input line in need of processing. If the test expression evaluates to **false**, then there is no input to process. Thus, the **while** loop iterates only if there is a nonempty text line to process.

Scanner methods

Class `Scanner` provides several "has" methods. Besides `hasNext()`, the other principal ones are `hasNextInt()`, `hasNextDouble()`, `hasNextBoolean()`, `hasNextLong()`, `hasNextShort()`, and `hasNextFloat()`. These methods report whether the next value is of the desired form. A complete description of class `Scanner` is given in Appendix E.

As Figure 6.2 shows, an empty line is not an indication that no text is being provided. Instead, an empty line corresponds to an empty string. To indicate that no more text is being provided, the user must enter an operating system-dependent escape sequence (sentinel). The Windows sentinel value is `Ctrl+z` and for most other operating systems it is `Ctrl+d`. For historic reasons regarding earlier programming languages, software developers commonly refer to the sentinel value as *end-of-file*.

The body of the **while** is comprised of two actions.

```
while (stdin.hasNext()) {
    // get next input line
    String currentLine = stdin.nextLine();

    // process current line
    String currentConversion = currentLine.toLowerCase();
    converted += (currentConversion + "\n");
}
```

It first defines and initializes a `String` variable `currentLine`. The initialization value is the current input string.

```
String currentLine = stdin.nextLine();
```

The processing of the current line requires that variable `converted` be updated. Its representation must be appended with the lowercase conversion of the current line.

The conversion is produced by `String` member method `toLowerCase()`. The conversion result initializes a `String` variable `currentConversion`.

```
String currentConversion = currentLine.toLowerCase();
```

The `String` append assignment operator += then uses that value in an update of variable `converted`.

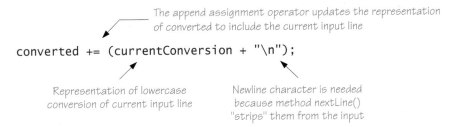

The append assignment operator updates the representation of converted to include the current input line

```
converted += (currentConversion + "\n");
```

Representation of lowercase conversion of current input line

Newline character is needed because method nextLine() "strips" them from the input

The append assignment completes the processing of the current line.

The **while** test expression then is reevaluated. If test expression (`stdin.hasNext()`) again evaluates to **true** then the loop body iterates to extract and process another input line. However, if the user has indicated end-of-file, then the test expression evaluates to **false** and the loop terminates.

When the loop is finished, the program displays the converted text.

```
// display result
System.out.println("\nThe conversion is:\n" + converted);
```

Although the **while** statement has sufficient flexibility to handle all iteration needs, Java provides two other iterative statements—the **for** and **do-while**. Programmers tend to use the three iterative statements for different types of tasks.

Loop design

It is especially important when you design a loop that you understand its purpose and its effects on other parts of the programs. Some good questions to consider in your design and analysis are the following.

- What initialization is necessary for the loop's test expression?
- What initialization is necessary for the loop's processing?
- What causes the loop to terminate?
- What actions should the loop perform?
- What actions are necessary to prepare for the next iteration of the loop?
- What conditions are true and what conditions are false when the loop is terminated?
- When the loop completes, what actions are need to prepare for subsequent program processing?

The **while** statement tends to be used when the number of necessary iterations is unknown. The **for** statement tends to be used when the number of iterations is known. The **do-while** tends to be used when at least one iteration is necessary but the number of additional iterations is unknown. We next consider the **for** statement.

6.2 FOR STATEMENT

The following annotated code segment demonstrates a **for** statement in use. The segment displays the value of 2^i for i in the interval 0 ... 4. That is, the segment displays the values 1, 2, 4, 8, 16.

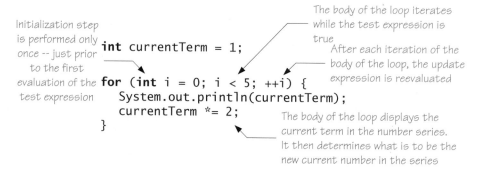

The code segment begins by defining an **int** variable currentTerm, which represents the current term to be displayed in the number series.

```
int currentTerm = 1;
```

The execution of the **for** loop then begins. There are four parts to a **for** loop, the first three of which occur within the parentheses that follow the keyword **for**. In order, these parts are the *initialization step*, the *test expression*, and the *update step*. The fourth part is the *body of the loop* and it occurs immediately after the parentheses.

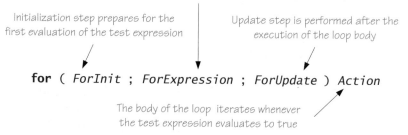

The initialization step is performed only once—at the start of the execution of the loop.

Next, the test expression is evaluated. If the test expression is initially **false**, then execution immediately continues with the next statement in the program. If the expression is **true**, the body of the loop is executed and then the update step is performed. The update step is permitted to be an assignment, method invocation, or omitted.

After the update step is performed, the test expression then is reevaluated. If the expression is again **true**, the execution of the loop body and update step is iterated. This process continues until the test expression evaluates to **false**. Execution then continues with the next statement in the program.

Figure 6.3 Semantic representation of a for statement.

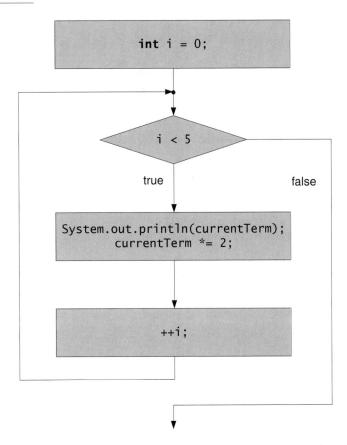

Every part has a purpose

Programmers tend to use the initialization step to do the work that is required to make sensible the first evaluation of the test expression and they tend to use the update step to make sensible the next evaluation of the test expression.

To better under the **for** loop, let's trace through the execution of the **for** loop from our example. (Its semantics are depicted in Figure 6.3.)

```
for (int i = 0; i < 5; ++i) {
    System.out.println(currentTerm);
    currentTerm *= 2;
}
```

The initialization step of the **for** loop defines and initializes an **int** variable i. In traditional programming terminology, i is known as the *index variable*—its value changes with each iteration. The value of i reflects the index of the current term in the number series. Because i is initialized to 0, variables `currentTerm` and i have representation

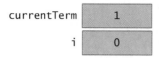

The test expression i < 5 determines if there are terms in the number series still needing to be displayed. If i is less than 5, then i is indexing a term that needs displaying. Because 0 is less than 5, the test expression evaluates initially to **true**.

The body of **for** loop displays `currentTerm` and then scales (multiplies) currentTerm by 2. The scaling causes `currentTerm` to represent the next term in the number series.

```
System.out.println(currentTerm);
currentTerm *= 2;
```

The output produced thus far is

```
1
```

The update step then is executed, causing index i to be incremented by 1. Variables `currentTerm` and i now have representation

currentTerm | 2
i | 1

The loop then reevaluates the test expression i < 5. Because 1 is less than 5, the **for** loop body is executed. In the loop body, `currentTerm` is redisplayed and rescaled by 2. The result is that `currentTerm` has value 4. The output produced thus far is

```
1
2
```

The update step ++i then is performed, causing index i to be incremented by 1. Variables `currentTerm` and i now have representation

currentTerm | 4
i | 2

The loop then reevaluates the expression i < 5. Because 2 is less than 5, the **for** loop body is again executed. In the body, `currentTerm` is again redisplayed and rescaled. The result is that `currentTerm` has value 8. The output produced thus far is

```
1
2
4
```

The update step ++i then is performed, causing index i to be incremented by 1. Variables currentTerm and i now have representation.

currentTerm	8
i	3

The loop then reevaluates the expression i < 5. Because 3 is less than 5, the **for** loop body executes again. The body of the loop redisplays and rescales currentTerm. The new value of currentTerm is 16. The output produced thus far is

```
1
2
4
8
```

The update step ++i then is performed, causing index i to be incremented by 1. Variables currentTerm and i now have representation

currentTerm	16
i	4

The loop then reevaluates the expression i < 5. Because 4 is less than 5, the **for** loop body executes again. The body of the loop redisplays and rescales currentTerm. The new value of currentTerm is 32. The output produced thus far is

```
1
2
4
8
16
```

The update step ++i then is performed, causing index i to be incremented by 1. Variables currentTerm and i now have representation

currentTerm	32
i	5

The loop then reevaluates the expression i < 5. Because 5 is not less than 5, the test expression evaluates to **false** and the loop is completed.

Infinite loops

All of the loop examples in this chapter include some action that causes the iteration statement to complete eventually. Without such an occurrence, the programs would have what is known as an *infinite loop*—they would continue to execute until some operating system command eventually terminated them. To avoid such a problem in your programs, make sure that you understand what is going on in your iteration statements. In particular, make sure that your iteration statements are designed to terminate.

6.2.1   INDEX VARIABLE SCOPE

Suppose we modified our code segment to display the value of i after the **for** loop has executed. What value gets displayed?

```java
int currentTerm = 2;

for (int i = 0; i < 5; ++i) {
   System.out.println(currentTerm);
   currentTerm *= 2;
}

System.out.println("i is " + i);
```

This question is a trick. The code segment does not compile. The *scope* of the index variable is limited to the **for** loop. Conceptually, i is a variable that is local only to the loop. We consider the notion of scope in more detail in Chapter 7.

6.2.2   COMPUTING THE NUMBER OF COMBINATIONS

Our next **for** loop example makes use of the products of nonnegative integers called *factorials*. Let n be a nonnegative integer, then the product of the integers 1 through n is denoted as $n!$ (pronounced "en-factorial"). Mathematically, $n!$ has definition

$$n! = \begin{cases} 1 & \text{if } n = 0 \\ 1 \times 2 \times \ldots \times n & \text{if } n \geq 1 \end{cases}$$

The computing of $n!$ is straightforward with a **for** loop.

```java
int nFactorial = 1;
for (int i = 2; i <= n; ++i) {
   nFactorial *= i;
}
```

In the preceding code segment, variable nFactorial is used to store the solution. An initial value of 1 ensures that nFactorial is set correctly for n equal to 0 or 1.

The **for** loop initialization step defines an index variable i that represents the next factor by which nFactorial needs to be multiplied. Index i is initialized to 2—the first factor required in a factorial computation.

The test expression i <= n determines whether i is part of n!. If it is, then the factor is used to scale nFactorial. Thus, the **for** loop considers in turn each of the factors 2, 3, ..., and n. When the loop is finished, nFactorial is set to the desired value.

Several factorial computations are performed by program Combination.java of Listing 6.3. Program Combination.java uses those computations to determine the number of different combinations that can be made by choosing n objects from a set of m objects. For example, with a standard deck of 52 playing cards there are 2,598,960 different possible poker hands that can be constructed by choosing 5 of the 52 cards.

Listing 6.3   **Combination.java**

```
1.  // Compute C(m,n) for user-specified m and n
2.
3.  import java.util.*;
4.
5.  public class Combination {
6.     // main(): application entry point
7.     public static void main(String[] args) {
8.        // set input stream
9.        Scanner stdin = new Scanner(System.in);
10.
11.       // prompt and extract user inputs
12.       System.out.print("Enter number of distinct objects: ");
13.       int m = stdin.nextInt();
14.       System.out.print("Enter desired subset size: ");
15.       int n = stdin.nextInt();
16.
17.       // compute the three needed factorials
18.       int mFactorial = 1;
19.       for (int i = 2; i <= m; ++i) {
20.          mFactorial *= i;
21.       }
22.
23.       int nFactorial = 1;
24.       for (int i = 2; i <= n; ++i) {
25.          nFactorial *= i;
26.       }
27.
28.       int mDiffNFactorial = 1;
29.       for (int i = 2; i <= m - n; ++i) {
30.          mDiffNFactorial *= i;
31.       }
32.
33.       // compute and display combinations
34.       int combinations = mFactorial
35.          / (mDiffNFactorial * nFactorial);
36.
37.       System.out.println("We can make " + combinations
38.          + " different combinations when choosing\n" + n
39.          + " objects from " + m + " different objects\n");
40.    }
41. }
```

The number of different combinations that can be made by choosing n objects from a set of m objects is written mathematically as $C(m, n)$. The formula for $C(m, n)$ is

$$C(m, n) = \frac{m!}{(m - n)!\,n!}$$

The first **for** loop in program Combination.java computes m!.

```
int mFactorial = 1;
for (int i = 2; i <= m; ++i) {
   mFactorial *= i;
}
```

and the second loop computes n!.

```
int nFactorial = 1;
for (int i = 2; i <= n; ++i) {
    nFactorial *= i;
}
```

and the third loop computes (m-n)!.

```
int mDiffNFactorial = 1;
for (int i = 2; i <= m - n; ++i) {
    mDiffNFactorial *= i;
}
```

The same but different

Although each of the **for** loops in Listing 6.3 uses an index variable i, they are different variables with the same name. The scope of a **for** loop index variable is limited to the loop.

Using the values mFactorial, nFactorial, and mDiffNFactorial we can compute and display the number of combinations.

```
int combinations = mFactorial
    / (mDiffNFactorial * nFactorial);

System.out.println("We can make " + combinations
    + " different combinations when choosing\n" + n
    + " objects from " + m + " different objects\n");
```

We now consider the remaining Java iterative statement—the **do-while** statement.

6.3	**DO-WHILE STATEMENT**

In some situations an action needs to be done at least once and possibly multiple times. For such situations, programs often use the **do-while** statement. The statement has the form

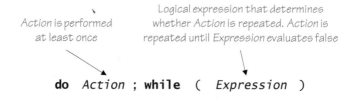

A **do-while** loop *begins* by executing the body of its loop. *Afterward*, the test expression is evaluated. If the test expression evaluates to **true**, then the body is repeated. This process continues until the test expression evaluates to **false**. The **do-while** semantics are demonstrated in Figure 6.4.

> ### Figure 6.4   Semantic representation of a do-while statement.

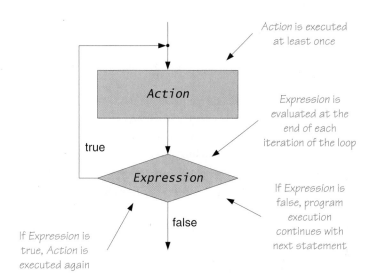

In the first example of this section, a **do-while** loop is used to display individually the digits of an **int** variable number. For pedagogic purposes, assume number has the value 141932.

```
do {
    int digit = number % 10;
    System.out.println(digit);
    number = number / 10;
} while (number != 0);
```

The current digit is acquired using the modulus operator %. After displaying the digit, number is divided by 10 to remove that digit from further consideration. Once number has value 0, all digits have been displayed. The following output is a sample run of the code segment.

```
2
3
9
1
4
1
```

Some programmers would be tempted to use a **while** loop rather than a **do-while** loop for this task. However, the **while** loop implementation that those programmers probably would consider first does not work.

```
while (n != 0) {
    int digit = n % 10;
    System.out.println(digit);
    n = n / 10;
}
```

While versus do-while

Use a **while** loop when the action can occur zero or more times; use a **do-while** loop when the action can occur one or more times.

This loop does not always produce the correct output. In particular, it does not handle correctly the case when n is 0. For this case, the **while** loop does not produce any output. However, the correct output is a single line displaying a 0.

The **do-while** is useful particularly in the processing of a user reply to a prompt. For example, the following code segment repeatedly issues a prompt and then expects a single character reply indicating yes or no. If a reply is not given, the code segment assumes no. If an incorrect response is given, it is ignored and the process is repeated.

```java
Scanner stdin = new Scanner(System.in);

char reply = 'n';
boolean stillDeciding = true;

do {
   System.out.print("Decision (y, n): ");
   if (stdin.hasNext()) {
      // process response
      String response = stdin.nextLine();
      if (response.length() == 1) {
         reply = response.charAt(0);
         reply = Character.toLowerCase(reply);
         if ((reply == 'y') || (reply == 'n')) {
            stillDeciding = false;
         }
      }
   }
   else {
      stillDeciding = false;
   }
} while (stillDeciding);
```

The code segment defines a **char** variable reply to indicate whether the user's reply indicated yes or no. Variable reply is initialized to `'n'` (i.e., no is the assumed response if no input is entered). A **boolean** variable stillDeciding is defined also. The variable indicates whether the user has yet to make a decision. Its initial value is **true**, because the decision has not yet been determined.

```java
char reply = 'n';
boolean stillDeciding = true;
```

The body of the **do-while** begins with an issuing of a prompt and the extraction of the response.

```java
System.out.print("Decision (y, n): ");
```

A test then determines whether there is input in response to the prompt. If so, then the response must be processed; otherwise, the user signaled end-of-file, in this case no is assumed and the decision is made implicitly.

```
if (stdin.hasNext()) {
    // process response …
}
else {
    stillDeciding = false;
}
```

To process the response, it is first extracted and its length is determined.

```
// process response
String response = stdin.nextLine();
if (response.length() == 1) {
    reply = response.charAt(0);
    reply = Character.toLowerCase(reply);
    if ((reply == 'y') || (reply == 'n')) {
        stillDeciding = false;
    }
}
```

If it is of the proper length (i.e., it is a single character), the code first grabs the character that makes up the string. To simplify the testing, the character is converted to its lower-case equivalent using `Character` class method `toLowerCase()`. If the character is a 'y' or an 'n', a decision has been made. If the character is something different, no explicit action needs to be taken—variable `stillDeciding` remains **true**, causing the loop test expression to evaluate to **true** and the loop to iterate.

If instead, the user provides a response that is greater than length 1, then the response is ignored. Because `stillDeciding` remains **true**, the loop test expression evaluates to **true** and the loop iterates.

The following output is a sample run of the code segment

```
Decision (y, n): not sure
Decision (y, n):
Decision (y, n): thinking
Decision (y, n): yeah
Decision (y, n): Y
```

Scope

The scope of variable `response` in the body of a **do-while** loop is limited to that body. Variables defined in the body *cannot* be used in the loop's test expression. For example, the following code segment does not compile because j is undefined in the test expression j != 6211954.

```
do {
    int j = stdin.nextInt();
} while (j != 6211954);   // j is undefined at this point
```

Our next series of examples nest one loop within another loop.

6.4   NESTED LOOPS

Consider the following code segment

```java
int m = 2;
int n = 3;
for (int i = 0; i < n; ++i) {
    System.out.println("i is " + i);
    for (int j = 0; j < m; ++j) {
        System.out.println("   j is " + j);
    }
}
```

Why does it produce this output?

```
i is 0
    j is 0
    j is 1
i is 1
    j is 0
    j is 1
i is 2
    j is 0
    j is 1
```

The statement

```java
System.out.println("i is " + i);
```

is part of the action associated with the **for** loop that begins on the third line of the segment. We say that this loop is the *outer* loop. The expression i < n that controls the iteration of the loop evaluates to **true** three times with i taking on in turn the values 0, 1, and 2. Thus, there are three lines of output that begin with "i is ". Each time there is such a display, the **for** loop beginning on the fifth line of the segment is executed. We say this loop is an *inner* or *nested* loop.

It is important to realize that an inner loop starts up once per iteration of its outer loop. For our example, each time the inner loop is executed, the expression j < m evaluates to **true** two times with j taking on, in turn, the values 0 and 1. Thus, it causes the output

```
j is 0
j is 1
```

to be displayed each time there is an output line beginning with "i is ".

Nesting one loop in another loop produces a multiplicative effect in terms of the number of statements that are executed. For our example, the outer **for** loop action is executed n times. Each one of those times, the inner **for** loop action is executed m times. As a result, the inner **for** loop action is performed a total of m × n times.

MultiplicationTable.java of Listing 6.4 uses nested loops to produce a standard multiplication table. The output of the program is

```
*  |  0  1  2  3  4  5  6  7  8  9 10 11 12
----------------------------------------------
 0 |  0  0  0  0  0  0  0  0  0  0  0  0  0
 1 |  0  1  2  3  4  5  6  7  8  9 10 11 12
 2 |  0  2  4  6  8 10 12 14 16 18 20 22 24
 3 |  0  3  6  9 12 15 18 21 24 27 30 33 36
 4 |  0  4  8 12 16 20 24 28 32 36 40 44 48
 5 |  0  5 10 15 20 25 30 35 40 45 50 55 60
 6 |  0  6 12 18 24 30 36 42 48 54 60 66 72
 7 |  0  7 14 21 28 35 42 49 56 63 70 77 84
 8 |  0  8 16 24 32 40 48 56 64 72 80 88 96
 9 |  0  9 18 27 36 45 54 63 72 81 90 99 108
10 |  0 10 20 30 40 50 60 70 80 90 100 110 120
11 |  0 11 22 33 44 55 66 77 88 99 110 121 132
12 |  0 12 24 36 48 60 72 84 96 108 120 132 144
```

Method main() of MultiplicationTable.java has two sections. The first section produces the header for the table.

```
// display table header
System.out.print("  * |");
for (int i = 0; i <= MAX_FACTOR; ++i) {
    System.out.printf("%4d", i);
}
System.out.println();
for (int i = 0; i <= MAX_FACTOR+1; ++i) {
    System.out.print("----");
}
System.out.println();
```

The display of the column headers makes use of System.out method printf(). This method allows *formatted printing*.

In its simplest form, method printf() expects two parameters. The first parameter is a *format string* that specifies how the second parameter is to be printed. In | Appendix C describes format strings in more detail

our example, the specifier "%4d" indicates that value i is to be displayed as a decimal integer using 4 characters. The '%' is the escape sequence character indicating a format specifier; the number following the % indicates how many characters are to be used in the

Listing 6.4   MultiplicationTable.java

```java
1.  // Produces standard times table
2.  import java.util.*;
3.
4.  public class MultiplicationTable {
5.      // main(): application entry point
6.      public static void main(String[] args) {
7.          final int MAX_FACTOR = 12;
8.
9.          // display table header
10.         System.out.print(" * |");
11.         for (int i = 0; i <= MAX_FACTOR; ++i) {
12.             System.out.printf("%4d", i);
13.         }
14.         System.out.println();
15.         for (int i = 0; i <= MAX_FACTOR+1; ++i) {
16.             System.out.print("----");
17.         }
18.         System.out.println();
19.
20.         // display table
21.         for (int i = 0; i <= MAX_FACTOR; ++i) {
22.             // display row label
23.             System.out.printf("%2d |", i);
24.
25.             // display row entries
26.             for (int j = 0; j <= MAX_FACTOR; ++j) {
27.                 // compute entry
28.                 int product = i * j;
29.
30.                 // pretty-print entry
31.                 System.out.printf("%4d", product);
32.             }
33.
34.             // finish up the row
35.             System.out.println();
36.         }
37.     }
38. }
```

display, and the 'd' indicates that the value is to be displayed as a decimal integer. If the value does not require 4 characters to be printed, then a sufficient number of leading blanks are used to pad the display so that 4 characters are printed.

The second section (lines 20–36) displays the various products that make up the multiplication table. Nested **for** loops display the products. The outer **for** loop manages index variable i, which represents the left operand for the current product of interest. The values of interest are 0 ... MAX_FACTOR, where MAX_FACTOR has value 12. The inner **for** manages index variable j, which represents the right operand for the current product of interest. The values of interest are again 0 ... MAX_FACTOR.

```
for (int i = 0; i <= MAX_FACTOR; ++i) { ...
    for (int j = 0; j <= MAX_FACTOR; ++j) { ...
    }
    ...
}
```

For each value of i, the program must display a row of the table. To do so, three actions must be performed: display the row label, display a row of products, and display a newline character to end the row.

To ensure that the various row labels are aligned correctly, the row label is displayed using method System.out.printf() with an appropriate format specifier.

```
System.out.printf("%2d |", i);
```

Here, the format string specifies, besides displaying i as integer decimal using 2 characters, that a trailing blank and vertical separator should also be displayed.

After displaying the label, the inner **for** loop iterates for each value j of interest.

```
// display row entries
for (int j = 0; j <= MAX_FACTOR; ++j) {
    // compute entry
    int product = i * j;

    // pretty-print entry
    System.out.printf("%4d", product);
}
```

With i and j both being set, the product can be computed and displayed. To ensure that the table entries are aligned, the product is displayed in a formatted manner.

```
System.out.printf("%4d", product);
```

To complete the processing of a row, a newline character is displayed. This action is accomplished with a println() statement.

```
// finish up the row
System.out.println();
```

6.5 SIMPLE FILE PROCESSING

Besides allowing access to standard input and standard output, Java libraries also provide support for program interactions with various file devices and file systems. With this support, a program can make I/O requests while being unconcerned how the requests are carried out. The I/O requests of the stream view are translated automatically by the compiler into file-level specific actions that accomplish the desired requests (e.g., reading data from a disk file on a hard disk or DVD).

While you may not have paid much attention to it, you have already seen and used two different input stream representations. In fact, we use two of them whenever we define a `Scanner` variable `stdin` for processing data from the standard input stream (e.g., `BMICalculator.java` of Listing 2.10).

```
Scanner stdin = new Scanner(System.in);
```

Besides using these input streams, our console programs also have used the output stream variable `System.out`. `System.out` references a `PrintStream` that converts the characters generated by `print()` and `println()` methods into a stream sequence of bytes.

The `System` class also provides the output stream variable `System.err` for sending error or status messages. Like `System.out`, `System.err` print requests are directed by default to the console window. Several example error messages are given below:

```
System.err.println("System being rebooted in 2 minutes");
System.err.println("Zero balance: withdrawal ignored");
System.err.println("Modem is not online, no call possible");
```

`System.err` is preferred over `System.out` for such messages, because operating systems often provide a way for specifying that a program's standard output commands go to a file rather than the console window.

The > is a command-line operator in Windows, Linux, and OS X. It instructs the operating system to send the program's standard output requests to the file specified by its right operand (Output.txt)

```
cmd: java DisplayForecast > Output.txt
cmd: type Output.txt
I think there is a world market for maybe five computers.
   Thomas Watson, IBM Chairman, 1943.
cmd:
```

Because the viewing of error or system status messages should not be delayed until the user gets around to looking at the output file, `System.err` is preferred over `System.out` for warnings.

Java provides several representations for files. For extracting input from a file, we will first use class `File` to specify the file of interest and then create a `Scanner` object that operates on that file. For sending output to a file we will use `FileWriter`. Both `File` and `FileWriter` are part of the `java.io` package. We begin our examination of file manipulation with data extraction.

There is one `File` constructor of particular interest.

```
File(String s)
```

> Creates a new system-independent representation for a file named s. The name can be either an absolute pathname or a pathname relative to the current working folder.

With a File, we can create a Scanner that is associated with the file of interest. For example, the following code segment displays the first line from the file blurb.txt.

```
File file = new File("blurb.txt");
Scanner fileIn = new Scanner(file);
String currentLine = fileIn.nextLine();
System.out.println(currentLine);
```

In the code segment, Scanner variable fileIn provides a stream view of the file referenced by file, where file is a representation of file blurb.txt from the current working folder.

Because fileIn references a Scanner, the segment can use segment method nextLine() to extract a line of text from the file. Program FileLister.java of Listing 6.5 expands upon this example to display the entire contents of a user-specified file.

The definition of method main() of FileLister.java includes a program element that we have not needed before—a **throws** *expression*.

```
public static void main(String[] args) throws IOException {
```

The **throws** IOException expression indicates that the method may generate an unhandled exception.

As discussed in Chapter 2, an exception is an abnormal event that occurs during program execution. If a program does not have code that *catches* (processes) the exception, then the program is terminated. Java requires that methods that do not handle input and output exceptions must explicitly indicate this potentiality.

Method main() begins by defining a Scanner variable stdin that is a reference to the standard input stream. The reference is needed as the name of the file comes from the standard input stream.

```
// set up standard input stream
Scanner stdin = new Scanner(System.in);
```

The program then prompts and extracts the filename and then defines a File variable file that references the associated file.

```
// determine file
System.out.print("File: ");
String name = stdin.nextLine();
File file = new File(name);
```

If the name represents a valid input file, the constructor produces a system-independent view of its filename. If the name does not represent a valid input file, the constructor throws an IOException.

Listing 6.5   **FileLister.java**

```
1.  // Lists contents of a user-specified file
2.
3.  import java.util.*;
4.  import java.io.*;
5.
6.  public class FileLister {
7.
8.      // main(): application entry point
9.      public static void main(String [] args) throws IOException {
10.         // set up standard input stream
11.         Scanner stdin = new Scanner(System.in);
12.
13.         // determine file
14.         System.out.print("File: ");
15.         String name = stdin.nextLine();
16.         File file = new File(name);
17.
18.         // set up file stream
19.         Scanner fileIn = new Scanner(file);
20.
21.         // process lines one by one
22.         while (fileIn.hasNext()) {
23.             // get next line
24.             String currentLine = fileIn.nextLine();
25.
26.             // display the line
27.             System.out.println(currentLine);
28.         }
29.     }
30. }
```

The `File` is then used to initialize a `Scanner` variable `fileIn` that references the file stream of interest.

```
Scanner fileIn = new Scanner(file);
```

The **while** loop begins by evaluating its test expression (`fileIn.hasNext()`).

```
while (fileIn.hasNext()) {
```

If there is data in the file, then the test expression evaluates to **true** and the next line is processed. If there is no data, the test expression is **false** indicating that the file is empty.

For the case of an input being present, the loop body first extracts the next line and then displays it.

```
// get next line
String currentLine = fileIn.nextLine();

// display the line
System.out.println(currentLine);
```

Once the data in the file is exhausted, the test expression (`fileIn.hasNext()`) evaluates to **false** and the loop terminates.

A sample run of program `FileReader.java` follows.

```
Filename: blurb.txt
It was a dark and stormy night; the rain fell in torrents--
except at occasional intervals, when it was checked by a violent
gust of wind which swept up the streets (for it is in London that
our scene lies), rattling along the housetops, and fiercely
agitating the scanty flame of the lamps that struggled against
the darkness.
```

In this program run, file `blurb.txt` contains the opening sentence from "Paul Clifford" by Edward George Bulwer-Lytton (1830).

As another example of file processing, program `FileAverage.java` of Listing 6.6 revisits the average problem considered by `NumberAverage.java` of Listing 6.1. This console program produces the average of the numeric inputs from a user-specified file.

Suppose the file `numbers.txt` contains the following values: 1, 4, 32, 5, 12, 28, 6, 21, 54, 4, 30, 54, 6, 9, 82, 11, 29, 85, 11, 28, 91, 1, 1, 1. Then when using that file, our program has the following input/output behavior.

```
Filename: numbers.txt
Average file data value: 25.25
```

Program `FileAverage.java` begins in the same manner as `FileLister.java`. The program first defines a `Scanner` variable `stdin` that is a reference to the standard input stream. It then prompts and extracts the filename. With the filename, the program defines a second `Scanner` variable `fileIn` that references the associated file.

From this point `FileAverage.java`'s behavior is analogous to `NumberAverage.java` of Listing 6.1. However, rather than processing the values from the standard input stream referenced by `stdin`, the program processes the values from the file input stream referenced by `fileIn`. In addition, `FileAverage.java` does not make use of a negative number sentinel—the operating system automatically provides an end-of-file sentinel.

Prior to any reading of the values, the number of values processed is 0 and the running total is 0.

```
// initially no values have been processed
int valuesProcessed = 0;
double valueSum = 0;
```

After the initialization of the two variables, the **while** loop processing begins. The **while** test expression evaluates whether there is any input to extract.

```
while (stdin.hasNextDouble()) {
```

`Scanner` method `hasNextDouble()` indicates whether the next value (if any) in the input stream is a **double** value.

If test expression (`stdin.hasNextDouble()`) evaluates to **true**, then there is an input value in need of processing. If the test expression evaluates to **false**, then there is no input to process. Thus, the **while** loop iterates only if there is data to process.

Listing 6.6   FileAverage.java

```
1.  // Compute the average of a user-specified file of data values
2.
3.  import java.util.*;
4.  import java.io.*;
5.
6.  public class FileAverage {
7.      // main(): application entry point
8.      public static void main(String[] args) throws IOException {
9.          // set up standard input stream
10.         Scanner stdin = new Scanner(System.in);
11.
12.         // determine filename
13.         System.out.print("Filename: ");
14.         String name = stdin.nextLine();
15.
16.         // get file stream for text processing
17.         File file = new File(name);
18.         Scanner fileIn = new Scanner(file);
19.
20.         // initially no values have been processed
21.         int valuesProcessed = 0;
22.         double valueSum = 0;
23.
24.         // process values one by one
25.         while (fileIn.hasNextDouble()) {
26.             // get the input value
27.             double value = fileIn.nextDouble();
28.             // add value to running total
29.             valueSum += value;
30.             // processed another value
31.             ++valuesProcessed;
32.         }
33.
34.         // ready to compute average
35.         if (valuesProcessed > 0) {
36.             double average = valueSum / valuesProcessed;
37.             System.out.println("Average file data value: " + average);
38.         }
39.         else {
40.             System.err.println(name + ": no values to average");
41.         }
42.     }
43. }
```

For the case of a value being present, the body of the loop extracts the input value; adds the value to running total; and increments the number of values processed.

```
while (fileIn.hasNextDouble()) {
    // get the input value
    double value = fileIn.nextDouble();
    // add value to running total
    valueSum += value;
    // processed another value
    ++valuesProcessed;
}
```

After the body completes, the test expression (`stdin.hasNextDouble()`) is reevaluated to determine whether there is another value to process. When there are no more values to process, the loop terminates.

An **if** statement then determines whether an average can be computed. If the number of values processed is nonzero, then there is an average to calculate.

```
double average = valueSum / valuesProcessed;
System.out.println("Average file data value: " + average);
```

If there were no values to process, then a message is displayed to the standard error stream indicating the problem.

```
System.err.println(name + ": no values to average");
```

This completes our analysis of `FileAverage.java`. We next turn our attention to the development of a simple API for keeping track of important characteristics of a data set.

| 6.6 | **CASE STUDY — DATA SET ANALYSIS** |

In analyzing a data set there are often four values of particular interest: the minimum, the maximum, the mean, and the standard deviation. Together the minimum and maximum let us know the range of the values; the mean is the average data set value, which often gives insight on what is a typical value; and the standard deviation gives insight on how clustered the data set values are around the average. (Our implementation of a data set representation DataSet.java leaves the computing of a standard deviation to the exercises.)

> The objective of this case study is to practice using conditional and iterative statements in the context of the design and implementation of a class

Table 6.1 lists an example data set for the number of Internet users per 100 people of population for 189 of the political entities recognized by the United Nations. The data set is for the year 2000 and comes from the United Nations' Department of Economic and Social Affairs. The mean value is approximately 8.28 and the standard deviation is approximately 13.01. The minimum value is 0.1 (Democratic Republic of the Congo, Myanmar, and Somalia) and the maximum value is 73.4 (Falkland Islands).

Table 6.1   **Internet use per 100 people of population for 189 entities.**

0.09	0.16	8.97	0.23	6.52	6.75	1.42	13.65	34.45	25.86
0.16	4.32	5.84	0.08	3.74	1.78	22.89	6.24	0.25	0.22
1.44	1.01	1.54	2.94	9.14	5.28	0.08	0.07	0.05	0.27
41.30	1.84	0.04	0.04	16.58	1.74	38.64	13.70	2.07	0.22
5.67	0.27	5.59	0.54	17.88	9.71	0.01	36.59	0.22	7.78
1.86	1.42	0.71	0.80	0.15	0.13	27.21	73.40	1.47	37.23
14.43	6.43	1.22	0.92	0.42	29.18	0.15	9.47	4.36	1.75
0.70	0.10	0.25	6.04	0.25	0.62	7.15	59.79	0.54	0.94
0.39	20.70	20.26	23.04	3.11	29.31	2.53	0.62	0.65	1.80
40.25	7.84	1.06	0.11	6.19	8.58	0.19	0.02	0.18	6.09
22.66	0.19	0.15	15.90	2.23	0.17	13.08	1.17	0.19	7.29
2.74	39.71	1.26	0.71	0.06	0.01	1.71	0.22	24.39	11.15
21.67	0.99	0.04	0.18	49.05	25.05	3.55	0.09	1.10	3.17
2.81	0.73	9.74	2.01	7.25	24.94	10.22	5.01	1.20	18.60
3.57	0.06	4.79	3.09	0.56	48.70	4.36	0.93	0.42	7.40
0.10	29.87	12.03	15.08	0.46	0.01	5.49	13.43	0.64	0.10
2.70	0.99	45.58	29.62	0.19	28.10	0.05	3.79	2.47	0.86
7.73	2.61	3.06	0.13	0.18	0.69	28.20	30.12	0.33	45.07
11.09	0.49	2.03	3.93	0.25	0.08	3.76	0.19	0.37	

Suppose x is a list of n values $x_1, x_2, \ldots x_n$, then its mean is written as $\bar{x}$, where the overline character " ̄" is the statistical mean symbol. Mean $\bar{x}$ has following definition.

$$\bar{x} = (x_1 + x_2 + \ldots + x_n) /\ n$$

As an example, the following data set represents the birth months of nine people familiar to authors.

4, 6, 6, 11, 11, 2, 3, 3, 12

The mean value is $(4 + 6 + 6 + 11 + 11 + 2 + 3 + 3 + 12) / 9$, which is approximately 6.444.

ANALYSIS AND DESIGN

In developing a representation `DataSet` for a data set it is clear that four methods are certainly necessary.

`public double` `getMinimum()`

> Returns the minimum value in the data set. If the data set is empty, then `Double.NaN` is returned, where `Double.NaN` is the Java **double** value representing the status *not-a-number*.

`public double` `getMaximum()`

> Returns the maximum value in the data set. If the data set is empty, then `Double.NaN` is returned.

`public double` `getAverage()`

> Returns the average value in the data set. If the data set is empty, then `Double.NaN` is returned.

`public double` `getStandardDeviation()`

> Returns the standard deviation value of the data set. If the data set is empty, then `Double.NaN` is returned.

But what constructors and what other behaviors should a data set representation have? Before reading on, determine your own answer to this question.

With regard to constructors, we believe two constructors are appropriate—a default constructor that represents a data set with no values and a *specific constructor* that represents a data set whose characteristics are determined from a file of values.

`public` `DataSet()`

> Initializes a representation of an empty data set.

`public` `DataSet(String s)` **throws** `IOException`

> Initializes the data set using the values from the file with name `s`. An exception is thrown if no file can be opened with name `s`.

In terms of member methods, we believe methods are appropriate for indicating the number of values in the data set, adding values to the data set being represented, clearing the values represented by the data set, and adding values from a file to the data set being represented.

`public int` `getSize()`

> Returns the number of values in the data set being represented.

`public void` `addValue(`**double** `x)`

> Adds the value `x` to the data set being represented.

`public void` `clear()`

> Sets the representation to that of an empty data set.

```
public void load(String s) throws IOException
```
Adds the values from the file with name **s** to the data set being represented. An exception is thrown if no file can be opened with name **s**.

To implement these behaviors, the following instance variables suffice.
```
private int n
```
Number of values in the data set being represented
```
private double minimumValue
```
Minimum value in the data set being represented.
```
private double maximumValue
```
Maximum value in the data set being represented.
```
private double xSum
```
The sum of values in the data set being represented

Program `DataSetTester.java` of Listing 6.7 demonstrates some uses of class `DataSet`. The program displays results regarding four data sets: `age.txt`, which contains the ages of 2,208 different women; `stature.txt`, which contains the height in centimeters of those same women; `foot-length.txt`, which contains the foot length in centimeters of those same women; and an empty data set. The original source for the first three data sets is a 1987 survey by the United States government. For each survey participant over 100 separate measurements were taken. The survey results are known as MIL-STD-1472D. The output produced by the program is given in Figure 6.5.

Figure 6.5   **Snapshot of a run of DataSetTester.java.**

```
cmd:    javac DataSet.java

cmd:    javac DataSetTester.java

cmd:    java DataSetTester

Minimum: 18.0
Maximum: 50.0
Mean: 26.182065217391305
Size: 2208

Minimum: 142.8
Maximum: 187.0
Mean: 162.93722826086938
Size: 2208

Minimum: 20.3
Maximum: 29.0
Mean: 24.438496376811592
Size: 2208

Minimum: NaN
Maximum: NaN
Mean: NaN
Size: 0

cmd:
```

Listing 6.7   **DataSetTester.java**

```
1.  // DataSet demonstration program
2.  import java.io.*;
3.
4.  public class DataSetTester {
5.     public static void main(String[] args) throws IOException {
6.        DataSet dataset = new DataSet("age.txt");
7.        System.out.println();
8.        System.out.println("Minimum: " + dataset.getMinimum());
9.        System.out.println("Maximum: " + dataset.getMaximum());
10.       System.out.println("Mean: " + dataset.getAverage());
11.       System.out.println("Size: " + dataset.getSize());
12.       System.out.println();
13.       dataset.clear();
14.       dataset.load("stature.txt");
15.       System.out.println("Minimum: " + dataset.getMinimum());
16.       System.out.println("Maximum: " + dataset.getMaximum());
17.       System.out.println("Mean: " + dataset.getAverage());
18.       System.out.println("Size: " + dataset.getSize());
19.       System.out.println();
20.       dataset.clear();
21.       dataset.load("foot-length.txt");
22.       System.out.println("Minimum: " + dataset.getMinimum());
23.       System.out.println("Maximum: " + dataset.getMaximum());
24.       System.out.println("Mean: " + dataset.getAverage());
25.       System.out.println("Size: " + dataset.getSize());
26.       System.out.println();
27.       dataset.clear();
28.       System.out.println("Minimum: " + dataset.getMinimum());
29.       System.out.println("Maximum: " + dataset.getMaximum());
30.       System.out.println("Mean: " + dataset.getAverage());
31.       System.out.println("Size: " + dataset.getSize());
32.       System.out.println();
33.    }
34. }
```

Because method `main()` of `DataSetTester.java` uses the `DataSet` specific constructor which throws an `IOException` if a bad filename is used, method `main()` can potentially throw `IOException`. Therefore, its definition specifies this possibility.

```
public class DataSetTester {
   public static void main(String[] args) throws IOException {
      ...
   }
}
```

IMPLEMENTATION

A straightforward implementation of `DataSet` is given in Listing 6.8. For example, the default constructor can be implemented by simply invoking method `clear()`.

```
// DataSet(): default constructor
public DataSet() {
   clear();
}
```

Listing 6.8 *DataSet.java*

```java
1.   // Data set summary representation
2.   import java.util.*;
3.   import java.io.*;
4.
5.   public class DataSet {
6.       // instance variables
7.       private int n;
8.       private double xSum;
9.       private double minimumValue;
10.      private double maximumValue;
11.
12.      // DataSet(): default constructor
13.      public DataSet() {
14.         clear();
15.      }
16.
17.      // DataSet(): specific constructor
18.      public DataSet(String s) throws IOException {
19.         load(s);
20.      }
21.
22.      // clear(): empties the data set
23.      public void clear() {
24.         n = 0;
25.         xSum = 0;
26.         minimumValue = Double.NaN;
27.         maximumValue = Double.NaN;
28.      }
29.
30.      // load(): adds the values from the file to set
31.      public void load(String s) throws IOException {
32.         // get a scanner for the file
33.         Scanner fileIn = new Scanner(new File (s));
34.
35.         // add values one by one
36.         while (fileIn.hasNextDouble()) {
37.            double x = fileIn.nextDouble();
38.            addValue(x);
39.         }
40.      }
41.
42.      // addValue(): adds the value to the set
43.      public void addValue(double x) {
44.         xSum += x;
45.         ++n;
46.         if (n == 1) {
47.            minimumValue = maximumValue = x;
48.         }
49.         else if (x < minimumValue) {
50.            minimumValue = x;
51.         }
52.         else if (x > maximumValue) {
53.            maximumValue = x;
54.         }
```

Listing 6.8   *DataSet.java (Continued)*

```
55.    }
56.
57.    // getAverage(): compute data set average
58.    public double getAverage() {
59.       if (n == 0) {
60.          return Double.NaN;
61.       }
62.       else {
63.          return xSum / n;
64.       }
65.    }
66.
67.    // getMinimum(): produce minimum data set value
68.    public double getMinimum() {
69.       return minimumValue;
70.    }
71.
72.    // getMaximum(): produce maximum data set value
73.    public double getMaximum() {
74.       return maximumValue;
75.    }
76.
77.    // getSize(): produce data set size
78.    public int getSize() {
79.       return n;
80.    }
81. }
```

Similarly, the specific constructor can be implemented by simply invoking method load().

```
// DataSet(): specific constructor
public DataSet(String s) throws IOException {
    load(s);
}
```

Because method load() throws an IOException if a bad filename is used, the specific constructor must indicate that it too can potentially throw an IOException.

Method clear() has the task of setting the representation to that of an empty data set. The task is accomplished by setting all of the instance variables to appropriate values. In particular, the size n of the data set is set to 0. Because there are no associated values for the data set, the sum of the values xSum is set to 0. Lastly, minimumValue and maximumValue are set to Double.NaN because there is no minimum or maximum value associated with an empty data set. (See Section 2.4 for a discussion of class Double class constants.)

```
// clear(): empties the data set
public void clear() {
    n = 0;
    xSum = 0;
    minimumValue = Double.NaN;
    maximumValue = Double.NaN;
}
```

Method `load()` uses its parameter s to create a `Scanner` associated with the file whose name is s. Because method `load()` throws an `IOException` if a bad filename is specified, its definition indicates this possibility.

```
// load(): adds the values from the file to set
public void load(String s) throws IOException {
    // get a scanner for the file
    Scanner fileIn = new Scanner(new File(s));

    // add values one by one
    while (fileIn.hasNextDouble()) {
        double x = fileIn.nextDouble();
        addValue(x);
    }
}
```

In the definition of method `load()`, the parameter to its invocation of the `Scanner` constructor is a new `File`, which is associated with filename s. We chose to create the `Scanner` this way rather than in the following manner.

```
File file = new File(s);
Scanner fileIn = new Scanner(file);
```

We did so because there is no need for variable `file` after the creation of the `Scanner`.

The values in the file are extracted one at a time with each value in turn being added to the data set. The values are added using method `addValue()`. Thus, this processing is very similar to the processing by `FileLister.java` of Listing 6.5 and `FileAverage.java` of Listing 6.6.

Method `addValue()` processes a new value x to be associated with the data set,

```
// addValue(): adds the value to the set
public void addValue(double x) {
    xSum += x;
    ++n;
    if (n == 1) {
        minimumValue = maximumValue = x;
    }
    else if (x < minimumValue) {
        minimumValue = x;
    }
    else if (x > maximumValue) {
        maximumValue = x;
    }
}
```

First, the new value is added to the sum variable xSum. In addition, the size n of the data set is incremented by 1.

Case analysis determines whether `minimumValue` or `maximumValue` requires updating. If the data set consists currently of a single value, then that value is both the minimum and the maximum value of the data set.

```
if (n == 1) {
    minimumValue = maximumValue = x;
}
```

Otherwise, the data set has more than one value and the new value may be smaller than the minimum. If it is smaller than the minimum, its value is now the minimum value of the data set.

```
else if (x < minimumValue) {
    minimumValue = x;
}
```

If it is not smaller than the minimum, it may be larger than the maximum. If it is larger than the maximum, its value is now the maximum value of the data set.

```
else if (x > maximumValue) {
    maximumValue = x;
}
```

Otherwise, there is no change in the minimum or maximum values of the data set.

The remaining member methods are sufficiently simple to warrant no further analysis.

TESTING

By comparing the results produced by program `DataSetTester.java` of Listing 6.7 to the published results for those three standard data sets, we develop confidence in the correctness of class `DataSet`. To further increase the level of confidence, additional data sets should be constructed and their results analyzed. These data sets should ensure that every statement is executed.

This discussion completes our introduction to iteration. In Chapter 7 we consider many of the nuances of method and class design in Java.

6.7   REVIEW

- The **while** statement has form

    while (*Expression*) *Action*

    When a **while** statement is executed, its test expression is evaluated first. If the expression evaluates to **true**, its body is executed, where the body is the action of the **while** statement. The evaluation process then is repeated. If the expression reevaluates to **true**, the body is executed again. This process is called looping, and it continues until the test expression evaluates to **false**. At that point, execution continues with the next statement in the program.

- If a **while** test expression initially evaluates to false, then its **while** body is never executed.

- The **for** statement has form

    for (*ForInit* ; *ForExpression* ; *ForUpdate*) *Action*

    The **for** initialization step is performed only once—at the start of the execution of the loop. Next, the test expression is evaluated. If the test expression is initially **false**, then execution immediately continues with the next statement in the program. If the expression is **true**, the body of the loop is executed and then the update step is performed. The update step is permitted to be an assignment, method invocation, or omitted. The test expression then is reevaluated. If the expression is again **true**, the execution of the loop body and update step is iterated. This process continues until the test expression evaluates to **false**. Execution then continues with the next statement in the program.

- The **do-while** has form

    do *Action* ; **while** (*Expression*)

    A **do-while** loop begins by executing its action. Afterward, the test expression is evaluated. If the test expression evaluates to **true**, then the action is repeated. This process continues until the test expression evaluates to **false**.

- Use a **while** loop when the action can occur zero or more times; use a **do-while** loop when the action can occur one or more times.

- It is important when you design a loop that you understand its purpose and its effects on other parts of the program.

- A loop whose test expression never evaluates to false is known as an infinite loop. Such loops continue to execute until some operating system command eventually terminates them.

- A common pitfall is writing a loop that never executes because the initialization work is incorrect.

- An off-by-one error occurs when the index variable for the loop is either not initialized properly (e.g., starting with a value of 1 when a value of 0 is needed) or where the test expression allows the body of the loop to iterate one time too many.

- Class Scanner provides several "has" methods. Besides hasNext(), the other principal ones are hasNextInt(), hasNextDouble(), hasNextBoolean(), hasNextLong(), hasNextShort(), and hasNextFloat(). These methods report whether the next value is of the desired form.

- The System class provides output stream System.err. Programs use this stream to display messages regarding abnormal situations.
- A stream is a hardware-independent view of a device.
- A stream view enables a program to issue generic I/O requests on flows of data while being unconcerned about how the requests are to be carried out.
- A file view captures the important physical characteristics of the device. The input/output requests of the stream view are translated automatically by the compiler into file-level specific actions that accomplish the desired requests.
- Java provides several representation for files. Class File provides a system-independent representation of a file name. With a File, a Scanner can be created to provide a text stream view of the file.

6.8 SELF-TEST

S6.1 Implement a program that produces the first n numbers in the Fibonacci sequence, where n is a user-specified integer value. The sequence starts with the following numbers: 1, 1, 2, 3, 5, 8, 13, 21. After the initial two 1s, each number in the sequence is the sum of the two previous numbers. For example, $1 + 1 = 2$, $1 + 2 = 3$, $2 + 3 = 5$, $3 + 5 = 8$, and so on.

S6.2 What is the output of the following code segment?

```
int counter1 = 0;
int counter2 = 0;
int counter3 = 0;
int counter4 = 0;
int counter5 = 0;
for (int i = 0; i < 5; ++i) {
   ++counter1;
   for (int j = 0; j < 10; ++j) {
      ++counter2;
      for (int k = 0; k < 2; ++k) {
         ++counter3;
      }
      ++counter4;
   }
   ++counter5;
}
System.out.println(counter1);
System.out.println(counter2);
System.out.println(counter3);
System.out.println(counter4);
System.out.println(counter5);
```

S6.3 What is the output of the following code segment?

```
int n = 10;
```

```
int i;
for (i = 0; i < n; ) {
    ++n;
    i += 3;
}
System.out.println(i);
```

S6.4 What is the output of the following code segment?

```
int n = 3;
while (n > 0) {
    System.out.println(n);
    --n;
}
int m = 3;
do {
    System.out.println(m);
    --m;
} while (m > 0);
```

6.9   EXERCISES

6.1 Redo `Combination.java` using the following equivalent form of $C(m, n)$.

$$C(m, n) = \frac{m \times (m-1) \times (m-2) \times \ldots \times (n+1)}{(m-n)!}$$

6.2 Geneticists use the symbols A, G, T, and C in writing a DNA sequence. Develop a program that extracts a user-specified DNA sequence and reports whether the sequence is composed of valid symbols.

6.3 Stirling's approximation for $n!$ is

$$n! \approx \sqrt{2\pi n}\left(\frac{n}{e}\right)^n$$

Develop a program that produces a table with m entries for a user-specified value of m. For each value n in the range $1 \ldots m$, the program should report the difference between $n!$ and Stirling's approximation. To calculate a square root use class method `Math.sqrt()`. To calculate a power use class method `Math.pow()`. To approximate π use double constant `Math.PI`. To approximate e use double constant `Math.E`.

6.4 Display prime numbers in the range $1 \ldots n$, where n is a user-specified value. A number i is prime if its only factors are 1 and itself.

6.5 Display perfect numbers in the range $1 \ldots n$, where n is a user-specified value. A number i is perfect if the sum of its factors is i.

6.6 Rearrange the following code segment so that it is indented properly.

```
if ((n > 0) && (m > 0)) { for (int i = 0; i < n;
++i) { for (int j = 0; j < m; ++j) { if (i ! =
j) { System.out.println("0"); } else {
```

```
System.out.println ("1"); } } } } else {
System.out.println("2"); }
```

6.7 Provide a code segment that prompts a user for an extracted positive integer value less than 10 million. The segment then displays the value in words. For example, if the input value is 21, then twenty-one is displayed.

6.8 What is the output of the following code segment?

```
int counter1 = 0;
int counter2 = 0;
int counter3 = 0;
int counter4 = 0;
int counter5 = 0;
for (int i = 0; i < 10; ++i) {
    ++counter1;
    for (int j = 0; j < 10; ++j) {
        ++counter2;
        if (i == j) {
            ++counter3;
        }
        else {
            ++counter4;
        }
    }
    ++counter5;
}
System.out.println(counter1 + " " + counter2 + " "
    + counter3 + " " + counter4 + " " + counter5);
```

6.9 Correct the following code segment so that it displays the number of inputs that are bigger than the first input.

```
Scanner stdin = new Scanner(System.in);
int firstValue = stdin.nextInt();
int sum = 1;
while (stdin.hasNextInt()) {
    int currentValue = stdin.nextInt();
    if (firstValue == currentValue) {
        ++sum;
    }
}
System.out.println(sum);
```

6.10 Provide a code segment that displays the sum of odd integers from 1 to n.

6.11 Provide a code segment that iteratively extracts *n* pairs of integers. For each extracted pair of integers *a* and *b*, the program displays the product $a \times a+1 \times \ldots b$.

6.12 Provide a code segment that displays the sum of integers from a to b.

6.13 Provide a code segment using nested loops that displays a daily calendar of form

```
 9:00
 9:15
 9:30
 9:45
10:00
10:15
```

```
10:30
10:45
...
5:00
```

6.14　Consider the following code segment:

```java
int i = 1;
while (i <= n) {
    if ((i % n) == 0) {
        ++i;
    }
}
System.out.println(i);
```

　a)　What is the output if n is 0?

　b)　What is the output if n is 1?

　c)　What is the output if n is 3?

6.15　Consider the following code segment:

```java
for (i = 0; i < n; ++i) {
    --n;
}
System.out.println(i);
```

　a)　What is the output if n is 0?

　b)　What is the output if n is 1?

　c)　What is the output if n is 3?

　d)　What is the output if n is 4?

6.16　Design and implement a program that counts the number of its inputs from the standard input stream in each of the categories positive, negative, and zero.

6.17　Design and implement a program that extracts values from the standard input stream and then displays the smallest and largest of those values to the standard output stream. The program should display appropriate messages for special cases where there are no inputs and only one input.

6.18　A sequence of numbers is monotonic increasing if the values are in sorted order. For example, 1, 1, 3, 4, 9 is a monotonic sequence, but 1, 3, 2, 4, 9 is not a monotonic sequence because 3 is greater than 2. Design and implement a program that determines whether its input sequence is in monotonic increasing order.

6.19　Design and implement a program that prompts its user for a nonnegative value n. The program then displays as its output:

```
1 2 3 ... n-1 n
1 2 3 ... n-1
...
1 2 3
1 2
1
```

6.20 A character is whitespace if it is a blank (`' '`), a tab (`'\t'`), a newline character (`'\n'`), or a formfeed (`'\f'`). Design and implement a program that counts the number of whitespace characters in standard input.

6.21 Design and implement a program that extracts lines from standard input and then reports the average line length.

6.22 Design and implement a program that prompts a user for a filename. The program verifies that each line in that file starts with a valid telephone number. For example, in the United States, a valid telephone number has syntax:

$D\ D\ D$ `'-'` $D\ D\ D$ `'-'` $D\ D\ D\ D$

where the first D cannot be a zero. For each invalid telephone number, the program should display the corresponding line to the standard error stream.

6.23 Design and implement a program that prompts a user for a filename and string. The program then counts the numbers of occurrences of that string in the specified file.

6.24 Design and implement a program that prompts a user for a filename. The program then displays the number of lines and characters in the file.

6.25 Modify `DataSet.java` so that the class also provides a method for computing the standard deviation of the data set. The formula for the standard deviation s of a data set with mean $\bar{x}$ and values $x_1, x_2, \ldots x_n$, is

$$s = \sqrt{\frac{(x_1 - \bar{x})^2 + (x_2 - \bar{x})^2 + \ldots + (x_n - \bar{x})^2}{n - 1}}$$

It can be shown mathematically that s also equals

$$s = \sqrt{\frac{((x_1 \cdot x_1) + (x_2 \cdot x_2) + \ldots + (x_n \cdot x_n)) - n\bar{x}\bar{x}}{n - 1}}$$

The second formulation is preferred because it means that the standard deviation can be computed knowing only the sum of the values

$$x_1 + x_2 + \ldots + x_n$$

and the sum of the squares of the values

$$(x_1 \cdot x_1) + (x_2 \cdot x_2) + \ldots + (x_n \cdot x_n).$$

6.10   PROGRAMMING PROJECT — FOUR HOBO PROBLEM

The following riddle dates back to the late 19th century. (Its revival is credited to Will Shortz, crossword puzzle editor of the *New York Times*.)

The objective of this case study is to practice using iteration with nested loops in the context of problem solving

PROBLEM STATEMENT

There were once four hoboes traveling across the country. During their journey they ran short on funds, so they stopped at a farm to look for some work. The

farmer said there were 200 hours of work that could be done over the next several weeks. The farmer went on to say that how they divided up the work was up to them. The hoboes agreed to start the next day. The following morning, one of the hoboes—who was markedly smarter and lazier than the other three—said there was no reason for them all to do the same amount of work. This hobo went on to suggest the following scheme: The hoboes would all draw straws. A straw would be marked with a number. The number would indicate both the number of days the drawer must work and the number of hours to be worked on each of those days. For example, if the straw was marked with a 3, the hobo who drew it would work 3 hours a day for 3 days. It goes without saying that the lazy hobo convinced the others to agree to this scheme and that through sleight of hand, the lazy hobo drew the best straw. The riddle is to determine the possible ways to divide up the work according to the preceding scheme.

ANALYSIS AND DESIGN

So what tasks must be accomplished to produce a Java program that solves the four hobo problem? The first task is to recognize what it means to be a possible solution to the problem. Knowing the solution form can give insight on how to generate possible solutions.

A solution to the riddle consists of four positive integer numbers a, b, c, and d such that $a^2 + b^2 + c^2 + d^2 = 200$. The necessity of having four numbers and examining the sum of the squares are *explicit constraints* of the problem.

So what does knowing the solution form tell us? Most importantly, it tells us some limits on the possible values involved in a solution. For one, the values of a, b, c, and d are each at least 1. For another, the values of a, b, c, and d can be at most 200; otherwise, the sum of their squares cannot be equal to 200. In fact, a, b, c, and d can be at most $\lfloor \sqrt{200} \rfloor$; that is, a, b, c, and d can be no bigger than the largest integer whose square is at most 200. That integer is 14. Thus, we know $1 \le a, b, c, d \le 14$. These conditions on a, b, c, and d are *implicit constraints*.

IMPLEMENTATION

You should name your program `FourHobo.java`. The class should be appropriately documented and laid out. For example, the code should make use of program header and method comments, whitespace, and a consistent indentation scheme.

Together the explicit and implicit constraints imply a way to solve the problem: systematically generate all combinations of four numbers, where each of the numbers is from the inclusive interval 1 ... 14, and check for each combination whether it has the property that the squares of the numbers sum to 200. Because there are only $14 \times 14 \times 14 \times 14 = 38{,}416$ such combinations to consider, this task is not too onerous—nested loops to generate the various values for a, b, c, and d with the innermost loop performing the test.

Nested loops, rather than consecutive loops, are the way to go, because for each value of a, we need to consider a collection of possibilities for b, c, and d. And for each sub-combination value of a and b, we need to consider a collection of possibilities for c and d. And for each subcombination value of a, b, and c, we need to consider a collection of values for d.

As we stated before 38,416 combinations is not an excessive number of combinations to consider. However, among the 38,416 combinations there are effectively many duplicates. For example, the combination ($a = 1$, $b = 1$, $c = 2$, $d = 2$) is equivalent to combinations (1, 2, 1, 2), (1, 2, 2, 1), (2, 1, 1, 2), (2, 1, 2, 1), and (2, 2, 1, 1). They all represent incorrect solutions of two straws of length 1 and two straws of length 2.

There are, in fact, 1,214 unique combinations. This number is significantly less than 38,416, so it is worthwhile to generate only the unique combinations. An easy way to ensure no duplications is to generate the combinations in ascending order. As a result, each generated combination will have the property that $a \leq b \leq c \leq d$.

TESTING

Testing for this problem can be rather complete. It should be possible to verify that all 1,214 unique combinations are generated. Furthermore, among puzzle solvers it is well known that there are only two unique combinations where $a^2 + b^2 + c^2 + d^2 = 200$. And if we assume the lazy hobo is both smart and dishonest, then one solution is preferred.

6.11	**SELF-TEST ANSWERS**

S6.1 `Fibonacci.java`

```java
import java.util.*;

public class Fibonacci {
    public static void main(String[] args)
    {
        Scanner stdin = new Scanner(System.in);

        System.out.print("Number of Fibonacci values: ");
        int n = stdin.nextInt();

        if ( n < 1 ) {
            System.out.println(n + ": illegal size");
        }
        else if ( n == 1 ) {
            System.out.println("1    1");
        }
```

```
            else {
                System.out.println("1    1");
                System.out.println("2    1");

                int prev1 = 1;
                int prev2 = 1;

                for (int i = 3; i <= n; ++i) {
                    int curr = prev1 + prev2;
                    System.out.println(i + "    " + curr);
                    prev2 = prev1;
                    prev1 = curr;
                }
            }
        }
    }
```

S6.2 The output is

```
5
50
100
50
5
```

S6.3 The output is

```
15
```

S6.4 The output is

```
3
2
1
3
2
1
```

I GUI–BASED PROGRAMMING

Graphical user interface–based programming is the dominant model in real-world programming. Its importance makes it imperative that all programmers have a basic familiarity with its concepts. This chapter provides a gentle introduction to graphical user interfaces (GUIs) by exploring the design and development of a windchill calculator. The program uses many of the major graphical elements of the Java packages `awt` and `swing`.

OBJECTIVES

- To introduce the awt and swing packages.
  - To introduce graphical user interfaces and event-driven programming.
    - To manipulate containers and components to build effective interfaces.
    - To demonstrate the purpose of a layout manager for organizing the placement of GUI components within a container.
  - To build containers similar in form to desktop windows.
- To gain practice manipulating and configuring labels and data entry areas.
- To develop action listeners and performers for GUI events such as button clicking.

G1.1 **GUI AND EVENT-DRIVEN PROGRAMMING**

Users prefer graphical user interface–based programs over console-based programs. Studies indicate that users find graphical user interfaces (GUIs) intuitively easier to use. The GUI ease of functionality comes at a programming price—GUI-based programs are more complex in their structure than console-based programs. This trade-off is illustrated in Figure G1.1.

Figure G1.1 **The trade-off between ease of use and software complexity.**

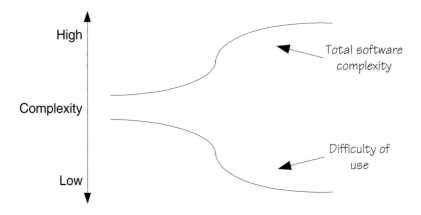

Despite the complexity of GUI programming, its dominance in real-world software development makes it imperative that GUI programming be considered even in an introductory text.

Our first example of a GUI is a program that calculates the *windchill* temperature for a user-specified temperature and windspeed. Windchill temperature is the temperature

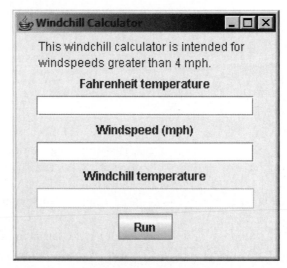

perceived by a person when taking into account the actual temperature and the wind-speed.

In terms of calculation complexity, a windchill GUI program is equivalent to the body mass index program `BMICalculator.java` of Listing 2.10. However, a windchill GUI program has other complexities. In addition to the values for performing the computation, there are also the objects that comprise the GUI. Our windchill calculator GUI has nine major graphical components: a window, a legend, three data labels, three data areas, and a run button. For a console-based windchill calculator, none of these components are present.

Besides having more objects to consider, a GUI program also has to deal with the interactions of its graphical components. For example, *whenever* a user clicks the wind-chill calculator run button, the button *dispatches* a signal. The GUI must have a *listener* for that signal that causes the current temperature and windspeed data entry values to be obtained, the windchill temperature to be calculated, and the result of that computation to be assigned to the windchill temperature entry area.

Java GUI-based programming typically makes use of the `swing` API. The `swing` API provides over 40 different types of graphical components and 250 classes to support the use of these components.

> Definitions of many swing components are available in Appendix E. For complete documentation see www.javasoft.com

In creating a GUI, the following `swing` classes are particularly useful:

`JFrame`
> Represents a titled, bordered window.

`JTextArea`
> Represents an editable multiline text entry component.

`JLabel`
> Represents a display area suitable for one or both of a single-line text or image.

`JTextField`
> Represents an editable single-line text entry component.

`JButton`
> Represents a push button.

Figure G1.2 illustrates the use of these classes in the windchill calculator GUI. The window containing the GUI has two major elements: a *title bar* that provides the functionality and a *content pane* that contains the GUI components. A detailed discussion of the classes representing these window elements and GUI components occurs in the next sections.

Besides having a different look and feel from console-based programs, GUI-based programs follow a different program execution paradigm—*event-driven programming*.

A comparison of the *flow of control* (program execution) of a console-based program to a GUI-based program shows similarities and differences. A console program begins and ends in its method `main()`. To solve the intended problem, the method `main()` statements are executed in order. After the last statement in `main()` executes, the program terminates.

The execution of a GUI-based program also begins in its method `main()`. However, method `main()` is responsible normally only for creating an *instance* (object) of the GUI.

Figure G1.2 **GUI with swing components annotated.**

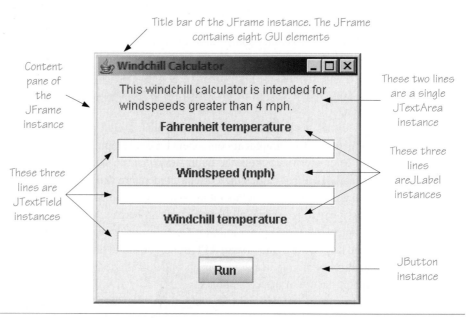

After creating the GUI, the flow of control goes from method main() to an *event-dispatching loop* that checks repeatedly for user interactions with the GUI (i.e., *action events*). When an action event occurs, an *action performer* method is invoked for each *listener* of that event. The performer then processes the interaction. After the performer *handles* the event, flow of control is given again to the event-dispatching loop to watch for future user interactions. This process continues until an action performer signals that the program has completed its task. The execution process is illustrated in Figure G1.3.

GUI-based programs typically have at least three methods. One method is the class method main() that defines an instance of the GUI. The creation of that object is accomplished by invoking a constructor that creates and initializes the components of the GUI. The constructor also registers any event listeners that handle any program-specific responses to user interactions.

The third method is an action performer instance method that processes the events of interest. For many GUIs there is a separate listener-performer object for each of the major components of the GUI. An action performer is always a **public** instance method with name actionPerformed().

GUI-based programs also have instance variables for representing the graphical components and the values necessary for its task. Thus, a GUI is a true object. Once constructed, a GUI has attributes and behaviors. The attributes are the graphical component instance variables and the behaviors are the actions taken by the GUI when events occur.

We now proceed with the development of windchill calculator program Windchill.java.

Figure G1.3 GUI and console-based execution process.

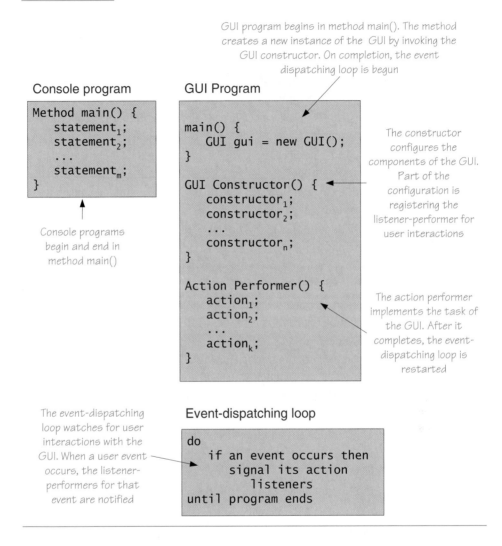

GUI program begins in method main(). The method creates a new instance of the GUI by invoking the GUI constructor. On completion, the event dispatching loop is begun

Console program

```
Method main() {
    statement₁;
    statement₂;
    ...
    statementₘ;
}
```

Console programs begin and end in method main()

GUI Program

```
main() {
    GUI gui = new GUI();
}

GUI Constructor() {
    constructor₁;
    constructor₂;
    ...
    constructorₙ;
}

Action Performer() {
    action₁;
    action₂;
    ...
    actionₖ;
}
```

The constructor configures the components of the GUI. Part of the configuration is registering the listener-performer for user interactions

The action performer implements the task of the GUI. After it completes, the event-dispatching loop is restarted

The event-dispatching loop watches for user interactions with the GUI. When a user event occurs, the listener-performers for that event are notified

Event-dispatching loop

```
do
    if an event occurs then
        signal its action
            listeners
until program ends
```

G1.2 WINDCHILL CALCULATOR

There are several formulas for calculating the windchill temperature t_{wc}. The one used by program `Windchill.java` is provided by the U.S. National Weather Service and is applicable for a windspeed greater than four miles per hour.

$$t_{wc} = 0.081(t - 91.4)(3.71\sqrt{v} + 5.81 - 0.25v) + 91.4$$

In this formula, variable t is the Fahrenheit temperature and variable v is the windspeed in miles per hour.

A `Windchill` GUI object has nine attributes and therefore nine instance variables. These variables are

- `window`: references a `JFrame` representing the window containing the other components of the GUI;

- `legendArea`: references a `JTextArea` representing the multiline program legend;

- `fahrTag`: references a `JLabel` representing the label for the data entry area supplying the temperature;

- `fahrText`: references a `JTextField` representing the data entry area supplying the temperature;

- `windTag`: references a `JLabel` representing the label for the data entry area supplying the windspeed;

- `windText`: references a `JTextField` representing the data entry area supplying the windspeed;

- `chillTag`: references a `JLabel` representing the label for the entry area giving the windchill;

- `chillText`: references a `JTextField` representing the entry area giving the windchill;

- `runButton`: references a `JButton` representing the button that signals a windchill calculation request.

In addition to these instance variables, the `Windchill` class also defines the following *class constants*. Class constants are common values to which all objects of the class *share* access.

> Class constants are considered in detail in Chapter 7.

- `WINDOW_WIDTH`: an **int** value giving the initial width of the GUI;

- `WINDOW_HEIGHT`: an **int** value giving the initial height of the GUI;

- `TEXT_WIDTH`: an **int** value giving the width of the text entry area and the text display;

- `LEGEND`: reference to the `String` representation of the program legend;

- `LAYOUT_STYLE`: reference to a `FlowLayout` that manages the layout of the GUI components within the window. In particular, a `FlowLayout` manager arranges the GUI components in a top-to-bottom, left-to-right manner in the order that they are added to the window.

The definition of program `Windchill.java` in Listing 1.1 is markedly different from our previous program definitions. The differences are apparent from the start of the `Windchill` class definition (line 7).

```
public class Windchill implements ActionListener {
```

The keyword indicates that the class will implement some interface specifications

ActionListener requires a method actionPerformed() be implemented for handling GUI action events

Listing G1.1 **Windchill.java**

```java
1.  // Windchill GUI
2.
3.  import javax.swing.*;
4.  import java.awt.*;
5.  import java.awt.event.*;
6.
7.  public class Windchill implements ActionListener {
8.     // class constants
9.     private static final int WINDOW_WIDTH = 275;   // pixels
10.    private static final int WINDOW_HEIGHT = 250;  // pixels
11.    private static final int TEXT_WIDTH = 20;      // characters
12.
13.    private static final FlowLayout LAYOUT_STYLE =
14.       new FlowLayout();
15.
16.    private static final String LEGEND = "This windchill "
17.       + "calculator is intended for velocities greater than 4 mph.";
18.
19.    // instance variables
20.
21.    // window for GUI
22.    private JFrame window = new JFrame("Windchill Calculator");
23.
24.    // legend
25.    private JTextArea legendArea = new JTextArea(LEGEND, 2,
26.       TEXT_WIDTH);
27.
28.    // user entry area for temperature
29.    private JLabel fahrTag = new JLabel("Fahrenheit temperature");
30.    private JTextField fahrText = new JTextField(TEXT_WIDTH);
31.
32.    // user entry area for windspeed
33.    private JLabel windTag = new JLabel("Windspeed (mph)");
34.    private JTextField windText = new JTextField(TEXT_WIDTH);
35.
36.    // entry area for windchill result
37.    private JLabel chillTag = new JLabel("Windchill temperature");
38.    private JTextField chillText = new JTextField(TEXT_WIDTH);
39.
40.    // run button
41.    private JButton runButton = new JButton("Run");
42.
43.    // Windchill(): constructor
44.    public Windchill() {
45.       // configure GUI
46.       window.setSize(WINDOW_WIDTH, WINDOW_HEIGHT);
47.       window.setDefaultCloseOperation(JFrame.EXIT_ON_CLOSE);
48.
49.       legendArea.setEditable(false);
50.       legendArea.setLineWrap(true);
51.       legendArea.setWrapStyleWord(true);
52.       legendArea.setBackground(window.getBackground());
53.
54.       chillText.setEditable(false);
```

Listing G1.1 **Windchill.java (Continued)**

```
55.          chillText.setBackground(Color.WHITE);
56.
57.          // register event listener
58.          runButton.addActionListener(this);
59.
60.          // arrange components in GUI
61.          window.setLayout(LAYOUT_STYLE);
62.          window.add(legendArea);
63.          window.add(fahrTag);
64.          window.add(fahrText);
65.          window.add(windTag);
66.          window.add(windText);
67.          window.add(chillTag);
68.          window.add(chillText);
69.          window.add(runButton);
70.
71.          // display GUI
72.          window.setVisible(true);
73.       }
74.
75.       // actionPerformed(): run button action event handler
76.       public void actionPerformed(ActionEvent e) {
77.          // get user's responses
78.          String response1 = fahrText.getText();
79.          double t = Double.parseDouble(response1);
80.          String response2 = windText.getText();
81.          double v = Double.parseDouble(response2);
82.
83.          // compute windchill
84.          double windchillTemperature = 0.081 * (t - 91.4)
85.                  * (3.71*Math.sqrt(v) + 5.81 - 0.25*v) + 91.4;
86.
87.          int perceivedTemperature =
88.              (int) Math.round(windchillTemperature);
89.
90.          // display windchill
91.          String output = String.valueOf(perceivedTemperature);
92.          chillText.setText(output);
93.       }
94.
95.       // main(): application entry point
96.       public static void main(String[] args) {
97.          Windchill gui = new Windchill();
98.       }
99.   }
```

Keyword **implements** indicates that the class definition satisfies the specifications of the *interfaces* that follow the keyword. Informally, an interface is a template describing features of a class. Java requires that action performers for GUI events implement the ActionListener interface.

Interfaces are discussed in Chapter 9

Most events are handled directly by the GUI component with which the user interacts (e.g., a JTextField object handles the entering and editing of data in its text box). How-

Figure G1.4 **Run button action-event processing.**

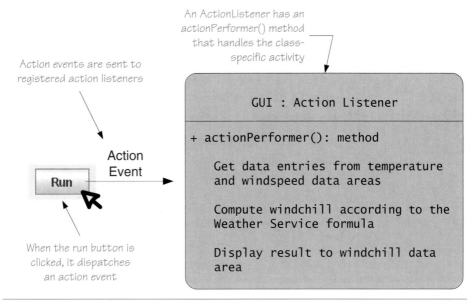

ever, an application-specific response is needed for a run-button event—the event must initiate the computing and displaying of the windchill. To define its response for that event, class `Windchill` implements the **ActionListener** interface. Figure G1.4 illustrates the `Windchill` event-handling process.

The `Windchill` class definition has four sections. The first section, lines 8–41, specifies a collection of **private** class constants and instance variables that are used elsewhere in the definition.

The second section, lines 43–73, defines the `Windchill` default constructor. The constructor configures the instance variable GUI components so that they are ready to perform the windchill computation upon user request.

The third section, lines 75–93, defines the event handler method `actionPerformed()`. Implementing this event handling method is the only requirement of the `ActionListener` interface. The interface requires the method have the form

```
public void actionPerformed(ActionEvent e)
```

where class `ActionEvent` is part of standard package `java.awt.event`. The `Action-Event` class is the basis for representing all `swing` windowing events.

The fourth section, lines 95–98, defines method `main()`, the application program's entry point. With GUI-based programs, method `main()` often is trivial to implement. For example, in this program it defines only a new instance of the class's GUI.

```
Windchill gui = new Windchill();
```

We now discuss each of the four sections in turn.

G1.2.1   CLASS CONSTANTS AND INSTANCE VARIABLES

The class constants and instance variables section begins with the definitions of five constants. The constants are used in configuring the various components of the windchill GUI. The indication that the five definitions are specifying class constants is their use of modifiers **final** and **static**. Modifier **final** indicates a constant is being defined; modifier **static** indicates that the element is common to the entire class rather than to just an individual object.

Constants WINDOW_WIDTH and WINDOW_HEIGHT are the initial dimensions of the GUI. Constant TEXT_WIDTH is the width of the legend and the text boxes for the inputs and output of the windchill computation.

```
// class constants
private static final int WINDOW_WIDTH = 350;    // pixels
private static final int WINDOW_HEIGHT = 185;   // pixels
private static final int TEXT_WIDTH = 20;        // characters
```

FlowLayout constant LAYOUT_STYLE describes how the components of the GUI are to be arranged in the window. In particular, a FlowLayout manager arranges GUI components in a top-to-bottom, left-to-right manner in the order that they are added to the window.

```
private static final FlowLayout LAYOUT_STYLE =
    FlowLayout();
```

Figure G1.5 shows that if the width of the JFrame is increased, the GUI components flow upward to fill the available space.

Figure G1.5   **Increased window width causes component rearrangement.**

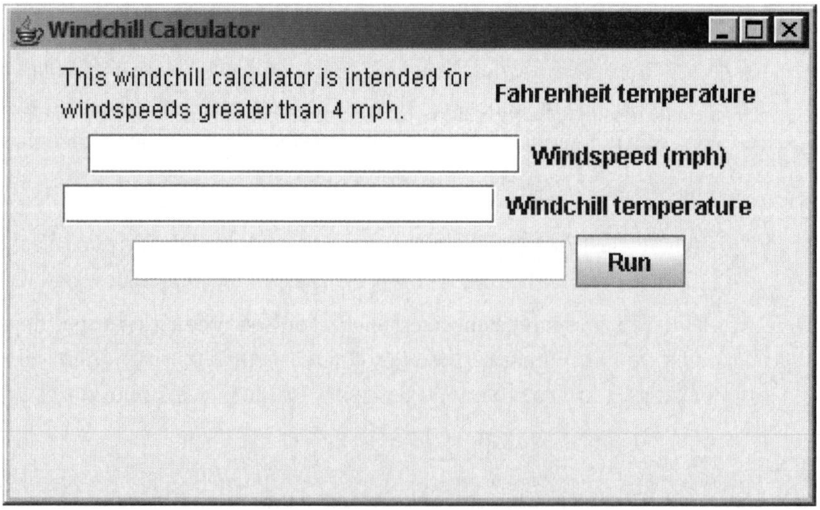

Figure G1.6 **Windchill GUI in the absence of a layout manager.**

If a window does not specify a layout manager, then the last component added to the window occupies the entire window. Figure G1.6 demonstrates how the windchill GUI would look if no layout manager was specified.

The last constant definition is for `String` constant `LEGEND` representing the text of the program legend.

```
private static final String LEGEND = "This windchill "
    + " calculator is intended for velocities greater than 4 mph."
```

Following the class constants come the instance variables definitions. The definitions initialize the instance variables of each new `Windchill` GUI object. Each `Windchill` GUI object has its own copy of the instance variables.

The first instance variable is the `JFrame` variable `window`. A `JFrame` acts as a *container* that holds the components of the GUI. A `JFrame` is similar in form to the other windows on your desktop (e.g, it has a frame and title bar) and can be manipulated like other windows (e.g., minimized, maximized, and moved).

Variable `window` references a new `JFrame` window object. The `JFrame` constructor titles the new window using its `String` parameter `"Windchill Calculator"`.

```
// window for GUI
private JFrame window = new JFrame("Windchill Calculator");
```

The second instance variable is `legendArea`. It references a new `JTextArea` object that acts as a multiline text box. The `JTextArea` constructor creating the object takes three parameters.

```
// legend
private JTextArea legendArea = new JTextArea(LEGEND, 2,
    TEXT_WIDTH);
```

The first parameter is the string to be displayed in its text box, which in this case is the String referenced by LEGEND. The second and third parameters are the dimensions of the new text box—the number of lines and the approximate number of characters per line. For legendArea, its JTextArea is a two-line text box that displays TEXT_WIDTH characters per line.

There is a pair of instance variables associated with each of the following: the input temperature, the input windspeed, and the windchill output. Each pair defines two new objects—a JLabel and a JTextField. The label clues the user on what information is needed or supplied, and the text entry area serves as the conduit between the user and the program.

For example, variable fahrTag references a new JLabel object whose label signals the user to supply the temperature of interest and variable fahrText references a new JTextField object that provides the text box in which the user enters that temperature.

```
// user entry area for temperature
private JLabel fahrTag = new JLabel("Fahrenheit temperature");
private JTextField fahrText = new JTextField(TEXT_WIDTH);
```

The label is produced using a JLabel constructor. The constructor uses its String parameter "Fahrenheit temperature" to set the text of its new label. The text entry area is produced using a JTextField constructor. This constructor uses its **int** parameter TEXT_WIDTH for the width of its new text box.

The text that makes up a JLabel is noneditable by the program user. However, the text fields of a JTextArea or JTextField are user-editable by default.

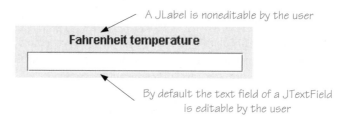

A JLabel is noneditable by the user

Fahrenheit temperature

By default the text field of a JTextField is editable by the user

The objects referenced by variables windTag and windText enable the user to supply the windspeed of interest. The objects referenced by variables chillTag and chillText provide the means for displaying the result of a windchill request.

```
// user entry area for windspeed
private JLabel windTag = new JLabel("Windspeed (mph)");
private JTextField windText = new JTextField(TEXT_WIDTH);

// entry area for windchill result
private JLabel chillTag = new JLabel("Windchill temperature");
private JTextField chillText = new JTextField(TEXT_WIDTH);
```

The last of the instance variables is runButton.

```
// run button
private JButton runButton = new JButton("Run");
```

Variable `runButton` references a new `JButton` object. The `JButton` constructor creating the object expects a single parameter that specifies the button's label. In this case, the new button has the label `"Run"`.

With these class constants and instance variables, the `Windchill` default constructor configures and displays the GUI so that whenever its run button is clicked, the `action-Performed()` method first accesses the entry areas that are referenced by `fahrText` and `windText` so that it can compute the associated windchill. Method `actionPerformed()` then displays the windchill in the entry area referenced by `chillText`.

We now turn our attention to `Windchill` default constructor `Windchill()`.

GI.2.2   GUI CONSTRUCTION

When a constructor begins execution, it configures, as necessary, the newly initialized copies of the instance variables for the object under construction. For the `Windchill` GUI, all nine instance variables require manipulation.

The `Windchill` constructor begins by sizing the window that will hold the GUI. For this purpose, the `Windchill` constructor signals the window through `JFrame` instance method `setSize()`. Method `setSize()` expects two parameters giving the width and height of the new window in pixels.

```
window.setSize(WINDOW_WIDTH, WINDOW_HEIGHT);
```

The constructor then configures the program to terminate when the window closes. It does so by invoking `JFrame` instance method `setDefaultCloseOperation()`.

```
window.setDefaultCloseOperation(JFrame.EXIT_ON_CLOSE);
```

The parameter `JFrame.EXIT_ON_CLOSE` is a `JFrame` class constant whose value indicates that the program is to be terminated when this `JFrame` is closed.

The legend for the GUI then is configured. Variable `legendArea` is associated with the `JTextArea` object that holds the program's legend. Because the user should not be allowed to alter the warning, the `JTextArea` object is signaled through its instance method `setEditable()` to make its text field *noneditable*.

```
legendArea.setEditable(false);
```

Method `setEditable()` expects a single **boolean** value as its parameter. The **boolean** value **false** indicates that the text field of the `JTextArea` is noneditable; the **boolean** value **true** indicates that the text field is editable. Figure G1.7 illustrates why a legend should be made noneditable.

The other configuring done with `legendArea` ensures that the legend is displayed properly within its entry area. By default, a `JTextArea` object does not wrap its text. To signal that wrapping is desired, its method `setLineWrap()` is invoked.

```
legendArea.setLineWrap(true);
```

Figure G1.7   **Dangers of an editable legend.**

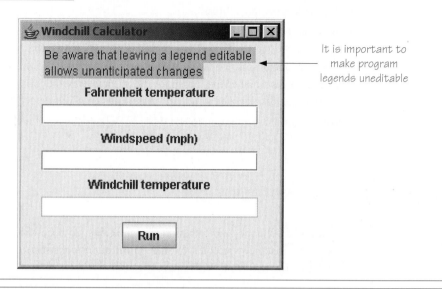

It is important to make program legends uneditable

Figure G1.8   **Bad line wrapping.**

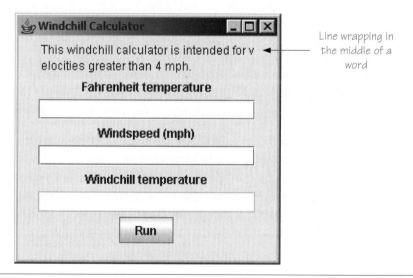

Line wrapping in the middle of a word

Method `setLineWrap()` expects a single **boolean** value as its parameter. The value **false** indicates that its text is not to be wrapped; a value of **true** indicates that its text is to be wrapped.

Simply requesting line wrapping is insufficient. The default line wrapping style is to break up text only when a text-field line is completely full. This style can cause a word to split over two lines (see Figure G1.8).

Abstract Window Toolkit

The package `java.awt` (*Abstract Window Toolkit*) was a solid first attempt at providing a portable graphics library for user interfaces. Because `awt` components generally require more work by the operating system than their `javax.swing` counterparts require, Java programmers tend to look to `swing` for graphical components. However, the `awt` is used by programmers and by `swing` for such things as color and font representation and drawing.

Definitions of many awt classes are available in Appendix E. For complete documentation go to www.javasoft.com

To ensure line wrapping only at word boundaries, a `JTextArea` object is signaled through its method `setWrapStyleWord()`.

```
legendArea.setWrapStyleWord(true);
```

Method `setWrapStyleWord()` expects a single **boolean** value as its parameter. The value **true** indicates that its text is to be wrapped at word boundaries; the value **false** indicates that its text is to wrapped when a text-field line is full.

The background color of the legend area can be altered to match the background color of the window (the default background color of a `JTextArea` is white). To signal a `JTextArea` background color change, its method `setBackground()` is invoked with a parameter specifying the desired color.

```
legendArea.setBackground(window.getBackground());
```

To match the two background colors, the color of the `JFrame` is obtained using its instance method `getBackground()`.

The `JTextField` associated with `chillText` should be made noneditable—it is the program that supplies the value, not the user.

```
chillText.setEditable(false);
```

The prohibition regarding the editing of the text field applies only to the user and not to the object itself.

Making it noneditable causes Java to change its background color from the standard `JTextField` background color. To override the color change, `JTextField` method `setBackground()` is invoked.

```
chillText.setBackground(Color.WHITE);
```

`Color.WHITE` is a class constant of class `java.awt.Color` representing the color white.

The action performer for a `JButton` then is specified using `JButton` instance method `addActionListener()`.

```
runButton.addActionListener(this);
```

The parameter to `addActionListener()` specifies the object whose method `action-Performed()` processes the clicking of the run button. The object in question is the GUI under construction; that is, it is the object currently being configured by the `Windchill` default constructor method. The parameter to addActionListener() is **this**. Keyword **this** is the Java mechanism for referencing the object being manipulated by a constructor or an instance method.

The arranging of the GUI components within the JFrame has two parts. The first part is a single statement setting the layout manager.

```
window.setLayout(LAYOUT_STYLE);
```

To complete the arrangement, the eight GUI components are added to the content pane portion of window using JFrame method add().

```
window.add(legendArea);
window.add(fahrTag);
window.add(fahrText);
window.add(windTag);
window.add(windText);
window.add(chillTag);
window.add(chillText);
window.add(runButton);
```

Once the configuration is complete, it is appropriate to make the window *visible*. Up until this point, the Windchill constructor has set up the graphical components that make up its interface, but it has not displayed them. To do so, the constructor uses JFrame method setVisible().

```
window.setVisible(true);
```

By default, JTextArea, JLabel, JTextField, and JButton instances are visible once the window in which they have been placed is made visible. Therefore, setting their visibility individually is not necessary. The display completes the construction of the GUI, so the Windchill default constructor is done.

G1.2.3   EVENT HANDLING AND ACTIONPERFORMED()

Implementing the button action performer method actionPerformed() is relatively straightforward. When invoked in response to the user selecting the run button, the performer first gets the user inputs from the text fields associated with JTextField variables fahrText and windText. Method actionPerformed() uses the two values to compute the associated windchill. The windchill value then is used to set the text field associated with variable chillText.

A JTextField has a method getText() that returns a copy of the text in its text field in String form. The String representation can be converted to a numeric representation using Double class method parseDouble(), where class Double is part of package java.lang. Class method parseDouble() expects a String parameter and

Figure GI.9 Depiction of a sample run of Windchill.java

returns a double value. Thus, to initialize a **double** variable t representing the temperature of interest, the Windchill action performer uses code segment

```
// compute windchill
String response1 = fahrText.getText();
double t = Double.parseDouble(response1);
```

For the GUI depicted in Figure G1.9, **double** variable t is initialized to 21.

The action performer uses a similar code segment to initialize a **double** variable v representing the windspeed of interest.

```
String response2 = windText.getText();
double v = Double.parseDouble(response2);
```

For the GUI depicted in Figure G1.9, **double** variable v is initialized to 6.

Given v and t, a **double** variable windchillTemperature can be defined and properly initialized. To translate the windchill formula

$$t_{wc} = 0.081(t - 91.4)(3.71\sqrt{v} + 5.81 - 0.25v) + 91.4$$

into a valid Java expression, a square root is needed. API Math provides a class method sqrt() for calculating square root values. With that method, the translation of the windchill formula can be accomplished.

```
// compute windchill
double windchillTemperature = 0.081 * (t - 91.4)
        * (3.71*Math.sqrt(v) + 5.81 - 0.25*v) + 91.4;
```

Because variable windchillTemperature is a **double** variable, its value can have a significant number of digits after the decimal point. These digits are uninteresting to most users. Therefore, the action performer uses `Math` class method `round()` to produce the integer value closest to `windchillTemperature`.

```
int perceivedTemperature =
    (int) Math.round(windchillTemperature);
```

As method `round()` returns a **long** value, the cast **(int)** converts that value to an **int** value. The cast is necessary because Java does not implicitly narrow a **long** value to an **int** value.

To display the windchill, the action performer converts the **int** value to a `String` representation using the `String` class method `valueOf()`. The method expects a single **int** value as its parameter and returns a `String` version of the number.

```
// display windchill
String output = String.valueOf(perceivedTemperature);
```

The action performer uses that string value as a parameter to `JTextField` method `setText()`. The method updates the text box associated with variable `chillText`. In particular, by invoking

```
chillText.setText(output);
```

the correct windchill output is displayed (e.g., see Figure G1.9).

The displaying of the windchill computation finishes the event handling for the button-clicking event. The program then continues with the event-dispatching loop until another action event occurs or the program is ended.

G1.2.4   METHOD MAIN()

Method `main()` of the `Windchill` program is trivial to implement. The method just defines a new instance of `Windchill`.

```
public static void main(String[] args) {
    Windchill gui = new Windchill();
}
```

No other work is needed, because the constructor handles the building and display of the GUI and the `actionPerformed()` method handles the user interaction.

If desired, method `main()` can be modified to create multiple `Windchill` GUIs. Each of the windchill calculators would be displayed simultaneously.

```
public static void main(String[] args) {
    Windchill gui1 = new Windchill();
    Windchill gui2 = new Windchill();
}
```

This scenario is depicted in Figure G1.10.

This discussion completes our introduction to GUIs.

Figure G1.10 Two instances of the windchill calculator.

G1.3   REVIEW

- The execution of a GUI-based program begins in its method `main()`. Method `main()` is responsible normally only for creating an instance (object) of the GUI. After creating the GUI, the flow of control goes from method `main()` to an event-dispatching loop that checks repeatedly for user interactions with the GUI (action events). When an action event occurs, an action performer method is invoked for each listener of that event. The performer then processes the interaction. After the performer handles the event, flow of control is again given to the event-dispatching loop to watch for future user interactions. The process continues until an action performer signals that the program has completed its task.

- A container is a GUI component that can hold other GUI components.

- A layout manager organizes the placement of GUI components within a container.

- The `awt` class `FlowLayout` arranges the GUI components of a container in a top-to-bottom left-to-right manner in the order that they were added to the container.

- `JFrame` is the `swing` class for representing a window. A `JFrame` is similar in form to the other windows on your desktop and can be manipulated like those other windows.

- A `JFrame` constructor takes a single string as its parameter, which is displayed as the window title.

- A `JFrame` can be displayed by invoking its instance method `setvisible()` with the **boolean** value **true** as its parameter.

- Most `swing` components have an instance method `setBackground()` that expects a `Color` value as its parameter. The value is used to set the background color of the component.

- `JLabel` is the `swing` class for representing a single-line label in a noneditable form.

- One `JLabel` constructor takes a `String` parameter that specifies the text to be displayed. By default, a `JLabel` object is visible once the container in which it has been placed is visible.

- `JTextField` is the `swing` class for representing a single-line text box by which the user can provide input information to the program.

- One `JTextField` constructor takes an **int** parameter that specifies the width of the text box in characters. By default a `JTextField` object is visible once the container in which it has been placed is visible.

- A `JTextArea` is the `swing` class for representing a multiline text box by which the user can provide input information to the program.

- One `JTextArea` constructor takes two **int** parameters. The first parameter is the number of rows of characters for the text box; the second parameter is the width of the text box in characters. By default a `JTextArea` object is visible once the container in which it has been placed is visible.

- `JTextField` and `JTextArea` both have an instance method `setEditable()`. Method `setEditable()` expects a single **boolean** value as its parameter. The value **false** indicates that the text is currently noneditable; a value of **true** indicates that the text is currently editable. By default, the text boxes of a `JTextField` and a `JTextArea` are editable.

- `JButton` is the `swing` class for representing a push button.
- One `JButton` constructor takes a `String` parameter that specifies the button label.
- A `JButton` has an instance method `addActionListener()` for specifying which object is responsible for implementing the action associated with the button. A button click generates an event that causes the indicated object's method `actionPerformed()` to be executed.
- An interface specifies what methods a class must define.
- The `ActionListener` interface requires the implementation of a method `actionPerformed()`. The method takes a parameter of class type `ActionEvent`.
- Objects that handle a button event must implement the `ActionListener` interface.
- `JTextField`, `JLabel`, and `JTextArea` all have an instance method `getText()`. The method returns a `String` that represents the associated object's text.
- `JTextField`, `JLabel`, and `JTextArea` all have an instance method `setText()`. The method expects a single `String` value as a parameter. The value is used to update the associated object's text.

GI.4 SELF-TEST

S1.1 Give a code segment that creates a new `JFrame` with dimensions 200 by 225. When this `JFrame` closes, it should terminate its program.

S1.2 Give a code segment that defines a new `JTextArea` that uses two lines to display the text "Ring around the rosey, a pocketful of posies." The `JTextArea` should not allow line wrapping that breaks up a word.

S1.3 Give a code segment that defines a window with the title `"By any other name"`. The window should contain a label `"Rose"`.

S1.4 Design and implement a program `TemperatureConverter.java` that implements the following GUI.

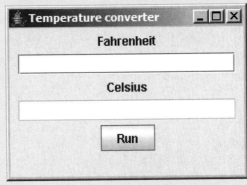

G1.5   EXERCISES

G1.1   Design and implement a program that produces the following window.

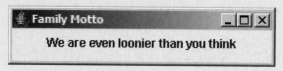

G1.2   Design and implement a program that inputs the weight of an object in pounds and outputs the weight of the object in kilograms. Your program should use a GUI similar to the following.

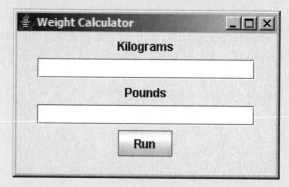

G1.3   Design and implement a program that computes the average of three numbers. Your program should use a GUI similar to the following.

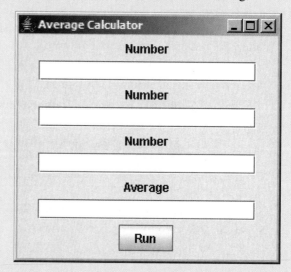

G1.4   Design and implement a GUI program that computes the volume of a requested object described in terms of its mass and density. The mass will be given in grams;

the density will be in grams per cubic centimeter. The relationship of mass, density, and volume of a variable is given by

$$Density = \frac{Mass}{Volume}$$

G1.5 Design and implement a GUI program that gets from its user the distance a train travels in miles and the time it takes to travel that distance. The program should compute and display the average speed of the train for that journey.

G1.6 Design and implement a GUI program that gets from its user a person's age and heart rate. The program computes and displays the number of heart beats since the person was born. Assume that there are 365 days in a year.

G1.7 Design and implement a GUI program that computes the monthly interest charge on a credit card account. The program should acquire the previous balance, the payment amount, the number of days in the billing cycle, the day of the billing cycle the payment was made, and the monthly interest rate. For a formula on credit card interest see Exercise 2.39.

G1.8 Design and implement a GUI program that processes a user-supplied date. The program should display the date's position in that year. For example, if the date is 12 29 2006, then the displayed number is 363.

G1.9 Design and implement a GUI program that processes a value in the interval 0 ... 99. The program displays the value in words. For example, if the input value is 21, then twenty-one is displayed.

G1.10 Design and implement a GUI program that processes two user-specified x- and y-coordinates. The program reports the slope and y-intercept of the associated lines.

G1.11 Design and implement a GUI program that processes two integer values as input. The program displays whether the inputs are both positive, both negative, or one positive and one negative.

G1.12 Design and implement a GUI program that processes a user-specified filename and string. The program displays the numbers of occurrences of that string in the specified file.

G1.13 Design and implement a program that processes a user-specified filename. The program displays the number of lines and characters in the file.

G1.6 PROGRAMMING PROJECT — TRAINING ZONES

There are two kinds of exercise—aerobic and anaerobic exercise. Normally, sustained activities such as bicycling, running, or swimming are aerobic exercises, while activities requiring bursts of activity such as weight lifting and tennis are anaerobic exercises. Both types of exercise have their advantages. For example, anaerobic exercise can stimulate

The object of this programming project is to design and implement a GUI-based program

muscle growth and aerobic exercise can raise your metabolism by stimulating the production of fat-burning enzymes.

For a sustained activity to be an aerobic exercise there needs to be an elevation in the heart rate. However, the elevation cannot be extreme. If the elevation is extreme then muscles are oxygen deprived and they burn sugars rather than fat. Research indicates that there is a heart beat rate training zone that should be kept in order to get the maximum aerobic effect from an exercise. The actual training zone for a person is based on many factors, such as the individual's normal heart rate, fitness, health, weight, etc. However, there are formulas indicating reasonable training zones for the majority of fit people with normal heart rates. The formula we use in this section comes from the USA President's Council on Fitness and Sports (`www.fitness.gov`). The formula works as follows: subtract the age of interest from 220; 65% of that value is the low end of the training zone range and 80% of that value is the high end of the training zone range.

The problem goal is a program that computes a training zone according to the following problem statement.

> *Provide a GUI-based training zone calculator that acquires an age of interest. The calculator then computes and displays the training zone for that age. The low end of the training zone is 65% of the difference between 220 and the specified age. The high end of the training zone is 80% of the difference between 220 and the specified age.*

ANALYSIS AND DESIGN

Before designing the necessary information structures and algorithm, you should depict a sample input/output behavior. A depiction should help clarify what information is being provided and what information is to be computed. Furthermore, if the software is being developed for a client, then it also aids you in verifying with the client that the proper problem is being solved. An example of a possible interface for the training zone calculator is given in Figure G1.11.

An analysis of the problem statement indicates that you need to acquire one piece of information from the user—the age of interest. From that information and the training zone formula you derive the lower and upper heart beat rates for the training zone associated with that age of interest. An analysis of the problem also indicates that in developing an algorithm three integer variables are appropriate: *ageOfInterest*, *lowBeatRate*, and *highBeatRate*. Also, three constants are appropriate: *BASE_RATE* with value 220, *LOW_ZONE_MULTIPLER* with value 65%, and *HIGH_ZONE_MULTIPLIER* with value 80%.

These calculation variables and constants are in addition to the GUI component variables that you decide to use. For the interface displayed in Figure G1.11, variables were used for the window, legend, labels, text fields, and run button.

IMPLEMENTATION

Producing a Java program `TrainingZone.java` from the problem statement can be done nicely with a single class `TrainingZone`. The class should be documented and laid out appropriately. For example, the code should make use of program header and method comments, whitespace, and a consistent indentation scheme.

Figure G1.11 **A possible training zone calculator GUI.**

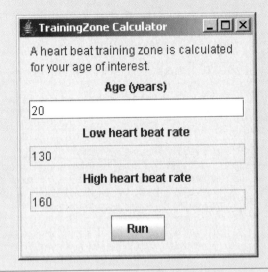

TESTING

One way to test a program informally is to do a *hand-check*—compute by hand what the output should be for several different ages. Then run your program using those same ages and compare the results. If there are any discrepancies, determine whether your program or hand calculation is incorrect. If the program is incorrect, review the formulas given above and your implementation of them. You may also consider adding some debugging statements or using a debugger to display intermediary results in an effort to determine where your program's correctness breaks down.

<table>
<tr><td>G1.7</td><td>**SELF-TEST ANSWERS**</td></tr>
</table>

S1.1 A possible code segment is

```
JFrame window = new JFrame("Window");
window.setSize(WINDOW_WIDTH, WINDOW_HEIGHT);
window.setDefaultCloseOperation(JFrame.EXIT_ON_CLOSE);
```

S1.2 A possible code segment is

```
JTextArea saying = new JTextArea("Ring around the rosey, "
    + "a pocketful of posies.", 2, 25);
saying.setLineWrap(true);
saying.setWrapStyleWord(true);
```

S1.3 A possible code segment is

```
JFrame window = new JFrame("By any other name");
JLabel roseLabel = new JLabel("Rose");
window.setLayout(new FlowLayout())
```

```
                    window.add(roseLabel);
```

S1.4   A possible program is

```java
import javax.swing.*;
import java.awt.*;
import java.awt.event.*;

public class TemperatureConverter implements
    ActionListener {
  private static final int WINDOW_WIDTH = 250;
  private static final int WINDOW_HEIGHT = 175;
  private static final int TEXT_WIDTH = 20;

  private JFrame window
    = new JFrame("Temperature converter");
  private JLabel fahrLabel = new JLabel("Fahrenheit");
  private JLabel celsiusLabel = new JLabel("Celsius");
  private JTextField fahrField
    = new JTextField(TEXT_WIDTH);
  private JTextField celsiusField
    = new JTextField(TEXT_WIDTH);

  private JButton runButton = new JButton("Run");

  public TemperatureConverter () {
    window.setDefaultCloseOperation(
      JFrame.EXIT_ON_CLOSE);
    window.setSize(WINDOW_WIDTH, WINDOW_HEIGHT);
    window.setLayout(new FlowLayout());
    celsiusField.setEditable(false);
    celsiusField.setBackground(Color.WHITE);

    runButton.addActionListener(this);

    window.add(fahrLabel);
    window.add(fahrField);
    window.add(celsiusLabel);
    window.add(celsiusField);
    window.add(runButton);

    window.setVisible(true);
  }

  public void actionPerformed(ActionEvent e) {
    int fahrenheit
      = Integer.parseInt(fahrField.getText());
    double celsius = 5 * (fahrenheit-32) / 9;

    celsiusField.setText(String.valueOf(celsius));
  }

  public static void main(String[] args) {
    TemperatureConverter gui
      = new TemperatureConverter();
  }
}
```

7 PROGRAMMING WITH METHODS AND CLASSES

To assist in the object-oriented design and implementation of software systems, Java provides many different class and method mechanisms. When properly applied, these mechanisms enable designers to produce effective data representations that enable information to be expressed and manipulated in an intuitive manner. This chapter explores Java mechanisms that support the manipulation and calculation of values through method invocations; the use of class and instance variables; and the implementation of constructors, accessors, mutators, and facilitators. The examination begins with the method invocation process.

OBJECTIVES

- Explain the method invocation process.
- Introduce the concepts of locality, scope, and nesting.
- Consider the nuances of method overloading and overriding.
- Explore the use of class methods and class constants and variables through the use of the static modifier.
- Explore the use of instance methods for accessing and manipulating object attributes.

7.1 MODIFIER STATIC

There are two types of methods in Java—instance methods and class methods. An instance method operates on a object (i.e., an *instance* of the class) and a class method is a service provided by a class that is not associated with a particular object.

Both instance and class methods are used in the following code segment.

```
String s = new String("Help every cow reach its potential!");
int n = s.length();   ◄─────────────────── Invoking instance method length()
String t = String.valueOf(n);   ◄───
                                      Invoking class method valueOf()
```

In the code segment, instance method `length()` is invoked with respect to the `String` object referenced by variable `s`. Therefore, when this invocation executes, it is the attributes of the `String` object referenced by `s` that are being examined. Because the length of that `String` is 35, **int** variable n is initialized to 35.

In the same code segment, method `valueOf()` is invoked. Because the invocation expression `String.valueOf(n)` starts with the class name rather than an object, it is clear that `valueOf()` is a class method. `String` class method `valueOf()` provides the service of returning a reference to a `String` representation of its actual parameter. As a result, `String` variable t references a `String` object representing "35".

Besides supporting class methods, Java also supports class variables and class constants. Each class variable or class constant is a common value to which all objects of the class share access. Class variables and class constants represent collective information that is not specific to individual objects of the class. For example, the standard Java package `math` provides the class constant `PI`. The value associated with a class variable or class constant is often referred to as a *class data field*.

Many of the standard Java classes make use of class variables and class constants. Examples include the predefined colors of class `Color` and the mathematical constants of class `Math`.

```
Color favoriteColor = Color.MAGENTA;   ◄───   Accessing Color class
                                              constant MAGENTA
double favoriteNumber = Math.PI - Math.E;   ◄───
                                              Accessing Math class
                                              constants PI and E
```

Because the `Color` and `Math` class constants are **public**, access to those constants is not limited to the respective classes.

In Java, class methods, variables, and constants are specified through the use of the modifier **static**. Examples of class methods and class constants are provided in class `Conversion` of Listing 7.1. We previously gave examples of class methods whenever we defined the method `main()` of an application program.

Class `Conversion` supports conversion between English and metric values. It provides several **public** class methods and **private** class constants that support standard conversions. The class make use of the following equivalencies.

- d degrees Fahrenheit = $(d - 32)/1.8$ degrees Celsius

Listing 7.1   Conversion.java

```
1.  // Conversion methods
2.
3.  public class Conversion {
4.      // conversion equivalencies
5.      private static final double KILOMETERS_PER_MILE = 1.609344;
6.      private static final double LITERS_PER_GALLON = 3.785411784;
7.      private static final double GRAMS_PER_OUNCE = 28.349523125;
8.      private static final double HECTARES_PER_ACRE = 0.40468564;
9.
10.     // temperature conversion methods
11.     public static double fahrenheitToCelsius(double fahrenheit) {
12.         return (fahrenheit - 32) / 1.8;
13.     }
14.
15.     public static double celsiusToFahrenheit(double celsius) {
16.         return 1.8 * celsius + 32;
17.     }
18.
19.     // length conversion methods
20.     public static double kilometersToMiles(double kilometers) {
21.         return kilometers / KILOMETERS_PER_MILE;
22.     }
23.
24.     public static double milesToKilometers(double miles) {
25.         return miles * KILOMETERS_PER_MILE;
26.     }
27.
28.     // mass conversion methods
29.     public static double litersToGallons(double liters) {
30.         return liters / LITERS_PER_GALLON;
31.     }
32.
33.     public static double gallonsToLiters(double gallons) {
34.         return gallons * LITERS_PER_GALLON;
35.     }
36.
37.     public static double gramsToOunces(double grams) {
38.         return grams / GRAMS_PER_OUNCE;
39.     }
40.
41.     public static double ouncesToGrams(double ounces) {
42.         return ounces * GRAMS_PER_OUNCE;
43.     }
44.
45.     // area conversion methods
46.     public static double hectaresToAcres(double hectares) {
47.         return hectares / HECTARES_PER_ACRE;
48.     }
49.
50.     public static double acresToHectares(double acres) {
51.         return acres * HECTARES_PER_ACRE;
52.     }
53. }
```

- 1 mile = 1.609344 kilometers
- 1 gallon = 3.785411784 liters
- 1 ounce (avdp) = 28.349523125 grams
- 1 acre = 0.0015625 square miles = 0.40468564 hectares

Using the provided formula for Fahrenheit to Celsius makes it straightforward to define a temperature conversion method

Modifier public indicates other classes can use the method

Modifier static indicates the method is a class method

```java
public static double fahrenheitToCelsius(double fahrenheit) {
    return (fahrenheit - 32) / 1.8;
}
```

Observe that there is no reference in the method to an attribute of an implicit Conversion object (i.e., a "this" object). This absence is a class method requirement. Class methods are invoked without respect to any particular object

and a complementary temperature conversion method.

```java
public static double celsiusToFahrenheit(double celsius) {
    return 1.8 * celsius + 32;
}
```

To perform the other conversions, class `Conversion` makes use of several constants that it represents as class constants.

```java
private static final double KILOMETERS_PER_MILE = 1.609344;
private static final double LITERS_PER_GALLON = 3.785411784;
private static final double GRAMS_PER_OUNCE = 28.349523125;
private static final double HECTARES_PER_ACRE = 0.40468564;
```

Java allows all methods of a class to use its class constants and class variables. Furthermore, if the class constants and class variables are **public**, classes elsewhere can use them. Because the `Conversion` class constants are **private**, only `Conversion` methods are permitted to use them.

With constant `KILOMETERS_PER_MILE`, it is straightforward to define length conversion methods.

```java
// length conversion methods
public static double kilometersToMiles(double kilometers) {
    return kilometers / KILOMETERS_PER_MILE);
}

public static double milesToKilometers(double miles) {
    return miles * KILOMETERS_PER_MILE;
}
```

When a Java compiler translates one of these methods and encounters an identifier (e.g., KILOMETERS_PER_MILE), it first determines whether the identifier has been defined in that method. If so, that definition is used. If there is no such definition in effect, the compiler then determines whether the identifier is the name of a class or instance variable. If so, then that definition is used. Otherwise the identifier must be defined in one of the packages that the source file has imported.

With class constants LITERS_PER_GALLON and GRAMS_PER_OUNCE, it is straightforward to define the mass conversion methods.

```
// mass conversion methods
public static double litersToGallons(double liters) {
    return liters / LITERS_PER_GALLON;
}

public static double gallonsToLiters(double gallons) {
    return gallons * LITERS_PER_GALLON;
}

public static double gramsToOunces(double grams) {
    return grams/ GRAMS_PER_OUNCE;
}

    public static double ouncesToGrams(double ounces) {
        return ounces * GRAMS_PER_OUNCE;
}
```

Similarly, with class constant HECTARES_PER_ACRE, the area conversion methods have straightforward definitions.

```
// area conversion methods
public static double hectaresToAcres(double hectares) {
    return hectares / HECTARES_PER_ACRE;
}

public static double acresToHectares(double acres) {
    return acres * HECTARES_PER_ACRE;
}
```

ConversionDemo.java of Listing 7.2 demonstrates a use of class Conversion. The program prompts a user for metric values and produces the English equivalents. A sample run of the program is displayed in Figure 7.1.

The conversion invocations occur in lines 26–29, where the values of actual parameters kilometers, liters, grams, and hectares are the user-supplied values.

```
double miles = Conversion.kilometersToMiles(kilometers);
double gallons = Conversion.litersToGallons(liters);
double ounces = Conversion.gramsToOunces(grams);
double acres = Conversion.hectaresToAcres(hectares);
```

If variables miles, gallons, ounces, and acres were displayed directly with a System.out.println(), then the conversion output would resemble the following rather than the display of Figure 7.1.

```
2.0 kilometers = 1.242742384474668 miles
3.0 liters = 0.7925161570744452 gallons
4.0 grams = 0.14109584779832166 ounces
5.0 hectares = 12.355269141746666 acres
```

Listing 7.2   ConversionDemo.java

```
1.  // Demonstrates some uses of class Conversion
2.
3.  import java.util.*;
4.
5.  public class ConversionDemo {
6.      // main(): application entry point
7.      public static void main(String[] args) {
8.          Scanner stdin = new Scanner(System.in);
9.
10.         System.out.println();
11.         System.out.print("Enter a length in kilometers: ");
12.         double kilometers = stdin.nextDouble();
13.
14.         System.out.println();
15.         System.out.print("Enter a mass in liters: ");
16.         double liters = stdin.nextDouble();
17.
18.         System.out.println();
19.         System.out.print("Enter a mass in grams: ");
20.         double grams = stdin.nextDouble();
21.
22.         System.out.println();
23.         System.out.print("Enter an area in hectares: ");
24.         double hectares = stdin.nextDouble();
25.
26.         double miles = Conversion.kilometersToMiles(kilometers);
27.         double gallons = Conversion.litersToGallons(liters);
28.         double ounces = Conversion.gramsToOunces(grams);
29.         double acres = Conversion.hectaresToAcres(hectares);
30.
31.         System.out.println();
32.         System.out.printf("%5.2f kilometers = ", kilometers);
33.         System.out.printf("%5.2f miles\n", miles);
34.         System.out.printf("%5.2f liters = ", liters);
35.         System.out.printf("%5.2f gallons\n", gallons);
36.         System.out.printf("%5.2f grams = ", grams);
37.         System.out.printf("%5.2f ounces\n", ounces);
38.         System.out.printf("%5.2f hectares = ", hectares);
39.         System.out.printf("%5.2f acres\n", acres);
40.         System.out.println();
41.     }
42. }
```

To avoid the display of uninteresting digits, method
System.out.printf() is used. As discussed in
Chapter 6, this print method will work with two param-
eters—a format specifier and a value. For each of the four conversions in Conversion-
Demo.java, two decimal places after the decimal is sufficient. The f in format specifier
"%5.2f" indicates that a decimal floating point value is to be display; the .2 indicates
that two places after the decimals are to be displayed; and the 5 indicates the total number
of columns to be used in displaying the number (leading blanks are used as necessary).

> Appendix C describes format
> strings in more detail

Figure 7.1 **Sample conversions.**

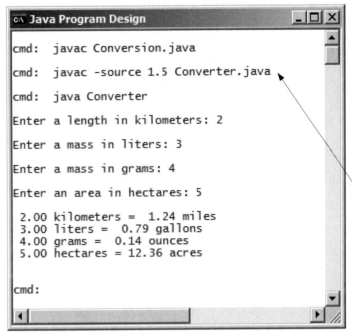

```
cmd:   javac Conversion.java

cmd:   javac -source 1.5 Converter.java

cmd:   java Converter

Enter a length in kilometers: 2

Enter a mass in liters: 3

Enter a mass in grams: 4

Enter an area in hectares: 5

 2.00 kilometers =  1.24 miles
 3.00 liters =  0.79 gallons
 4.00 grams =  0.14 ounces
 5.00 hectares = 12.36 acres


cmd:
```

As the text book is being developed, the parameters -source 1.5 are necessary for a compilation that makes use of Java 1.5 syntax. For program Converter.java, its use of method printf() requires a Java 1.5 compilation.

Listing 7.3 **Demonstration.java**

```
1.  public class Demonstration {
2.      static private int counter = 0;
3.      public Demonstration() {
4.          ++counter;  // another construction has been performed
5.      }
6.      // main(): application entry point
7.      public static void main(String[] args) {
8.          Demonstration d1 = new Demonstration();
9.          Demonstration d2 = new Demonstration();
10.         Demonstration d3 = new Demonstration();
11.         System.out.println(Demonstration.counter);
12.     }
13. }
```

Although class `Conversion` made use of only class constants, Java also allows class variables. For example, program `Demonstration.java` of Listing 7.3 uses a class variable count to maintain the number of class constructions that the program has performed.

Because there are three invocations of the `Demonstration` constructor within the program, its output is

3

Class methods and instance variables

Because a class method is associated with its class and not a particular object, any use of an instance variable within it must indicate explicitly the associated object. The following class `StaticDemo` illustrates this requirement.

```
public class StaticDemo {
    private int number;
        public StaticDemo(int n) {
        number = n;
    }
    static void print1(StaticDemo v) {
        System.out.println(v.number);   // display v's attribute
    }
    void print2() {
        System.out.println(number);     // display attribute of
    }                                    // invoking object
}
```

Class `StaticDemo` has methods `print1()` and `print2()` for printing the `number` attribute of a `StaticDemo`. Because method `print1()` is a class method, it requires a `StaticDemo` as a parameter to indicate which `number` attribute should be displayed. Because method `print2()` is an instance method, there is automatically a `StaticDemo` object associated with its code—the `StaticDemo` that invoked the method.

This analysis completes our discussion of modifier **static** and its effect on methods, constants, and variables. We now turn our attention to examining the nuances of parameter passing.

7.2   PARAMETER PASSING

We start our discussion of parameter passing with a review of what happens during a method invocation. In this example, we make use of class methods `add()`, `multiply()`, and `main()` from program `Demo.java` of Listing 7.4. Method `add()` computes a sum and `multiply()` computes a product. The two methods are invoked by method `main()` to compute the sum and product of 8 and 11.

In method `main()`, variable `sum` is initialized through the invocation `add(a,b)` and variable `product` is initialized through the invocation `multiply(a, b)`. In both invocations, the actual parameters `a` and `b` have values 8 and 11.

Actual parameters provide information that is otherwise unavailable to a method. For methods `add()` and `multiply()`, the two parameters supply the operands of interest. Without them, `add()` would not know what to sum and `multiply()` would not know what to multiply.

Listing 7.4 Demo.java

```
1.  // Parameter passing demonstration
2.
3.  public class Demo {
4.      // add(): returns the sum of its parameters
5.      public static double add(double x, double y) {
6.          double result = x + y;
7.          return result;
8.      }
9.
10.     // multiply(): returns the product of its parameters
11.     public static double multiply(double x, double y) {
12.         x = x * y;
13.         return x;
14.     }
15.
16.     // main(): application entry point
17.     public static void main(String[] args) {
18.         System.out.println();
19.         double a = 8;
20.         double b = 11;
21.         double sum;
22.         double product;
23.
24.         sum = add(a, b);
25.         System.out.println(a + " + " + b + " = " + sum);
26.
27.         product = multiply(a, b);
28.         System.out.println(a + " * " + b + " = " + product);
29.     }
30. }
```

Whenever a method is invoked, flow of control is transferred temporarily to that method. The actual parameters in the invocation are used to initialize the formal parameters in the method's definition. For *each* method invocation, Java sets aside memory—known as the *activation record*—for that *particular* invocation. The activation record stores, among other things, the values of the formal parameters.

Java uses value parameter passing in an invocation. Once the actual parameters have been used to initialize the formal parameters, the actual parameters and formal parameters are independent of each other. If a method updates the value of a formal parameter, the change does not affect the actual parameter. The change is limited to the activation record containing the value of the formal parameter. As an example, we trace through a run of program Demo.java. The output of the program is displayed in Figure 7.2.

Figure 7.2   **Program Demo output.**

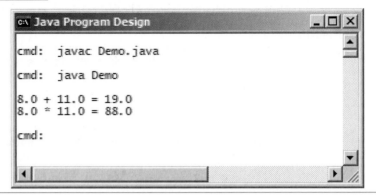

The definition of method `add()` specifies the names of its formal parameters to be x and y. Therefore, the invocation `add(a, b)` causes `add()` to be executed with its formal parameters x and y initialized respectively to the values of a and b.

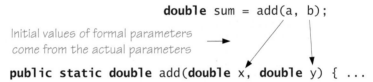

Immediately prior to the `add()` invocation to initialize sum, the activation record for method `main()` would have depiction

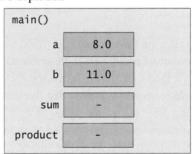

With the invocation, a new activation record is created for method `add()` and the flow of control is transferred to the method. In creating this activation record, formal parameter x is initialized to the value of the actual parameter a, which in this case is the value 8.0, and formal parameter y is initialized to the value of the actual parameter b, which in this case is the value 11.0.

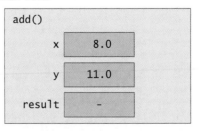

Therefore, if add() updates the value of its formal parameters, the change is visible only within add()—the actual parameters are left unchanged.

Formal parameters x and y are used in the initialization of variable result.

double result = x + y;

After the definition of result, the activation record for add() has depiction

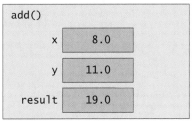

The **return** statement for add()

return result;

then is evaluated. The return value is the value of result, which is the **double** value 19.0.

The method's completion causes the memory associated with its activation record to be released. The flow of control is returned to method main(), where the add() return value is used to initialize sum. The activation record associated with main() now has depiction

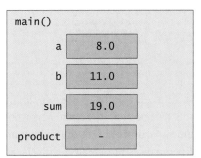

A println() invocation then displays the first line of program output.

8.0 + 11.0 = 19.0

Method multiply() is invoked to initialize variable product.

product = multiply(a, b);

This invocation causes a transfer of the flow of control to multiply() with its formal parameters x and y initialized respectively to the values a and b. Because of the transfer, an activation record is created for method `multiply()`. The new activation record has depiction

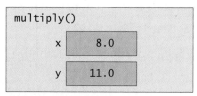

Parameters x and y are used in an assignment to x.

```
x = x * y;
```

After the assignment, the current activation records have depiction

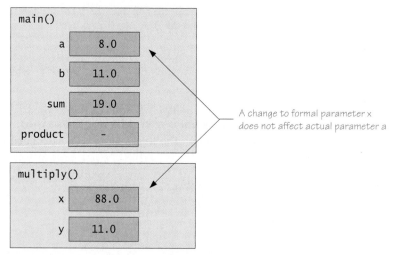

Because a formal parameter is essentially a variable local to its method, a change to a formal parameter does not affect the corresponding actual parameter. The assignment to formal parameter x of `multiply()` did not affect actual parameter a of `main()`.

Formal parameters are created with the invocation of their method, their values are accessible only within the method, and they are destroyed when their method completes. The only difference between the formal parameters and the other variables defined by a method is that the formal parameters are initialized using the values of the actual parameters.

```
double product = multiply(a, b);
```

Initial values of formal parameters come from the actual parameters →

```
public static double multiply(double x, double y) {
    x = x * y;
    return x;
}
```

Changes to formal parameters do not affect the actual parameters

The **return** statement for `multiply()` is evaluated then.

```
return x;
```

Clarity

Method `multiply()` of Listing 7.4 was written to demonstrate that parameters can be modified. If that had not been our intention, the method would be better expressed as

```java
public static double multiply(double x, double y) {
    double product = x * y;
    return product;
}
```

The return value is the value of the expression x, which is 88.0. The method's completion causes the memory associated with its activation record to be released. The flow of control is returned to method `main()`, where the `multiply()` return value is used to initialize `product`. The activation record associated with `main()` now has depiction

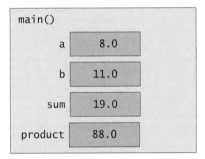

The last statement in method `main()` then is executed. This statement displays the result of the `multiply()` invocation.

```java
System.out.println(a + " * " + b + " = " + product);
```

The output of the statement verifies our statement regarding the independence of actual and formal parameters—the display of variable a shows that it has the same value after the invocation as it had before the invocation.

```
8.0 * 11.0 = 88.0
```

Regardless of the type of parameter, Java uses the value parameter passing style. Therefore, no matter whether the parameters are primitive values or references, the value of an actual parameter does not change. This property is demonstrated in `PassingReferences.java` of Listing 7.5. The output of the program is depicted in Figure 7.3.

The program consists of three class methods: `f()`, `g()`, and `main()`.

- Method `f()` has a single formal parameter v. The method assigns to v a reference to a new `Point` representing (0, 0).

- Method `g()` also has a single formal parameter v. However, this method does not make an assignment to its parameter v. Instead, `g()` changes the object to which v refers. In particular, that object has its location attribute set to (0, 0).

- Method `main()` invokes methods `f()` and `g()`.

By analyzing the results of the method `main()` invocations, a deeper understanding of the possible effects of passing references can be obtained.

Listing 7.5 **PassingReferences.java**

```java
1.  // Parameter passing demonstration
2.
3.  import java.awt.*;
4.
5.  public class PassingReferences {
6.      // f(): set the value of the formal parameter
7.      public static void f(Point v) {
8.          v = new Point(0, 0);
9.      }
10.
11.     // g(): modifies the contents of the referred to object
12.     public static void g(Point v) {
13.         v.setLocation(0, 0);
14.     }
15.
16.     // main(): application entry point
17.     public static void main(String[] args) {
18.         Point p = new Point(10, 10);
19.         System.out.println(p);
20.
21.         f(p);
22.         System.out.println(p);
23.
24.         g(p);
25.         System.out.println(p);
26.     }
27. }
```

Figure 7.3 **Program PassingReferences output.**

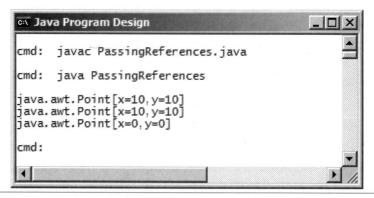

Method `main()` begins by initializing and displaying a `Point` variable p. Variable p references an object referencing the location (10, 10).

```java
Point p = new Point(10, 10);
System.out.println(p);
```

The output produced by the first `println()` invocation is

```
java.awt.Point[x=10,y=10]
```

After completing the initial segment, the activation record for method `main()` has depiction

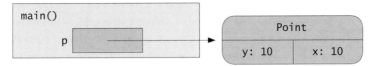

Observe that although variable p is part of the activation record for method `main()`, the memory for the `Point` to which it refers is not part of the activation record. Java divides the memory allocated to a program into two portions—the *stack* and the *heap*. Activation records are maintained in the stack and the space for objects comes from the heap.

Method `f()` then is invoked with p as the actual parameter.

```
f(p);
```

With its invocation, an activation record is created and flow of control is transferred to it. The depiction of the activation records is now

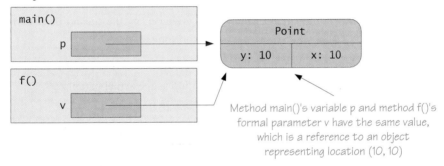

Method main()'s variable p and method f()'s formal parameter v have the same value, which is a reference to an object representing location (10, 10)

Because Java performs value parameter passing, the actual and formal parameters p and v have the same value, that is, they reference the same `Point` object.

The assignment statement in method `f()` is executed then.

```
v = new Point(0, 0);
```

The assignment gives `f()` formal parameter v a new value, that is, v now references a new `Point` object representing the location (0, 0). This assignment does not modify method `main()` variable p because variable p has its own memory where it stores its value.

The depiction of the activation records is now

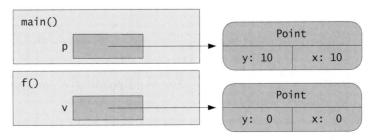

> ## Every class has a constructor
>
> If a class does not define at least one constructor, then Java will create a default constructor for the class. The provided default constructor will invoke the default constructor of the *superclass* (parent class) for the new class. If the class does not explicitly define a superclass, then the superclass is class `Object`. Chapter 9 considers the nuances of deriving classes from a class other than `Object`.

The activation record for `f()` then is released and the flow of control is transferred back to method `main()` where the `println()` statement is executed.

```
System.out.println(p);
```

The activation records now have depiction

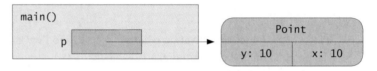

An examination of the output produced by the second `println()` invocation confirms our analysis—there has been no change in p.

```
java.awt.Point[x=10,y=10]
```

Method `g()` then is invoked with p as the actual parameter.

```
g(p);
```

With its invocation, an activation record is created and flow of control is transferred to it. The depiction of the activation records is now

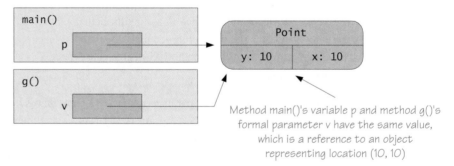

Method main()'s variable p and method g()'s formal parameter v have the same value, which is a reference to an object representing location (10, 10)

The actual and formal parameters p and v have the same value, that is, they reference the same `Point` object.

The `Point` instance method invocation is executed then.

```
v.setLocation(0, 0);
```

This invocation causes an update to the `Point` object to which parameter v refers. The update changes the representation to that of (0, 0).

Observe that this update changed neither actual parameter p nor formal parameter v. However, the object to which they both refer has been updated and its change is visible through them. The activation records now have depiction

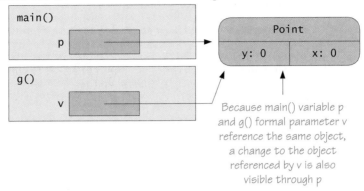

Because main() variable p
and g() formal parameter v
reference the same object,
a change to the object
referenced by v is also
visible through p

With the update in location, flow of control is transferred then back to method main() and the println() statement is executed.

```
System.out.println(p);
```

An examination of the output produced by the final println() invocation confirms our analysis—the Point object which p references has undergone change.

```
java.awt.Point[x=0,y=0]
```

In summary, the value of an actual parameter does not change with method invocation. However, if the actual parameter is a reference, then the object to which the actual parameter refers can be modified in a method invocation.

We now turn our attention to the use of the keyword **this** and some methods that should be present in almost any class implementation. In the accompanying discussion, a class Triple is used to illustrate these programming concepts.

7.3 THIS

Class Triple of Listing 7.6 supports the representation of objects with three numeric attributes. The class defines a default and specific constructor; an accessor getValue(); mutator setValue(); and facilitators toString(), clone(), and equals().

    public Triple()

        Constructs a default Triple value representing three zeros.

    public Triple(**int** a, **int** b, **int** c)

        Constructs a representation of the values a, b, and c.

    public int getValue(**int** i)

        Returns the ith element of the associated Triple.

    public void setValue(**int** i, **int** value)

        Sets the ith element of the associated Triple to value.

    public String toString()

        Returns a textual representation of the associated Triple.

Listing 7.6   Triple.java

```
1.  // Purpose: Support the representation of a three-tuple.
2.
3.  public class Triple {
4.      // instance variables for the three attributes
5.      private int x1;      // first value
6.      private int x2;      // second value
7.      private int x3;      // third value
8.
9.      // Triple(): default constructor
10.     public Triple() {
11.         this(0, 0, 0);
12.     }
13.
14.     // Triple(): specific constructor
15.     public Triple(int a, int b, int c) {
16.         setValue(1, a);
17.         setValue(2, b);
18.         setValue(3, c);
19.     }
20.
21.     // getValue(): attribute accessor
22.     public int getValue(int i) {
23.         switch (i) {
24.             case 1: return x1;
25.             case 2: return x2;
26.             case 3: return x3;
27.             default:
28.                 System.err.println("Triple: bad get: " + i);
29.                 System.exit(i);
30.                 return i;
31.         }
32.     }
33.
34.     // setValue(): attribute mutator
35.     public void setValue(int i, int value) {
36.         switch (i) {
37.             case 1: x1 = value; return;
38.             case 2: x2 = value; return;
39.             case 3: x3 = value; return;
40.             default:
41.                 System.err.println("Triple: bad set: " + i);
42.                 System.exit(i);
43.                 return;
44.         }
45.     }
46.
47.     // toString(): string representation facilitator
48.     public String toString() {
49.         int a = getValue(1);
50.         int b = getValue(2);
51.         int c = getValue(3);
52.
53.         return "Triple[" + a + ", " + b + ", " + c + "]";
54.     }
```

Listing 7.6   **Triple.java (Continued)**

```
55.
56.     // clone(): duplicate facilitator
57.     public Object clone() {
58.        int a = getValue(1);
59.        int b = getValue(2);
60.        int c = getValue(3);
61.
62.        return new Triple(a, b, c);
63.     }
64.
65.     // equals(): equals facilitator
66.     public boolean equals(Object v) {
67.        if (v instanceof Triple) {
68.           int a1 = getValue(1);
69.           int b1 = getValue(2);
70.           int c1 = getValue(3);
71.
72.           Triple t = (Triple) v;
73.           int a2 = t.getValue(1);
74.           int b2 = t.getValue(2);
75.           int c2 = t.getValue(3);
76.
77.           return (a1 == a2) && (b1 == b2) && (c1 == c2);
78.        }
79.        else {
80.           return false;
81.        }
82.     }
83. }
```

public Object clone()

>   Returns a new Triple whose representation is the same as the associated Triple.

public boolean equals(Object v)

>   Returns whether v is equivalent to the associated Triple.

The default constructor for class Triple is syntactically interesting—it uses the specific constructor to initialize a new Triple object.

```
// Triple(): default constructor
public Triple() {
   this(0, 0, 0);
}
```

The new Triple object (the this object) is constructed by invoking the Triple constructor expecting three int values as actual parameters

Keyword **this** is a reference to the object being acted upon. It provides a notation for an object to refer to itself. In a constructor, **this** references the object under construction; in an instance method, **this** references the object being manipulated. Thus, for the Triple class, **this** is a reference to the Triple object being acted upon by one of its constructors or methods.

Our use of **this** in the Triple default constructor signifies that the object under construction is to be configured with zeros for its attribute values. The configuration is performed by invoking the `Triple` constructor whose signature matches the invocation (i.e., the `Triple` specific constructor expecting three **int** values as parameters).

This type of construction is common in defining Java constructors. Typically, one constructor has a detailed initialization process. The other constructors then use that definition by invoking it with appropriate values. By using that single detailed initialization process, it is less likely that some aspect of object configuration is omitted.

If another constructor of the class assists the initialization, Java requires that the **this**() invocation be at the beginning of the statement body. Therefore, the following constructor definition is illegal.

```
public Triple() {
        int a = 0;
        int b = 0;
        int c = 0;
        this(a, b, c);   ◄───── Illegal this() invocation. A this() invocation
}                                must begin its statement body
```

The `Triple` specific constructor of Listing 7.6 uses its three actual parameters to initialize the attributes of the `Triple` object under construction. It does so through the use of the `Triple` mutators.

```
// Triple(): specific constructor
public Triple(int a, int b, int c) {
   setValue(1, a);
   setValue(2, b);
   setValue(3, c);
}
```

The `Triple` specific constructor could have used explicit **this** references to indicate that it is the object under construction whose `setValues()` mutators are being invoked.

```
// Triple(): specific constructor - alternative definition
public Triple(int a, int b, int c) {
   this.setValue(1, a);
   this.setValue(2, b);
   this.setValue(3, c);
}
```

However, in practice Java programmers tend generally to omit explicit **this** references. It is understood implicitly that the methods being invoked are acting upon the object under consideration.

7.4   INHERITED METHODS AND OVERRIDING

Class `Triple` like every other Java class is automatically an *extension* of the standard class `Object`; that is, class `Object` specifies some basic behaviors common to all objects. In object-oriented programming terminology these behaviors are said to be

Chapter 9 considers inheritance in detail

inherited. One of the methods that `Triple` inherits from `Object` is method `toString()`.

It generally is recommended that every class *override* the `toString()` definition provided by `Object` (i.e., provide a different implementation). By doing so, `System.out.println()` can display a meaningful representation of all of the attributes of the object rather than just its `Object` attributes. This capability can be quite useful when debugging a program.

Consider the following code segment.

```
Triple p = new Triple(1, 1, 2);
Triple q = new Triple(3, 5, 8);

System.out.println(p);  // displays string version of object p
System.out.println(q);  // displays string version of object q
```

Without the override, the code segment would produce as its output

```
Triple@187c6c7
Triple@10b62c9
```

Such output is not of use to most programmers.

For a `Triple` object, a reasonable `String` representation would be a listing of its three attributes. The class `Triple` implementation is

```
// toString(): string representation facilitator
public String toString() {
    int a = getValue(1);
    int b = getValue(2);
    int c = getValue(3);

    return "Triple[" + a + ", " + b + ", " + c + "]";
}
```

With this method, code segment

```
Triple p = new Triple(1, 1, 2);
Triple q = new Triple(3, 5, 8);

System.out.println(p);  // displays string version of object p
System.out.println(q);  // displays string version of object q
```

produces reasonable output.

```
Triple[1, 1, 2]
Triple[3, 5, 8]
```

Observe that the name of the class was displayed as part of the representation. This practice is quite common if the expected use of `toString()` is to provide debugging information.

The other `Triple` methods of interest are `clone()` and `equals()`. Like method `toString()`, methods `clone()` and `equals()` are overrides of methods inherited from class `Object`.

Copy construction

While Java programmers tend to use a `clone()` method to produce a duplicate of an object, programmers in other object-oriented languages such as C++ tend to use a *copy constructor*. A copy constructor expends a single parameter of its class type and creates a duplicate of that object. Although the two mechanisms are different in syntax, they are equivalent.

Method `clone()` returns a new `Triple` object that is a duplicate of the current object.

```
// clone(): duplicate facilitator
public Object clone() {
    int a = getValue(1);
    int b = getValue(2);
    int c = getValue(3);

    return new Triple(a, b, c);
}
```

Because it is an override, the method has the return type of `Object`, which is the return type of the `clone()` method defined by class `Object`.

Creating a `Triple` clone is straightforward. First variables a, b, and c are initialized with the attribute values of the `Triple` object that invoked method `clone()`. The return value is produced by creating a new `Triple` object with attribute values a, b, and c. The following code segment makes use of method `clone()` to initialize variable t2.

```
Triple t1 = new Triple(9, 28, 29);
Triple t2 = (Triple) t1.clone();
System.out.println("t1 = " + t1);
System.out.println("t2 = " + t2);
```

Although `Triple` method `clone()` returns a `Triple` object, its return type is `Object`. Therefore, the return value must be cast to `Triple` to use that value appropriately.

The segment output shows that the objects referenced by t1 and t2 have the same attributes.

```
t1 = Triple[9 , 28 , 29]
t2 = Triple[9 , 28 , 29]
```

To complete our discussion of class `Triple`, we turn our attention to its override of method `equals()`.

The `Triple` class definition overrides the `Object` class `equals()` method because the inherited `equals()` does not meet our purposes. Consider the following code segment that defines `Triple` variables t1 and t2 that reference similarly constructed objects.

```
Triple t1 = new Triple(9, 28, 29);
Triple t2 = new Triple(9, 28, 29);
```

The representation of t1 and t2 would be

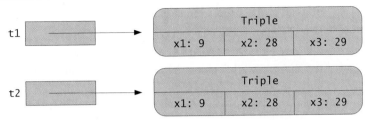

The inherited Object class equals() method reports if the two object references are the same rather than reporting whether the referenced objects have equivalent attributes. With Object class equals() method in effect, the following code segment displays **false**—variables t1 and t2 contain different references.

```
System.out.println(t1.equals(t2));
```

Object method equals() is equivalent to the == operator. Both test whether the objects in question are in fact the same object.

The Triple implementation of equals() instead determines whether its parameter is a Triple object with attributes that are *equivalent* to the invoking Triple object. Because it is an override, the parameter to the method is of type Object, which is the type of parameter specified by the equals() method of class Object.

The Triple implementation follows the standard form of an equals() method.

```
// equals(): equals facilitator
public boolean equals(Object v) {
    if (v instanceof Triple) {
        int a1 = getValue(1);
        int b1 = getValue(2);
        int c1 = getValue(3);

        Triple t = (Triple) v;
        int a2 = t.getValue(1);
        int b2 = t.getValue(2);
        int c2 = t.getValue(3);

        return (a1 == a2) && (b1 == b2) && (c1 == c2);
    }
    else {
        return false;
    }
}
```

The implementation begins by testing whether its parameter v references a Triple object. Operator **instanceof** returns **true** when the type of object referenced by the left operand is either that of the right operand or derived from the right operand; otherwise, the operator returns **false**. (The **null** reference is never considered an instance of a class.)

If v is not referencing a Triple object, then the test expression evaluates to **false** causing the **else** part to be executed. The **else** part returns **false** as the object cannot be equal to the Triple object invoking the equals() method.

If the test expression evaluates to **true**, then v is referencing a non-**null** Triple object. As such, the method can determine whether the corresponding attributes of the two Triple objects match.

Variables a1, b1, and c1 and a2, b2, and c2 represent respectively the attributes of the object invoking the equals() method and the Triple object referenced by parameter v.

```
int a1 = getValue(1);
int b1 = getValue(2);
int c1 = getValue(3);

Triple t = (Triple) v;
int a2 = t.getValue(1);
int b2 = t.getValue(2);
int c2 = t.getValue(3);
```

By testing whether a1 equals a2, b1 equals b2, and c1 equals c2, the method can signal whether the two objects represent objects with identical attribute values.

```
return (a1 == a2) && (b1 == b2) && (c1 == c2);
```

You may have wondered why the code defines a variable t that is a cast of v. Although it must be the case at this point in the method that parameter v references a Triple object, Java still requires an explicit cast to treat v as something other than an Object. Therefore, the statement

```
int a2 = v.getValue(1);
```
← *The invocation does not compile because the apparent type of the object referenced by v is Object, which does not have a method getValue()*

would not compile—an Object does not have a method getValue(). The cast allows the Triple attributes of the object referenced by v to be obtained.

Consider the following code segment.

```
Triple e = new Triple(4, 6, 10);
Triple f = new Triple(4, 6, 11);
Triple g = new Triple(4, 6, 10);
Triple h = new Triple(4, 5, 11);

boolean flag1 = e.equals(f);
boolean flag2 = e.equals(g);
boolean flag3 = g.equals(h);
```

Keep things private

When designing your own classes, keep in mind that instance variables are declared normally to be **private**. This convention requires that any access or modification to the instance variables by other classes be through the accessors and mutator methods. This information hiding helps ensure the integrity of the variables and also normally makes it possible to update or correct the class without requiring changes to other classes that use your class.

Method equals()

In implementing an `equals()` method, the Java standard suggests that the following properties hold typically:

- *Reflexivity*: `x.equals(x)` should be always true.
- *Symmetry*: If `x.equals(y)` is true, then `y.equals(x)` should be true.
- *Transitivity*: If `x.equals(y)` and `y.equals(z)` are true then `x.equals(z)` should be true.
- *Consistency*: While the objects to which `x` and `y` refer are unchanged, repeated evaluations of `x.equals(y)` should return the same value.
- *Physicality*: `x.equals(`**null**`)` should return **false**.

Before reading on, determine the values to which variables `flag1`, `flag2`, and `flag3` are initialized.

Based on their initialization, variables e, f, g, and h have representations

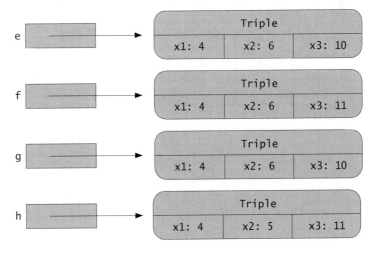

The objects referred to by e and f are different because their x3 attributes are different ($10 \neq 11$). The objects referred to by e and g are equivalent because the corresponding attribute values are the same. The objects referred to by g and h are different because both their x2 and x3 attributes are different ($6 \neq 5$ and $10 \neq 11$). Thus, variables `flag1`, `flag2`, and `flag3` have depiction

flag1	false
flag2	true
flag3	false

This discussion concludes our analysis of overriding `toString()`, `clone()`, and `equals()`. We now turn our attention to scope and name reuse.

7.5 SCOPE AND NAME REUSE

Consider the following class definition. Why doesn't the program compile?

```java
// Illegal variable referencing
class Scope {
  public static void main(String[] args) {
    int i = 10;                       // local definition
    f(i);                             // invoking f() with i as parameter
    System.out.println(a);  // illegal reference
    System.out.println(b);  // illegal reference
  }

  public static void f(int a) {
    int b = 1;                        // local definition
    System.out.println(a);  // print 10
    a = b;                            // update a
    System.out.println(a);  // print 1
  }
}
```

The program does not compile, because the references to variables a and b in method main() are illegal as seen in the activation record for main().

Variables a and b do not exist in the *scope* of method main(). According to the Java language specification, a method's parameters and variables can be used only within the method itself. The parameters and variables are said to be *local* to the method. Depending on where the definition occurs and what other definitions occur within the method, other scope rules can further limit a local variable to particular sections of code within the method.

7.5.1 LOCAL SCOPE RULES

A *block* is a list of statements nested within braces. By this definition, a method body is a block. It is legal in Java to put a statement block anywhere a statement would be legal, and there is no restriction on what type of statements a block can include. This flexibility enables us to have a block within a block within a block and so on. A block contained within another block is called a *nested* block.

The statement list that comprises a block is delimited naturally, or *terminated* in Java terminology, from the statement that follows it by the right brace. Thus, no semicolon is needed after the right brace.

The termination property is shown in the following example:

```
{
    int a = 1;  // semicolon is necessary
}               // semicolon is not necessary
int b = 2;      // semicolon is necessary
```

Java's scope rules state that a local variable can be used only in the block and in the nested blocks of the block in which it has been defined. In particular, a local variable can be used only in a statement or nested block that occurs after its definition. Java considers a formal parameter to be defined at the beginning of its associated method body. That is why a formal parameter can be used throughout its method.

7.5.2 NAME REUSE

There is a scope rule that limits the statements in which a variable can be used. The limitation has to do with the reuse of a variable's name. Although name reuse often seems disconcerting to beginning programmers, imagine how difficult it would be to write programs if name reuse was not permitted. Programmers would then need to be aware of the name of every variable used in every method in the software project, regardless of the method's author. Not only would this task tend to be unmanageable; it would encourage poor names for the sake of uniqueness.

Informally, Java allows an identifier name to be reused as long as the blocks containing the duplicate declarations are not nested one within the other. This policy means that the following class definition is legal.

```
class Scope2 {
    public static void main(String[] args) {
        int a = 10;                    // local definition
        f(a);                          // invoking f() with a as parameter
        System.out.println(a);         // print 10
    }

    public static void f(int a) {
        System.out.println(a);         // print 10
        a = 1;                         // update a
        System.out.println(a);         // print 1
    }
}
```

Method `main()`'s local variable a is different from the formal parameter a of method `f()`. The local variable a of `main()` exists only within `main()`'s statement block, and the formal parameter a of `f()` exists only within `f()`'s statement block.

The name reuse is reflected in the activation records for the two methods. They both contain entries for an a, but the a in one method is independent of the a in the other method. The activation records would have the following depiction immediately after the last statement in method f () executes.

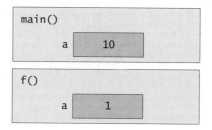

The output of the program is

```
10
1
10
```

Name reuse within the same method is permitted as long as the reuse occurs in distinct blocks. For example, while it is hard to understand, method g () is legal Java.

```java
public void g() {
    {
        int j = 1;                   // define j
        System.out.println(j);       // print 1
    }
    {
        int j = 10;                  // define a different j
        System.out.println(j);       // print 10
    }
    {
        char j = '@';                // define a different j
        System.out.println(j);       // print '@'
    }
}
```

The three variable j's are defined in three different blocks none of which are nested with respect to the others.

Because the three variable j's exist only within their respective blocks, we cannot move the println () statements to display their values as in method h ().

```java
public void h() {
    {
        int j = 1;                   // define j
    }
    System.out.println(j);           // illegal: no j in scope
    {
        int j = 10;                  // define a different j
    }
    System.out.println(j);           // illegal: no j in scope
    {
        char j = '@';                // define a different j
    }
    System.out.println(j);           // illegal: no j in scope
}
```

Shadowing

Name reuse is permitted within nested blocks if one of the blocks is a class definition block. The following class ShadowDemo demonstrates this practice.

```
public class ShadowDemo {
    static int n = 0;
    public static void main(String[] args) {
        int n = 0;      // local n shadows the class variable n
        n = 10;         // local n is updated
        System.out.println(n);
        System.out.println(ShadowDemo.n);
    }
}
```

ShadowDemo has a class variable n and its method main() has a local variable n. Within method main(), the name n by itself refers to the local variable. We say that the local variable n *shadows* (obscures) the class variable n. Access to the class variable requires its class specification (i.e., ShadowDemo.n). Therefore, the assignment in method main() updates the local variable and not the class variable. The program output is therefore

```
10
0
```

Because of its potential for reader and programmer confusion, the shadowing of variables is not recommended generally.

In the next example, method k() does not compile because one of the definitions of j is nested within a block that has already defined j.[†]

```
public void k() {
    int j = 1;
    {
        int j = 10;      // illegal: j already defined locally
        System.out.println(j);
    }
    System.out.println(j);
}
```

Now consider the following **for** loop using a local variable j. What is its output?

```
for (int i = 0; i < 3; ++i) {
    int j = 0;
    ++j;
    System.out.println(j);
}
```

The segment output is

```
1
1
1
```

[†]   Java naming requirements are more restrictive than those of other languages (e.g., C++).

The scope of variable j is the body of the **for** loop. Variable j is not in scope when the **for** post expression ++i and test expression i < 3 are evaluated. Therefore, variable j is redefined and reinitialized with each iteration of the loop.

Just because name reuse is permitted does not mean that it should be used. Variable names should reflect their intended purpose and name reuse within a method should be limited normally to loop index variables.

7.6   OVERLOADING

In Chapter 2, we discussed how Java has *overloaded* operators. That is, what an operator does depends on the type of its operands. For example, the division operator (/) performs integer or floating-point division depending on whether its operands are respectively integer or floating-point. Similarly, the plus operator (+) is overloaded. If its operands are numeric then addition is performed; and if its operands are strings then concatenation is performed.

Java also supports *method overloading*. It allows us to create methods that have the same name but behave differently. Method overloading is useful when we need to write methods that perform similar tasks but need to operate on either different types or on different numbers of parameters. Java allows a method name to be overloaded as long as the signature of the new definition is different from the other methods for the class to which it belongs (i.e., the two signatures must differ in the names, types, number, or order of the parameters).

For example, package `java.lang.Math` overloads the method name `min()` four times—there are methods operating on **int**, **long**, **float**, and **double** parameters. Their signatures are respectively `min(`**int, int**`)`, `min(`**long, long**`)`, `min(`**float, float**`)`, and `min(`**double, double**`)`.

The `min(`**int, int**`)` and `min(`**double, double**`)` methods are demonstrated in the following code segment.

```
Scanner stdin = new Scanner(System.in);

System.out.println("Enter two integers:");
int i1 = stdin.nextInt();
int i2 = stdin.nextInt();
int imin = Math.min(i1, i2);
System.out.println("Min of " + i1 + " and " + i2 + " is "
      + imin);

System.out.println("Enter two decimal values: ");
double d1 = stdin.nextDouble();
double d2 = stdin.nextDouble();
double dmin = Math.min(d1, d2);
System.out.println("Min of " + d1 + " and " + d2 + " is "
      + dmin);
```

Continuing with the `min()` example, the class `Tools` of Listing 7.7 defines in part two methods named `min()`. These two methods are class methods that operate respectively with three and four **int** parameters.

The use of these `min()` methods is demonstrated in `MinDemo.java` of Listing 7.8. When the compiler encounters a call to a method `Tools.min()` in method `main()`, there is no ambiguity on which method to invoke—the compiler examines the parameter list of the method call, and it invokes the method whose signature best matches the actual parameter list. The process of determining which method to invoke is known as *overloading resolution*. For class `Tools`, there is only one method `min()` with a three-parameter signature and only one method `min()` with a four-parameter signature. Thus, the `Tools` method with signature

```
min(int, int, int)
```

is invoked in statement

```
int imin = Tools.min(i1, i2, i3);
```

and the `Tools` method with signature

```
min(int, int, int, int)
```

is invoked in the statement

```
int jmin = Tools.min(j1, j2, j3, j4);
```

It is interesting to observe that the `Tools` three-parameter method `min()` makes two uses of `Math.min()` to achieve its result.

```
return Math.min(a, Math.min(b, c));
```

The method returns whatever is minimum—a or the minimum of b or c. This method also demonstrates that a return value can be an arbitrary expression and not just a variable.

The four-parameter method `min()` uses both the `Math.min()` and the `Tools` three-parameter `min()` to achieve its result.

```
return Math.min(a, min(b, c, d));
```

The four-parameter `min()` method returns whatever is minimum—a or the minimum of b, c, or d. There is no need to write the **return** statement as

```
return Math.min(a, Tools.min(b, c, d));
```

Because the default scope is the class scope, the Tools scope specifier is unnecessary

because by default, the `Tools` class uses `Tools` methods.

As another example of method overloading, class `Tools` defines two methods named `power()` that calculate x^n. One method has an integer base parameter x and the other

---

Listing 7.7   Tools.java

```java
1.  // Defines some helpful methods
2.
3.  public class Tools {
4.      // min(): returns the min of its three parameters
5.      public static int min(int a, int b, int c) {
6.          return Math.min(a, Math.min(b, c));
7.      }
8.
9.      // min(): returns the min of its four parameters
10.     public static int min(int a, int b, int c, int d) {
11.         return Math.min(a, min(b, c, d));
12.     }
13.
14.     // power(): returns x ^ n
15.     public static int power(int x, int n) {
16.         int result = 1;
17.         for (int i = 1; i <= n; ++i) {
18.             result *= x;
19.         }
20.         return result;
21.     }
22.
23.     // power(): returns x ^ n
24.     public static double power(double x, int n) {
25.         double result = 1;
26.         for (int i = 1; i <= n; ++i) {
27.             result *= x;
28.         }
29.         return result;
30.     }
31.
32.     // isInteger(): returns whether s is a number
33.     public static boolean isInteger(String s) {
34.         // is there a nonempty string to consider
35.         if ((s == null) || (s.length() == 0)) {
36.             return false;
37.         }
38.
39.         // ignore sign if there is one
40.         if ((s.charAt(0) == '+') || (s.charAt(0) == '-')) {
41.             s = s.substring(1);
42.             // make sure what's left is nonempty
43.             if (s.length() == 0) {
44.                 return false;
45.             }
46.         }
47.
48.         // make sure the rest is digits
49.         for (int i = 0; i < s.length(); ++i) {
50.             // is current character a digit
51.             if (! Character.isDigit(s.charAt(i))) {
52.                 return false;
53.             }
54.         }
```

Listing 7.7   Tools.java (Continued)

```
55.
56.        // number checked out
57.        return true;
58.     }
59. }
```

Listing 7.8   MinDemo.java

```
1. // Demonstrates overloading method usage
2.
3. import java.util.*;
4.
5. public class MinDemo {
6.
7.     // main(): application entry point
8.     public static void main(String[] args) {
9.         Scanner stdin = new Scanner(System.in);
10.
11.         System.out.println("Enter three integers: ");
12.         int i1 = stdin.nextInt();
13.         int i2 = stdin.nextInt();
14.         int i3 = stdin.nextInt();
15.         int imin = Tools.min(i1, i2, i3);
16.         System.out.println("Min of " + i1 + ", "+ i2 + ", and " + i3
17.             + " is " + imin);
18.
19.         System.out.println("Enter four integers: ");
20.         int j1 = stdin.nextInt();
21.         int j2 = stdin.nextInt();
22.         int j3 = stdin.nextInt();
23.         int j4 = stdin.nextInt();
24.         int jmin = Tools.min(j1, j2, j3, j4);
25.         System.out.println("Min of " + j1 + ", "+ j2 + ", " + j3
26.             + ", and " + j4 + " is " + jmin);
27.     }
28. }
```

method has a floating-point base parameter x. In addition, both power() methods require an integer exponent parameter n. (Both methods assume implicitly n is positive.)

```java
public static int power(int x, int n) {
    int result = 1;
    for (int i = 1; i <= n; ++i) {
        result *= x;
    }
    return result;
}

public static double power(double x, int n) {
    double result = 1;
    for (int i = 1; i <= n; ++i) {
        result *= x;
    }
    return result;
}
```

Listing 7.9   **PowerDemo.java**

```
1.  // Demonstrates method overloading usage
2.
3.  import java.util.*;
4.
5.  public class PowerDemo {
6.
7.      // main(): application entry point
8.      public static void main(String[] args) {
9.          Scanner stdin = new Scanner(System.in);
10.
11.         System.out.print("Enter an integer base: ");
12.         int i1 = stdin.nextInt();
13.         System.out.print("Enter a positive integer power: ");
14.         int i2 = stdin.nextInt();
15.         int ipow = Tools.power(i1, i2);
16.         System.out.println(i1 + " to the power "+ i2 + " is "
17.             + ipow);
18.
19.         System.out.print("Enter a floating-point base: ");
20.         double d = stdin.nextDouble();
21.         System.out.print("Enter a positive integer power: ");
22.         int n = stdin.nextInt();
23.         double dpow = Tools.power(d, n);
24.         System.out.println(d + " to the power "+ n + " is " + dpow);
25.     }
26. }
```

Even though both power() methods take two parameters, they have different signatures: power(**int**, **int**) and power(**double**, **int**).

Program PowerDemo.java of Listing 7.9 uses both Tools methods power(). Its method main() first invokes the Tools method power() requiring two **int** parameters.

```
System.out.print("Enter an integer base: ");
int i1 = stdin.nextInt();
System.out.print("Enter a positive integer power: ");
int i2 = stdin.nextInt();
int ipow = Tools.power(i1, i2);
System.out.println(i1 + " to the power "+ i2 + " is "
    + ipow);
```

Method main() then invokes the Tools method power() requiring a **double** parameter and an **int** parameter.

```
System.out.print("Enter a floating-point base: ");
double d = stdin.nextDouble();
System.out.print("Enter a positive integer power: ");
int n = stdin.nextInt();
double dpow = Tools.power(d, n);
System.out.println(d + " to the power "+ n + " is " + dpow);
```

As it was for `MinDemo.java` with the `min()` methods, there is no problem for the compiler in determining which method `power()` is to be invoked in statement

```
int ipow = Tools.power(i1, i2);
```

and in statement

```
double dpow = Tools.power(d, n);
```

When the compiler encounters the invocation `Tools.power(i1, i2)` in method `main()`, clearly the best match is the `Tools` method `power()` with two **int** parameters. Thus, the `Tools` method with signature

```
power(int, int)
```

is used to calculate `Tools.power(i1, i2)`.

Similarly, when the compiler encounters the invocation `Tools.power(d, n)` in method `main()`, there is again no ambiguity on which method to invoke—the best match is the `Tools` method `power()` with one **double** parameter and one **int** parameter; that is, the `Tools` method with signature

```
power(double, int)
```

Now consider the program `OverloadingDemo.java` of Listing 7.10. The program defines two methods `f()`. One `f()` method requires two **int** parameters and the other requires two **double** parameters. The `f()` method with two **int** parameters displays the sum of its parameters; the `f()` method with two **double** parameters displays the difference of its second parameter from its first parameter.

Listing 7.10 OverloadingDemo.java

```
1.  // Demonstrates method overloading
2.
3.  public class OverloadingDemo {
4.
5.      // main(): application entry point
6.      public static void main(String[] args) {
7.          int i = 19;
8.          double x = 54.0;
9.
10.         f(i, x);      // which f() is invoked?
11.     }
12.
13.     // f(): display a + b
14.     public static void f(int a, int b) {
15.         System.out.println(a + b);
16.     }
17.
18.     // f(): display a - b
19.     public static void f(double a, double b) {
20.         System.out.println(a - b);
21.     }
22. }
```

So which of the `f()` methods gets invoked at line 10 of method `main()`?

```
f(i, x);
```

Unlike our previous overloading examples, there is no perfect match in terms of the invocation and the method signatures. However, there is a best match. The compiler would cause the method `f()` with signature

```
f(double, double)
```

to be invoked. It does so because there is an automatic conversion that maps the **int** value i to the **double** version of i. This conversion produces parameters suitable for method `f(`**double** `a,` **double** `b)`. This match is the best match because there are no automatic conversions that could produce parameters suitable for method `f(`**int** `a,` **int** `b)`. Thus, the output of the program is

```
-35.0
```

A good programming practice is to not rely on automatic conversion. Instead make explicit conversions. That way readers of the code have an easier time determining which method is being invoked. For example, line 10 of method `main()` from `Overloading-Demo.java` can be written as

```
f((double) i, x);
```

Overloading

When method overloading, Java requires that the parameter lists for the methods be different. Therefore, the following class BadDemo does not compile.

```java
public class BadDemo {
    public double f(int a, int b) {
        return 2.5 * (a + b);
    }

    public int f(int a, int b) {  // illegal overloading
        return (a + b);
    }

    public static void main(String[] args) {
        double x = f(2, 4);
        int i = f(2, 4);
    }
}
```

Java does not consider the different return types of the two methods `f()` as a distinguishing factor for allowing the overloading.

ILLUSTRATIONS

We next present several small classes for illustrative purposes. Each of the classes demonstrates a nuance with regard to class behavior in Java.

First consider class A. Class A has four instance variables named `data1`, `data2`, `data3`, and `data4`. These four variables are of type **int**, **double**, **boolean**, and **String**, respectively, and the latter three variables have no explicit initialization. There is also a default constructor that performs no explicit work and accessors for each of the instance variables.

```java
public class A {
    private int data1 = 1;
    private double data2;
    private boolean data3;
    private String data4;

    public A() {
        // no body used
    }

    public int getData1() {
        return data1;
    }

    public double getData2() {
        return data2;
    }

    public boolean getData3() {
        return data3;
    }

    public String getData4() {
        return data4;
    }
}
```

Before reading our analysis try to determine the output of the following program `ADemo.java`. Understanding what output is produced should reinforce your understanding of instance variable initialization.

```java
public class ADemo {
    public static void main(String[] args) {
        A a = new A();
        System.out.println(a.getData1());
        System.out.println(a.getData2());
        System.out.println(a.getData3());
        System.out.println(a.getData4());
    }
}
```

As noted previously, immediately before a constructor begins executing its statement body, its instance variables are initialized. If the instance variable definition includes an explicit initialization value as does the definition of data1, then that value is used. If a variable definition does not specify an explicit initialization value, then it is initialized to 0 if it is a primitive numeric variable, to **false** if it is a **boolean** variable, or to **null** if it is a reference type variable.

```java
private int data1 = 1;
private double data2;
private boolean data3;
private String data4;
```

Thus, in regard to the new object to which variable a refers, **int** instance variable data1 is initialized explicitly to 1; **double** instance variable data2 is default initialized to 0.0, **boolean** instance variable data3 is default initialized to **false**, and String instance variable data4 is default initialized to **null**. The result is that program ADemo.java outputs

```
1
0.0
false
null
```

Now consider the following class B with a class variable counter1 and an instance variable counter2.

```java
public class B {
    private static int counter1 = 0;
    private int counter2;

    public B(int n) {
        counter2 = n;
    }

    public void incrementCounter1() {
        ++counter1;
    }

    public void incrementCounter2() {
        ++counter2;
    }

    public int getCounter1() {
        return counter1;
    }

    public int getCounter2() {
        return counter2;
    }
}
```

Before reading our analysis try to determine the output of program BDemo.java that uses class B. If you understand what output it produces, you should understand the important difference between class and instance variables.

```java
public class BDemo {
    public static void main(String[] args) {
        B b1 = new B(0);
```

```
        B b2 = new B(0);

        b1.incrementCounter1();
        b1.incrementCounter2();
        b1.incrementCounter2();
        b1.incrementCounter2();

        b2.incrementCounter1();
        b2.incrementCounter2();

        System.out.println(b1.getCounter1());
        System.out.println(b1.getCounter2());
        System.out.println(b2.getCounter1());
        System.out.println(b2.getCounter2());
    }
}
```

Program BDemo.java begins by defining two B reference variables b1 and b2. The variables reference distinct newly created B objects. These objects each have an instance variable counter2 with value 0. These same objects share access to a class variable counter1 with value 0. A series of incrementCounter1() and incrementCounter2() invocations then is made.

The effect of invocations

```
b1.incrementCounter1();
b1.incrementCounter2();
b1.incrementCounter2();
b1.incrementCounter2();
```

is to increment class variable counter1 from 0 to 1 and to increment the instance variable counter2 of the object to which b1 refers from 0 to 3.

The effect of invocations

```
b2.incrementCounter1();
b2.incrementCounter2();
```

is to further increment class variable counter1 from 1 to 2 and to increment instance variable counter2 of the object to which b2 refers from 0 to 1.

Therefore, the output of the program is

```
2
3
2
1
```

The output confirms our analysis. Because counter1 is a class variable, regardless of whether it is accessed via b1 or b2 it is the same value being manipulated. As this class variable was incremented two times over the course of the program, its value went from 0 to 2. Because counter2 is an instance variable, each B object has its own counter2 data field to hold its value. As b1 and b2 reference different objects, their increment operations affected different instances of counter2. Because three increments were applied to the object referenced by b1 and one increment was applied to the object referenced by b2, their counter2 values are respectively 3 and 1 at the end of the program.

Next suppose class C has definition

```
public class C {
    private int count = 0;

    public C(int n) {
        count = n;
    }

    public void f(int n) {
        count = n;
    }

    public void g(int n) {
        int count = n;
        count += n;
    }
}
```

Our interest in this class concerns its manipulation of the **private** instance variable count. Before reading our analysis try to determine your own answers to the following questions.

- Which methods in class C are in principle allowed to access instance variable count?
- Which of the methods in class C legally set instance variable count?
- Which of the methods in class C illegally attempt to set the instance variable count?
- Which of the methods in class C do not make any attempt to modify the instance variable count?

The answer to the first question is that all of the methods are in principle allowed to modify instance variable count. They are allowed to do so because all of the methods are instance methods, and regardless of the access attribute of an instance method (e.g., **public** or **private**), an instance method is allowed to access any instance variable of its class.

To determine the answers to the other questions, we first make several observations. Both constructor C() and method f() consist of the single statement

```
count = n;
```

The count being used here is the instance variable count of the invoking object. This association is the case because of the following facts: count was not declared previously within either the C() constructor or method f(), and every C object has an instance variable count.

The definition of method g() defines a local variable count. Furthermore, the assignment that follows increments that local variable.

```
int count = n;
count += n;
```

It increments the local variable rather than the instance variable because the local definition takes precedence over definitions from other scopes (i.e., it shadows them). Thus, method g() does not reference instance variable count.

Based on our observations, we know that methods C() and f() manipulate instance variable count, method g() does not manipulate instance variable count, and none of the methods have any illegal statements.

We next consider two classes D and E. It will be the case that both of these classes define a String instance variable named data and a method get(). Furthermore, the definitions of get() methods are identical—they return the value of their instance variable data. However, the two classes do define different overridings of a clone() method. The definition of class D is

```java
public class D {
    private String data;

    public D(String s) {
        data = s;
    }

    public String get() {
        return data;
    }

    public Object clone() {
        String val = get();
        return new D(val);
    }
}
```

and the definition of class E is

```java
public class E {
    private String data;

    public E(String s) {
        data = s;
    }

    public String get() {
        return data;
    }

    public Object clone() {
        String str = get();
        String val = new String(str);
        return new E(val);
    }
}
```

Before reading the analysis that follows, try to determine the output of the following program DEDemo.java that uses classes D and E. Understanding what output it produces should reinforce your understanding of cloning.

```java
public class DEDemo {
    public static void main(String[] args) {
        String word = "strengths";
        D d1 = new D(word);
        E e1 = new E(word);
```

```
                          D d2 = (D) d1.clone();
                          E e2 = (E) e1.clone();

                          boolean flag1 = d1.get() == d1.get();
                          boolean flag2 = d1.get() == d2.get();
                          boolean flag3 = e1.get() == e1.get();
                          boolean flag4 = e1.get() == e2.get();

                          System.out.println(flag1);
                          System.out.println(flag2);
                          System.out.println(flag3);
                          System.out.println(flag4);
               }
      }
```

The program begins by defining two D reference variables d1 and d2, and two E reference variables e1 and e2. The object to which d2 refers is a clone of d1 and the object to which e2 refers is a clone of e1. All four objects have a String instance variable string that refers to a representation of "strengths". Three of these instance variables refer to the same String object and one does not.

In creating the object to which d1 refers, its instance variable data is initialized to reference the same object as word.

```
      data = s;
```

This assignment value occurs because the actual value of formal constructor parameter s is the value of word. The depiction of memory at this point is

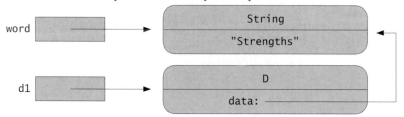

This depiction is correct because d1 references a new D object. This new object has an instance variable data of type String, which references the same String as word.

For similar reasons, the object to which e1 refers has an instance variable data that is initialized to reference the same instance variable as word.

```
      data = s;
```

Localization

The use of accessors and mutators rather than direct access of instance variables insulates an implementation. This localization generally makes it simpler to incorporate changes in the data representation. It also ensures consistent checking for the validity of new instance variable values.

Thus, after this construction, variables `word`, `d1.data`, and `e1.data` all reference the same object. The depiction of memory at this point is

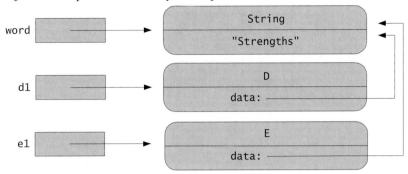

In creating the clone of the object to which `d1` refers, a new D object is created. This new D object has an instance variable `data` that references the same object as `clone()` method local variable `val` references.

```
String val = get();
return new D(val);
```

But, `val` references the same `String` object as that which `d1.data` references. It does so because the value of the current object is the value of `d1`, which means the `get()` operation returns `d1.data`. Therefore, variables `word`, `d1.data`, `d2.data`, and `e1.data` all reference the same object. The depiction of memory at this point is

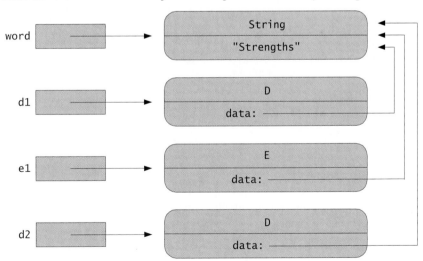

In creating the clone of the object to which `e1` refers, a new E object is created. This new E object has an instance variable `data` that references the same `String` object as `val` references.

```
String str = get();
String val = new String(str);
return new E(val);
```

However, `val` does not reference the same `String` object that `e1.data` does. While `str` references the same object that `e1.data` does; variable `val` references a new object. Although this new object has the same representation as the object to which `e1.data` references, it is a different object. Therefore `e2.data` is not referencing the same `String` as `e1.data`.

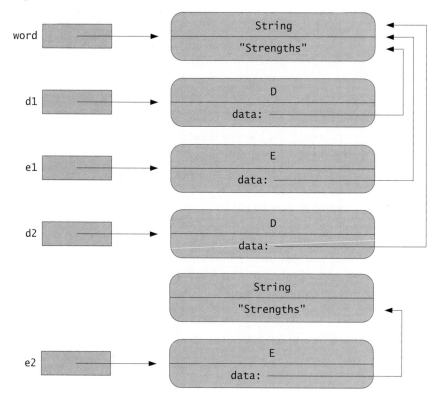

Thus, the output of the program is

```
true
true
true
false
```

We now turn our attention to a feature of Java that was introduced with the release of Java 5.0—generics.

7.8   GENERIC CLASSES

If we asked experts to list the necessary features of an object-oriented language, their replies would generally be the same. Their answers would state that the most important feature of an object-oriented language is its ability to allow both data and behavior to be encapsulated in a single object. Class and inheritance mechanisms would also appear in all the answers. These three features—objects, classes, and inheritance—are the core of object-oriented programming. If the experts were to agree on one more necessary feature, it would likely be *polymorphism*.

Java provides three forms of polymorphism—*primitive polymorphism*, *true polymorphism*, and *generic polymorphism*. Method overloading is an example of primitive polymorphism. With overloading we can *repeatedly* define methods with the same name (e.g., methods name `min()` taking different numbers of parameters. True polymorphism is considered in Chapter 9, which discusses Java's inheritance mechanisms. In this chapter we now consider generic polymorphism. Generics offer a syntactic convenience making use of a class template that looks like polymorphism. Once the particulars are supplied, the class is generated. The power of generics is that they allow common functionality to be supplied to different types of values.

For example, the following code example defines a generic class named `Wrapper` for storing and displaying a single value. The generic formal type parameter T is a placeholder for the type of value to be represented.

T is the formal type parameter. It is a placeholder for the type of interest

```
class Wrapper<T> {
    // instance variable
    private T tValue;
    // Wrapper(): specific constructor
    public Wrapper(T t) {
        tValue = t;
    }

    // get(): accessor
    public T get() {
        return tValue;
    }

    // set(): mutator
    public void set(T t) {
        tValue = t;
    }

    // toString(): text representation facilitator
    public String toString() {
        return tValue.toString();
    }
}
```

Each Wrapper has an instance variable named tValue. The type of tValue depends upon the instantiation of the generic class.

Each Wrapper has a specific constructor that requires a formal parameter of type T

Each Wrapper has an accessor get(). The return type of get() depends upon the instantiation of the generic class

Each Wrapper has a mutator set() that requires a formal parameter of type T

Each Wrapper overloads toString() to produce a textual representation of its object.

In defining a generic class, the formal parameters are listed within angled brackets after the class name. The formal parameters can be used through the class definition as placeholders for the actual type of interest.

To generate a class from a class template, you provide actual parameters for the formal parameters. The actual parameters are provided after the class name within angled brackets, where an actual type parameter is a known nonprimitive type. For example, the following code segment uses the generic `Wrapper` to define variables `x1` and `x2`. These variables are respectively of type `Wrapper<Rectangle>` and `Wrapper<String>`.

```
Rectangle r1 = new Rectangle(4, 30, 6, 21);

Wrapper<Rectangle> x1 = new Wrapper<Rectangle>(r);

Wrapper<String> x2 = new Wrapper<String>("rehabilitative");
```

Variable `x1` references a `Wrapper<Rectangle>` object that has a `Rectangle` instance variable `tValue`, an accessor method `get()` that returns a `Rectangle` and a **void** mutator method `set()` that expects a `Rectangle` as a parameter. Variable `x2` references a `Wrapper<String>` object that has a `String` instance variable `tValue`, an accessor method `get()` that returns a `String` and a **void** mutator method `set()` that expects a `String` as a parameter. Both `x1` and `x2` reference objects that have a `String` method `toString()`.

Thus, the following statements are all legal

```
String s = x2.get();
x2.set("verisimilitude");
x1.set(new Rectangle(6, 9, 11, 29));
Rectangle t = x1.get();
System.out.println(x1 + " " + x2);
```

and the following statements are all illegal

```
Rectangle r2 = x2.get();              // illegal: returns String
x2.set(new Rectangle(1,1,2,8));       // illegal: expects String
x1.set("overelaborates");             // illegal: expects Rectangle
String t = x1.get();                  // illegal: returns Rectangle
```

We revisit generics in Chapter 8, which discusses the *Java Collections Framework*. This framework provides a variety of list representations and associated algorithms all of which make use of generics.

This discussion completes our introduction to classes and methods.

| 7.9 | **REVIEW** |

- There are two types of methods in Java—instance methods and class methods. An instance method operates on an object and a class method is a service provided by a class that is not associated with a particular object.
- When a method is invoked, flow of control is transferred temporarily to that method. The actual parameters in the invocation are used to initialize the formal parameters in the method's definition.
- For each method invocation, Java sets aside memory—known as the activation record—for that particular invocation. The activation record stores, among other things, the values of the formal parameters.
- Java uses value parameter passing in an invocation. Once the actual parameters have been used to initialize the formal parameters, the actual parameters and formal parameters are independent of each other. If a method updates the value of a formal parameter, the change does not affect the actual parameter. The change is limited to the activation record containing the value of the formal parameter.
- Java divides the memory allocated to a program into two portions—the stack and the heap. Activation records are maintained in the stack and the space for objects comes from the heap.
- A method's parameters and variables can be used only within the method itself. The parameters and variables are said to be local to the method.
- To invoke a method, a programmer supplies actual parameters of the correct types. If the actual parameters do not match the types of the formal parameters, the compiler attempts to perform conversions to put the actual parameters in the correct form.
- Instance variables are declared normally to be **private**. This convention requires that any access or modification to the instance variables by other classes be through the accessors and mutator methods. This information hiding helps ensure the integrity of the variables and also normally makes it possible to update or correct the class without requiring changes to other classes that use your class.
- A class normally uses its accessors and mutators to manipulate its instance variables. This localization makes it simpler to incorporate changes in the data representation. It also ensures consistent checking for the validity of new instance variable values.
- A statement block is a list of statements within braces.
- A nested block is a statement block occurring within another statement block.
- A local variable is a variable defined within a statement block.
- Names can be reused as long as the declarations associated with the names occur in different blocks (i.e., neither of the blocks is nested within the other).
- Method overloading occurs when two or more methods defined in a class have the same name. Java allows a method name to be overloaded as long as the signature of the new definition is different from the other methods for the class to which it belongs (i.e., there must be a difference in the types, number, or order of the parameters).
- The compiler resolves overloaded method calls by calling the method whose signature best matches that of the invocation.

- Keyword **this** is a reference to the object being acted upon. In a constructor, **this** references the object under construction; in an instance method, **this** references the object being manipulated.

- A constructor of a class can invoke another constructor of its class to assist in the creation of the new object. Java requires that such assistance be at the beginning of the statement body. To invoke another constructor for assistance, keyword **this** is used.

- If a class does not define any constructors, then Java will create a default constructor for the class. The provided default constructor will invoke the default constructor of the direct superclass for the new class.

- A facilitator method performs a task that depends in part on the attributes of an object.

- Methods with the modifier **static** are known as class methods; methods without the modifier **static** are instance methods.

- A class variable or class constant is a common value to which all objects of the class share access. Class variables and class constants represent collective information that is not specific to individual objects of the class. The modifier **static** indicates that the value being represented is a class variable or constant.

- An instance method can access both class variables and the instance variables of the object on which the method operates.

- It is generally the responsibility of a mutator to validate manipulation requests.

- Operator **instanceof** returns **true** when the type of its left operand is either the right operand or derived from the right operand; otherwise, the operator returns **false**.

- All classes inherit methods toString(), equals(), and clone(). It is standard for a class to override these three methods.

- In overriding the clone() method, the return type is Object, which is the return type of the clone() method defined for the class Object.

- It is generally expected when implementing an equals() method that the following properties will hold:
  - Reflexivity: For any object x, x.equals(x) should be true.
  - Symmetry: For any objects x and y, if x.equals(y) then y.equals(x).
  - Transitivity: For any objects x, y, and z, if x.equals(y) and y.equals(z), then x.equals(z).
  - Consistency: For any unchanging objects x and y, repeated evaluations of x.equals(y) should return the same value.
  - Physicality: For any object x, x.equals(**null**) should return **false**.

- Generics offer a syntactic convenience making use of a class template that looks like polymorphism. Once the particulars are supplied, the class is generated.

- In defining a generic class, the formal parameters are listed within angled brackets after the class name. The formal parameters can be used through the class definition as placeholders for the actual types of interest.

■ To generate a class from a class template, you provide actual parameters for the formal parameters. The actual parameters are provided after the class name within angled brackets, where an actual type parameter is a known nonprimitive type.

S7.1 Rewrite Listing 7.7's method `min()` with signature

```
min(int, int, int, int)
```

so that the method body uses only `Math.min()`.

S7.2 What is the output of the following program? Explain.

```java
public class CounterTest {
    public static void f(int counter) {
        ++counter;
    }

    public static void g(int counter) {
        f(counter);
        f(counter);
    }

    public static void h(int counter) {
        f(counter);
        g(counter);
        f(counter);
    }

    public static void main(String[] args) {
        int counter = 0;
        f(counter);
        System.out.println(counter);
        g(counter);
        System.out.println(counter);
        h(counter);
        System.out.println(counter);
    }
}
```

S7.3 The formula for a line is given normally as $y = mx + b$. Write a method `line()` that expects three **double** parameters, a slope m, a y-intercept b, and an x-coordinate x. The method computes the y-coordinate associated with the line specified by m and b at x-coordinate x.

S7.4 Can you write a **void** method `swap()` that swaps the values of its two actual parameters? For example, the desired output of the following code segment

```java
int a = 1;
int b = 2;
swap(a, b);
System.out.println(a + " "+ b);
```

is

2 1

S7.5 Design and implement a console-based program `TriangleArea.java` that prompts and extracts for the sides *a*, *b*, and *c* of a triangle. If the sides do not represent a triangle, then an appropriate message is displayed. Otherwise, the program displays the area of the associated triangle. The program should define and use a method `area()`. Method `area()` takes three parameters representing the sides of a possible triangle. The sides represent a valid triangle if they are positive and the sum of the lengths for any two sides is greater than the length of the remaining side. The area of a triangle can be computed from its sides using the formula

$$\sqrt{s(s-a)(s-b)(s-c)}$$

where *s* is half of the sum of the sides (i.e., it is half the perimeter).

S7.6 Develop a class `Cast.java` that offers conversions from the fundamental types to its string representation and vice versa. For example, `Cast.toInt(s)` returns the **int** value represented by `String` variable `s`.

S7.7 Consider the following class declaration.

```java
public class C {
    private int data1 = 0;
    private int data2 = 0;
    public int data3 = 0;
    public C() {
        // no body used
    }
    public void setData1(int n) {
        data1 = n;
    }
    public void getData2() {
        return data2;
    }
    public void getData3() {
        return data3;
    }
    private void setData3(int n) {
        data3 = n;
    }
}
```

Explain all errors in classes `C` and `CDemo.java`.

```java
public class CDemo {
    public static void main(String[] args) {
        C c1 = new C();
        C c2 = new C(1, 2, 3);
        c1.setData1(4);
        c1.setData3(5);
        int n1 = c1.getData2();
        int n2 = c1.getData3();
        int n3 = c1.data1;
        int n4 = c1.data2;
```

```
                    int n5 = c1.data3;
                }
            }
```

7.11   EXERCISES

7.1 What is the purpose of name reuse?

7.2 Describe what happens during a method invocation.

7.3 What is an activation record?

7.4 What is a local variable?

7.5 What is a signature?

7.6 Can the name of a formal parameter be the same name as an actual parameter? Explain.

7.7 Discuss the transfers of flow of control during method invocation and completion.

7.8 Speculate on possible parameter-passing styles other than pass by value. Discuss how they could be effective.

7.9 Why is the information-hiding principle so important to the object-oriented programming paradigm?

7.10 What methods does a client program have access to? Why?

7.11 Does every class have a constructor? Why?

7.12 Should a **void** method necessarily contain a **return** statement? Explain.

7.13 Can a non-**void** method have a **return** statement? Explain.

7.14 What is it called when two methods have the same name? Under what situations can two methods have the same name?

7.15 Write a method barrelsToTeaspoons() with a **double** parameter **b** representing a number of barrels of petroleum. The method returns the equivalent number of teaspoons of oil. For your information,

- 1 barrel petroleum = 158.98729 liters
- 1 teaspoon = 0.004928922 liters

7.16 Write a method pointsToMeters() with a **double** parameter **p** representing a number of points. The method returns the distance in meters. For your information,

- 1 typographical point = 0.3514598 millimeters

7.17 Write an **int** method cube() that returns the cube of its single **int** formal parameter n.

7.18 Write a **double** method triangle() that computes the area of a triangle using its two **double** formal parameters h and w, where h is the height and w is the length of the base of the triangle.

7.19 Write a **double** method `rectangle()` that computes and returns the area of a rectangle using its two **double** formal parameters h and w, where h is the height and w is the width of the rectangle.

7.20 Write a **void** method `doubleSpace()` that inserts two newline characters (`'\n'`) to standard output.

7.21 Write a **void** method `endLine()` with a single **int** formal parameter n that indicates the number of newline characters to be displayed to standard output by the method.

7.22 Write a **boolean** method `intersect()` with four **double** parameters m1, b1, m2, and b2. The parameters come conceptually in two pairs. The first pair contains the coefficients describing one line; the second pair contains coefficients describing a second line. The method returns **true** if the two lines intersect; otherwise, the method returns **false**.

7.23 Write a **boolean** method `parallel()` with four **double** parameters m1, b1, m2, and b2. The parameters come conceptually in two pairs. The first pair contains the coefficients describing one line; the second pair contains coefficients describing a second line. The method returns **true** if the two lines are parallel; otherwise, the method returns **false**. Why does the method take four parameters?

7.24 Write a **boolean** method `isPrime()` that has a single parameter i of type integer. The method returns **true** if i is a prime number; otherwise, the method returns **false**.

7.25 Write a **boolean** method `isEndOfSentence()` that has a single value **char** parameter c. The method returns **true** if c is either a period, a question mark, or an exclamation point; otherwise, the method returns **false**.

7.26 Write an **int** method `sum()` that expects a single integer number as its parameter. The method should return the sum of the integers from 1 to that number.

7.27 Write a **void** method `printChar()` that expects two parameters: a character object c and an integer amount n. The method should make n copies of the character c to the standard output stream.

7.28 Write a **double** method `evaluateQuadraticPolynomial()` that expects four **double** parameters a, b, c, and x. The method should return the value

$$ax^2 + bx + c$$

7.29 Write a **double** method `cubicArea()` that computes the area under the curve for the cubic polynomial $a_3x^3 + a_2x^2 + a_1x + a_0$ along the x-interval (s, t).

7.30 Write a **double** method `quarticArea()` that computes the area under the curve for the quartic polynomial $a_4x^4 + a_3x^3 + a_2x^2 + a_1x + a_0$ along the x-interval (s, t).

7.31 An angle is measured normally in either degrees or in radians where 360 degrees equal 2π radians. Write **double** methods `degreesToRadians()` and `radiansToDegrees()` that each expect a single **double** parameter. Method `degreesToRadians()` treats its parameter as a value in degrees and returns the equivalent number of radians. Method `radiansToDegrees()` treats its parameter as a value in radians and returns the equivalent number of degrees.

7.32 Write a method `stripVowels()` that extracts and processes the current input line. The method returns, as a string, the consonant portion of the input.

7.33 Write a method `distanceToLightYears()` that takes a distance in kilometers and returns the amount in light-years to travel that distance. The speed of light is approximately $2.997925 * 10^8$ meters per second. What types should the parameter and return value be? Why?

7.34 Write a `String` method `pigLatin()` with a single parameter w of type `String`. The method returns the translation of the word represented by w into Pig Latin. Pig Latin translates words in the following way: words that start with consonants have the consonants stripped and added as a suffix along with the string "ay"; words that start with a vowel are appended with the string "ay".

7.35 Suppose you must create a library to facilitate computer-assisted telephone calls. What methods should be in the library to support client applications?

7.36 Suppose you must create a library to facilitate computer-assisted checkbook management. What methods should be in the library to support client applications?

7.37 Specify two application areas other than telephony and checkbook management where computing assistance is appropriate. What methods should be in these libraries to support client applications?

7.38 Write methods for the following tasks. Discuss your choice of which values are parameters, which values are local constants, and what their types should be.

   a) `speed()`: Compute the speed of an object after t seconds of acceleration given that the object was traveling initially at v_0 meters per second and then accelerated at a meters per second per second, where $speed = v_0 + at$.

   b) `distance()`: Compute the distance traveled in t seconds by an object that started at rest and then accelerated at a meters per second per second, where $distance = at^2/2$.

7.39 Write a program `CompoundInterest.java` that gets from its users a deposit amount, an interest rate, and a term of deposit. The program then computes and displays how the principal will change. The program should define and use a method `compoundAnnual()` with three parameters: a starting amount, an interest rate represented as a percentage, and the number of years. After acquiring these values, the program then computes and displays how the principal will change. The formula for computing interest compounded on an annual basis is as follows:

$$StartingAmount(1 + InterestRate/100)^{Years}$$

7.40 Write a program `SwissCheese.java` that gets from its user eight values that specify the characteristics of a rectangular hunk of cheese: width w, length l, height h, m internal spherical air bubbles of radius b, and n surface cylindrical holes of radius r and height d. The program then computes and displays the volume of the associated hunk of Swiss cheese. In developing the program, you should define and use methods

- `cylinderVolume()`: computes using its radius and height parameters, the volume of the associated cylinder. The volume of a cylinder with radius r and height h is $\pi r^2 h$.

- `barVolume()`: computes using its width, height, and length parameters, the volume of the associated bar. The volume of a bar is the product of its width, height, and length.

- `sphereVolume()`: computes using its radius parameter, the volume of the associated sphere. The volume of sphere with radius r is $4\pi r^3/3$.

7.41 Develop a program `Euler.java` that uses the method `factorial()` to compute an approximation of e (Euler's number). Base your approximation on the following formula for e:

$$1 + \frac{1}{1!} + \frac{1}{2!} + \frac{1}{3!} + \dots$$

For Exercises 7.42 – 7.44 consider the following class `Overload.java`.

```java
public class Overload {
    public static void f(int a, double b) {
        System.out.println("f(int, double): a = " + a);
        System.out.println("f(int, double): b = " + b);
    }

    public static void f(int a, int b) {
        System.out.println("f(int, int): a = " + a);
        System.out.println("f(int, int): b = " + b);
    }

    public static void f(double a, double b) {
        System.out.println("f(double, double): a = " + a);
        System.out.println("f(double, double): b = " + b);
    }
}
```

7.42 What is output (if any) by the following program? Explain.

```java
public class OverloadDemo1 {
    public static void main(String[] args) {
        int i = 1;
        int j = 2;
        double x = 3.5;
        double y = 10.2;
        Overload.f(i, j);
        Overload.f(i, y);
        Overload.f(y, x);
    }
}
```

7.43 What is output (if any) by the following program? Explain.

```java
public class OverloadDemo2 {
```

```java
    public static void main(String[] args) {
        Overload.f(1, 2.3);
        Overload.f(2, 4);
        Overload.f(2.6, 10.5);
    }
}
```

7.44 What is output (if any) by the following program? Explain.

```java
public class OverloadDemo3 {
    public static void main(String[] args) {
        Overload.f(1, 2.3);
        Overload.f(2.3, 4);
        Overload.f(2.6, 10.5);
    }
}
```

7.45 Rewrite our method min() with signature

min(int, int, int)

from Listing 7.7 using **if** statements.

7.46 Rewrite our method min() with signature

min(int a, int b, int c, int d)

from Listing 7.7 using **if** statements.

7.47 Reimplement power() so that if the values of its parameters require it, the method appropriately returns values Double.NaN, Double.NEGATIVE_INFINITY, and Double.POSITIVE_INFINITY.

7.48 Explain why two classes referenced by the same program can have methods with identical names.

7.49 Explain why two classes referenced by the same program can have constructors with identical names.

For Exercises 7.50 – 7.53 the following definition is in effect.

```java
class A {
    private int count = 0;
    public A(int n) {
        count = n;
    }
    public static void d() {
        count = 5;
    }
    public void e(int n) {
        { count = n; }
    }
    public void f(int n) {
        { int count = n; }
        ++count;
    }
    public static void g(int n) {
        count = n;
    }
    public static void h(int n) {
```

```
                count = n;
            }
        }
```

7.50   Which of the methods in A are in principle allowed to modify the instance variable count? Why?

7.51   Which of the methods in A, if any, legally modify the instance variable count? Why?

7.52   Which of the methods in A, if any, illegally attempt to modify the instance variable count? Why?

7.53   Which of the methods in A, if any, do not make any attempt to modify the instance variable count. Why?

7.54   Suppose class B1 has definition

```java
public class B1 {
    private String string = "";
    public B1(String s) {
        string = s;
    }
    public String getS() {
        return string;
    }
    public Object clone() {
        return new B1(getS());
    }
}
```

and class B2 has definition

```java
public class B2 {
    private String string = "";
    public B2(String s) {
        string = s;
    }
    public String getS() {
        return string.clone();
    }
    public Object clone() {
        return new B2(getS());
    }
}
```

What is the output of the following program? Why?

```java
public class BDemo
    public static void main(String[] args) {
        String s = "tsktsking";
        B1 u1 = new B1(s);
        B1 u2 = u1.clone();
        B2 u3 = new B2(s);
        B2 u4 = u3.clone();
        boolean flag1 = (u1.getS() == u3.getS());
        boolean flag2 = (u2.getS() == u4.getS());

        System.out.println(flag1);
```

```
                    System.out.println(flag2);
                }
            }
```

7.55 Suppose class C has definition

```
        public class C {
            private int data1;
            private int data2;
            private Point data3;
            private Point data4 = new Point();
            public C() {
                data2 = 1;
            }
            public int getData1() {
                return data1;
            }
            public int getData2() {
                return data2;
            }
            public Point getData3() {
                return data3;
            }
            public Point getData4() {
                return data4.toString();
            }
        }
```

What is the output of the following program? Why?

```
        public class CDemo {
            public static void main(String[] args) {
                C c = new C();
                System.out.println(c.getData1());
                System.out.println(c.getData2());
                System.out.println(c.getData3());
                System.out.println(c.getData4());
            }
        }
```

7.56 Suppose class D has definition

```
        public class D {
            private static int counter1 = 0;
            private int counter2 = 0;
            public D() {
                // no body needed
            }
            public void increment() {
                ++counter1;
                ++counter2;
            }
            public int getCounter1() {
                return counter1;
            }
            public int getCounter2() {
                return counter2;
            }
```

```
                    }
```

What is the output of the following program? Why?

```
public static class DDemo {
    public void main(String[] args) {
        D d1 = new D();
        D d2 = new D();
        d1.increment();
        d1.increment();
        d2.increment();
        d2.increment();
        System.out.println(d1.getCounter1());
        System.out.println(d1.getCounter2());
        System.out.println(d2.getCounter1());
        System.out.println(d2.getCounter2());
    }
}
```

For Exercises 7.57 and 7.58 the following definition is in effect

```
public class E {
    private int data = 0;
    public E() {
        // no body used
    }
    public void f() {
        data = 1;
        // f comment
    }
    public void g() {
        data = 2;
        // g comment
    }
}
```

7.57 If the comment in method f() is replaced with the following statement will class E successfully compile? Why?

```
g();
```

7.58 If the comment in method g() is replaced with the following statement will class E successfully compile? Why?

```
f();
```

7.59 Design and implement a data abstraction for representing the days of the week. Justify why your design and implementation are reasonable.

7.60 Reimplement the power() methods of Listing 7.7 to work for an arbitrary integer power *n*.

7.12   PROGRAMMING PROJECT — AUTOMOBILE FINANCING

Suppose you want borrow an amount d to purchase an automobile and your lending institution offers you a loan with n monthly payments at annual interest rate of $i\%$. The formula to determine your monthly payment p is

> The objective of this case study is to practice the design and development of methods

$$p = \frac{d(a-1)a^n}{a^n - 1}, \text{ where } a = 1 + i/12$$

If your automobile loan is a *simple interest* loan, then your interest charge each month is based on your current balance. Your balance $b(m)$ after the month m is

$$b(m) = da^m - \frac{p(a^m - 1)}{a - 1}$$

If you decided to make a balloon payment of $b(m)$ at month m (a final payment that finishes off the loan), then your total interest charges $c(m)$ would have been

$$c(m) = pm - d + b(m)$$

Table 7.1 provides an *amortization table* for a \$10,000 simple interest loan at 7% for 36 months. Each row in the table indicates for the given month: opening balance, monthly payment, amount of payment applied to principal, amount of payment applied to interest, and closing balance. Thus, if you decided to retire the loan at the 12th month you would have paid previously the amount $11 \times \$308.77 = \$3,396.47$ and would have to make a balloon payment of \$7,163.41. Your total outlay would be \$10,559.88.

Many automobile loans are not simple interest loans. They are instead *precomputed loans*. For such loans, the total interest to be paid is more front loaded. The loading is based on the *Rule of 78s*. (Because of the excessive prepayment penalties associated with the Rule of 78s, the United States has banned its use for loans with terms longer than 61 months.)

The term Rule of 78s arose in how the interest is charged for a precomputed loan with a twelve-month term. If such a loan goes its full term, then the total interest to be paid is $c(12)$, which is the same amount for a simple loan. However, with precomputed loans, the lender requires that 12/78 of $c(12)$ be paid in interest the first month, 11/78 of $c(12)$ be paid the second month, 10/78 of $c(12)$ be paid in the third month, and so on, leaving the last month to pay 1/78 of $c(12)$. (78 is the sum of $1 + 2 + \ldots + 12$.) For example, in the first three payments of a twelve-month loan, the borrower is obligated to pay 42.3% of the finance charges $(0.423 \cong (12 + 11 + 10)/78)$.

The Rule of 78s can be generalized for a loan with a term of t months. For such loans, $t/(t(t+1)/2)$ of $c(t)$ is paid the first month, $(t-1)/(t(t+1)/2)$ of $c(t)$ is paid the second month, $(t-2)/(t(t+1)/2)$ of $c(t)$ is paid the third month, and so on. As a result of how interest is charged, a precomputed loan's monthly balance formula $f(m)$ is different

Table 7.1   Simple interest 7% loan calculation using CarLoan.java.

```
Amortization table for a simple 7.00% loan of $10000.00
for 36 months

Month   Opening  Payment  Debt    Interest  Closing
        Balance           Paid    Paid      Balance
========================================================
   1    10000.00  308.77  250.44   58.33    9749.56
   2     9749.56  308.77  251.90   56.87    9497.66
   3     9497.66  308.77  253.37   55.40    9244.30
   4     9244.30  308.77  254.85   53.93    8989.45
   5     8989.45  308.77  256.33   52.44    8733.12
   6     8733.12  308.77  257.83   50.94    8475.29
   7     8475.29  308.77  259.33   49.44    8215.96
   8     8215.96  308.77  260.84   47.93    7955.11
   9     7955.11  308.77  262.37   46.40    7692.75
  10     7692.75  308.77  263.90   44.87    7428.85
  11     7428.85  308.77  265.44   43.33    7163.41
  12     7163.41  308.77  266.98   41.79    6896.43
  13     6896.43  308.77  268.54   40.23    6627.89
  14     6627.89  308.77  270.11   38.66    6357.78
  15     6357.78  308.77  271.68   37.09    6086.10
  16     6086.10  308.77  273.27   35.50    5812.83
  17     5812.83  308.77  274.86   33.91    5537.96
  18     5537.96  308.77  276.47   32.30    5261.50
  19     5261.50  308.77  278.08   30.69    4983.42
  20     4983.42  308.77  279.70   29.07    4703.72
  21     4703.72  308.77  281.33   27.44    4422.39
  22     4422.39  308.77  282.97   25.80    4139.41
  23     4139.41  308.77  284.62   24.15    3854.79
  24     3854.79  308.77  286.28   22.49    3568.50
  25     3568.50  308.77  287.95   20.82    3280.55
  26     3280.55  308.77  289.63   19.14    2990.91
  27     2990.91  308.77  291.32   17.45    2699.59
  28     2699.59  308.77  293.02   15.75    2406.57
  29     2406.57  308.77  294.73   14.04    2111.83
  30     2111.83  308.77  296.45   12.32    1815.38
  31     1815.38  308.77  298.18   10.59    1517.20
  32     1517.20  308.77  299.92    8.85    1217.28
  33     1217.28  308.77  301.67    7.10     915.61
  34      915.61  308.77  303.43    5.34     612.18
  35      612.18  308.77  305.20    3.57     306.98
  36      306.98  308.77  306.98    1.79       0.00
------------------------------------------------------
Totals          11115.75 10000.00 1115.75
```

Table 7.2 Amortization for precomputed interest 7% loan.

Amortization table for a precomputed interest 7.00% loan
of $10000.00 for 36 months

Month	Opening Balance	Payment	Debt Paid	Interest Paid	Closing Balance
1	10000.00	308.77	248.46	60.31	9751.54
2	9751.54	308.77	250.14	58.64	9501.40
3	9501.40	308.77	251.81	56.96	9249.59
4	9249.59	308.77	253.49	55.29	8996.11
5	8996.11	308.77	255.16	53.61	8740.95
6	8740.95	308.77	256.84	51.93	8484.11
7	8484.11	308.77	258.51	50.26	8225.60
8	8225.60	308.77	260.19	48.58	7965.41
9	7965.41	308.77	261.86	46.91	7703.55
10	7703.55	308.77	263.54	45.23	7440.01
11	7440.01	308.77	265.21	43.56	7174.80
12	7174.80	308.77	266.89	41.88	6907.91
13	6907.91	308.77	268.56	40.21	6639.35
14	6639.35	308.77	270.24	38.53	6369.11
15	6369.11	308.77	271.91	36.86	6097.19
16	6097.19	308.77	273.59	35.18	5823.60
17	5823.60	308.77	275.26	33.51	5548.34
18	5548.34	308.77	276.94	31.83	5271.40
19	5271.40	308.77	278.62	30.16	4992.78
20	4992.78	308.77	280.29	28.48	4712.49
21	4712.49	308.77	281.97	26.80	4430.53
22	4430.53	308.77	283.64	25.13	4146.89
23	4146.89	308.77	285.32	23.45	3861.57
24	3861.57	308.77	286.99	21.78	3574.58
25	3574.58	308.77	288.67	20.10	3285.91
26	3285.91	308.77	290.34	18.43	2995.57
27	2995.57	308.77	292.02	16.75	2703.55
28	2703.55	308.77	293.69	15.08	2409.86
29	2409.86	308.77	295.37	13.40	2114.49
30	2114.49	308.77	297.04	11.73	1817.44
31	1817.44	308.77	298.72	10.05	1518.73
32	1518.73	308.77	300.39	8.38	1218.33
33	1218.33	308.77	302.07	6.70	916.26
34	916.26	308.77	303.75	5.03	612.52
35	612.52	308.77	305.42	3.35	307.10
36	307.10	308.77	307.10	1.68	0.00
Totals		11115.75	10000.00	1115.75	

from the formula for the monthly balance $b(m)$ of a simple loan. For a precomputed loan, the balance $f(m)$ is

$$f(m) = d - pm + c(t)\left(1 - \frac{(t-m)(t-m+1)}{t(t+1)}\right).$$

Table 7.2 provides an amortization table for a $10,000 precomputed interest loan at 7% for 36 months. If you compare the difference in entries with Table 7.1, you will see that there is an interest penalty associated with the early payback of a precomputed interest loan as compared to what happens with a simple interest loan. For example, the balloon payment for the loan at the twelfth month is $7,174.80. For a comparable simple interest loan the balloon payment was only $7,163.41.

PROBLEM STATEMENT

For this case study, implement an automobile loan calculator. The calculator should expect the user to provide: a loan amount, interest rate, term, and indication of whether the finance charges are simple interest or precomputed interest. The program should display an amortization table for the loan.

IMPLEMENTATION

Your program should be named `CarLoan.java`. Your program should consist of an application entry point method `main()`. Method `main()` manages the program interaction. In doing its work it invokes several other methods. At a minimum you need to make the following methods available.

`static double balanceSimple(double d, double i, double n, double m)`

> Computes the balance $b(m)$ at m months for a simple interest loan of amount d at annual interest i with a term of n months

`static double payment(double d, double i, double n)`

> Computes the monthly payment p for a loan of amount d at annual interest i with a term of n months

`static double cumulative(double d, double i, double t, double m)`

> Computes the total interest paid $b(m)$ at m months for a simple interest loan of amount d at annual interest i with a term of t months.

`static double balanceNonsimple(double d, double i, double n, double m)`

> Computes the balance $f(m)$ at m months for a precomputed interest loan of amount d at annual interest i with a term of n months

TESTING

The World Wide Web has many sites that provide loan calculators that compute amortization tables. Search the Web for such calculators, and compare your calculator's results to one of the calculators that you find. Document the various test cases that you considered and the calculator that was used in the comparison.

DOCUMENTATION

You should document both your design and implementation. In documenting your design, justify the access specification of all members. You should also justify your approach and explain the behaviors and nuances of your methods. This documentation requirement has been added to the case study because of the complexity of your design task. Previous case studies were specified to such a degree that class members were specified fully.

SELF-TEST ANSWERS

S7.1 Method `min()` can be reimplemented in the following manner:

```java
min(int a, int b, int c, int d) {
    return Math.min(Math.min(a, b), Math.min(c, d));
}
```

S7.2 The output of the program is

```
0
0
0
```

This output is produced because Java uses value parameters. The value of the actual **int** parameter is unaffected by changes to the formal **int** parameter.

S7.3 Method `line()` can be implemented in the following manner

```java
public double line(double m, double b, double x) {
    return m*x + b;
}
```

S7.4 No. Because Java uses call-by-value parameter passing, the actual parameters cannot be affected by a method invocation.

S7.5 `TriangleArea.java` can be implemented in the following manner.

```java
import java.util.*;

public class TriangleArea {
    public static void main(String[] args) {
        Scanner stdin = new Scanner(System.in);

        System.out.println("Enter triangle sides: ");
        double a = stdin.nextDouble();
        double b = stdin.nextDouble();
        double c = stdin.nextDouble();

        double val = area(a, b, c);

        if (! Double.isNaN(val)) {
            System.out.println("A triangle with sides "
                + a + ", " + b + ", and " + c
                + " has area " + val);
        }
        else {
            System.out.println(a + ", " + b + ", and " + c
                + " do not represent sides of a triangle");
        }
    }
```

```java
        public static double area(double a, double b,
                double c){
            boolean ok = (a > 0) && (b > 0) && (c > 0)
                && (a + b > c) && (a + c > b) && (b + c > a);

            if (ok) {
                double s = (a + b + c) / 2;
                return Math.sqrt(s*(s - a)*(s - b)*(s - c));
            }
            else {
                return Double.NaN;
            }
        }
    }
```

S7.6 Class Cast can be implemented in the following manner.

```java
    public class Cast {

        static public char toChar(String s) {
            return s.charAt(0);
        }

        static public boolean toBoolean(String s) {
            return Boolean.parseBoolean(s);
        }

        static public short toShort(String s) {
            return Short.parseShort(s);
        }

        static public int toInt(String s) {
            return Integer.parseInt(s);
        }

        static public long toLong(String s) {
            return Long.parseLong(s);
        }

        static public float toFloat(String s) {
            return Float.valueOf(s);
        }

        static public double toDouble(String s) {
            return Double.valueOf(s);
        }

        static public String toString(short val) {
            return String.valueOf(val);
        }

        static public String toString(int val) {
            return String.valueOf(val);
        }

        static public String toString(long val) {
            return String.valueOf(val);
```

```
        }

        static public String toString(float val) {
            return String.valueOf(val);
        }

        static public String toString(double val) {
            return String.valueOf(val);
        }

        static public String toString(char val) {
            return String.valueOf(val);
        }

        static public String toString(boolean val) {
            return String.valueOf(val);
        }
    }
```

S7.7 With regard to CDemo.java:

- The definition of c1 is legal because C has a **public** default constructor.
- The definition of c2 is illegal because C does not have a constructor taking three parameters.
- The invocation c1.setData1(4) is legal because C mutator method setData1() is **public** and takes one integer parameter. It makes no difference that the mutator is setting a **private** instance variable.
- The invocation c1.setData3(4) is illegal because C mutator method setData3() is **private**. It makes no difference that the mutator is setting a **public** instance variable.
- The definition of n1 is legal because C accessor method getData2() is **public**.
- The definition of n2 is legal because C accessor method getData3() is **public**.
- The definition of n3 is illegal because C instance variable data1 is **private**.
- The definition of n4 is illegal because C instance variable data2 is **private**.
- The definition of n5 is legal because C instance variable data3 is **public**.

8

ARRAYS AND COLLECTIONS

A programmer often needs the ability to represent a group of values as a list. For such tasks, Java provides several list representation alternatives. Our examination of lists begins with the array, which is the basic Java list mechanism. Java arrays have features that make them more robust than arrays in other common programming languages: the size of an array can be specified at run time; automatic bounds checking ensures that any reference to an array element is valid; and a data field `length` specifies the number of elements in the list. Furthermore, because an array is an object, an array also has the features common to all other objects (e.g., the ability to clone). Our examination of lists also considers the `java.util` collection classes. The collection classes are important to programmers because they provide advanced data structures and algorithms that are useful in many problem-solving situations.

OBJECTIVES

- Define and initialize one-dimensional and multidimensional arrays.
- Reference and manipulate entire arrays and individual array elements.
- Use arrays and array elements as parameters to methods.
- Present algorithms for sorting and searching arrays.
- Consider the various collection classes.
- Explore the use of ArrayList<T>.
- Explore the use of the collections algorithms.

8.1   BASIC LIST REQUIREMENTS

Suppose we want to find the minimum value of five integers represented by **int** variables `value1`, `value2`, through `value5`. The following code segment computes that value for us.

```
int minimumSoFar = value1;
if (value2 < minimumSoFar) {
    minimumSoFar = value2;
}
if (value3 < minimumSoFar) {
    minimumSoFar = value3;
}
if (value4 < minimumSoFar) {
    minimumSoFar = value4;
}
if (value5 < minimumSoFar) {
    minimumSoFar = value5;
}
```

Notice that a separate **if** statement is used for each value in the list—although the variable names are similar, each variable is independent of the other variables.

Now suppose that we need the minimum value of 1,000 integers represented by variables `value1` through `value1000`. Because of the variable independence, we cannot simply introduce iteration into the solution as was done for the number averaging problem of Chapter 6. And if we proceed as above, with a separate **if** statement for each individual value, the resulting very large code segment would be both clumsy and error prone. Instead what we require is a Java mechanism that enables us to create an object that can represent a list of values. Furthermore, we require the ability to manipulate collectively and individually the elements of a list in an intuitive manner.

Our examination of list types begins with the array, which is the basic Java mechanism for representing a list of values. Because Java considers an array to be an object, an array has the features common to all other objects. In particular, the value of an array variable is a reference to an array rather than being an array itself.

8.2   ONE-DIMENSIONAL ARRAYS

The individual values that make up an array are known as *elements*. Array elements can be referenced collectively or individually. They can be of any fundamental type, a previously defined class type, or an array type. One important language restriction on arrays is that all elements of an array have the same type, which is known as the *element type*.

8.2.1   DEFINITIONS

Arrays can be defined with or without initialization. If there is no initialization, then the definition has the form

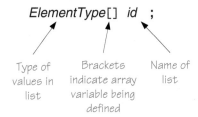

$$ElementType[] \ \ id \ \ ;$$

Type of values in list	Brackets indicate array variable being defined	Name of list

where *ElementType* is the type of the individual elements in the array and *id* is an identifier naming the array.

Our next code segment defines three local array variables a, b, and c without specifying initial values for these variables.

```
int[] a;
char[] b;
double[] c;
```

Like other local variable definitions that do not specify initial values, the values of these variables are undefined. Our representation of these variables is

An array variable definition can specify the array which the variable refers. The most common such form is

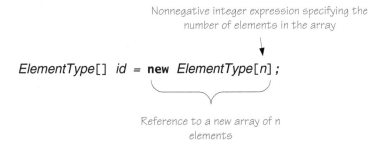

Nonnegative integer expression specifying the number of elements in the array

$$ElementType[] \ \ id \ = \ \textbf{new} \ \ ElementType[n] \ ;$$

Reference to a new array of n elements

The following code segment defines in part, three array variables number, value, and s. The variable definitions specify the arrays to which they refer.

```
Scanner stdin = new Scanner(System.in);
int[] number = new int[3];
int n = stdin.nextInt();
double[] value = new double[n];
```

```
String[] s = new String[n];
```

Variable `number` references a new array of three elements with element type **int**, variable `value` references a new array of n elements with element type **double**, and variable `s` references a new array of n elements with element type `String`, where the value for n has been extracted from the standard input stream. Each of the arrays is a collection of individual *array elements*. Each of the array elements can be used like a variable of the underlying element type.

If the value extracted for n is 5, then `number`, `value`, and `s` have representation

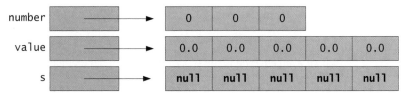

Variable `number` refers to a list of three elements and variables `value` and `s` both refer to lists of five elements. Because no initial values are specified for the elements themselves, the elements of the three arrays are default initialized. By default, numeric elements are initialized to 0; **boolean** elements are initialized to **false**; and object elements are initialized to **null**.

Suppose d and e are both **int** array variables, where d references an array with three elements whose values are initialized to 10, 20, and 30 and e references an array of two elements whose values are initialized to 40 and 50. Also suppose that f is a two-element **double** array whose elements are initialized to 1.1 and 2.2.[†] Our depiction of these arrays is

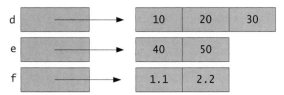

Because d and e are both of the same type, we can assign one to the other. For example, if

```
d = e;
```

is executed, then the new value of d is the value of e; i.e., d and e now reference the same array of elements. Our depiction of the arrays is now

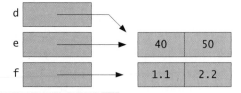

---

† Explicit array initialization is considered in Section 8.2.3.

(The three-element array that d previously referenced is returned automatically to the system by the Java garbage collector.)

The assignment

```
f = e;      // illegal
```

is illegal. Arrays e and f have different element types—e is an array of **int** values and f is an array of **double** values. Because the arrays have different types, one cannot be assigned to the other.

Unless it would cause confusion with regard to the particular example, in subsequent array depictions, we use a more succinct representation that does not explicitly show the reference. For example, if g is a three-element **char** array whose elements are 'a', 'b', and 'c', then our standard depiction of g is

g | 'a' | 'b' | 'c' |

Bracket placement

Java permits the brackets indicating an array variable definition to be placed alternatively after the variable name. Thus, array definition

```
double[] x;
```

can also be specified in the following manner

```
double x[];
```

It is our practice to use only the first form. This convention is the one followed by most Java programmers.

Remember array variables are reference variables

Beginning Java programmers sometimes forget that an array type variable holds a reference to an object. They mistakenly assume that the definition of the array type variable automatically provides the list of elements that are to be manipulated.

8.2.2   ELEMENT ACCESS

The act of referring to an individual array element is called *subscripting* or *indexing*. Just as brackets are used in a definition to indicate that an array is being created, so too are brackets used to subscript a particular element of an array. Each element of an array has its own subscript value. The first element of an array has subscript value 0, the second element of an array has subscript value 1, and so on. For array v defined below,

```
int[] v = new int[10]; // elements default initialized to 0s
```

the last element has a subscript value 9. The following figure shows a representation of v.

The elements of array v can be referenced via the expressions v[0], v[1], v[2], ..., v[9].

A subscript can be a nonnegative integer expression. For example, v[(low + high)/2], refers to the element of v with subscript value (low + high)/2. If low has value 0 and high has value 9, then v[(low + high)/2] refers to v[4].

In the following code segment, all references to array elements are legal.

```
int i = 7;
int j = 2;
int k = 4;
v[0] = 1;                          // element 0 of v given value 1
v[i] = 5;                          // element i of v given value 5
v[j] = v[i] + 3;                   // element j of v given value
                                   // of element i of v plus 3
v[j+1] = v[i] + v[0];             // element j+1 of v given value
                                   // of element i of v plus
                                   // value of element 0 of v
v[v[j]] = 12;                      // element v[j] of v given
                                   // value 12
System.out.println(v[2]);          // element 2 of v is displayed
v[k] = stdin.nextInt();           // element k of v given next
                                   // extracted value
```

If the value extracted from the standard input was the value 3, then the effect of executing the preceding code segment is

v	1	0	8	6	3	0	0	5	12	0
	v[0]	v[1]	v[2]	v[3]	v[4]	v[5]	v[6]	v[7]	v[8]	v[9]

Unlike many other programming languages, Java automatically checks that proper array subscripts are used. If a subscript is determined to be invalid, an exception of type IndexOutOfBoundsException is generated. For example, the following code segment contains two misuses of array b.

```
int[] b = new int[100];    // b has 100 elements: b[0], ... b[99]
b[-1] = 0;                 // illegal: subscript too small
b[100] = 0;                // illegal: subscript too large
```

Unless a program provides exception handling code, an IndexOutOfBoundsException exception causes the program to terminate.

Exception handling is considered in Chapter 10

If the element type of an array is an object type, then the elements hold either the value **null** or references to element type values rather than holding element type values themselves. This situation is illustrated in the following example that defines and then initializes a two-element String array s.

```
String[] s = new String[2];
s[0] = "cats";
s[1] = "dogs";
```

Element s[0] is a reference to a String representing "cats" and element s[1] is a reference to a String representing "dogs". Array s has depiction

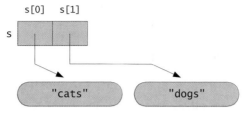

In our next example, we use awt class Point.

```
Point[] p = new Point[3];
p[0] = new Point(0, 0);
p[1] = new Point(1, 1);
p[2] = new Point(2, 2);
```

Array p has depiction

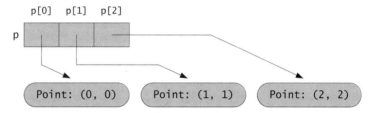

Because p[0], p[1], and p[2] are Point reference variables, they have access to Point member methods. For example, code segment

```
p[0].setX(1);
p[1].setY(p[2].getY());
```

causes the following update of p.

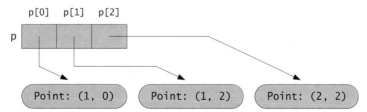

The update occurs in this manner:

- Expression p[0].setX(1) causes the object that p[0] references to set its x-coordinate data field to 1.

- Expression p[1].setY(p[2].getY()) causes the object that p[1] references to set its y-coordinate to the value of the y-coordinate of the object referenced by p[2].

The elements of **p** hold references. Therefore, an assignment to one of its elements modifies what that element references rather than modifying the object that had been referenced. For example, consider the following code segment that further updates array **p**.

```
Point vertex = new Point(4,4);
p[1] = p[0];
p[2] = vertex;
```

The assignment of **p[0]** to **p[1]** causes **p[1]** to refer to the same object as **p[0]**; the assignment of **vertex** to **p[2]** causes **p[2]** to refer to the same object as **vertex**. Thus, memory has depiction

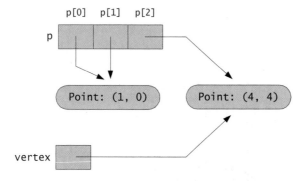

(Because **Point** objects (1, 2) and (2, 2) no longer have any variables referencing them, their memory is reclaimed automatically by the Java garbage collector.)

8.2.3   EXPLICIT INITIALIZATION

Java also provides a declaration form to specify explicitly the initial values of the elements of an array.

id references an array of *n* elements. *id[0]* has
value *exp$_0$*, *id[1]* has value *exp$_1$*, and so on.

$$\textit{ElementType[] } \textit{id} = \{ \textit{ exp}_0 \textit{ , exp}_1 \textit{ , } ... \textit{ exp}_{n\text{-}1} \};$$

Each *exp$_i$* is an expression that
evaluates to type *ElementType*

By using this feature, the following code segment specifies the initial values for the arrays referenced by variables **fibonacci**, **puppy**, and **unit**.

```
int[] fibonacci = { 1, 1, 2, 3, 5, 8, 13, 21, 34, 55 };
String[] puppy = { "nilla", "buffer", "darby", "galen" };
int[] unit = { 1 };
```

The declaration of `fibonacci` causes it to reference an **int** array of 10 elements, the declaration of `puppy` causes it to reference a `String` array of four elements, and the declaration of `unit` causes it to reference an **int** array of one element. Functionally, the three declarations are equivalent to the following.

```
int[] fibonacci = new int[10];
fibonacci[0] = 1;
fibonacci[1] = 1;
fibonacci[2] = 2;
fibonacci[3] = 3;
fibonacci[4] = 5;
fibonacci[5] = 8;
fibonacci[6] = 13;
fibonacci[7] = 21;
fibonacci[8] = 34;
fibonacci[9] = 55;

String[] puppy = new String[4];
puppy[0] = "nilla";
puppy[1] = "buffer";
puppy[2] = "darby";
puppy[3] = "galen";

int[] unit = new int[1];
unit[0] = 1;
```

A single element list, like `unit`, is an array and is treated consistently by Java in that manner.

8.2.4   CONSTANT ARRAYS

As in other declarations, the modifier **final** can be applied in an array declaration. The modifier has the usual effect—after its initialization, the array variable is treated as a constant. In this case, the array variable cannot change which array it references. For example, the following declaration defines and initializes a constant two-element array B.

```
final int[] B = { 10, 100 };
```

Our depiction for B is

where the lock indicates that the value of the reference cannot be changed. With the constant declaration in effect, the following statement is invalid.

```
B = new int[2];           // illegal: a final object cannot be
                          // the target of an assignment
```

However, the values of the elements of the array can be changed.

```
B[1] = 20;                // legal: B[1] is not final
```

8.2.5 MEMBERS

Because an array is a Java object, an array has associated with it all of the member methods of an `Object` (e.g., `clone()` and `equals()`). However, the array `clone()` method is overridden specifically for arrays. In addition to member methods, an array also has a **public final** data field `length` specifying the number of elements in the array.

The Java language designers were particularly helpful to programmers by including array data field `length`—it is a convenience not found with arrays in many other programming languages. In the next code segment, we make use of the feature in the test expression of a **for** loop. The loop displays the elements of the array `puppy` to standard output.

```
for (int i = 0; i < puppy.length; ++i) {
    System.out.println(puppy[i]);
}
```

In the loop, i iteratively takes on the values 0, 1, 2, 3, and 4. Because the values 0, 1, 2, and 3 are all less than `puppy.length`, the statement

```
System.out.println(puppy[i]);
```

is executed four times. Each time a successive element of `puppy` is displayed. When i is 4, the expression i < `puppy.length` is **false**, which causes the loop to be exited.

Array method `clone()` returns a duplicate of the array. The new array object has the same number of elements as the invoking array. The values of these elements are duplicates of the invoking array. A clone produced in this manner is known as a *shallow copy*. The corresponding elements in the two arrays reference the same objects. The shallowness can be seen by viewing the representations of the array variables u and v defined in the following code segment.

```
Point[] u = { new Point(0, 0), new Point(1, 1),
                    new Point(2, 2) };
Point[] v = u.clone();
```

The code segment makes array v a clone of array u. Arrays u and v have representation

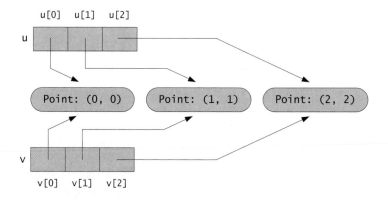

The shallowness of array cloning is further highlighted by the effect of the following statement on the arrays u and v.

```
u[2].setX(3);
```

Because elements u[2] and v[2] reference the same Point, the change to u[2] is visible through v[2].

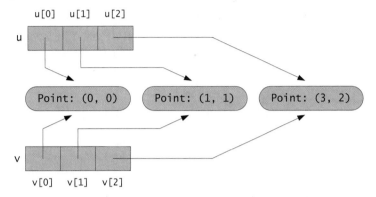

Although array v was created to be a clone to array u, there is no requirement that the elements of v reference the same Point objects as u.

For example, if statement

```
v[2] = new Point(4, 30);
```

is executed, then changes to u[2] do not affect v[2] and vice versa. This independence is in effect because u[2] and v[2] reference different objects.

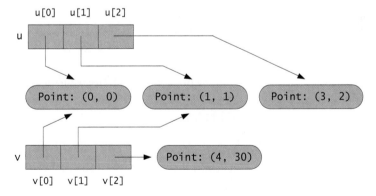

If a distinct element-by-element clone w of array u is needed, it can be created in the following manner.

```
Point[] w = new Point[u.length];
for (int i = 0; i < u.length; ++i) {
   w[i] = u[i].clone();
}
```

In this code segment, the definition of w causes a new array of the proper length to be created. Distinct copies of the elements of u are created by individually cloning its elements.

For this example, we say that array w is a *deep copy* of u—arrays u and w do not share any memory.

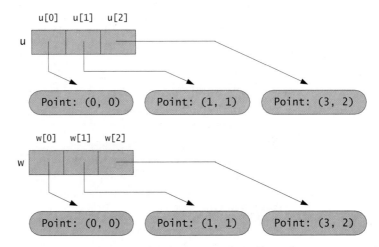

The next example demonstrates that using method clone() on an array with a primitive element type automatically produces a deep copy.

```
int[] x = { 0, 1, 2 };
int[] y = x.clone();
```

The two arrays have depiction

```
       x[0]   x[1]   x[2]
   x |   0  |   1  |   2  |

   y |   0  |   1  |   2  |
       y[0]   y[1]   y[2]
```

Because the elements of the two arrays hold **int** values and not **int** references, a change to array x does not affect array y and vice versa. A change to an element affects only its value. For example, if x[1] is modified

```
x[1] = 3;
```

then y[1] is unaffected (i.e., there are no side effects to the assignment of x[1]).

```
       x[0]   x[1]   x[2]
   x |   0  |   3  |   2  |

   y |   0  |   1  |   2  |
       y[0]   y[1]   y[2]
```

8.3 ITERATOR FOR LOOP

With the release of version 5.0, Java now provides a **for** loop that provides an *iterator* approach to accessing the elements of an array, where an iterator is an object that sequentially takes on the values of the elements of a list.

Suppose `String` array `townList` has the following definitions.

```
String[] townList = { "Brooklyn", "Glen Rock", "Memphis",
                      "Wichita Falls" };
```

If our task was to display the elements of `townList`, then the following **for** loop demonstrates the pre-5.0 way to display them.

```
for (int i = 0; i < townList.length; ++i) {
    System.out.println(townList[i]);
}
```

With Java 5.0, the display can be performed in the following manner.

```
for (String town : townList) {
    System.out.println(town);
}
```

In the iterator **for** loop, an *iterator variable* is specified for representing the current array element of interest. The array of interest is also specified. Separating the iterator and the array is a colon (:).

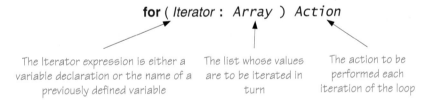

The body of the iterator **for** loop executes once for each element in the array. On the first iteration, the iterator takes on the value of the first element of the array; on the second iteration, the iterator takes on the value of the second element of the array; and so on.

Thus, the iterator **for** loop

```
for (String town : townList) {
    System.out.println(town);
}
```

produces output

```
Brooklyn
Glen Rock
Memphis
Wichita Falls
```

On the first execution of the **for** loop body, memory has depiction

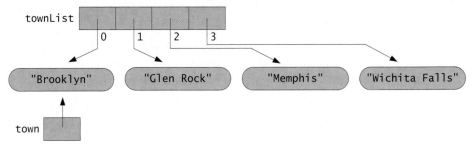

The figure shows that iterator `town` has the same value as `townList[0]`; i.e., they reference the same `String` representation of `"Brooklyn"`.

After the next execution of the **for** loop body, memory has been updated.

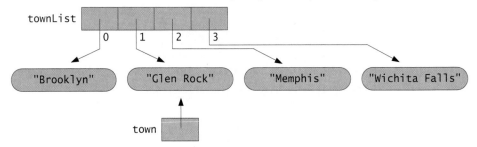

Iterator `town` now has the same value as `townList[1]`. They both reference a representation of `"Glen Rock"`.

After the next execution of the **for** loop body, memory has again been updated.

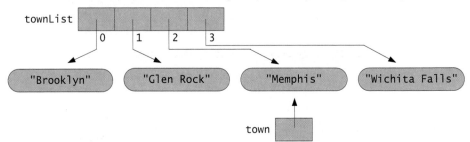

Iterator `town` now has the same value as `townList[2]`; i.e., it references a representation of `"Memphis"`.

After the next execution of the **for** loop body, memory has again been updated.

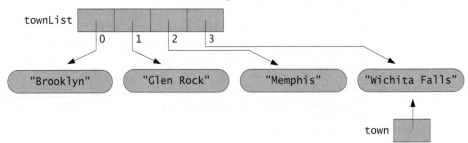

Iterator `town` now has the same value as `townList[3]`; i.e., it references a `String` representation of `"Wichita Falls"`. As `townList` only has four elements, this iteration completes the loop.

Because the iterator and the list element are distinct (separate locations hold their values), a change to the value of the iterator does not change the value of the associated list element and vice-versa. The following code segment makes use again of array `townList` and iterator `town`. Its evaluation makes the distinctness property obvious.

```
for (String town : townList) {
    town = "Shangri-La";
}
```

Immediately before the first execution of the assignment statement in the **for** loop body, memory has depiction

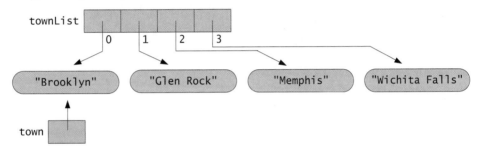

As expected iterator `town` refers to the same memory location as `townList[0]`.

Because an assignment to iterator `town` is just that, an assignment updates its value

```
town = "Shangri-La";
```

and leaves the list elements alone. In particular the value of `townList[0]` is unchanged.

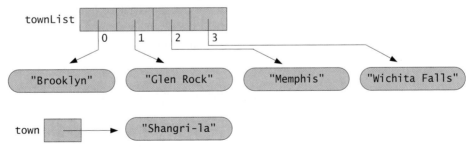

The other iterations of the **for** loop each cause iterator `town` to start with the value of another element in `townList`. The assignment in the **for** loop body then updates the iterator and leaves the list elements unchanged. An iterator is like a value parameter—once it is initialized, it is independent from the source of the value.

We now turn our attention to other array processing activities.

Which loop construct to use?

Because the iterator **for** loop is new to Java, code developed before Java 5.0 does not make use of it. Therefore, it is important that you be familiar with both the traditional and iterator style of accessing elements. Because the iterator **for** loop ensures that only valid array elements are even considered, we expect that in the future it will be the preferred loop form for sequentially processing array elements. However, the huge existing code base of Java applications might cause the iterator **for** loop to remain a programming curiosity. It is our expectation that the iterator **for** loop will become the popular form—but not for a while.

In the remaining discussion of arrays, we shall use the traditional **for** loop when accessing elements. However, our Section 8.10 discussion of generic class **Array-List<T>** makes use of iterator **for** loops. Class **ArrayList<T>** is part of the Java *collections framework*. This framework provides a variety of lists representations of which **ArrayList<T>** is one and an extensive collection of algorithms for examining and manipulating list representations.

8.4   SIMPLE ARRAY PROCESSING

We now consider a series of code segments that accomplish three common tasks when using arrays. The segments illustrate

- Extraction of input values to set up an array;
- Searching an array of values to determine if a particular value is present;
- Finding the minimum value in an array.

Each of these tasks is important and has many applications. For example, an online retailer needs to be able to read a list of merchandise in response to a user query. From that list, the merchandise matching the query request needs to be displayed with special attention given typically to the merchandise of least cost.

8.4.1   EXTRACTION

The following code segment extracts up to MAX_LIST_SIZE values from the standard input stream. Upon completion of the segment, the extracted values are represented by the elements of array `data`, where `data.length` equals the number of extracted values. In setting up array `data`, an array `buffer` temporarily stores the extracted values.

```java
final int MAX_LIST_SIZE = 1000;

int[] buffer = new int[MAX_LIST_SIZE];

int listSize = 0;
```

```
for (int i = 0; (stdin.hasNextInt()) && (i < MAX_LIST_SIZE);
        ++i) {
  buffer[i] = stdin.nextInt();
  ++listSize;
}

int[] data = new int[listSize];
for (int i = 0; i < data.length; ++i) {
  data[i] = buffer[i];
}
```

Because the user does not necessarily provide MAX_LIST_SIZE values, a variable listSize keeps track of the number of elements in buffer that have been assigned extracted values. Variable listSize is initialized to zero to reflect that no values have been extracted as of yet.

A **for** loop processes the extractions. The loop iterates only while there are values to extract *and* there is an unassigned element in buffer. Each execution of the **for** loop body assigns another element of buffer (the first iteration assigns buffer[0], the second iteration assigns buffer[1], and so on).

```
buffer[i] = stdin.nextInt();
++listSize;
```

To complete the processing of the current input, variable listSize is incremented to reflect that another input value has been assigned to array buffer.

Suppose the input stream contains three values: 4, 9, and 5. The first time through the loop, i is 0, so buffer[0] is assigned the input value 4. The memory associated with buffer and listSize looks like the following

	0	1	2	3	4	5	6	7	8	9
buffer	4	0	0	0	0	0	0	0	0	0

listSize	1

where the elements buffer[1] through buffer[9] contain 0s from the default initialization of the elements of buffer.

In the next iteration, i is incremented to 1, and buffer[1] is assigned the input value 9. The variable depiction is now

	0	1	2	3	4	5	6	7	8	9
buffer	4	9	0	0	0	0	0	0	0	0

listSize	2

In the last iteration, i is incremented to 2, and buffer[2] and is assigned 5.

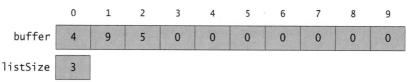

Because with our example the user does not supply any more values and instead indicates end-of-file, the **for** loop text expression evaluates to **false** and the loop terminates.

At this point listSize indicates the number of elements that data is to represent and the first listSize elements of buffer have the values of interest.

The code segment then copies the input values to array data. Array data is created to hold listSize elements. The elements are copied in turn from array buffer.

```
int[] data = new int[listSize];
for (int i = 0; i < data.length; ++i) {
   data[i] = buffer[i];
}
```

After the segment has completed, arrays buffer and data have the following depiction.

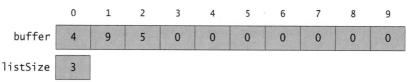

In particular, data is a correctly sized array holding the extracted input values.

You might have been tempted to say that we have accomplished our task of extracting the input values once the first **for** loop completes. However, array buffer has buffer.length elements and the number of extracted elements is listSize. These two values are not necessarily the same.

It normally is incumbent upon a programmer to have the size of an array reflect the number of elements that have been assigned to it. It is easy to imagine that the input values will undergo significant and varied processing. In such cases, a list whose length does not reflect the number of elements to be processed can be misused. Thus in support of good programming practice, we copy the assigned elements of buffer to data.

8.4.2 SEARCHING FOR A KEY VALUE

In our next example, array data is searched for a particular value. The variable holding the value to be searched is called the *key*. As indicated at the start of this section, searching is an important list processing activity. For many applications the presence of a value indicates availability; for other applications the presence of a value indicates the list has a particular property associated with it.

```
System.out.println("Enter the search value (number): ");
int key = stdin.nextInt();

int i;
for (i = 0; i < data.length; ++i) {
    if (key == data[i]) {
        break;
    }
}

if (i != data.length) {
    System.out.println(key + " is element " + i + " in the list");
}
else {
    System.out.println(key + " is not in the list");
}
```

The code uses index variable i to represent the current subscript value. The value of i must be available after the loop, so variable i cannot be declared as part of the **for** loop. The loop examines in turn array elements data[0] through data[data.length - 1].

Each iteration, another element of the array is tested for equivalence to the key value. If data[i] does not match the key value, then the loop proceeds with the next iteration. If data[i] does match the key value, then the **break** statement is executed. As in a **switch** statement, the **break** in a looping construct indicates that the construct is finished. Execution continues immediately at the statement following the loop.

By examining the value of i after the **for** loop has completed, the code determines whether one of the array elements of data has the same value as key.

If i does not have the value of data.length, then it must be the case that the **for** loop terminated because (key == data[i]) was **true** for some i with a value between 0 and data.length - 1. In this case, data[i] is the key value, and the appropriate message is inserted to the standard output stream.

If i has the value data.length, then the loop was terminated because there were no more elements to consider. (Remember that data[0] through data[data.length - 1] are the elements to consider.) In this case, the key value is not present, and an appropriate message is inserted to the output stream.

We now trace through the code segment using the following representation for data, key, and i.

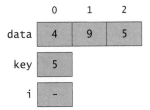

In terms of execution, we are about to begin the **for** loop.

The initialization step of the **for** loop is first executed, and index i is assigned value 0.

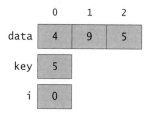

The **for** test expression then is evaluated. Because i < data.length (i.e., 0 < 3), the **for** loop body is executed. Because data[i] does not equal key (i.e., 4 != 5), the loop does not terminate automatically. Index i then is incremented to 1 to prepare for the next evaluation.

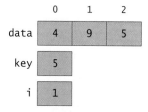

The test expression is reevaluated. Because i < data.length (i.e., 1 < 3), the **for** loop body is executed again. Because data[i] does not equal key (i.e., 9 != 5), the loop does not terminate automatically. Index i then is incremented to 2 to prepare for the next evaluation.

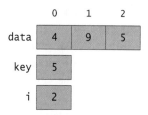

The test expression is reevaluated. Because i < data.length (i.e., 2 < 3), the **for** loop body is executed again. Because data[i] equal key (i.e., 5 = 5), the **break** statement is executed and the loop is terminated.

The **if** statement following the **for** loop then is evaluated, and its test expression is found to be **true** (2 != 3). As a result, the following output occurs.

```
5 is element 2 in the list
```

8.4.3   SEARCHING FOR THE MINIMUM VALUE

The key value search code segment is typical of array processing. There is initialization to prepare for the processing of the array, a loop to process each array element in turn, and a check to see how the list processing completed. For example, the next code segment finds the minimum value of a list `sample` where the list size of `sample` is at least 1.

```java
int minimumSoFar = sample[0];
for (int i = 1; i < sample.length; ++i) {
   if (sample[i] < minimumSoFar) {
      minimumSoFar = sample[i];
   }
}
```

To find the minimum value in an array requires examining each element in turn. If the code segment keeps track of the minimum array element value seen so far, the lesser of that value and the current element is the minimum value seen so far. If this processing is done for each array element, then after the last array element has been considered, the minimum value seen so far is in fact the minimum. Observe that our code segment for finding the minimum of an arbitrarily sized list is even smaller than the code segment presented at the start of this chapter for finding the minimum of five values!

We now turn our attention to using arrays and array elements as method parameters and as return values. By providing methods for list manipulations, the previous code segments can be put to general use.

8.5   ARRAYS AND METHODS

The syntax for expressing an array parameter definition is no different from that of a normal variable definition. An array parameter has form

ElementType[] *ParameterName*

A formal array parameter must include its name as part of its declaration

A formal array parameter must include its array type as part of its declaration

Evidence of this fact has been in all of our programs. For example, listing

```java
// Authors: J. P. Cohoon and J. W. Davidson
// Purpose: display a quotation in a console window

public class DisplayForecast {

   // main(): application entry point
   public static void main(String[] args) {
      System.out.print("I think there is a world market for");
      System.out.println(" maybe five computers.");
      System.out.println("   Thomas Watson, IBM, 1943.");
   }
}
```

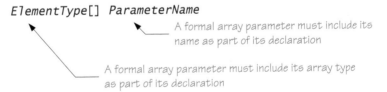

An array formal parameter specifies its element type, brackets, and parameter name

reproduces `DisplayForecast.java` of Listing 1.1—the first program that we considered. As required by Java, its method `main()` has a single array parameter `args` with an element type of `String`.

Our consideration of methods using arrays as parameters or producing arrays as return values begins with methods `sequentialSearch()` and `binarySearch()`. These two methods for searching lists are part of `ArrayTools.java` that we develop in this chapter. Class `ArrayTools` is an API for accomplishing some common list tasks. For example, the API also contains methods to sort and display lists. All of the methods in this API are **static**; that is, each method is a class method.

<table>
<tr><td>**8.5.1**</td><td>## SEQUENTIAL AND BINARY SEARCH</td></tr>
</table>

Method `sequentialSearch()` of Listing 8.1 has two formal parameters—the first parameter is an **int[]** array `data` and the second parameter is the search value `key`.

Listing 8.1   **sequentialSearch() from ArrayTools.java**

```
 1.  // sequentialSearch(): search an unsorted list for a key
 2.  public static int sequentialSearch(int[] data, int key) {
 3.      for (int i = 0; i < data.length; ++i) {
 4.          if (data[i] == key) {
 5.              return i;
 6.          }
 7.      }
 8.
 9.      return -1;
10.  }
```

Method `sequentialSearch()` is similar in form to the code segment that searched an array for a key value in Section 8.4.2. However, `sequentialSearch()` does not display a message indicating whether it found the value. If `sequentialSearch()` finds the key value in the array, it returns the subscript of the first matching element. If the key value is not among the array element values, `sequentialSearch()` returns the number of elements in the array. Because the array elements occupy subscript positions 0 through `data.length-1` in the array, the value -1 indicates that the key value is not in the array.

Suppose the array `score` has the following definition.

```
int[] score = { 6, 9, 82, 11, 29, 85, 11, 28, 91 };
```

Its depiction is

	0	1	2	3	4	5	6	7	8
score	6	9	82	11	29	85	11	28	91

In the following code segment, the array `score` is searched for two values.

```
int i1 = ArrayTools.sequentialSearch(score, 11);  // 3
int i2 = ArrayTools.sequentialSearch(score, 30);  // -1
```

Listing 8.2   binarySearch() from ArrayTools.java

```
1.  // binarySearch(): search a sorted list for a key
2.  public static int binarySearch(char[] data, char key) {
3.      int left = 0;
4.      int right = data.length - 1;
5.      while (left <= right) {
6.          int mid = (left + right)/2;
7.          if (data[mid] == key) {
8.              return mid;
9.          }
10.         else if (data[mid] < key) {
11.             left = mid + 1;
12.         }
13.         else {
14.             right = mid - 1;
15.         }
16.     }
17.
18.     return -1;
19. }
```

The first invocation initializes i1 to 3 because the first match of the value 11 in the array score is with score[3]. The second invocation initializes i2 to –1, because none of array elements score[0] through score[8] have value 30.

Although subscripts are not used when an array is used as an actual parameter, subscripts are used when an individual array element is passed as an actual parameter. The use of brackets is necessary because it is the subscript that enables a particular element to be specified. For example, consider the following code segment that uses class method max() from the java.lang.Math API to display the larger of array elements score[0] and score[2].

```
System.out.println(Math.max(score[0], score[2]));
```

Method max() expects two **int** parameters. Because the element type of array score is **int**, passing two score array elements to max() is appropriate.

When the values of a list are in sorted order, there are better searches than method sequentialSearch() for determining if a particular value is in the list. For example, when you look up a name in the phone book, you do not start in the beginning and scan through until you find the name—you use the fact that the names are listed in sorted order and use some intelligence to jump quickly to the right page and then start scanning.

Method binarySearch() of Listing 8.2 conducts a series of tests that enable it to reduce repeatedly the portion of its array parameter data that possibly can contain the value of parameter key. The method follows the same convention as sequentialSearch(). If the key value is present, then binarySearch() returns the index of a matching element; if the key value is not present, then binarySearch() returns –1.

> The standard Java class Collections method binarySearch() behaves differently than our method—if the key is not in the list, that method returns the index where the key value should be located

The portion of the list that can contain the key value is represented by the indexes left and right. Prior to the first **if** test, any list element can contain the key value. For this reason, left is initialized to 0, and right is initialized to data.length-1. Suppose the list and key value have representation

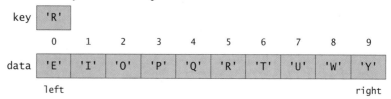

A **while** loop performs repeated tests to update indexes left and right. The loop iterates until either the key value has been found or it has been determined that no portion of the list contains the key value.

The **while** loop body starts by assigning the average of the current values of left and right to variable mid. If element data[mid] equals key, then mid is returned.

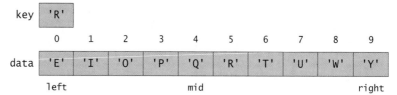

If element data[mid] is less than key, then because the list is sorted, all elements to the left of data[mid] are also less than key. If the value of key is to be in the list, it must occur to the right of data[mid]. Therefore, index left is reset to be to the immediate right of mid; that is, left becomes mid + 1. For our example, the value of key, which is 'R', is greater than the value of data[mid], which is 'Q'. After the updating of mid at the start of the next iteration, the variables have depiction

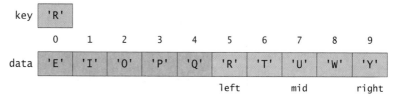

The grayed portion indicates that those elements are no longer in consideration in finding the value of key.

If element data[mid] is neither equal to nor less than key, it must be greater than the key. As the list is sorted, all elements to the right of data[mid] are also greater than key. If the value of key is to be in the list, it must occur to the left of data[mid]. Therefore, in this case index right is reset to be to the immediate left of mid; that is, right becomes mid - 1. For the previously depicted situation, the value of key, which is 'R', is less than the value of data[mid], which is 'U'. After the updating of mid at the start of the next iteration, the variables have depiction

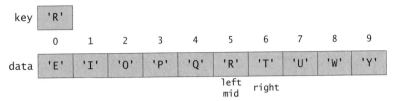

With this situation, the values of key and data[mid] test equal, so the method returns the value of mid.

It can be shown in the worst case that binarySearch() performs approximately $2 \cdot \log_2 n$ comparisons to process a list of *n* elements. Consequently, for a sorted list of 1,000 elements, 20 comparisons are sufficient for binarySearch() to determine whether the key value is present. It also means that for a sorted list of 1 million elements, binarySearch() can determine whether a particular value is present using no more than 40 comparisons! This ability is even more impressive when compared to **sequentialSearch()**, which can need up to 1 million comparisons! For interactive applications, the fast response time of binarySearch() is what users expect.

We next turn our attention to some of the implications of having an array reference be a parameter of a method.

8.5.2   ZEROING

Consider program ArrayDemo.java of Listing 8.3. In particular, pay attention to methods zeroInt() and zeroArray(). What is the output of the program? Do not examine the output until you have tried to determine it yourself.

The output of the program is

```
int i: 1
array z: 1 2 3
int i: 1
array z: 0 0 0
```

Why has z changed but not i? From previous chapters, you know that in the invocation of zeroInt(i) a copy of the **int** value of actual parameter i is passed to zeroInt() to initialize its formal parameter val. It is that copy that method zeroInt() modifies, leaving method main() variable i untouched. The following figure depicts the activa-

---

Listing 8.3 **ArrayDemo.java**

```
1.  // Demonstrates array parameter nuances
2.  public class ArrayDemo {
3.      public static void main(String[] args) {
4.          int i = 1;
5.          int[] z = { 1, 2, 3 };
6.
7.          System.out.println("int i: " + i);
8.          System.out.println("array z: " + z[0] + " " + z[1] + " "
9.                  + z[2]);
10.
11.         zeroInt(i);
12.         zeroArray(z);
13.
14.         System.out.println("int i: " + i);
15.         System.out.println("array z: " + z[0] + " " + z[1] + " "
16.                 + z[2]);
17.     }
18.
19.     public static void zeroInt(int val) {
20.         val = 0;
21.     }
22.
23.     public static void zeroArray(int[] list) {
24.         for (int j = 0; j < list.length; ++j) {
25.             list[j] = 0;
26.         }
27.     }
28. }
```

---

tion records for methods `main()` and `zeroInt()` immediately before `zeroInt()` completes.

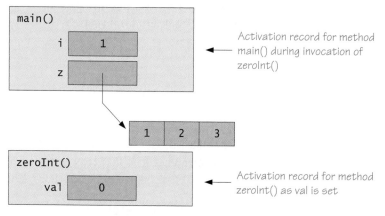

However, in invocation `zeroArray(z)`, a copy of the reference value of variable `z` is used to initialize parameter `list` of `zeroArray()`. In particular, the value is a reference to an array of three **int** elements. Thus, when method `zeroArray()` is executing, list is referencing the same list as z. As a result, the activation records for main() and zeroArray() have the following depiction.

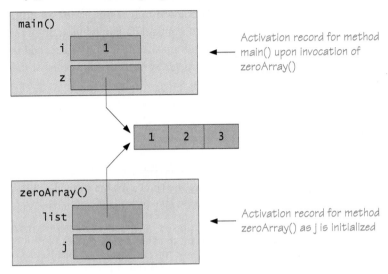

Therefore, whenever the **for** statement body is executed,

```
list[j] = 0;
```

method zeroArray() is changing the jth element of array z. The changes brought about by the **for** loop cause the activation records for methods main() and zeroArray() to have the following depiction as method zeroArray() completes.

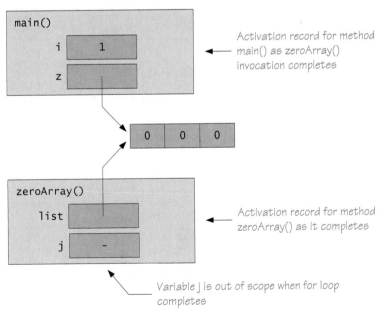

We make use of this ability of methods to change the elements of the actual array parameter in Section 8.6.1 when we present a method to sort the values in an array.

We now consider three other methods from API `ArrayTools`. These methods are `putList()`, `getList()`, and `reverse()`. The first two of these methods are probably the most needed ones when doing list processing. Method `putList()` displays the elements of its array parameter to standard output; method `getList()` extracts a list of values from standard input and returns the list in array form; and method `reverse()` takes the elements of its array parameter and reverses the order of the values. The three methods are defined in Listing 8.4.

8.5.3 DISPLAY

Method `putList()` of `ArrayTools` is a useful method to have around. It is convenient when debugging a program to display the contents of an array.

```
// putList(): produces a string representation
public static void putList(int[] data) {
    for (int i = 0; i < data.length; ++i) {
        System.out.println(data[i]);
    }
}
```

This **void** method has a single parameter `data` of type `int[]`. The method uses a **for** statement to display iteratively the elements of the array one per line to standard output. As an example of its use, suppose array `score` has the following depiction.

	0	1	2	3	4	5	6	7	8
score	6	9	82	11	29	85	11	28	91

Then invocation

```
ArrayTools.putList(score);
```

displays the elements of the array `score`, one per line to standard output.

```
6
9
82
11
29
85
11
28
91
```

Variable arity

Java now supports an alternative notation for specifying that a formal array parameter is an array. An ellipsis . . . (i.e., three consecutive periods) can be used rather than []. When the ellipsis is used, the formal array parameter is known as a *vararg* parameter.

The following example provides an alternative definition for ArrayTools method putList().

```java
public static void putList(int... data) {
    for (int i = 0; i < data.length; ++i) {
        System.out.println(data[i]);
    }
}
```

When ellipsis syntax is used, code segments such as the following

```java
int day1 = 9;
int day2 = 29;
int day3 = 28;
int day4 = 21;
int day5 = 30;
int[] days = { day1, day2, day3, day4, day5 };
ArrayTools.putList(days);
```

still work as expected

```
9
29
28
21
30
```

In addition, method putList() can now be invoked with an explicit list of **int** values as its parameter list.

```java
ArrayTools.putList(day1, day2, day3, day4, day5);
```

Such an invocation also produces the output

```
9
29
28
21
30
```

In performing an invocation of a method using vararg capabilities, Java constructs a temporary array whose elements are initialized using the list. This construction is known as *boxing* the actual parameters. The temporary array is then used as the parameter to the method. The System.out.printf() method makes use of this capability to support the display of multiple values in a single printf() invocation.

It is because the number of values passed to the method can vary with the invocation that the array formal parameter is known as the vararg (i.e., variable arguments).

Java allows only a single vararg parameter to be defined per method. Furthermore, the vararg parameter must be the last formal parameter in the method definition.

Listing 8.4 **putList(), getList(), and reverse() from ArrayTools.java**

```java
1.  // class constant
2.  private static final int MAX_LIST_SIZE = 1000;
3.
4.  // putList(): produces a string representation
5.  public static void putList(int[] data) {
6.     for (int i = 0; i < data.length; ++i) {
7.        System.out.println(data[i]);
8.     }
9.  }
10.
11. // getList(): extract up to MAX_LIST_SIZE values and returns them
12. public static int[] getList() {
13.    Scanner stdin = new Scanner(System.in);
14.
15.    int[] buffer = new int[MAX_LIST_SIZE];
16.
17.    int listSize = 0;
18.
19.    for (int i = 0; (stdin.hasNextInt()) && (i < MAX_LIST_SIZE);
20.                    ++i) {
21.       buffer[i] = stdin.nextInt();
22.       ++listSize;
23.    }
24.
25.    int[] data = new int[listSize];
26.    for (int i = 0; i < data.length; ++i) {
27.       data[i] = buffer[i];
28.    }
29.
30.    return data;
31. }
32.
33. // reverse(): reverses the order of the element values
34. public static void reverse(int[] list) {
35.    int n = list.length;
36.
37.    for (int i = 0; i < n/2; ++i) {
38.       // swap element from front of list with corresponding
39.       // element from the end of the list
40.       int rmbr = list[i];
41.       list[i] = list[n-1-i];
42.       list[n-1-i] = rmbr;
43.    }
44. }
```

8.5.4   EXTRACTION AND REVERSAL

Method getList() of Listing 8.4 is the input extraction segment of Section 8.4 embedded in a method body. The method warrants no further discussion. The exercises consider alternative implementations.

Method reverse() of Listing 8.4 takes the elements of its array parameter and reverses the order of the values. The method has a **for** loop whose index variable i iterates over the first half of the array referenced by parameter list. The ith element from the front of the list is swapped with the ith element from the end of the list. The ith element from the end of the list has index n-i-1, where n is the number of elements in the list.

Methods getList(), putList(), and reverse() are used in program Demo.java of Listing 8.5. An example of the program's input and output behavior is depicted in Figure 8.1.

Listing 8.5   Demo.java

```
 1.  // Extracts and displays a list in forward and reverse order
 2.
 3.  public class Demo {
 4.      // main(): application entry point
 5.      public static void main(String[] args) {
 6.          System.out.println("");
 7.          System.out.println("Enter a list of integers:");
 8.          int[] number = ArrayTools.getList();
 9.
10.          System.out.println("");
11.          System.out.println("Your list");
12.          ArrayTools.putList(number);
13.
14.          ArrayTools.reverse(number);
15.          System.out.println("");
16.          System.out.println("Your list in reverse");
17.          ArrayTools.putList(number);
18.          System.out.println();
19.      }
20.  }
```

8.5.5   INCREASING REPRESENTATION CAPACITY

In some problem-solving situations, the case arises where new values need to be added to a list but the list is full. For example, suppose merchandise is a String array with definition

```
String[] merchandise = { "Music", "Books", "Magazines",
    "DVDs" };
```

Figure 8.1   **Demo snapshot.**

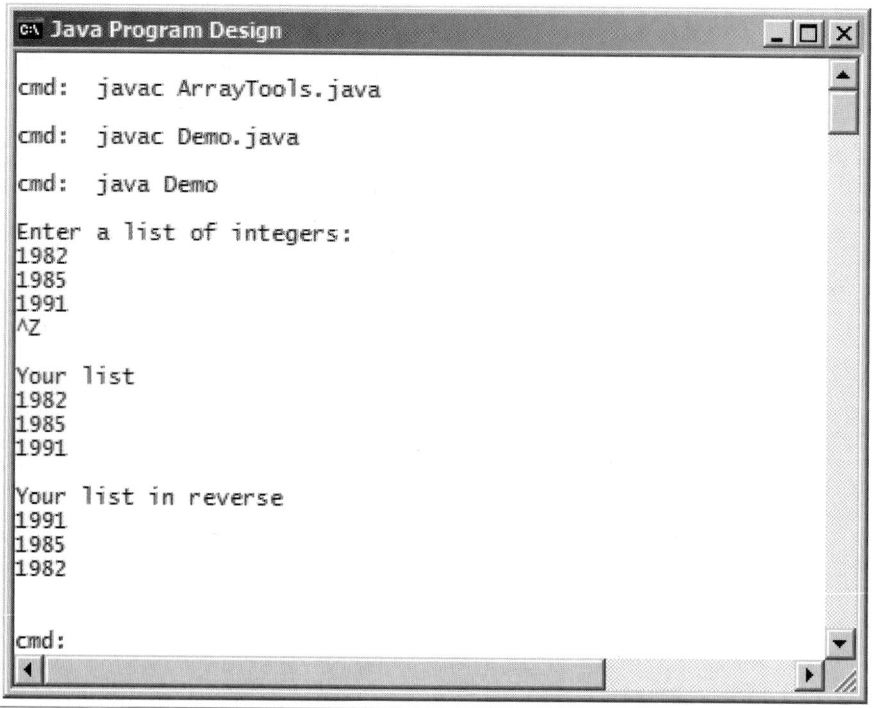

Listing 8.6   **doubleCapacity() from ArrayTools.java**

```
1.  // doubleCapacity(): create a duplicate list with extra capacity
2.  public static String[] doubleCapacity(String[] currList) {
3.      int n = currList.length;
4.      String[] biggerList = new String[2*n]; // get a bigger list
5.
6.      for (int i = 0; i < n; ++i) {
7.          biggerList[i] = currList[i];        // copy existing values
8.      }
9.
10.     return biggerList;
11. }
```

There is no room to add additional items to list merchandise. Each element of the array already references a value. This problem can be alleviated with method doubleCapacity() of Listing 8.6. The method takes an array currList as its parameter and returns a new array with twice the capacity of currList, where the first half of the new array is initialized to the values of currList.

With method doubleCapacity(), the following actions are possible

```
merchandise = doubleCapacity(merchandise);
merchandise[4] = "Clothes";
merchandise[5] = "Shoes";
```

The depiction of merchandise before the code segment is

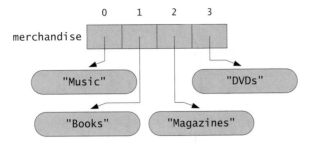

The depiction of merchandise after the code segment is

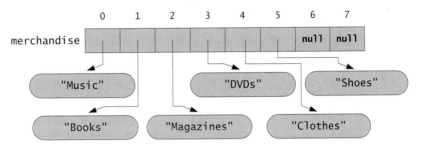

Method `doubleCapacity()` begins by determining the size of array represented by its formal parameter.

```
int n = currList.length;
```

A new bigger array then is created with twice the capacity.

```
String[] biggerList = new String[2*n]; // get a bigger list
```

The elements then are copied from the old list to the new bigger array.

```
for (int i = 0; i < n; ++i) {
    biggerList[i] = currList[i];       // copy existing values
}
```

To complete its task, the method needs only to return the new list.

```
return biggerList;
```

8.6   SORTING

Chapter 5 introduced the notion of sorting in `SortTwo.java` and `SortThree.java`, which respectively displayed two and three input values in nondecreasing order. We used the term nondecreasing rather than increasing to allow for duplicate values. Here we consider the general sorting problem of arranging the values in a list of arbitrary size into nondecreasing order.

Clarity

Even the most experienced programmers are tempted to optimize their programs so they run faster. While efficiency is important, clarity and correctness are more important. Who wants to use a program that runs fast but produces incorrect results or is so difficult to understand that its correctness cannot be verified? Thus, we should not sacrifice clarity and correctness for efficiency. Furthermore, it is hard for a programmer to "tweak" a program so that it runs measurably faster. One rule of thumb in programming is that 90 percent of a program's running time is spent in 10 percent of the code. Consequently, without some idea of where a program spends most of its time, most changes to a program to speed it up will have little effect on the overall running time. If efficiency becomes an issue, a more effective approach is to wait until the program is complete and then use a special tool called a *profiler* to identify the program's hot spots. *Hot spots* are where the programs spends most of its time running. These areas of the program can be tuned to reduce the running time of the program.

A sort is often an iterative process such that each iteration rearranges some of the values in the list `v` to be sorted. For example, on iteration `i` the method known as `selectionSort()` finds the element containing the `i`th smallest value of its list `v` and exchanges that element with `v[i]`. As another example, on iteration `i` the method known as `insertionSort()` correctly places the value of `v[i]` with respect to the values stored in elements `v[0]` through `v[i-1]`.

In the next section, we present an implementation of `selectionSort()`. Method `insertionSort()` is considered in the exercises. In the discussion that follows, we assume that the list to be sorted is an array of **char** values. The sort can be modified easily to handle other types of values.

8.6.1 METHOD SELECTIONSORT()

As discussed in the previous section, on iteration `i`, `selectionSort()` finds the element containing the `i`th smallest value of array `v` and exchanges that element with element `v[i]`; that is, on the first iteration, the smallest element is placed correctly; on the second iteration, the second smallest element is placed correctly; and so on.

In looking for the smallest element, `selectionSort()` must consider all of the elements. The element containing the smallest considered value then is exchanged with `v[0]`. For example, suppose the list to be sorted is

	0	1	2	3	4	5	6	7	8	9
v	'Q'	'W'	'E'	'R'	'T'	'Y'	'U'	'I'	'O'	'P'

then v[2], which contains an 'E', is exchanged with v[0], which contains a 'Q'. The result is

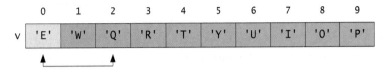

The yellow shading indicates that the element has been determined to be set correctly in the sorting of v.

In looking for the second smallest element, selectionSort() need not consider the element containing the smallest value. Because the element containing the smallest value is v[0], to find the second smallest element, selectionSort() needs only to find the smallest value among elements v[1] through v[n-1]. The element containing the smallest considered value then is exchanged with v[1]. In our example, v[7], which contains an 'I', is exchanged with v[1], which contains a 'W'. The result is

The yellow shading continues to indicate the elements that have been determined to be set correctly.

In looking for the third smallest element, selectionSort() need not consider the elements containing the smallest and second smallest values. Because the element containing the smallest value is v[0] and the element containing the second smallest value is v[1], to find the third smallest element, selectionSort() needs only to find the smallest value among elements v[2] through v[n-1]. The element containing the smallest considered value then is exchanged with v[2]. In our example, v[8], which contains an 'O', is exchanged with v[2], which contains a 'Q'. The result is

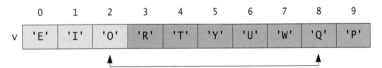

In general, looking for the ith smallest element, selectionSort() needs only to find the smallest value among elements v[i] through v[n-1]. The element containing the smallest considered value then is exchanged with v[i]. The following code segment correctly finds the element containing the smallest value among elements v[i] through v[n-1].

```
// guess the location of the ith smallest element
int guess = i;
for (int j = i+1; j < v.length; ++j) {
    if (v[j] < v[guess]) // is guess ok?
        // update guess with index of smaller element
        guess = j;
```

```
}
```

```
// guess is now correct, so swap elements v[guess] and v[i]
```

The code is similar to our other array processing code. In particular, the code is most similar to the code that searches an array. The code segment begins defining **int** index variable guess. Variable guess represents where we believe the ith smallest element can be found. The definition initializes guess to i. The code segment then determines whether the value of guess is correct. The **for** loop body repeatedly tests whether v[j] < v[guess], with j iteratively taking on the values i + 1 through v.length - 1.

If it is determined that v[j] < v[guess], then our value for guess is wrong and it is updated with the value of j. At this point, guess is the index of the smallest value among elements v[i] through v[j]. Thus, completing the **for** loop assures that guess is the index of the ith smallest element.

To place the ith smallest element correctly, the values of v[i] and v[guess] are interchanged.

```
char rmbr = v[i];
v[i] = v[guess];
v[guess] = rmbr;
```

The outer **for** loop ends when i equals v.length-1; that is, no additional work is needed to place the largest element correctly once the other elements have been placed correctly. For our example, after placing the second largest element the array has depiction

	0	1	2	3	4	5	6	7	8	9
v	'E'	'I'	'O'	'P'	'Q'	'R'	'T'	'U'	'W'	'Y'

Because the search for the largest value in the array needs only to consider the final element, no additional work is needed—the largest value is already placed correctly.

	0	1	2	3	4	5	6	7	8	9
v	'E'	'I'	'O'	'P'	'Q'	'R'	'T'	'U'	'W'	'Y'

Based on this analysis, we present method selectionSort() from Array-Tools.java in Listing 8.7.

8.6.2   QUALITY OF SELECTIONSORT()

In analyzing a sorting algorithm, software developers are concerned normally with the total number of element comparisons and the total number of element copies/assignments performed by the sort. When i is 0 for selectionSort(), there are $n - 1$ element comparisons and 3 element copies/assignments, where n is the number of elements in array v. When i is 1, there are $n - 2$ element comparisons and 3 element copies/assignments.

Listing 8.7   Method selectionSort() of ArrayTools.java

```
1.  // selectionSort(): sorts the elements of a
2.  public static void selectionSort(char[] v) {
3.      for (int i = 0; i < v.length-1; ++i) {
4.      // guess the location of the ith smallest element
5.          int guess = i;
6.          for (int j = i+1; j < v.length; ++j) {
7.              if (v[j] < v[guess]) { // is guess ok?
8.              // update guess with index of smaller element
9.                  guess = j;
10.             }
11.         }
12.
13.     // guess is now correct, so swap elements v[guess] and v[i]
14.         char rmbr = v[i];
15.         v[i] = v[guess];
16.         v[guess] = rmbr;
17.     }
18. }
```

When i is 2, there are $n - 3$ element comparisons and 3 element copies/assignments. In general, on iteration i, there are $n - (i + 1)$ element comparisons and 3 element copies/assignments.

The total number of element comparisons is therefore $n-1 + n-2 + \dots + 2 + 1$, which is proportional to n^2. The total number of element copies/assignments is at most $3 + 3 + \dots + 3$, which is proportional to n. Because the number of element comparisons is proportional to the square of the number of elements, we say that method selectionSort() has *quadratic* performance with respect to element comparisons. Because the number of element copies/assignments is proportional to the number of elements, we say that the algorithm has *linear* performance with respect to element copies/assignments. Because $n^2 > n$, we say that the overall algorithm performs a quadratic number of element operations.

8.7   COMMAND-LINE PARAMETERS

Many operating systems (e.g., Linux and Windows) provide command-line interpreters. These interpreters enable a user to type a command and then have the operating system execute it. For example, the following instruction uses the Linux/Windows command cd to change the current folder to folder code.

    cmd: cd code

In the instruction, the string "code" is a *command-line parameter* to the command cd.

Figure 8.2   **Command-line parameter associations.**

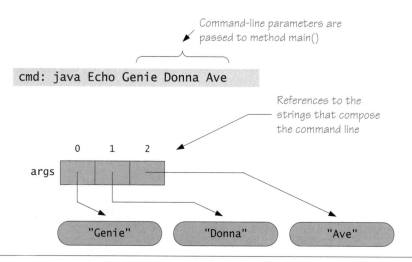

As another example, the following instruction runs the Java program Echo with the strings Genie, Donna, and Ave as its command-line parameters.

    java Echo Genie Donna Ave

This program displays its parameters to standard output.

    Genie Donna Ave

Thus, its operation is the same as the Linux/Windows commands echo.

Java provides a method for creating programs that use command-line parameters. The command-line parameters are communicated to a program via its method main(). To make this communication straightforward, Java requires that a program view the command-line parameters as an array of strings. The first element in the array is the first command-line parameter, the second element in the array is the second command-line parameter, and so on. For the Echo example, the array consists of references to the strings "Genie", "Donna", and "Ave".

Access to the array of strings representing the command-line parameters is through method main()'s array parameter.

public static void main(String[] args)

When a program is run, elements args[0] through args[args.length - 1] are initialized automatically to reference the strings representing the command-line parameters to the program. This initialization is depicted for the Echo example in Figure 8.2.

Listing 8.8 supplies the code for Echo.java. The command-line parameters passed to the program are displayed iteratively using a **for** loop that iterates once for each command-line parameter. Each parameter is displayed individually using method print().

Listing 8.8   Echo.java

```
1.  // Mimics operating system command echo.
2.
3.  public class Echo {
4.      // main(): application entry point
5.      public static void main(String[] args) {
6.          // display parameters one after the other
7.          for (int i = 0; i < args.length; ++i) {
8.              System.out.print(args[i] + " ");
9.          }
10.
11.         System.out.println();
12.     }
13. }
```

Once the loop is finished, method `println()` causes a newline character to be displayed.

We now turn our attention to multidimensional arrays.

Another program parameter example

Chapter 10 presents a version of the Windows command `type` (in Linux it is known as `cat`). We delay its coverage until then because of its use of exception handling.

8.8   MULTIDIMENSIONAL ARRAYS

In addition to defining one-dimensional arrays, it is also possible to define multidimensional arrays. There are a great many problems whose solutions can be determined through the manipulation of multidimensional arrays. The application domains include matrices, graphical animation, economic forecast models, map representation, time studies of population change, and microprocessor design to name just a few.

The following definition initializes m to reference a two-dimensional array.

```
int[][] m = new int[3][4];
```

Two-dimensional array m should be viewed as consisting of three *component* arrays m[0], m[1], and m[2] with each of these components consisting of a four-element array. The *component type* of m is **int**[] and the element type of each of m[0], m[1], and m[2] is **int**. To be explicit, our definition of m is shorthand for

```
int[][] m = new int[3][];
m[0] = new int[4];
m[1] = new int[4];
m[2] = new int[4];
```

The components of a two-dimensional array are known as *rows*. To refer to an individual element of a row, an additional subscript is used. For example, m[i][j] is the jth element of the ith row in m. Array m has representation

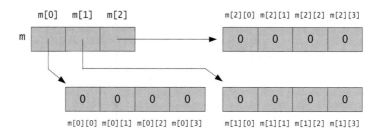

The representation indicates explicitly that m[0], m[1], and m[2] are all references to four-element arrays whose elements are default initialized to zero.

Suppose we wanted to set the elements of a two-dimensional array m using standard input. To do so, we would use nested **for** loops. The outer **for** loop would iterate once per subarray. For each such iteration, the inner **for** loop would iterate once for each element of the current subarray. Such nesting is demonstrated in the following code segment.

```java
for (int r = 0; r < m.length; ++r) {
    for (int c = 0; c < m[r].length; ++c) {
        System.out.print("Enter a value: ");
        m[r][c] = stdin.nextInt();
    }
}
```

Notice that the outer **for** loop test expression is r < m.length, where r is the current row index. The expression term m.length has meaning because m consists of three one-dimensional subarrays. Similarly, the term m[r].length from the inner **for** loop test expression c < m[r].length has meaning because component m[r] is an **int**[] array.

Java does not require that the subarrays of a two-dimensional array have the same length. For example, the following code segment defines a two-dimensional array s of type String[][]. Array s consists of four rows. The first two rows both have two elements; the last two rows have four and three elements respectively.

```java
String[][] s = new String[4][];
s[0] = new String[2];
s[1] = new String[2];
s[2] = new String[4];
s[3] = new String[3];
```

Array s has representation

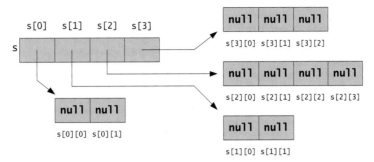

Arrays with more than two dimensions are also possible. However, in practice, arrays with three dimensions are used infrequently, and arrays with more than three dimensions are used rarely.

The definition of a multidimensional array can include initialization by specifying a block of values with each component of the array having its own initialization specification. For example, the following definitions initialize both b and c to be **int**[][] arrays.

```
int b[][] = {{1, 2, 3}, {4, 5, 6}, {7, 8, 9}};
int c[][] = {{1, 2}, {3, 4}, {5, 6}, {7, 8, 9}};
```

Array b consists of three components each of which is a three-element array.

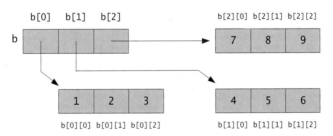

Array c consists of four components, the first three of which are two-element arrays and the fourth is a three-element array.

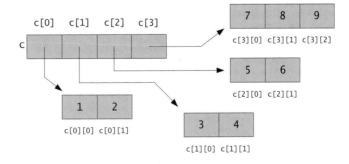

Methods with parameters that are multidimensional arrays are permitted. For example, the following method `zero()` sets to 0 all of the elements of the subarrays of its two-dimensional **int**`[][]` parameter array a.

```
public void zero(int[][] a) {
   for (int r = 0; r < a.length; ++r)
      for (int c = 0; c < a[r].length; ++c)
         a[r][c] = 0;
}
```

It is also possible to use a subarray of a multidimensional array as a parameter. For example, we can invoke ArrayTools method `sequentialSearch()` on each of the components of the two-dimensional array m that was defined at the beginning of this section.

```
System.out.println(ArrayTools.sequentialSearch(m[0], key));
System.out.println(ArrayTools.sequentialSearch(m[1], key));
System.out.println(ArrayTools.sequentialSearch(m[2], key));
```

We can make these invocations using the rows of m because each row of a two-dimensional array is a one-dimensional array.

The following example demonstrates a three-dimensional array alpha. Each element in alpha is assigned a value equal to the sum of its subscripts.

```
int[][][] alpha = new int[10][5][3];
for (int i = 0; i < alpha.length; ++i) {
   for (int j = 0; j < alpha[i].length; ++j) {
      for (int k = 0; k < alpha[i][j].length; ++k) {
         alpha[i][j][k] = i + j + k;
      }
   }
}
```

8.8.1   MATRICES

A two-dimensional array is sometimes known as a *matrix* because it resembles that mathematical concept. A matrix a with m rows and n columns is represented mathematically in the following manner:

In the programming project of Section 8.16, a class Matrix is developed for matrix representation and manipulation

$$\begin{bmatrix} a_{1,1} & a_{1,2} & \dots a_{1,n} \\ a_{2,1} & a_{2,2} & \dots a_{2,n} \\ \dots & & \dots \\ a_{m,1} & a_{m,2} & \dots a_{m,n} \end{bmatrix}$$

Addition is defined for matrices whose dimensions match. If a and b are both matrices with m rows and n columns, then their sum c has the following form:

$$\begin{bmatrix} a_{1,1} + b_{1,1} & a_{1,2} + b_{1,2} & \dots a_{1,n} + b_{1,n} \\ a_{2,1} + b_{2,1} & a_{2,2} + b_{2,2} & \dots a_{2,n} + b_{2,n} \\ \dots & \dots & \\ a_{m,1} + b_{m,1} & a_{m,2} + b_{m,2} & \dots a_{m,n} + b_{m,n} \end{bmatrix}$$

Matrix addition is implemented in the following method add() whose body is a doubly nested **for** loop.

```
public static double[][] add(double[][] a, double[][] b) {
    // determine number of rows in solution
    int m = a.length;
    // determine number of columns in solution
    int n = a[0].length;

    // create the array to hold the sum
    double[][] c = new double[m][n];

    // compute the matrix sum row by row
    for (int i = 0; i < m; ++i) {
        // produce the current row
        for (int j = 0; j < n; ++j) {
            c[i][j] = a[i][j] + b[i][j];
        }
    }

    return c;
}
```

The outer **for** loop of add() supplies the index variable i to process the current row. The inner **for** loop supplies the index variable j to process the current column in the current row. Together the two indices enable the sum of a pair of elements from arrays a and b to be calculated and assigned to the corresponding array element of c. (A robust method add() would test that arrays a and b are sized consistently; that is, both arrays have m rows with n columns per row.)

If a is a matrix with m rows and n columns and b is a matrix with n rows and p columns, then the product of matrices a and b is a matrix c with n rows and p columns, where element $c_{i,j}$ has definition

$$c_{i,j} = a_{i,1}b_{1,j} + a_{i,2}b_{2,j} + \dots + a_{i,n}b_{n,j}$$

Conceptually, element $c_{i,j}$ is the sum of terms produced by multiplying the matrix a elements in row i times the corresponding matrix b elements in column j.

Matrix multiplication is implemented in the following method multiply() whose body is a triply nested **for** loop.

```
public static double[][] multiply(double[][] a, double[][] b) {
    // determine the size of the matrices
    int m = a.length;
    int n = a[0].length;
    int p = b[0].length;
```

```
// create array to hold the product
double[][] c = new double[m][p]; // elements are initially 0

// create the product row by row
for (int i = 0; i < m; ++i) {
    // produce the current row
    for (int j = 0; j < p; ++j) {
        for (int k = 0; k < n; ++k) {
            c[i][j] += a[i][k] * b[k][j];
        }
    }
}

return c;
}
```

(A robust method `multiply()` would test that arrays a and b are sized consistently; that is, array a has m rows and n columns per row and array b has n rows with p columns per row.) The exercises consider other matrix operations.

We now turn our attention to the collections framework. This framework is a collection of classes and interfaces that support list representation and manipulation. Informally, an *interface* is a template describing features of a class. Interfaces are discussed in Section 9.5.

| 8.9 | **COLLECTIONS FRAMEWORK** |

Although arrays in Java are more robust than arrays in other languages they suffer from the traditional shortcoming—they cannot be resized; that is, there are no Java array operations that support the insertion of new elements or the deletion of existing elements.

For software projects being developed in other languages, the restrictions on arrays often forced developers to use nonportable alternative list representations. The cost of using nonportable representations can be quite high because developers must create and support multiple versions of their software.

Through its *collections framework*, Java provides a rich set of list representations that do not have the restrictions that are imposed on arrays. The framework also provides an extensive collection of algorithms for

> As of Java 5.0, the collections framework makes use of generics (see Section 7.8).

examining and manipulating its list representations. Together the list representations and algorithms allow software developers to concentrate their resources on the problem-specific aspects of their project.

There are two types of list representations in the collections framework—those that implement the interface `java.util.Collection` and those that implement the interface `java.util.Map`.

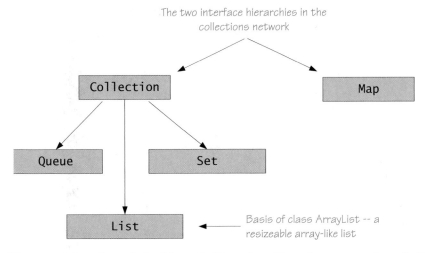

The generic interfaces derived from `Collection<T>` each support a view of a list as a group of elements. These interfaces are `List<T>`, `Queue<T>`, and `Set<T>`. Interface `List<T>` specifies the expected behaviors for representing an ordered collection of values; interface `Set<T>` specifies the expected behaviors for representing a collection of values without duplicates; and interface `Queue<T>` specifies the expected behaviors for representing a collection of values awaiting processing. Classes that implement the `Map<K, V>` interface or its derived interface `HashMap<K, V>` take a more associative view; that is, these classes provide the means to associate "keys" with values. The `Map<K, V>`-based classes also provide the means to determine the value associated with a key and vice versa.

8.10   ARRAYLIST<T>

Our focus here will be on the generic class `ArrayList<T>`. Class `ArrayList<T>` is an implementation of the `List` interface and it provides a resizeable list representation that implements the `List` interface. The name `ArrayList<T>` is intended to be suggestive. An `ArrayList<T>` uses an array to represent the elements of its list. `ArrayList<T>` has been designed so that its element accessor and mutator methods are guaranteed to be very efficient. In computer science parlance, we say that the element accessor and mutator methods run in *constant time*.

A complete description of `ArrayList<T>` is provided in Appendix E

Associated with each `ArrayList<T>` is a *capacity*, which is the maximum number of elements that the list can store without growing. The capacity is the size of the array the `ArrayList<T>` uses to store the elements of the list. If the capacity of that array

---

Table 8.1   **Selected ArrayList<T> constructors and methods.**

`public ArrayList<T>()`

Constructs an empty list representation. The representation has an initial capacity of ten elements.

`public ArrayList<T>(int n)`

Constructs an empty list representation with an initial capacity for n elements.

`public void add(int i, T v)`

Inserts value v into the list such that v has index i. Any preexisting elements with indices i or greater are shifted rightward by one element position.

`public boolean add(T v)`

Appends the list with a new element with value v and returns **true**.

`public void clear()`

Removes all elements from the list.

`public Object clone()`

Returns a shallow copy of this list.

`public T get(int i)`

If i is a valid index, it returns the ith element; otherwise an exception is generated.

`public boolean isEmpty()`

Returns **true** if there are no elements; otherwise, it returns **false**.

`public T remove(int i)`

If i is a valid index, it removes the ith element from the list by shifting leftward elements i + 1 and on. In addition, the removed value is returned. Otherwise, an exception is generated.

`public T set(int i, T v)`

If i is a valid index, then the ith element is set to v and the previous value of the element is returned. Otherwise, an exception is thrown.

`public int size()`

Returns the numbers of elements in the list.

---

becomes insufficient, then a new array is created with greater capacity for the `Array-List<T>` and the values from the old list are copied to it. The operation is much like method `doubleCapacity()` of Listing 8.6.

In addition to accessor and mutator methods, `ArrayList<T>` also provides the ability to add (*append*) an element to the end of the list. The append operation is guaranteed to be fast on average (i.e., an append operation operates in constant time on average). The class also provides a number of other methods for inserting and deleting elements. These other methods can require time proportional to the number of elements in the list to perform their tasks. In computer science parlance, we say that these methods run in *linear time*. A partial list of the capabilities of `ArrayList<T>` is provided in Table 8.1.

The following code segment defines and initializes `ArrayList<String>` variables `city`, `bush`, and `number`. We shall use these variables in subsequent code segments.

```
ArrayList<String> city = new ArrayList<String>();
ArrayList<String> bush = new ArrayList<String>(20);
ArrayList<Integer> number = new ArrayList<Integer>();
```

Variable `city` references a new `ArrayList<String>`. This list has no elements. A default constructed `ArrayList<T>` has the ability to represent up to 10 elements before it needs to update its internal capacity.

Variable `bush` references another new `ArrayList<String>`, which also has no elements. In terms of its internal configuration, this new `ArrayList<String>` has been set up so that it has the ability to represent up to 20 elements before it needs to update its internal capacity.

Variable `number` references a new `ArrayList<Integer>`. This list has no elements with a default initial capacity of 10 elements before it needs to update its internal capacity.

Suppose we wanted to add two elements to the list referenced by `city`, where these elements represent the strings `"Madrid"` and `"Cairo"`. The following code will accomplish this task.

```
city.add("Madrid");
city.add("Cairo");
```

Based on the two `add()` invocations, `ArrayList<String>` variable `city` has representation

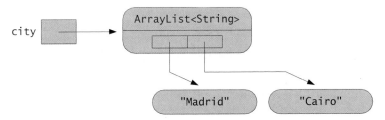

The representation indicates that variable `city` references an `ArrayList<String>` object. This object represents a list with two `String` elements. The first element references the string `"Madrid"` and the second element references the string `"Cairo"`.

The code segment

```
bush.add("Forsythia");
bush.add("Azalea");
bush.add("Rhododendron");
```

causes `bush` to have representation

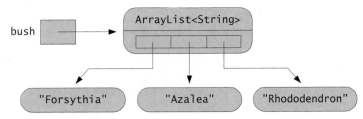

The `ArrayList<String>` object represents a list with three `String` elements. The first element references the string `"Forsythia"`, the second element references the string `"Azalea"`, and the third element references the string `"Rhododendron"`.

ArrayList<T> method `set()` can be used to change the value of an element, where the elements of an ArrayList<T> are numbered in the same manner as the elements of an array—the first element has index 0, the second element has index 1, and so on. The following code segment uses method `set()` to change the value of the second element in bush.

```
bush.set(1, "Lilac");
```

The representation of d after the invocation is

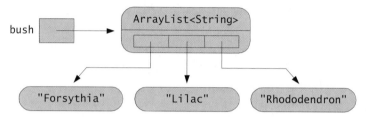

Because variables city and bush are of the same type—ArrayList<String>— one of these variables can be assigned to the other.

```
city = bush; // legal: city and bush have the same type
bush = city; // legal: city and bush have the same type
```

However, because ArrayList<Integer> variable number is of a different type than city and bush, variable number can be assigned to neither city nor bush or vice-versa.

```
number = city; // illegal: number and city have different types
bush = number; // illegal: bush and number have different types
```

Suppose we wanted variable number to reference a list whose elements represented the integers 0, 1, and 2. The following code segment accomplishes this task.

```
for (int i = 0; i < 3; ++i) {
    number.add(i);
}
```

Although i is an **int** and not an Integer, we can syntactically pass i rather than the Integer representation of i (i.e., Integer.valueOf(i)). We can do so because Java automatically performs the conversion. This type of conversion is called *primitive type autoboxing*.

Based on the preceding code segment, ArrayList<Integer> variable number has representation

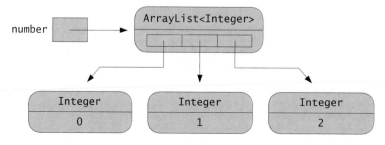

The representation indicates that variable number references an ArrayList<Integer> object. This object represents a list with three elements. The first element references an Integer representing the value 0, the second element references an Integer representing the value 1, and the third element references an Integer representing the value 2.

To access a particular element of an ArrayList<T> we can use method get(). This method behaves in practice like the array subscript operator []. For example, the following code segment displays the elements of e.

```java
for (int i = 0; i < number.size(); ++i) {
    System.out.println(number.get(i));
}
```

Observe that we used ArrayList<T> member method size() in the **for** loop test expression. Method size() returns the number of elements represented by the list.

As it does for arrays, Java provides an iterator **for** loop for its Collection classes (e.g., ArrayList<T>). So the preceding code segment can be rewritten as

```java
for (Integer element : number) {
    System.out.println(element);
}
```

Java provides for automatic *unboxing* to the primitive types. The following code segment uses unboxing in computing the sum of the elements represented by e.

```java
int sum = 0;

for (Integer element : number) {
    sum += element;
}
```

Setting up an ArrayList<Integer> object to represent numeric values from standard input is straightforward given the capabilities of this collection class. For example, the following code segment defines an ArrayList<Integer> variable data and initializes it to represent the integer values from standard input.

```java
Scanner stdin = new Scanner(System.in);

ArrayList<Integer> data = new ArrayList<Integer>();

while (stdin.hasNextInt()) {
    int number = stdin.nextInt();
    data.add(number);
}
```

Thus, its purpose is similar to method getList() of Listing 8.4. However, its implementation is far simpler. The simplicity is possible because of the capabilities of the ArrayList<T> methods. The append behavior of method add() enables each additional input value to be incorporated easily into the list.

If standard input contains the following values

```
28 9
29
```

then the code segment results in variable `data` having representation

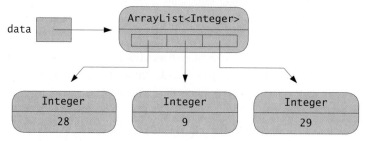

COLLECTIONS ALGORITHMS

As indicated at the beginning of our collections framework discussion, the framework includes algorithms for performing standard list operations. The algorithms are implemented as class methods of the class `java.util.Collections`. A summary of some of the most commonly useful methods is included in Table 8.2.

> A complete list of `Collections` capabilities is provided in Appendix E

Several of the `Collections` methods make use of the interface `java.lang.Comparable` for examining list elements (e.g., `min()`, `binarySearch()`, and `sort()`). Interface Comparable<T> calls for a method `compareTo()` with the following characteristics.

> `public int compareTo(T v)`
>
> > Returns a negative value if the invoking object is less than v; returns zero if the two objects are equal; and returns a positive value if the invoking object is greater than v2.

Many of the standard classes implement the `Comparable` interface including `String`, `Integer`, and `Double`. The comparison methods for these classes work as you would expect. For example, the `compareTo()` methods of the numeric classes (e.g., `Integer` and `Double`) order values numerically and the `compareTo()` method of `String` orders values lexicographically.

Program `CollectionsTest.java` of Listing 8.9 demonstrates some of the `Collections` algorithms. The program begins by defining an ArrayList<Integer> variable a that references an ArrayList<Integer> whose Integer elements represent the integer values 0 ... 9.

```java
ArrayList<Integer> number = new ArrayList<Integer>();
for (int i = 0; i < 10; ++i) {
    number.add(i);
}
```

Table 8.2   Some Collections<T> algorithms.

`static boolean disjoint(Collection<?> a, Collection<?> b)`

Returns whether the two collections do not have any common elements. The specification ? indicates that there is no restriction to the type of elements maintained by collections a and b with respect to class T.

`static void fill(List<? super T> a, T v)`

Sets all elements of collection a to v. The specification ? **super** T requires that the type of elements maintained by collection a be a superclass of class T. The creation of subclasses and superclasses is discussed in Chapter 9.

`static int frequency(Collection<?> a, Object v)`

Returns the number of elements in collection a that are equal to v. The specification ? indicates that there is no restriction to the type of elements maintained by collection a with respect to class T.

`static T max(Collection<? extends T> a)`

Returns the maximum-valued element of collection a. Class T is required to implement the `Comparable` interface. The determination of the value is based on the natural ordering of the elements (i.e., the ordering based on `Comparable` interface method `compareTo()`). The specification ? **extends** T requires that the type of elements maintained by collection a be a subclass of class T. The creation of subclasses and superclasses is discussed in Chapter 9.

`static T min(Collection<? extends T> a)`

Returns the minimum-valued element of collection a. Class T is required to implement the `Comparable` interface. The determination of the value is based on the natural ordering of the elements (i.e., the ordering based on `Comparable` interface method `compareTo()`). The specification ? **extends** T requires that the type of elements maintained by collection a be a subclass of class T. The creation of subclasses and superclasses is discussed in Chapter 9.

`static void reverse(List<?> a)`

Reverses the order of the elements in list a. The specification ? indicates that there is no restriction to the type of elements maintained by collection a with respect to class T.

`static void shuffle(List<?> a)`

Randomly permutes list a. The specification ? indicates that there is no restriction to the type of elements maintained by collection a with respect to class T.

`static void sort(List<T> a)`

Sorts list a into its natural ordering of the elements (i.e., the ordering based on their `Comparable` interface method `compareTo()`). Class T is required to implement the `Comparable` interface.

`static void swap(List<?> a, int i, int j)`

Swaps the elements at positions i and j in list a. The specification ? indicates that there is no restriction to the type of elements maintained by collection a with respect to class T.

Listing 8.9 **Collections Test.java**

```
 1. // Demonstrate Collections usefulness
 2.
 3. import java.util.*;
 4.
 5. public class CollectionsTest {
 6.    // main(): application entry point
 7.    public static void main(String[] args) {
 8.       // initialize number to represent the integers 0 … 9
 9.       ArrayList<Integer> number = new ArrayList<Integer>();
10.       for (int i = 0; i < 10; ++i) {
11.          number.add(i);
12.       }
13.
14.       // display number to demonstrate its current configuration
15.       System.out.println("Original: " + number + "\n");
16.
17.       // put number into reverse order
18.       Collections.reverse(number);
19.
20.       // display number to demonstrate its current configuration
21.       System.out.println("Reversed: " + number + "\n");
22.
23.       // put number into random order
24.       Collections.shuffle(number);
25.
26.       // display number to demonstrate its current configuration
27.       System.out.println("Shuffled: " + number + "\n");
28.
29.       // sort number
30.       Collections.sort(number);
31.
32.       // display number to demonstrate its current configuration
33.       System.out.println("Sorted:   " + number + "\n");
34.    }
35. }
```

The program then displays the `ArrayList<Integer>` using a `println()` invocation.

```
System.out.println("Original: " + number);
```

The values of the elements then are put into reverse order using `Collections` method `reverse()`.

```
Collections.reverse(number);
```

The program then redisplays the `ArrayList<Integer>` using another `println()` invocation.

```
System.out.println("Reverse: " + number);
```

The values of the elements are rearranged randomly using `Collections` method `shuffle()`.

```
Collections.shuffle(number);
```

The program then redisplays the `ArrayList<Integer>` using another `println()` invocation.

```
System.out.println("Shuffled: " + number);
```

In a sample run of the program, the program output up to this point was

```
Original: [0, 1, 2, 3, 4, 5, 6, 7, 8, 9]

Reversed: [9, 8, 7, 6, 5, 4, 3, 2, 1, 0]

Shuffled: [3, 0, 1, 9, 5, 2, 8, 6, 7, 4]
```

The output indicates that the elements of the `ArrayList<Integer>` were configured, reversed, and scrambled correctly.

Program `CollectionsTest.java` then sorts the values by using `Collections` method `sort()`.

```
Collections.sort(number);
```

Finally, the program redisplays the `ArrayList<Integer>` a last time.

```
System.out.println("Sorted: " + number);
```

For the same run depicted only partially before, the complete output of the program was

```
Original: [0, 1, 2, 3, 4, 5, 6, 7, 8, 9]

Reversed: [9, 8, 7, 6, 5, 4, 3, 2, 1, 0]

Shuffled: [3, 0, 1, 9, 5, 2, 8, 6, 7, 4]

Sorted:   [0, 1, 2, 3, 4, 5, 6, 7, 8, 9]
```

The output shows that the elements of the `ArrayList<Integer>` end up being sorted.

This discussion completes our introduction to the collections framework. We now turn our attention to data visualization. That example will complete our introduction to array and list mechanisms.

8.12   CASE STUDY — PIE CHARTS

Visualization of data is an important area of computing and statistical research. Two standard visualization techniques are histograms and pie charts. We consider a pie chart representation here and leave a histogram representation to the exercises. An array will be used to store the data. Therefore, methods will be needed for extracting inputs and converting those inputs to a pie chart representation.

> The objective of this case study is practice with arrays, and class design and implementation in the context of data visualization

A pie chart shows graphically the relative sizes of a set of numeric values. Each value is represented as a slice of pie with the size of a slice proportional to the ratio of the associated value to the sum of the values. Accompanying the pie is a legend describing the data set.

As an example of a data set, consider Table 8.3, which reports preferred musical tastes as reported by the Recording Industry Association of America. A pie chart for this data is given in Figure 8.3. The pie chart was produced by program `MusicChart.java` of Listing 8.10. The program makes use of a class `PieChart` that we design and develop.

Table 8.3   **USA musical preferences.**

Genre	%	Genre	%
Classical	3.2	Religious	6.7
Country	10.5	Rock	24.4
Jazz	3.4	Urban and R&B	10.6
Pop	12.1	Other	17.7
Rap and Hip-Hop	11.4		

The pie chart does a better job of showing the various similarities and disparities. When analyzing data, a visual representation typically enables relationships to be recognized more easily.

ANALYSIS AND DESIGN

If you consider how users may want to generate pie charts, you will see the utility of at least two types of constructors—a constructor where just the data and legend information are supplied and a constructor that also requires coloring information.

`public PieChart(double[] d, String[] s)`

Generates a default-color pie chart representation for data list `d`, where `s[i]` is the legend text associated with value `d[i]`.

`public PieChart(double[] d, String[] s, Color[] c)`

Generates a pie chart representation for data list `d`, where `s[i]` is the legend text associated with value `d[i]` and `c[i]` is the color associated with `d[i]`.

Figure 8.3   Pie chart produced by MusicChart.java.

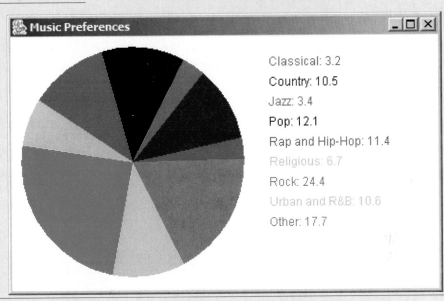

In the implementation that we develop here, only array representations are considered for the data, legend, and color lists. The exercises consider constructors where the data, legend, and color lists are represented using `ArrayList<T>` objects.

A variety of accessors, mutators, and facilitators should be present if the `PieChart` representation is to have general utility. For example, the class should provide the means for getting and setting the various pie chart characteristics including such characteristics as pie position, radius, and legend position. The class should also provide the means for rendering the entire pie chart and the individual rendering of the pie and the legend.

We leave the implementation of accessors and mutators to the exercises. Our discussion concentrates on implementing the constructors and the following rendering facilitators.

`public void paint(Graphics g)`

Renders a graphical representation of the pie chart to graphical context `g`.

`public void paintPie(Graphics g, int x, int y, int r)`

Renders a graphical representation of the pie to graphical context `g`, where the radius of the pie is `r` and the upperleft-hand corner of the bounding box of the pie is (`x`, `y`).

`public void paintLegend(Graphics g, int x, int y, int delta)`

Renders a graphical representation of the pie legend to graphical context `g`, where the first line of the legend begins at location (`x`, `y`) and successive lines are each offset by an additional `delta` pixels downward.

In support of these rendering behaviors, the following `PieChart` attributes are appropriate.

`private double[] data`

Reference to the list of numeric values being represented in the pie chart.

Listing 8.10 **MusicChart.java**

```
1.  // Produces a pie chart of music preferences
2.
3.  import java.awt.*;
4.  import javax.swing.*;
5.  import java.util.*;
6.
7.  public class MusicChart {
8.      // main()" application entry point
9.      public static void main(String[] args) {
10.         JFrame w = new JFrame("Music Preferences");
11.         w.setSize(450, 280);
12.         w.setVisible(true);
13.         w.setDefaultCloseOperation(JFrame.EXIT_ON_CLOSE);
14.         Container c = w.getContentPane();
15.         c.setBackground(Color.WHITE);
16.         Graphics g = c.getGraphics();
17.
18.         double[] choice = { 3.2, 10.5, 3.4, 12.1, 11.4, 6.7, 24.4,
19.                             10.6, 17.7 };
20.         String[] genre = { "Classical", "Country", "Jazz", "Pop",
21.                 "Rap and Hip-Hop", "Religious", "Rock",
22.                             "Urban and R&B", "Other" };
23.
24.         System.out.println("Hit enter when ready");
25.         Scanner stdin = new Scanner(System.in);
26.         stdin.nextLine();
27.
28.         PieChart chart = new PieChart(choice, genre);
29.         chart.paint(g);
30.     }
31. }
```

---

private String[] name

Reference to the list of names to be used in the pie chart, where name[i] is the basis for the legend entry for value data[i].

private Color[] color

Reference to the list of colors to be used in the pie chart, where the color associated with value data[i] is color[i].

private int radius

The radius of the pie in the pie chart.

private Point pieLocation

Reference to the location where the pie is to be placed in the pie chart.

private Point legendLocation

Reference to the location where the legend is to be placed in the pie chart.

private int lineSpacing

Number of pixels separating successive legend lines in the pie chart.

IMPLEMENTATION

Because one of the `PieChart` constructors automatically assigns the colors in the pie chart, it is appropriate for the class `PieChart` to maintain a list of available colors. The list can be represented using a class constant DEFAULT_PIE_COLORS.

```
private static final Color[] DEFAULT_PIE_COLORS = {
    Color.RED, Color.BLUE, Color.MAGENTA, Color.BLACK,
    Color.GREEN, Color.YELLOW, Color.CYAN, Color.PINK,
    Color.GRAY, Color.ORANGE, Color.DARK_GRAY, Color.WHITE };
```

To make the construction of a pie chart simple for a `PieChart` user, it is also appropriate to have constants that specify default layout characteristics of the pie chart.

```
private static final int DEFAULT_RADIUS = 115;
private static final int DEFAULT_LINE_SPACING = 20;
private static final int DEFAULT_PIE_LOCATION
                        = new Point (10, 10);
private static final int DEFAULT_LEGEND_LOCATION
                        = new Point (495, 35);
```

(The exercises investigate alternatives to using these values through the use of mutator methods.) These class constants serve the following purposes:

- DEFAULT_RADIUS: the default pie radius;

- DEFAULT_LINE_SPACING: the default spacing in pixels between successive lines of the legend;

- DEFAULT_PIE_LOCATION: the default location of the upperleft-hand corner of the bounding box of the pie;

- DEFAULT_LEGEND_LOCATION: the default location of the upperleft-hand corner of the bounding box of the legend.

With DEFAULT_PIE_COLORS, the initialization required of the first `PieChart` constructor can be accomplished through an invocation of the other `PieChart` constructor.

```
// PieChart(): constructor for case when colors are not supplied
public PieChart(double[] d, String[] s) {
    this(d, s, DEFAULT_PIE_COLORS);
}
```

Defining one constructor in terms of another is a standard software engineering practice.

The other `PieChart` constructor uses its parameters to set respectively the data values, legend text, and colors to be used in the pie chart. The class constants are used to set the other attributes of the pie chart.

```
// PieChart(): constructor using given data, names, colors
public PieChart(double[] d, String[] s, Color[] c) {
    if ((d.length == 0) || (d.length > s.length)
                || (d.length > c.length)) {
        System.err.println("PieChart: invalid data");
        System.exit(1);
    }

    data = d;
    name = s;
```

```
    color = c;

    radius = DEFAULT_RADIUS;
    pieLocation = DEFAULT_PIE_LOCATION;
    legendLocation = DEFAULT_LEGEND_LOCATION;
    lineSpacing = DEFAULT_LINE_SPACING;
}
```

As an examination of the constructor body indicates, the implementation is straightforward. A test first determines whether the parameters are sensible. If there are no data values or an insufficient number of legend entries or colors, then the constructor issues an error message and terminates the program. Otherwise, the constructor sets the various attributes of the pie chart.

We now turn our attention to implementing the three rendering facilitators specified in the problem design section. As a reminder, renderer paint() displays the complete pie chart; renderer paintPie() displays the pie itself; and renderer paintLegend() displays the legend associated with the pie chart.

Renderer method paint() needs to display the pie chart in the graphical context specified by its parameter g. It can do so by invoking rendering methods paintPie() and paintLegend() with appropriate parameters.

```
// paint(): render chart and legend
public void paint(Graphics g) {
    // set pie chart characteristics
    int r = getRadius();
    Point pie = getPieLocation();
    Point legend = getLegendLocation();
    int spacing = getLineSpacing();

    // paint the chart
    paintPie(g, pie.x, pie.y, r);
    paintLegend(g, legend.x, legend.y, spacing);
}
```

Our implementation of method paint() begins by using PieChart accessors getRadius() and getPieLocation() to determine the size of the pie and its location.[†]

```
int r = getRadius();
Point pie = getPieLocation();
```

It then uses accessors getPieLocation() and getLegendSpacing() to determine the location of the legend and the number of pixels separating successive legend lines.

```
Point legend = getLegendLocation();
int spacing = getLineSpacing();
```

[†] The accessors are considered in the self-test section with their implementation included in Listing 8.11, which starts on page 456. Listing 8.11 provides a complete definition of PieChart.java.

With these values, the pie renderer `paintPie()` and the legend renderer `paintLe-gend()` then can be invoked to display the pie chart.

```
paintPie(g, pie.x, pie.y, r);
paintLegend(g, legend.x, legend.y, spacing);
```

The implementation of method `paintPie()` iteratively displays the slices one at a time.

```
// paintPie(): render the pie
public void paintPie(Graphics g, int x, int y, int r) {
    final int CIRCLE_DEGREES = 360;

    // determine number of values
    int n = getSampleSize();

    // compute sum of the values
    double dataSum = 0;
    for (int i = 0; i < n; ++i) {
        dataSum += getData(i);
    }

    // draw slices one by one starting from origin
    int startAngle = 0;

    for (int i = 0; i < n; ++i) {
        // how much of the pie does the next slice take
        double percent = getData(i) / dataSum;
        int arcAngle = (int) Math.round(percent * CIRCLE_DEGREES);

        // set the slice color
        Color c = getColor(i);
        g.setColor(c);

        // render the slice
        g.fillArc(x, y, 2*r, 2*r, startAngle, arcAngle);

        // record where next slice starts
        startAngle += arcAngle;
    }
}
```

In doing its slice display, the `paintPie()` implementation makes use of one local constant. The constant specifies the number of degrees in a circle.

```
final int CIRCLE_DEGREES = 360;
```

Because the size of a slice is proportional to the ratio of its associated value to the sum of the values, `paintPie()` first uses `PieChart` accessors to determine the number of data values n and the sum `dataSum` of the data values.

```
// determine number of values
int n = getSampleSize();

// compute sum of the values
double dataSum = 0;
for (int i = 0; i < n; ++i) {
```

```
        dataSum += getData(i);
}
```

The implementation uses a variable `startAngle` to represent the starting angle orientation of the next slice to be displayed, where the first slice has a starting orientation of 0 degrees.

```
// draw slices one by one starting from origin
int startAngle = 0;
```

Method `paintPie()` uses a **for** loop to display the slices, with the `i`th iteration displaying the slice associated with the `i`th data value. Each iteration begins by determining the width `arcAngle` of the current slice in degrees.

```
// how much of the pie does the next slice take
double percent = getData(i) / dataSum;
int arcAngle = (int) Math.round(percent * CIRCLE_DEGREES);
```

The width of the angle equals the product of the number of degrees in a circle and the relative size of the current data value to the sum of the data values.

The **for** loop body then sets the color of the slice in the desired graphical context.

```
// set the slice color
Color c = getColor(i);
g.setColor(c);
```

The slice then is rendered using `Graphics` member method `fillArc()`.

```
// render the slice
g.fillArc(x, y, 2*r, 2*r, startAngle, arcAngle);
```

`Graphics` method `fillArc()` expects six parameters. The first two parameters specify the x- and y-coordinates of the upperleft-hand corner of the bounding box associated with the oval that contains the slice. The next two parameters specify width and height of that rectangle. The next parameter specifies the starting angle of the slice and the last parameter specifies the width of the angle. The method renders the slice counterclockwise from the start angle. The roles of the parameters are demonstrated in Figure 8.4.

In the `paintPie()` invocation of `fillArc()`, the coordinates of the upperleft-hand corner of the bounding box come from parameters x and y of `paintPie()`. Because the pie is to be a circle, the width and height values are both `2*r`, where r is also one of the parameters of `paintPie()`. The starting angle and the width angle are respectively `startAngle` and `arcAngle`.

To prepare for the display of the next slice, the **for** loop body ends with an updating of `startAngle`. Its new value is to be where the last slice ended.

```
// record where next slice starts
startAngle += arcAngle;
```

Figure 8.4　**Method fillArc() rendering.**

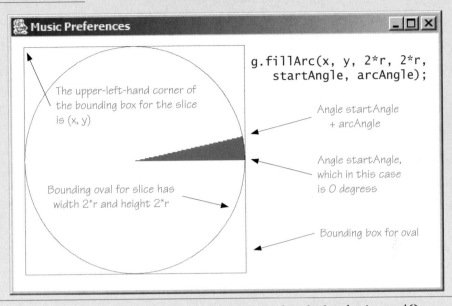

Like method `paintPie()`, the implementation of method `paintLegend()` uses a **for** loop to iteratively display its elements.

```
// paintLegend(): render the legend for the pie
public void paintLegend(Graphics g, int x, int y, int delta) {
    // determine number of values
    int n = getSampleSize();

    for (int i = 0; i < n; ++i) {
        // set up the current legend line
        Color c = getColor(i);
        String s = getName(i) + ": " + getData(i);

        // render the line
        g.setColor(c);
        g.drawString(s, x, y);

        // set up the y-coordinate location of the next line
        y += delta;
    }
}
```

Its parameters x and y specify the starting location for the first line of the legend and its parameter `delta` specifies how far apart are successive legend lines.

For each of the n values in the data set, the associated color and entry for the legend is determined.

```
// set up the current legend line
Color c = getColor(i);
String s = getName(i) + ": " + getData(i);
```

The legend line is rendered using `Graphics` method `drawString()`.

```
// render the line
g.setColor(c);
g.drawString(s, x, y);
```

Method `drawString()` takes three parameters. The first parameter supplies the string to be rendered and the next two parameters specify where the rendering is to begin.

This discussion completes both our analysis of class `PieChart` and our introduction to Java array and list mechanisms. A complete definition of `PieChart` is given in Listing 8.11 of the self-test answer section.

8.13 REVIEW

- An array is the basic Java list mechanism. Because Java considers an array to be an object, it has the features common to other objects.

- The value of an array variable is a reference to an array rather than being an array itself.

- The individual objects that make up an array are known as elements. Array elements can be accessed collectively or individually. They can be of any fundamental type, a previously defined class type, or even an array type.

- An important language restriction on arrays is that all elements of an array must have the same type, which is known as the element type.

- An array element can be used like a variable of the underlying element type.

- An array whose elements are arrays is a multidimensional array.

- An array variable definition does not automatically provide a list of elements to be manipulated.

- Like other objects, arrays can be defined either with or without initialization. If there is no initialization, then the definition has the form

  ElementType[] *id* ;

  where *ElementType* is the type of the individual elements in the array and *id* is an identifier that is the name of the array.

- An array variable definition can specify the initial array that the variable is to reference. The most common such form is

  ElementType[] *id* = **new** *ElementType*[*exp*] ;

- Java also provides a declaration form to specify initial values for a new array.

  ElementType[] *id* = { exp_0 , exp_1 , ... exp_{n-1} };

- The act of referring to an individual array element is called *subscripting* or *indexing*. A subscript can be a nonnegative integer expression. Just as brackets are used in a definition to indicate that an array is being created, so too are brackets used to subscript a particular element of an array. Each element of an array has its own subscript value. The first element of an array has subscript value 0, the second element of an array has subscript value 1, and so on.

- Unlike many other programming languages, Java automatically checks that proper array subscripts are used. If a subscript is determined to be invalid, an exception of type IndexOutOfBoundsException is generated.

- If the element type of an array is an object type, then the elements of the array hold references to values of the element types.

- An array has a **public final** data field length that specifies the number of elements in the array.

- Because an array is an object, an array has associated with it all of the methods of class `Object`. The `clone()` method of an array is one tailored specifically for arrays to produce a shallow copy of the array.

- There are no methods to resize an array—an array's size is fixed at its creation.

- When used as a parameter, a reference to the array is passed. If code modifies the elements of that formal parameter, the changes are visible to the elements of the actual parameter.

- Java provides a method for creating programs that use command-line parameters. The command-line parameters are communicated to a program via its method `main()`. To make this communication straightforward, Java requires that a program view the command line parameters as an array of strings.

- A sort is often an iterative process such that each iteration rearranges some of the values in the list to be sorted. For example, on iteration `i`, the method known as `selectionSort()` finds the element containing the `i`th smallest value of the list and exchanges that element with the `i`th element.

- The total number of element comparisons made by `selectionSort()` is proportional to n^2, where n is the number of elements in array `a`. Because the number of element comparisons is proportional to the square of the number of elements, we say that method `selectionSort()` has quadratic performance with respect to element comparisons. Because the number of element copies/assignments is proportional to the number of elements, we say that the algorithm has linear performance with respect to element copies/assignments. Overall, the algorithm has quadratic performance.

- The components (subarrays) of a two-dimensional array are known as rows. To refer to an individual element of a row, an additional subscript is used. For example, `m[i][j]` is the `j`th element of the `i`th row in `m`.

- A two-dimensional array is sometimes known as a matrix because it resembles that mathematical concept.

- Java does not require that the components of a two-dimensional array have the same length.

- The definition of a multidimensional array can include initialization. For a two-dimensional array whose base type is a fundamental type, the array initialization is given as collections of initial row values.

- Arrays in Java suffer from the traditional shortcoming—they cannot be resized—there are no Java array operations that support the insertion of new elements or the deletion of existing elements.

- Java also provides a rich set of alternative list representations, known as the collections framework. There are two types of list representations in the collections framework—those that implement the interface `java.util.Collection` and those that implement the interface `java.util.Map`.

- Classes that implement one of the derived `Collection` generic interfaces `List<T>`, `Queue<T>`, and `Set<T>` represent lists as we normally would imagine them. Such classes support a view of a list as a group of elements. Classes that implement the Map<K, V> interface or its derived interface HashMap<K, V> take a more associative view; that is, these classes provide the means to associate "keys" with values. The Map<K, V>-based classes also provide the means to determine the value associated with a key and vice versa.

- Generic class ArrayList<T> provides a resizeable list representation that implements the List<T> interface. The name ArrayList<T> is intended to be suggestive doubly. An ArrayList<T> uses an array to represent the elements of its list. In addition, an ArrayList<T> has been designed so that its element accessor and mutator methods are guaranteed to run in constant time.

- ArrayList<T> provides the ability to append an element to the end of the list. The append operation takes a constant amount of time on average. The class also provides a number of other methods for inserting and deleting elements. These other methods are guaranteed to run in at most linear time.

- The collections framework through its class Collections provides a collection of algorithms for performing standard list operations. For example, the class provides methods that search, copy, reverse, and shuffle a list. There are also methods to determine the minimum and maximum and methods to swap individual elements.

8.14   SELF-TEST

S8.1   Assume that a and b are **int** arrays that have been initialized and that i, j, and k are **int** variables that have been initialized.

- Write the statement that adds 6 to element k of a.
- Write the statement that copies element i of b to element k+1 of b.
- Write the statement that sums elements i and k of a and places the result in element j+5 of b.

S8.2   Write the appropriate definitions.

- Define an array named stackElements that can hold 50 values of type **double**.
- Define an array named testData that can hold 500 values of type String.

S8.3   Write an array definition for an array coefficient that is initialized with the following values: 1.4, 4.30, 5.12, 6.9, 6.21, 7.31, 11.4, 11.28, and 11.29.

S8.4   Implement a method max() that takes an array of integers as its parameter. The method returns the largest value in the list.

S8.5   Implement a method called isSorted() that takes an integer array as a parameter. The method returns **true** if the list is in nondecreasing order; otherwise it returns **false**.

S8.6   Because of its simplicity, a popular sorting algorithm is *BubbleSort*. Bubblesort is so named because the smallest item "bubbles" to the top of the array when the algorithm is applied. The basic idea is to successively compare adjacent elements and swap them if they are out of order. If we are sorting the list into ascending order (smallest elements appear first in the array), the smaller elements slowly "bubble" to the top, while the largest elements sink to the bottom. After the first pass through the elements, the maximal value is guaranteed to be in its correct position. After the second pass, the next most maximal element is guaranteed to be in its correct position, and so on. Implement a Java version of `bubbleSort()`.

S8.7 Implement a program `ExpressionEvaluate.java` that evaluates its three command-line parameters as a binary arithmetic expression. An example sample run could be

```
java ExpressionEvaluate 12.3 * 4.56
```

S8.8 Implement a `void` method `printMatrix()` that prints the values of its integer matrix parameter row by row.

S8.9 What happens if the following code using class `PieChart` is executed?

```
double[] d = null;
String[] s = null;
PieChart piechart = new PieChart(d, s);
JFrame w = new JFrame("Test");
Graphics g = w.getContentPane().getGraphics();
piechart.paint(g);
```

How should class `PieChart` be modified to correct this problem?

S8.10 Implement the following accessors for class `PieChart`.

`public double getData(int i)`

Returns the `i`th value from the data set being represented.

`public String getName(int i)`

Returns the associated legend name for the `i`th value from the data set being represented.

`public Color getColor(int i)`

Returns the associated color for the `i`th value from the data set being represented.

`public int getRadius()`

Returns the radius of the pie chart.

`public Point getPieLocation()`

Returns the location of the upperleft-hand corner of the bounding box for the pie.

`public Point getLegendLocation()`

Returns the location of where the display of the legend is to start.

`public int getLineSpacing()`

Returns the interline spacing in pixels between successive legend lines.

8.15   EXERCISES

8.1   Which operator is used to refer to a particular element of an array?

8.2   Can an array represent more than one type of value? Explain.

8.3   Can an array be a parameter? Explain.

8.4 Does a local array with a base type that is a fundamental type have its elements automatically initialized? Explain.

8.5 Write a code segment that does the following:

a) Defines a constant MAX_SIZE equal to 20.

b) Defines an array list with MAX_SIZE elements.

c) Sets the first element of list to the value 19.

d) Sets the last element of list to the value 54.

e) Sets the other elements of list to 0.

f) Displays list.

8.6 Write a code segment that does the following:

a) Defines an array score with 40 elements. The element type of the array is **double**.

b) Sets the value of each element in score so that it matches its subscript value.

c) Displays the values of the last five elements of scores.

d) Is the value 3.1415 a legal element value for score? Explain.

e) Is the value 3.1415 a legal subscript value for score? Explain.

8.7 Explain why a[3] does not access the third element of the array a.

8.8 What is the output of the following program fragment?

```
int[] a = new int[5];
a[0] = 0;
for (int i = 1; i <= 4; ++i) {
    a[i] = a[i-1] + i;
}
System.out.println(a[3]);
```

8.9 Write a code segment that does the following:

a) Defines constants MAX_ROWS equal to 25 and MAX_COLUMNS equal to 10.

b) Defines a two-dimensional **boolean** array Data with 25 rows, where each row consists of 10 elements.

c) Initializes array data so that the elements whose row subscript values are odd have the value **true** and initializes the other elements to **false**.

For Exercises 8.10–8.21, suppose the following definitions are in effect.

■ a is an **int** array with 10 elements;

■ b and c are **int** arrays with 20 elements;

■ d is a **double** array with 20 elements.

8.10 Is the following legal? Explain.

```
a[1] = a[9];
```

8.11 Is the following legal? Explain.

```
a[1] = a[10];
```

8.12 Is the following legal? Explain.

```
a[1] = b[1];
```

8.13 Is the following legal? Explain.

```
a[1] = d[1];
```

8.14 Is the following legal? Explain.

```
d[1] = a[1];
```

8.15 Is the following legal? Explain.

```
b = c;
```

8.16 Is the following legal? Explain.

```
a = b;
```

8.17 Is the following legal? Explain.

```
b = a;
```

8.18 Is the following legal? Explain.

```
d = b;
```

8.19 Is the following legal? Explain.

```
b = d;
```

8.20 Is the following legal? Explain.

```
int m = a.length;
```

8.21 Is the following legal? Explain.

```
int n = a.size();
```

The following definition of method f() is in effect for Exercises 8.22–8.25.

```java
public int f() {
    Scanner stdin = new Scanner(System.in);
    int[] a = new int[10];
    for (int i = 0; i < a.length; ++i) {
        a[i] = stdin.nextInt();
    }
    int guess = -1;
    for (int i = 0; i < a.length; ++i) {
        if (guess < a[i]) {
            guess = a[i];
        }
    }
    return guess;
}
```

8.22 If the values in a are all positive, does method f() correctly determine the maximum value in a? Explain.

8.23 If the values in a are all negative, does method f() correctly determine the maximum value in a? Explain.

8.24 If the definition of guess is replaced with the following statement, does method f() determine correctly the maximum value in a? Explain.

```
int guess = a[0];
```

8.25 If the definition of guess is replaced with the following statement, does method f() determine correctly the maximum value in a? Explain.

```
int guess = a[9];
```

8.26 Design and implement a **double** method min() with formal parameter **double** array a. The method returns the minimum element value in a.

8.27 Design and implement a String[] method deepCopy() with a formal parameter String array s. The method returns a deep copy of s.

8.28 Design and implement a **void** method initialize() with two formal parameters: an **int** array a and an **int** value v. The method sets each of the n elements of a to val.

8.29 Design and implement an **int** method numberLessThan() with two formal parameters: an **int** array a and an **int** value v. The method returns the number of elements in a that are less than v.

8.30 Design and implement the following statistical methods. Each of the methods returns a **double** value and has an **int** array a.

   a) Method mean(): returns the average of the n values in the list.

   b) Method median(): returns the middle value of the values in the list if the size of the list is odd; otherwise, it returns the average of the two middle values of the list. In performing its computation, the method does not alter the elements of a (i.e., it makes a copy of a and manipulates the copy).

   c) Method mode(): returns a value in the list that occurs most frequently. If there is more than one such value, any of the possible modes can be returned.

8.31 Implement a variant of searching method sequentialSearch(). The variant method has four formal parameters: **int** array a and **int** parameters key, m, and n. The variant searches elements a[m] through a[n] for the key value. If the value is present, then the method returns the minimal index k in m … n such that a[k] equals key. If the value is not present, then the method returns n+1.

8.32 Design and implement a **void** method listAll() that has two formal parameters: an **int** array a and an **int** value key. Method listAll() displays the indexes of all elements in a that are equal to key. Method listAll() accomplishes its task through a series of iterative calls to the modified method sequentialSearch() of Exercise 8.31.

8.33 Implement the iterative sorting method insertionSort(). The method has one formal parameter: **int** array a. On its ith iteration, this method correctly places the value of a[i] with respect to elements a[0] through a[i-1].

8.34 Implement a variant of sorting method insertionSort(). The variant method has three formal parameters: **int** array a and **int** parameters m and n. The variant sorts only elements a[m] through a[n].

8.35 Implement a method `zeroMatrix()` that takes two **int** parameters m and n. The method returns a two-dimensional array with m rows and n columns with element type **double**. All elements are initialized to 0.

8.36 Implement a method `identityMatrix()` that takes one **int** parameter m. The method returns a two-dimensional array with m rows and columns with element type **double**. All elements are initialized to 0 except for those elements on the *main diagonal* (i.e., elements whose row index equals its column index). Elements on the main diagonal are initialized to 1.

8.37 Implement a **boolean** method `isUpperTriangular()` that takes one **double**[][] parameter m. The method returns **true** if all elements below the main diagonal are 0 and returns **false**, otherwise. (See Exercise 8.36 for a definition of main diagonal.)

8.38 Redesign and reimplement `getList()` so that it takes account that there is no need to copy the elements of `buffer` to `data` when `listSize` equals `MAX_LIST_SIZE`. For this case, it is sufficient to return the value of `buffer` to accomplish the method's task.

8.39 Redesign and reimplement `getList()` so that it takes one **int** parameter n. The parameter specifies the maximum number of values to extract.

8.40 Redesign and reimplement `ArrayTools` method `getList()` so that it can extract all remaining values from standard input. Hint: you may find a method like `doubleCapacity()` helpful.

8.41 Implement the following constructors for class `PieChart`. Your implementation of the constructors should neither introduce any additional instance variables nor require modification to any of the `PieChart` methods.

    a) **public** `PieChart(ArrayList<Double> d, ArrayList<String> s)`: Generates a default-color pie chart representation for data list d, where s[i] represents the legend text associated with the value d[i].

    b) **public** `PieChart(ArrayList<Double> d, ArrayList<String> s, ArrayList<Color> c)`: Generates a pie chart representation for data list d, where s[i] represents the legend text associated with value d[i] and c[i] represents the color associated with d[i].

8.42 Implement the following methods for class `PieChart`.

    a) **public double** `setData(int i, double v)`: sets the ith value of the data set being represented to v.

    b) **public double** `setName(int i, String s)`: sets the associated legend name for the ith value of the data set being represented to s.

    c) **public double** `setColor(int i, Color c)`: sets the associated color for the ith value of the data set being represented to c.

    d) **public void** `setRadius(int r)`: sets the radius of the associated pie chart to r.

    e) **public void** `setPieLocation(Point p)`: sets the location of the bounding box for the pie slices of the associated pie chart to p.

f) **public void** setLegendLocation(Point p): sets the location of the legend of the associated pie chart to p.

g) **public void** setLineSpacing(**int** n): sets the interline spacing between successive legend lines to n pixels.

8.43 Implement the following methods for class PieChart. As part of your implementation ensure that the rendering methods attempt only to paint a sensible pie chart representation.

a) **public double** setData(**double**[] d): sets the data set being represented to d.

b) **public double** setName(String[] s): sets the legend names for the data set being represented to s.

c) **public double** setColor(Color[] c): sets the colors for the data set being represented to c.

8.44 In class PieChart, the pie slice rendered for each data value may be only an approximation. Inaccuracy can be introduced both because an integer angle width is being derived from a floating-point data value and because the angle widths and data values come from different numeric ranges. In the case of the music chart data of Table 8.3, the last rendered pie slice paints over the first rendered pie slice by one degree. This condition is demonstrated in the following diagram.

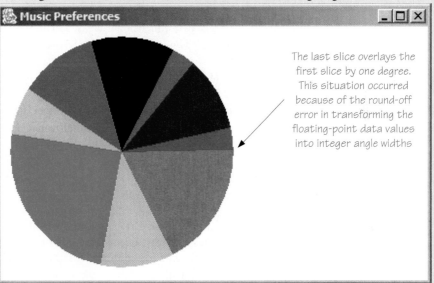

For other data sets, the last slice may not complete the circle. Reimplement method paintPie() of PieChart so that a complete pie with no overlap is rendered. One possibility is to render the last slice outside of the loop and have that slice complete the pie. Another possibility is to render the largest slice last. To do so, use one **for** loop to render pie slices counterclockwise toward the largest slice and use another loop to render pie slices clockwise toward the largest slice. The largest slice is rendered in the unfilled section of the circle. Why might one of these possible implementations be preferred over the other?

8.45 Reimplement constructor `PieChart(double[], String[], Color[])` so that the constructor checks whether formal parameters `d`, `s`, and `c` are all non-**null** array references before it checks whether the lengths of the associated arrays are sensible.

8.46 Design and implement a class `Histogram` with functionality similar to `PieChart`. A histogram displays its values as height-varying rectangles with unit width. The height of a rectangle is proportional to its value.

| 8.16 | PROGRAMMING PROJECT — MATRICES |

Our representation of matrices in Section 8.8.1 did not take an object-oriented design approach. This programming project takes an object-oriented view of a matrix.

> The objective of this case study is practice with arrays and class design in implementing a matrix representation

As indicated there, a matrix is a collection of numeric values arrange in rows. In a given matrix, each row has the same number of columns.

ANALYSIS AND DESIGN

To represent a matrix, you need to represent its rows and columns with the natural underlying representation being a two-dimensional array. For this project, the elements of a matrix are represented using a two-dimensional **double** array `element`.

`private double[][] element`

Represents the element values of the matrix, where `element[i][j]` represents the value in the `j`th column of the `i`th row.

Previous experience with matrices, numbers, and other Java APIs tells us that the `Matrix` abstraction should provide methods to initialize and manipulate a matrix in at least the following ways:

`public Matrix()`

Construct a new matrix of size 10×10 (i.e., 10 rows with 10 columns per row). Each element in the matrix has value 0.

`public Matrix(int m, int n)`

Construct a new matrix of size $m \times n$, where `m` and `n` represent the number of rows and columns respectively. Each element in the matrix has value 0.

`public Matrix(int m, int n, double v)`

Construct a new matrix of size $m \times n$, where `m` and `n` represent the number of rows and columns respectively. Each element in the matrix has value `v`.

`public Matrix(double[][] a)`

Construct a new matrix of size $m \times n$ whose elements are initialized using two-dimensional array parameter `a`, where `m` is the number of rows in array `a` and `n` is the number of columns per row.

`public Matrix add(Matrix a)`

Returns the matrix addition of this matrix and matrix `a`.

`public Matrix multiply(Matrix a)`

Returns the matrix product of this matrix and matrix `a`.

```
public int getNumberRows()
```
Returns the number of rows of this matrix.
```
public int getNumberColumns()
```
Returns the number of columns of this matrix.
```
public double get(int i, int j)
```
Returns the value of the element in the jth column of the ith row of this matrix.
```
public Object clone()
```
Returns a new matrix that is a duplicate of this matrix.
```
public String toString()
```
Returns a text representation of this matrix.
```
public boolean equals(Object v)
```
Returns whether object v is a matrix of the same dimensions as this matrix and whose element values correspond to the element values of this matrix.
```
public void fill(double v)
```
Sets all elements of this matrix to v.
```
public static Matrix identityMatrix(int m)
```
Returns a new square **Matrix** with m rows and columns. All elements are initialized to 0 except for those elements on the *main diagonal* (i.e., elements whose row index equals its column index). Elements on the main diagonal are initialized to 1.
```
public static Matrix createMatrix(int m, int n, Scanner s)
```
Returns a new **Matrix** with m rows and n columns. The element values for the matrix are extracted from **Scanner** stream s. The input values fill in the new matrix in a row by row manner.

TESTING AND DOCUMENTATION

In addition, develop a test program MatrixDemo.java that illustrates and tests all of the constructors and methods of your class Matrix. The test program should also highlight the robustness of your constructors and methods.

In documenting your implementation, be sure to explain the behaviors and nuances of your methods. Also explain how you ensured that your methods are robust.

8.17   SELF-TEST ANSWERS

S8.1 The statements are

```
a[k] += 6;
b[k+1] = b[i];
b[j+5] = a[i] + a[k];
```

S8.2 The definitions of stackElements and testData are

```
double[] stackElements = new double[50];
String[] testData = new String[500];
```

S8.3 Array coefficient can be defined as follows.

```
double[] coefficient = {1.4, 4.30, 5.12, 6.9, 6.21, 7.31,
```

$$11.4, \ 11.28, \ 11.29\};$$

S8.4 Method max() can be implemented as follows.

```java
public static int max(int[] a) {
    int guess = a[0];
    for (int i = 1; i < a.length; ++i) {
        if (guess < a[i]) {
            guess = a[i];
        };
    }
    return guess;
}
```

S8.5 Method isSorted() can be implemented as follows.

```java
public static boolean isSorted(int[] a) {
    for (int i = 0; i < a.length - 1; ++i) {
        if (a[i] > a[i+1]) {
            return false;
        }
    }

    return true;
}
```

S8.6 Method bubbleSort() can be implemented as follows.

```java
public static void bubbleSort(int[] a) {
    boolean bubbling;
    do {
        bubbling = false;
        for (int i = 0; i < a.length - 1; ++i) {
            if (a[i+1] < a[i]) {
                int rmbr = a[i];
                a[i] = a[i+1];
                a[i+1] = rmbr;
                bubbling = true;
            }
        }
    } while (bubbling);
}
```

S8.7 Program ExpressionEvaluate.java can be implemented as follows.

```java
public class ExpressionEvaluate {
    public static void main(String args[]) {
        if (args.length == 3) {
            double op1 = Double.parseDouble(args[0]);
            double op2 = Double.parseDouble(args[2]);
            if (args[1].length() != 1) {
                System.err.println("Unrecognized operator: "
                        + args[1]);
                return;
            }
            char operator = args[1].charAt(0);
            double result;
            switch ( operator ) {
                case '+':
```

```
                    result = op1 + op2;
                    break;
                case '-':
                    result = op1 - op2;
                    break;
                case '*':
                    result = op1 * op2;
                    break;
                case '/':
                    result = op1 / op2;
                    break;
                default:
                    System.err.println("Illegal operation");
                    return;
            }
            System.out.println(args[0] + " " + args[1]
                + " " + args[2] + " = " + result);
        }
        else {
            System.err.println("Malformed expression");
        }
    }
}
```

S8.8 Method `printMatrix()` can be implemented as follows.

```
public static void printMatrix(int[][] a) {
    for (int i = 0; i < a.length; ++i) {
        for (int j = 0; j < a[i].length; ++j) {
            System.out.print(a[i][j] + " ");
        }
        System.out.println();
    }
}
```

S8.9 The code segment generates an exception (error) in constructor `PieChart(double[], String[], Color[])` while attempting to access the length of a nonexistent array. The situation can be corrected by first ensuring that the formal parameters d, s, and c are all non-**null** array references and then checking whether the lengths of the associated arrays are sensible.

S8.10 The implementation of the requested accessors is included in the definition of `PieChart.java` of Listing 8.11.

Listing 8.11 PieChart.java

```
1.   // Supports the representation of a statistical pie chart
2.
3.   import java.awt.*;
4.
5.   public class PieChart {
6.      // default characteristics
7.      private static final Color[] DEFAULT_PIE_COLORS = {
8.         Color.RED, Color.BLUE, Color.MAGENTA, Color.BLACK,
9.         Color.GREEN, Color.ORANGE, Color.CYAN, Color.PINK,
10.        Color.GRAY, Color.YELLOW, Color.DARK_GRAY, Color.WHITE };
11.
12.     private static final int DEFAULT_RADIUS = 115;
13.     private static final int DEFAULT_LINE_SPACING = 20;
14.     private static final Point DEFAULT_PIE_LOCATION
15.                                  = new Point (10, 10);
16.     private static final Point DEFAULT_LEGEND_LOCATION
17.                                  = new Point (265, 35);
18.
19.     // individual pie chart characteristics
20.     private double[] data;         // data to be represented
21.     private String[] name;         // legend names for data
22.     private Color[] color;         // colors representing data
23.     private int radius;            // radius of the pie
24.     private Point pieLocation;     // pie location
25.     private Point legendLocation;  // legend location
26.     private int lineSpacing;       // spacing between legend lines
27.
28.     // PieChart(): default constructor
29.     public PieChart(double[] d, String[] s) {
30.        this(d, s, DEFAULT_PIE_COLORS);
31.     }
32.
33.     // PieChart(): constructor using given data, names, colors
34.     public PieChart(double[] d, String[] s, Color[] c) {
35.        if ((d.length == 0) || (d.length > s.length)
36.               || (d.length > c.length)) {
37.           System.err.println("PieChart: invalid data");
38.           System.exit(1);
39.        }
40.
41.        data = d;
42.        name = s;
43.        color = c;
44.
45.        radius = DEFAULT_RADIUS;
46.        pieLocation = DEFAULT_PIE_LOCATION;
47.        legendLocation = DEFAULT_LEGEND_LOCATION;
48.        lineSpacing = DEFAULT_LINE_SPACING;
49.     }
50.
51.     // getSampleSize(): return the number of data values
52.     public int getSampleSize() {
53.        return data.length;
54.     }
```

Listing 8.11   PieChart.java (Continued)

```java
55.
56.       // getColor(): return the ith color
57.       public Color getColor(int i) {
58.          return color[i];
59.       }
60.
61.       // getData(): return the ith data value
62.       public double getData(int i) {
63.          return data[i];
64.       }
65.
66.       // getName(): return the ith legend name
67.       public String getName(int i) {
68.          return name[i];
69.       }
70.
71.       // getRadius(): return the pie radius
72.       public int getRadius() {
73.          return radius;
74.       }
75.
76.       // getPieLocation(): return the location of the pie
77.       public Point getPieLocation() {
78.          return pieLocation;
79.       }
80.
81.       // getLegendLocation(): return the location of the legend
82.       public Point getLegendLocation() {
83.          return legendLocation;
84.       }
85.
86.       // getLineSpacing(): return space between legend lines
87.       public int getLineSpacing() {
88.          return lineSpacing;
89.       }
90.
91.       // paint(): render chart and legend
92.       public void paint(Graphics g) {
93.          // get pie chart characteristics
94.          int r = getRadius();
95.          Point pie = getPieLocation();
96.          Point legend = getLegendLocation();
97.          int spacing = getLineSpacing();
98.
99.          // paint the chart
100.         paintPie(g, pie.x, pie.y, r);
101.         paintLegend(g, legend.x, legend.y, spacing);
102.      }
103.
104.      // paintPie(): render the pie
105.      public void paintPie(Graphics g, int x, int y, int r) {
106.         final int CIRCLE_DEGREES = 360;
107.
108.         // determine number of values
```

Listing 8.11 **PieChart.java (Continued)**

```
109.        int n = getSampleSize();
110.
111.        // compute sum of the values
112.        double dataSum = 0;
113.        for (int i = 0; i < n; ++i) {
114.            dataSum += getData(i);
115.        }
116.
117.        // draw slices one by one starting from origin
118.        int startAngle = 0;
119.
120.        for (int i = 0; i < n; ++i) {
121.            // how much of the pie does the next slice take
122.            double percent = getData(i) / dataSum;
123.            int arcAngle = (int) Math.round(percent * CIRCLE_DEGREES);
124.
125.            // set the slice color
126.            Color c = getColor(i);
127.            g.setColor(c);
128.
129.            // render the slice
130.            g.fillArc(x, y, 2*r, 2*r, startAngle, arcAngle);
131.
132.            // record where next slice starts
133.            startAngle += arcAngle;
134.        }
135.    }
136.
137.    // paintLegend(): render the legend for the pie
138.    public void paintLegend(Graphics g, int x, int y, int delta) {
139.        // determine number of values
140.        int n = getSampleSize();
141.
142.        for (int i = 0; i < n; ++i) {
143.            // set up the current legend line
144.            Color c = getColor(i);
145.            String s = getName(i) + ": " + getData(i);
146.
147.            // render the line
148.            g.setColor(c);
149.            g.drawString(s, x, y);
150.
151.
152.            // set up the y-coordinate location of the next line
153.            y += delta;
154.        }
155.    }
156. }
```

INHERITANCE AND POLYMORPHISM

Inheritance and polymorphism are two powerful mechanisms of object-oriented languages. *Inheritance* is the ability to define a new class using an existing class as a basis. The new class, called the *subclass*, inherits the attributes and behaviors of the class on which it is based, the *superclass*. The subclass also *extends* the superclass representation by introducing new attributes and behaviors that are specific to the subclass. Polymorphism is a programming language behavior where the same code expression can invoke different methods depending on the types of the objects using the code. In this chapter, we begin our introduction of these two mechanisms by extending the standard class `Point`.

OBJECTIVES

- Explore the role of inheritance in object-oriented design.
- Demonstrate the power of polymorphism and the late binding of methods.
- Develop a series of classes demonstrating the power of the inheritance and polymorphism mechanisms.
- Explore the nuances of superclasses and subclasses in Java.
- Consider the roles of protected access and default access in information hiding.
- Introduce abstract classes and interfaces.
- Provide an appreciation for the use of modifier final with classes and methods.

9.1   OBJECT-ORIENTED DESIGN

We are all familiar with the concept of biological inheritance. Living things inherit characteristics from their ancestors. For example, you may have one parent's eye color and the other parent's smile. These characteristics may have been unique to your parents, or ones your parents inherited from their parents.

The concept of inheritance is important in the design of software systems. It provides a way of organizing the components of the system in a hierarchical manner. The hierarchy helps us understand the system. In addition, it provides a framework for reusing code.

Inheritance is used typically to organize abstractions in a top-down fashion from most general to least general. For example, Figure 9.1 contains a partial outline of a hierarchical organization for different types of musical instruments. The hierarchy is organized according to how the instruments make their sound. Understanding the hierarchy enables us to recognize and distinguish shared and differing musical instrument characteristics.

As the figure indicates, musical instruments fall into one of five categories: idiophones, membranophones, aerophones, chordophones, or electrophones.

- Idiophones: Solid instruments that are intrinsically sonorous, e.g., bell and cymbal;
- Membranophones: Instruments with taut membranes, e.g., drum and kazoo;
- Aerophones: Instruments that enclose and free masses of air, e.g., clarinet and whistle;
- Chordophones: Instruments with stretched strings, e.g., lyre and violin;
- Electrophones: Instruments with oscillating electric circuits, e.g. synthesizer and electric piano.

Figure 9.1   **A partial outline of a musical instrument hierarchy.**

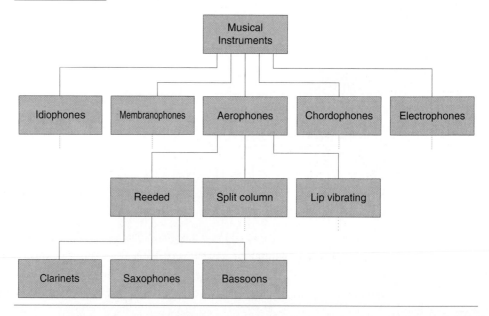

We can refine our notions of each of the categories. For example, aerophones are classified into three subcategories: reeded, split column, and lip vibrating. Clarinets and saxophones are examples of reeded aerophones; whistles and flutes are examples of split-column aerophones; and tubas and trumpets are lip-vibrating aerophones. As another example, chordophones are classified into one of three subcategories: flat-bodied, necked, and plucked. Zithers and dulcimers are examples of flat-bodied chordophones; violins and guitars are examples of necked chordophones; and lyres and harps are examples of plucked chordophones.

In object-oriented programming languages, a class created by extending another class is known as a *subclass*. The class used as a basis for a subclass is its *superclass*. A superclass is also referred to as the *base* class and the subclass is also referred to as the *derived* class. In general, a subclass can provide both additional data fields and methods. Figure 9.2 shows the subclass and superclass relationships between clarinets, reeded instruments, membranophones, and musical instruments.

Figure 9.2   **Some relationships in the musical hierarchy.**

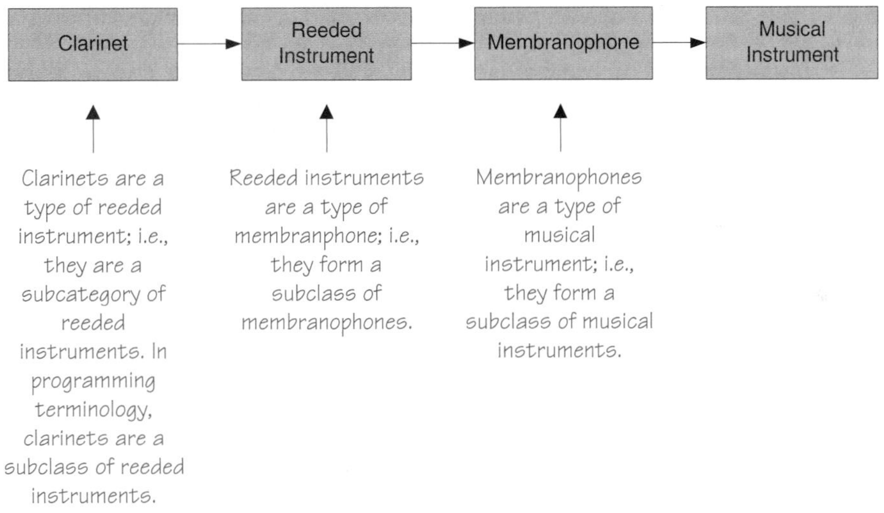

One complication with regard to inheritance for beginning programmers is the fact that a subclass object has multiple types. The subclass object *is* a specialized superclass type object. Therefore, the subclass object is of both the subclass and superclass types. With inheritance, we say there is an *is-a relationship* between the subclass type and its superclass type. A clarinet is a reeded instrument and it is a membranophone.

Now that you understand the concept of inheritance, we turn our attention to using inheritance as a programming mechanism. In our first examples, we extend the awt class to support several different application needs. In particular, we use inheritance to extend Java's Point class to create a three-dimensional point class and a colored point class.

9.1.1   THREEDIMENSIONALPOINT

The awt class `Point` provides a representation of a two-dimensional point that we have used several times throughout the text. With inheritance, it is easy to build upon this two-dimensional point representation to create a three-dimensional point class representation, `ThreeDimensionalPoint`. The new class `ThreeDimensionalPoint` *extends* class `Point` by adding a new property that the `Point` class does not have—a z-coordinate value.

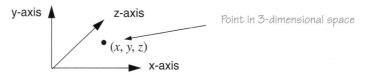

The property can be maintained using a **public** data field z. To support encapsulation and information hiding, the class `ThreeDimensionalPoint` provides an accessor method `getZ()` and a mutator method `setZ()` for the new z-coordinate property.

As we are extending class `ThreeDimensionalPoint` from `Point`, `ThreeDimensionalPoint` inherits the `Point` x-coordinate and y-coordinate attributes and `Point` accessor and mutator methods `getX()`, `getY()`, `setX()`, and `setY()`. We will use the accessors and mutators methods in our implementation of `ThreeDimensionalPoint`. The use of these methods is not strictly necessary because the `Point` class makes its attributes **public** (and this is why we made z a **public** data field). Our implementation uses them because the use of the accessors and mutators is good practice—superclass attributes are almost always **private** (`Point` is a rare exception to the rule). In the typical case, a subclass cannot directly access the attributes, and instead must use the available superclass accessors and mutators to manipulate the superclass attributes.

Unless we indicate otherwise, the `ThreeDimensionalPoint` class also inherits the `Point` facilitators, e.g., `translate()`, `toString()`, `equals()`, and `clone()`. However, these `Point` facilitators are unsuitable for a three-dimensional context—they are not cognizant of the z-coordinate value. Therefore, the `ThreeDimensionalPoint` class must provide its own versions of these methods.

For the `ThreeDimensionalPoint` method `translate()`, there will be three parameters. The parameters represent the increment in x-coordinate value, increment in y-coordinate value, and increment in z-coordinate value by which the point will be shifted. Because the method signatures of the `ThreeDimensionalPoint` and `Point` versions of `translate()` are different, the method name `translate()` is overloaded in the `ThreeDimensionalPoint` class. Thus, with a `ThreeDimensionalPoint` object both methods are available. Java determines which method is in use by the number of parameters in the given invocation.

```
ThreeDimensionalPoint a = new ThreeDimensionalPoint(6, 21, 54);
a.translate(1, 1);      // invocation of superclass translate()
a.translate(2, 2, 2);   // invocation of subclass translate()
```

It's all inheritance

Remember that all classes are either explicitly or implicitly an extension of the class `Object`. The relationship between `ThreeDimensionalPoint`, `Point`, and `Object` are illustrated by the following diagram.

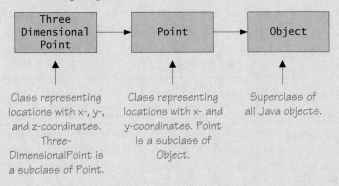

Class `Object` provides basic versions of several methods. In particular, it has methods `toString()`, `equals()`, and `clone()`. It also has methods `finalize()`, `get-Class()`, `hashCode()`, `notify()`, `notifyAll()`, and `wait()`. These are all inherited by the subclasses of `Object`.

The `ThreeDimensionalPoint` versions of `toString()`, `equals()`, and `clone()` should *not* have different signatures from the `Point` versions. By having the same signatures as their superclass counterparts, the subclass methods override the superclass definitions for `ThreeDimensionalPoint` objects. The overriding enables the subclass-specific nature of the `ThreeDimensionalPoint` objects to be considered.

```
ThreeDimensionalPoint c = new ThreeDimensionalPoint(1, 4, 9);

ThreeDimensionalPoint d = (ThreeDimensionalPoint) c.clone();

String s = c.toString();

boolean b = c.equals(d);
```

Cast is necessary as return type of subclass method clone() is Object

Invocation of subclass toString() method

Invocation of subclass equals() method

Now that the subclass requirements are clear, we give the definition of `ThreeDimensionalPoint.java` in Listing 9.1.

`ThreeDimensionalPoint.java` begins with a **package** statement. A **package** statement indicates that the definitions that follow are part of a bigger collection known as a *package*. In particular, `ThreeDimensionalPoint` is part of the package `geometry`.

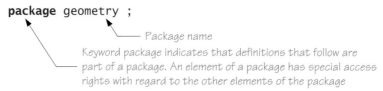

package geometry ;

Package name

Keyword package indicates that definitions that follow are part of a package. An element of a package has special access rights with regard to the other elements of the package

We have used packages (e.g., `swing`, `awt`, `math`, `io`) in many of our programs. However, class `ThreeDimensionalPoint` is the first class that we have defined to be part of a package.

Programmers put classes and interfaces into a package for two basic reasons—*organization* and *special access to members*. By organizing classes and interfaces with a related purpose into a package, you make it easier for users to find them—classes and interfaces with the same package name are stored in the same folder. In addition, Java puts the classes of one package in a different *namespace* (scope) than it puts the classes of another package. As a result, the names in a package do not conflict with names in other packages.

When defining members of a class or interface, Java does not require an explicit access specification. The implicit specification is known as *default access*. Members of a class with default access can be accessed only by members of the package.

If a Java file does not begin with a **package** statement, then all definitions in that file are considered to be part of a **package** unique to that file.

The next statement in Listing 9.1 of `ThreeDimensionalPoint` begins the class definition of `ThreeDimensionalPoint`.

public class ThreeDimensionalPoint **extends** Point {

Keyword extends indicates that class ThreeDimensionalPoint is a subclass of its superclass Point

Keyword **extends** is Java's mechanism for deriving a new class from an existing class. Programmers often read this statement as "`ThreeDimensionalPoint` is a kind of `Point`." Except for the use of the **extends**, defining a subclass is not very different from defining a superclass. When differences do arise, they are found normally in the constructor definitions.

Listing 9.1   ThreeDimensionalPoint.java

```java
1.  // Represents a three-dimensional point
2.
3.  package geometry;
4.
5.  import java.awt.*;
6.
7.  public class ThreeDimensionalPoint extends Point {
8.      // private class constant
9.      private final static int DEFAULT_Z = 0;
10.
11.     // private instance variable
12.     public int z = DEFAULT_Z;
13.
14.     // ThreeDimensionalPoint(): default constructor
15.     public ThreeDimensionalPoint() {
16.         super();
17.     }
18.
19.     // ThreeDimensionalPoint(): specific constructor
20.     public ThreeDimensionalPoint(int a, int b, int c) {
21.         super(a, b);
22.         setZ(c);
23.     }
24.
25.     // getZ(): z-coordinate accessor
26.     public double getZ() {
27.         return z;
28.     }
29.
30.     // setZ(): y-coordinate mutator
31.     public void setZ(int value) {
32.         z = value;
33.     }
34.
35.     // translate(): shifting facilitator
36.     public void translate(int dx, int dy, int dz) {
37.         translate(dx, dy);
38.
39.         int zValue = (int) getZ();
40.
41.         setZ(zValue + dz);
42.     }
43.
44.     // toString(): conversion facilitator
45.     public String toString() {
46.         int a = (int) getX();
47.         int b = (int) getY();
48.         int c = (int) getZ();
49.         return getClass() + "[" + a + ", " + b + ", " + c + "]";
50.     }
51.
52.     // equals(): equality facilitator
53.     public boolean equals(Object v) {
54.         if (v instanceof ThreeDimensionalPoint) {
```

Listing 9.1   ThreeDimensionalPoint.java (Continued)

```
55.            ThreeDimensionalPoint p = (ThreeDimensionalPoint) v;
56.            int z1 = (int) getZ();
57.            int z2 = (int) p.getZ();
58.
59.            return super.equals(p) && (z1 == z2);
60.        }
61.        else {
62.            return false;
63.        }
64.    }
65.
66.    // clone(): clone facilitator
67.    public Object clone() {
68.        int a = (int) getX();
69.        int b = (int) getY();
70.        int c = (int) getZ();
71.
72.        return new ThreeDimensionalPoint(a, b, c);
73.    }
74. }
```

The ThreeDimensionalPoint class first defines a **private** class constant DEFAULT_Z and a **public** instance variable z. Adding a member to a subclass does not require special syntax.

```
// private class constant
private final static int DEFAULT_Z = 0;

// private instance variable
public int z = DEFAULT_Z;
```

The definition of instance variable z includes its initialization value. As first discussed in Chapter 4, providing an initialization value is optional. If none is specified, Java uses **null** for reference variables, **false** for **boolean** variables, and zero for numeric variables. The initialization of instance variables and constants for an object occurs immediately before the constructor is invoked to complete its configuration. The initialization of class constants and variables occurs before any object is created.

The definitions of the ThreeDimensionalPoint constructors differ from the definitions of previous constructors in their use of keyword **super**.

```
// ThreeDimensionalPoint(): default constructor
public ThreeDimensionalPoint() {
        super();  ◄─────────── Default superclass constructor invocation
    }
```

```
// ThreeDimensionalPoint(): specific constructor
public ThreeDimensionalPoint(int a, int b, int c) {
        super(a, b);  ◄─────────── Specific superclass constructor invocation
        setZ(c);
    }
```

Because a ThreeDimensionalPoint object is an extended version of a Point object, the construction of a ThreeDimensionalPoint object begins with the construction of its superclass attributes (i.e., x- and y-coordinate values). To initialize these attributes, a superclass constructor must be invoked. The superclass invocation can be explicit or implicit.

As we discussed, a subclass is a specialization of the superclass. Consequently, a constructor for the superclass must be invoked to create a superclass object before the constructor for the subclass can do its specialization. If you think about what inheritance means for a moment, this sequence makes sense. The superclass object must exist before it can be turned into a specialized subclass object.

To explicitly invoke a superclass constructor for the object under construction, we use the keyword **super**. Keyword **super** is the Java mechanism for viewing the current object as an instance of the superclass. Therefore, statement

```
super();
```

from the `ThreeDimensionalPoint` default constructor definition is an invocation of the superclass's default constructor on the object under construction. Because the superclass of `ThreeDimensionalPoint` is `Point`, it is the `Point` default constructor that is invoked for the object under construction. The `Point` default constructor takes care of the initialization of the x- and y-coordinate values. This action is the only explicit work required for the initialization process, because the z-coordinate instance variable definition specifies the initial value for instance variable z.

The other `ThreeDimensionalPoint` constructor initializes the object under construction to the given x-, y-, and z-coordinate values. This constructor also explicitly invokes a superclass constructor.

```
super(a, b);
```

The invocation uses the `Point` constructor to properly set the x- and y-coordinate values. To complete the initialization, the z-coordinate is set to the desired value using mutator `setZ()`.

```
setZ(c);
```

If a subclass constructor does not explicitly invoke a superclass constructor, then Java automatically invokes the superclass's default constructor to initialize the superclass attributes. Therefore, we could have written our `ThreeDimensionalPoint` default constructor definition without explicitly invoking **super()**.

```
public ThreeDimensionalPoint() {
    // implicit super() invocation before mutator invocation
}
```

Because it is simpler to omit the explicit invocation than to key it in, most constructor code makes use of the implicit invocation of **super()**.

An interesting thing to observe about these constructors is that they are very short. It is possible to be succinct because we are able to reuse the code that we developed for the superclass. Although with this simple subclass the savings are not that great, it is important to realize that with more complex classes, the savings can be substantial.

The Listing 9.1 definitions of accessor `getZ()`, mutator `setZ()` and facilitator `clone()` are all straightforward and warrant no special analysis except to remark that method `getZ()` returns a **double** to make it consistent with superclass methods `getX()` and `getY()`. Because the definitions of `toString()`, `equals()`, and `translate()` are each interesting in their own right, we consider them next.

Method `toString()` of class `ThreeDimensionalPoint` makes use of its `Object` inherited method `getClass()` in displaying its debugging representation.

```
// toString(): conversion facilitator
public String toString() {
    int a = (int) getX();         Casts are necessary as Point
    int b = (int) getY();         accessors return the int-valued
    int c = (int) getZ();         data fields as double values
    return getClass() + "[" + a + ", " + b + ", " + c + "]";

}
```

Method `getClass()` returns a `String` description of the object's type. For example, the following code segment

```
ThreeDimensionalPoint p = new ThreeDimensionalPoint();
System.out.println(p);
```

displays

```
class geometry.ThreeDimensionalPoint[0, 0, 0]
```

String produced by invocation
getClass()

`ThreeDimensionalPoint` method `equals()` uses superclass method `equals()` in determining whether parameter `v` is the same as the **this** object.

```
// equals(): equality facilitator
public boolean equals(Object v) {
    if (v instanceof ThreeDimensionalPoint) {
        ThreeDimensionalPoint p = (ThreeDimensionalPoint) v;
        int z1 = (int) getZ();
        int z2 = (int) p.getZ();

        return super.equals(p) && (z1 == z2);
    }
    else {                              Invocation of superclass
        return false;                   method equals()
    }
}
```

For the `ThreeDimensionalPoint` method `equals()` to use its superclass `Point` method `equals()`, a special syntax is needed. Special syntax is required because by default the subclass version overrides normal access to the superclass version. Using the keyword **super** indicates explicitly that the superclass member is to be referenced.

`ThreeDimensionalPoint` method `translate()` uses the superclass method `translate()` to assist in the shifting of position. However, keyword **super** is not required to invoke the superclass `translate()`. Because the superclass version uses two parameters and the subclass version uses three parameters, Java can tell by context that it is the superclass method `translate()` being invoked within the definition.

```java
// translate(): shifting facilitator
public void translate(int dx, int dy, int dz) {
    translate(dx, dy);
    int zValue = (int) getZ();
    setZ(zValue + dz);
}
```

Because there are two parameters present, it is the superclass method translate() being invoked

The following code segment demonstrates some uses of class `ThreeDimensionalPoint`.

```java
ThreeDimensionalPoint c = new ThreeDimensionalPoint();
c.translate(2, 2, 2);
ThreeDimensionalPoint d = new ThreeDimensionalPoint(1, 2, 3);
ThreeDimensionalPoint e = (ThreeDimensionalPoint) d.clone();

System.out.println(c);
System.out.println(d);
System.out.println(e);

System.out.println(d.equals(c));
System.out.println(d.equals(e));
```

The segment produces output

```
class geometry.ThreeDimensionalPoint[2, 2, 2]
class geometry.ThreeDimensionalPoint[1, 2, 3]
class geometry.ThreeDimensionalPoint[1, 2, 3]
false
true
```

9.1.2   COLOREDPOINT

Suppose an application calls for the use of colored points. For example, we can use colored points to represents the pixels of some images. It makes sense to consider using inheritance to create a class to represent colored points. Listing 9.2 of `Colored-Point.java` defines a class `ColoredPoint` that extends `Point` in the natural manner to provide a representation of a colored point. The class adds data field `color` to represent the color attribute and an appropriate accessor and mutator for that property. The class also provides overrides of `equals()`, `clone()`, and `toString()`.

The following code segment demonstrates some uses of class `ColoredPoint`.

```java
ColoredPoint c = new ColoredPoint();
ColoredPoint d = new ColoredPoint(1, 2, Color.BLACK);
ColoredPoint e = (ColoredPoint) d.clone();
```

```
System.out.println(c);
System.out.println(d);
System.out.println(e);
System.out.println(d.equals(c));
System.out.println(d.equals(e));
```

The segment produces output

```
class geometry.ColoredPoint[0, 0, java.awt.Color[r=0,g=0,b=255]]
class geometry.ColoredPoint[1, 2, java.awt.Color[r=0,g=0,b=0]]
class geometry.ColoredPoint[1, 2, java.awt.Color[r=0,g=0,b=0]]
false
true
```

Suppose we are now interested in colored, three-dimensional points. The question to be asked is whether there is a way to create a class `Colored3DPoint` that extends from *both* `ThreeDimensionalPoint` and `ColoredPoint`? The answer is no. Java supports *single inheritance* but does not support *multiple inheritance*. Because of its complexity, Java language designers decided explicitly not to support multiple inheritance. For example, suppose we were to create `Colored3DPoint` by extending it from both `ThreeDimensionalPoint` and `ColoredPoint`. Should our new class have two sets of x- and y-coordinate values because `ThreeDimensionalPoint` and `ColoredPoint` both have x- and y-coordinate values or should it have one set of x- and y-coordinate values because `ThreeDimensionalPoint` and `ColoredPoint` are both extended from `Point`? Rather than making programmers deal with such issues, Java does not permit multiple inheritance.

So if we want a colored three-dimensional point representation `Colored3DPoint`, we would either extend `ThreeDimensionalPoint` to provide a color attribute or extend `ColoredPoint` to provide a z-coordinate attribute. The former alternative is demonstrated in Listing 9.3.

Listing 9.2 ColoredPoint.java

```java
1.  // Represents a colored two-dimensional point
2.
3.  package geometry;
4.
5.  import java.awt.*;
6.
7.  public class ColoredPoint extends Point {
8.      // instance variable
9.      Color color;
10.
11.     // ColoredPoint(): default constructor
12.     public ColoredPoint() {
13.         setColor(Color.BLUE);
14.     }
15.
16.     // ColoredPoint(): specific constructor
17.     public ColoredPoint(int x, int y, Color c) {
18.         super(x, y);
19.         setColor(c);
20.     }
21.
22.     // getColor(): color property accessor
23.     public Color getColor() {
24.         return color;
25.     }
26.
27.     // setColor(): color property mutator
28.     public void setColor(Color c) {
29.         color = c;
30.     }
31.
32.     // clone(): clone facilitator
33.     public Object clone() {
34.         int a = (int) getX();
35.         int b = (int) getY();
36.         Color c = getColor();
37.         return new ColoredPoint(a, b, c);
38.     }
39.
40.     // toString(): string representation facilitator
41.     public String toString() {
42.         int a = (int) getX();
43.         int b = (int) getY();
44.         Color c = getColor();
45.         return getClass() + "[" + a + ", " + b + ", " + c + "]";
46.     }
47.
48.     // equals(): equal facilitator
49.     public boolean equals(Object v) {
50.         if (v instanceof ColoredPoint) {
51.             Color c1 = getColor();
52.             Color c2 = ((ColoredPoint) v).getColor();
53.             return super.equals(v) && c1.equals(c2);
54.         }
```

Listing 9.2   **ColoredPoint.java (Continued)**

```
55.        else {
56.            return false;
57.        }
58.    }
59. }
```

Why not add rather than extend?

You may have already asked yourself, why bother with inheritance. Why not just modify the existing class to cover the new features? For example, we could give the Point class a z-coordinate value. However, the approach of adding features is generally not the preferred one, and sometimes it is not even an option.

Simply adding features can make a class too complex to understand or build. Imagine if such an approach were taken with musical instruments—whenever a new sound is desired, an existing instrument is modified to also make that sound. Such a combined musical instrument would be too unwieldy to use effectively.

Another factor discouraging addition is user confidence and cost. Complex classes are difficult to build, maintain, and test. Programmers are understandably skeptical regarding the use of a massive API. Furthermore, if the source code for an existing class is not available, then adding new features to that class is not an option. Consider the fact that most libraries are distributed as compressed archives or as .class files with the .java versions unavailable—developers often keep the .java versions to themselves to protect their intellectual investment.

Listing 9.3   Colored3DPoint.java

```java
1.  // Represents a colored, three-dimensional point
2.
3.  package geometry;
4.
5.  import java.awt.*;
6.
7.  public class Colored3DPoint extends ThreeDimensionalPoint {
8.      // instance variable
9.      Color color;
10.
11.     // Colored3DPoint(): default constructor
12.     public Colored3DPoint() {
13.         setColor(Color.BLUE);
14.     }
15.
16.     // Colored3DPoint(): specific constructor
17.     public Colored3DPoint(int a, int b, int c, Color d) {
18.         super(a, b, c);
19.         setColor(d);
20.     }
21.
22.     // getColor(): color property accessor
23.     public Color getColor() {
24.         return color;
25.     }
26.
27.     // setColor(): color property mutator
28.     public void setColor(Color c) {
29.         color = c;
30.     }
31.
32.     // clone(): clone facilitator
33.     public Object clone() {
34.         int a = (int) getX();
35.         int b = (int) getY();
36.         int c = (int) getZ();
37.         Color d = getColor();
38.         return new Colored3DPoint(a, b, c, d);
39.     }
40.
41.     // toString(): string representation facilitator
42.     public String toString() {
43.         int a = (int) getX();
44.         int b = (int) getY();
45.         int c = (int) getZ();
46.         Color d = getColor();
47.         return getClass() + "[" + a + ", " + b + ", " + c + ", "
48.             + d + "]";
49.     }
50.
51.     // equals(): equal facilitator
52.     public boolean equals(Object v) {
53.         if (v instanceof Colored3DPoint) {
54.             Color c1 = getColor();
```

Listing 9.3 **Colored3DPoint.java (Continued)**

```
55.            Color c2 = ((Colored3DPoint) v).getColor();
56.            return super.equals(v) && c1.equals(c2);
57.        }
58.        else {
59.            return false;
60.        }
61.    }
62. }
```

<table><tr><td>**9.2**</td></tr></table> **POLYMORPHISM**

We use all four point classes—Point, ThreeDimensionalPoint, ColoredPoint, and Colored3DPoint—in the program PolymorphismDemo.java of Listing 9.4. The **for** loop of method main() in conjunction with the program output demonstrates one of the important features of object-oriented programming—*a code expression can invoke different methods depending on the types of objects using the code*. This language feature is known as *polymorphism.*

Some people view method overloading and generics as *syntactic* or *primitive* polymorphism. With syntactic polymorphism, Java can determine which method to invoke or class to create at compile time. However, true polymorphism—or as it is sometimes known, *pure* polymorphism—generally requires the decision to be delayed until run time.

The polymorphic code in the **for** loop is invocation expression p[i].toString().

```
String s = p[i].toString();
```

In Java, *it is not the variable type that determines the invocation, but the type of object at the location to which the variable refers.* The code is polymorphic because array p is a *heterogeneous* list; that is, its elements reference values of different types.

That array p is a heterogeneous list is a result of how its elements are set. For example, Point variable p[0] is set using statement

```
p[0] = new Colored3DPoint(4, 4, 4, Color.BLACK);
```

The assignment makes sense because Colored3DPoint has an *is-a* relationship with Point. Colored3DPoint extends from ThreeDimensionalPoint, which extends from Point. Thus, Point variable p[0] refers to a Colored3DPoint object.

Similarly, the assignment

```
p[1] = new ThreeDimensionalPoint(2, 2, 2);
```

causes variable p[1] to refer to a ThreeDimensionalPoint object. The other two assignments cause p[2] and p[3] to refer respectively to ColoredPoint and Point

---

Listing 9.4   PolymorphismDemo.java

```
1.  // Demonstrates polymorphism using various point classes
2.
3.  import java.awt.*;
4.  import geometry.*;
5.
6.  public class PolymorphismDemo {
7.      // main(): application entry point
8.      public static void main(String[] args) {
9.          Point[] p = new Point[4];
10.
11.         p[0] = new Colored3DPoint(4, 4, 4, Color.BLACK);
12.         p[1] = new ThreeDimensionalPoint(2, 2, 2);
13.         p[2] = new ColoredPoint(3, 3, Color.RED);
14.         p[3] = new Point(4, 4);
15.
16.         for (int i = 0; i < p.length; ++i) {
17.             String s = p[i].toString();
18.             System.out.println("p[" + i + "]: " + s);
19.         }
20.
21.         return;
22.     }
23. }
```

objects.

```
p[2] = new ThreeDimensionalPoint(3, 3, Color.RED);
p[3] = new Point(4, 4);
```

Because array p is heterogeneous, the toString() method that is invoked in expression p[i].toString() depends on the type of Point object to which p[i] refers. For i equal to 0, the expression p[i].toString() invokes the Colored3DPoint method toString(); for i equal to 1, expression p[i].toString() invokes the ThreeDimensionalPoint method toString(); for i equal to 2, the expression p[i].toString() invokes the ColoredPoint method toString(); and for i equal to 3, the expression p[i].toString() invokes the Point method toString().

Therefore, the program outputs

```
class geometry.Colored3DPoint[4, 4, 4, java.awt.Color[r=0,g=0,b=0]]
class geometry.ThreeDimensionalPoint(2, 2, 2)
class geometry.ColoredPoint[3, 3, java.awt.Color[r=255,g=0,b=0]]
java.awt.Point[x=4,y=4]
```

Flexibility for future enhancements

With polymorphism, the decision on which method to invoke in an expression may have to be determined at run time. This capability makes it possible to compile a method that performs a method invocation in its body even though the subclass eventually supplying the method has not yet been implemented or even defined!

Design with inheritance in mind

When designing a collection of new but related classes, pay attention to what are the common behaviors and characteristics. This process is known as *factorization*. Then try to create a coherent base class that provides this commonality. From this base class, subclasses can be defined to provide the special behaviors and characteristics. Your current work effort should be reduced as common behaviors are implemented just once. Future work efforts should also be minimized as new features can be added by extending the existing classes.

9.3 INHERITANCE NUANCES

Before developing a data abstraction, we first present several small classes for illustrative purposes. Each of the classes demonstrates some important nuance with regard to inheritance behavior in Java. Our examination begins with construction.

Consider the following class B composed of two constructors. Both constructors produce output when invoked.

```java
public class B {
    // B(): default constructor
    public B() {
        System.out.println("Using B's default constructor");
    }

    // B(): specific constructor
    public B(int i) {
        System.out.println("Using B's int constructor");
    }
}
```

Before reading the analysis that follows, try to determine the output of the following program C.java whose class C extends B. If you understand what output it produces, you should better understand how object construction is always a two-step process. The first step constructs the superclass view of the object. The second step constructs the subclass view of the object.

```java
public class C extends B {
    // C(): default constructor
    public C() {
        System.out.println("Using C's default constructor");
        System.out.println();
    }

    // C(int a): specific constructor
    public C(int a) {
        System.out.println("Using C's int constructor");
        System.out.println();
    }
}
```

```
// C(int a, int b): specific constructor
public C(int a, int b) {
   super(a + b);
   System.out.println("Using C's int-int constructor");
   System.out.println();
}

// main(): application entry point
public static void main(String[] args) {
   C c1 = new C();
   C c2 = new C(2);
   C c3 = new C(2,4);
   return;
}
}
```

Method main() of program C.java begins by defining three C variables c1, c2, and c3. Each of the objects is constructed using a different C constructor. Because construction is a two-step process, the construction of each C object begins with the construction of its superclass attributes. Neither of the constructors for the objects referenced by c1 and c2 explicitly invoke a superclass constructor. Therefore, Java automatically invokes C's superclass default constructor for these objects.

Because the constructor of the object referenced by c3 explicitly invokes a superclass constructor, Java does not automatically invoke C's superclass default constructor for that object. Therefore, the program produces the following output.

```
Using B's default constructor
Using C's default constructor

Using B's default constructor
Using C's int constructor

Using B's int constructor
Using C's int-int constructor
```

9.3.1   CONTROLLING ACCESS

Up to this point our member variables and methods have always had either **public** or **private** access rights. A **public** member has no restrictions on access to it. A **private** member can be used only by the class that defines that member. With respect to **public** and **private** access rights, a subclass is treated no differently than any other Java class—a subclass can access the superclass's **public** members and cannot access the superclass's **private** members. Java also supports two other access rights. They are **protected** access and default access.

Besides being accessible in its own class, a **protected** variable or method can be used by subclasses of its class.

For example, consider class P from package demo with a **private** instance variable data, a **public** default constructor, a **public** accessor getData(), a **protected** mutator setData(), and a facilitator print() with default access.

```
package demo;

public class P {
   // instance variable
   private int data;

   // P(): default constructor
   public P() {
      setData(0);
   }

   // getData(): accessor
   public int getData() {
      return data;
   }

   // setData(): mutator
   protected void setData(int v) {
      data = v;
   }

   // print(): facilitator
   void print() {
      System.out.println(getData());
   }
}
```

Class Q, which extends P, can invoke P's default constructor, accessor getData(), and mutator setData(). However, class Q cannot directly access P's instance variable data.

```
import demo.P;

public class Q extends P {
   // Q(): default constructor
   public Q() {
      super();          ◄——————  Q can access superclass's public default constructor
   }

   // Q(): specific constructor
   public Q(int v) {
      setData(v);       ◄——————  Q can access superclass's protected mutator
   }

   // toString(): string facilitator
   public String toString() {
      int v = getData();   ◄——————  Q can access superclass's public
      return String.valueOf(v);                         accessor
   }

   // invalid1(): illegal method
   public void invalid1() {
```

```
        data = 12;          ◄────────  Q cannot directly access superclass's private data
    }                                   field

    // invalid2(): illegal method
    public void invalid2() {
        print();            ◄────────  Q cannot directly access superclass's default access
    }                                   method print()
}
```

With regard to default access, only two classes in the same package can access each other's default-access members. Therefore, class Q, which is not part of package demo, cannot access P facilitator print().

Now consider class R of package demo: R's methods can invoke P's **public** default constructor and accessor getData(), **protected** mutator setData(), and default-access facilitator print(). However, class R cannot directly access P's **private** instance variable data.

```
    package demo;

    public class R {
        // instance variable
        private P p;

        // R(): default constructor
        public R() {
            p = new P();        ◄────────  R can access P's public default constructor
        }

        // set(): mutator
        public void set(int v) {
            p.setData(v);       ◄────────  R can access P's protected mutator
        }

        // get(): accessor
        public int get() {
            return p.getData();     ◄────────  R can access P's public accessor
        }

        // use(): facilitator
        public void use() {
            p.print();          ◄────────  R can access P's default access method
        }

        // invalid(): illegal method
        public void invalid() {
            p.data = 12;        ◄────────  R cannot directly access P's private data field
        }
    }
```

Next consider class S that is neither part of package demo nor is it extended directly or indirectly from class P. Therefore, class S can invoke only P's **public** default constructor and accessor getData().

```
    import demo.P;

    public class S {
```

```
// instance variable
private P p;

// S(): default constructor
public S() {
    p = new P();      ◄──────  S can access P's public default constructor
}

// get(): inspector
public int get() {
    return p.getData();   ◄──────  S can access P's public accessor
}

// illegal1(): illegal method
public void illegal1(int v) {
    p.setData(v);     ◄──────  S cannot directly access P's protected mutator
}

// illegal2(): illegal method
public void illegal2() {
    p.data = 12;      ◄──────  S cannot directly access P's private data field
}

// illegal3(): illegal method
public void illegal3() {
    p.print();        ◄──────  S cannot directly access P's default access print()
}
}
```

Access rights of classes are summarized in Table 9.1.

Table 9.1   **Class access rights.**

Member Restriction	this	Subclass	Package	General
public	√	√	√	√
protected	√	√	√	—
default	√	—	√	—
private	√	—	—	—

9.3.2   DATA FIELDS

Consider the following class D with a single **protected int** instance variable d. Because the variable is **protected**, classes extending D have direct access to it. The D default constructor explicitly sets d to 0. The other D constructor sets d to the value of its parameter v. We will use class D as the base class for classes E and F.

```java
public class D {
    // D instance variable
    protected int d;

    // D(): default constructor
    public D() {
        d = 0;
    }

    // D(): specific constructor
    public D(int v) {
        d = v;
    }

    // printD(): facilitator
    public void printD() {
        System.out.println("D's d: " + d);
        System.out.println();
    }
}
```

Although class E extends D, it does not introduce any new instance variables. However, class E does define a single constructor and a method printE().

```java
public class E extends D {
    // E(): specific constructor
    public E(int v) {
        d = v;                   ⎫  For class E, both d and super.d
        super.d = v*100;         ⎭  access superclass instance variable d
    }

    // printE(): facilitator
    public void printE() {
        System.out.println("D's d: " + super.d);
        System.out.println("E's d: " + this.d);
        System.out.println();
    }
}
```

In contrast, class F both extends D and introduces a new instance variable. Because the new variable has the same name d as the superclass instance variable, the superclass variable is *hidden* in class F. Class F also defines a constructor, facilitator, and class method main() that enables the class to serve as an application program.

Before reading our analysis, determine the output of program F.java.

```java
public class F extends D {
    // F instance variable
    int d;

    // F(): specific constructor
    public F(int v) {
        d = v;
        super.d = v*100;
```

```
        }

        // printF(): facilitator
        public void printF() {
            System.out.println("D's d: " + super.d);
            System.out.println("F's d: " + this.d);
            System.out.println();
        }

        // main(): application entry point
        public static void main(String[] args) {
            E e = new E(1);
            F f = new F(2);
            e.printE();
            f.printF();
            return;
        }
    }
```

Because E does not define any instance variables itself, the instance variable it manipulates is its superclass's instance variable. Thus, the two assignments in constructor

```
        public E(int v) {
            d = v;              ⎤  Two separate modifications to the
            super.d = v*100;    ⎦  superclass (D) instance variable d
        }
```

are both manipulating the same variable. When the constructor completes, the value of that variable is based on the second assignment. The fact that d and **super**.d are referencing the same variable means that E's facilitator

```
        public void printE() {
            System.out.println("D's d: " + super.d);
            System.out.println("E's d: " + this.d);
            System.out.println();
        }
```

prints the same value twice. In the case of the E object referenced by e from F's method main(), the value 100 is displayed twice.

```
        E e = new E(1);
```

Because F defines an instance variable d, that definition results in the superclass instance variable being hidden. Inside an F method, the expression d refers to the F instance variable and not the superclass instance variable. Thus, the two assignments in constructor

```
                    Modification to the this class (F) instance variable d
        public F(int v) {
            d = v;                ◄───────────┐
            super.d = v*100;  ◄───────────    │
        }
                    Modification to the superclass (D) instance variable d
```

manipulate different instance variables. When the constructor completes, the value of the object's F variable d is equal to v and the value of the object's superclass variable d is equal to 100*v. So unless v equals 0, when method `printF()`

Accessing the superclass (D) instance variable d

```
public void printF() {
    System.out.println("D's d: " + super.d);
    System.out.println("E's d: " + this.d);
    System.out.println();
}
```

Accessing the this class (F) instance variable d

is invoked, two different values are displayed. In the case of the F object referenced by `f` from F's method

```
F f = new F(2);
```

`main()`, the values 200 and 2 are displayed. So the output produced by the program is

```
D's d: 100
E's d: 100

D's d: 200
F's d: 2
```

9.3.3   TYPING

Consider the following class X. Class X provides a default constructor, a **boolean** class method `isX()` that reports whether its parameter v is of type X, and a **boolean** class method `isObject()` that reports whether its parameter v is of type `Object`.

```
public class X {
    // default constructor
    public X() {
        // no body needed
    }

    // isX(): class method
    public static boolean isX(Object v) {
        return (v instanceof X);
    }

    // isObject(): class method
    public static boolean isObject(X v) {
        return (v instanceof Object);
    }
}
```

Now consider program `Y.java`. Class Y extends class X. Besides defining method `main()`, class Y provides a default constructor and a **boolean** class method `isY()` that reports whether its parameter v is of type Y.

Before reading the analysis that follows, determine the output of program Y.java. Understanding what output is produced should contribute to your understanding of inheritance with respect to object types.

```java
public class Y extends X {
    // Y(): default constructor
    public Y() {
        // no body needed
    }

    // isY(): class method
    public static boolean isY(Object v) {
        return (v instanceof Y);
    }

    public static void main(String[] args) {
        X x = new X();
        Y y = new Y();
        X z = y;

        System.out.println("x is an Object: " + X.isObject(x));
        System.out.println("x is an X: " + X.isX(x));
        System.out.println("x is a Y: " + Y.isY(x));
        System.out.println();

        System.out.println("y is an Object: " + X.isObject(y));
        System.out.println("y is an X: " + X.isX(y));
        System.out.println("y is a Y: " + Y.isY(y));
        System.out.println();

        System.out.println("z is an Object: " + X.isObject(z));
        System.out.println("z is an X: " + X.isX(z));
        System.out.println("z is a Y: " + Y.isY(z));
        return;
    }
}
```

The definition of variable x assigns it to a new object of type X. Because all classes in Java are extensions of class Object, both X.isObject(x) and X.isX(x) report true. Class X is not extended directly or indirectly from class Y, so Y.isY(x) reports false.

Because variable y is defined to be of class type Y, where Y is a subclass of X, each of X.isX(y), Y.isY(y), and X.isObject(y) reports true.

Although the apparent type of z is X, the object referenced by z is the same object that y references. Therefore, variable z references a Y object and the tests regarding z report the same results as the tests regarding y. Therefore, the program outputs

```
x is an Object: true
x is an X: true
x is a Y: false

y is an Object: true
y is an X: true
y is a Y: true

z is an Object: true
```

```
z is an X: true
z is a Y: true
```

9.3.4   LATE BINDING

Consider the following class L.

```java
public class L {
    // L(): default constructor
    public L() {
        // no body needed
    }

    // f(): facilitator
    public void f() {
        System.out.println("Using L's f()");
        g();
    }

    // g(): facilitator
    public void g() {
        System.out.println("using L's g()");
    }
}
```

Also consider class M that extends L. Together, classes L and M further demonstrate the power of polymorphism in Java.

```java
public class M extends L {
    // M(): default constructor
    public M() {
        // no body needed
    }

    // g(): facilitator
    public void g() {
        System.out.println("Using M's g()");
    }

    // main(): application entry point
    public static void main(String[] args) {
        L l = new L();
        M m = new M();
        l.f();
        m.f();
        return;
    }
}
```

The statements of interest in method main() are

```
l.f();
m.f();
```

Because class M does not override superclass method f(), both f() invocations are invocations of L's method f(). However, the invocations produce different results!

The invocation 1.f() causes statements

```
System.out.println("Using L's f()");
g();
```

from the L definition of f() to be executed with respect to the object referenced by variable 1. Because 1 references an L object, it is L method g() that is invoked. Thus, the first two output lines produced by the program are

```
Using L's f()
using L's g()
```

The invocation m.f() again causes statements

```
System.out.println("Using L's f()");
g();
```

from the L definition of f() to be executed. They are executed with respect to the object referenced by variable m. Because m references an M object, it is M method g() that is invoked. Thus, the program output is

```
Using L's f()
using L's g()
Using L's f()
Using M's g()
```

Late binding demonstrates the power of Java—a code expression can invoke different methods depending on the types of objects using the code. We now turn our attention to a new use of keyword **final**.

9.3.5   FINALITY

Just as Java permits a constant data field to be defined through the use of the keyword **final**, so it permits **final** methods and classes. A **final** class is a class that cannot be extended. A **final** method is a method that cannot be overridden.

The developer of a class might make it **final** for economic or security reasons. If clients have access only to the `.class` version of a **final** class, then they must look to the developer for additional features. As another example, a class or method may be crucial to a system. By declaring the class or method in question to be **final**, it is harder to tamper with the system by introducing classes that override the existing code.

For example, the following class U is a **final** class. Therefore, class U cannot be extended.

```
final public class U {
    // U(): default constructor
    public U() {
    }
```

```
    // f(): facilitator
    public void f() {
        System.out.println("f() can't be overridden: U is final");
    }
}
```

As another example, method f() of class V is a **final** method. Therefore, f() cannot be overridden if V is extended.

```
public class V {
    // V(): default constructor
    public V() {
    }

    // f(): facilitator
    final public void f() {
        System.out.println("f() can't be overridden: it is
final");
    }
}
```

9.4   ABSTRACT BASE CLASSES

When doing program development, a need sometimes arises for defining a superclass where for some of its methods there are no sensible definitions; that is, it is necessary to make some methods part of the superclass so that other code can exploit Java's polymorphic capabilities. Such classes are known as *abstract* classes. For example, in developing a geometric shape hierarchy, a suitable superclass GeometricObject for the hierarchy might have two data fields:

Point position

Northwest corner of the shape's bounding box.

Color color

Color of the shape.

The following methods are reasonable for the superclass GeometricObject. (Other methods could also be reasonable.)

public Point getPosition()

Returns the upper northwest corner of the shape's bounding box.

public void setPosition(Point p)

Sets the upper northwest corner of the shape's bounding box to p.

public Color getColor()

Returns the color of the shape.

public void setColor(Color c)

Sets the color of the shape to c.

public void paint(Graphics g)

Renders the shape in graphics context g.

However, we can define sensible implementations only for methods getPosition(), setPosition(), getColor(), and setColor().

```
    // getPosition(): return object position
    public Point getPosition() {
```

```
    return position;
}
// setPosition(): update object position
public void setPosition(Position p)
    position = p;
}
// getColor(): return object color
public Color getColor() {
    return color;
}
// setColor(): update object color
public void setColor(Color c) {
    color = c;
}
```

Method `paint()` has no sensible implementation because it is shape-specific—the rendering of a rectangle is different from the rendering of a line, which is different from the rendering of a circle. Because there is no sensible implementation for `paint()`, it makes sense to use the Java modifier **abstract** to make `GeometricObject` an **abstract** class and to make its method `paint()` and an **abstract** method. A complete definition of the abstract class `GeometricObject` is given in Listing 9.5. Definitions of its subclasses `Box` and `Circle` are given in Listing 9.6 and Listing 9.7.

The keyword **abstract** at the start of a class definition indicates that the class cannot be instantiated; i.e., we cannot directly create a new `GeometricObject`.

The keyword **abstract** at the front of a method declaration indicates that the definition of the method will not be supplied. Non-**abstract** subclasses of the **abstract** superclass *must* provide their own definitions of the **abstract** method, which would not have been the case if the superclass had instead defined the method with an empty statement list for its method body.

Because classes `Box` and `Circle` both define a method `paint()`, the classes are non-**abstract** and can be instantiated.

```
Circle c = new Circle(1, new Point(0, 0), Color.BLUE);
Box r = new Box(1, 2, new Point(3, 4), Color.RED);
```

Abstract classes are valid types. Therefore, we can initialize a variable of an **abstract** type to reference an existing subclass object of that type.

```
GeometricObject g = c;    // A Circle is a GeometricObject
```

We can also use an abstract base type to define a polymorphic method.

```
public void renderShapeInBlue(Graphics g, GeometricObject s) {
    g.setColor(Color.BLUE);
    s.paint(g);      // drawing is based on s's subclass type
}
```

Here the method will set the color for current graphical context `g` to blue and then draw the object referenced by `s` in that context. Because Java invokes the `paint()` method for the type of object to which parameter `s` refers, the type of drawing depends on the `GeometricObject` subclass type of `s`.

Listing 9.5 **GeometricObject.java**

```
1.  // GeometricObject: abstract superclass for geometric shapes
2.
3.  import java.awt.*;
4.
5.  abstract public class GeometricObject {
6.      // instance variables
7.      Point position;
8.      Color color;
9.
10.     // getPosition(): return object position
11.     public Point getPosition() {
12.         return position;
13.     }
14.
15.     // setPosition(): update object position
16.     public void setPosition(Point p) {
17.         position = p;
18.     }
19.
20.     // getColor(): return object color
21.     public Color getColor() {
22.         return color;
23.     }
24.
25.     // setColor(): update object color
26.     public void setColor(Color c) {
27.         color = c;
28.     }
29.
30.     // paint(): render the shape to graphics context g
31.     abstract public void paint(Graphics g);
32. }
```

Listing 9.6 **Box.java**

```
1.  // Box: rectangle shape representation
2.
3.  import java.awt.*;
4.
5.  public class Box extends GeometricObject {
6.      // instance variables
7.      int length;
8.      int height;
9.
10.     // Box(): default constructor
11.     public Box() {
12.         this(0, 0, new Point(), Color.BLACK);
13.     }
14.
15.     // Box(): specific constructor
16.     public Box(int l, int h, Point p, Color c) {
17.         setLength(l);
18.         setHeight(h);
19.         setPosition(p);
```

Listing 9.6   **Box.java (Continued)**

```
20.         setColor(c);
21.     }
22.
23.     // getLength(): get the rectangle length
24.     public int getLength() {
25.         return length;
26.     }
27.
28.     // getHeight(): get the rectangle height
29.     public int getHeight() {
30.         return height;
31.     }
32.
33.     // setLength(): set the rectangle length to l
34.     public void setLength(int l) {
35.         length = l;
36.     }
37.
38.     // setHeight(): set the rectangle height to h
39.     public void setHeight(int h) {
40.         height = h;
41.     }
42.
43.     // paint(): render the rectangle to graphics context g
44.     public void paint(Graphics g) {
45.         Point p = getPosition();
46.         Color c = getColor();
47.         int   l = getLength();
48.         int   h = getHeight();
49.
50.         g.setColor(c);
51.         g.fillRect((int) p.getX(), (int) p.getY(), l, h);
52.     }
53. }
```

Listing 9.7   **Circle.java**

```
1. // Circle: circle shape representation
2.
3. import java.awt.*;
4.
5. public class Circle extends GeometricObject {
6.     // instance variable
7.     int radius;
8.
9.     // Circle(): default constructor
10.    public Circle() {
11.        this(0, new Point(), Color.BLACK);
12.    }
13.
14.    // Circle(): specific constructor
15.    public Circle(int r, Point p, Color c) {
16.        setRadius(r);
17.        setPosition(p);
```

Listing 9.7   **Circle.java**

```
18.        setColor(c);
19.     }
20.
21.     // getRadius(): get the circle radius
22.     public int getRadius() {
23.        return radius;
24.     }
25.
26.     // setRadius(): set the circle radius to r
27.     public void setRadius(int r) {
28.        radius = r;
29.     }
30.
31.     // paint(): render the circle to graphics context g
32.     public void paint(Graphics g) {
33.        Point p = getPosition();
34.        Color c = getColor();
35.        int   r = getRadius();
36.
37.        g.setColor(c);
38.
39.        g.fillOval((int) p.getX(), (int) p.getY(), r, r);
40.     }
41. }
```

9.5   INTERFACES

Besides allowing programmers to define **abstract** classes, Java also allows programmers to define *interfaces*. An **interface** is not a class but is instead a partial template of what must be in a class that *implements* the interface. An **interface** is a Java type and can be used as such.

```
public interface name {
        // constants        ◄─────────    All variables are either
                                          explicitly or implicitly public
        // method declarations            class constants (i.e., public
                                          static final )
    }
                                 ◄─────────   All listed methods are either
                                              explicitly or implicitly public
```

An interface definition differs from an **abstract** class definition in three important ways.

- An **interface** cannot specify any method implementations;

- All of the methods of an **interface** are **public**;

- All of the variables defined in an **interface** are **public**, **final**, and **static**.

Listing 9.8   Colorable.java

```
1.  package geometry;
2.
3.  import java.awt.*;
4.
5.  public interface Colorable {
6.     // getColor(): return the color of the object
7.     public Color getColor();
8.     // setColor(): set the color of the object
9.     public void setColor(Color c);
10. }
```

So why use an **interface** when an **abstract** class offers greater flexibility? The answer is twofold. First, Java allows a class to implement more than one **interface**, whereas a class can extend only one superclass. Second, because an **interface** is not a class, it is not part of a class hierarchy. Two unrelated classes can implement the same interface with objects of those unrelated classes having the same type—the **interface** their class types implement.

As an example, consider **interface** Colorable of Listing 9.8. Implementing the interface requires two methods—getColor() and setColor(). The methods' intended purposes are to serve respectively as a color accessor and mutator. Classes ColorablePoint and Colorable3DPoint of Listing 9.9 and Listing 9.10 are respectively reworkings of classes ColoredPoint and Colored3DPoint of Listing 9.2 and Listing 9.3. Except for the cosmetic differences of ColorablePoint versus ColoredPoint and Colorable3DPoint versus Colored3DPoint, the only other difference is that ColorablePoint and Colorable3DPoint indicate that they implement Colorable.

Because both ColorablePoint and Colorable3DPoint indicate they implement interface Colorable, a polymorphic code segment such as the following is possible

```
ColorablePoint u = new ColorablePoint();
Colorable3DPoint v = new Colorable3DPoint();
Colorable w = u;
w.setColor(Color.BLACK);          ColorablePoint method
w = v;                            setColor() is invoked
w.setColor(Color.RED);            Colorable3DPoint method
                                  setColor() is invoked
```

In this segment, variable w is used in the invocation of two different setColor() methods. This polymorphic circumstance is possible because points u and v share the common interface type Colorable.

Similarly, a polymorphic method can be defined to take advantage of interface-implemented commonality. Consider the following class Blue with polymorphic class method setBlue().

```
public class Blue {
    public static void setBlue(Colorable p) {
        p.setColor(Color.BLUE);
    }
}
```

Listing 9.9   ColorablePoint.java

```java
1.  package geometry;
2.
3.  import java.awt.*;
4.
5.  public class ColorablePoint extends Point implements Colorable {
6.      // instance variable
7.      Color color;
8.
9.      // ColorablePoint(): default constructor
10.     public ColorablePoint() {
11.         setColor(Color.BLUE);
12.     }
13.
14.     // ColorablePoint(): specific constructor
15.     public ColorablePoint(int x, int y, Color c) {
16.         super(x, y);
17.         setColor(c);
18.     }
19.
20.     // getColor(): color property accessor
21.     public Color getColor() {
22.         return color;
23.     }
24.
25.     // setColor(): color property mutator
26.     public void setColor(Color c) {
27.         color = c;
28.     }
29.
30.     // clone(): clone facilitator
31.     public Object clone() {
32.         int x = (int) getX();
33.         int y = (int) getY();
34.         return new ColorablePoint(x, y, getColor());
35.     }
36.
37.     // toString(): string representation facilitator
38.     public String toString() {
39.         Color c = getColor();
40.         return "[" + super.toString() + ", " + c.toString() + "]";
41.     }
42.
43.     // equals(): equal facilitator
44.     public boolean equals(Object v) {
45.         if (v instanceof ColorablePoint) {
46.             Color c1 = getColor();
47.             Color c2 = ((ColoredPoint) v).getColor();
48.             return super.equals(v) && c1.equals(c2);
49.         }
50.         else {
51.             return false;
52.         }
53.     }
54. }
```

Listing 9.10 **Colorable3DPoint.java**

```
1.  package geometry;
2.
3.  import java.awt.*;
4.
5.  public class Colorable3DPoint extends ThreeDimensionalPoint
6.                                  implements Colorable {
7.      // instance variable
8.      Color color;
9.
10.     // Colorable3DPoint(): default constructor
11.     public Colorable3DPoint() {
12.         setColor(Color.BLUE);
13.     }
14.
15.     // Colorable3DPoint(): specific constructor
16.     public Colorable3DPoint(int x, int y, int z, Color c) {
17.         super(x, y, z);
18.         setColor(c);
19.     }
20.
21.     // getColor(): color property accessor
22.     public Color getColor() {
23.         return color;
24.     }
25.
26.     // setColor(): color property mutator
27.     public void setColor(Color c) {
28.         color = c;
29.     }
30.
31.     // clone(): clone facilitator
32.     public Object clone() {
33.         int x = (int) getX();
34.         int y = (int) getY();
35.         int z = (int) getZ();
36.         return new Colorable3DPoint(x, y, z, getColor());
37.     }
38.
39.     // toString(): string representation facilitator
40.     public String toString() {
41.         Color c = getColor();
42.         return "[" + super.toString() + ", " + c.toString() + "]";
43.     }
44.
45.     // equals(): equal facilitator
46.     public boolean equals(Object v) {
47.         if (v instanceof Colorable3DPoint) {
48.             Color c1 = getColor();
49.             Color c2 = ((Colorable3DPoint) v).getColor();
50.             return super.equals(v) && c1.equals(c2);
51.         }
52.         else {
53.             return false;
54.         }
```

Listing 9.10 Colorable3DPoint.java (Continued)

```
55.    }
56. }
```

Class method `setBlue()` can have either a `ColorablePoint` or a `Colorable3DPoint` as its actual parameter, both of which are demonstrated in the following code segment.

```
ColorablePoint a = new ColorablePoint();
Colorable3DPoint b = new Colorable3DPoint();
Blue.setBlue(a);
Blue.setBlue(b);
```

Thus, the `setColor()` method invoked with `setBlue()` depends on the actual type of the `Colorable` parameter.

Even though both `ColoredPoint` and `Colored3DPoint` implement `getColor()` and `setColor()` methods, comparable code segments with `ColoredPoint` and `Colored3DPoint` being used is not possible. `ColoredPoint` and `Colored3DPoint` are not of type `Colorable`, whereas `ColorablePoint` and `Colorable3DPoint` are.

```
ColoredPoint c = new ColoredPoint();
Colored3DPoint d = new Colored3DPoint();
Colorable e = c;          ◄——————— Illegal: c does not reference a Colorable object
e.setColor(Color.black);
e = d;                    ◄——————— Illegal: d does not reference a Colorable object
e.setColor(Color.red);
Blue.setBlue(c);          ◄——————— Illegal: c does not reference a Colorable object
Blue.setBlue(d);          ◄——————— Illegal: d does not reference a Colorable object
```

9.6 CASE STUDY — PREPARING THE AQUARIUM

One of the examples that we will consider in Chapter 12 is an aquarium simulation. For the simulation to be interesting, it will need to be able to draw fish and plants. To help in that task, we create now an interface `Drawable`. Implementing interface `Drawable` of Listing 9.11 requires three methods: `getX()`, `getY()`, and `paint()`. The purposes of methods `getX()` and `getY()` are to return respectively the x- and y-coordinates of the position of the object. The purpose of the method `paint()` is to render its object in the graphics context specified by its parameter.

Listing 9.11   **Drawable.java**

```
1.  import java.awt.*;
2.
3.  public interface Drawable {
4.      // getX(): returns the x-coordinate of the object
5.      public int getX();
6.
7.      // getY(): returns the y-coordinate of the object
8.      public int getY();
9.
10.     // paint(): draw the object in context g at coordinate
11.     // (getX(), getY())
12.     public void paint(Graphics g);
13. }
```

We will use interface `Drawable` in our definition of the class `Fish`. For our purposes, a fish is a drawable shape of specified color located at a particular position. To specify the color and shape, we use awt classes `Color` and `Polygon`. To specify the x- and y-coordinates, we use **int** values.

Before describing class `Fish`, we briefly review class `Polygon`. Class `Polygon` represents a shape using an ordered list of points. For example, with three points a triangle can be represented (e.g., `ColoredTriangle` of Chapter 5), with four points a quadrilateral can be represented, and so on. To support the creation of shapes, class `Polygon` has a constructor that takes three parameters—an array of x-coordinates, and an array of y-coordinates, and the number of points.

```
public Polygon(int[] x, int[] y, int n)
```

> Constructs a polygon whose ith endpoint has location (x[i], y[i]). The number of points in the new polygon is n.

The following code segment uses `Polygon` to define both an equilateral triangle and a house-shaped pentagon.

```
int[] triangleX = { 10, 20, 30 };
int[] triangleY = { 20, 10, 20 };
Polygon triangle = new Polygon(triangleX, triangleY, 3);
int[] pentalateralX = { 100, 100, 150, 200, 200 };
int[] pentalateralY = { 200, 100,  75, 100, 200 };
Polygon house = new Polygon(pentalateralX, pentalateralY, 5);
```

Among its members, a `Polygon` has three **public** instance variables—xpoints, ypoints, and npoints. These instance variables represent respectively the array of x-coordinates, the array of y-coordinates, and the number of points in the polygon.

As indicated, one of the data fields of a Fish is a Polygon. In particular, instance variable fishShape references a Polygon. The other Fish instance variables are fishColor, currentX and currentY.

> **private** Color fishColor
>> Represents the color of the fish.
>
> **private** Polygon fishShape
>> Represents the shape of the fish.
>
> **private int** currentX;
>> Represents the current x-coordinate of the fish's position.
>
> **private int** currentY;
>> Represents the current y-coordinate of the fish's position.

To support the construction of fish, the class provides two constructors.

> **public** Fish()
>> Creates a default fish using class method makeRandomColoredFish().
>
> **public** Fish(Color c, Polygon p, **int** x, **int** y)
>> Creates a fish with color c and shape p at coordinate (x, y).

To support information hiding, the class provides accessors and mutators for fish attributes.

> **public** Color getColor()
>> Returns the color of the fish.
>
> **public void** setColor(Color c)
>> Sets the color of the fish to c.
>
> **public** Polygon getShape()
>> Returns the shape of the fish.
>
> **public void** setShape(Polygon p)
>> Sets the shape of the fish to be a clone of p.
>
> **public int** getX()
>> Returns the x-coordinate of the fish's position.
>
> **public void** setX(**int** x)
>> Sets the x-coordinate of the fish's position to x.
>
> **public int** getY()
>> Returns the y-coordinate of the fish's position.
>
> **public void** setY(**int** y)
>> Sets the y-coordinate of the fish's position to y.
>
> **public void** setPosition(**int** x, **int** y)
>> Sets the fish's position to (x, y).

Because the class implements the interface Drawable, it also defines method paint(). (Methods getX() and getY() have already been accounted for.)

> **public void** paint(Graphics g)
>> Draws a representation of the fish to context g at position (getX(), getY()).

In addition to its instance variables and member methods, there is the single class method makeRandomColoredFish().

> **public static** Fish makeRandomColoredFish()
>> Creates a "fishy" shape of random color that is positioned at coordinate (0, 0).

The definition of class `Fish` is given in Listing 9.12. Based on the preceding specifications, the implementation of most of the methods is straightforward. Discussion is warranted only for methods `paint()` and `makeRandomColoredFish()`.

In drawing its fish, member method `paint()` must recognize that the `Polygon` referenced by `fishShape` represents only a template for describing the outline of the fish. In particular, the points that make up that `Polygon` represent the *relative* positions of the line segment endpoints to each other. To draw the fish at its current position, those relative positions must be offset by its current position. For example, if the tip of the fish's nose has relative coordinate (130, 30) and the fish's current position is given by coordinate (50, 75), then the tip of the nose is rendered at $(130+50, 30+75) = (180, 105)$.

The figure shifting is accomplished by method `paint()`. It first copies the arrays of x-coordinates and y-coordinates that represent the shape of the fish. The copies are made by cloning **the public** data fields `xpoints` and `ypoints` for the `Polygon` describing the fish shape. Clones are made because the shifting should be evident only in `paint()`.

```
Polygon p = getShape();
int[] x = (int[]) p.xpoints.clone();
int[] y = (int[]) p.ypoints.clone();
int n = p.npoints;
```

A **for** loop then shifts the copies of the x-coordinates and y-coordinates by `getX()` and `getY()` respectively .

```
for (int i = 0; i < n; ++i) {
    x[i] += getX();
    y[i] += getY();
}
```

A new polygon then is constructed using the shifted points.

```
p = new Polygon(x, y, n);
```

To do the actual drawing, the color of the fish is determined; the graphical context has its active color set to that color, and a filled polygon is rendered.

```
Color c = getColor();
g.setColor(c);
g.fillPolygon(p);
```

Class method `makeRandomColoredFish()` operates in the following manner. It first defines array variables `x` and `y` that are initialized respectively with the x- and y-coordinates of the points that make up the polygon describing the shape of the fish.

```
int[] x = {    0,   30,   40,   50,  60,  70,  90, 100, 115,
             130,  115,  100,   90,  70,  60,  50,  40,  30,
               0,   15 };
int[] y = {    5,   15,   10,    7,   0,   7,  12,  15,  22,
              25,   28,   35,   40,  43,  50,  43,  40,  35,
              45,   25 };
```

The method then constructs an object of type `Random` that is referenced by variable `die`.

```
Random die = new Random();
```

Listing 9.12 Fish.java

```
1.  // Representation of a fish
2.
3.  import java.awt.*;
4.  import java.util.*;
5.
6.  public class Fish implements Drawable {
7.      // instance variables
8.      Color fishColor;
9.      Polygon fishShape;
10.     int currentX;
11.     int currentY;
12.
13.     // Fish(): default constructor
14.     public Fish() {
15.         Fish fish = makeRandomColoredFish();
16.         setColor(fish.getColor());
17.         setShape(fish.getShape());
18.         setPosition(fish.getX(), fish.getY());
19.     }
20.
21.     // Fish(): constructor for specified color, shape, and position
22.     public Fish(Color c, Polygon p, int x, int y) {
23.         setColor(c);
24.         setShape(p);
25.         setPosition(x, y);
26.     }
27.
28.     // getColor(): returns the color of the fish
29.     public Color getColor() {
30.         return fishColor;
31.     }
32.
33.     // setColor(): sets the color of the fish to c
34.     public void setColor(Color c) {
35.         fishColor = c;
36.     }
37.
38.     // getShape(): returns the shape of the fish
39.     public Polygon getShape() {
40.         return fishShape;
41.     }
42.
43.     // setShape(): sets the shape of the fish to a clone of p
44.     public void setShape(Polygon p) {
45.         fishShape = new Polygon(p.xpoints, p.ypoints, p.npoints);
46.     }
47.
48.     // getX(): returns the fish's x-coordinate position
49.     public int getX() {
50.         return currentX;
51.     }
52.
53.     // setX(): sets the fish's x-coordinate position
54.     public void setX(int x) {
```

Listing 9.12 Fish.java (Continued)

```
55.         currentX = x;
56.     }
57.
58.     // getY(): returns the fish's y-coordinate position
59.     public int getY() {
60.         return currentY;
61.     }
62.
63.     // setY(): sets the fish's y-coordinate position
64.     public void setY(int y) {
65.         currentY = y;
66.     }
67.
68.     // setPosition(): sets the fish's x- and y-coordinate position
69.     public void setPosition(int x, int y) {
70.         setX(x);
71.         setY(y);
72.     }
73.
74.     // paint(): draws the fish in graphical context g
75.     public void paint(Graphics g) {
76.         Polygon p = getShape();
77.         int[] x = (int[]) p.xpoints.clone();
78.         int[] y = (int[]) p.ypoints.clone();
79.         int n = p.npoints;
80.
81.         for (int i = 0; i < n; ++i) {
82.             x[i] += getX();
83.             y[i] += getY();
84.         }
85.
86.         p = new Polygon(x, y, n);
87.
88.         Color c = getColor();
89.         g.setColor(c);
90.         g.fillPolygon(p);
91.     }
92.
93.     // makeRandomColoredFish(): create fish with random color
94.     public static Fish makeRandomColoredFish() {
95.         int[] x = {   0,  30,  40,  50,  60,  70,  90, 100, 115,
96.                     130, 115, 100,  90,  70,  60,  50,  40,  30,
97.                       0,  15 };
98.         int[] y = {   5,  15,  10,   7,   0,   7,  12,  15,  22,
99.                      25,  28,  35,  40,  43,  50,  43,  40,  35,
100.                      45,  25 };
101.
102.        Random die = new Random();
103.        int red = die.nextInt(255);
104.        int yellow = die.nextInt(255);
105.        int green = die.nextInt(255);
106.
107.        Color c = new Color(red, yellow, green);
108.
```

Listing 9.12   **Fish.java (Continued)**

```
109.        Polygon p = new Polygon(x, y, x.length);
110.
111.        return new Fish(c, p, 0, 0);
112.    }
113. }
```

Random values

Random number sequences have an important role in many computer applications. For example, they are used in games to ensure that players do not experience the same situations each time they play the game. Random number sequences are also used in the design of complex systems such as a new highway. Before a highway is constructed, it is typically modeled and simulated on a computer. By using random number sequences that reflect the expected frequency and behavior of automobiles on the proposed highway, designers can estimate the impact of adding a lane or an interchange.

A particularly useful random number sequence is the *uniform random number sequence*. A uniform random number sequence has a specified set of numbers from which the sequence takes or *draws* its random numbers. In each position of the random number sequence, any number from the set is equally likely to occur.

Suppose you wanted to create a uniformly distributed random number sequence drawn from the set {1, 2, 3, 4, 5, 6}. One way to do so is to get a normal six-sided die that has each of its sides labeled with a different element from that set. When the die is thrown, one of its sides will be facing up after the throw. For any given throw, each side is equally likely to be facing up. The sequence of values appearing on the face-up side will be a uniform random number sequence from the set {1, 2, 3, 4, 5, 6}.

Because a random number sequence is supposed to be random, there cannot be any computer algorithm that iteratively computes truly random numbers. The instructions that constitute an algorithm are deterministic rules—knowing them tells you the next number. However, there are methods that produce sequences of numbers that appear to be random. These sequences are more properly called *pseudorandom number sequences*, although most people are imprecise and drop the prefix *pseudo*.

Standard Java class `Random` provides the means to generate pseudorandom numbers. The class `Random` is part of the Java package `java.util`.

The `Random` object referenced by `die` is used to generate **int** values in the interval 0 ... 255.

```
int red = die.nextInt(256);
int yellow = die.nextInt(256);
int green = die.nextInt(256);
```

This interval corresponds to the legal values for the three settings in a `Color` representation. The `Random` method used to generate the values is one of several `nextInt()` class methods. The particular `nextInt()` method takes a value *n* and returns a pseudorandom value from the interval 0 ... *n*−1.

> See Appendix E for a complete description of class Random

Listing 9.13 FishDemo.java

```java
1.  // Demonstrates fish and canvas features
2.
3.  import java.awt.*;
4.  import javax.swing.*;
5.  import java.util.*;
6.
7.  public class FishDemo {
8.      // main(): application entry point
9.      public static void main(String[] args) {
10.         JFrame window = new JFrame("Fish still life");
11.         window.setDefaultCloseOperation(JFrame.EXIT_ON_CLOSE);
12.         window.setSize(200, 200);
13.         window.setVisible(true);
14.
15.
16.         Canvas canvas = new Canvas();
17.         canvas.setSize(200, 200);
18.         canvas.setBackground(Color.BLUE);
19.
20.         Container c = window.getContentPane();
21.
22.         FlowLayout manager = new FlowLayout();
23.         c.setLayout(manager);
24.
25.         c.add(canvas);
26.
27.         System.out.print("\nEnter any character when ready.");
28.         Scanner stdin = new Scanner(System.in);
29.         stdin.nextLine();
30.
31.         Graphics g = canvas.getGraphics();
32.
33.         Fish fish = new Fish();
34.         fish.setPosition(12, 25);
35.         fish.paint(g);
36.         fish.setPosition(45, 95);
37.         fish.paint(g);
38.     }
39. }
```

By generating three pseudorandom values, a pseudorandom color can be constructed.

```java
Color c = new Color(red, yellow, green);
```

Using c and a polygon constructed from x, y, and x.length, a fish with pseudorandom color can be generated, where the fish is positioned at the origin.

```java
Polygon p = new Polygon(x, y, x.length);
return new Fish(c, p, 0, 0);
```

To illustrate the drawing process of a fish, program FishDemo.java of Listing 9.13 first creates a window and a *canvas* in that window, where a canvas is a rectangular drawing area to which drawing commands can be issued. The program then creates a fish and

Figure 9.3 **FishDemo window.**

draws the fish on the canvas at two different positions. A sample window produced by the program is depicted in Figure 9.3.

The canvas is produced using awt class `Canvas`. A `Canvas` object can be sized using member method `setSize()` and its background can be colored using member method `setBackground()`.

```
Canvas canvas = new Canvas();
canvas.setSize(200, 200);
canvas.setBackground(Color.BLUE);
```

To make the canvas a part of the window we must *add* the canvas to the window. In particular, we must add the canvas to the content part of the window.

```
Container c = window.getContentPane();

FlowLayout manager = new FlowLayout();
c.setLayout(manager);

c.add(canvas);
```

Although our program only adds one element to the `Container` representing the content pane, there are generally multiple elements added to a `Container`. To arrange its elements, a `Container` uses a layout manager. Program `FishDemo.java` uses awt class `FlowLayout` for element positioning. A `FlowLayout` manager arranges the elements in a top-to-bottom, left-to-right manner in the order in which they are added to the window.

Figure 9.4 depicts that same window of Figure 9.3 as part of a desktop. The window is obscured partially by the console window that initiated the program. Figure 9.5 shows that same desktop after the console window has been moved. Observe that the fish rendering is no longer complete. The reason the now exposed portions of the fish are missing is that the program had not been configured to *repaint* the canvas with the two fish ren-

Figure 9.4   **FishDemo window obscured partially by console window.**

Figure 9.5   **FishDemo window after console window has shifted.**

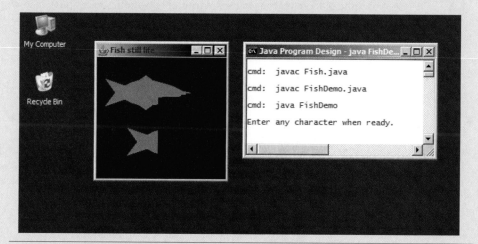

derings whenever an exposure event occurs. As written, the program displays the two fish only once.

Although every `Canvas` object has a method `paint()` that is invoked automatically whenever an exposure event occurs in relation to the object, the `paint()` method defined by `Canvas` performs no actions. It is a placeholder that is to be overridden by a specialized `Canvas` for the task at hand.

As an example of a specialized canvas, Listing 9.14 gives `FishCanvas.java`. Class `FishCanvas` extends `Canvas` so that it produces a picture of a fish centered within the canvas. For that purpose, the class defines an instance variable `fish` of type `Fish`. The `FishCanvas` default constructor both configures the canvas (i.e., size and background) and positions the fish for the canvas. `FishCanvas` member method `paint()` simply draws the fish in the current graphical context.

Listing 9.14 FishCanvas.java

```java
1.   // Demonstrates specialized canvas redrawing
2.
3.   import java.awt.*;
4.   import javax.swing.*;
5.
6.   public class FishCanvas extends Canvas {
7.
8.      // instance variables
9.      Fish fish = new Fish();
10.
11.     // FishCanvas(): default constructor
12.     public FishCanvas() {
13.        // configure canvas attributes
14.        setSize(200, 200);
15.        setBackground(Color.BLUE);
16.
17.        // position fish
18.        int fishWidth =
19.            (int) fish.getShape().getBounds().getWidth();
20.        int fishHeight =
21.            (int) fish.getShape().getBounds().getHeight();
22.        int w = getWidth();
23.        int h = getHeight();
24.        fish.setPosition((w - fishWidth)/2, (h - fishHeight)/2);
25.     }
26.
27.     // paint(): draw the fish
28.     public void paint(Graphics g) {
29.        fish.paint(g);
30.     }
31.
32.     // main(): application entry point
33.     public static void main(String[] args) {
34.        FishCanvas fishCanvas = new FishCanvas();
35.
36.        JFrame window = new JFrame("Canvas demo");
37.        window.setSize(200, 200);
38.        window.setDefaultCloseOperation(JFrame.EXIT_ON_CLOSE);
39.
40.        Container c = window.getContentPane();
41.
42.        FlowLayout manager = new FlowLayout();
43.        c.setLayout(manager);
44.
45.        c.add(fishCanvas);
46.
47.        window.setVisible(true);
48.     }
49.  }
```

To demonstrate its specialization, FishCanvas provides a class method main() that defines an instance of FishCanvas and adds that canvas to a JFrame. Figure 9.6 shows the program window as part of a desktop. In the figure, the program is obscured partially by the console window. Figure 9.7 shows the program window after the console window

Figure 9.6   **FishCanvas window obscured partially by console window.**

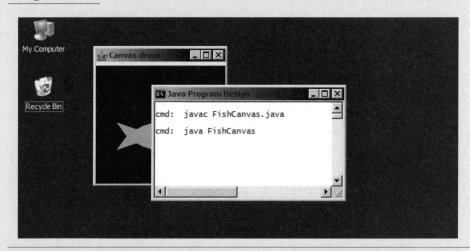

Figure 9.7   **FishCanvas window after console window has shifted.**

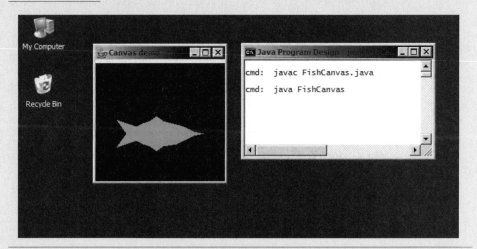

has been shifted rightward on the desktop. Observe that `FishCanvas` method `paint()` correctly handled the rendering of the canvas after the exposure event occurred.

This analysis completes our introduction to inheritance and polymorphism.

9.7   REVIEW

- Inheritance is a powerful mechanism in the object-oriented design methodology. Inheritance is the ability to define a new class using an existing class as a basis. The new class, called the subclass, inherits the attributes and behaviors of the class on which it is based, the superclass. The subclass also extends the superclass representation by introducing new attributes and behaviors that are specific to the subclass.

- Keyword **extends** is Java's mechanism for deriving a new class from an existing class.

- Inheritance is often used to organize abstractions in a top-down fashion from most general to least general.

- A superclass is also referred to as the base class and the subclass is also referred to as the derived class.

- A subclass can provide additional data fields and methods.

- A subclass object has multiple types. The subclass object is a specialized superclass type object. Therefore, the subclass object is of both the subclass and superclass types.

- With inheritance, there is an is-a relationship between the subclass type and its superclass.

- All classes are either explicitly or implicitly extensions of the class `Object`.

- A subclass method overrides a superclass method if the two methods have the same signature.

- A subclass constructor essentially adds to a superclass object the features needed to make that object into a subclass object; that is, a subclass is a specialization of the superclass. A superclass constructor must be called to create a superclass object before the subclass constructor can do its job.

- To explicitly invoke a superclass constructor for the object under construction, we use the keyword **super**. Keyword **super** is the Java mechanism for viewing the current object as an instance of the superclass.

- If a subclass constructor does not explicitly invoke a superclass constructor, then Java automatically invokes the superclass's default constructor to initialize the superclass attributes.

- If a subclass overrides a method, the subclass can access the overridden method through the use of the keyword **super**.

- Java supports single inheritance but does not support multiple inheritance; that is, a subclass can be extended directly from only one class.

- A code expression is polymorphic if it can invoke different methods depending on the types of objects using the code.

- In Java, it is not the variable type that determines which method is invoked, but the type of object at the location to which the variable refers.

- Java's support for polymorphism makes it possible to compile a method that performs a method invocation in its body even though the subclass that eventually will supply the method has not yet been implemented or even defined. This capability is important for software vendors who design libraries where the source code is to be kept proprietary. A library client can extend classes and have them make use of the vendor methods without the client needing access to vendor implementation files.

- Object construction is always a two-step process. The first step constructs the superclass view of the object. The second step constructs the subclass view of the object.

- With respect to **public** and **private** access rights, a subclass is treated no differently than any other Java class—a subclass can access the superclass's **public** members and cannot access the superclass's **private** members.

- Besides being accessed by its own class, a **protected** variable or method can be used by subclasses of its class.

- A **package** statement indicates that the definitions that follow are part of a bigger collection known as a package. Programmers put classes and interfaces into a package for two basic reasons—organization and special access to members. By organizing classes and interfaces with a related purpose into a package, you make it easier for users to find them—classes and interfaces with the same package name are stored in the same folder.

- Java puts the classes of one package in a different namespace (scope) than it puts the classes of another package. As a result, the names in a package do not conflict with names in other packages.

- When defining members of a class or interface, Java does not require an explicit access specification. The implicit specification is known as default access or package access. Members of a class with default access can be accessed only by members of the package.

- If a Java file does not begin with a **package** statement, then Java automatically considers all definitions in that file to be part of a **package** unique to that file.

- Two classes that are part of the same package can access each other's **public**, **protected**, and default access members.

- Just as Java permits a constant data field to be defined through the use of the keyword **final**, so it permits **final** methods and classes. A **final** class is a class that cannot be extended. A **final** method is a method that cannot be overridden.

- Developers of classes sometimes make them **final** for economic or security reasons.

- The keyword **abstract** at the start of a class definition indicates that the class is not to be instantiated. The class exists to be a superclass of other classes. By having a common base for the specialized classes, the inheritance and polymorphism mechanisms can be exploited.

- The keyword **abstract** at the front of a method declaration indicates that the definition of the method will not be supplied. Non-**abstract** subclasses of the **abstract** superclass must provide their own definitions.

- Because **abstract** classes are valid types, we can initialize a variable of an **abstract** type variable to reference an existing subclass object of that type.

- Besides allowing programmers to define **abstract** classes, Java also allows programmers to define and implement interfaces. An **interface** is not a class but is instead a partial template of what must be in a class.

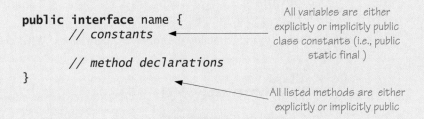

```
public interface name {
        // constants
        // method declarations
}
```

All variables are either explicitly or implicitly public class constants (i.e., public static final)

All listed methods are either explicitly or implicitly public

- An **interface** differs from an **abstract** class in three important ways.

  - An **abstract** class can have complete method definitions, while an **interface** cannot specify any method implementations;

  - The methods and variables of an **abstract** class can have different access specifications, while the methods and variables of an interface are all **public**;

  - There are no restrictions on the kinds of variables an **abstract** class defines, while any variables defined in **interface** are **final** and **static**.

- A class can extend only one class, but it can implement multiple interfaces.

- Most applications that use class Canvas extend its definition to include an application-specific paint() method.

9.8   SELF-TEST

S9.1 What is the relationship that implies inheritance? A class that is created from another class via inheritances is called a _____. The class at the top of the inheritance hierarchy is known as the _____.

S9.2 Fill in the following table to show how the different inheritance access specifiers affect the ability of the derived class's member functions to access a base class's members.

Member Restriction	this	Subclass	Package	General
public				
protected				
default				
private				

S9.3 Consider classes D and F from Section 9.3.2. What is the output of the following code segment? Why?

```
F f = new F(2);
D d = f;
d.printD();
f.printF();
```

S9.4 Suppose U.java contains the following definitions. What does the program output?

```
class S {
    private int value;

    public S(int x) {
        value = x;
        System.out.println("Made an S: " + value);
    }

    public int getValue() {
        return value;
    }
}

class T {
    private S s;

    public T(int x) {
        s = new S(x);
    }

    protected S getValue() {
        return s;
    }
}

public class U extends T {
    private U(int y) {
        super(y);
    }

    private void print() {
        S s = getValue();
        System.out.println(s.getValue());
    }

    public static void main(String[] args) {
        U u = new U(1128);
        u.print();
    }
}
```

| **9.9** | **EXERCISES** |

9.1 Design a hierarchy of toys. Examples of possible specialized subclasses are stuffed toy, battery-powered toy, and mechanical toy. Illustrate your hierarchy by drawing a diagram like the one in Figure 9.1.

9.2 Design an inheritance hierarchy for lights. For example, there are electric lights, combustible lights (kerosene lanterns, propane lanterns, etc.), and electroluminescent lights. Illustrate your hierarchy by drawing a diagram like the one in Figure 9.1.

9.3 Design an inheritance hierarchy for shoes. The first level of your hierarchy should be men's and women's shoes. Illustrate your hierarchy by drawing a diagram like the one in Figure 9.1.

9.4 Design an inheritance hierarchy of clocks. After you have designed the hierarchy, design classes for each type of clock. Do not implement the member functions of the classes.

9.5 Consider the classes A and B. Identify the errors and explain them.

```
1. public class A {
2.    private int n;
3.    protected int m;
4.
5.    public A() {
6.       super(0, 0);
7.    }
8.
9.    private A(int a) {
10.       this(a, 0);
11.    }
12.
13.    protected A(int a, int b) {
14.       super(a, b);
15.    }
16. }
17.
18. public class B {
19.    public A() {
20.       super(0);
21.    }
22.
23.    public B(int a) {
24.       this(a, 0);
25.    }
26.
27.    private B(int a, int b) {
28.       A(a, b);
29.    }
30. }
```

9.6 Consider the following file C.java.

```
public class C {
```

```
        protected int m;
        private int n;

        public C() {
            this(0, 0);
        }

        C(int n) {
            this(n, 0);
        }

        protected C(int a, int b) {
            this(n, 0);
        }

        int look1() {
            return m;
        }
        int look2() {
            return n;
        }
    }
```

Suppose class D is extended from C. Which members of C can be accessed by D? How would your answer change (if at all), if class D was defined in the same file as C?

9.7   Suppose class X has the following definition.

```
    public class X {
        private int data;
        public X(int n) {
            data = n;
        }

        public int getData() {
            return data;
        }
    }
```

Also suppose Y has the following definition.

```
    public class Y {
        private int value;
        public Y(int n) {
            value = n;
        }

        public int getValue() {
            return value;
        }
    }
```

If it is necessary, correct the following class definition that attempts to define a class Z that has two data fields representing respectively X and Y objects.

```
    public class Z extends X, Y {
        public Z(int x, int y) {
```

```
        super.X(x);
        super.Y(y);
    }
}
```

9.8   Suppose class F has the following definition

```
public class F {
    private int value;
    public F(int x) {
        value = x;
        System.out.println("Made F: " + value);
    }
}
```

What is the output of the following program?

```
public class G extends F {
    private F value;

    public G(int x, int y) {
        super(x);
        value = new F(y);
    }

    public static void main(String[] args) {
        G g = new G(11, 28);
    }
}
```

9.9   Consider class E from Section 9.3.2. How many times is its instance variable set during the construction process? Explain.

9.10   Defend Java's decision not to give subclasses special access rights with regard to **private** members.

9.11   Defend Java's decision to give subclasses special access rights with regard to **protected** members.

9.12   Does awt class Polygon support encapsulation and information hiding?

9.13   Defend Java's decision to give the classes of a package special access rights with regard to default access members.

9.14   Consider class Y in Section 9.3.3. Which of the following statements could be the fourth statement in method main()? Explain.

a) x = y;

b) x = (X) y ;

c) y = x;

d) y = (Y) x;

9.15   Suppose the following method main() was added to class Colored3DPoint. What would the program output be?

```
public static void main(String[] args) {
    Colored3DPoint c = new Colored3DPoint();
    Colored3DPoint d =
        new Colored3DPoint(1, 2, 3, Color.BLACK);
```

```
            Colored3DPoint e = (Colored3DPoint) d.clone();
            System.out.println(c);
            System.out.println(d);
            System.out.println(e);
            System.out.println(d.equals(c));
            System.out.println(d.equals(e));
            return;
    }
```

9.16 Why is the decision on which method to invoke often made at run time rather than at compile time?

9.17 Extend class `Polygon` by defining a subclass `Triangle` that implements the `Drawable` interface for representing triangles embedded in coordinate space.

9.18 Speculate on why abstract methods are used rather than methods that simply do an immediate return. Consider what would happen if a derived class did not have an overriding definition.

9.19 Our concern here is developing a representation for vehicles.

a) Design an interface hierarchy for the types of vehicle ownership: commercial, individual, or governmental.

b) Define a movement interface hierarchy: wheeled and nonwheeled.

c) Define a class hierarchy for vehicles based on energy source—fossil fuel, solar, chemical, steam, electric, or nuclear—that also takes into account ownership and movement. Further develop the hierarchy for classes for snowmobiles, school buses, and station wagons. Justify which classes and methods are **abstract** or **final** (if any).

9.20 Use instances of classes `Polygon`, `Circle`, and `Box` along with `Triangle` from Exercise 9.17 to paint a canvas with the following image.

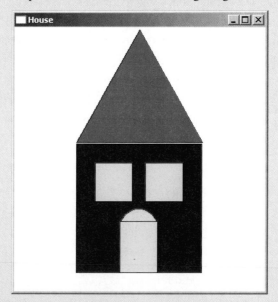

9.21 Use instances of classes `Polygon`, `Circle`, and `Box` along with `Triangle` from Exercise 9.17 to paint a canvas with the following image whenever an exposure event occurs.

9.10 PROGRAMMING PROJECT — CHANGE MAKER

In this case study, we explore the notion of inheritance by developing a collection of coin classes and then use those classes in producing a change-making program. The utility of a change-making algorithm is evident whenever we use a commercial food or beverage dispenser. After inserting coins and making our selection, we expect both the right product and the correct amount of change.

The objective of this case study is to design and implement a hierarchy structure in the context of problem solving

A major part of this assignment is documenting your design decisions regarding the classes you create. This case study gives you more of a chance to be a designer than previous case studies did. With a good design for this assignment, the methods you specify will have straightforward implementations.

ANALYSIS AND DESIGN

Suppose the superclass for your collection of coin classes is `Coin`. What attributes (if any) should be associated with class `Coin`? In particular, should there be attributes `valueOf` and `name` or should only the classes derived from `Coin` have attributes `valueOf` and `name`? Should the attributes be instance variables, class variables, instance constants, or class constants?

What methods (if any) should be associated with class `Coin`? For example, should there be an accessor and a mutator giving and setting the coin's worth? For the methods that do exist, should they have **public**, **private**, **protected**, or default access? There are other questions to consider in regard to class `Coin`. For example, should the `Coin` class be abstract?

From class `Coin` you should derive the unit coin for your monetary system (e.g., the cent in the United States and the centavo in Mexico).

The other coin types from your monetary system should also be derived. It is up to you whether they are derived from `Coin` or from the unit coin class. However, your documentation should justify this design decision. Also document whether the classes are part of a package.

To facilitate the change-making program, you should also develop a class `Change`. Class `Change` has an instance variable associated with each of the coin types of your monetary system. The instance variable associated with a particular coin type indicates the number of its coins that are part of the change.

IMPLEMENTATION

As part of its definition, class `Change` should have a constructor that takes a single **int** parameter n. The constructor initializes the object so that its instance variables are configured to make change for the amount n. In configuring the instance variables, the minimum number of coins should be used for the specified amount. For example, if we are using the U.S. monetary system and n has the value 138, then the `Change` object should be initialized to indicate one dollar, no half-dollars, one quarter, one dime, no nickels, and three cents. Any other way of making change for 138 uses more coins.

In designing your classes, take care to consider what superclass and `Object` methods (if any) they should override (e.g., `clone()`, `equals()`, and `toString()`)?

Demonstrate a use of your classes by also developing a program `Change-Maker.java` that displays how to make change for a user-specified amount. Possible interfaces are depicted in Figure 9.8 and Figure 9.9.

TESTING

We recommend *unit testing* for this assignment. In unit testing, each class is tested separately for correctness. If the classes have been implemented correctly, and encapsulation and information hiding is practiced, then their use in combinations should also be correct. Thus, before testing `ChangeMaker.java`, it is important that you know class `Change` is correct. Because the correctness of class `Change` is dependent on the correctness of your implementation of the coin hierarchy, the coin hierarchy classes must also be tested.

Although exhaustively testing all these classes is not possible, there is a reasonable test that will give confidence of the correctness of many of the methods of your `Change`

Figure 9.8   Changemaker screen shot.

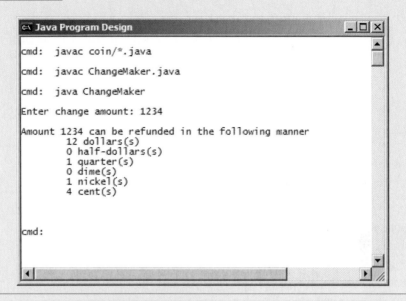

Figure 9.9   Changemaker screen shot.

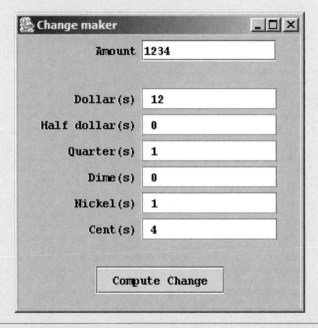

and coin classes. The test involves a **for** loop that iterates for all amounts i in the interval $0 \ldots 2n$, where n is the value of your largest coin. For each amount i, construct a Change object with i as its parameter and then display that object. You can then manually verify the correctness of the output. Testing and debugging are considered in detail in Chapter 13.

POSSIBLE EXTENSIONS

In practice, a change maker is constrained to make change using the coins held in storage. As such, the optimal way to make change may not be possible using the available coins.

Modify class Change so that its initialization supports specifying the number of coins for each coin type that are available. The algorithm for making change should take into account coin availability.

DOCUMENTATION

Besides documenting all design decisions and methods, also document your testing process.

9.11	**SELF-TEST ANSWERS**

S9.1 The relationship is is-a. A class created from another class via inheritances is called a subclass. The class at the top of an inheritance hierarchy is known as the superclass.

S9.2 The table has the following specification.

Member Restriction	this	Subclass	Package	General
public	√	√	√	√
protected	√	√	√	—
default	√	—	√	—
private	√	—	—	—

S9.3 The segment displays

```
D's d: 200
D's d: 200
F's d: 2
```

S9.4 The program displays

```
1128
```

GUI-BASED PROGRAMMING

This chapter continues our gentle introduction to graphical user interfaces (GUIs) by first exploring the object-oriented design and development of a psychometric-like tool for estimating a user's psychological type. The chapter then continues with the initial stages of the object-oriented design and development of a guessing game. The completion of the game is left as a programming project.

OBJECTIVES

- To consider two significant GUI-based tools using the principles of object-oriented programming.

G2.1   CASE STUDY — PERSONALITY TYPING

We now turn our attention to the development of a GUI-based program `TypeIndica-tor.java` that attempts to estimate the user's psychological type. The examination is intended for fun and to gain experience with program design and implementation. The program is not a true psychometric tool. We caution that the development of a true tool requires significant interaction with psychologists and extensive testing in controlled environments to calibrate the validity of the tool. Screen snapshots of the tool are depicted in Figure G2.1 and Figure G2.2.

Figure G2.1   **Screen snapshot of TypeIndicator.java's first query.**

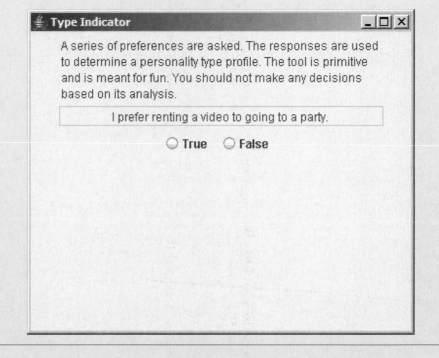

G2.1.1   BACKGROUND

A major activity of psychological research is developing a psychological type model for explaining the structure of human personality. An early major effort was conducted by Carl Jung in the 1920s. Jung believed people primarily differed in whether they were *extroverted* or *introverted*; that is, whether they preferred to be outward or inward look-ing. Jung believed that two other important ways of categorizing people were according to their preferences regarding perception and judgment. In particular, he thought that judgments tended to arise from processes that were based primarily on either *thinking* or

Figure G2.2 **Screen snapshot of TypeIndicator.java's analysis.**

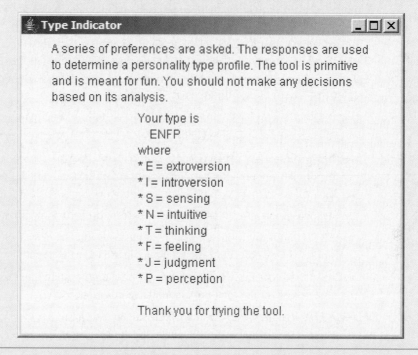

feeling. He also believed that people tended to have a preference for perception that was based primarily on either *physical sensing* or *intuition.*

Another major psychological typing effort began in the 1940s. This effort was conducted by Isabel Myers-Briggs and her mother Katherine Briggs. Their model classified people according to four preferences. Besides using Jung's three preferences, Myers-Briggs and Briggs also classified people with respect to their attitude toward life—whether *perception* or *judgment* was dominant. Based on the dominating characteristic for each of these four preferences, they would classify people into 1 of 16 personality types. Myers-Briggs and Briggs also developed a test now known as the MBTI for determining a person's personality type. The test proved to be enormously popular and remains today an important psychometric tool. Research on improving the MBTI and other type indicator tests such as the Keirsey Temperament Sorter is an important psychology research activity.

The 16 Myers-Briggs and Briggs personality types are ISTJ, ISTP, ISFJ, ISFP, INTJ, INTP, INFJ, INFP, ESTJ, ESTP, ESFJ, ESFP, ENTJ, ENTP, ENFJ, and ENFP, where I indicates introversion is dominant to extroversion, E indicates extroversion is dominant to introversion, S indicates sensing is dominant to intuition, N indicates intuition is dominant to sensing, T indicates that thinking is dominant to feeling, F indicates feeling is dominant to thinking, J indicates judgment is dominant to perception, and P indicates perception is dominant to judgment.

A major consequence of accepting the existence of these various types is being to able make inferences regarding individuals' interests and behaviors. Of course, caution must be taken in making such inferences—people are unique and their specific actions and reactions are a holistic sum of their entire makeup. However, a person's tendencies can sometimes be understood by knowing her or his personality type. The following summaries of the 16 Myers-Briggs and Briggs personality types are based on the work *Gifts Differing: Tenth Anniversary Edition* by Isabel Myers-Briggs with Peter Briggs, Consulting Psychologists Press, 1980.

- ENFJ: Forceful, outstanding leader; can be aggressive at helping others. Five percent of the total population have this type.

- ENFP: Empathic; uncanny sense of the motivations of others; views life as an exciting drama; emotionally warm. Five percent of the total population have this type.

- ENTJ: Enjoys leading and problem solving; basic driving force is to lead; tends to seek positions of responsibility. Five percent of the total population have this type.

- ENTP: Innovative nonconformist; enthusiastic interest in everything; sensitive to possibilities. Five percent of the total population have this type.

- ESFJ: Most sociable type; nurturer of harmony; outstanding host or hostesses. Thirteen percent of the total population have this type.

- ESFP: Radiates warmth and optimism; witty, charming, clever; generous. Thirteen percent of the total population have this type.

- ESTJ: In touch with external environment; very responsible; pillar of strength. Thirteen percent of the total population have this type.

- ESTP: initiator; fiercely competitive; entrepreneur; uses shock effect to get attention; effective negotiator. Thirteen percent of the total population have this type.

- INFJ: Motivated and fulfilled by helping others; complex personality. One percent of the total population have this type.

- INFP: High capacity for caring. Calm and pleasant face to the world. Sense of honor comes from internal values. One percent of the total population have this type.

- INTJ: Very self-confident and pragmatic; decisions made easily; builder of systems and the applier of theoretical models. One percent of the total population have this type.

- INTP: Great precision in thought and language; readily discerns contradictions and inconsistencies; world exists to be understood. One percent of the total population have this type.

- ISFJ: Desires to be of service and to minister to individual needs; extremely loyal. Six percent of the total population have this type.

- ISFP: Interested in the fine arts; expression through action or art form; keen senses. Five percent of the total population have this type.

- ISTJ: Decisive in practical affairs; protector of institutions; dependable. Six percent of the total population have this type.

- ISTP: Impulsive, fearless, spontaneous; action is an end to itself; craves excitement; master of tools. Five percent of the total population have this type.

ANALYSIS AND DESIGN

The tool should have the following features.

> The objective of this case study is to practice the design and development of a significant class

- Is GUI-based.
- Presents introductory information on the tool and its limitations.
- Quizzes the user about preferences regarding extroversion versus introversion, sensing versus intuition, thinking versus feeling, and perception versus judgment.
- Analyzes and displays the results of the testing to estimate the associated personality type. The display indicates the associated personality type along with a summary of that type. Included in the description is a caveat warning of the tool's limitations.

These requirements indicate that the following elements should be part of the `TypeIndicator` GUI (i.e., they are `TypeIndicator` instance variables).

`private JFrame window`

Represents the window displaying the GUI.

`private JTextArea legendArea`

Represents the text message displaying tool usage and limitations.

`private JTextArea resultArea`

Represents the text message summary of the personality type test.

`private JTextField statementPad`

Represents the text for the current preference being determined.

`private JRadioButton trueButton`

Represents the toggle indicating a true response to the current preference.

`private JRadioButton falseButton`

Represents the toggle indicating a false response to the current preference.

The button objects are of class type `JRadioButton`, which is a class that we have not used previously. `JRadioButton` is a `swing` button class whose behavior is like that of a toggle. The class name was chosen because the button supports the selection of mutually exclusive options—like the different buttons on an automobile radio cause different radio stations to be selected.

○ **True**　○ **False**

A `JRadioButton` is in one of two *states—selected* or *unselected*. By default, a `JRadioButton` is unselected when initialized.

To assist applications that require at most one `JRadioButton` object to be selected at a time, the `swing` API provides the class `ButtonGroup` for defining a logical grouping of buttons. When some button in a `ButtonGroup` is selected, the previously selected button from the group is made unselected.

As a reply to a trait query requires that a single response be selected, it is appropriate for class `TypeIndicator` to have a `ButtonGroup` element.

> **private** ButtonGroup buttonGroup
>
> > Manages button selection behavior.

Once some button is selected from its group, a ButtonGroup requires that there be a selected button. Because we want neither the true button nor the false button to be selected when a new trait query is presented initially, TypeIndicator uses a third JRadioButton to be the selected button when a new query is made.

> **private** JRadioButton hiddenButton
>
> > Represents the hidden alternative to true and false.

This JButton is never added to the GUI, so its presence is unknown to a program user. The user just sees and must pick from one of the other two radio buttons.

> I prefer renting a video to going to a party.
>
> ○ True   ○ False

In addition to the GUI elements, the results of the trait testing must be available to the TypeIndicator object so that it can create the appropriate display. Because the results are specific to the particular testing, they too are instance variables.

> **private boolean** introvert
>
> > Indicates whether testing shows introversion is dominant to extroversion.
>
> **private boolean** senser
>
> > Indicates whether testing shows sensing is dominant to intuition.
>
> **private boolean** thinker
>
> > Indicates whether testing shows thinking is dominant to feeling.
>
> **private boolean** judger
>
> > Indicates whether testing shows judging is dominant to perception.

We now turn our attention from TypeIndicator instance variables to TypeIndicator behaviors.

The TypeIndicator class is not intended to be of use to other classes. It is a standalone class whose purpose is to administer and determine the results of its personality type test. Thus, it is sufficient for the class's **public** interface to consist of two methods—a default constructor that carries out an occurrence of the testing process and a class method main() that defines an instance of the class.

> **public** main(String[] args)
>
> > Creates an instance of the TypeIndicator class.
>
> **public** TypeIndicator()
>
> > Conducts a personality type indicator test.

For simplicity, we suggest the following *top-level* algorithm for the default constructor.

- Configure and display GUI.

- Test whether extroversion or introversion is dominant.

- Test whether sensing or intuition is dominant.

- Test whether thinking or feeling is dominant.

- Test whether perception or judgment is dominant.

- Display testing summary.

Programmers commonly expect that high-level activities correspond to the major methods of the class's implementation. We take such a view for `TypeIndicator`. The six steps are handled by different instance methods.

`private configureAndDisplayGUI()`

Configures and displays the initial representation of the GUI.

`private boolean isIntroversionDominant()`

Determines and reports whether introversion is dominant over extroversion.

`private boolean isSensingDominant()`

Determines and reports whether sensing is dominant over intuition.

`private boolean isThinkingDominant()`

Determines and reports whether thinking is dominant over feeling.

`private boolean isJudgingDominant()`

Determines and reports whether judging is dominant over thinking.

`private void presentResults()`

Displays the result of the test.

The methods are all **private** as their use outside the class does not make sense.

To determine whether the user has a particular characteristic (e.g., introversion), the program presents the user with a series of five statements. For each statement, the user selects one of two responses in reaction. By summarizing the responses we can get an indication of the dominant trait. A summary value of **true** means the trait in question is dominant and a summary value of **false** means the alternative trait is dominant (e.g., extroversion). By using a summary value as the return value for a trait test, the personality type instance variables can be initialized properly.

```
introvert = isIntroversionDominant();

senser = isSensingDominant();

thinker = isThinkingDominant();

judger = isJudgingDominant();
```

If you think about it, you should be able to see that the trait testers are doing the same type of work but asking different questions. This commonality suggests that the class have an instance method `doTraitTest()` that performs the trait testing. Through its parameters, it can be given the specific queries to be used in the current trait test. Furthermore, because a trait test involves making repeated queries, an instance method `getTrueOrFalseResponse()` is appropriate—the method poses an individual query and returns the response. Method `doTraitTest()` can accomplish its testing through five invocations of `getTrueOrFalseResponse()`.

`private boolean doTraitTest(String s1, String s2, String s3,`
`    String s4, String s5)`

Conducts a trait test. The five statements involved in the five trait queries are represented by s1, s2, s3, s4, and s5. The method returns **true**, if the majority of the trait queries return **true**; otherwise, the method returns **false**.

`private boolean getTrueOrFalse(String statement)`

Displays a trait query and determines the user's response. The method returns a **boolean** value reflecting that response.

Listing G2.1 TypeIndicator.java

```
1.   // A simple psychometric-like type tool
2.
3.   import javax.swing.*;
4.   import java.awt.*;
5.   import java.awt.event.*;
6.
7.   public class TypeIndicator {
8.      // class constants
9.      private final int WINDOW_WIDTH = 400;
10.     private final int WINDOW_HEIGHT = 325;
11.     private final int TEXT_WIDTH = 30;
12.
13.     private final String LEGEND =
14.        "A series of preferences are asked. The responses are "
15.      + "used to determine a personality type profile. The tool "
16.      + "is primitive and is meant for fun. You should not make "
17.      + "any decisions based on its analysis. ";
18.
19.     // instance GUI variables
20.     private JFrame window = new JFrame("Type Indicator");
21.     private JTextArea legendArea =
22.           new JTextArea(LEGEND, 4, TEXT_WIDTH);
23.     private JTextArea resultArea = new JTextArea();
24.     private JTextField statementPad =
25.           new JTextField("", TEXT_WIDTH);
26.     private JRadioButton trueButton = new JRadioButton("True ");
27.     private JRadioButton falseButton = new JRadioButton("False");
28.     private JRadioButton hiddenButton = new JRadioButton("");
29.     private ButtonGroup buttonGroup = new ButtonGroup();
30.
31.     // instance test variables
32.     private boolean introvert;
33.     private boolean senser;
34.     private boolean thinker;
35.     private boolean judger;
36.
37.     // main(): application entry point
38.     public static void main(String[] args) {
39.        TypeIndicator testInstrument = new TypeIndicator();
40.     }
41.
42.     // TypeIndicator(): default constructor
43.     public TypeIndicator() {
44.        configureAndDisplayGUI();
45.
46.        introvert = isIntroversionDominant();
47.
48.        senser = isSensingDominant();
49.
50.        thinker = isThinkingDominant();
51.
52.        judger = isJudgingDominant();
53.
54.        presentResults();
```

Listing G2.1 TypeIndicator.java (Continued)

```java
55.    }
56.
57.     // configureAndDisplayGUI(): set up the GUI
58.     private void configureAndDisplayGUI() {
59.       // configure elements
60.       window.setSize(WINDOW_WIDTH, WINDOW_HEIGHT);
61.       window.setDefaultCloseOperation(JFrame.EXIT_ON_CLOSE);
62.
63.       legendArea.setEditable(false);
64.       legendArea.setLineWrap(true);
65.       legendArea.setWrapStyleWord(true);
66.       legendArea.setBackground(window.getBackground());
67.
68.       statementPad.setVisible(false);
69.       statementPad.setEditable(false);
70.       statementPad.setHorizontalAlignment(SwingConstants.CENTER);
71.       statementPad.setBackground(window.getBackground());
72.
73.       trueButton.setVisible(false);
74.       falseButton.setVisible(false);
75.       buttonGroup.add(trueButton);
76.       buttonGroup.add(falseButton);
77.       buttonGroup.add(hiddenButton);
78.
79.       resultArea.setEditable(false);
80.       resultArea.setBackground(window.getBackground());
81.
82.       // add elements to window's content pane
83.       window.setLayout(new FlowLayout());
84.
85.       window.add(legendArea);
86.       window.add(statementPad);
87.       window.add(trueButton);
88.       window.add(falseButton);
89.       window.add(resultArea);
90.
91.       // ready to display GUI
92.       window.setVisible(true);
93.     }
94.
95.     // isIntroversionDominant(): is introversion dominant to
96.     // extroversion
97.     private boolean isIntroversionDominant() {
98.       String s1 = "I prefer renting a video to going to a party.";
99.       String s2 = "I am happy when house guests leave.";
100.      String s3 = "Meeting new people makes me tense.";
101.      String s4 = "I enjoy being alone.";
102.      String s5 = "Crowds suck the life out of me.";
103.      return doTraitTest(s1, s2, s3, s4, s5);
104.    }
105.
106.    // isSensingDominant(): is sensing dominant to intuition
107.    private boolean isSensingDominant() {
108.      String s1 = "Facts are more interesting than ideas.      ";
```

Listing G2.1 **TypeIndicator.java (Continued)**

```
109.         String s2 = "I need the details more than the big picture.";
110.         String s3 = "I always measure, I never estimate.";
111.         String s4 = "Seeing is believing.";
112.         String s5 = "If you cannot touch it, it's not real.";
113.         return doTraitTest(s1, s2, s3, s4, s5);
114.     }
115.
116.     // isThinkingDominant(): test whether thinking is dominant to
117.     // feeling
118.     private boolean isThinkingDominant() {
119.         String s1 = "I prefer page 1 to the comics in a newspaper.";
120.         String s2 = "I think therefore I am.";
121.         String s3 = "I am not an emotional person.";
122.         String s4 = "Tears will not cause me to change my mind.";
123.         String s5 = "I'd rather be Data than Troi.";
124.         return doTraitTest(s1, s2, s3, s4, s5);
125.     }
126.
127.     // isJudgingDominant(): is judging dominant to perceiving
128.     private boolean isJudgingDominant() {
129.         String s1 = "It is easy to make a decision.";
130.         String s2 = "My first impressions are usually right.";
131.         String s3 = "Wrong decisions are better than none.";
132.         String s4 = "I seldom have second thoughts.";
133.         String s5 = "Uncertainty makes me uncomfortable.";
134.         return doTraitTest(s1, s2, s3, s4, s5);
135.     }
136.
137.     // doTraitTest(): test for dominant response for a type category
138.     private boolean doTraitTest(String s1, String s2, String s3,
139.             String s4, String s5) {
140.         // create running totals for responses
141.         int choiceTrue = 0;
142.         int choiceFalse = 0;
143.
144.         // pose queries and get responses
145.         if (getTrueorFalseResponse(s1)) {  // do query 1
146.             ++choiceTrue;
147.         }
148.         else {
149.             ++choiceFalse;
150.         }
151.
152.         if (getTrueorFalseResponse(s2)) {  // do query 2
153.             ++choiceTrue;
154.         }
155.         else {
156.             ++choiceFalse;
157.         }
158.
159.         if (getTrueorFalseResponse(s3)) {  // do query 3
160.             ++choiceTrue;
161.         }
162.         else {
```

Listing G2.1 TypeIndicator.java (Continued)

```
163.              ++choiceFalse;
164.          }
165.
166.          if (getTrueorFalseResponse(s4)) {   // do query 4
167.              ++choiceTrue;
168.          }
169.          else {
170.              ++choiceFalse;
171.          }
172.
173.          if (getTrueorFalseResponse(s5)) {   // do query 5
174.              ++choiceTrue;
175.          }
176.          else {
177.              ++choiceFalse;
178.          }
179.
180.          // produce test result
181.          return choiceTrue > choiceFalse;
182.      }
183.
184.      // getTrueorFalseResponse(): pose a statement and get response
185.      private boolean getTrueorFalseResponse(String statement) {
186.
187.          statementPad.setText(statement);
188.          hiddenButton.setSelected(true);
189.          statementPad.setVisible(true);
190.          trueButton.setVisible(true);
191.          falseButton.setVisible(true);
192.
193.          for (; ;) {
194.              if (trueButton.isSelected() || falseButton.isSelected()) {
195.                  break;
196.              }
197.          }
198.
199.          statementPad.setVisible(false);
200.          trueButton.setVisible(false);
201.          falseButton.setVisible(false);
202.
203.          return trueButton.isSelected();
204.      }
205.
206.      // presentResults(): display testing results
207.      private void presentResults() {
208.          // setup text
209.          String result = "Your type is\n"
210.              + "      "
211.
212.              + ((introvert) ? "I" : "E")
213.              + ((senser)    ? "S" : "N")
214.              + ((thinker)   ? "T" : "F")
215.              + ((judger)    ? "J" : "P")
216.              + "\n"
```

Listing G2.1 TypeIndicator.java (Continued)

```
217.
218.             + "where\n"
219.             + "* E = extroversion \n"
220.             + "* I = introversion \n"
221.             + "* S = sensing \n"
222.             + "* N = intuitive \n"
223.             + "* T = thinking \n"
224.             + "* F = feeling \n"
225.             + "* J = judgment \n"
226.             + "* P = perception \n"
227.             + "\n"
228.
229.             + "Thank you for trying the tool.";
230.
231.         // display text and quit button
232.         resultArea.setText(result);
233.
234.         window.setVisible(true);
235.     }
236. }
```

We now consider some of the important implementation details.

IMPLEMENTATION

`TypeIndicator.java` is given in Listing G2.1. In terms of intellectual content, methods `isIntroversionDominant()`, `isSensingDominant()`, `isThinkingDominant()`, and `isJudgingDominant()` are all equivalent. Therefore, we discuss only `isIntroversionDominant()`. We also discuss `configureAndDisplayGUI()`, `doTraitTest()`, and `getTrueOrFalseResponse()`. The other methods do not warrant specific discussion. The method examination begins with `configureAndDisplayGUI()`.

Our particular interest in method `configureAndDisplayGUI()` (lines 57–93 of `TypeIndicator.java`) is its initial configuring of the GUI elements involved in assessing personality traits.

```
statementPad.setVisible(false);
statementPad.setEditable(false);
statementPad.setHorizontalAlignment(SwingConstants.CENTER);
statementPad.setBackground(window.getBackground());

trueButton.setVisible(false);
falseButton.setVisible(false);
buttonGroup.add(trueButton);
buttonGroup.add(falseButton);
buttonGroup.add(hiddenButton);
```

`JTextField` variable `statementPad` represents the `JTextField` that is reset repeatedly with the current preference query.

```
I prefer renting a video to going to a party.
```

This `JTextField` is configured to be invisible initially. It is made visible only when there is a query to be made. Because the code executes so fast, the user is unaware of the delay between the initial display of the GUI and the start of the first trait test. The text in the `JTextField` is always centered because of invocation

```
statementPad.setHorizontalAlignment(SwingConstants.CENTER);
```

Besides defining constant `CENTER` for centering, there are also swing constants for other alignments: `LEFT`, `RIGHT`, `LEADING`, and `TRAILING`.

For the same reason, the `JRadioButton` objects are configured to be invisible initially. Because only one response is permitted, the two buttons are put in the `Button-Group` referenced by variable `buttonGroup`. The buttons are added one at a time using `ButtonGroup` instance method `add()`. Because a `ButtonGroup` is a logical grouping rather than a physical grouping, the group is not added to the GUI as an entity in itself.

We now consider methods `isIntroversionDominant()` and `doTraitTest()`.

In order to conduct its test, method `isIntroversionDominant()` (lines 95–104 of Listing G2.1) defines several `String` variables to represent statements that an introvert might find true.

```
String s1 = "I prefer renting a video to going to a party.";
String s2 = "I am happy when house guests leave.          ";
String s3 = "Meeting new people makes me tense.           ";
String s4 = "I enjoy being alone.                         ";
String s5 = "Crowds suck the life out of me.              ";
```

The method then invokes `doTraitTest()` (lines 137–182 of Listing G2.1) using the five statements as parameters. The return value of the invocation is the return value for testing whether introversion is dominant.

```
return doTraitTest(s1, s2, s3, s4, s5);
```

For each invocation, method `doTraitTest()` first defines two **int** variables `choiceTrue` and `choiceFalse`.

```
int choiceTrue = 0;
int choiceFalse = 0;
```

The variables are used to represent respectively the number of true responses and false responses to the statements in the current trait test.

The method then processes the first query of the current trait test.

```
// pose queries and get responses
if (getTrueorFalseResponse(s1)) {  // do query 1
   ++choiceTrue;
}
else {
   ++choiceFalse;
}
```

The invocation `getTrueorFalseResponse(s1)` causes in part `statementPad`'s text label to be set to `s1`. The method returns **true** if the user indicated true to the new query and returns **false** if the user instead indicated false to the new query. Thus, based on the return value of the invocation, `choiceTrue` or `choiceFalse` can be updated appropriately.

The method then repeats this process four times to handle the other parts of this trait test using s2, s3, s4, and s5 as the statements to be displayed.

```
if (getTrueorFalseResponse(s2)) {  // do query 2
   ++choiceTrue;
}
else {
   ++choiceFalse;
}

if (getTrueorFalseResponse(s3)) {  // do query 3
   ++choiceTrue;
}
else {
   ++choiceFalse;
}

if (getTrueorFalseResponse(s4) {  // do query 4
   ++choiceTrue;
}
else {
   ++choiceFalse;
}

if (getTrueorFalseResponse(s5)) {  // do query 5
   ++choiceTrue;
}
else {
   ++choiceFalse;
}
```

The result of the current trait test then is reported by comparing `choiceTrue` and `choiceFalse`.

```
// produce test result
return choiceTrue > choiceFalse;
```

We now consider method `getTrueOrFalseResponse()` (lines 184–204 of Listing G2.1). The method begins by configuring the GUI elements related to trait testing—the objects referenced by instance variables `statementPad`, `trueButton`, `falseButton`, and `hiddenButton`.

```
statementPad.setText(statement);
hiddenButton.setSelected(true);
statementPad.setVisible(true);
trueButton.setVisible(true);
falseButton.setVisible(true);
```

The `JTextArea` referenced by `statementPad` has its text set to the statement specified by parameter `statement`, where `statement` is the current statement to which the user is to respond. The radio button referenced by `hiddenButton` then is set to the selected state. Because the three radio buttons are all part of the same button group, this selection has the effect of causing the true and false buttons to be unselected. To complete the configuration, the query statement, true button, and false button are made visible to the user.

A **for** loop then iterates until one of the buttons referenced by trueButton or falseButton has been selected.

```
for (; ;) {
    if (trueButton.isSelected() || falseButton.isSelected()) {
        break;
    }
}
```

Because an empty **for** test expression is equivalent to **true**, loop termination must come from the body of the **for** loop. The **if** statement in the loop body uses JRadioButton instance method isSelected() to test whether the radio button referenced by true-Button or the radio button referenced by falseButton has been selected. If one of those buttons has been selected, then the **break** statement executes and the loop terminates. Otherwise the loop continues to iterate. Because there is effectively no pause between the repeated evaluations of the **if** statement, this type of loop is known as a *busy-wait loop*.

Once the user has made a response, the GUI elements related to the query are made invisible.

```
statementPad.setVisible(false);
trueButton.setVisible(false);
falseButton.setVisible(false);
```

The return value for getTrueorFalseResponse() is based on expression true-Button.isSelected().

```
return trueButton.isSelected();
```

The expression returns **true** if the true has been selected by the user and returns **false** otherwise (i.e., the false button has been selected indicating a false indication to the statement).

This discussion completes our analysis of the code.

TESTING AND ETHICS

To determine whether our effort was more than an exercise in developing a Java program, you can test the program on willing participants. Because of the nature of the program, you must tell them of its limitations—it was developed by computer scientists rather than psychologists and that it has not been calibrated. If you do such testing, you must treat your participants confidentially.

When using human subjects for your own software projects, you should take similar care to give full disclosure. For information on how a professional computer scientist should behave visit http://www.acm.org/constitution/code.html.

REFERENCES

For further information on psychological typing, the following references should prove helpful.

■ Association for Psychological Type, http://www.aptcentral.org/, 2002.

- Center for the Applications of Personality Type, `http://www.capt.org/`, 2001.
- Collected Works of C. G. Jung: Volume 6. Psychological Types, Carl Jung, Editors and translators: Gerhard Adler and R.F.C. Hull, Princeton University Press, 1976.
- Do What You Are: Second Edition, Paul Tieger and Barbara Barron-Tieger, Little Brown & Company, 2001.
- Please Understand Me II: Temperament, Character, and Intelligence, David Keirsey, Prometheus Books, 1998.

We now turn our attention to the design and partial development of a word guessing game.

G2.2   PROGRAMMING PROJECT — SMILEY GUESSING GAME

The Smiley guessing game follows the same rules as the popular word guessing game Hangman. The player makes repeated attempts at trying to guess the letters in a mystery word. Each guess must be a single letter. If the guessed letter is part of the word, then all occurrences of the letter are revealed. If the guessed letter is not part of the word, then a face feature is drawn.

> The objective of this case study is to practice the design and development of a significant class

If the word is guessed correctly before the face is drawn completely, then the game ends and the player wins. If instead, the word is not guessed correctly before the face is drawn completely, then the game ends and the player loses.

In the Smiley game, the face is drawn completely with the seventh errant guess. The first errant guess draws the contour of a face, the second errant guess draws the left eye, the third errant guess draws the left eyebrow, the fourth errant guess draws the right eye, the fifth errant guess draws the right eyebrow, the sixth errant guess draws the nose, and the last errant guess draws the mouth to complete the face. Some snapshots of the game are given in Figure G2.3.

To implement the game, you will need a GUI to represent the game display, update mechanisms, and an initialization process. We consider each of these needs in turn.

Our implementation uses a single class. However, given the complexity of the problem being solved, a design and implementation using two or more classes could be appropriate. For example in an alternative implementation, there can be one class for the GUI display and another class for controlling the flow of the game.

ANALYSIS AND DESIGN

We envision the game display as consisting of several graphical elements along with the window that holds them. The elements represent the mystery word, the current guess, an update signaller, the face, the past guesses, a quit signaler, and a status message.

The entries for the mystery word, current guess, and past guesses can all be represented using class `JTextField` and the labels for those entries using class `JLabel`. The face can be drawn on a `Canvas` using the rendering methods of class `Graphics`. The game update signal can be generated using a `JButton`. Last, the game status message can be represented using class `JLabel`.

    `private JFrame window`
        Represents the container for Smiley game GUI.
    `private JTextField answerPad`
        Represents the current state of the mystery word solution.
    `private JTextField guessPad`
        Represents the entry area for entering a guess of a letter.
    `private JButton updateButton`
        Signaler for making a guess.
    `private Canvas facePad`
        Represents the drawing area for indicating bad guesses.

Figure G2.3 **Screen snapshots of the Smiley game.**

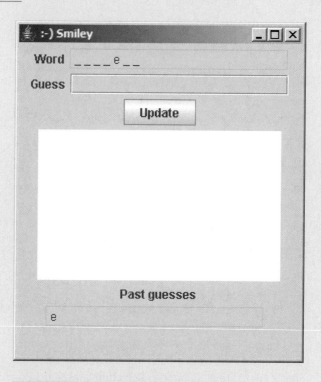

```
private JTextField pastPad
```

Represents the list of past guesses.

```
private JLabel resultPad
```

Represents a status message on the outcome of the game.

```
private JLabel answerLabel
```

Provides a label identifying the entry area for the current state of the mystery word solution.

```
private JLabel guessLabel
```

Provides a label identifying the entry area where a letter guess is made.

```
private JLabel pastLabel
```

Provides a label identifying the entry area for past guesses

To assist in the initialization of these instance variables, the following class constants should prove helpful. `String` constant `WORD_LIST` represents the name of the file containing the lists of possible words to be guessed. Constant `TEXT_WIDTH` represents the width of the `JTextField` entry areas. Constants `CANVAS_WIDTH` and `CANVAS_HEIGHT` represent the width and height respectively of the drawing area for the face. Constants `WINDOW_WIDTH` and `WINDOW_HEIGHT` represent the width and height respectively of the window containing the GUI. Constant `SKY_BLUE` represents the background color of the components of the GUI. `OFFSET` represents a pixel offset for drawing parts of the face. We discuss the role of `OFFSET` later.

```
private final static String WORD_LIST = "words.txt";
private final static int OFFSET = 2;
private final static int TEXT_WIDTH = 20;
private final static int CANVAS_WIDTH = 250;
private final static int CANVAS_HEIGHT = 150;
private final static int WINDOW_WIDTH = 300;
private final static int WINDOW_HEIGHT = 340;
private final static Color SKY_BLUE = new Color(217,217, 255);
```

When the player clicks the `JButton`, the player is signaling a request to update the game using the new guess. If the new guess is a previously unseen letter, then either the mystery word or the face requires updating. In addition, the display of past guesses requires updating. If instead the new guess is not a previously unseen letter, then it is to be ignored. These activities can be supported through instance methods.

```
private boolean isValid(String s)
```

Determines whether s represents a new valid guess.

```
private void updateAnswer()
```

Displays occurrences of the new guess in the mystery word and the number of letters still to be guessed. If there are no occurrences of the guess in the mystery word, then the number of errant guesses has increased by one.

```
private void updateFace()
```

Updates drawing of the face based on the number of errant guesses.

```
private void updatePast()
```

Adds the current guess to the list of past guesses.

To support the drawing of the various features required by `updateFace()`, the following instance methods are appropriate.

`private void` drawContour()

> Draws the basic shape of the face.

`private void` drawRightEye()

> Draws the right eye.

`private void` drawLeftEye()

> Draws the left eye.

`private void` drawRightEyebrow()

> Draws the right eyebrow.

`private void` drawLeftEyebrow()

> Draws the left eyebrow.

`private void` drawNose()

> Draws the nose.

`private void` drawMouth()

> Draws the mouth.

To support debugging and analysis, inherited method `toString()` should be overridden.

`public` toString()

> Returns a `String` representation of the state of the game.

To make the game interesting, there must be some mechanism to choose a random mystery word.

`private` String getRandomWord()

> Returns a random mystery word.

Therefore, the game must have access to a list of words. Our list is in the file `words.txt`. The first line of the file is the number of words that follows. The words occur one per line and there are approximately 200 listed words.

In addition to the GUI instance variables listed previously, the methods we have proposed need access to the following *state information* about the game: the word to be guessed, what portion of the word has been guessed so far, the current guess, how many errant guesses have there been, how many letters are left to be guessed, and whether the game is over. This information on the state of the game can be maintained using instance variables

`String` word

> Represents word to be guessed.

`StringBuffer` answer

> Represents the portion of word guessed so far.

`char` guess

> Current letter guess.

`int` errors

> Indicates how many bad guesses so far.

`int` lettersLeft

> Indicates how many letters still needed.

`boolean` gameOver

> Indicates has the game been won or lost.

A `StringBuffer` representation of the guessed portion of the word is maintained with variable `answer`. A `StringBuffer` is used because the display of the mystery word needs to be modified as the user makes correct guesses. Using a `String` would also be possible, however, keeping track of the updates is simpler with a `StringBuffer`.

Class `StringBuffer` provides a *mutable* representation of a character sequence; that is, there are methods that allow the representation to be modified (e.g., instance method `setCharAt()` allows the character at a specified index to be modified).

Three other methods of interest in regard to Smiley are accessors `charAt()` and `length()`, and facilitator `toString()`.

```
public void setCharAt(int i, char c)
```

Sets the character in the sequence with index `i` to `c`.

```
public char charAt(int i)
```

Returns the character at index `i` in the sequence.

```
public int length()
```

Returns the number of characters in the sequence.

```
public String toString()
```

Returns a `String` representation of the character sequence.

To play the game, we must be able to create instances of it. We suggest two constructors.

```
public Smiley()
```

Invokes **this(null)**.

```
public Smiley(String w)
```

Creates an instance of the Smiley game. If w is non-**null**, then it is the word to be guessed. If instead w is **null**, then a random word from WORD_LIST is used as the mystery word.

While it may seem strange to have a constructor where the mystery word is known, such a constructor is convenient for code debugging.

We now turn our attention to game implementation.

IMPLEMENTATION

The implementation of the class is in part your responsibility. We briefly describe versions of several `Smiley` methods. These methods are

```
public Smiley(String w)
private boolean isValid(String s)
private void updateAnswer()
private void drawContour()
private void drawLeftEye()
```

The constructor `Smiley(String w)` begins by processing its parameter w.

```
// process parameter
if (w != null) {
   word = w;
}
else {
   word = getRandomWord();
}
```

If parameter w is non-**null**, then it represents the mystery word to be guessed. If instead w is **null**, then a random word is used as the mystery word.

The constructor then creates the initial state of the game.

```
// initialize state information

// record number of letters still unfound
lettersLeft = word.length();

// current guess placeholder
guess = ' ';

// no errant guesses as of yet
errors = 0;

// the game is not over
gameOver = false;

// create mystery word representation, e.g., _ _ _ _ _ _ _
String s = "";
for (int i = 0; i < word.length(); ++i) {
    s += " _";
}
answer = new StringBuffer(s);
```

With this state information, the GUI can be configured. The configuration begins with the window that holds the other GUI components. In particular, the window is sized, colored, and has its closing policy set.

```
// configure GUI
window.setSize(WINDOW_WIDTH, WINDOW_HEIGHT);
window.setDefaultCloseOperation(JFrame.EXIT_ON_CLOSE);
window.setBackground(SKY_BLUE);
```

The components of the GUI are then colored to match the window.

```
window.getContentPane().setBackground(window.getBackground());
guessPad.setBackground(window.getBackground());
answerPad.setBackground(window.getBackground());
resultPad.setBackground(window.getBackground());
pastPad.setBackground(window.getBackground());
updateButton.setBackground(window.getBackground());
```

The first of these six colorings is interesting syntactically.

```
window.getContentPane().setBackground(window.getBackground());
```

The content of a GUI lies in the content pane. This pane lies within the window. The window and the content pane can have distinct background colors. This statement ensures that they are the same. The subexpression `window.getContentPane()` evaluates to the content pane. The subexpression `setContentPane(window.getBackground())` then operates on the content pane to set its color to the overall background color. The next five statements set the background of other GUI components to the overall background color.

The GUI elements requiring configuration are then set.

```
answerPad.setText(answer.toString());
```

```
updateButton.addActionListener(this);

facePad.setSize(CANVAS_WIDTH, CANVAS_HEIGHT);
facePad.setBackground(Color.WHITE);

answerPad.setEditable(false);
pastPad.setEditable(false);

window.setLayout(new FlowLayout());
```

To complete the GUI, the configured elements are added to its content pane and the GUI is made visible.

```
window.add(answerLabel);
window.add(answerPad);
window.add(guessLabel);
window.add(guessPad);
window.add(updateButton);
window.add(facePad);
window.add(pastLabel);
window.add(pastPad);
window.add(resultPad);

window.setVisible(true);
```

Facilitator method isValid() determines whether the new input guess is valid. The method begins the validation by examining the string s in the text area of guessPad.

```
// input guess must be a single unseen letter
if (input.length() != 1) {
  // not a single character
  return false;
}
else if (! Character.isLetter(input.charAt(0))) {
  // not a letter
  return false;
}
else { // it's a letter -- is it previously unseen
  String past = pastPad.getText();
  input = input.toLowerCase();
  // indexOf() only returns -1 if the s is not there
  return (past.indexOf(input) == -1);
}
```

If the length of the new guess is not equal to 1, then the guess does not correspond to a single character and **false** is returned. Also, if the guess is not a letter, **false** is returned. Otherwise, a lowercase version of the guess is compared to the previous guesses. The return value for this case is based on whether the guess can be found among the previous guesses.

The purpose of method updateAnswer() is to update the state instance variables and answerPad with respect to the current guess. The method begins by assuming the guess is not part of the mystery word by setting local variable foundMatch to **false**.

```
// assume the character is not there
boolean foundMatch = false;
```

A **for** loop then considers the mystery word letter-by-letter. If the current letter in the word matches the guess, then foundMatch is set to **true** and the corresponding position in instance variable answer is set to the guess, thus revealing the letter to the user. In addition, the number of letters left to be guessed is decremented by one.

```
// go through word character by character and look for
// matches with guess
for (int i = 0; i < word.length(); ++i) {
    if (word.charAt(i) == guess) { // got a match
        foundMatch = true;
        --lettersLeft;
        answer.setCharAt(2*i + 1, guess);
    }
}
```

After the loop is finished, a test determines whether the number of errant guesses needs to be increased.

```
// update errors and gameOver as needed
if (! foundMatch) {
    ++errors;
}
else if (lettersLeft == 0) {
    gameOver = true;
}
```

If foundMatch is **false**, then the guess was not part of the mystery word and instance variable errors is incremented by one. If instead a match was found, then it may be the case that all letters have been guessed. If this condition is **true**, then instance variable gameOver is set to **true**.

Once these cases have been processed, all that remains for updateAnswer() to do is to use the updated value of answer to set the text area of answerPad.

```
// update GUI
answerPad.setText(answer.toString());
```

We next consider how to draw the face contour and the left eye. The face contour is an oval drawn by method drawContour(). The oval is to be slightly smaller than the size of the drawing canvas represented by Canvas instance variable facePad.

```
// drawContour(): draw the outline of the face
private void drawContour() {
    int w = facePad.getWidth();
    int h = facePad.getHeight();
    int ow = w - 2*OFFSET;
    int oh = h - 2*OFFSET;
    Graphics g = facePad.getGraphics();
    g.setColor(window.getBackground());
    g.fillOval(OFFSET, OFFSET, ow, oh);
}
```

Using facePad methods getWidth() and getHeight(), we can determine the width w and height h of the drawing canvas. The upperleft-hand corner of the oval's bounding box will be at coordinate (OFFET, OFFSET) of the Canvas. By making the oval

Figure G2.4 A use of OFFSET for drawing.

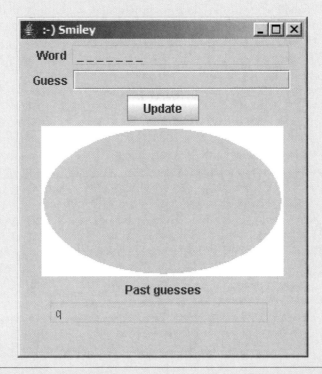

width ow equal to w - 2*OFFSET and the oval height oh equal to h - 2*OFFSET, the oval will be centered in the drawing canvas. (The use of OFFSET is depicted in Figure G2.4.)

To draw the oval, the graphics context g of the canvas is first determined using method getGraphics(). By then invoking Graphics methods setColor() and fillOval() appropriately, the drawing color can be set and the oval can be rendered on the canvas.

Method drawLeftEye() is used to draw a left eye. The method draws an oval that is 1/8 of the width and height of the drawing canvas. The upperleft-hand corner of the oval's bounding box is positioned 1/4 of the way down and 1/4 of the way over from the upper-left-hand corner of the oval representing the face contour. The actual rendering follows the same scheme as drawContour().

```java
// drawLeftEye(): draw the draw left eye
private void drawLeftEye() {
    int w = facePad.getWidth();
    int h = facePad.getHeight();
    int ow = w / 8;
    int oh = h / 8;
    Graphics g = facePad.getGraphics();
    g.setColor(Color.white);
    g.fillOval(OFFSET + w/4, OFFSET + h/4, ow, oh);
}
```

Method `drawNose()` is used to draw a nose. The method draws an oval that is 1/8 of the width and height of the drawing canvas. The upperleft-hand corner of the oval's bounding box is positioned approximately 1/2 of the way down and 1/2 of the way over from the upperleft-hand corner of the oval representing the face contour. The rendering follows the same scheme as `drawContour()` and `drawLeftEye()`.

```
// drawNose(): draw the nose for our face
private void drawNose() {
    int w = facePad.getWidth();
    int h = facePad.getHeight();
    int ow = w / 8;
    int oh = h / 8;
    Graphics g = facePad.getGraphics();
    g.setColor(Color.white);
    g.fillOval(OFFSET + w/2 - ow/2, OFFSET + h/2, ow, oh);
}
```

IMPLEMENTATION RESPONSIBILITIES

Complete the partial implementation provided in Listing G2.2. In particular, the following methods require design and implementation.

```
public Smiley()
public void actionPerformed(ActionEvent e)
private void updatePast()
private void resetGuess()
private void updateStatus()
private void updateFace()
private void drawLeftEyebrow()
private void drawRightEye()
private void drawRightEyebrow()
private void drawMouth()
private String getRandomWord()
```

Of these methods, we discuss only `getRandomWord()`. Method `getRandomWord()` must return a random mystery word from file `"words.txt"`. There are two simple ways to accomplish this task. One way is to assign the possible words to an `ArrayList` and then use `Collections` class method `shuffle()` to arrange the words into a random order. Method `getRandomWord()` can then return the first word in the list. A second way is to choose a random number *i* from the interval 1 ... *n*, where *n* is the number of words in the file. The *i*th word in the file can then be returned. To generate the value of *i*, a `java.util.Random` object can be used. A `Random` object has several methods named `nextInt()` that should prove useful in initializing *i*.

TESTING

You should document any changes to our design and document your implementation. Also, document your program's behavior with print-screen snapshots of games in progress.

You may consider modifying method `main()` to support selection of the word to be guessed. That way the program can be tested easily for correctness—the tester knows ahead of time whether a guess should be valid and in what positions it appears.

Listing G2.2 Smiley.java

```
1.  // Plays a game similar to hangman
2.
3.  import java.io.*;
4.  import java.util.*;
5.  import java.awt.*;
6.  import java.awt.event.*;
7.  import javax.swing.*;
8.
9.  public class Smiley implements ActionListener {
10.
11.     // class constants
12.     private final static String WORD_LIST = "words.txt";
13.     private final static int OFFSET = 2;
14.     private final static int TEXT_WIDTH = 20;
15.     private final static int CANVAS_WIDTH = 250;
16.     private final static int CANVAS_HEIGHT = 150;
17.     private final static int WINDOW_WIDTH = 300;
18.     private final static int WINDOW_HEIGHT = 340;
19.     private final static Color SKY_BLUE = new Color(217, 217, 255);
20.
21.     // GUI instance variables
22.
23.     // window: frame for GUI
24.     private JFrame window = new JFrame(" :-) Smiley");
25.
26.     // answerLabel and answerPad: area for displaying mystery word
27.     private JLabel answerLabel = new JLabel(" Word");
28.     private JTextField answerPad = new JTextField(TEXT_WIDTH);
29.
30.     // guessLabel and guessPad: entry area to make a guess
31.     private JLabel guessLabel = new JLabel("Guess");
32.     private JTextField guessPad = new JTextField(TEXT_WIDTH);
33.
34.     // updateButton: signaler that a new guess has been made
35.     private JButton updateButton = new JButton("Update");
36.
37.     // facePad: drawing area for face
38.     private Canvas facePad = new Canvas();
39.
40.     // pastLabel and pastPad: area for displaying past guesses
41.     private JLabel pastLabel = new JLabel("Past guesses");
42.     private JTextField pastPad = new JTextField(" ", TEXT_WIDTH);
43.
44.     // resultPad: status area for game result
45.     private JLabel resultPad = new JLabel(" ");
46.
47.     // game instance variables
48.     private String word;              // word to be guessed
49.     private StringBuffer answer;      // portion of word guessed so far
50.     private char guess;               // current letter guess
51.     private int errors;               // how many bad guesses so far
52.     private int lettersLeft;          // how many letters still needed
53.     private boolean gameOver;         // has the game been won or lost
54.
```

Listing G2.2 **Smiley.java (Continued)**

```java
55.     // Smile(): word-specified constructor
56.     public Smiley(String w) {
57.         // process parameter
58.         if (w != null) {
59.             word = w;
60.         }
61.         else {
62.             word = getRandomWord();
63.         }
64.
65.         // initialize state information
66.
67.         // record number of letters still unfound
68.         lettersLeft = word.length();
69.
70.         // current guess placeholder
71.         guess = ' ';
72.
73.         // no errant guesses as of yet
74.         errors = 0;
75.
76.         // the game is not over
77.         gameOver = false;
78.
79.         // create mystery word representation, e.g., _ _ _ _ _ _ _
80.         String s = "";
81.         for (int i = 0; i < word.length(); ++i) {
82.             s += " _";
83.         }
84.         answer = new StringBuffer(s);
85.
86.         // configure GUI
87.         window.setSize(WINDOW_WIDTH, WINDOW_HEIGHT);
88.         window.setDefaultCloseOperation(JFrame.EXIT_ON_CLOSE);
89.         window.setBackground(SKY_BLUE);
90.
91.         window.getContentPane()
92.                 .setBackground(window.getBackground());
93.         guessPad.setBackground(window.getBackground());
94.         answerPad.setBackground(window.getBackground());
95.         resultPad.setBackground(window.getBackground());
96.         pastPad.setBackground(window.getBackground());
97.         updateButton.setBackground(window.getBackground());
98.
99.         answerPad.setText(answer.toString());
100.
101.         updateButton.addActionListener(this);
102.
103.         facePad.setSize(CANVAS_WIDTH, CANVAS_HEIGHT);
104.         facePad.setBackground(Color.WHITE);
105.
106.         answerPad.setEditable(false);
107.         pastPad.setEditable(false);
108.
```

Listing G2.2   Smiley.java (Continued)

```
109.          window.setLayout(new FlowLayout());
110.
111.          window.add(answerLabel);
112.          window.add(answerPad);
113.          window.add(guessLabel);
114.          window.add(guessPad);
115.          window.add(updateButton);
116.          window.add(facePad);
117.          window.add(pastLabel);
118.          window.add(pastPad);
119.          window.add(resultPad);
120.
121.          window.setVisible(true);
122.      }
123.
124.      // isValid(): is current input guess valid
125.      private boolean isValid(String input) {
126.          // input guess must be a single unseen letter
127.          if (input.length() != 1) {
128.              // not a single character
129.              return false;
130.          }
131.          else if (! Character.isLetter(input.charAt(0))) {
132.              // not a letter
133.              return false;
134.          }
135.          else { // it's a letter -- is it previously unseen
136.              String past = pastPad.getText();
137.              input = input.toLowerCase();
138.              // indexOf() only returns -1 if the s is not there
139.              return (past.indexOf(input) == -1);
140.          }
141.      }
142.
143.      // updateAnswer(): see where current guess fits in word
144.      private void updateAnswer() {
145.          // assume the character is not there
146.          boolean foundMatch = false;
147.
148.          // go through word character by character and look for
149.          // matches with guess
150.          for (int i = 0; i < word.length(); ++i) {
151.              if (word.charAt(i) == guess) { // got a match
152.                  foundMatch = true;
153.                  --lettersLeft;
154.                  answer.setCharAt(2*i + 1, guess);
155.              }
156.          }
157.
158.          // update errors and gameOver as needed
159.          if (! foundMatch) {
160.              ++errors;
161.          }
162.          else if (lettersLeft == 0) {
```

Listing G2.2 Smiley.java (Continued)

```
163.          gameOver = true;
164.        }
165.
166.        // update GUI
167.        answerPad.setText(answer.toString());
168.      }
169.
170.      // drawContour(): draw the outline of the face
171.      private void drawContour() {
172.        int w = facePad.getWidth();
173.        int h = facePad.getHeight();
174.        int ow = w - 2*OFFSET;
175.        int oh = h - 2*OFFSET;
176.        Graphics g = facePad.getGraphics();
177.        g.setColor(window.getBackground());
178.        g.fillOval(OFFSET, OFFSET, ow, oh);
179.      }
180.
181.      // drawLeftEye(): draw the draw left eye
182.      private void drawLeftEye() {
183.        int w = facePad.getWidth();
184.        int h = facePad.getHeight();
185.        int ow = w / 8;
186.        int oh = h / 8;
187.        Graphics g = facePad.getGraphics();
188.        g.setColor(Color.white);
189.        g.fillOval(OFFSET + w/4, OFFSET + h/4, ow, oh);
190.      }
191.
192.      // drawNose(): draw the nose for our face
193.      private void drawNose() {
194.        int w = facePad.getWidth();
195.        int h = facePad.getHeight();
196.        int ow = w / 8;
197.        int oh = h / 8;
198.        Graphics g = facePad.getGraphics();
199.        g.setColor(Color.white);
200.        g.fillOval(OFFSET + w/2 - ow/2, OFFSET + h/2, ow, oh);
201.      }
202.
203.      // main(): application entry point
204.      public static void main (String[] args) {
205.        Smiley game = new Smiley();
206.      }
207.
208.      // ***************** methods to be completed ******************
209.
210.      // default constructor
211.      public Smiley() {
212.        // to be completed
213.      }
214.
215.      // getRandomWord(): choose a random word from word file. file
216.      // begins with number of words n, followed by n words
```

Listing G2.2 Smiley.java (Continued)

```
217.    private String getRandomWord() {
218.        // to be completed
219.    }
220.
221.    // actionPerformed(): process interaction
222.    public void actionPerformed(ActionEvent e) {
223.        // to be completed
224.    }
225.    // updatePast(): add current guess to list of guesses
226.    private void updatePast() {
227.        // to be completed
228.    }
229.
230.    // resetGuess(): blank out current guess
231.    private void resetGuess() {
232.        // to be completed
233.    }
234.
235.    // updateStatus(): if game is over, report results
236.    private void updateStatus() {
237.        // to be completed
238.    }
239.
240.    // updateFace(): update the face based on error count
241.    private void updateFace() {
242.        // to be completed
243.    }
244.
245.    // drawLeftEyebrow(): draw the draw left eyebrow
246.    private void drawLeftEyebrow() {
247.        // to be completed
248.    }
249.
250.    // drawRightEye(): draw the draw right eye
251.    private void drawRightEye() {
252.        // to be completed
253.    }
254.
255.    // drawRightEyebrow(): draw the draw right eyebrow
256.    private void drawRightEyebrow() {
257.        // to be completed
258.    }
259.
260.    // drawMouth(): draw the mouth for our face
261.    private void drawMouth() {
262.        // to be completed
263.    }
264. }
265.
```

10 EXCEPTIONS

When a program is running, abnormal events can arise that prevent the intended program execution. Such events are known as *exceptions*. For example, suppose a program that computes quotients is given a denominator with value zero. Rather than producing an undefined result, Java generates—or in programming parlance, *throws*—an exception that indicates the arithmetic operation cannot be performed. Unless a program has been designed to *catch* and *handle* this exception, the program automatically terminates when the exception is thrown.

OBJECTIVES

- Consider some of the abnormal events that can occur during program execution.
- Explore the use of try blocks for code that may generate exceptions.
- Explore the use of catch blocks as exception handlers.
- Encourage robust programs that always end gracefully.

10.1   EXCEPTION HANDLING

An *exception* is an abnormal event that occurs during program execution. Some examples of abnormal events are attempts to manipulate nonexistent files, improper array subscripting, and improper arithmetic operations such as a divide by zero.

If an exception occurs and an *exception-handler* code segment is in effect for that exception, then flow of control is transferred to the handler. If an exception occurs and there is no handler for it, the program terminates.

Consider program A.java of Listing 10.1 that prompts and extracts the name of a file. From that file, two integer values are extracted, and their quotient is computed and displayed.

Listing 10.1   A.java

```
1.  import java.util.*;
2.  import java.io.*;
3.
4.  public class A {
5.      // main(): application entry point
6.      public static void main(String[] args) throws IOException {
7.          // get filename
8.          Scanner stdin = new Scanner(System.in);
9.          System.out.print("Filename: ");
10.         String s = stdin.nextLine();
11.
12.         // set up file stream for processing
13.         File file = new File(s);
14.         Scanner fileIn = new Scanner(file);
15.
16.         // extract values and compute quotient
17.         int numerator = fileIn.nextInt();
18.         int denominator = fileIn.nextInt();
19.
20.         int quotient = numerator / denominator;
21.         System.out.println();
22.         System.out.println(numerator + " / " + denominator + " = "
23.                 + quotient);
24.
25.         return;
26.     }
27. }
```

There is a **throws** expression in the method main() signature for class A. In fact, all of our previous programs that manipulate files have **throws** expressions in their method main() signatures (e.g., FileLister.java of Listing 6.5). Java requires this **throws** expression of any method that does not handle the I/O (input/output) exceptions it may generate. Its inclusion is a warning to users of the method. The warning is important because if an invoked method does not handle an exception, then the exception is given to the invoking method to handle. If the invoking method does not handle the exception, then the *unwinding* process continues up the *call chain* (i.e., the sequence of invoking methods) to find a method that handles the exception. If no handling method is found during the unwinding, the program terminates.

Suppose program A.java is run and that the user specifies the file of interest to be a file numbers.txt containing the values 12 and 4 on successive lines. The I/O behavior of the program would be the following

```
cmd: java A
Filename: numbers.txt

12 / 4 = 3
```

In this run, the program's execution proceeded as planned—the user supplied a valid filename and the quotient was computed and displayed.

Now consider a program run, where the user misspells the intended filename.

```
cmd: java A
Filename: mumbers.txt
Exception in thread "main" java.io.FileNotFoundException:
    mumbers.txt (The system cannot find the file specified)
        at java.io.FileInputStream.open(Native Method)
        at java.io.FileInputStream.<init>(Unknown Source)
        at java.util.Scanner.<init>(Unknown Source)
        at A.main(A.java:14)
```

Because file mumbers.txt does not exist, it cannot be opened for input processing. Therefore, the Scanner creation at line 14 of A.java cannot complete successfully. Under such circumstances, Java throws an exception of type java.io.FileNotFound-Exception, where FileNotFoundException is a subclass of IOException.

When an exception is thrown and not handled, Java generates a message to the standard error stream indicating where the exception occurred. When examining an exception message, it is sometimes easier to start with the last line of the message and work toward the first message line. The last line indicates the start of the process that caused the throwing of the exception.

The last message line in our example indicates that the exception was generated when executing line 14 of A.java. That line defines a Scanner variable fileIn. In reading the other message lines we see that in creating the Scanner, a FileInputStream was needed. The FileInputStream was to be the source of the extractions. This FileInputStream used a method open() that interacted with the file system. Because of the misspelled name, the file could not be opened. An exception reporting this problem was generated that eventually *propagated* to method main(). Because method main() did not handle the exception, the Java interpreter terminated the program.

For this example, the program did not end *gracefully*—a user does not want to read the jargon of an exception message. An alternative is to use Java's **try-catch** mechanism. With this mechanism, code that deals with situations in which exceptions can arise is put in a **try** block, where a **try** block is a statement block with the keyword **try** preceding it. If an exception arises in a **try** block, Java will transfer control to the appropriate *exception handler* to handle the problem.

The exception handlers are **catch** blocks and they immediately follow the **try** block. A **catch** block is a statement block that begins with the keyword **catch** followed by a single parameter that specifies the type of exception to be handled by the block. There is usually a **catch** handler for each type of exception that can occur within the **try** block. The **catch** blocks are executed only if an exception is generated.

try { *Action* } catch (*ExceptionType Parameter*) { *Handler* }

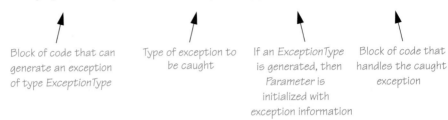

Block of code that can generate an exception of type *ExceptionType*

Type of exception to be caught

If an *ExceptionType* is generated, then *Parameter* is initialized with exception information

Block of code that handles the caught exception

If an exception is thrown in a **try** block, then the first associated **catch** block whose parameter type matches the generated exception is used. If no **catch** block parameter matches the exception, then the invocation process is unwound automatically to find the appropriate exception handler. The unwinding process is depicted in Figure 10.1.

If a **catch** block is executed, then its parameter is initialized with information regarding the specifics of the exception. If the **catch** block does not end the program, then after the **catch** block completes, program execution continues with the statement following the **try-catch** construct.

As an example, the following code segment from program B.java of Listing 10.2 catches the exception generated by an invalid filename.

```
// set up file stream for processing
File file = new File(s);
Scanner fileIn = null;

try {
    fileIn = new Scanner(file);
}
catch (FileNotFoundException e) {
    System.err.println(s + ": cannot be opened for reading");
    System.exit(0);
}
```

The code segment defines the Scanner variable fileIn before the **try-catch** blocks so that it is available after the code segment. Like other block definitions, the scope of the definitions in a **try** or **catch** block is limited to that block.

The **try** block attempts to assign variable fileIn, a reference to a Scanner associated with the file indicated by variable file. If the Scanner construction runs as planned (i.e., the file can be opened), then program execution continues with the statement that follows the **try-catch** construct (line 25). The result is an I/O behavior similar to A.java.

```
cmd: java B
Filename: numbers.txt

12 / 4 = 3
```

Figure 10.1   Exception-handling process.

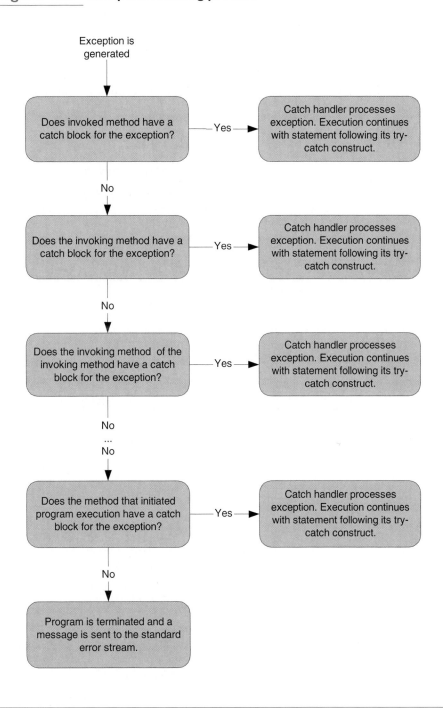

Listing 10.2 **B.java**

```
1.  import java.util.*;
2.  import java.io.*;
3.
4.  public class B {
5.      // main(): application entry point
6.      public static void main(String[] args) throws IOException {
7.          // get filename
8.          Scanner stdin = new Scanner(System.in);
9.          System.out.print("Filename: ");
10.         String s = stdin.nextLine();
11.
12.         // set up file stream for processing
13.         Scanner fileIn = null;
14.
15.         try {
16.             File file = new File(s);
17.             fileIn = new Scanner(file);
18.         }
19.         catch (FileNotFoundException e) {
20.             System.err.println(s + ": cannot be opened for reading");
21.             System.exit(0);
22.         }
23.
24.         // extract values and compute quotient
25.         int numerator = fileIn.nextInt();
26.         int denominator = fileIn.nextInt();
27.
28.         int quotient = numerator / denominator;
29.         System.out.println();
30.         System.out.println(numerator + " / " + denominator + " = "
31.                 + quotient);
32.
33.         return;
34.     }
35. }
```

If instead the `Scanner` creation results in the throwing of a `FileNotFoundExcep-`tion, then the program handles the exception with its **catch** block. Because it does not make sense for the program to proceed without a valid filename, the **catch** block generates an error message and exits the program.

```
cmd: java B
Filename: mumbers.txt
mumbers.txt: cannot be opened for reading
```

A question you may have asked yourself is "Why does method `main()` of `B.java` have a **throws** expression if it is catching the `FileNotFoundException`?" It does so because it is possible for constructor `Scanner(File)` to throw a general `IOException` if there is a file system error in the act of creating the `Scanner`.

To remove the necessity of having the **throws** expression as part of the method `main()` signature, a second **catch** block needs to be added. Program `C.java` of Listing

Listing 10.3 C.java

```
 1.  import java.util.*;
 2.  import java.io.*;
 3.
 4.  public class C {
 5.      // main(): application entry point
 6.      public static void main(String[] args) {
 7.          // get filename
 8.          Scanner stdin = new Scanner(System.in);
 9.          System.out.print("Filename: ");
10.          String s = stdin.nextLine();
11.
12.          // set up file stream for processing
13.          Scanner fileIn = null;
14.
15.          try {
16.              File file = new File(s);
17.              fileIn = new Scanner(file);
18.          }
19.          catch (FileNotFoundException e) {
20.              System.err.println(s + ": cannot be opened for reading");
21.              System.exit(0);
22.          }
23.          catch (IOException e) {
24.              System.err.println("File system error on "+ s);
25.              System.exit(0);
26.          }
27.
28.          // extract values and compute quotient
29.          int numerator = fileIn.nextInt();
30.          int denominator = fileIn.nextInt();
31.
32.          int quotient = numerator / denominator;
33.          System.out.println();
34.          System.out.println(numerator + " / " + denominator + " = "
35.              + quotient);
36.
37.          return;
38.      }
39.  }
```

10.3 has two **catch** blocks for its **try** block. The first **catch** block catches errant file-name entering; the other **catch** block catches general file system errors.

With its IOException handling ability, it *appears* that program C.java is well-engineered to handle user miscues. However, suppose we run the program using the file values.txt, where values.txt consists of the lines

```
12
b
```

A program run using this file generates the following I/O behavior.

```
cmd: java C
Filename: values.txt
Exception in thread "main" java.util.InputMismatchException
```

```
            java.util.Scanner.throwFor(Unknown Source)
        at java.util.Scanner.next(Unknown Source)
        at java.util.Scanner.nextInt(Unknown Source)
        at java.util.Scanner.nextInt(Unknown Source)
        at C.main(C.java:31)
```

The problem is one of input format—character 'b' is not the representation of an integer.

Suppose we run the program with the file **one.txt** that contains only the value 12. A program run using this file generates the following I/O behavior.

```
cmd: java C
Filename: one.txt
Exception in thread "main" java.util.NoSuchElementException
        java.util.Scanner.throwFor(Unknown Source)
        at java.util.Scanner.next(Unknown Source)
        at java.util.Scanner.nextInt(Unknown Source)
        at java.util.Scanner.nextInt(Unknown Source)
        at C.main(C.java:30)
```

The problem here is one of existence—there is no second integer to extract.

Suppose we run the program using the file **data.txt**, where **data.txt** contains the values 12 and 0. A program run using this file generates the following I/O behavior.

```
cmd: java C
Filename: data.txt
Exception in thread "main" java.lang.ArithmeticException: / by
    zero
        at C.main(C.java:32)
```

The problem is now one of illegal arithmetic—division is not defined for a denominator with value 0.

The *format, missing,* and *arithmetic exceptions* arising in the preceding cases are examples of *runtime exceptions*. The superclass for all runtime exceptions is **java.lang.RuntimeException**. Because runtime exceptions can occur throughout a program and because the cost of implementing handlers for them can exceed the expected benefit, Java makes it optional for a method to catch them or to specify that it throws them.

Because runtime exceptions need not be caught, they are also known as *unchecked exceptions*. All other exceptions are known as *checked exceptions*. The checked exceptions that a method may generate must be either caught by one of its exception handlers or listed in the **throws** expression of the method.

Program **D.java** of Listing 10.4 continues with our quotient-calculating example and handles the three possible runtime exceptions that **C.java** did not handle. For this particular problem, the handling of these runtime exceptions is appropriate because well-crafted programs ensure the validity of their input. Program **D.java**'s handling of the

---

Listing 10.4 D.java

```java
1.  import java.util.*;
2.  import java.io.*;
3.
4.  public class D{
5.      // main(): application entry point
6.      public static void main(String[] args) {
7.          // get filename
8.          Scanner stdin = new Scanner(System.in);
9.          System.out.print("Filename: ");
10.         String s = stdin.nextLine();
11.
12.         // set up file stream for processing
13.         Scanner fileIn = null;
14.
15.         try {
16.             File file = new File(s);
17.             fileIn = new Scanner(file);
18.         }
19.         catch (FileNotFoundException e) {
20.             System.err.println(s + ": cannot be opened for reading");
21.             System.exit(0);
22.         }
23.         catch (IOException e) {
24.             System.err.println("File system error on "+ s);
25.             System.exit(0);
26.         }
27.
28.         // extract values and compute quotient
29.         try {
30.             int numerator = fileIn.nextInt();
31.             int denominator = fileIn.nextInt();
32.
33.             int quotient = numerator / denominator;
34.             System.out.println();
35.             System.out.println(numerator + " / " + denominator + " = "
36.                 + quotient);
37.         }
38.         catch (InputMismatchException e) {
39.             System.err.println(s + ": contains nonnumeric inputs");
40.             System.exit(0);
41.         }
42.         catch (NoSuchElementException e) {
43.             System.err.println(s + ": doesn't contain two inputs");
44.             System.exit(0);
45.         }
46.         catch (ArithmeticException e) {
47.             System.err.println(s + ": unexpected 0 input value");
48.             System.exit(0);
49.         }
50.
51.         return;
52.     }
53. }
```

input validity exceptions is accomplished with an additional **try** block for the extracting of the inputs and computing the quotient.

```
// extract values and compute quotient
try {
   int numerator = fileIn.nextInt();
   int denominator = fileIn.nextInt();

   int quotient = numerator / denominator;
   System.out.println();
   System.out.println(numerator + " / " + denominator + " = "
         + quotient);
}
```

The first **catch** block handler processes an InputMismatchException, which occurs with malformed input.

```
catch (InputMismatchException e) {
   System.err.println(s + ": contains nonnumeric inputs");
   System.exit(0);
}
```

The handler displays an appropriate error message and terminates the program.

The second **catch** block handler processes a NoSuchElementException, which occurs because of missing input.

```
catch (NoSuchElementException e) {
   System.err.println(s + ": doesn't contain two inputs");
   System.exit(0);
}
```

This handler also displays an appropriate error message and terminates the program.

The third **catch** block handler processes an ArithmeticException. For the **try** block, this exception is generated only if a divide-by-0 is attempted.

```
catch (ArithmeticException e) {
   System.err.println(s + ": unexpected 0 input value");
   System.exit(0);
}
```

The following I/O behavior shows three runs of program D.java using the previously described files one.txt, data.txt. and values.txt.

```
cmd: java D
Filename: one.txt
one.txt: doesn't contain two inputs

cmd: java D
Filename: data.txt
data.txt: unexpected 0 input value

cmd: java D
Filename: values.txt
values.txt: contains nonnumeric inputs
```

At this point, we can claim that we have a well-engineered solution to the quotient problem.

10.2   FINALLY AND THE COMMAND TYPE

Although not strictly necessary, Java provides a syntax for a handler block that is *always* run after the **try** block or **catch** handler have completed their tasks. The special handler is introduced through the keyword **finally**.

A **finally** handler is used by program Type.java of Listing 10.5. The program displays to standard output the contents of the files whose names are given to the program as command-line parameters. Thus, the program mimics the operation of the Windows command type and the Unix/Linux command cat.

The program begins with a **for** loop that iterates once for each of the command-line parameters to the program. At the start of each iteration i, a Scanner variable fileIn is defined.

```
Scanner fileIn = null;
```

A **try** block then attempts to display the file stream whose name is specified by args[i].

```
try {
   fileIn = null;
   File file = new FileReader(args[i]);
   Scanner fileIn = new Scanner(file);
   // args[i] is a readable filename
   ...
}
catch (FileNotFoundException e) {
   // args[i] is not a valid filename
   System.err.println(args[i] + ": cannot be opened");
}
```

If the file stream cannot be opened, the **try** block throws a FileNotFoundException that is caught by the **catch** handler. The handler then displays an appropriate error message. If the file stream can be opened, then the contents of the file referenced by fileIn is displayed using a **while** loop that iterates while String variable s is non-**null**.

```
while (fileIn.hasNext()) {
   String s = fileIn.nextLine();
   System.out.println(s);
}
```

The second catch handler catches any general file system failures that may arise.

```
catch (IOException e) {
   System.err.println(args[i] + ": processing error");
}
```

Regardless whether the file is displayed successfully or an exception is thrown during its processing, a non-**null** file stream should be closed when either the **try** or **catch** block has completed. The **finally** block handles this activity. By using a **finally**

Listing 10.5 *Type.java*

```
1.   // Mimics operating system command type
2.
3.   import java.util.*;
4.   import java.io.*;
5.
6.   public class Type {
7.
8.       // main(): application entry point
9.       public static void main(String[] args) {
10.          // each command-line parameter is treated as a filename
11.          // whose contents are displayed to standard output
12.          for (int i = 0; i < args.length; ++i) {
13.              Scanner fileIn = null;
14.              // open input stream associated with i-th file parameter
15.              try {
16.                  fileIn = null;
17.                  File file = new File(args[i]);
18.                  fileIn = new Scanner(file);
19.                  // args[i] is a readable filename
20.
21.                  while (fileIn.hasNext()) {
22.                      String s = fileIn.nextLine();
23.                      System.out.println(s);
24.                  }
25.              }
26.              catch (FileNotFoundException e) {
27.                  // args[i] is not a valid filename
28.                  System.err.println(args[i] + ": cannot be opened");
29.              }
30.              catch (IOException e) {
31.                  System.err.println(args[i] + ": processing error");
32.              }
33.              finally {
34.                  if (fileIn != null) {
35.                      fileIn.close();
36.                  }
37.              }
38.          }
39.      }
40.  }
```

block we do not need to repeat the close() invocation in both of the inner **try** and **catch** blocks.

```
finally {
    if (fileIn != null) {
        fileIn.close();
    }
}
```

We next turn our attention to the throwing of exceptions to indicate a malformed request.

> ## *Why exception handle?*
>
> Although Java's exception-handling mechanism sometimes appears excessive to the beginning programmer, the mechanism truly is needed if programs are to follow the object-oriented programming paradigm. For example, suppose an error occurred within a method f() that was invoked by a method g() that was invoked by a method h(). Suppose further that to correct the error, method h() that initiated this invocation sequence must regain the flow of control. Without the exception-handling mechanism it would be extremely difficult to unwind the method invocations to enable corrective action to take place at the true problem source.

10.3 CREATING AND THROWING EXCEPTIONS

To generate an exception, a **throw** statement is performed

> **throw** *exception* ;

where *exception* specifies the necessary exception information. Our next example, class `BankAccount` makes use of this signaling mechanism. Class `BankAccount` throws `NegativeAmountException` exceptions, where class `NegativeAmountException` is a class that we also will define.

Class `BankAccount` maintains a bank account balance. Its constructors and methods throw a `NegativeAmountException` if there is an attempt to make the balance negative, deposit a negative amount, or withdraw a negative amount.

Class `BankAccount` supports two constructors—creating a new bank account with an empty balance and creating a new bank account with a positive balance.

> **public** `BankAccount()`
>> Creates a new bank account with an empty balance.
>
> **public** `BankAccount(`**int** `n)` **throws** `NegativeAmountException`
>> Attempts to create a new bank account with an initial balance of n. If n is negative, a `NegativeAmountException` is thrown.

The class uses instance variable `balance` to keep track of the current bank account balance.

> **private** `balance`
>> Represents the balance of this bank account.

Class `BankAccount` provides three instance methods to support balance access and manipulation.

> **public** **int** `getBalance()`
>> Returns the balance of this bank account.
>
> **public** **void** `addFunds(`**int** `n)` **throws** `NegativeAmountException`
>> Attempts to deposit a positive amount n into this bank account. If n is positive, the balance is increased by amount n. If n is negative, a `NegativeAmountException` is thrown.

```
public void removeFunds(int n) throws NegativeAmountException
```

Attempts to withdraw a positive amount n from this bank account. If n is negative, a NegativeAmountException is thrown. If n is positive and less than or equal to the current balance, then the balance is decreased by amount n; otherwise, a NegativeAmountException is thrown.

Class NegativeAmountException of Listing 10.6 is a specialized exception class for indicating abnormal bank account manipulation.

Listing 10.6 **NegativeAmountException.java**

```
1. // Represents an abnormal bank account event
2.
3. public class NegativeAmountException extends Exception {
4.     // NegativeAmountException(): creates exception with message s
5.     public NegativeAmountException(String s) {
6.         super(s);
7.     }
8. }
```

The behaviors wanted of a NegativeAmountException are just the normal exception behaviors. Therefore, the definition of this subclass needs only to define a specific constructor.

```
public NegativeAmountException(String s)
```

Creates a new NegativeAmountException with message s.

The definition of the NegativeAmountException specific constructor is straightforward. It invokes the constructor of its superclass Exception with s as the message for the new exception.

Listing 10.7 gives the definition of class BankAccount. With the existence of class NegativeAmountException, the BankAccount constructors and methods all have simple implementations. For example, the specific BankAccount constructor needs only to examine its parameter n to determine if a new bank account is to be created with balance n or whether an exception is being thrown.

```
// BankAccount(): specific constructor for a new balance n
public BankAccount(int n) throws NegativeAmountException {
    if (n >= 0) {
        balance = n;
    }
    else {
        throw new NegativeAmountException("Bad balance");
    }
}
```

If the constructor is given a negative value for n, then **throw** statement

```
throw new NegativeAmountException("Bad balance");
```

is executed. This **throw** statement generates a new NegativeAmountException. Associated with the exception is the message "Bad Balance".

Listing 10.7 **BankAccount.java**

```java
1.  // Represents a bank account balance
2.
3.  public class BankAccount {
4.      // instance variable
5.      int balance;
6.
7.      // BankAccount(): default constructor for a new empty balance
8.      public BankAccount() {
9.          balance = 0;
10.     }
11.
12.     // BankAccount(): specific constructor for a new balance n
13.     public BankAccount(int n) throws NegativeAmountException {
14.         if (n >= 0) {
15.             balance = n;
16.         }
17.         else {
18.             throw new NegativeAmountException("Bad balance");
19.         }
20.     }
21.
22.     // getBalance(): return the current balance
23.     public int getBalance() {
24.             return balance;
25.     }
26.
27.     // addFunds(): deposit amount n
28.     public void addFunds(int n) throws NegativeAmountException {
29.         if (n >= 0) {
30.             balance += n;
31.         }
32.         else {
33.             throw new NegativeAmountException("Bad deposit");
34.         }
35.     }
36.
37.     // removeFunds(): withdraw amount n
38.     public void removeFunds(int n) throws NegativeAmountException {
39.         if (n < 0) {
40.             throw new NegativeAmountException("Bad withdrawal");
41.         }
42.         else if (balance < n) {
43.             throw new NegativeAmountException("Overdrawn");
44.         }
45.         else {
46.             balance -= n;
47.         }
48.     }
49. }
```

Similarly, method addFunds() needs only to examine its parameter n to determine
if a deposit should be entered or whether an exception should be thrown.

```java
// addFunds(): deposit amount n
public void addFunds(int n) throws NegativeAmountException {
```

```
    if (n >= 0) {
       balance += n;
    }
    else {
       throw new NegativeAmountException("Bad deposit");
    }
}
```

If the deposit is negative, then statement

```
throw new NegativeAmountException("Bad deposit");
```

is executed. This **throw** statement generates a new NegativeAmountException with message "Bad deposit".

Method removeFunds() processes a withdrawal. There are two ways a withdrawal can be improper: the withdrawal amount is negative or the withdrawal amount makes the balance negative.

```
// removeFunds(): withdraw amount n
public void removeFunds(int n) throws NegativeAmountException {
    if (n < 0) {
       throw new NegativeAmountException("Bad withdrawal");
    }
    else if (balance < n) {
       throw new NegativeAmountException("Overdrawn");
    }
    else {
       balance -= n;
    }
}
```

A negative withdrawal amount is handled by throwing an exception with message "Bad withdrawal".

```
throw new NegativeAmountException("Bad withdrawal");
```

And a withdrawal that would leave the balance negative is handled by throwing an exception with message "Bad balance".

```
throw new NegativeAmountException("Overdrawn");
```

A demonstration of classes BankAccount and NegativeAmountException is given in program Deposits.java of Listing 10.8. The program creates a new BankAccount and then processes two deposit requests. Runs of the program are shown in Figure 10.2. The second run shows what happens if a negative deposit is made. The self-exercises consider adding a **try-catch** block construct to Deposits.java to handle NegativeAmountException exceptions.

This discussion ends our introduction to exceptions. We revisit exception handling in Chapter 12. That chapter introduces thread programming. In Java, threads make extensive use of exceptions to control program flow.

Listing 10.8 Deposits.java

```
1.  // Demonstrates use of BankAccount and NegativeAmountException
2.
3.  import java.util.*;
4.
5.  public class Deposits {
6.     // main(): application entry point
7.     public static void main(String[] args)
8.           throws NegativeAmountException {
9.        Scanner stdin = new Scanner(System.in);
10.
11.       BankAccount savings = new BankAccount();
12.
13.       System.out.print("\nEnter first deposit: ");
14.       int deposit = stdin.nextInt();
15.       savings.addFunds(deposit);
16.
17.       System.out.print("\nEnter second deposit: ");
18.       deposit = stdin.nextInt();
19.       savings.addFunds(deposit);
20.
21.       System.out.println("\nClosing balance: "
22.          + savings.getBalance());
23.    }
24. }
```

Figure 10.2 **Sample Deposits.java runs.**

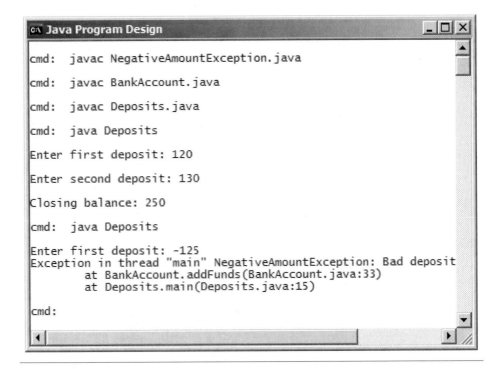

10.4 REVIEW

- An exception is an abnormal event that occurs during program execution. If an exception occurs and an exception handler code segment is in effect for that exception, then flow of control is transferred to the handler. If an exception occurs and there is no handler for it, the program terminates.

- Java requires a **throws** expression for any method that does not handle the exceptions it may generate. If the invoking method does not handle the exception, then an exception-unwinding process continues with the method that did the invoking of the invoking method, and so on. If no method is found in the unwinding process to handle the exception, then the program terminates.

- When an exception is thrown and not handled, Java generates a message to the standard error stream indicating where the exception occurred.

- Programs should end gracefully. Users should not need to read the jargon of an exception message.

- Code that deals with situations in which exceptions can arise can be put in a **try** block. Following the **try** block should be a **catch** exception handler block for each type of exception that can occur within the **try** block.

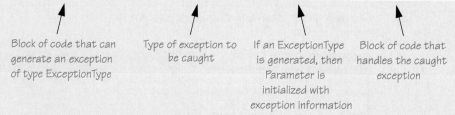

- If an exception is thrown in a **try** block, then the first associated **catch** block whose parameter type matches the generated exception is used. If no **catch** block parameter matches the exception, then the invocation process is unwound automatically to find the appropriate exception handler.

- If a **catch** block is executed, then its parameter is initialized with information regarding the specifics of the exception. If the **catch** block does not end the program, then after the **catch** block completes, program execution continues with the statement following the **try-catch** construct.

- The superclass for all runtime exceptions is `java.lang.RuntimeException`. Because runtime exceptions can occur throughout a program and because the cost of implementing handlers for them typically exceeds the expected benefit, Java makes it optional for a method to catch them or to specify that it throws them.

- Format and arithmetic exceptions are examples of runtime exceptions.

- Runtime exceptions are also known as unchecked exceptions. All other exceptions are known as checked exceptions. The checked exceptions that a method may generate must be either caught by one of its exception handlers or listed in the **throws** expression of the method.

■ Java provides a syntax for a handler block that is always run after the **try** block or **catch** handler have completed their tasks. The special handler is introduced through the keyword **finally**.

<table>
<tr><td>**10.5**</td><td>**SELF-TEST**</td></tr>
</table>

S10.1 Identify where exceptions can be generated in program AverageFive.java of Listing 2.11.

S10.2 Reimplement FileAverage.java of Listing 6.6 so that its method main() does not have a **throws** expression.

S10.3 What is the purpose of a **throws** clause?

S10.4 What is an unchecked exception?

S10.5 Modify Deposits.java to catch NegativeAmountException exceptions.

<table>
<tr><td>**10.6**</td><td>**EXERCISES**</td></tr>
</table>

10.1   What is an exception? How do exceptions come about?

10.2   What is a **try** block?

10.3   What is a **catch** block?

10.4   What is a **finally** block?

10.5   What is a runtime exception?

10.6   What happens if an unchecked exception is not caught?

10.7   What happens if a checked exception is not caught?

10.8   Argue why using **if** statements to determine data validity is insufficient in robust programming.

10.9   Reimplement class ColoredTriangle of Listing 5.7 to make proper use of exceptions in its implementation.

10.10 Implement a program whose method main() does not have a **throws** expression that accomplishes the following task. The program should prompt its user for a file-name *s* and a number of values *n*. The program should then extract *n* input lines from *s*. Finally, it should echo back to standard output copies of the *n* input lines.

10.7   PROGRAMMING PROJECT — A SECOND LOOK

Reimplement the class DataSet of Listing 6.8 to make proper use of exceptions in its implementation. In the resulting class any remaining error message displays should be initiated by an exception handler.

> The objective of this case study is to practice exception handling and software modification

You should also develop test sets that demonstrate the exception handling abilities of your implementations. Document why your exception handling is sufficient for robust programming.

10.8   SELF-TEST ANSWERS

S10.1 Each of the five stdin.nextInt() invocations can throw either an InputMismatchException or a NoSuchElementException depending on whether the user respectively mis-enters the numbers or signals end-of-file.

S10.2 The following definition has the desired property.

```java
import java.util.*;
import java.io.*;

public class FileAverage {
    // main(): application entry point
    public static void main(String[] args) {
        // set up standard input stream
        Scanner stdin = new Scanner(System.in);

        // determine filename
        System.out.print("Filename: ");
        String filename = stdin.nextLine();

        // get file stream for text processing
        Scanner fileIn = null;
        try {
            File file = new File(filename);
            fileIn = new Scanner(file);
        }
        catch (FileNotFoundException e) {
            System.err.println(filename + ": cannot be opened");
            System.exit(0);
        }
        catch (IOException e) {
            System.err.println("File system error on "
                + filename);
            System.exit(0);
        }

        // initially no values have been processed
        int valuesProcessed = 0;
        double valueSum = 0;
```

```
                // process values one by one
                while (fileIn.hasNextDouble()) {
                    // get the input value
                    double value = fileIn.nextDouble();
                    // add value to running total
                    valueSum += value;
                    // processed another total
                    ++valuesProcessed;
                }

                // ready to compute average
                if (valuesProcessed > 0) {
                    double average = valueSum / valuesProcessed;
                    System.out.println("Average file data value: "
                            + average);
                }
                else {
                    System.err.println(filename
                            + ": no values to average");
                }
            }
        }
```

S10.3 A **throws** clause of a method specifies the uncaught exceptions that the method may generate—either directly or through invocation.

S10.4 Runtime exceptions are known as unchecked exceptions. The adjective unchecked refers to the fact that a method need not catch the exception or list its **throws** expression. Java does not require their handling because such exceptions can occur throughout a program and because the cost of implementing handlers for them typically exceeds the expected benefit.

S10.5 The following version of program `Deposits.java` catches abnormal bank account events.

```
// Demonstrates BankAccount & NegativeAmountException

import java.util.*;

public class Deposits {
    // main(): application entry point
    public static void main(String[] args) {
        Scanner stdin = new Scanner(System.in);

        BankAccount savings = new BankAccount();

        System.out.print("\nEnter first deposit: ");
        int deposit = stdin.nextInt();

        try {
            savings.addFunds(deposit);
        }
        catch (NegativeAmountException e) {
            System.err.println("Bad deposit: " + deposit);
            System.exit(deposit);
```

```
        }

        System.out.print("\nEnter second deposit: ");
        deposit = stdin.nextInt();

        try {
            savings.addFunds(deposit);
        }
        catch (NegativeAmountException e) {
            System.err.println("Bad deposit: " + deposit);
            System.exit(deposit);
        }

        System.out.println("\nClosing balance: "
            + savings.getBalance());
    }
}
```

RECURSIVE PROBLEM SOLVING

In this chapter we explore an elegant and powerful approach to problem solving—recursive problem solving. Recursive problem solving involves breaking a problem into identical, but smaller or simpler problem instances and solving those to obtain a solution to the original problem. Most programming languages, including Java, support the use of recursion to solve problems.

OBJECTIVES

- Explain the concept of a recursive definition.
- Learn to think recursively.
  - Develop an understanding and appreciation of recursive problem solving.
  - Explain the basic components of a recursive algorithm.
  - Learn to use recursion in Java to solve problems.
  - Develop an appreciation of the trade-offs between recursion and iteration.

11.1 RECURSIVE METHODS

A concise and elegant way to define a term or concept is to use a recursive definition. A recursive definition defines something in terms of itself. For example, a recursive definition of the term "descendants" is "A person's descendants are the person's children and all their descendants." Similarly, a concise and elegant method for solving a large class of problems is to use a recursive algorithm. A recursive algorithm is an algorithm that invokes or calls itself with smaller or simpler problem instances. The solution to the original problem is then obtained by applying simple operations to the solution of the smaller or simpler problem instances.

Java supports the use of recursion to solve problems. *Recursion* is the ability of a method to call itself. To illustrate what we mean by recursion and its use, let's reconsider the implementation of the factorial function. Our earlier definition of factorial

$$n! = \begin{cases} 1 & \text{if } n = 0 \\ n \times (n-1) \times ..\times 1 & \text{if } n \geq 1 \end{cases}$$

is not mathematically precise because we use an ellipsis (…). The ellipsis tells readers to use their intuition to recognize the pattern. A formal definition of factorial removes any ambiguity.

$$n! = \begin{cases} 1 & \text{if } n = 0 \\ n \times (n-1)! & \text{if } n > 0 \end{cases}$$

In the preceding formal definition, we see that factorial is defined in terms of itself. That is, if $n > 0$, then $n!$ is $n \times (n-1)!$. You should be able to verify that the two definitions are equivalent.

Using recursion, we can write a short and simple method that computes factorials. The method is

```java
public static int factorial(int n) {
    if (n == 0) {
        return 1;
    }
    else {
        return n * factorial(n-1);
    }
}
```

This method mirrors the mathematical definition of factorial. If the value of n is 0, the value 1 is returned. If the value of n is not equal to 0, the product of n and `factorial(n-1)` is returned.

To understand how recursion works, it is useful to visualize what is happening when a method calls itself. One way to do so is to picture the activation records that are created for each recursive call. Let's assume that we have the following method `main()` invoking `factorial()`

```java
public static void main(String[] args) throws IOException {
    Scanner stdin = new Scanner(System.in);
```

```
        System.out.print("Enter a positive integer: ");
        int n = stdin.nextInt();
        System.out.println(n + "! = " + factorial(n));
    }
```

In this initial invocation of factorial(), n is 3, so the **else** part

> **return** n * factorial(n-1);

of the **if** statement is executed. The activation records are

Activation records

```
System.out.println(n + "! + " + factorial(n));
```

invoke factorial(3)

n = 3   factorial(3) = 3 * factorial(2)

The **else** part invokes factorial() again, this time with an actual parameter with value 2. The activation records are

Activation records

```
System.out.println(n + "! + " + factorial(n));
```

invoke factorial(3)

n = 3   factorial(3) = 3 * factorial(2)

invoke factorial(2)

n = 2   factorial(2) = 2 * factorial(1)

In this recursive invocation of factorial(), n is 2, so the **else** part

> **return** n * factorial(n-1);

of the **if** statement is executed with an actual parameter with value 1. As shown in Figure 11.1, the recursive invocation process continues until n equals 0. At this point, the **if** test expression evaluates to true, and

> **return** 1;

is executed. The statement causes the recursion to start *unwinding* (i.e., no more recursive calls).

As the recursion unwinds, values are returned to the calling invocation of the method. In effect, the return value is substituted for the call. The process of the recursion unwinding is illustrated in Figure 11.2. Using the returned value, the factorial of the n (for this invocation) is computed and returned to the next level. This process continues until the call to factorial() from main() returns to main() with the value of 3! which is 6.

Figure 11.1   **Activation records for recursive invocations of factorial.**

Activation records

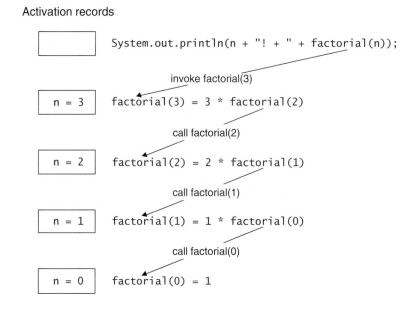

Figure 11.2   **Unwinding the recursive invocations of factorial.**

Activation records

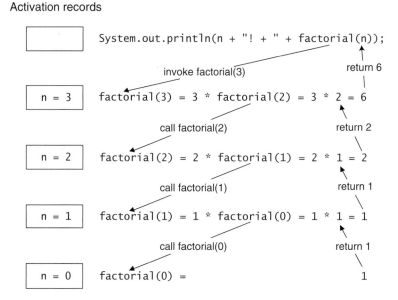

When the first call to `factorial()` returns to `main()`, the insertion statement produces the following output:

```
3! = 6
```

One of the nice things about recursion is that it is a succinct way of expressing certain mathematical formulas, and the corresponding Java implementation is equally short. A recursive method generally has two parts:

- A termination part that stops the recursion. This is called the base case. The base case should have a simple or trivial solution.

- One or more recursive calls. This is called the recursive case. The recursive case calls the same method but with simpler or smaller arguments.

In the factorial code, the recursive call and the termination part were the two action parts of the **if-else** statement.

$$
\left. \begin{array}{l}
\textbf{if } (\text{n} == 0) \\
\qquad \textbf{return } 1;
\end{array} \right\} \textit{Base case}
$$

$$
\textit{Recursive case} \left\{ \begin{array}{l}
\textbf{else} \\
\qquad \textbf{return } \text{n} * \text{factorial}(\text{n} - 1);
\end{array} \right.
$$

Let's now consider the development of a recursive implementation of method `power()` to compute x^n, where x and n are both integers.

We know that x^0 is 1 for all x. This fact will be the base case of our recursive method. We also know that $x^n = x \times x^{n-1}$ when $n > 0$, which will be the recursive part. Observe that because n is getting smaller, the recursion is sure to terminate. Writing the recursive version of the power method is simple.

```java
public static int power(int x, int n) {
    if (n == 0) {
        return 1;
    }
    else {
        return x * power(x, n-1);
    }
}
```

11.1.1   FIBONACCI NUMBERS AND SQUARES

Our final example of simple recursion considers the Fibonacci sequence. We previously saw this number sequence in the self-test section of Chapter 6, when we developed iterative code to display the first *n* Fibonacci numbers. The sequence starts with the following numbers: 1, 1, 2, 3, 5, 8, 13, 21, 34, 55, 89, and 144. After the initial two 1s, each number in the sequence is the sum of the two previous numbers. For example, $1 + 1 = 2$, $1 + 2 = 3$, $2 + 3 = 5$, $3 + 5 = 8$, and so on.

Recursive algorithm design

A recursive algorithm always consists of at least two parts.
- A *base case* that deals with the simplest instance of the problem.
- A *recursive case* that deals with a simpler or smaller version of the problem.

There must always be one base case and one recursive case, but there can be more.

The Fibonacci numbers are interesting scientifically and socially because they model many things in nature. For example, they model the reproductive behavior of bees, the number of branches in a tree, and the number of petals on a flower (e.g., buttercups have 5 petals; some asters have 21 petals; and there are daisies with 34, 55, and 89 petals).

The first known investigation into the Fibonacci sequence was by the Italian mathematician Leonardo Pisano in 1202. Pisano was investigating how fast rabbits could breed under idealized circumstances. He assumed that a pair of male and female rabbits always breed and produce another pair of male and female rabbits. He also assumed that a rabbit becomes sexually mature after one month, and that the gestation period is also one month. With these assumptions, a pair of rabbits produces one new pair every month from its second month on. Pisano wanted to know the answer to the question how many rabbits would there be after one year?

We can work out a solution by hand. At the end of the first month, there is still only one pair. At the end of the second month, another pair is born so there are now two pairs. At the end of the third month, the original pair produces another pair, and the second pair has just matured, so there are only three pairs. At the end of the fourth month, the original pair has produced another pair and so has the second pair, so now there are five pairs. At the end of the fifth month, there will be eight pairs. In the sixth month, there will be 13 pairs. The sequence being generated is

   1, 1, 2, 3, 5, 8, 13, 21, 34, ...

That is, the number of pairs for a month is the sum of the number of pairs in the two previous months. Therefore, at the end of one year, there will be 144 pairs of rabbits.

The mathematical definition of the nth Fibonacci number f_n is given by the recurrence

$$f_n = \begin{cases} f_n = 1 & \text{if } n = 1 \\ f_n = 1 & \text{if } n = 2 \\ f_n = f_{n-1} + f_{n-2} & \text{if } n > 2 \end{cases}$$

The definition is more complicated than our previous recursive methods, but we can still use the same strategy. The pattern for our previous recursive methods has been

```
if ( termination code satisfied ) {
    return value;
}
else {
    make simpler recursive call;
}
```

and this pattern also works for computing Fibonacci numbers. The code for the method is

```
public static int fibonacci(int n) {
```

```
    if (n <= 2) {
        return 1;
    }
    else {
        return fibonacci(n-1) + fibonacci(n-2);
    }
}
```

The main difference between the current code and the code for the previous recursive methods is that the current code makes two recursive calls. We know that both of these recursive calls eventually unwind because every recursive call has a parameter that is less than the parameter of the invocation that spawned the call. Figure 11.3 depicts the recursive calls made by the method when computing f_5.

Figure 11.3 **Computation of f_5.**

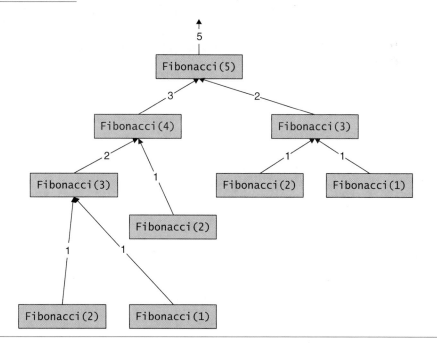

Fibonacci numbers arise in the rendering of some geometric art. Consider the picture in Figure 11.4(a). The squares have a Fibonacci relationship, which is made more explicit in the picture in Figure 11.4(b). The pictures are drawn by starting with two squares of size 1, one drawn to left of the other. Below these two squares, a square is drawn whose size is the sum of the two previously drawn squares (i.e., a square of size 2). Each succeeding square's size is the sum of the sizes of the two most previously drawn squares and its position is related in a counterclockwise manner to the square most previously drawn. Development of a program FibonacciSquares.java to produce a Fibonacci square picture is left to the exercises.

Figure 11.4 Fibonacci art.

(a) Geometric art.

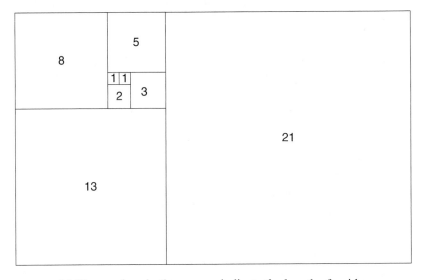

(b) The numbers in the squares indicate the length of a side.

Infinite recursion

A common programming error when using recursion is to not stop making recursive calls. The program will continue to recurse until it runs out of memory. Be sure that your recursive calls are made with simpler or smaller subproblems, and that your algorithm has a base case that terminates the recursion.

CASE STUDY — RECURSIVE BINARY SEARCH

We have all looked up a name in the telephone directory or a word in the dictionary. The fact that the directory or dictionary entries are in sorted order helps us find the number or word quickly. One fast strategy for finding an entry in a sorted list is called binary search. The basic idea is as follows. First, you compare the entry to the middle element of the list. If the entry matches the mid-

> The objective of this case study is to demonstrate the development of a recursive algorithm to solve a common problem—searching for an entry in a list.

dle element, the desired entry has been located and the search is over. If the entry doesn't match, then if the entry is in the list it must be either to the left or right of the middle element. The correct sublist can be searched using the same strategy. This binary search strategy is illustrated by the diagram in Figure 11.5.

Figure 11.5   **Searching a sorted list.**

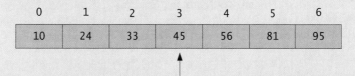

Compare entry to this element. If the entry matches, the search is successful. If the entry is less than 45, then the entry, if it is in the list, must be to the left in elements 0-2. If the entry is greater than 45, then the entry, if it is in the list, must be to the right in elements 4-6.

Consider searching for the number 24 in the list in Figure 11.5. The first comparison is with the middle element containing the value 45. Since $24 \neq 45$ and $24 < 45$, we know that we should search the sublist to the left of element 3. We can apply the same search technique to the sublist consisting of elements 0 through 2. Again, we pick the middle element—element 1 in this case. The entry, 24, is equal to the value in `element[1]` so the search is successful.

The preceding search strategy can be implemented elegantly using recursion. The base case occurs when the entry is located or the sublist to search is empty. The previous paragraph discussed the case where the entry is located. Now we consider the case where the entry is not found. For example, if we searched the list in Figure 11.5 for 83, we would search the right sublist consisting of elements 4 through 6. Because 83 is greater than 81, we next search the sublist consisting of element 6, which also fails. There is no sublist to the left of element 6, so the search fails.

The recursive case is to search the appropriate sublist. Because a sublist is smaller than the size of the list, the condition that the recursive call has simpler or smaller sub-problem is satisfied.

To illustrate recursive binary search, we develop a class for searching a list of names and telephone numbers for a name. If the name is found, we print out the associated telephone number.

The following class defines an address book entry.

```java
public class AddressEntry {
    private String personName;
    private String telephoneNumber;
    // default constructor
    public AddressEntry(String name, String number) {
        personName = name;
        telephoneNumber = number;
    }
    public String getName() {
        return personName;
    }
    public String getNumber() {
        return telephoneNumber;
    }
    public void setName(String Name) {
        personName = Name;
    }
    public void setTelephoneNumber(String number) {
        telephoneNumber = number;
    }
}
```

The class declaration follows our standard pattern for implementing a data abstraction. The class contains the standard inspector and mutator methods.

ANALYSIS AND DESIGN

We are now ready to begin the design of the recursive binary search class. Our class will not contain any instance variables. The job of this class is to provide a method for searching an array of `AddressEntry` objects when a name is provided. We will call the array an address book.

Our first step is to develop the interface to the method that initiates a search for a name in an address book. This step involves determining what arguments the method should accept and what type the method should return. Because the method is to locate the address entry for a person, it is appropriate that the search method return an `AddressEntry`. The method's parameters are the address book to search and the name of the person to look up. Thus, an appropriate interface to the search function is

```java
public static AddressEntry recSearch(AddressEntry[]
  addressBook, String name)
```

We are now ready to design the interface to the recursive method that will perform the search and the algorithm to perform the search. The recursive method also returns an `AddressEntry`. The recursive method will also take as parameters the address book to search and the name to look up. In addition to those two parameters, the method will accept two integer parameters that indicate the sublist of the address book to search. Successive recursive calls to the method will search shorter and shorter sublists.

```
private static AddressEntry recSearch(AddressEntry[]
  addressBook, String name, int first, int last)
```

As we noted earlier, the base case of the algorithm consists of two subcases—the element is located and the list to search has length zero. In both cases, the recursion terminates. The recursive case also consists two subcases—the element, if it exists, is in the left half of the list or it is in the right half of the list. The algorithm then can be stated as follows:

Step 1. If the list has no elements
return null

Step 2. Compute the midpoint of the list

Step 3. If the name matches the name in the midpoint element
return the midpoint element

Step 4. If the name is lexically less than the name in the midpoint element
recursively search the sublist to the left of the midpoint

Step 5. Else the name is lexically greater than the name in the midpoint element
recursively and search the sublist to the right of the midpoint

Now that we have the interface and the high-level algorithm, the implementation will be easy.

IMPLEMENTATION

Listing 11.1 contains the implementation of method `recSearch()`. The implementation of the public method `recSearch()` simply calls the private method with the length of the list.

```
public static AddressEntry recSearch(
  AddressEntry[] addressBook, String name) {
    return recSearch(addressBook, name, 0,
      addressBook.length-1);
}
```

The private method `recSearch()` does all the work. The first **if** statement decides whether the sublist to search is empty. If the list is empty, the method returns null. Otherwise, the midpoint of the sublist is computed and the name is compared to the name at the midpoint. If the names are the same, the method returns the address book entry. If the names are not the same, the code determines which side of the midpoint to search recursively. To determine the sublist to search `recSearch()` uses `String` method `compareToIgnoreCase()`. This method compares two strings, but ignores whether their letters are upper- or lowercase. Method `compareToIgnoreCase()` returns a negative if the string parameter is lexically greater than this string, zero if the string argument is equal to this string, and a positive if the string argument is less than this string.

TESTING

Method `recSearch()` is simple and elegant, but its operation is subtle. We should carefully test our implementation. To do so, we need to develop a set of cases to thoroughly test the code. After some consideration, we come up with the following situations that should be tested.

Listing 11.1 Recursive binary search method

```
1.  public static AddressEntry recSearch(AddressEntry[] addressBook,
2.   String name) {
3.      return recSearch(addressBook, name, 0, addressBook.length-1);
4.  }
5.
6.  private static AddressEntry recSearch(AddressEntry[] addressBook,
7.   String name, int first, int last) {
8.      // base case: if the array section is empty, not found
9.      if (first > last)
10.        return null;
11.     else {
12.        int mid = (first + last) / 2;
13.        // if we found the value, we're done
14.        if (name.equalsIgnoreCase(addressBook[mid].getName()))
15.           return addressBook[mid];
16.        else if (name.compareToIgnoreCase(
17.          addressBook[mid].getName()) < 0) {
18.             // if value is there at all, it's in the left half
19.             return recSearch(addressBook, name, first, mid-1);
20.        }
21.         else { // array[mid] < value
22.             // if value is there at all, it's in the right half
23.             return recSearch(addressBook, name, mid+1, last);
24.        }
25.     }
26. }
```

1. Locate a name that is in the first element of the address book.
2. Locate a name that is in the last element of the address book.
3. Attempt to locate a name that is not in the address book.
4. Locate a name that is in the middle of the address book.

Listing 11.2 gives the corresponding test harness. The first part of the code (lines 3–12) creates and initializes a list to search. The elements of the list are in sorted order because this is required by the binary search algorithm. The next parts of the code test various situations by searching for various names. The test harness searches for a name that is at the beginning of the list, then it searches for a name in the middle, and then a name at the end of the list. The final test makes sure the code works properly when searching for a name that is not in the address book.

The listed created in the test harness contains eight elements. To thoroughly test the code, a test should be created where a list containing an odd number of elements is created. Creating this additional test case is left to the exercises.

The binary search algorithm is very efficient. The efficiency of the search algorithm is represented by the binary tree in Figure 11.6. This tree is a full binary tree because no more nodes can be added without increasing the number of levels. If we think of each node in the tree as representing a comparison, we can use this tree to reason about the efficiency of binary search. At the top of the tree, a comparison divides the tree in half and similarly for subsequent levels until either the node is found or a leaf of the tree is reached. Hence the number of levels or height of the tree is the worst-case number of comparisons needed to find an entry in a sorted list. We can see from Figure 11.6 that a

Listing 11.2 Recursive binary search test harness

```
1.  public static void main(String[] args) {
2.      // list must be in sorted order
3.      AddressEntry addressBook[] = {
4.          new AddressEntry("Audrey", "434-555-1215"),
5.          new AddressEntry("Emily" , "434-555-1216"),
6.          new AddressEntry("Jack"  , "434-555-1217"),
7.          new AddressEntry("Jim"   , "434-555-2566"),
8.          new AddressEntry("John"  , "434-555-2222"),
9.          new AddressEntry("Lisa"  , "434-555-3415"),
10.         new AddressEntry("Tom"   , "630-555-2121"),
11.         new AddressEntry("Zach"  , "434-555-1218")
12.     };
13.     AddressEntry p;
14.     // first element
15.     p = recSearch(addressBook, "Audrey");
16.     if (p != null) {
17.         System.out.println("Audrey's telephone number is " +
18.             p.getNumber());
19.     }
20.     else {
21.         System.out.println("No entry for Audrey");
22.     }
23.     // middle element
24.     p = recSearch(addressBook, "Jim");
25.     if (p != null) {
26.         System.out.println("Jim's telephone number is " +
27.             p.getNumber());
28.     }
29.      else {
30.         System.out.println("No entry for Jim");
31.     }
32.     // last element
33.     p = recSearch(addressBook, "Zach");
34.     if (p != null) {
35.         System.out.println("Zach's telephone number is " +
36.             p.getNumber());
37.     }
38.     else {
39.         System.out.println("No entry for Zach");
40.     }
41.     // non existent entry
42.     p = recSearch(addressBook, "Frank");
43.     if (p != null) {
44.         System.out.println("Frank's telephone number is " +
45.             p.getNumber());
46.     }
47.     else {
48.         System.out.println("No entry for Frank");
49.     }
50. }
```

binary tree with 31 nodes has a height of 5. Indeed, a binary tree that contains *n* nodes has a height of $\log_2 (n + 1)$. For example, this says that we can search a sorted list with up to 1 billion numbers with at most 30 comparisons.

Figure 11.6 **Efficiency of the binary search algorithm.**

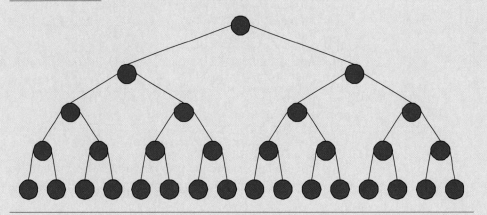

11.3	**METHOD MERGESORT()**

Although method `selectionSort()` described in Chapter 8 has reasonable performance characteristics, we can do better. In particular, time-critical client applications often use the `mergeSort()` or `quickSort()` methods. In this section, we discuss the `mergeSort()` method in `ArrayTools.java`. In the exercises, we consider how to develop `quickSort()`.

Method `mergeSort()` is a recursive sort that conceptually divides its list of n elements to be sorted into two sublists of size $n/2$. If a sublist contains more than one element, the sublist is sorted by a recursive call to `mergeSort()`. After the two sublists of size $n/2$ are sorted, they are merged together to produce a single sorted list of size n. This type of strategy is known as a *divide-and-conquer* strategy—the problem is divided into subproblems of lesser complexity and the solutions of the subproblems are used to produced the overall solution. The running time of method `mergeSort()` is proportional to $n\log n$. This performance is sometimes known as *linearithmic* performance.[†]

Suppose we are to again sort the following array:

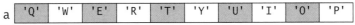

If we first sort the left and right sublists, the array would then look like

We are now left with the simpler task of merging the two sublists to produce the sorted array

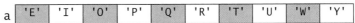

For a client to invoke `mergeSort()` to sort array `a`, the invocation would be

`mergeSort(a);`

In our implementation of `mergeSort()`, this invocation will in turn cause the invocation

`mergeSort(a, 0, a.length - 1);`

to occur. As you can tell, our implementation overloads the name `mergeSort`. We do so, for client ease—a client should not need to worry about the mechanics of the sort. It is the responsibility of the API programmer to use the supplied information to accomplish the task at hand. In this case, the API translates the request to sort array `a` into the specific request of sorting from its first element through its last element; that is, elements `a[0]` through `a[9]`, where 9 equals `a.length - 1`.

[†]   Linearithmic is a portmanteau of linear and logarithm coined by Robert Sedgwick.

Because this invocation will sort the array, there is nothing left for that method to do. Thus, its definition is straightforward.

```
public static void mergeSort(char[] a) {
    mergeSort(a, 0, a.length - 1);
}
```

We now consider the other method `mergeSort()`, the method that does the actual sorting. This method has three parameters: the array `a` to be sorted and indices `left` and `right` that demark the portion of `a` to be sorted.

The method must first determine whether the sorting request involves any true work; i.e., are there are least two elements to consider. This determination can be made by testing whether `left < right`. If so, then there are at least two elements to consider.

```
if (left < right) {
    // there are multiple elements to sort.

        ...

}
```

If there are multiple elements to consider, we first recursively sort the left and right sublists. To do so, we calculate the middle index `mid` in the range `left ... right`. Index `mid` has the value `(left + right) / 2`. Subrange `left ... mid` are the indices of the left sublist and subrange `mid + 1 ... right` are the indices of the right sublist.

```
// first, recursively sort the left and right sublists
int mid = (left + right) / 2;
mergeSort(a, left, mid);
mergeSort(a, mid+1, right);
```

Although it is possible to merge the two sublists in place, it is far simpler to merge the sublists into another array `temp` and then copy array `temp` into a. Array `temp` needs to be only big enough to store the portion of `a` that we are sorting. Therefore, `temp` needs to be able to store only `right - left + 1` elements.

```
// next, merge the sorted sublists into array temp
char[] temp = new char[right - left + 1];
```

Our code must keep track of which elements are left to consider in the left and right sublists. We will use index `j` to indicate the location of the smallest-valued element from the left sublist to be copied and index `k` to indicate the location of the smallest-valued element from the right sublist to be copied.

```
int j = left;       // index of left sublist smallest element
int k = mid + 1;    // index of right sublist smallest element
```

A **for** loop can then be used to copy the elements from the two sublists into `temp`. The **for** loop will iterate `temp.length` times, where in each iteration the appropriate value from the sublists is copied into `temp`.

```
for (int i = 0; i < temp.length; ++i) {
    // store the next smallest element
    // from the sublists into temp
```

```
      ...
}
```

Case analysis is performed to determine where to get the next value to store into temp. If j ≤mid and k ≤right, then both sublists have elements to be considered. If this is not the case, then only one of the sublists still has unconsidered elements.

```
if ((j <= mid) && (k <= right)) {
    // need to grab the smaller of a[j] and a[k]
    ...
}
else if (j <= mid) { // can grab only from left half
    ...
}
else { // can grab only from right half
    ...
}
```

For the case where both sublists have values to consider, a[j] is the least uncopied value of the left sublist and a[k] is the least uncopied value from the right sublist. The lesser of these two values needs to be copied into temp.

```
if (a[j] <= a[k]) { // left has the smaller element
    temp[i] = a[j];
    ++j;
}
else { // right has the smaller element
    temp[i] = a[k];
    ++k;
}
```

If a[j] is the lesser value then besides copying it to temp[i], we must also increment j. The increment reflects that another element from the left sublist has been copied. If instead a[k] is the lesser value, then in addition to copying it to temp[i], we must also increment k. The increment reflects that another element from the right sublist has been copied.

If this case does not apply (i.e., only one sublist has uncopied elements), then it must be determined which sublist has uncopied elements. If j ≤mid then, it is the left sublist.

```
else if (j <= mid) { // can only grab from left half
    temp[i] = a[j];
    ++j;
}
```

Otherwise, it is the right sublist that has uncopied elements.

```
else { // can only grab from right half
    temp[i] = a[k];
    ++k:
}
```

Once all the elements have been copied into `temp`, all that remains to complete the sorting of `a[left]` through `a[right]` is to copy `temp` into that portion of `a`. The copying can be done in a straightforward manner using a **for** loop.

```
// lastly, copy temp into a
for (int i = 0; i < temp.length; ++i) {
    a[left + i] = temp[i];
}
```

Listing 11.3 contains the complete definitions of methods `mergeSort(`**char**`[] a)` and `mergeSort(`**char**`[] a,` **int** `left,` **int** `right)`. As we indicated previously, the methods are part of `ArrayTools.java`.

Figure 11.7 illustrates all the invocations of `mergeSort()` to arrange our list correctly. Each entry shows the values of parameters `left` and `right` at the start of an invocation. The invocation information is also presented in the following list. The invocations are listed in the order that they occur in the program. Like the figure, each entry provides the range of elements to be sorted by that invocation and the contents of the array immediately before and after the associated invocation.

```
0 ... 9:   QWERTYUIOP   EIOPQRTUWY
0 ... 4:   QWERTYUIOP   EQRTWYUIOP
0 ... 2:   QWERTYUIOP   EQWRTYUIOP
0 ... 1:   QWERTYUIOP   QWERTYUIOP
0 ... 0:   QWERTYUIOP   QWERTYUIOP
1 ... 1:   QWERTYUIOP   QWERTYUIOP
2 ... 2:   QWERTYUIOP   QWERTYUIOP
3 ... 4:   EQWRTYUIOP   EQWRTYUIOP
3 ... 3:   EQWRTYUIOP   EQWRTYUIOP
4 ... 4:   EQWRTYUIOP   EQWRTYUIOP
5 ... 9:   EQRTWYUIOP   EQRTWIOPUY
5 ... 7:   EQRTWYUIOP   EQRTWIUYOP
5 ... 6:   EQRTWYUIOP   EQRTWUYIOP
5 ... 5:   EQRTWYUIOP   EQRTWYUIOP
6 ... 6:   EQRTWYUIOP   EQRTWYUIOP
7 ... 7:   EQRTWUYIOP   EQRTWUYIOP
8 ... 9:   EQRTWIUYOP   EQRTWIUYOP
8 ... 8:   EQRTWIUYOP   EQRTWIUYOP
9 ... 9:   EQRTWIUYOP   EQRTWIUYOP
```

Listing 11.3   Mergesorting methods of SortandSearching.java

```java
1.   // mergeSort(): sorts the elements of a
2.   public static void mergeSort(char[] a) {
3.      mergeSort(a, 0, a.length - 1);
4.   }
5.
6.   private static void mergeSort(char[] a, int left,
7.    int right) {
8.      if (left < right) {
9.         // there are multiple elements to sort.
10.
11.        // first, recursively sort the left and right sublists
12.        int mid = (left + right) / 2;
13.        mergeSort(a, left, mid);
14.        mergeSort(a, mid+1, right);
15.
16.        // next, merge the sorted sublists into array temp
17.        char[] temp = new char[right - left + 1];
18.
19.        int j = left;       // index of left sublist smallest element
20.        int k = mid + 1;    // index of right sublist smallest element
21.
22.        for (int i = 0; i < temp.length; ++i) {
23.           // store the next smallest element into temp
24.           if ((j <= mid) && (k <= right)) {
25.              // need to grab the smaller of a[j] and a[k]
26.              if (a[j] <= a[k]) { // left has the smaller element
27.                 temp[i] = a[j];
28.                 ++j;
29.              }
30.              else { // right has the smaller element
31.                 temp[i] = a[k];
32.                 ++k;
33.              }
34.           }
35.           else if (j <= mid) { // can only grab from left half
36.              temp[i] = a[j];
37.              ++j;
38.           }
39.           else { // can only grab from right half
40.              temp[i] = a[k];
41.              ++k;
42.           }
43.        }
44.
45.        // lastly, copy temp into a
46.        for (int i = 0; i < temp.length; ++i) {
47.           a[left + i] = temp[i];
48.        }
49.     }
50.  }
```

Figure 11.7 Trace of mergeSort() when sorting string QWERTYUIOP.

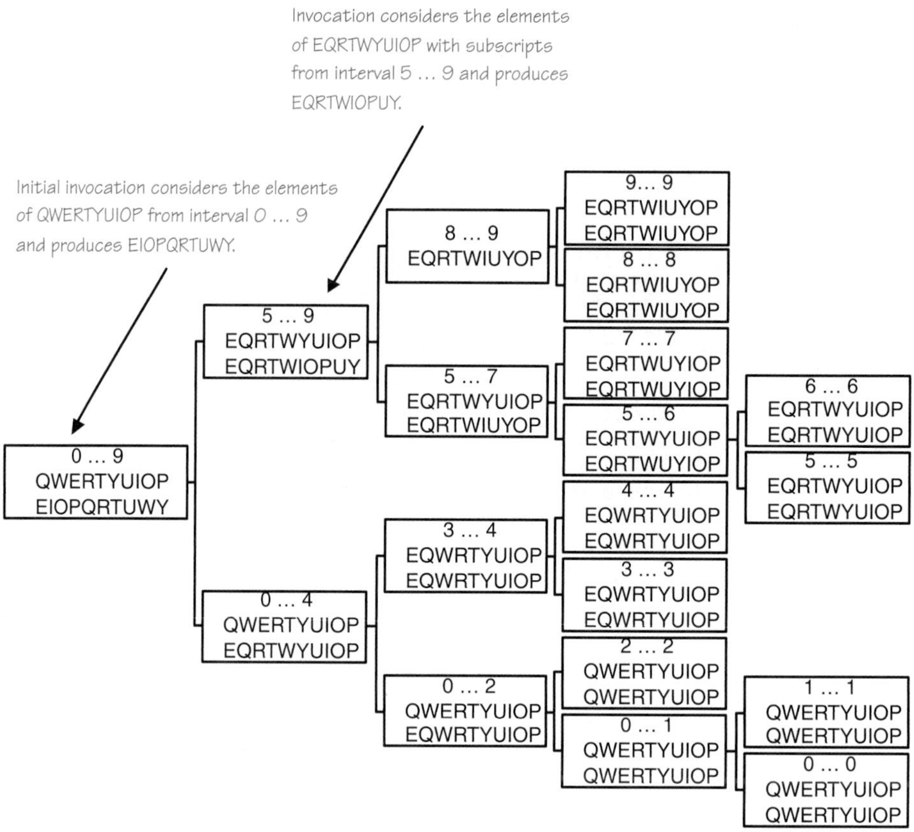
Invocation considers the elements of EQRTWYUIOP with subscripts from interval 5 ... 9 and produces EQRTWIOPUY.
Initial invocation considers the elements of QWERTYUIOP from interval 0 ... 9 and produces EIOPQRTUWY.
0 ... 9 QWERTYUIOP EIOPQRTUWY
5 ... 9 EQRTWYUIOP EQRTWIOPUY
0 ... 4 QWERTYUIOP EQRTWYUIOP
8 ... 9 EQRTWIUYOP
5 ... 7 EQRTWYUIOP EQRTWIUYOP
3 ... 4 EQWRTYUIOP EQWRTYUIOP
0 ... 2 QWERTYUIOP EQWRTYUIOP
9... 9 EQRTWIUYOP EQRTWIUYOP
8 ... 8 EQRTWIUYOP EQRTWIUYOP
7 ... 7 EQRTWUYIOP EQRTWUYIOP
5 ... 6 EQRTWYUIOP EQRTWUYIOP
4 ... 4 EQWRTYUIOP EQWRTYUIOP
3 ... 3 EQWRTYUIOP EQWRTYUIOP
2 ... 2 QWERTYUIOP QWERTYUIOP
0 ... 1 QWERTYUIOP QWERTYUIOP
6 ... 6 EQRTWYUIOP EQRTWYUIOP
5 ... 5 EQRTWYUIOP EQRTWYUIOP
1 ... 1 QWERTYUIOP QWERTYUIOP
0 ... 0 QWERTYUIOP QWERTYUIOP

11.4 HOW FAST CAN WE SORT?

It is clear that `mergeSort()` is an improvement over `selectionSort()`. The question remains, however, can we create an even better performing sorting method. It turns out that all sorting algorithms that use comparisons to determine the ordering of the elements must perform at least $n \log n$ element operations in the worst case. This fact about sorting algorithms can be shown using what is known as an *information-theoretic* argument.

If a list is composed of n distinct values, then there are $n!$ possible orderings of the values. When the first element comparison is made, one-half of the $n!$ orderings are still candidates to be the sorted ordering. For example, if the *i*th element is smaller than the *i*th element, then all orderings where the value of the *i*th element precedes the value of the *i*th element are valid possibilities. After the second comparison, in the worst-case performance at least one-fourth of the $n!$ orderings are still candidates to be the sorted ordering. After the third comparison, in the worst case at least one-eighth of the $n!$ orderings still need to be considered. In a worst-case performance, we need at least $n \log n$ comparisons before only a single candidate ordering might remain to be considered. Therefore, any comparison-based sorting algorithm has a worst-case performance that is at least linearithmic in the number of comparisons.

11.5   RECURSION VERSUS ITERATION

How do we decide when to use iteration and when to use recursion? To get a handle on answering this question we need to understand the costs of recursion.

A recursive program accomplishes its task by making successive recursive calls with smaller subprograms. As we discussed in Chapter 4, a method call involves several steps. Three of these steps are to arrange for the values of the actual parameters to be passed to the invoked method, to create a new activation record, and to transfer control to the called method. When the called method returns, the return value (if any) is passed back to the calling method, the activation record must be removed, and control must be returned to the calling method. Combined these operations make method invocation relatively expensive compared to simple operations like evaluating an expression or looping to repeat a sequence of statements.

A second issue is the amount of memory used by a recursive program. Each time we make a recursive call a new activation record is created. If the program recurses deeply and the activation records for the method are large, substantial amounts of memory may be consumed. Depending on the amount of memory on the machine, this could be a potential problem.

To see concretely the potential inefficiency of a recursive solution, Table 11.1 gives some data about the execution characteristics of our Fibonacci code. The table gives the number of recursive calls made and the depth of the recursion (i.e., the number of activation records simultaneously on the stack). For an input value of 36, the program makes over 29 million recursive calls and the depth of the stack grows to 35.

Table 11.1   Fibonacci execution statistics.

n	Calls made	Call depth
5	9	4
6	15	5
12	287	11
18	5,167	17
24	92,735	23
30	1,664,079	29
36	29,860,703	35

For Fibonacci numbers, we can create a much more efficient solution through iteration. The following method computes the *n*th Fibonacci number iteratively.

```java
public static int fibonacci(int n) {
    if (n <= 2) {
        return 1;
    }
    else {
        int f = 1;
        int f1 = 1;
        int f2 = 1;
        for (int i = 2; i <= n; ++i) {
            f = f1 + f2;
            f1 = f2;
            f2 = f;
        }
        return f;
    }
}
```

This solution is quite efficient and is also straightforward to understand.

So does this mean that one should avoid recursive solutions to problems? Not at all. Sometimes the easiest and least error-prone solution to a problem is a recursive one. Put another way, sometimes an iterative solution to a problem is much more difficult than a recursive solution. As an example, try solving the Towers of Hanoi problem in the exercises using iteration. An iterative solution is challenging, whereas the recursive solution is simple. Generally, our approach is to favor the solution that is easiest to understand. Later, if the chosen solution is inefficient to the extent it noticeably affects the overall performance of the application, we can investigate using a different solution approach. With today's modern compilers and the speed of machines, it is rare that a recursive solution is not fast enough.

　　## CASE STUDY — STRING PERMUTATION

The Daily Jumble® is a popular two-part puzzle that
appears every day in many newspapers. Figure 11.8
reproduces a sample Daily Jumble puzzle. The first part
of the puzzle gives a list of strings to be rearranged—
each string in the list is to be unscrambled so that it
forms a word. The second part of the puzzles poses a

> The objective of this case
> study is to demonstrate the
> development of both a
> recursive algorithm and an
> iterator

riddle regarding an accompanying cartoon. The answer to the riddle is formed by using
selected letters from the words found in the first part.

Figure 11.8　**Daily Jumble. Copyright, 2000, Tribune Media Services, Inc.
All rights reserved. Reprinted with permission.**

ANALYSIS AND DESIGN

Our interest in the puzzle lies in how to automate unscrambling the letters to find the
word. One approach is to generate all possible permutations of the letters in the scrambled word and then scan the list for legal words. For a string of length 5, the number of
permutations can be computed as follows. There are five possibilities for the first letter.

This leaves four possibilities for the second letter, three possibilities for the third letter, two possibilities for the fourth letter, and one possibility for the last letter. Thus there are $5 \times 4 \times 3 \times 2 \times 1$ or 120 permutations of five letters. This computation should be familiar. It is just the computation of 5!. Indeed, in general, the number of permutations in a string of length n is $n!$.

For example, if we generate the 120 permutations of the first scrambled word *mezia* we get the following list of 120 words.

mezia	mezai	meiza	meiaz	meazi
meaiz	mzeia	mzeai	mziea	mziae
mzaei	mzaie	mieza	mieaz	mizea
mizae	miaez	miaze	maezi	maeiz
mazei	mazie	maiez	*maize*	emzia
emzai	emiza	emiaz	emazi	emaiz
ezmia	ezmai	ezima	eziam	ezami
ezaim	eimza	eimaz	eizma	eizam
eiamz	eiazm	eamzi	eamiz	eazmi
eazim	eaimz	eaizm	zmeia	zmeai
zmiea	zmiae	zmaei	zmaie	zemia
zemai	zeima	zeiam	zeami	zeaim
zimea	zimae	ziema	zieam	ziame
ziaem	zamei	zamie	zaemi	zaeim
zaime	zaiem	imeza	imeaz	imzea
imzae	imaez	imaze	iemza	iemaz
iezma	iezam	ieamz	ieazm	izmea
izmae	izema	izeam	izame	izaem
iamez	iamze	iaemz	iaezm	iazme
iazem	amezi	ameiz	amzei	amzie
amiez	amize	aemzi	aemiz	aezmi
aezim	aeimz	aeizm	azmei	azmie
azemi	azeim	azime	aziem	aimez
aimze	aiemz	aiezm	aizme	aizem

Scanning the list of permutations we locate the word maize.

Thus our plan for solving the Daily Jumble is to create a class called `PermuteString` that generates all permutations of a given string. We can then scan the generated list for legal English words. The exercises contain some problems that further automate our technique.

IMPLEMENTATION

Class `PermuteString` will be designed to be an iterator. An iterator is a type of class that produces successive values. For our problem, the successive values to generate are the permutations of the word. Typically, an iterator has the following methods.

- A constructor to create the generator.
- A method for returning the next value.
- A method that indicates if there are any more values to return.

Class `PermuteString` will have three methods.

`public PermuteString(String s)`

Default constructor that creates the permutation generator for `String s`.

`public String nextPermutation()`

Returns the next permutation of `String s`.

```
public boolean morePermutations()
```

>Returns **false** if all permutations have been generated; otherwise **true** is returned.

Recall that to create a recursive solution we need two cases—the base case and the recursive case. For the permutation problem, the base case is the trivial case of a string that consists of a single letter. The permutation of a string of length one is the string. The recursive case is a little more complicated, but not much more. To generate the permutations of a string, we will select each letter of the string and concatenate it with all the permutations of the remaining letters (we will call this the substring). Notice that this definition satisfies the recursive case requirement that the recursive call have an argument that is simpler or smaller. The recursive call is being made with the substring that has one less character than the word.

To implement the permutation generator, we need to maintain state information to track the permutations generated thus far. We will need the following variables.

```
String word
```

>The string being permuted.

```
int index
```

>The position within the word of the character being selected to add to the permutations of the substring.

```
PermuteString substringGenerator
```

>A reference to the **PermuteString** generator for the substring of the word.

The constructor for **PermuteString** is:

```java
// PermuteString: default constructor
public PermuteString(String s) {
    word = s;
    index = 0;
    if (s.length() > 1) {
        substringGenerator =
          new PermuteString(s.substring(1));
    }
}
```

The constructor initializes word to the string being permuted, and it sets index to 0. If the length of the string is greater than one, a **PermuteString** object is created for the substring of the word. Notice that this is a recursive call. Basically, when a **PermuteString** generator is created for a string, **PermuteString** generators are created for every substring of the word. For example, the invocation

```java
PermuteString p = new PermuteString("ath");
```

creates the following objects.

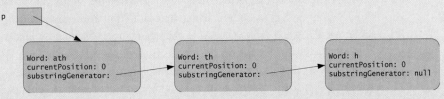

The two generators for the substrings "th" and "h" will be invoked by method next-Permutation() to create permutations of these substrings as needed.

We now turn our attention to method morePermutations(). This method returns false if all permutations have been produced. The way we can tell whether all the permutations have been generated is by comparing index to the length of word. If we have selected every letter from instance variable word, then all permutations have been generated. Remember, our technique for generating the permutations is to select each letter of word and concatenate it with all the permutations of the substring. Consequently, the implementation of method morePermutations() is quite simple.

```
public boolean morePermutations() {
    return index < word.length();
}
```

When index is less than the length of word (i.e., there are still more characters in word to select), method morePermutations() returns **true**.

Now it is time to tackle method nextPermutation(), which is given in Listing 11.4. Like the constructor, method nextPermutation() will be recursive. The base case is when the instance variable word is length one (lines 17–21). For the base case, the instance variable word is the permutation. To indicate that there are no more permutations for this case, index is incremented so that it is equal to the size of the word.

For the recursive case, the code generates the permutation to return by taking the character at position index and concatenates it with the next permutation of the substring. This permutation is obtained by invoking the nextpermutation() method of the substring object (lines 22–23).

If there are no more permutations of the substring, then we need to advance index to the next character of word. If we are not at the end of the word, then we pick the character at that position, create the new substring (i.e., all the other characters in word), and create a PermuteString object for the new substring. Instance variable substring-Generator is a reference to the newly created PermuteString object. These steps are accomplished by lines 24–32. The final step is to return the permutation that was created by lines 23–24.

Listing 11.4 contains the complete implementation for class PermuteString. To help understand class PermuteString's operation, Figure 11.9 traces the production of the permutations of the string "tocs". A permutation can be found by tracing a path from the starting point on the left to a node on the right and reading off the letters in red. For example, the top path traces out the permutation "tocs", the next path (again starting from the left) traces out the permutation "tosc". Successive words can be found by reading the traces from the top to bottom. Thus, the last permutation generated would be "scot." The diagram illustrates how successive characters are chosen and a recursive call is made to create a generator for the resulting substring. For example, we see to produce the permutation "scot" that the last letter, "s" is selected from the original word "tocs" and a recursive call is made to generate the permutations of the remaining letters, "toc."

Listing 11.4 PermuteString.java

```
1.  // generate the permutations of a string
2.
3.  public class PermuteString {
4.      private String word;
5.      private int index;
6.      private PermuteString substringGenerator;
7.
8.      // PermuteString: default constructor
9.      public PermuteString(String s) {
10.         word = s;
11.         index = 0;
12.         if (s.length() > 1)
13.             substringGenerator = new PermuteString(s.substring(1));
14.     }
15.
16.     // nextPermutation: return next permutation of word
17.     public String nextPermutation() {
18.         if (word.length() == 1) {
19.             ++index;
20.             return word;
21.         }
22.         else {
23.             String r = word.charAt(index)
24.              + substringGenerator.nextPermutation();
25.             if (!substringGenerator.morePermutations()) {
26.                 ++index;
27.                 if (index < word.length()) {
28.                     String tailString = word.substring(0, index)
29.                      + word.substring(index + 1);
30.                     substringGenerator = new PermuteString(tailString);
31.                 }
32.             }
33.             return r;
34.         }
35.     }
36.
37.     // morePermutations: return true of more permutations available
38.     public boolean morePermutations() {
39.         return index < word.length();
40.     }
41. }
```

Figure 11.9 **Generations of the permutations of string "tocs".**

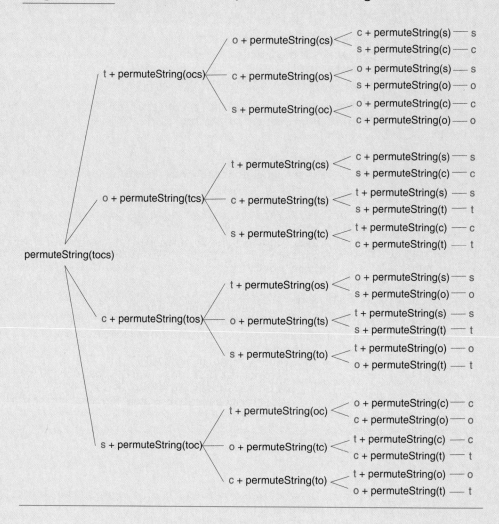

11.7 REVIEW

- Recursion is when a function calls itself. A recursive function must have two parts. It has a termination part that ends the recursion and a recursive call with simpler parameters.

- The termination part of a recursive algorithm is called the base case.

- The recursive part of a recursive algorithm is called the recursive case.

- Time-critical client applications with a sorting substep often use the `mergeSort()` method.

- Method `mergeSort()` is a recursive sort that conceptually divides its list of *n* elements to be sorted into two sublists of size *n*/2. If a sublist contains more than one element, the sublist is sorted by a recursive call to `mergeSort()`. After the two sublists of size *n*/2 are sorted, they are merged together to produce a single sorted list of size *n*. The running time of method `mergeSort()` is proportional to *n*log*n*. This performance is sometimes known as *linearithmic* performance.

- The `mergeSort()` strategy is known as a *divide-and-conquer* strategy—the problem is divided into subproblems of lesser complexity and the solutions of the subproblems are used to produce the overall solution.

- Any comparison-based sorting algorithm has a worst-case performance that is at least linearithmic in the number of comparisons. It can also be shown using an information-theoretic argument that any comparison-based searching algorithm is at least logarithmic in the number of comparisons.

- The binary search algorithm requires at most $\log_2 (N + 1)$ comparisons to search a sorted list with *N* elements.

- The height of a full binary tree of *N* nodes is $\log_2 (N + 1)$.

- The number of permutations of *n* distinct items is *n*!.

11.8 SELF-TEST

S11.1 What is the output of the following program?

```java
public class SelfCheck1 {
    public static int f(int n) {
        if (n <= 1)
            return n;
        else
            return f(n-1) + f(n-2);
    }
    public static void main(String[] args) {
        System.out.println(f(4));
    }
}
```

S11.2 Write a recursive function `reverse()` that accepts two string arguments, s and r. Function `reverse()` uses recursion to reverse the characters in string s and place the reversed string in string r.

S11.3 Write a recursive function `printNumber()` that accepts an integer argument. Function `printNumber()` uses recursion to print out the value of its argument a digit at a time.

S11.4 Give the names of the two types of cases every recursive algorithm must have.

S11.5 A full binary tree has 1023 nodes. What is the height of the tree?

11.9	EXERCISES

11.1 In the definition, "A person's descendants are the person's children and all their descendants," identify the base case and the recursive case.

11.2 Develop a recursive formula for the number of recursive calls made by `fibonacci()` in computing the *n*th Fibonacci number.

11.3 Rewrite method `fibonacci()` so that it performs the computation only if its parameter is nonnegative.

11.4 Redo the permutation generator using an iterative solution. Which solution is easier to understand?

11.5 Development a program `FibonacciSquares.java` to produce a Fibonacci square as depicted in the Figure 11.4. The number of squares to be displayed should be a user-supplied value. The colors of the squares should cycle through `Color.red`, `Color.yellow`, `Color.green`, and `Color.blue`, and the squares should be generated in a counterclockwise manner.

11.6 If we take the ratio of successive numbers in the Fibonacci sequence, we see that the ratio is approaching a particular value. For example, 5/3 is 1.66666...; 8/5 is 1.6; and 13/8 is 1.625. The value to which these ratios are converging is called the *golden ratio* or *golden mean*. Develop a program to compute an approximation of the golden mean. To get an accurate estimation of its value, compute the golden mean of successive pairs of Fibonacci numbers until the difference between the computed golden means is less than 0.0005.

11.7 Develop a program that prompts a user for a number *n* and then computes and displays for integer values *i* in the interval 1 through *n* the nearest integer to the expression

$$\frac{1}{\sqrt{5}}\left(\left(\frac{1+\sqrt{5}}{2}\right)^i - \left(\frac{1-\sqrt{5}}{2}\right)^i\right)$$

Compare the output of the program with the output of method `fibonacci()` for the same values. Discuss their similarity.

11.8 Rewrite function `factorial()` so that it returns a double value.

11.9 Develop a program that uses the function `factorial()` of Exercise 11.8 to compute an approximation of *e* (Euler's number). Base your approximation on the following formula for *e*:

$$1 + \frac{1}{1!} + \frac{1}{2!} + \frac{1}{3!} + \cdots$$

11.10 Write a recursive function to compute the greatest common divisor (gcd) of two integers. The gcd of two integers is the largest integer that divides them both. A working definition of gcd is

$$\gcd(m, n) \ = \ \begin{cases} n & \text{if } n \text{ divides } m \\ \gcd(n, \text{remainder of } m \text{ divided by } n) & \text{otherwise} \end{cases}$$

11.11 Implement a method `pivot()` with three formal parameters: **int** array a and **int** parameters m and n, where m is less than n. If a[n] is less than a[m], then the values of elements a[m] and a[n] are interchanged.

11.12 Develop an application that gives a solution to the Towers of Hanoi problem. There are three pegs with *n* disks on one of the pegs as in the following diagram.

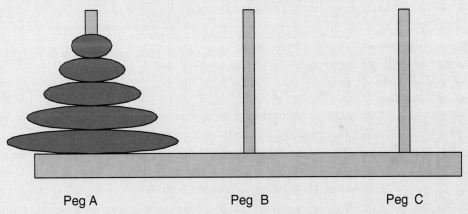

Peg A   Peg B   Peg C

The problem to be solved is to come up with a set of moves that transfers the disks from Peg A to Peg C. A move must obey the following rules.

- Only one disk can be moved at a time, and this disk must be top disk on a tower.
- A larger disk cannot be placed on the top of a smaller disk.

Your application should print out the moves necessary to move all the disks from Peg A to Peg C. The moves generated by the application should be of the form:

```
move a disk from Peg A to Peg B
```

11.13 Implement a method `partition()` with three formal parameters: **int** array a and **int** parameters m and n, where m is less than n. Method `partition()` first invokes method `pivot()` of Exercise 11.11. The list is then rearranged into three sublists or *partitions*. The middle sublist is composed of an element whose value is the *pivot value* a[m]; the values of the elements in the left sublist are no larger than the pivot value, and the values of the elements in the right sublist are no smaller than the pivot value. The method returns the location of the pivot value after the partitioning has completed.

11.14 Implement the `quickSort()` sorting method that uses in part, method `partition()` of Exercise 11.13. The method has three formal parameters: **int** array a and **int** parameters m and n. The method sorts elements a[m] through a[n] of a. If m ≥ n, the method simply returns. If m+1 equals n, then the method sorts the sublist directly. Otherwise, the method invokes `partition()`. Let k be the return value of the `partition()` invocation. To complete the sorting, method `quickSort()` makes two recursive calls to sort sublists a[m] through a[k-1] and a[k+1] through a[n].

11.15 Modify method `mergeSort()` so that it invokes the variant of `insertionSort()` of Exercise 8.33 if the number of elements to be sorted is 20 or less.

11.16 Modify method `quickSort()` of Exercise 11.14 so that it invokes the variant of `insertionSort()` of Exercise 8.33 if the number of elements to be sorted is 20 or less.

11.17 Create an additional test harness for the binary search method that searches a list with an odd number of elements.

11.18 A palindrome is a string that is identical to its reverse when differences in spacing, case of letters, and punctuation is ignored. Examples of palindromes are "level", "Was it a rat I saw", and "A man, a plan, a canal: Panama". Implement and test a Java method

public static boolean isPalindrome(String phrase)

Method `isPalindrome()` returns true if its argument is a palindrome; otherwise it returns false. Include a test harness for your method.

11.19 Write a recursive method `sum(int m, int n)` that computes the sum of the integers m through n (i.e., m + (m + 1) + (m + 2) + ... + (n −2) + (n −1) + n). Write a test harness to exercise your code.

11.20 Modify the permutation generator so that it eliminates duplicate permutations. That is, the generator never returns the same string twice.

11.10   **PROGRAMMING PROJECT — SIERPINSKI FRACTAL**

Fractals are geometric patterns where the curves or surfaces are independent of scale or self-similar. What that means from a visual standpoint is that if you took a fractal and magnified a section of it, the section would appear identical to the original.

> The objective of this programming project is to practice using recursion to create an interesting graphics image

Fractals have many uses in describing the mathematical properties of complex objects. However, most of us are more familiar with some of the beautiful images created using fractals. Figure

Figure 11.10 **Mandelbrot fractal.**

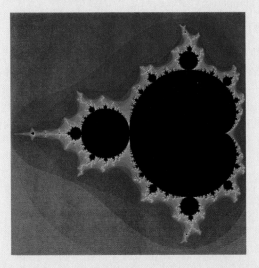

11.10 contains an image of a famous fractal named after the mathematician Benoit Mandelbrot.

In this programming case study, you will create a recursive program that renders another well known fractal—the Sierpinski fractal.

PROBLEM STATEMENT

A Sierpinski fractal or gasket is formed using the following algorithm.

Step 1.   *Draw a triangle.*

Step 2.   *Compute the midpoint of each of the triangle's sides.*

Step 3.   *Repeat for each smaller triangle that is formed by one vertex of the original triangle and the two closest midpoints. Stop when a predetermined number of steps is completed.*

The following diagram illustrates two levels of recursion.

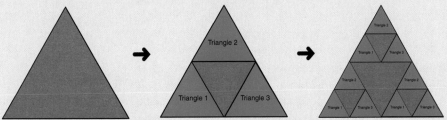

Design and develop a program to render a Sierpinski fractal. Your program should prompt for and accept the depth of recursion from the console.

ANALYSIS AND DESIGN

Because we are developing a recursive solution, you should first determine the base and inductive cases. The base case occurs when the program has recursed to the depth input by the user. The recursive case draws the specified triangle, computes the midpoints of the triangle's three sides, and makes three recursive calls for each of the three new triangles. To make the image interesting and colorful looking, your program should alternate the colors used to render the triangles.

IMPLEMENTATION

Your program's name should be `SierpinskiFractal.java`.

What objects and methods do you need to create your Sierpinski fractal? Obviously, your program needs the capability to render a triangle. For this capability, it makes sense to use the `ColoredTriangle` class developed in Chapter 5. Class `ColoredTriangle` can be used to create and draw the necessary triangles. Recall that class `ColoredTriangle` has the following public methods:

`public ColoredTriangle()`

> Constructs a default triangle representation. The default representation is a black triangle with points at coordinates (1, 1), (2, 2), and (3, 3).

`public ColoredTriangle(Point v1, Point v2, Point v3, Color c)`

> Constructs a triangle using color `c` whose endpoints are equivalent to the points referenced by `p1`, `p2`, and `p3`.

`public Point getPoint(int i)`

> Returns the `i`th point of the associated triangle.

`public void setPoint(int i, Point v)`

> Sets the `i`th point of the associated triangle so that its value is equivalent to the point referenced by `v`.

`public Color getColor()`

> Returns the color of the associated triangle.

`public void setColor(Color c)`

> Sets the color of the associated triangle to `c`.

`public void paint(Graphics g)`

> Renders the triangle to graphic context `g`.

The Sierpinski algorithm requires that we compute the midpoints of the sides of a triangle. Consequently, a method that computes the midpoint of a line segment will be useful. Method `midPoint` has the following prototype:

`public static Point midPoint(Point p1, Point p2)`

> Compute the midpoint of the line segment defined by endpoints `p1` and `p2`.

The two other methods necessary are method `main` and method `Sierpinski`. Method `main()` will prompt for and read the number of levels of triangles that should be drawn (i.e., the depth of recursion). It will then invoke the method `Sierpinski()`. Method `Sierpinski()` will do all the work. Its prototype is:

`public static void Sierpinski(Graphics g, Point p1, Point p2, Point p3, Color c, int depth)`

This method will draw a triangle of color `c` with points `p1`, `p2`, and `p3` in the graphics context `g`. The triangle should be color `c`. Parameter `depth` is the current depth of recursion. The method will recursively call itself to draw three new triangles.

The following diagram shows a Sierpinski fractal rendered using the colors blue and orange recursing to a depth of 6.

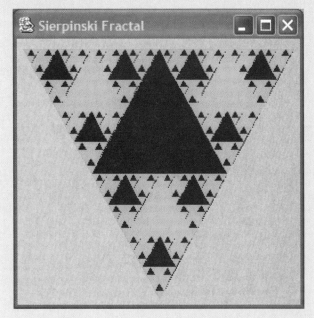

TESTING

Because you were able to reuse class `ColoredTriangle`, your program `Sierpinski-Fractal.java` is short and simple. Consequently, testing the program is straightforward. You should make sure your program does something reasonable if the recursion depth input is less than zero, zero, and one. You should also test to see what happens if different kinds of triangles are used. The previous diagram shows an equilateral triangle. Try an obtuse triangle. Does your program still work?

11.11   SELF-TEST ANSWERS

S11.1 The program outputs 3.

S11.2

```java
public class SelfCheckReverse {
    public static String reverse(String s) {
    if (s.length() <= 1) {
       return s;
    }
    else {
       return reverse(s.substring(1, s.length()))
          + s.substring(0,1);
    }
}
```

```
                    public static void main(String[] args) {
                        System.out.println(reverse("hello"));
                    }
                }
```

S11.3

```
        public class SelfCheckPrintNumber {
            public static void printNumber(int n) {
                if (n < 10) {
                    System.out.print(n % 10);
                }
                else {
                    printNumber(n / 10);
                    System.out.print(n % 10);
                }
            }
            public static void main(String[] args) {
                printNumber(231);
            }
        }
```

S11.4 Every recursive algorithm must have at least one base case and at least one recursive case.

S11.5 The height of the tree is 10.

12 THREADS

In state-of-the-art software, a program can be composed of multiple independent flows of control, where these flows of control are known commonly as *processes* or *threads*. For example, many document processing suites use multiple threads. The suites often use one thread to print a document while another thread enables a user to enter and format text. By separating these tasks into different flows of control, a user can continue to edit and format a document as it prints. In this chapter, we examine several Java mechanisms for creating, scheduling, managing, and running threads.

OBJECTIVES

- Develop programs with multiple, concurrent flows of control using threads.
  - Create threads that run at a time relative to the current time.
  - Create threads that run repeatedly.
  - Create threads that run at designated times.
- Schedule programs to pause for some specific time or event.
- Consider standard classes Timer, TimerTask, and Thread.
- Consider standard classes Date and Calendar.

12.1	SCHEDULING

Our programs thus far have consisted of single flows of control. For example with console-based programs, the flow of control started in the first statement of method `main()` and worked its way statement by statement to the last statement of method `main()`. Flow of control could be passed temporarily to other methods through invocations, but the control returned to `main()` after their completion. Programs with single flows of control are known as *sequential processes*.

```
Single-threaded Program {
    Statement 1;
    Statement 2;    ◄─────────
    ...
    Statement k;
}
```
Although the statements within a single flow of control may invoke other methods, the next statement is not executed until the current statement completes

The ability to run more than one process at the same time is an important characteristic of modern operating systems such us Linux, OS X, and Windows. For example, a user desktop may be running a browser, programming IDE, music player, and document preparation system. Figure 12.1 shows two snapshots of a Windows task manager: Figure 12.1(a) displays a list of applications running on some machine. Figure 12.1(b) displays some of the operating system and application processes required to run those applications.

Java supports the creation of programs with *concurrent* flows of control. These independent flows of control are called *threads*. Because threads run within a program and make use of its resources in their execution, these individual flows of control are also called *lightweight processes*. Figure 12.2 depicts a scenario where the main flow of control for a program spawns two threads to assist in the completion of its task. One of these threads spawns yet another thread to assist in its subtask.

Java has several classes that support the creation and scheduling of threads. Classes `java.util.Timer` and `java.util.TimerTask` are generally the easiest to use. They allow a thread to be created and run either at a time relative to the current time or at some specific time.

Class `Timer` has three methods named `schedule()` for creating threads after either some specified delay or at some specific time.

```
public void schedule(TimerTask task, long m)
```
Runs `task.run()` after waiting m milliseconds.

```
public void schedule(TimerTask task, long m, long n)
```
Runs `task.run()` after waiting m milliseconds. It then repeatedly reruns `task.run()` every **n** milliseconds.

```
public void schedule(TimerTask task, Date t)
```
Runs `task.run()` at the time indicated by date t.

By extending **abstract** class `TimerTask` and specifying a definition for its **abstract** method `run()`, an application-specific thread can be created.

Figure 12.1 Task manager snapshot.

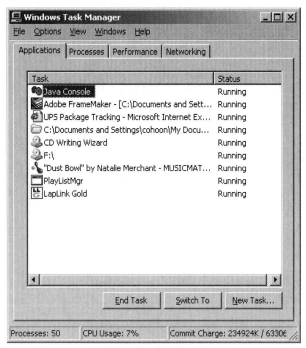

(a) Application listing.

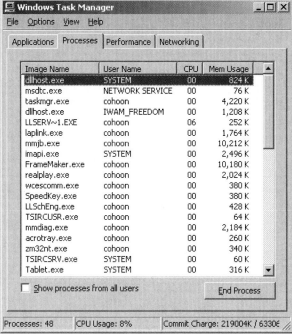

(b) Process listing.

Figure 12.2 **A multithreaded program.**

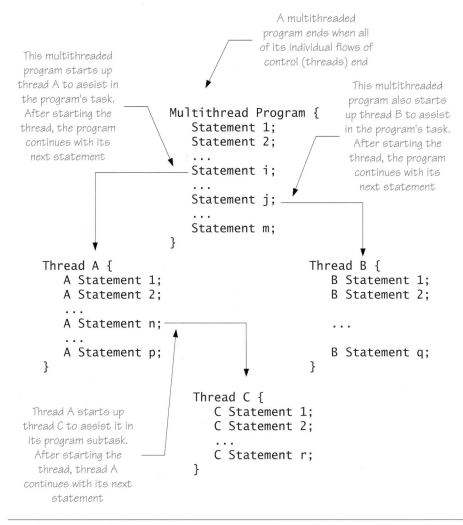

```
abstract void run()
```

Implements the action to be performed by this task.

RUNNING AFTER A DELAY

For our first thread example, we define a class `DisplayCharSequence` in Listing 12.1 that extends `TimerTask` to support the creation of a thread that displays 20 copies of some desired character (e.g., "H", "A", or "N").

Listing 12.1 **DisplayCharSequence.java**

```
1.  // Displays characters in separate threads
2.
3.  import java.util.*;
4.
5.  public class DisplayCharSequence extends TimerTask {
6.      // instance variables
7.      private char displayChar;
8.      Timer timer;
9.
10.     // DisplayCharSequence(): construct a c displayer
11.     public DisplayCharSequence(char c) {
12.         displayChar = c;
13.         timer = new Timer();
14.         timer.schedule(this, 0);
15.     }
16.
17.     // run(): display the occurrences of the character of interest
18.     public void run() {
19.         for (int i = 0; i < 20; ++i) {
20.             System.out.print(displayChar);
21.         }
22.
23.         timer.cancel();
24.     }
25.
26.     // main(): application entry point
27.     public static void main(String[] args) {
28.         DisplayCharSequence s1 = new DisplayCharSequence('H');
29.         DisplayCharSequence s2 = new DisplayCharSequence('A');
30.         DisplayCharSequence s3 = new DisplayCharSequence('N');
31.     }
32. }
```

To assist with its behavior, a DisplayCharSequence object has two instance variables. They are **char** variable displayChar and Timer variable timer.

private char displayChar

The character to be displayed by the thread. Its value is specified during DisplayCharSequence construction.

private Timer timer

Represents the timer that schedules the thread.

The DisplayCharSequence class defines a single constructor.

public DisplayCharSequence(**char** c)

Schedules a thread whose task is to display 20 copies of the character c to standard output. The thread is scheduled to start after a delay of zero milliseconds; i.e., immediately.

Because class DisplayCharSequence extends TimerTask to support thread creation, DisplayCharSequence must define a method run().

public void run()

Displays 20 copies of displayChar.

To demonstrate its use as a thread creator, class DisplayCharSequence also defines a **static** method main() as a program entry point.

Figure 12.3   **DisplayCharSequence.java execution runs.**

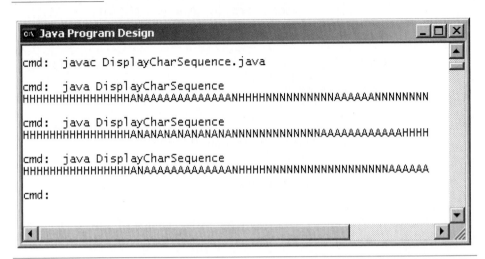

public static void main(String[] args)

Creates three DisplayCharSequence that display respectively the characters 'H', 'A', and 'N'.

By examining different runs of program DisplayCharSequence.java, it becomes obvious that there are different processes operating and producing output. Figure 12.3 depicts three runs of DisplayCharSequence.java. Each run produced a different output sequence.

The method definitions are worth analyzing. The DisplayCharSequence constructor configures the instance variables and schedule the thread.

```
// DisplayCharSequence(): construct a c displayer
public DisplayCharSequence(char c) {
    displayChar = c;
    timer = new Timer();
    timer.schedule(this, 0);
}
```

The value of instance variable displayChar is given by parameter c; and the value of variable timer is obtained by constructing a new Timer. The new Timer then is used to schedule a thread based on the new DisplayCharSequence object. Because the thread is to be based on the DisplayCharSequence object under construction, the first schedule() parameter is **this**. To schedule the new thread to run after a zero-millisecond delay from the current time, the second schedule() parameter has value 0.

A subclass implementation of TimerTask's **abstract** method run() typically has two parts. The first part defines the application-specific action the thread is to perform. The second part ends the thread. The thread is ended, because the application-specific

Timesharing

Most computer systems have a single central processing unit (CPU). On such systems, there can only be one process using the CPU at a time; i.e., there cannot be multiple processes running simultaneously. To simulate multiprocessing, uniprocessor computing systems normally practice *timesharing*. A timesharing computer system repeatedly gives each process a slice of time to use the CPU to make progress with respect to its action. Because the time slices are typically small and occur so frequently, the computing system has the appearance of simultaneous behavior.

action has completed. `DisplayCharSequence` method `run()` follows the standard form.

```java
// run(): display the occurrences of the character of interest
public void run() {
    for (int i = 0; i < 20; ++i) {
        System.out.print(displayChar);
    }
    timer.cancel();
}
```
Desired action to be performed by thread

Desired action is completed so thread is canceled

A **for** loop displays 20 copies of `displayChar`. Because the display completes the action wanted of the thread, the next statement uses `Timer` method `cancel()` to end the thread.

For class method `main()` to create the three character displaying threads, it needs only to define three instances of `DisplayCharSequence`.

```java
// main(): application entry point
public static void main(String[] args) {
    DisplayCharSequence s1 = new DisplayCharSequence('H');
    DisplayCharSequence s2 = new DisplayCharSequence('A');
    DisplayCharSequence s3 = new DisplayCharSequence('N');
}
```

12.1.2   RUNNING REPEATEDLY

Our next example demonstrates how to schedule a thread to run multiple times. We do so in `SimpleClock.java` of Listing 12.2. This program updates the display of a GUI-based clock every second.

Listing 12.2   SimpleClock.java

```
1.  // displays current time
2.
3.  import javax.swing.JFrame;
4.  import java.util.*;
5.  import java.text.*;
6.  import java.awt.*;
7.
8.  public class SimpleClock extends TimerTask {
9.     // class constants
10.    final static long MILLISECONDS_PER_SECOND = 1000;
11.
12.    // instance variables
13.    private JFrame window = new JFrame("Clock");
14.    private Timer timer = new Timer();
15.    private String clockFace = "";
16.
17.    // SimpleClock(): default clock constructor
18.    public SimpleClock() {
19.       // configure GUI
20.       window.setDefaultCloseOperation(JFrame.EXIT_ON_CLOSE);
21.       window.setSize(200, 60);
22.       Container c = window.getContentPane();
23.       c.setBackground(Color.WHITE);
24.       window.setVisible(true);
25.
26.       // update GUI every second starting immediately
27.       timer.schedule(this, 0, 1*MILLISECONDS_PER_SECOND);
28.    }
29.
30.    // run(): updates clock display
31.    public void run() {
32.       Date time = new Date();
33.
34.       Graphics g = window.getContentPane().getGraphics();
35.
36.       g.setColor(Color.WHITE);
37.       g.drawString(clockFace, 10, 20);
38.
39.       clockFace = time.toString();
40.       g.setColor(Color.BLUE);
41.       g.drawString(clockFace, 10, 20);
42.    }
43.
44.    // main(): application entry point
45.    public static void main(String[] args) {
46.       SimpleClock clock = new SimpleClock();
47.    }
48. }
```

In producing its display, program SimpleClock.java makes uses of standard Java class Date. Class Date provides the following constructor and method of interest to us.

```
public Date()
```

Creates a date representation reflecting the current time to the millisecond.

```
public String toString()
```
Returns a textual representation of the date of the form

w c d h:m:s z y

where

- *w*: three-character representation of the day of the week;
- *c*: three-character representation of the calendar month of the year;
- *d*: two-digit representation of the day of the month;
- *h*: two-digit representation of the hour of the day;
- *m*: two-digit representation of the minute within the hour;
- *s*: two-digit representation of the second within the minute;
- *z*: three-character representation of the zone specification;
- y: four-character representation of the year.

Like `DisplayCharSequence.java`, program `SimpleClock.java` extends `TimerTask`. Class `SimpleClock` has three instance variables.

```
private JFrame window
```
Represents the window containing the GUI.

```
private String clockFace
```
Represents a string representation of the current date.

```
private Timer timer
```
Represents the timer that schedules this `SimpleClock` thread to run repeatedly every second.

The `SimpleClock` default constructor has two tasks: configure the GUI and schedule a thread whose task is to update the GUI every second.

```
// SimpleClock(): default clock constructor
public SimpleClock() {
    // configure GUI
    window.setSize(200, 60);
    Container c = window.getContentPane();
    c.setBackground(Color.WHITE);
    window.setDefaultCloseOperation(JFrame.EXIT_ON_CLOSE);
    window.setVisible(true);

    // update GUI every second starting immediately
    timer.schedule(this, 0, 1*MILLISECONDS_PER_SECOND);
}
```

The GUI configuration of its window is straightforward—the window is sized properly, its background color is set, its closing policy is set, and it is made visible.

With the GUI arranged, `Timer` method `schedule()` then is used to schedule a thread that runs every second to update the GUI.

```
timer.schedule(this, 0, 1*MILLISECONDS_PER_SECOND);
```

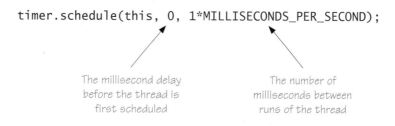

The millisecond delay before the thread is first scheduled

The number of milliseconds between runs of the thread

The `schedule()` method invoked by `SimpleClock` is different from the method invoked by `DisplayCharSequence`. That `schedule()` method initiated a single thread run. The `schedule()` method invoked by `SimpleClock` causes a thread to be first run after a delay of 0 milliseconds (i.e., immediately) and then rerun every second.

The thread action associated with a `SimpleClock` is specified by its method `run()`.

```java
// run(): updates clock display
public void run() {
    Date time = new Date();

    Graphics g = window.getContentPane().getGraphics();

    g.setColor(Color.WHITE);
    g.drawString(clockFace, 10, 20);

    clockFace = time.toString();
    g.setColor(Color.BLUE);
    g.drawString(clockFace, 10, 20);
}
```

Method `run()` first determines the current time by invoking a `Date` constructor.

```java
Date time = new Date();
```

The GUI then is updated to reflect the current time. To do so, the method first redraws the previous time display using the background color. The redrawing effectively erases the previous time display.

```java
Graphics g = window.getContentPane().getGraphics();

g.setColor(Color.WHITE);
g.drawString(clockFace, 10, 20);
```

Instance variable `clockFace` then is updated to reflect the current time and the new time then is rendered using the foreground color.

```java
clockFace = time.toString();
g.setColor(Color.BLUE);
g.drawString(clockFace, 10, 20);
```

There is no subsequent cancellation of the thread, because GUI updates are to occur every second.

For method `main()` of program `SimpleClock.java` to accomplish its task, it only needs to create a `SimpleClock` instance.

```java
// main(): application entry point
public static void main(String[] args) {
    SimpleClock clock = new SimpleClock();
}
```

Standard class Timer and standard class Timer

Java provides two different standard classes named `Timer`. The class we have been using is part of the `util` API. There is also a `Timer` class that is part of `swing` API. In importing classes into `SimpleClock.java` we were careful not to import both `Timer` classes. The inclusion of both classes would make it ambiguous which `Timer` class was being used at line 14 of the program.

```java
private Timer timer = new Timer();
```

Although we cannot import both `Timer` classes into a single Java source file, we can use both `Timer` classes in the same Java source file. The **import** statement exists to allow a syntactic shorthand when using Java resources; i.e., an **import** statement is not required to make use of Java resources. For example, by using fully qualified class names, the following code segment unambiguously uses both `Timer` classes.

```java
java.util.Timer t1 = new java.util.Timer();
javax.swing.Timer t2 = new javax.swing.Timer();
```

12.1.3   RUNNING AT A CHOSEN TIME

Our next thread example schedules two separate alerts for different times. The alerts are for two activities for the current day.

- Meeting of a prospective student at 9:30 AM.

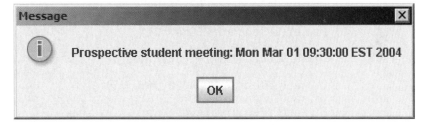

- Leave for dance recital at 6:15 PM.

The alerts are produced by program `DisplayAlert.java` of Listing 12.3. Class `DisplayAlert` provides a constructor that schedules the display of a message via a popup window. The parameters to the constructor are the message and the time the popup window is to appear.

Listing 12.3 DisplayAlert.java

```java
1.  // Displays alert at specified time
2.
3.  import javax.swing.JOptionPane;
4.  import java.awt.*;
5.  import java.util.*;
6.
7.  public class DisplayAlert extends TimerTask {
8.      // instance variables
9.      private String message;
10.     private Timer timer;
11.
12.     // DisplayAlert(): display alert s at date/time t
13.     public DisplayAlert(String s, Date t) {
14.         message = s + ": " + t;
15.         timer = new Timer();
16.         timer.schedule(this, t);
17.     }
18.
19.     // run(): pop up alert
20.     public void run() {
21.         JOptionPane.showMessageDialog(null, message);
22.         timer.cancel();
23.     }
24.
25.     // main(): application entry point
26.     public static void main(String[] args) {
27.         Calendar c = Calendar.getInstance();
28.
29.         c.set(Calendar.HOUR_OF_DAY, 9);
30.         c.set(Calendar.MINUTE, 30);
31.         c.set(Calendar.SECOND, 0);
32.
33.         Date studentTime = c.getTime();
34.
35.         c.set(Calendar.HOUR_OF_DAY, 18);
36.         c.set(Calendar.MINUTE, 15);
37.         c.set(Calendar.SECOND, 0);
38.
39.         Date danceTime = c.getTime();
40.
41.         DisplayAlert alert1 = new DisplayAlert(
42.             "Prospective student meeting", studentTime);
43.         DisplayAlert alert2 = new DisplayAlert(
44.             "Dance recital", danceTime);
45.     }
46. }
```

```
public DisplayAlert(String s, Date t)
```

Displays a popup dialog window giving alert s at the time indicated by date t.

To support its activities, class DisplayAlert has two instance variables message and timer.

```
private String message
```

References the alert message to be displayed.

```
private Timer timer
```

References the timer that schedules the display of the alert.

The definition of the `DisplayAlert` constructor uses yet another of the `Timer` methods named `schedule()`.

```
// DisplayAlert(): display alert s at date/time t
public DisplayAlert(String s, Date t) {
   message = s + ": " + t;
   timer = new Timer();
   timer.schedule(this, t);
}
```

This `schedule()` method arranges a thread to be run at the time referenced by parameter `t`. If the indicated time has already passed, then the thread is run immediately.

The `DisplayAlert` thread defined by its method `run()` creates a popup dialog of type `JOptionPane`.

```
// run(): pop up alert
public void run() {
   JOptionPane.showMessageDialog(null, message);
   timer.cancel();
}
```

`Swing` class `JOptionPane` provides a rich collection of class methods for displaying dialogs of various standard forms. Class `DisplayAlert` creates the `JOptionPane` using `JOptionPane` class method `showMessageDialog()`. This method displays an *information-message* `JOptionPane`, where an information-message `JOptionPane` displays a stylized letter *i* icon along with the message of interest.

```
public static void showMessageDialog(Component c, Object s)
   throws HeadlessException
```

Displays an information popup dialog with message `s` in the frame of component `c`. If `c` is either **null** or has no associated frame, then a default frame is created for the dialog. A runtime `java.awt.HeadlessException` is thrown if the current environment does not support a keyboard, mouse, and display.

An alert demonstration is given by `DisplayAlert` class method `main()`.

```
// main(): application entry point
public static void main(String[] args) {
   Calendar c = Calendar.getInstance();

   c.set(Calendar.HOUR_OF_DAY, 9);
   c.set(Calendar.MINUTE, 30);
   c.set(Calendar.SECOND, 0);

   Date studentTime = c.getTime();

   c.set(Calendar.HOUR_OF_DAY, 18);
   c.set(Calendar.MINUTE, 15);
   c.set(Calendar.SECOND, 0);

   Date danceTime = c.getTime();

   DisplayAlert alert1 = new DisplayAlert(
      "Prospective student meeting", studentTime);
```

```
        DisplayAlert alert2 = new DisplayAlert(
           "Dance recital", danceTime);
    }
```

Method `main()` creates alerts for two different times. The times are set by using standard class `java.util.Calendar`. Class `Calendar` is an **abstract** class that provides several class methods for manipulating calendar and date information. Its methods of interest to us are

`static public Calendar getInstance()`

> Returns a new calendar representing the current time using the default time zone and locale.

`public void set(int f, int v) throws` `ArrayIndexOutOfBoundsException`

> Sets the time field indicated by `f` to value `v`. The method throws an `ArrayIndexOutOfBoundsException` if `f` is not a valid time field indicator. The valid time field and associated values are given in Table 12.1.

`public Date getTime()`

> Returns a `Date` object representing the time of this `Calendar`.

To issue its alerts, method `main()` first creates a `Calendar` object representing the current time.

```
Calendar c = Calendar.getInstance();
```

To set up its two times alerts, method **main()** then modifies the time associated with `Calendar` variable `c`. The modifications are achieved using a `Calendar` member method `set()`.

The fields of interest for scheduling our alerts are `Calendar.HOUR`, `Calendar.MINUTE` and `Calendar.SECOND`. By first setting those fields respectively to 9, 30, and 0, the time for the prospective student appointment alert can be set.

```
c.set(Calendar.HOUR_OF_DAY, 9);
c.set(Calendar.MINUTE, 30);
c.set(Calendar.SECOND, 0);
```

The `Calendar` time then is converted to a `Date` representation suitable for scheduling a thread.

```
Date studentTime = c.getTime();
```

The calendar fields then are reset to arrange for the other alert.

```
c.set(Calendar.HOUR_OF_DAY, 18);
c.set(Calendar.MINUTE, 45);
c.set(Calendar.SECOND, 0);

Date danceTime = c.getTime();
```

Finally, two `DisplayAlert` objects are created.

```
DisplayAlert alert1 = new DisplayAlert(
   "Prospective student meeting", studentTime);

DisplayAlert alert2 = new DisplayAlert(
   "Dance recital", danceTime);
```

Their creation schedules the threads that cause the alerts to appear on the desktop at the designated times.

Table 12.1 **Calendar fields and fields values.**

Field	Purpose
AM_PM	Indicator whether the hour is before or after noon
DAY_OF_WEEK	Day of the week
MONTH	Month
DATE	Day of the month
HOUR	Hour of the morning or afternoon
MINUTE	Minute within the hour
SECOND	Second within the minute
MILLISECOND	Millisecond within the second
YEAR	Year
ZONE_OFFSET	Raw offset from GMT
WEEK_OF_MONTH	Week number within the month
WEEK_OF_YEAR	Week number within the year
DST_OFFSET	Daylight savings offset in milliseconds
ERA	Era (e.g., Gregorian.AD)
DAY_OF_WEEK_IN_MONTH	Day of the week within the month

Field Constant	Value
AM	Indicator of period midnight to just before noon
JANUARY	First month of the year
FEBRUARY	Second month of the year
APRIL	Fourth month of the year
MARCH	Third month of the year
MAY	Fifth month of the year
JULY	Seventh month of the year
JUNE	Sixth month of the year
AUGUST	Eighth month of the year
SEPTEMBER	Ninth month of the year
OCTOBER	Tenth month of the year
NOVEMBER	Eleventh month of the year
DECEMBER	Twelfth month of the year
UNDECIMBER	Thirteenth month of the lunar year
SUNDAY	Sunday
MONDAY	Monday
TUESDAY	Tuesday
WEDNESDAY	Wednesday
THURSDAY	Thursday
FRIDAY	Friday
SATURDAY	Saturday

| 12.2 | **SLEEPING** |

Thus far, our threads have performed some action. Threads are also used to pause a program for a time. For example, standard class `java.lang.Thread` has a class method `sleep()` for pausing a flow of control.

public static void sleep(**long** n) **throws** InterruptedException

> Pauses the current thread for n milliseconds. It then throws an `Interrupted-Exception`.

For example, the following code segment twice gets and displays the current time. The two time acquisitions are separated by 10 seconds.

```
Date t1 = new Date();
System.out.println(t1);
try {
   Thread.sleep(10000);
}
catch (InterruptedException e) {
}
Date t2 = new Date();
System.out.println(t2);
```

A sample running of this code segment produced output

```
Fri Jan 31 19:29:45 EST 2003
Fri Jan 31 19:29:55 EST 2003
```

Observe that the two times were indeed acquired 10 seconds apart.

For programming convenience, Listing 12.4 defines a class `Sleep` as part of package ez. The class has two class methods `pauseSeconds()` and `pauseMilliseconds()`. The methods enable a programmer to pause the flow of control for a specified number of seconds or milliseconds respectively. Besides being a syntactic shorthand, the invocations of the methods do not require user code to catch an `InterruptedException`.

public static void pauseSeconds(**long** n)

> Pauses the flow of control for n seconds.

public static void pauseMilliseconds(**long** n)

> Pauses the flow of control for n milliseconds.

For example, with `pauseSeconds()`, the previous code segment can be rewritten as

```
Date t1 = new Date();
System.out.println(t1);
ez.Sleep.pauseSeconds(10);
Date t2 = new Date();
System.out.println(t2);
```

The definitions of two `Sleep` methods are as expected. For example, method `pauseMilliseconds()` examines its parameter n to determine whether its nonnegative.

```
// pauseMilliseconds(): pauses n milliseconds
public static void pauseMilliseconds(long n) {
   if (n <= 0) {
      return;
   }
```

```
        else {
          try {
            Thread.sleep(n);
          }
          catch (java.lang.InterruptedException e) {
            return;
          }
        }
      }
```

If the value is negative, then the method immediately returns because no pause is required. Otherwise, a **try** block is entered and a Thread.sleep() invocation is made for n milliseconds. When the InterruptedException is thrown, the **catch** block performs a **return**.

We next turn our attention to the development of GUI-based programs with dynamic displays. In producing their animations, the programs make use of the Sleep class to introduce delays between display updates.

Listing 12.4 Sleep.java

```
1.  // Supports waiting
2.
3.  package ez;
4.
5.  public class Sleep {
6.      // class constant
7.      private static final int MILLISECONDS_PER_SECOND = 1000;
8.
9.      // pauseMilliseconds(): pauses n milliseconds
10.     public static void pauseMilliseconds(long n) {
11.         if (n <= 0) {
12.             return;
13.         }
14.         else {
15.             try {
16.                 Thread.sleep(n);
17.             }
18.             catch (java.lang.InterruptedException e) {
19.                 return;
20.             }
21.         }
22.     }
23.
24.     // pauseSeconds(): pauses n seconds
25.     public static void pauseSeconds(long n) {
26.         pauseMilliseconds(n*MILLISECONDS_PER_SECOND);
27.     }
28. }
```

12.3   CASE STUDY — ANIMATION

Besides making use of the Sleep class, our animations will also make use of class Step of Listing 12.5. Class Step provides the constructors and methods to generate random, but directed, changes in position. In particular, the Step class provides member methods xShift() and yShift() that return pseudorandom values from particular x- and y-intervals. These values can be used as offsets by which an object is moved.

For example, the following definition creates a Step object where pseudorandom shifts in the x-coordinate come from the integer interval 0 ... 1 and where pseudorandom shifts in the y-coordinate come from interval –1 ... 1.

```
Step step = new Step(0, 1, -1, 1);
```

With this Step object, we iteratively can invoke its xShift() and yShift() methods to generate a series of positions that when plotted correspond to a rightward pseudorandom walk.

```
int x = 0;
int y = 100;
System.out.println("Starting position: (" + x + ", " + y + ")");

for (int i = 0; i < 5; ++i) {
    // determine change in x and y
    x += step.xShift();
    y += step.yShift();

    System.out.println("New position: (" + x + ", " + y + ")");
}
```

One sample run produced output

```
Starting position: (0, 100)
New position: (1, 99)
New position: (1, 100)
New position: (2, 100)
New position: (3, 100)
New position: (4, 101)
```

and another sample run produced output

```
Starting position: (0, 100)
New position: (0, 99)
New position: (1, 98)
New position: (2, 99)
New position: (2, 99)
New position: (2, 98)
```

An examination of the Step listing indicates the following class elements.

```
public Step(int lx, int ux, int ly, int uy)
```

> Produces a Step where the pseudorandom generated x-coordinate offsets come from the interval lx ... ux and where the pseudorandom generated y-coordinate offsets come from the interval ly ... uy.

Listing 12.5 Step.java

```
1.  // generates changes in x and y from specified intervals
2.
3.  import java.util.*;
4.
5.  public class Step {
6.      // attributes and constant
7.      private static final Random DIE = new Random();
8.      private int minDeltaX;
9.      private int maxDeltaX;
10.     private int minDeltaY;
11.     private int maxDeltaY;
12.
13.     // Step(): step generator
14.     public Step(int lx, int ux, int ly, int uy) {
15.         minDeltaX = lx;
16.         maxDeltaX = ux;
17.         minDeltaY = ly;
18.         maxDeltaY = uy;
19.     }
20.
21.     // xShift(): returns a pseudorandom value from the x-interval
22.     public int xShift() {
23.         int a = getMinX();
24.         int b = getMaxX();
25.         return DIE.nextInt(b - a + 1) + a;
26.     }
27.
28.     // yShift(): returns a pseudorandom value from the y-interval
29.     public int yShift() {
30.         int a = getMinY();
31.         int b = getMaxY();
32.         return DIE.nextInt(b - a + 1) + a;
33.     }
34.
35.     // getMinX(): minimum change in x-coordinate
36.     public int getMinX() {
37.         return minDeltaX;
38.     }
39.
40.     // getMaxX(): maximum change in x-coordinate
41.     public int getMaxX() {
42.         return maxDeltaX;
43.     }
44.
45.     // getMinY(): minimum change in y-coordinate
46.     public int getMinY() {
47.         return minDeltaY;
48.     }
49.
50.     // getMaxY(): maximum change in y-coordinate
51.     public int getMaxY() {
52.         return maxDeltaY;
53.     }
54. }
```

```
public int xShift()
```

Returns a pseudorandom value from the interval `getMinX() ... getMaxX()`.

```
public int yShift()
```

Returns a pseudorandom value from the interval `getMinY() ... getMaxY()`.

```
public int getMinX()
```

Returns the minimum pseudorandom value that can be generated by `xShift()`.

```
public int getMaxX()
```

Returns the maximum pseudorandom value that can be generated by `xShift()`.

```
public int getMinY()
```

Returns the minimum pseudorandom value that can be generated by `yShift()`.

```
public int getMaxY()
```

Returns the maximum pseudorandom value that can be generated by `yShift()`.

In implementing these actions, class `Step` makes use of the following class constant and instance variables.

```
private static final Random DIE
```

Represents a pseudorandom number generator.

```
private minDeltaX
```

Represents the minimum pseudorandom x-coordinate offset to be generated.

```
private maxDeltaX
```

Represents the maximum pseudorandom x-coordinate offset to be generated.

```
private minDeltaY
```

Represents the minimum pseudorandom y-coordinate offset to be generated.

```
private maxDeltaY
```

Represents the maximum pseudorandom y-coordinate offset to be generated.

With these variables, the implementations of the `Step` constructor and member methods are straightforward and warrant no further discussion.

Listing 12.6 of program `Wiggler.java` and Listing 12.7 of program `Slider.java` demonstrate two uses of class `Step`. Both programs repeatedly render red circles after a brief delay. The points that position the circles are generated with `Step` methods `xShift()` and `yShift()`.

The step size in `Wiggler.java` is the same as the step size in the earlier code segment. Its graphic display shows a circle sequence that does not vary very much in its vertical orientation. A running of the program gives the illusion of a growing line that is wiggling through the window. The **while** loop in `Wiggler.java` iterates until the

---

Listing 12.6 Wiggler.java

```
1.  // generate a series of slightly shifted circles
2.
3.  import javax.swing.*;
4.  import java.awt.*;
5.  import ez.Sleep;
6.
7.  public class Wiggler {
8.     // main(): application entry point
9.     public static void main(String[] args) {
10.        // define animation constants
11.        final Color BACKGROUND_COLOR = Color.WHITE;
12.        final Color FOREGROUND_COLOR = Color.RED;
13.        final int PAUSE_TIME = 10;
14.        final int CIRCLE_DIAMETER = 10;
15.
16.        // set up display
17.        JFrame window = new JFrame("Wiggling");
18.        window.setSize(200, 200);
19.        window.setDefaultCloseOperation(JFrame.EXIT_ON_CLOSE);
20.        window.setBackground(BACKGROUND_COLOR);
21.        window.setVisible(true);
22.        window.setBackground(BACKGROUND_COLOR);
23.
24.        // set up and draw first circle
25.        Graphics g = window.getGraphics();
26.        g.setColor(FOREGROUND_COLOR);
27.
28.        int x = 0;
29.        int y = window.getHeight()/2;
30.
31.        g.fillOval(x, y, CIRCLE_DIAMETER, CIRCLE_DIAMETER);
32.
33.        // set up generator for subsequent offsets
34.        Step step = new Step (0, 1, -1, 1);
35.
36.        // draw the shifted circles
37.        while (x < window.getWidth()) {
38.           x += step.xShift();
39.           y += step.yShift();
40.           g.fillOval(x, y, CIRCLE_DIAMETER, CIRCLE_DIAMETER);
41.           Sleep.pauseMilliseconds(PAUSE_TIME);
42.        }
43.     }
44.  }
```

---

upper-left-hand corner of the bounding box of the current circle lies beyond the right edge of the window.

```
// draw the shifted circles
while (x < window.getWidth()) {
   x += step.xShift();
   y += step.yShift();
   g.fillOval(x, y, CIRCLE_DIAMETER, CIRCLE_DIAMETER);
   Sleep.pauseMilliseconds(PAUSE_TIME);
}
```

To give the illusion of growth, the program pauses fifteen milliseconds after each circle rendering. Figure 12.4 gives a representative snapshot of each `Wiggler.java`.

Figure 12.4 **Snapshot of Wiggler.java.**

Program `Slider.java` of Listing 12.7 is similar to `Wiggler.java`. The only consequential difference between the two programs occurs in the **while** loop body.

```
// draw the "sliding" circles
while (x < window.getWidth()) {
  // erase previously rendered circle
  g.setColor(BACKGROUND_COLOR);
  g.fillOval(x, y, CIRCLE_DIAMETER, CIRCLE_DIAMETER);
  g.setColor(FOREGROUND_COLOR);

  // draw the circle at its new position
  x += step.xShift();
  y += step.yShift();
  g.fillOval(x, y, CIRCLE_DIAMETER, CIRCLE_DIAMETER);
  Sleep.pauseMilliseconds(PAUSE_TIME);
  }
}
```

In program `Slider.java`, the **while** loop body performs three additional statements at the start of each iteration.

```
// erase previously rendered circle
g.setColor(BACKGROUND_COLOR);
g.fillOval(x, y, CIRCLE_DIAMETER, CIRCLE_DIAMETER);
g.setColor(FOREGROUND_COLOR);
```

These statements assist the "movement" of the circle. The first two of these statements render a new circle at the position of interest (x, y). Thus, the new circle replaces what previously was displayed. Because the new circle is displayed in the background color, the old circle is effectively gone and the new circle is not distinguishable with the background. The other new statement resets the rendering color to the foreground color.

Listing 12.7 Slider.java

```java
1.  // simulate a sliding circle
2.
3.  import javax.swing.*;
4.  import java.awt.*;
5.  import ez.Sleep;
6.
7.  public class Slider {
8.      // main(): application entry point
9.      public static void main(String[] args) {
10.         // define animation constants
11.         final Color BACKGROUND_COLOR = Color.WHITE;
12.         final Color FOREGROUND_COLOR = Color.RED;
13.         final int PAUSE_TIME = 10;
14.         final int CIRCLE_DIAMETER = 10;
15.
16.         // set up display
17.         JFrame window = new JFrame("Sliding");
18.
19.         window.setSize(200, 200);
20.         window.setDefaultCloseOperation(JFrame.EXIT_ON_CLOSE);
21.
22.         window.setBackground(BACKGROUND_COLOR);
23.         window.setVisible(true);
24.
25.         window.setBackground(BACKGROUND_COLOR);
26.
27.         Graphics g = window.getGraphics();
28.         g.setColor(FOREGROUND_COLOR);
29.
30.         // set up and draw first circle
31.         int x = 0;
32.         int y = window.getHeight()/2;
33.
34.         g.fillOval(x, y, CIRCLE_DIAMETER, CIRCLE_DIAMETER);
35.
36.         // set up generator for subsequent offsets
37.         Step step = new Step (0, 1, -1, 1);
38.
39.         // draw the "sliding" circles
40.         while (x < window.getWidth()) {
41.             // erase previously rendered circle
42.             g.setColor(BACKGROUND_COLOR);
43.             g.fillOval(x, y, CIRCLE_DIAMETER, CIRCLE_DIAMETER);
44.             g.setColor(FOREGROUND_COLOR);
45.
46.             // draw the circle at its new position
47.             x += step.xShift();
48.             y += step.yShift();
49.             g.fillOval(x, y, CIRCLE_DIAMETER, CIRCLE_DIAMETER);
50.             Sleep.pauseMilliseconds(PAUSE_TIME);
51.         }
52.     }
53. }
```

A new position of interest (x, y) then is calculated and a new circle is rendered at that position in the foreground color.

```
// draw the circle at its new position
x += step.xShift();
y += step.yShift();
g.fillOval(x, y, CIRCLE_DIAMETER, CIRCLE_DIAMETER);
```

The new position is a very slight shifting of the previous position. Because the old and new positions are so close to each other and because the background-colored and foreground-colored circles are rendered in a manner that appears to be simultaneous, the visual effect is that of the circle sliding to its new position. The process is depicted in Figure 12.5.

Figure 12.5 Rendering in an iteration of Slider.java.

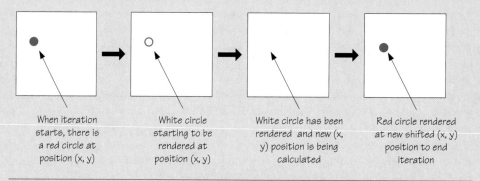

When iteration starts, there is a red circle at position (x, y) → White circle starting to be rendered at position (x, y) → White circle has been rendered and new (x, y) position is being calculated → Red circle rendered at new shifted (x, y) position to end iteration

The short millisecond program pause between circle slides causes the perceived motion to be occurring at a reasonable rate.

```
Sleep.pauseMilliseconds(PAUSE_TIME);
```

As a result, when program Slider.java is run, its display has the appearance of a red ball moving erratically across the window. Listing 12.7 contains the code for Slider.java.

We now our attention to the final example of the chapter—the simulation of three swimming fish.

12.4 CASE STUDY — SWIMMING FISH

In order to have three fish swimming, we need an aquarium. For now, our aquarium representation will be quite simple—it will be a window whose background is colored sea green. In the exercises, we consider some alternatives for producing more interesting aquariums. Our aquarium representation is named Aquarium.

The objective of this case study is to practice using threads and animation in the design and implementation of a class

ANALYSIS AND DESIGN

Class `Aquarium` is extended from `JFrame` and it provides a default constructor and two methods. It does not maintain any additional attributes.

`public Aquarium()`

> Initializes and displays a sea-green colored window of appropriate size.

`public Color getWaterColor()`

> Returns the color of the aquarium water.

`public Graphics getGraphicsContext()`

> Returns the graphics context in which the elements (i.e., fish) of the aquarium should be rendered.

The definition of class `Aquarium` is given in Listing 12.8. The constructor and methods are sufficiently simple to not warrant any analysis.

Listing 12.8 Aquarium.java

```java
1.  // Represents an aquarium
2.
3.  import java.awt.*;
4.  import javax.swing.*;
5.
6.  class Aquarium extends JFrame {
7.      private static final int AQUARIUM_WIDTH = 400;
8.      private static final int AQUARIUM_HEIGHT = 400;
9.      private static final Color SEA_BLUE = new Color(109,171,177);
10.
11.     public Aquarium() {
12.         super("Fishy swim");
13.         setDefaultCloseOperation(JFrame.EXIT_ON_CLOSE);
14.         getContentPane().setBackground(SEA_BLUE);
15.         setSize(AQUARIUM_WIDTH, AQUARIUM_HEIGHT);
16.         setVisible(true);
17.     }
18.
19.     public Color getWaterColor() {
20.         return SEA_BLUE;
21.     }
22.
23.     public Graphics getGraphicsContext() {
24.         return getContentPane().getGraphics();
25.     }
26. }
```

The simplest approach to produce a moving fish is to extend class `Fish` of Listing 9.12. This approach is taken with class `MovingFish` of Listing 12.9. A `MovingFish` object has one additional attribute that a plain `Fish` object does not have—a `stroke`. The `MovingFish` instance variable `stroke` is of type `Step` and it represents how the fish can change its position in a single swim stroke.

`private Step stroke`

> Describes the possible range of motion for a single swim stroke of the fish.

Class `MovingFish` should provide constructors that correspond to the `Fish` constructors and it should provide constructors that allow the swimming stroke to be speci-

---

Listing 12.9 MovingFish.java

```
1.  // Represent a moving fish
2.
3.  import java.awt.*;
4.
5.  public class MovingFish extends Fish {
6.      // movement attribute
7.      private Step stroke;
8.
9.      // MovingFish(): default fish with default movement
10.     public MovingFish() {
11.         stroke = new Step(0, 1, -1, 1);
12.     }
13.
14.     // swim(): move the fish
15.     public void swim() {
16.         int x = getX();
17.         int y = getY();
18.
19.         x += stroke.xShift();
20.         y += stroke.yShift();
21.         setPosition(x, y);
22.     }
23. }
```

---

fied. The MovingFish implementation of Listing 12.9 is a basic one and supplies only a default constructor. Other constructors are left to the exercises.

```
public MovingFish()
```

Constructs a pseudorandomly colored fish with swim stroke x-coordinate movement coming from the interval 0 ... 1 and swim stroke y-coordinate movement coming from the interval –1 ... 1.

To implement a default MovingFish constructor is simple. The default superclass constructor is used to configure the Fish attributes of the new MovingFish object. The stroke attribute then is configured by constructing a new Step with appropriate x- and y-axis intervals.

```
// MovingFish(): default fish with default movement
public MovingFish() {
    stroke = new Step(0, 1, -1, 1));
}
```

Because our implementation is minimal, only one MovingFish mutator is defined—swim(). Method swim() updates the position of the fish by making a single pseudorandom stroke.

```
public void swim()
```

Updates the position of the fish through the generation of x- and y-coordinate offsets. The offsets are generated using the Step shifting methods. The new position of the fish is shifting of its previous position with respect to the offsets.

To implement the behavior required of method swim(), the current position (x, y) of the fish must be determined.

```
// swim(): move the fish
public void swim() {
   int x = getX();
   int y = getY();

   x += stroke.xShift();
   y += stroke.yShift();
   setPosition(x, y);
}
```

The new position then can be determined by incrementing x by stroke.xShift() and incrementing y by stroke.yShift(). The new value (x, y) then can be used to update the position attribute of the fish.

IMPLEMENTATION

We now turn our attention to the actual aquarium simulation. Our approach is again one of minimality. Our simulation will animate 1000 swim strokes for each of the three fish. The fish will not "react" to swimming into the sides of the aquarium by changing course. Instead they will continue their course and disappear. (The exercises consider how to implement a bumping reaction.) A snapshot of the simulation is depicted in Figure 12.6.

The simulation will have two parts. The first part will set up the aquarium and place the fish. The second part will simulate the 1000 swim strokes.

To set up the animation, we will need an Aquarium representation and three MovingFish.

```
Aquarium aquarium = new Aquarium()
MovingFish[] fish = { new MovingFish(), new MovingFish(),
                      new MovingFish() };
```

For reason of aesthetics, the fish should be positioned in different areas of the aquarium.

```
fish[0].setPosition(   0, 100);
fish[1].setPosition(  50, 200);
fish[2].setPosition(-100, 300);
```

The positioning we prefer starts with only two of the fish being visible initially.

In order to simulate movement, the fish need to be rendered both in their true color and in the background color. Thus, the animation needs access to the graphic context of the aquarium and to the color of its water.

```
Graphics g = aquarium.getGraphicsContext();
Color water = aquarium.getWaterColor();
```

Because one of the rendering operations requires a resetting of a fish to its true color, it is appropriate to maintain a Color array c of the true fish colors.

```
Color[] c = new Color[fish.length];
for (int i = 0; i < fish.length; ++i) {
   c[i] = fish[i].getColor();
}
```

Figure 12.6 **Snapshot of ThreeSwimmingFish.java display.**

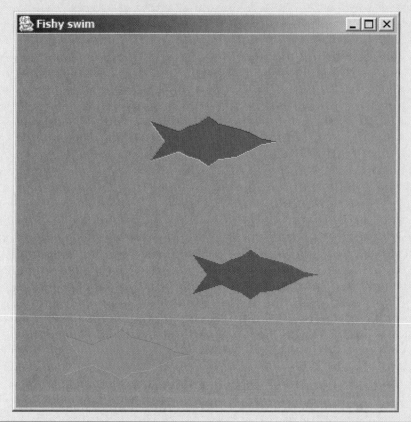

With the previously described actions in place, fish movement then can be simulated. The animation should follow the form of SimpleClock.java and Slider.java; that is, for each scene in the animation the following activities should occur.

- Erase the current renderings of the changeable elements (i.e., the fish at their current positions);

- Update the changeable elements (i.e., have each fish swim a stroke);

- Render the changeable elements (i.e., the fish at their new positions);

- Pause the animation to allow the change to be perceived.

Each of the first three activities can be implemented using a **for** loop that iterates once for each fish. For the first activity, the fish need to be rendered in the color of the water.

```
// erase the previous position
for (int j = 0; j < fish.length; ++j) {
    fish[j].setColor(water);
    fish[j].paint(g);
}
```

For the second activity, the fish need to swim a stroke.

```
// have each fish swim a stroke
for (int j = 0; j < fish.length; ++j) {
   fish[j].swim();
}
```

For the third activity, the fish need to be rendered in their true colors.

```
// paint the fish at their new positions
for (int j = 0; j < fish.length; ++j) {
   fish[j].setColor(c[j]);
   fish[j].paint(g);
}
```

The last activity can be accomplished by having the animation sleep for several milliseconds.

```
// pause to allow the movement to be perceived
ez.Sleep.pauseMilliseconds(5);
```

A complete implementation of the preceding animation description is given in program ThreeFishSwimming.java of Listing 12.10.

Listing 12.10 ThreeSwimmingFish.java

```
1.  // Represent three swimming fish
2.
3.  import java.awt.*;
4.
5.  public class ThreeSwimmingFish {
6.     public static void main(String[] args) {
7.        // set up the animation
8.        Aquarium aquarium = new Aquarium();
9.        MovingFish[] fish = { new MovingFish(), new MovingFish(),
10.                             new MovingFish() };
11.
12.       fish[0].setPosition(   0, 100);
13.       fish[1].setPosition(  50, 200);
14.       fish[2].setPosition(-150, 300);
15.
16.       Graphics g = aquarium.getGraphicsContext();
17.       Color water = aquarium.getWaterColor();
18.
19.       Color[] c = new Color[fish.length];
20.       for (int i = 0; i < fish.length; ++i) {
21.          c[i] = fish[i].getColor();
22.       }
23.
24.       // start the animation
25.       for (int i = 0; i < 1000; ++i) {
26.          // erase the previous position
27.          for (int j = 0; j < fish.length; ++j) {
28.             fish[j].setColor(water);
29.             fish[j].paint(g);
30.          }
31.
32.          // have each fish swim a stroke
```

Listing 12.10 ThreeSwimmingFish.java (Continued)

```
33.          for (int j = 0; j < fish.length; ++j) {
34.              fish[j].swim();
35.          }
36.
37.          // paint the fish at their new positions
38.          for (int j = 0; j < fish.length; ++j) {
39.              fish[j].setColor(c[j]);
40.              fish[j].paint(g);
41.          }
42.
43.          // pause to allow the movement to be perceived
44.          ez.Sleep.pauseMilliseconds(5);
45.      }
46.   }
47. }
```

This analysis completes our introduction to threads.

12.5 REVIEW

- Programs with single flows of control are known as sequential processes.

- Java supports programs with concurrent flows of control. These independent flows of control are called threads.

- Because threads run within a program and make use of its resources in their execution, threads are also called lightweight processes.

- To simulate multiprocessing, uniprocessor computing systems normally practice timesharing. A timesharing computer system repeatedly gives each process a slice of time on the processor to make progress with respect to its action. Because the time slices are so small and occur so frequently, the computing system has the appearance of simultaneous behavior.

- Java has several classes that support the creation and scheduling of threads. Classes `java.util.Timer` and `java.util.TimerTask` are generally the easiest to use. They allow a thread to be created and run either at a time relative to the current time or at some specific time.

- Class `Timer` has methods named `schedule()` for creating threads either after some specified delay or at some specific time.

  `public void` schedule(TimerTask task, `long` m)

  Runs `task.run()` after waiting m milliseconds.

  `public void` schedule(TimerTask task, `long` m, `long` n)

  Runs `task.run()` after waiting m milliseconds. It then repeatedly reruns `task.run()` every **n** milliseconds.

  `public void` schedule(TimerTask task, Date t)

  Runs `task.run()` at the time indicated by date t.

- By extending **abstract** class `TimerTask` and specifying a definition for its **abstract** method run(), an application-specific thread can be created.

  `abstract void` run()

  Implements the action to be performed by this task.

- A subclass implementation of `TimerTask`'s **abstract** method run() has typically two parts. The first part defines the application-specific action the thread is to perform. The second part ends the thread using its method cancel().

- Class `Date` is Java's principal class for time representation. Some of its constructors and methods include

  `public` Date()

  Creates a date representation reflecting the current time to the millisecond.

  `public` String toString()

  Returns a textual representation of the date.

- `Swing` class `JOptionPane` provides a rich collection of class methods for displaying dialog windows of various standard forms. One such method is showMessageDialog().

public static void showMessageDialog(Component c, Object s)
  throws HeadlessException

Displays an information popup dialog with message s in the frame of component c. If c is **null** or has no associated frame, then a default frame is created for the dialog. A runtime java.awt.HeadlessException is thrown if the current environment does not support a keyboard, mouse, and display.

■ Class Calendar is an **abstract** class that provides several methods named getInstance() for creating calendar times. The primary purpose of class Calendar is to support the setting and conversion of Date information. Some of its methods include

static public Calendar getInstance()

Returns a new calendar representing the current time using the default time zone and locale.

public void set(**int** f, **int** v) **throws**
  ArrayIndexOutOfBoundsException

Sets the time field indicated by f to value v. Throws an **ArrayIndexOutOf-BoundsException** if f is not a valid time field indicator. The valid time field and associated values are given in Table 12.1.

■ Class java.lang.Thread has a class method sleep() for pausing a flow of control.

public static void sleep(**long** n) **throws** InterruptedException

Pauses execution for n milliseconds. It then throws an **InterruptedException**.

| 12.6 | **SELF-TEST** |

S12.1 Suppose t is a Timer and task is a specialized TimerTask. Schedule two immediate occurrences of threads that run task.

S12.2 Suppose t is a Timer and task is a specialized TimerTask. Schedule an immediate occurrence of a thread that runs task. Also schedule an occurrence of a thread that runs task three seconds later.

S12.3 Suppose t is a Timer and task is a specialized TimerTask. Schedule an immediate occurrence of a thread that runs task two seconds from the current time. Reoccurrences of the thread start every second.

S12.4 Extend class Sleep to provide a method pauseMinutes() with a single **int** parameter n that pauses execution for n minutes.

| 12.7 | **EXERCISES** |

12.1 What is a thread?

12.2 What happens when a thread runs?

12.3 Do programs with a graphical user interface automatically have more than one thread?

The following definitions are in effect for Exercises 12.4–12.6.

```
DisplayCharSequence c = new DisplayCharSequence("J");
Timer t = new Timer();
```

12.4 When is the thread scheduled in the following statement?

```
t.schedule(c, 2000);
```

12.5 When is the thread scheduled in the following statement?

```
t.schedule(c, -100);
```

12.6 When is the thread scheduled in the following statement?

```
t.schedule(c, 2000, 1500);
```

12.7 Modify `SimpleClock.java` to display the time using a format appropriate to your locale.

12.8 Modify `SimpleClock.java` to support user selection of the display format.

12.9 Add accessor methods to class `Step`.

12.10 Add mutator methods to class `Step`.

12.11 Add `toString()`, `equals()`, and `clone()` methods to class `Step`.

12.12 Develop a program `CalendarAlert.java` that reads from a file `calendar.txt`. The file contains data in the format: *month day hour* : *event*, where month, day, and hour are integers and event is a string. The program should pop up an alert message that warns about the event. The alert should appear 15 minutes before the scheduled time of the event. The following listing represents a possible data file for the program.

```
 1  4  9 : Sing happy birthday to mom
 4 15  5 : Pay taxes
 5 12  9 : Sing happy birthday to dad
10 31 19 : Go trick-or-treating
```

12.13 Create a program `Butterfly.java` based on program `Wiggle.java` that displays a polygon in the shape of a butterfly rather than a circle.

12.14 Develop the following `MovingFish` constructors.

```
public MovingFish(Color c, Polygon p, int x, int y)
```
Creates a fish with color `c` and shape `p` at coordinate (`x`, `y`). The fish should have the same type of movement as a default-constructed fish.

```
public MovingFish(Step s)
```
Creates a fish with default shape and position, and movement `s`.

```
public MovingFish(Color c, Polygon p, int x, int y, Step s)
```
Creates a fish with color `c`, shape `p` at coordinate (`x`, `y`) and movement `s`.

12.15 Develop the following `MovingFish` facilitator.

public void paint(Color c, Graphics g)

Renders the fish in color c in graphics context g.

12.16 How might paint() method of Exercise 12.15 be used to simplify ThreeMov-ingFish.java?

12.17 Design and implement a class UnderwaterPlant for representing plants. Provide a class method makePlant() that creates a basic underwater plant. The default constructor should make use of the method.

12.18 Design and implement a class Aerator for representing an aquarium air bubbler. Provide a class makeAerator() that creates a basic aerator. The default constructor should make use of the method. An aerator releases bubbles in a regular manner that slowly rise to the surface.

12.19 Design and implement a class Sand for representing the gravel surface often found in aquariums. Provide a class method makeSand(). The default constructor should make use of the method.

12.20 Redesign and reimplement class Aquarium so that it supports both different-sized aquariums and the presence of sand, plants, and aerators. The implementation should make use of the classes UnderwaterPlant, Aerator, and Sand from Exercises 12.17–12.19.

12.21 Modify ThreeSwimmingFish.java so that rather than erasing the changeable elements, the stationary elements of the aquarium are redrawn. Such a change should allow for a complex background as produced by the modified aquarium representation of Exercise 12.20.

12.8   PROGRAMMING PROJECT — BETTER FISH

Aquarium.java of Listing 12.8 is only a first step at creating an aquarium simulator. For example, Exercises 12.14–12.21 propose changes that enable a more realistic aquarium background to be represented.

> The objective of this case study is to practice using threads and animation in the design and implementation of a class

Our interest here is to develop a more realistic fish that has capability to change course when it reaches the limit of its territory. In support of this development, you will design and implement classes Territory and BoundaryBehavior.

Class Territory supports objects that maintain and give access to four values: a minimum x-coordinate, a maximum x-coordinate, a minimum y-coordinate, and a maximum y-coordinate. In implementing the constructors and methods make use of the following instance variables.

private int xMin

Represents the minimum x-coordinate value.

private int xMax

Represents maximum x-coordinate value.

> `private int` yMin
>
> Represents the minimum y-coordinate value.
>
> `private int` yMax
>
> Represents maximum y-coordinate value.

These instance variables should also be used in implementing the following behaviors.

> `public boolean` inside(`int` x, `int` y)
>
> Indicates whether location (x, y) lies inside or on the edge of the territory.
>
> `public boolean` outside(`int` x, `int` y)
>
> Indicates whether location (x, y) lies neither inside nor on the edge of the territory.
>
> `public boolean` atLimit(`int` x, `int` y)
>
> Indicates whether location (x, y) lies on the edge of the territory.

Class `BoundaryBehavior` should provide six **public** class constants of type `BoundaryBehavior`. It should also provide a **protected** default constructor that performs no action. The constants will correspond to common behaviors with regard to an object's continued motion when it reaches a vertical or horizontal boundary:

- `BoundaryBehavior.Freeze`: When a vertical or horizontal boundary is reached by the object, its motion pauses.
- `BoundaryBehavior.Wraparound`: When a vertical or horizontal boundary is reached by the object, motion continues from the same relative position on the opposite boundary.
- `BoundaryBehavior.Reverse`: When a vertical or horizontal boundary is reached by the object, motion continues in the opposite direction from the current position.
- `BoundaryBehavior.Ignore`: When a vertical or horizontal boundary is reached by the object, it is ignored.
- `BoundaryBehavior.Clockwise`: When a vertical or horizontal boundary is reached by the object, motion continues from the current position in the direction that is clockwise to the reached boundary.
- `BoundaryBehavior.CounterClockwise`: When a vertical or horizontal boundary is reached by the object, motion continues from the current position in the direction that is counter-clockwise to the reached boundary.

Design and implement a class `BetterFish` that extends `MovingFish`. A `BetterFish` provides two additional fish attributes—a `Territory` and a `BoundaryBehavior`. Class `BetterFish` should at a minimum provide the following constructors.

> `public` BetterFish()
>
> Creates a fish with default shape, position, and movement. The territory of the fish should be boundless. Although it does not matter, its boundary behavior is reversal.
>
> `public` MovingFish(Step s)
>
> Creates a fish with default shape, position, territory, and boundary behavior. The stroke of the fish should be s.
>
> `public` MovingFish(Territory t, BoundaryBehavior b)
>
> Creates a fish with default shape, position and movement. The territory of the fish should be t and its boundary behavior should be b.

```
public MovingFish(Color c, Polygon p, int x, int y, Step s,
  Territory t, BoundaryBehavior b)
```
Creates a fish with color c, shape p at coordinate (x, y), movement s, territory t, and boundary behavior b.

The class should also provide accessors and mutators for its `Territory` and a `BoundaryBehavior` attributes.

Most importantly, the class should also override `MovingFish` method `swim()`. The new `swim()` method should respond appropriately when a stroke would bring a fish outside of its territory.

```
public void swim()
```
Makes a stroke. If the stroke would leave the bounding box for the fish completely within its territory, the new position is accepted. If the stroke does not allow the bounding box of the fish to remain within its territory, then one or more of the following actions are performed as necessary depending upon the boundary behavior of the fish and which boundary(s) would be crossed.

- Reverse the stroke;
- Update the stroke in a clockwise manner;
- Update the stroke in a counterclockwise manner;
- Shift the position of the fish in a wrap-around manner;
- Flip the outline of the fish right-to-left.

Each of these possible actions should be implemented as a **protected** method.

Lastly, develop a program `ThreeSwimmingBetterFish.java` that demonstrates your fish in action. The loop that runs the animation should be an infinite loop.

12.9   SELF-TEST ANSWERS

S12.1 The following code segment suffices.

```
t.schedule(task, 0);
t.schedule(task, 0);
```

S12.2 The following code segment suffices.

```
t.schedule(task, 0);
t.schedule(task, 3000);
```

S12.3 The following code segment suffices.

```
t.schedule(task, 2000, 1000);
```

S12.4 The following definition suffices.

```
import ez.Sleep;

public class MoreSleep extends Sleep {
    // pauseMinutes(): pauses n minutes
    public static void pauseMinutes(long n) {
        pauseSeconds(n*60);
    }
}
```

13 TESTING AND DEBUGGING

Two important aspects of software development are testing and debugging. The purpose of testing is to identify any problems before the software is put to use. Software testing is a major aspect of producing quality software. For large software projects, testing and debugging are 40 to 50 percent of the overall project costs. For major software projects, a large software company might employ as many as one or two testers for every development programmer. Debugging is the process of locating and repairing a problem identified by testing or reported by a user. Debugging is a two-step process—you locate the problem; and then you fix it. If not done properly, testing and debugging can consume significant time and resources. In this chapter, we discuss the basics of testing software and strategies for debugging once a problem has been recognized.

OBJECTIVES

- Introduce various testing techniques including black-box testing, white-box testing, unit testing, integration testing, and system testing.
- Present and explain the value of inspections and code reviews.
- Introduce techniques for developing effective and efficient test cases such as statement coverage, path coverage, and equivalence partitioning.

13.1   TESTING

We have all encountered bugs or problems in programs we have used. If you have ever had your word processor crash after entering a particularly long passage of text, you know how irritating bugs can be. Some bugs are so costly that they make the newspaper headlines. The crash of the Mars Polar Lander on the surface of Mars in 1999 is a recent example. In this incident, a 165 million dollar mission was lost because of a problem that went undetected despite extensive testing. The story of why the Polar Lander crashed illustrates the difficulties of thorough testing.

The landing was supposed to go like this: As the lander entered the atmosphere of Mars, a parachute would deploy to slow the lander's descent. As it neared the surface, the parachute would be discarded, the lander's three legs would snap into position for landing, and the lander's 12 engines would fire to slow the craft to a speed where it could land safely. Each of the lander's three legs had a sensor that would send a signal to the on-board computer to turn off the spacecraft's landing engines when at least one of the legs touched the surface.

Using a similar lander, investigators determined that when the legs were deployed for landing, vibrations could have caused the leg sensors to send spurious signals. In this scenario, the engines would shut down when the craft was about 130 feet high, and the lander would hit the surface at 50 miles per hour.

So how did this problem go undetected? Various postcrash investigations showed that tests of individual systems would not have exposed the problem. One full-scale system test was conducted that should have revealed the presence of the problem. However, the sensors were improperly wired for that test, and the problem went undetected. After the wiring was corrected, a full-scale test was not repeated because of budgetary constraints and time pressures.

The Mars Polar Lander illustrates why thorough testing is so difficult to do. While all the components work correctly when tested individually (unit testing), the system may not work correctly when tested as a whole (system testing). Thus, one must do both thorough unit testing as well as thorough system testing. Because of budgetary constraints and deadlines, however, all too often we convince ourselves that, even though some aspect of the system has changed, further testing is not warranted. Careful programmers *always* retest before delivering software even after the most trivial changes.

After you have written a program, how do you convince yourself that the program works correctly? The not-so-careful programmer runs the program with a few test inputs and then checks to see if the answers are correct. For the simplest programs, running a few tests may be enough, but this approach is hardly adequate even for a program of moderate complexity, and it surely will not be sufficient for a complex program of more than 1,000 lines.

In this chapter we discuss some strategies for testing the software that you design and implement. Unfortunately, a thorough discussion of testing is beyond the scope of this book. There are many excellent texts devoted just to the theory, science, and art of testing software. Section 13.4 lists several of the texts that we have found to contain helpful information about testing strategies and procedures.

We note before proceeding that testing is not a panacea for producing high-quality software. There is a well-known quote by the late computer scientist Edgar Dijkstra that gets to the heart of the problem. He observed that "Program testing can be used to show the presence of bugs, but never to show their absence."

High-quality software can be achieved only by applying testing along with a number of other software engineering techniques. These techniques include formal and informal reviews of the software specification, the proposed design or architecture of the system, as well as the actual code. Indeed, software engineering studies have shown that a disciplined, systematic review process is more effective at avoiding bugs in shipped software than testing. Another important element is the ability to manage and track evolving software effectively. Source-code control systems and software for tracking bugs are commonly used to help automate these tasks. These subjects are covered in depth in software engineering courses.

13.1.1   TESTING — AN EXAMPLE

The first thing to realize about bugs and testing is that the earlier problems are found, the better. Software engineering studies have shown that the costs of finding and fixing a problem grow exponentially with time. For example, a bug found early during the specification phase may cost little or nothing to repair. For the sake of argument, let's say it costs a dollar to fix. That same bug, if discovered during the final testing of the software, may cost hundreds or thousands of dollars to fix.

The high cost of fixing bugs discovered late in the software development process means that we should test code as we write it. This approach makes sense from a number of standpoints. Let's say we are designing and coding one particular function that is part of a larger system we are working on. At this point in time, we are enmeshed in the details of the problem. This is a good point to test this module. If a problem is discovered, because of our immediate familiarity with the code, we can most likely fix it quickly. On the other hand, if the problem crops up months later, we will need to refamiliarize ourselves with the code before we can diagnose and fix the problem. Furthermore, it's likely the method or class has grown over time, which again will make finding the bug harder. The process of testing a single module or function is known as *unit testing*.

To illustrate the process of testing, and unit testing in particular, let's begin development of an LED timer for displaying elapsed time. LED clocks are used in many consumer electronic devices such as microwave ovens, digital watches, clock radios, and VCRs to display numbers and time (time of day, elapsed time, etc.). An LED timer could be a handy class for building games that have a time limit, developing a computerized scoreboard, and so forth.

Our initial task is to develop the LED class that we will need to build the clock. As we will see, unit testing of our LED class will not only help us find any problems before we tackle larger problems, but it will also help us refine the interface to the object early: before it is used in a larger project and modification becomes more costly.

Following our object-oriented design approach, we must determine the attributes and behaviors of an LED. Obviously we need to control the value displayed. Our approach for realizing an LED is to use GIF images of digits to display a number. (GIF stands for Graphics Interchange Format, a common format for images.) For example, the image of the GIF for the number three looks like this:

$$3$$

Our website has GIF images for the numerals zero through nine.

The Swing API class `JLabel`, besides being useful for displaying short text strings, can also be used for displaying images. Class `JLabel` supports display of GIF and JPEG images. Because class `JLabel` already has the basic attributes and behaviors we need to realize an abstraction of an LED, we decide it would be smart to extend `JLabel` via inheritance.

For our initial cut at designing class LED, we determine that in addition to all the attributes and behaviors of class `JLabel`, class LED needs the following additional attributes.

- `value`—an integer value that the LED should display.
- `images`—a class array that contains a GIF image for each possible digit.

For the public interface, we will need an inspector and mutator for the `value` attribute. Our initial declaration for class LED is given in Listing 13.1.

Our use of inheritance makes the implementation of class LED quite simple. The only interesting part of the implementation is definition of the array `images` to hold the GIF images for each digit. This array is defined to be a **private final static** array. By making the array **final static**, we are indicating that the GIF images are to be immutable and shared across all instantiations of class LED. This sharing of images between instantiations of LED objects will save space.

Now that we have a preliminary version of class LED, we have a choice. We can continue to develop the code for the clock, or we can stop and test class LED to make sure it works properly by doing unit testing. As we mentioned earlier, it is much easier to test and find problems now, while we are familiar with the code, rather than waiting for problems to crop up down the road. However, how do we test our class given that we haven't written the program yet? We must provide a *test harness* or *test stub* to exercise our code. A test harness is a small piece of code written to test or exercise the code being developed.

Writing test harnesses is a standard subtask of unit testing. It is tempting to discard these code fragments after testing is completed, but the modest time and effort it takes to save these stubs is an investment that will pay off later when a bug is uncovered. You will already have a set of test harnesses available to help locate the bug and then ensure that

---

Listing 13.1 Class LED

```
1.   // Class LED: simulates an LED for a clock or timer
2.   import javax.swing.*;
3.
4.   public class LED extends JLabel {
5.
6.       // instance variables
7.       private int value;
8.
9.       // class constant holding images of digits
10.      private static final Icon images[] = {
11.        new ImageIcon("digit0.gif"),
12.        new ImageIcon("digit1.gif"),
13.        new ImageIcon("digit2.gif"),
14.        new ImageIcon("digit3.gif"),
15.        new ImageIcon("digit4.gif"),
16.        new ImageIcon("digit5.gif"),
17.        new ImageIcon("digit6.gif"),
18.        new ImageIcon("digit7.gif"),
19.        new ImageIcon("digit8.gif"),
20.        new ImageIcon("digit9.gif")
21.      };
22.
23.      // LED(): default constructor
24.      LED(int i) {
25.          setValue(i);
26.      }
27.
28.      // getValue(): get the LED value
29.      public int getValue() {
30.          return value;
31.      }
32.
33.      // setValue(): set the LED to a new value
34.      public void setValue(int i) {
35.          value = i;
36.          setIcon(images[i]);
37.      }
38.  }
```

---

the fix did not break something else. We often create a test directory where the various test harnesses we have written for a project are kept.

Listing 13.2 contains a test harness code for the LED class. The code creates a JFrame object, creates an LED with value zero, adds it to the frame, and then makes the frame visible. When we compile and run this code, the following window appears.

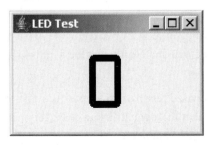

Listing 13.2 LED test harness — version 1

```
 1.  // Test harness for class LED
 2.  import java.awt.*;
 3.  import javax.swing.*;
 4.
 5.  public class LEDTest {
 6.      // instance constants and variables
 7.      private static final int WINDOW_WIDTH = 200;
 8.      private static final int WINDOW_HEIGHT = 125;
 9.
10.      // main(): application entry point
11.      public static void main(String[] args) {
12.          JFrame w1 = new JFrame("LED Test");
13.          w1.setSize(WINDOW_WIDTH, WINDOW_HEIGHT);
14.          w1.setLayout(new FlowLayout());
15.
16.          LED digit = new LED(0);
17.          w1.add(digit);
18.          w1.setVisible(true);
19.      }
20.  }
```

Our code worked! Depending on what we are planning to do, this amount of testing might be enough. However, for code used in a commercial application, we are not even close to being done. To test this code thoroughly, we need to think about how the code will be used and what could possibly go wrong. What we need is a systematic approach to unit testing.

First off, we need test cases that demonstrate that the code satisfies its requirements. What are the requirements of class LED? Unfortunately, we did not formally write these down. In a real software project, the first step is to write down formal specifications of what a class is supposed to do. However, we do have an informal idea of the capabilities class LED should provide because it is to be used to develop clock type objects, calculators, and other objects requiring a numeric display.

- Class LED should be capable of displaying the digits 0 through 9.

- The value that an LED object is displaying can be changed.

Using this informal specification, we can design a more comprehensive set of tests. Basically we need to ensure that class LED satisfies the stated requirements. Our test cases should make sure that class LED supports displaying each digit correctly, and we should also include tests to make sure that we can change the value displayed by an LED object. With a little work, we can write one test harness that does all this in a single run. After some trial and error to get the window sized correctly, we produce the code in Listing 13.3.

The revised test harness creates a frame to hold the LED objects (lines 21–22) and indicates that the default layout manager should be used to control the display of the objects in the container.

Listing 13.3 LED test harness – version 2

```
1.  // GUI test harness for class LED
2.  import java.awt.*;
3.  import javax.swing.*;
4.
5.  public class LEDTest {
6.      // instance constants and variables
7.      private static final int WINDOW_WIDTH = 350;
8.      private static final int WINDOW_HEIGHT = 200;
9.
10.     public static void sleep(int time) {
11.         try {
12.             Thread.sleep(time);
13.         }
14.         catch (Exception e) {
15.             // No body
16.         }
17.     }
18.
19.     // main(): application entry point
20.     public static void main(String[] args) {
21.         JFrame w1 = new JFrame("LED Test");
22.         w1.setSize(WINDOW_WIDTH, WINDOW_HEIGHT);
23.
24.         w1.setLayout(new FlowLayout());
25.
26.         LED digit[] = new LED[10];
27.         for (int i = 0; i < 10; ++i) {
28.             digit[i] = new LED(i);
29.             w1.add(digit[i]);
30.         }
31.
32.         w1.setVisible(true);
33.
34.         sleep(5000);
35.         for (int i = 0; i < 10; ++i) {
36.             digit[i].setValue(9-i);
37.         }
38.     }
39. }
```

The next segment of code creates an array to hold 10 LED objects. The **for** loop initializes array element *i* to have an LED that displays value *i* and adds the element to the window. The frame is then displayed.

We want this test case to demonstrate that the values displayed by an LED can be changed. To accomplish this aspect of the test, using our knowledge of threads, we create a simple sleep function (lines 10–17 of Listing 13.3) that enables us to suspend execution for some number of milliseconds. We use this function to suspend execution for 5,000 milliseconds (i.e., 5 seconds), then we change the values displayed by the LEDs. After 5 seconds, the frame is updated to the following.

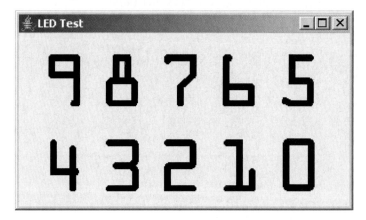

The not-so-careful programmer would be done at this point. However, the careful programmer also tests for what happens when the object is used in a way not permitted by the requirements. One of the benefits of this process is that as you think about unit test cases, bugs are often discovered before you even run the test cases. For example, as we think about test cases to ensure the object behaves appropriately when illegal values are requested, we realize immediately that class LED does not handle this case at all. Class LED will crash if a value less than 0 and greater than 9 is passed to it. We had better fix that. Again, it's much easier to fix it now rather than later.

To address this issue, we modify member function `setValue()` to indicate that it may throw an `ArrayIndexOutOfBoundsException`. This throwing indicates that it is up to the users of class LED to decide how they want to handle the error. This approach is more flexible than having method `setValue()` detect the error and exit. The revised member function is:

```
// setValue(): set the LED to a new value
public void setValue(int i)
 throws ArrayIndexOutOfBoundsException {
    myValue = i;
    setIcon(Images[i]);
}
```

We generate some test cases to make sure that the error detection code works. One test case passes a value less than 0; the other test case passes a value greater than 9. When we test, we run all the tests to make sure that all the test cases, both the new ones and the old ones, still pass.

So far, so good. However, we are still not done. Class LED will be used to build clocks. To test whether class LED will work in this application, we can do a quick prototype of a clock display. Prototyping is a common activity—you build a mock-up of the thing you plan to build to work out how it should look. In this case, we will produce a static clock face—the time will not change. This activity makes us realize that class LED is missing some features. To display a clock time like 12:30 P or 11:00 A, class LED needs the ability to display a colon and the letters *A* and *P* to denote an ante meridiem (i.e., A.M.) and a post meridiem time (i.e., P.M.), respectively. Again, we revise the implementation of class LED to include these features. The display produced by a possible test harness is shown here. The actual harness is left as an exercise for the reader.

The prototype unit test process makes us realize we have another problem with class LED. How do we display a time like 1:30 P? We need a way to display a blank (i.e., an unlit LED). Again, adding this new capability is easy at this stage as we are very familiar with class LED (maybe too familiar!). Listing 13.4 contains the final implementation of class LED.

Listing 13.4 Class LED (final version)

```
1.  // Class LED: simulates an LED for a clock or timer
2.  import javax.swing.*;
3.
4.  public class LED extends JLabel {
5.
6.      // instance variables
7.      private int myValue;
8.      // class constant holding images of digits
9.      private final static Icon myImages[] = {
10.       new ImageIcon("digit0.gif"),
11.       new ImageIcon("digit1.gif"),
12.       new ImageIcon("digit2.gif"),
13.       new ImageIcon("digit3.gif"),
14.       new ImageIcon("digit4.gif"),
15.       new ImageIcon("digit5.gif"),
16.       new ImageIcon("digit6.gif"),
17.       new ImageIcon("digit7.gif"),
18.       new ImageIcon("digit8.gif"),
19.       new ImageIcon("digit9.gif"),
20.       new ImageIcon("colon.gif"),
21.       new ImageIcon("leta.gif"),
22.       new ImageIcon("letm.gif"),
23.       new ImageIcon("letp.gif"),
24.       new ImageIcon("blank.gif")
25.     };
26.
27.     public final static int COLON = 10;
28.     public final static int LETA  = 11;
29.     public final static int LETM  = 12;
30.     public final static int LETP  = 13;
31.     public final static int BLANK = 14;
32.
33.     // LED(): default constructor
34.     LED(int i) {
35.         myValue = i;
36.         setIcon(myImages[i]);
37.     }
38.
39.     // getValue(): set the LED to a new value
40.     public int getValue() {
41.         return myValue;
42.     }
43.
44.     // setValue(): set the LED to a new value
45.     public void setValue(int i)
46.      throws ArrayIndexOutOfBoundsException {
47.         myValue = i;
48.         setIcon(myImages[i]);
49.     }
50. }
```

Listing 13.5 LED clock face test

```
1.  // Clock face test harness for class LED
2.  import java.awt.*;
3.  import javax.swing.*;
4.
5.  public class LEDTest {
6.      // instance constants and variables
7.      private static final int WINDOW_WIDTH = 400;
8.      private static final int WINDOW_HEIGHT = 125;
9.
10.     // main(): application entry point
11.     public static void main(String[] args) {
12.         JFrame w1 = new JFrame("Clock LED Test");
13.         w1.setSize(WINDOW_WIDTH, WINDOW_HEIGHT);
14.
15.         w1.setLayout(new FlowLayout());
16.
17.         LED clock[] = new LED[6];
18.         clock[0] = new LED(LED.BLANK);
19.         clock[1] = new LED(2);
20.         clock[2] = new LED(LED.COLON);
21.         clock[3] = new LED(5);
22.         clock[4] = new LED(8);
23.         clock[5] = new LED(LED.LETA);
24.
25.         for (int i = 0; i < 6; ++i) {
26.             w1.add(clock[i]);
27.         }
28.
29.         w1.setVisible(true);
30.     }
31. }
```

After we add the new capability, we add another test program to our growing suite of programs that test the functioning of the new capability. This test program given in Listing 13.5 produces the following display, which verifies that we can produce a blank.

We should emphasize that each time we make a change to class LED we rerun the entire suite of test programs. This practice avoids introducing a bug that is discovered only after a series of changes have been made. It is much easier to understand what went wrong when only one set of changes is involved.

After our exercise with testing class LED, you can see why testing is such a time-consuming and expensive part of software development. Running a comprehensive test suite

Prototyping

Building a prototype or mock-up is a widely used technique in engineering and design disciplines. Architects build models so customers can see what the building will look like and how it will fit in to its surroundings. Engineers build models of airplanes, automobiles, bridges, etc. so the design can be tested and evaluated before significant resources have been expended building the real artifact. Designers often build mock-ups of products so the utility of the design can be evaluated before the product goes into production.

Prototyping is also an important software development technique. A prototype helps customers and developers understand and refine the requirements for the system. For example, a customer can experiment with a prototype to see if the system will meet their needs. A prototype also helps expose misunderstandings between the users and the developers. In some cases, the prototype can serve as a starting point for building the real system.

Thus, prototyping has many benefits, which include:

- refinement and clarification of system requirements,
- delivered system is more likely to meet users' needs,
- missing capabilities can be identified, and
- reduced development time and cost.

after each change is time-consuming, but there are some things we can do to make it less painful. Programmers typically write "scripts" that automatically run the test suite and report any errors. Using scripts means running the tests is as simple as invoking a command. As new test programs are written, the script is modified so the new test program is included. These scripts, along with documentation on their use, are included with the test programs so that other developers know how to run the test programs. Thus, the script serves as documentation for future developers and testers.

13.1.2 TESTING FUNDAMENTALS

As we mentioned earlier, testing is a serious discipline that is a key to producing high-quality, robust software. Thus it should come as no surprise that testing is a well-studied area with its own terminology and research results. As a beginning programmer, devoting some time to understanding the fundamentals of testing will reward you handsomely in the years to come.

As Section 13.1.1 explained, the purpose of testing is to find bugs as early as possible in the development process and to make sure they get fixed before the software is shipped. Exactly what is a bug? Certainly, when a program crashes (e.g., blue-screen of death), that's a bug. However, there are many other types of bugs that are just as serious and not so obvious. For example, suppose the user manual for a document editor says that the way to set a word in boldface type is to highlight it and then click the bold button on the toolbar. Suppose you do this, and the selected word remains unchanged. Is this a bug?

The program didn't crash, it just did not perform as advertised. Not performing as specified is also a bug.

If we practice sound software engineering techniques, then we will write a complete and detailed specification of what the software is supposed to do, how it will operate, the features it will and will not support, and its performance requirements. In general, a bug is when the program does not meet the specification. However, testers and most programmers classify bugs into the following four broad categories:

- software crashes or data corruption;
- failure to meet or satisfy the specification;
- poor or unacceptable performance; and
- hard or difficult to use.

A software crash is when a program fails in a noticeable way. Examples of software crashes include when the program exits unexpectedly or it stops responding to commands and has to be manually terminated via operating system commands.

Data corruption occurs when a program writes bad data to a file. Suppose you were editing a file with your favorite word processor or editor, and after you saved the file you discovered the file contained gibberish. This situation is an example of a data corruption bug. Data corruption bugs are particularly insidious because they can go undetected easily. The error can propagate to other data files, and if the error goes undetected for a long period of time, it can be difficult to restore the corrupted files to a correct state.

An important component of a software specification is the features the system will provide. A list of features helps everybody, including the customer, know when the system is complete functionally. For example, the specification for a calculator program may state that the program should provide operations for converting between various number bases. If this feature gets left out or is incomplete (e.g., you can only convert to binary), then there is a bug.

A performance bug is present when the program fails to meet the performance requirements contained in the specification, or the program performs so poorly that it, in effect, does not satisfy the specification. As an example of a performance bug, suppose your e-mail system includes a feature for searching your archive of saved messages. While the feature works, a search takes so long that you never use the feature. In effect, it is as if the e-mail system did not provide the feature.

Modern user interfaces have made software easier to use than ever. However, we also expect software to do more and more. Designing software that is easy for people of various skill levels to use is a very difficult task. Indeed, the area of user interfaces and usability are subdisciplines of computer science. If the design of a program makes accomplishing a task overly difficult, this too is a bug—a bug in the design of the user interface. This type of bug can be very expensive to fix as a project is nearing completion. Consequently, it is very important to do early testing of the user interface to ensure that the program is easy to use or, as some people like to say, user-friendly.

Interestingly, when you are testing a program, crashes and data corruption are the best kind of bugs to encounter. The behavior is clearly an error, and it is often pretty obvious what has gone wrong. On the other hand, bugs where the program has an odd quirk,

Types of programming errors

Program errors generally fall into three categories—compilation errors, runtime errors, and logic errors.

- *Compilation errors.* A compilation error is an error detected by the compiler during the compilation process. Compilation errors are the easiest type of error to fix. A common type of compilation error is a *syntax error*. A syntax error is when the form of a statement or expression is not constructed according to the rules of the language. Typical syntax errors include forgetting a semicolon at the end of a statement, leaving off a closing curly brace, misspelling a keyword, etc. Another kind of compilation error is a *semantic error*. A semantic error is when the syntax of the statement or expression is correct, but the meaning of the statement is invalid according to the rules of the language. Examples of semantic errors are using a floating-point value to index an array and forgetting to define an object before using it.

- *Runtime errors.* As the name indicates, a runtime error is an error that occurs when the program is running. Runtime errors are harder than compilation errors to diagnose and fix. Fortunately, Java's runtime checks and exception mechanism provide information that is useful for identifying and fixing the error. Typical runtime errors include many of the exceptions caught by Java: `NullPointerException`, `IoException`, `IndexOutOfBoundsException`, and `ArithmeticException`.

- *Logic errors.* A logic error is when the program runs (i.e., no runtime errors) but it produces incorrect output or it fails in some other unanticipated way. A logic error is typically the hardest kind of error to find and fix. Logic errors are hard to characterize. Sometimes the error can be caused by a simple typographical error that does not create a compilation error (e.g., typing a constant incorrectly), or it can be because the programmer's algorithm had a flaw (e.g., the algorithm does not handle a case that sometimes arises). Using the scientific method of debugging described in Section 13.2 is the preferred approach for finding logic errors.

is slow, or is difficult to use are much more subjective. A developer may argue that the quirk is not a bug, but a feature; that the program is not that slow; or that the program is really not that hard to use.

It is important to understand the limitations of testing. Testing cannot show or prove a program is bug free. It only can show or expose bugs. Furthermore, for all but the most trivial programs it is impossible to test a program completely. The problem is that the number of inputs to most programs is very large, and the number of possible paths through the program is also very large. To simplify the problem, let's just talk about the number of paths in a program. Consider a simple program whose control flow graph is shown in Figure 13.1.

Each circle represents a block of statements. To test this program completely, we must cause the program to execute every possible permutation of statements because any sequence could potentially fail. Disregarding the loop, there are three distinct paths through the program. If the loop executes 20 times, there are 3^{20} different sequences of

Figure 13.1   Program control flow graph.

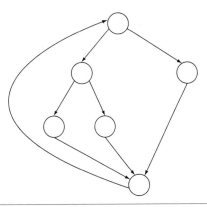

execution of the statements. That is about 3 billion different test cases! Exhaustively testing all possible executions of a program is impossible.

Clearly, we need some good procedures and strategies for testing so that as many bugs as possible are found before the software is delivered, yet testing is done efficiently.

13.1.3   REVIEWS AND INSPECTIONS

Recall our earlier comment that the sooner you find bugs the better. The goal of design and code reviews is to find bugs even before the code is run. Reviews of a design or code can run the spectrum from an informal meeting where one programmer explains the design or code to another programmer to a rigorous formal process. Whether the review is informal or formal the goal is the same—to identify bugs or problems early in the development process. However, reviews, if done and managed properly, can have other benefits.

A review can be a learning process for all involved. During a review, you may see a particularly elegant or effective design or technique for solving a problem. Similarly, you may see bad design or a poor implementation identified along with an explanation of why it is bad. We learn from successes as well as mistakes.

Reviews can help entry-level programmers learn the expectations and coding standards of the company. When working on a large project, it is vital that each programmer adheres to the coding standard that has been chosen. A coding standard specifies how the program is to be laid out (i.e., the indentation to use for the various language constructs, expectations for the form and content of comments, constructs that are not permitted, etc.). Uniform use of a coding standard produces code that is more reliable and easier to maintain.

Reviews are also useful for project management. Reviews help managers assess the skills of the project members. These assessments can be used to determine the assignment of tasks to project members and to form effective teams. Reviews can also help management assess the progress of the project. This information can also be used to take corrective action such as shifting resources, adding more resources, or allocating more time to certain aspects of the project.

Software engineering studies have shown that reviews are very effective at bug detection—more so than other kinds of testing. A study of a large software organization showed that reviews led to a 14 percent increase in productivity and a 90 percent decrease in defects. Another study found that reviews are at least twice as effective as unit testing.

A review process that has been shown to be very effective is the *inspection*. An inspection is a formal process where the personnel involved are assigned specific roles. Inspections were first employed by IBM in 1976. This pioneering work showed that design and code inspections typically remove 60 percent of the bugs in a product.

One characteristic that distinguishes an inspection from other types of reviews is that an inspection is highly structured. Each person involved in the inspection is assigned one of four roles. Furthermore, each participant receives training on how inspections are carried out and what her or his duties are. A participant in an inspection serves in one of four roles: moderator, inspector, author, or scribe.

Moderator. The moderator is in charge of running the inspection. The moderator's most important job is ensuring that the inspection proceeds at a reasonable pace. The inspection should be thorough so that as many problems as possible are identified, but it should not drag out so as to be unproductive. A very important aspect of being moderator is making sure that the inspection participants treat each other with respect and courtesy. In addition to running the inspection, the moderator is also responsible for distributing the code or design being reviewed to the inspection participants, scheduling the time and place of the inspection, reporting the inspection results, and making sure any action items generated as a result of the inspection are completed.

Inspector. An inspector, or reviewer, is someone other than the author who has some interest in the design or code (e.g., using the code to build a component, implementing the design, testing, etc.). The job of the inspector is to carefully scrutinize the design or code to find any potential problems. The inspection of the code is done prior to the inspection meeting.

Author. The author of the code or the design plays a minor role in the inspection. If the author has done her or his job, the code will be well-documented, easy to understand, and bug free. If the reviewers detect problems or the code is unclear in certain areas, an action item is generated directing the author to remedy the situation. Sometimes what may be perceived as an error by an inspector is in fact not an error. In this situation, the author can explain why the code is correct.

Scribe. The role of the scribe is to record all the errors that are detected and keep a list of action items generated.

Interestingly, managers are excluded from inspections. Software inspections are technical reviews with the goal of finding as many problems as possible, as early as possible. The presence of management personnel can change the tenor of the inspection. Inspection participants may become more defensive or less likely to speak up if they feel they are being evaluated.

Another characteristic that distinguishes an inspection from other types of reviews is that it consists of five well-defined phases or steps.

Planning. During the planning step, the portion of code to be inspected is chosen, and the moderator assigns tasks to the inspectors. Inspectors may be assigned different parts of the code to review, or they may be asked to review the code from a certain perspective (e.g., testability, extensibility, performance, etc.). Checklists are created to focus the inspectors' attention on certain areas that are known to be critical or that have caused problems in past projects. The moderator also chooses one of the inspectors to be the presenter. During the inspection step, the presenter will walk through the code, presenting it to the inspection team.

Overview. At the overview the author describes any high-level aspects of the project that may have affected the design or code being reviewed. If all of the project participants are familiar with these aspects of the project, the overview can be skipped.

Preparation. Working alone, each inspector carefully reviews the code using the supplied checklists as a guide. The inspectors note any problems or deficiencies in the code and come to the inspection meeting prepared to present their results. The inspector chosen as presenter uses the preparation plans to present the code or design during the inspection meeting. Studies of the inspection process have shown that this phase should last no more than a couple of hours. Reading code is hard work, and after two hours inspectors become tired and errors can go undetected.

Inspection meeting. At the inspection meeting, the presenter walks through the code line by line, explaining what the code does. As the presenter reads and explains the code, any problems for that portion of code are identified and discussed. The scribe records all the errors detected and the action items associated with them. The moderator makes sure that the inspection proceeds at a reasonable pace and the inspection stays focused. For example, it is tempting to discuss how a problem might be fixed. Fixing problems is not the goal of an inspection. Like the preparation phase, the inspection meeting should not last longer than a couple of hours.

Inspection report. After an inspection meeting, the moderator prepares a written report that identifies the work that needs to be done and who is responsible for each task. Depending on the magnitude of changes, an inspection of the revised code may be scheduled. The inspection report may suggest additions or changes to the checklist based on the results of the inspection. This information can improve the effectiveness of subsequent inspections.

Inspections are effective because they provide a structured environment for having the code read and understood. Left to their own devices, most people find reading code rather boring. As you read code, it is easy to slip into a mode in which you are just skimming the code and not fully understanding what the code is doing. Inspections help people read code in a focused, productive way. Inspections are also effective because they provide feedback about common problems. Integrating this information into checklists for future inspections improves the effectiveness of subsequent inspections.

BLACK-BOX AND WHITE-BOX TESTING

Two other testing strategies for delivering robust, high-quality software are black-box and white-box testing. The testing of class LED at the beginning of this chapter is an example of white-box testing. The term *white-box testing* indicates that we can "see" or examine the code as we devise our test cases. The term *black-box testing* indicates that we cannot examine the code as we devise test cases. The code is hidden in a black box we cannot see through.

How can you test code when you cannot see it? Why would you want to test code that you cannot see? There are good answers to both these questions. With black-box testing, although you do not know how the code works, the specification tells you what the code is supposed to do. You can create inputs, get output, and check the results for correctness without having access to the source code. The answer to the second question is that white-box testing can bias the testing toward finding errors in the code. If the code does not implement the specification, white-box testing is unlikely to expose that type of bug. The advantage to white-box testing is that knowledge of how the code works can help you test more effectively by avoiding redundant test cases.

Because black-box and white-box testing are complementary, both techniques are used on large software projects. Because this text is about programming, we will focus our discussion on white-box testing. However, the techniques we discuss apply to black-box testing as well.

The key to successful, efficient testing is producing good test cases—test cases that are most likely to expose bugs. This task is hard because the input possibilities accepted by a nontrivial program are, for all practical purposes, infinite. Thus we must find a way to reduce the number of possible test cases into a smaller, more manageable set that is still effective at exposing any potential bugs. The process of weeding out unnecessary or redundant test cases is called *equivalence partitioning*.

The basic idea behind equivalence partitioning is that if two inputs test the same portions of code, you only need one of the inputs in your test set. From a testing standpoint, the two inputs are equivalent. For example, suppose you are developing a calculator program. You have just implemented the addition operation and you are developing test cases to make sure addition works properly before implementing other operations. You try the test cases $1 + 2$, $2 + 1$, $0 + 3$, and $0 + 0$. The calculator produces the correct sums for these test cases. Do you think it will be useful to add the test case $1 + 3$? No, because on any reasonable platform test case $1 + 3$ is in the same equivalence class as $1 + 2$. If test case $1 + 2$ worked, test case $1 + 3$ will work. A good test case to add would be $-1 + 3$. This test case is in a new equivalence class because the first operand is negative. The self-check exercises ask you to develop additional test cases for the calculator program that are in new equivalence classes.

There are several strategies programmers and testers use to generate effective test cases. One of the most common strategies is boundary testing. The motivation for boundary testing is that program bugs occur most often at boundaries. Furthermore, if the code works properly at the boundaries, it probably works correctly elsewhere. One analogy sometimes used is that if you can walk along an edge of a cliff on a plateau without falling off, you can probably walk in the middle of the plateau. There are several types of boundaries depending on the code. There are loop boundaries—does the loop do the right thing at the beginning and the end; data boundaries—does the code do the right thing when handling data that is at the boundary of allowable values; and capacity boundaries—does the code correctly handle the situation when the array is full and empty.

With white-box testing, we can examine the code to look for boundary conditions. For example, Listing 13.6 contains function `binarySearch()` introduced in Chapter 8. Initial inspection of this code suggests that the boundary conditions are when the key value being searched for is located at the beginning of the array or at the end of the array. If the code works for those situations, it will likely work when the key is located somewhere in the middle of array `data`.

Listing 13.6 binarySearch method

```
1.  public static int binarySearch(char[] data, char key) {
2.      int left = 0;
3.      int right = data.length - 1;
4.      while (left <= right) {
5.          int mid = (left + right)/2;
6.          if (data[mid] == key) {
7.              return mid;
8.          }
9.          else if (data[mid] < key) {
10.             left = mid + 1;
11.         }
12.         else {
13.             right = mid - 1;
14.         }
15.     }
16.
17.     return data.length;
18. }
```

An example of a capacity boundary condition is whether the code works when the size of array `data` is one or zero. We should include tests for these two cases. Test cases like these two are testing degenerate situations. *Degenerate situations* are ones that would not arise in typical use of the code, but if they occur the program should work. Because the loop is controlled by the size of the list, these tests also serve as loop boundary tests. If array `data` is empty, the loop will not be executed at all. Does this code work when array `data` has size one? What about when its size is zero?

As another example of boundary testing, consider the following code fragment from the Chapter 5 program that computes the days in a given month and year.

```
// validate input
if ((year < CALENDAR_START) || (month < 1) || (month > 12)) {
    System.output.println("Bad request: " + year + " "
        + month);
    return;
}
```

Examination of the code shows that the code checks the validity of the input year and month. The code outputs an error message if the input year is less than `CALENDAR_START` or the month is not between one and twelve. The error checks immediately suggest the data boundary test cases in Table 13.1.

Table 13.1   Boundary values for DaysInMonth.java.

Input Year	Input Month
1582	2
1583	0
1583	13
1583	1
1583	12

The first test case checks whether the program detects an error when the input year is invalid and the month is valid. The second test case checks whether the program detects an error when the input year is just valid but the month is less than one. The third test is similar, but it checks to make sure an error is detected if the month entered is too large. Finally, the last two tests check the valid ranges of the month given a valid year.

The test cases can be partitioned into two equivalence classes. The first three test cases are invalid inputs, while the last two are valid inputs. Thus, the first three test cases should cause the program to generate an error message. If the program does not generate an error message, then we have exposed a bug. The program should produce correct output for the last two test cases. The tester should make sure that the output produced is indeed correct. In general, it is a good idea to classify all test cases as to whether they are valid inputs and the program should produce valid output, or whether they are invalid inputs and the program should generate an error message.

Another approach for generating test cases is to produce a set of test cases that cause each statement in the program to be executed at least once. This is known as *statement* or *code coverage testing*. The basic idea is that unless you have executed every line of code at least once you have not thoroughly tested the code. Of course, statement coverage testing can miss bugs because you may not execute a particular sequence of statements that exposes a bug. Also, for complicated programs, the number of test cases needed to guarantee complete code coverage can be quite high. Nonetheless, code coverage is a technique that is sometimes used. To support code coverage testing, there are software tools available that instrument the code and produce reports that show which program statements have been executed.

There are other techniques for test set generation. One approach is to generate a test set that causes each edge of the program's controlflow graph to be executed. This technique is called *path coverage* or *path testing*. To illustrate path testing, consider the following code fragment.

```
if (x != 3) {
    y = 5;
}
else {
```

```
    z = z - x;
}
if (z > 1) {
    z = z / x;
}
else {
    z = 0;
}
```

The controlflow graph of this program is shown in Figure 13.2. A set of tests that cause each edge to be traversed is <x = 0, z = 1> and <x = 3, z = 3>. The first test case causes paths A, B, G, H to be executed. The second test case causes paths E, F, C, D to be executed. The problem with this test set is that important cases have been missed. For example, what happens when test case <x = 0, z = 3> is executed? To address this problem, we would need to test every possible path, which we have seen, in general, is infeasible. However, path testing can identify portions of code that may need closer inspection.

Figure 13.2 Controlflow graph of two if-else statements.

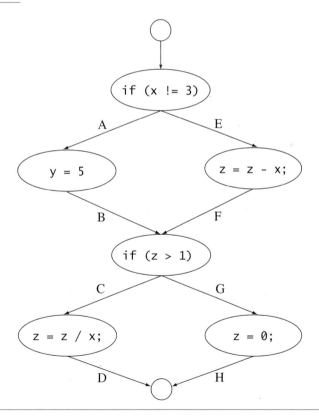

Regardless of the amount of testing and the strategy used to produce the test cases, an important component of testing is automation. As the software is developed, tests will need to be rerun periodically. Thus, it is important to set up an automated procedure for running the tests, capturing the output, and comparing the actual output to the expected output. Developing automated procedures promotes running *regression tests* periodically. A regression test compares the operation of the new version of the software to the operation of a previous version. The idea is that the behavior of the program should not change in unanticipated ways. If something that once worked no longer works, you have a regression. Regression testing ensures that you do not introduce new bugs or resurrect old ones!

The other reason to automate testing is that the testing procedure will serve to document how to run the tests. Taking these steps now makes testing easier when a bug is reported and fixed several years after the software is released. Without an automated testing procedure, you would have to remember how to run all the tests and which were supposed to pass and which were supposed to fail.

In summary, testing software is an integral and key component of the software development process. The size, complexity, and importance of today's software systems demand the application of effective testing techniques.

Testing tips

The following are some general tips for effective testing.

- *Test early.* The sooner you find bugs, the easier they are to fix. Also, it is easier and more effective to generate tests cases as you develop the code. Unit tests are an effective way to find bugs early in individual components or modules.
- *Use inspections.* Inspections are extremely effective at exposing bugs and other deficiencies in the software. Even if a formal inspection process is not practical, sitting down and explaining your code to another programmer can be productive.
- *Test boundaries.* Look for boundary conditions in your code and make sure you have test cases that test on the boundary and around the boundary. Off-by-one errors are fairly common, so it pays to test for them specifically.
- *Test exceptional conditions.* Try to think of situations that shouldn't happen, and then add tests for them. Typical situations include empty files, no data entered, invalid data, too little data, and too much data. A robust program should handle all these cases.
- *Make testing repeatable.* Set up an automated procedure for running your tests and comparing the actual output to the expected output. Scripting languages and shell languages are useful tools for this purpose.

13.1.5   INTEGRATION AND SYSTEM TESTING

Unit testing focuses on a single function, module, or component. Testing done as the pieces of the software are put together is called *integration testing*. *System testing* is testing done when the whole system is put together. Good unit testing simplifies integration and system testing. Because we are confident that the individual pieces work, we can focus our efforts on testing the interfaces between the pieces or components. Furthermore, if a test fails then we can focus our effort to find the problem on the interfaces between the components.

The guidelines for developing good unit tests apply to integration and system testing. The difference is the focus. With integration testing the focus is on testing the interaction between the software components. Thus, the test inputs you develop should focus on exercising that aspect of the system. Similarly with system testing, the test inputs should look to test overall system behavior, not the behavior of an individual component. That was accomplished by unit testing.

Such a modular approach to testing is necessary because as components are assembled to build larger components and the final system, testing the entire system becomes infeasible.

13.2   DEBUGGING

Testing is the process of detecting the existence of a bug. *Debugging* is the process of revealing what the bug is and removing it. Sometimes when a test case exposes a bug, the reason for the bug is obvious. Those are the easy bugs. Other times discovering why a program does not work correctly can be a tedious and time-consuming task—especially if an undisciplined approach is used. In Section 13.2.1, we describe an approach to debugging based on the scientific method. In Section 13.2.2 we give other advice and tips about debugging that experienced programmers often use.

13.2.1   SCIENTIFIC METHOD

Finding that last elusive bug before an assignment is due or the software is shipped can be a frustrating and stressful experience, sometimes so much so that otherwise bright programmers resort to making random changes to their code in hopes that insight into the problem will emerge. Such an approach is not very productive. In this section we introduce the notion of applying the scientific method to debugging.

The *scientific method* is a systematic way of reaching a conclusion based on inductive logic. The scientific method uses the following steps.

- *Gather data.* Observe facts and look for patterns in the data.
- *Develop a hypothesis.* Formulate a plausible explanation that accounts for or explains the observed facts. This explanation is the hypothesis.
- *Predict new facts.* Using the hypothesis, predict new facts or new behaviors that have not yet been observed.
- *Perform experiments.* Design experiments to observe the new facts. Run the experiments and collect data.
- *Prove or disprove the hypothesis.* If the predicted facts are observed, the hypothesis is assumed to be true. If observations do not support the hypothesis, the process is

repeated by developing an alternative hypothesis. Additional data may need to be collected to formulate an alternative hypothesis.

Here's a simple example to illustrate the application of the scientific method to debugging. A program is throwing an exception because of a division by zero in an arithmetic statement. You observe that the value used as the divisor in the offending statement is computed by a loop that counts the number of nonzero values in an array. Based on this observation, you hypothesize that the array must not contain any nonzero values.

Using the hypothesis, you predict that if you insert code to print the array right before the loop the output will contain all zeros. Running the modified code is the experiment. If the output shows the array contained only zeros, your hypothesis is true. If the output has nonzero values, the result of the experiment did not support the original hypothesis, and you need to formulate another hypothesis to explain why the divisor is zero.

This process sounds time-consuming, but it is really not. Often, the experiment to test the hypothesis can be carried out using a debugger. A debugger is a program that allows a programmer to control the execution of another program. Typical debuggers allow programmers to suspend execution of a program at a particular statement in the program. This operation is called setting a *breakpoint*. When the program executes the statement with the breakpoint, control is transferred to the debugger. Debuggers also allow program values to be displayed including the activation record. Sun Microsystems provides a Java debugger called `jdb` with the JDK.

In the previous example, instead of inserting code and recompiling the program, you could have used a *debugger* to set a breakpoint before the loop and then printed the array. The important point is that we need to reason about the code and not go willy-nilly changing statements without some clear idea of what we hope to discover.

Here's another example to illustrate the power of the scientific method applied to debugging. Sally Code and Chuck Hacker (the names have been changed to protect the innocent) have been asked to create a simple statistical analysis program, `FileStats.java`, that processes a list of numbers and produces various statistics such as the mean, median, and mode, etc. They are confident they can do this task and they produce the code shown in Listing 13.7.

The implementation is partial (it computes only the average) as they plan to add more features after they get this part working. The partial implementation is a sign they are good programmers—they develop their code incrementally.

Another indication that Sally and Chuck are good programmers is that after they created and implemented the initial version of `FileStats`, they developed a test input to make sure the preliminary version of `FileStats` worked correctly. If there are any problems with `FileStats`, debugging now will be easier than later when the implementation is more complex. The test input is contained in a file named `test1.dat` and it contains the following list of numbers: 10, 10, 20, 4.

To their surprise, when Sally and Chuck run their program, the behavior shown in the screen snapshot of Figure 13.3 occurs. The program seems to hang and produces no output at all.

It must be a simple error. Sally and Chuck decide to employ the scientific method to find the bug. Chuck comes up with the following hypothesis. He thinks that the program

---

Listing 13.7 Compute the statistics on a file of numbers

```
1.  // Compute the statistics on a user-specified file of data values
2.
3.  import java.util.*;
4.  import java.io.*;
5.
6.  public class FileStats {
7.
8.      // main(): application entry point
9.      public static void main(String[] args) throws IOException {
10.         // set up standard input stream
11.         Scanner stdin = new Scanner(System.in);
12.
13.         // determine filename
14.         System.out.print("Filename: ");
15.         String filename = stdin.next();
16.
17.         // open file stream for text processing
18.         File file = new File(filename);
19.         Scanner filein = new Scanner(file);
20.
21.         // initially no values have been processed
22.         int valuesProcessed = 0;
23.         double valueSum = 0;
24.
25.         // process values one by one
26.         while (stdin.hasNext()) {
27.             // get the next input
28.             double value = filein.nextInt();
29.             // add value to running total
30.             valueSum += value;
31.             // processed another total
32.             ++valuesProcessed;
33.         }
34.
35.         // ready to compute average
36.         if (valuesProcessed > 0) {
37.             double average = valueSum / valuesProcessed;
38.             System.out.println("Average file data value: " + average);
39.         }
40.         else {
41.             System.err.println(filename + ": no values to average");
42.         }
43.
44.         return;
45.     }
46. }
```

is not executing the loop at all. The program is just exiting without reading any data. Sally points out that even if this was the case, they would see some output. Chuck sees the logic of what Sally says. Even though Sally and Chuck did not run the code, they still did an experiment. In this case, Sally and Chuck ran a "thought experiment." Running thought experiments when appropriate is much faster than setting up experiments and running code.

Figure 13.3 **Running program FileStats.**

Sally and Chuck need more data to help formulate a plausible hypothesis. Sally suggests printing out the values read inside the loop. They insert the following statement inside the while loop immediately after line 29.

```
System.out.println("value is " + value);
```

When they run the program, they observe the behavior shown in Figure 13.4. The program is reading one value and then stopping. This observation eliminates the code before the loop that opens the file and reads the first value as the problem. The problem must be with the loop. Careful inspection of the loop shows that the hasNext() is being invoked for input stream stdin rather than filein. So that explains it! The program is waiting for input from the console.

Figure 13.4 **Running program FileStats with a debug statement.**

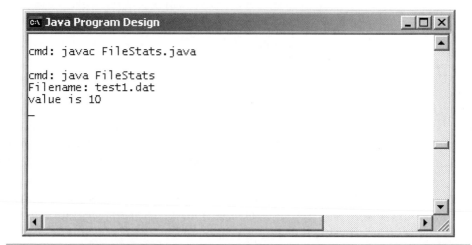

Chuck now remembers that he was doing some testing and he had changed all the input manipulations to use stream `stdin` so he could type in input rather than creating different test files. He must have forgotten to change one back. Fortunately, Sally and Chuck were able to find and fix the error before the code they were developing got too large. After correcting this line of code, Chuck and Sally retest the program and this time it works correctly.

13.2.2   DEBUGGING TIPS AND TECHNIQUES

The most powerful weapon in your arsenal against bugs is your ability to reason. There are also some handy techniques and tips that can reduce the time spent debugging. Many of these techniques help you apply the scientific method more efficiently.

Simplify the problem. Try to come up with the smallest amount of code that still exhibits the error. You can do this by removing calls to methods that are unnecessary and removing statements that should have no bearing on the problem. Anything you can do to reduce the complexity of the code you are debugging can be helpful. As you are removing code, you probably want to periodically run the code to make sure the bug is still there. If it goes away, you have discovered valuable information that you can use to reason about the cause of the bug. As you remove code, *be sure to retain a copy* of the original code.

Along these same lines, you should produce the smallest input that still causes the bug. If the program is interactive, try to find the shortest sequence of commands that cause the error to occur. Knowing the precise input that causes the problem is useful information.

Stabilize the error. Bugs that occur sporadically are some of the hardest to track down. If the bug does not happen consistently, work to make the bug appear reliably. If the bug is a hard one to track down, you will probably be running the program over and over again. In this case, you want each run to be productive.

How you make the bug appear reliably depends on the program; you will have to be resourceful. Here are some common techniques programmers use, depending on the situation.

Determine the exact sequence of inputs or the precise conditions that cause the bug to occur. If you are using a random number generator, make sure the seed is set to the same value on each run.

If the bug only occurs after the program has been running a long time, figure out ways to simulate that behavior. Perhaps the bug only occurs when data structures grow large. Simulate this behavior by writing a function that builds large dummy data structures. Call the function at the beginning of the program to simulate the effect of the program running a long time.

Dump the state of the program periodically. That is, print out key values and data structures. Use this last "state" information you've collected to initialize the program so it fails quickly and reliably.

Locate the error. Try to determine what function or section of code is causing the problem. To do this, print data values and observe at what point in the execution incorrect values are produced. It also helps to try different input values and observe the effect on the code. Sometimes with the right inputs you can "triangulate" the location of the error in the code. Figure 13.5 illustrates the process of triangulating the location of a bug.

Figure 13.5   Triangulating the location of a bug.

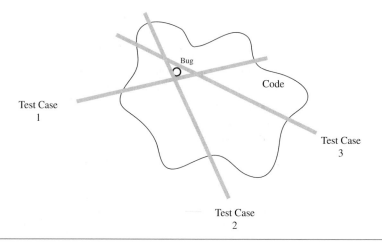

Locating a bug via triangulation often requires running a handful of test cases to narrow the location of the bug down to a region of code small enough to be helpful. The problem is that each test set may identify a large region of code. Consequently, more than two or three test cases are needed to zero in on the location of the bug.

Explain the bug to someone else. In the `FileStats` example, explaining the code to someone else could have caught the error. Hopefully, the person you explain the code to has a different mindset or different mental model of what's going on and will immediately see the problem that you were blind to.

If you have worked at a help desk, you have probably experienced the phenomena known as "confessional debugging." A person is explaining the problem and as they do so, it suddenly dawns on them what the problem is. The act of explaining the code to someone makes you think a little more clearly, not skip steps, and so on. Confessional debugging is surprisingly effective.

Recognize common bugs. Some common bugs have specific symptoms. Knowing the symptoms of commonly occurring bugs can help you identify them quickly.

A common bug is *oversubscripting or undersubscripting an array.* Java throws an `ArrayIndexOutOfBoundsException` if an array is improperly accessed. A common cause of an `ArrayIndexOutOfBoundsException` is an off-by-one-error in a loop—the loop iterates one time too many, or the loop starts off with the index initialized improperly.

Dereferencing null is another classic bug. This bug occurs when the program attempts to access an object through a reference variable and the variable has value **null**.

Again, Java will throw a `NullPointerException` when a program attempts to dereference **null**. The real issue, however, is why is the pointer null. Sometimes the variable is legitimately null, and you just forgot to guard the statement dereferencing the variable with an if-statement. Other times, you have a live bug that you need to remove. In these cases, using the scientific method of debugging to locate the bug is the best course of action.

Recompile everything. Modern IDEs are extremely useful, but sometimes they can get confused. If you have been making lots of changes to the code looking for a bug and the code is not behaving the way you think it should, or changes you have made do not seem to be having an effect, rebuild the entire project from scratch and rerun the code.

Gather more information. If you are stuck and cannot seem to understand what's going on, generate more data. Some standard actions taken by experienced programmers include running different test cases, using the debugger to observe the program's flow of execution, printing out intermediate results, and displaying data structures. You need to be selective and only print as much as you can reasonably digest. Sifting through mountains of data can be like searching for a needle in a haystack.

Pay attention to the compiler. Modern compilers are very good at detecting certain types of errors. However, they tend to be conservative and sometimes produce warning messages that end up being spurious. When you are searching for a bug, it's a good time to pay attention to all those warning messages you have been ignoring. If the compiler reports an object is used before being set, then that problem is something worth investigating.

Many compilers allow the programmer to control the level at which error and warning messages are issued. Setting the compiler to the strictest level can sometimes yield information that is helpful in searching for a bug.

Fix bugs as you find them. It often happens that when you are looking for a bug, you discover another bug. This bug seems unrelated to the bug you are trying to find. It is tempting to put off doing something about the bug just discovered since you are in the middle of tracking down the original bug. You do not want the trail to go cold.

Generally, it is good practice to fix bugs as you find them. The bug you just found could be related to the one you were originally trying to find. Fixing this bug could make the other bug go away. This phenomenon happens quite often. On the other hand, if you are sure the newly found bug is unrelated to the bug you were originally searching for, then it may be worthwhile to keep searching.

Take a break. Sometimes you get nowhere with a bug despite spending hours trying different strategies to locate it. While perseverance is a valuable programmer trait, knowing when to take a break and get away from a problem is also valuable. Experienced problem solvers know how important it is to get away and do something that lets the mind wander—jog, listen to music, take a walk, stare out the window, and so on. As you relax, the solution to the problem might just come to you.

Most experienced programmers have war stories about bug hunts. A common story is the "debugger's epiphany." The story goes something like this. Sally has been hunting a particularly nasty bug for days. None of the tried-and-true techniques for finding the bug have worked. Sally decides to take a break and hit the hills for some mountain biking action. When Sally is flying down a hill with trees whizzing by, the last thing she is thinking about is the elusive bug in the Web browser. After a great afternoon, Sally heads home for a shower. As she showers, she starts to think about the bug again, and it hits her—the solution to the browser problem suddenly becomes crystal clear. Sally heads to work to run an experiment to validate her hypothesis, but she's confident she's got it.

Stories like Sally's are common. Of course, the best stories always have the programmer doing something unusual when the epiphany occurs!

Think outside the box. It is very easy to get locked into a particular way of looking at or attacking a problem. If you are getting nowhere with a problem, try thinking outside the box. Try something unusual or new that you have not tried before. For example, do the opposite of what you have been doing and see what happens.

Debugging is an important part of the programming process. As you gain experience with programming, you will no doubt develop your own personal style of debugging—favorite techniques, tricks, tools, and so forth. You will also learn to use a source-level debugger. A source-level debugger integrated into a modern IDE is a powerful tool for tracking down bugs. However, the most important point to remember is that the key to effective debugging is to follow a disciplined process. Together, disciplined testing and disciplined debugging ensure that high-quality software is delivered on time and within budget.

13.3 REVIEW

- Testing cannot prove that software has no bugs. It can only show the presence of bugs.
- Bugs fall into four broad categories: software crashes or data corruption, failure to meet or satisfy the specification, poor or unacceptable performance, and difficulty of use.
- Test early in the development process. It is cheaper and easier to fix bugs when they are identified early.
- It is generally impossible to test a program completely.
- Develop prototypes to test functional requirements.
- A code inspection is a rigorous process of reading code to find errors and flaws before testing.
- Testing without knowledge of how the code works is called black-box testing.
- Testing with knowledge of how the code works is called white-box testing.
- Equivalence partitioning helps develop smaller, more effective test suites.
- Good test suites include inputs that test the software's boundary conditions.
- Statement coverage testing creates test inputs so that every statement in the software is executed at least once.
- Path coverage testing creates inputs so that every controlflow edge in the software is executed at least once.
- Set up automated procedures for running and checking the results of your tests. Automating test procedures will make testing go faster, and it also serves to document the testing process for future developers and maintainers.
- Use the scientific method for debugging.
- Take time to fix a bug properly. Resist the temptation to apply a quick fix to get the code running. Time spent fixing a bug properly early in the software development process is an investment that will pay off in the future.
- When debugging, try to produce the simplest input that causes the problem. Be sure to add the input to your set of test cases.
- Work to make the error consistently repeatable. This will help you understand the bug, and it will speed the debugging process.
- Learn to recognize the symptoms of common bugs.

13.4 REFERENCES

There are many excellent texts that discuss testing and debugging. The student interested in learning more about testing can begin with the following texts.

- Sandra Bartlett, Ann Ford, Toby Teorey, Gary Tyson, *Practical Debugging in Java*, Upper Saddle River, NJ: Prentice Hall, 2003.

- Brian Kernighan and Rob Pike, *The Practice of Programming,* Reading, MA: Addison-Wesley, 1999.
- Steve McConnell, *Code Complete: A Practical Handbook of Software Construction*, Redmond, WA: Microsoft Press, 1993.
- Glenford Myers, *The Art of Software Testing*, New York: Wiley, 1979.
- Ron Patton, *Software Testing,* Indianapolis: Sams Publishing, 2001.

13.5 SELF-TEST

S13.1 Typically, what percentage of a project is devoted to testing and debugging?

S13.2 Explain the difference between testing and debugging.

S13.3 What is a unit test?

S13.4 What is a test harness?

S13.5 Name the four roles used in an inspection.

S13.6 With many inspection methodologies, the presenter is someone other than the author of the code. Why should someone other than the author be the presenter?

S13.7 Explain the difference between black-box testing and white-box testing.

S13.8 What is statement coverage testing?

S13.9 What is path coverage testing?

S13.10 Devise test cases that cause each statement in the following method to be executed at least once.

```java
public int Euclid(int x, int y) {
    while (x != y) {
        if (x > y) {
            x = x - y;
        }
        else {
            x = y - x;
        }
    }
    return 0;
}
```

S13.11 Describe the steps of the scientific method.

S13.12 What kind of logic, inductive or deductive, does the scientific method use?

13.6 EXERCISES

13.1 The crash of the Ariane 5 was the result of poor testing practices. Using your library or Internet research facilities, find out about the Ariane 5 crash, and explain how the test procedure was flawed.

13.2 Develop test inputs to test the program of Listing 5.4. Your test inputs should achieve full statement coverage of the program. That is, the test inputs should cause every statement in the program to be executed at least once.

13.3 Revise the test harness for class LED that displayed all the numerals to include the blank, the A, the P, and the colon.

13.4 Test data is often partitioned into inputs that test for error conditions and inputs that test that the program works when given valid data. Examine the program of Listing 5.5. Develop one set of test inputs for error conditions and a separate set of inputs to demonstrate the program works.

13.5 Set up a test harness for the binary search function, and test it thoroughly. Report any errors you found.

13.6 How many unique paths are there in the following controlflow graph?

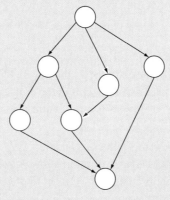

13.7 Develop a test harness, and test input for the class `Box.java` given in Listing 10.8.

13.8 With four other classmates, perform an inspection of the `DataSet.java` presented in Listing 6.8. Prepare an inspection report that describes any problems that the inspection discovered.

13.9 Explain why it is a good idea to have someone other than the programmer responsible for testing a program.

13.10 Use the Internet to research the Therac-25 accidents. Describe what happened.

13.7	**PROGRAMMING PROJECT — GETLIST()**

In this programming project, we exercise our testing and debugging skills by testing and debugging a method developed for reading a list of numbers into an array. The code for the method is given in Listing 13.8. Users of this code have reported that the method sometimes does not return the correct list. The users report that the error seems to occur when the method is invoked multiple times on the same file.

> The objective of this case study is to develop and practice testing and debugging skills

Listing 13.8 getList() method

```
1.  public static int[] getList(int maxListSize) {
2.      Scanner stdin = new Scanner(System.in);
3.      int[] input = new int[maxListSize];
4.      int n = 0;
5.      String currentInput = stdin.nextLine();
6.      while ((n < maxListSize) && stdin.hasNext()) {
7.          input[n] = Integer.parseInt(currentInput);
8.          ++n;
9.          currentInput = stdin.nextLine();
10.     }
11.     int[] values = new int[n];
12.     for (int i = 0; i < values.length; ++i) {
13.         values[i] = input[i];
14.     }
15.     return values;
16. }
```

ANALYSIS

The first step is to walk through the code and gain an understanding of its operation. An examination of the code shows that the method getList() receives a single **int** parameter called maxListSize. This is the number of numbers to attempt to read. The method then allocates a temporary array, input, to hold the values. The method then reads integers until it has read maxListSize integers or there are no more values.

The method then allocates another array, values, and copies the elements from array input to array values. It returns the array values. Overall the code looks straightforward, but there is a bug and we must find it.

IMPLEMENTATION

To locate the bug, we need to do extensive testing. To efficiently test the code, we should develop a test harness. The test harness we develop should invoke method getList() and verify that the list returned is correct. To this end, it might be appropriate to have the test harness code accept, as a command line argument, the test file to read. This will facilitate running different test cases.

Implementing the part of the test harness that verifies that the list returned is correct requires careful thought. You should consider how you might accomplish checking the list returned by method getList() is correct without having to read a separate list. Devising an efficient scheme now will pay off later when you begin testing the code.

TESTING

Because users have reported errors when method getList() is invoked multiple times on the same file, we definitely need to develop test cases that exercise using method getList() in this way. After you have developed the necessary test cases, the next step is to reproduce the bug.

If your initial set of test cases does not expose the bug, you will need to develop additional test cases. You should develop a hypothesis to explain the erroneous behavior and develop test cases to prove or disprove your hypothesis. You should always use the scientific method as you seek to find and fix bugs.

After you have found the bug, you should fix the bug and rerun all the test cases to ensure they still work properly. Sometimes we fix one bug, but we introduce another, so it is important to always test the code if it has been modified. Furthermore, it is always appropriate to consider the adequacy of the test set. Indeed, users have reported that `getList()` fails when small lists are read (e.g., one value). You should develop test cases to diagnose this bug.

13.8   SELF-TEST ANSWERS

S13.1   Typically 40 to 50 percent of a project is devoted to debugging and testing.

S13.2   The purpose of testing is to identify problems or errors in the software prior to delivery. The purpose of debugging is to locate and fix a problems and errors identified by testing or reported by users.

S13.3   A unit test tests a small component in isolation before the component is integrated into the larger system being constructed.

S13.4   A test harness is a small piece of code written to test or exercise the code being developed.

S13.5   The roles during an inspection are: moderator, inspector, author, scribe.

S13.6   Having the presenter be someone other than the author has a neutral person (i.e., someone who does not have ego involved in the code inspection) presenting the code.

S13.7   With black-box testing, the tester creates test cases without having seen the code. With white-box testing, the tester is able to inspect the code and use knowledge of the internal workings of the code to create test cases.

S13.8   Statement coverage testing creates test inputs so that every statement in the software is executed at least once.

S13.9   Path coverage testing creates inputs so that every controlflow edge in the software is executed at least once.

S13.10   Two test cases suffice: $x = 2$, $y = 3$, and $x = 5$, $y = 2$.

S13.11   The steps of the scientific method are: 1) gather data, 2) develop a hypothesis, 3) predict new facts, 4) perform experiments, and 5) prove or disprove hypothesis.

S13.12   The scientific method uses inductive logic.

A TABLES AND OPERATORS

This appendix presents information on the Unicode character set, reserved words, operators, and their precedence.

| A.I | | UNICODE CHARACTER SET |

Most traditional programming languages use the ASCII character set as their base character set. This character set is English-centric, although it does support many diacritical variants on the English alphabet. And even for English, ASCII does not support all of the punctuation marks and technical symbols in use. These limitations arise because ASCII uses a single byte for a character—allowing only 256 characters to be represented. Java uses the Unicode character set, which is the international character set standard. Unicode uses a 2-byte representation. Therefore, it can represent over 65,000 characters. This number is sufficiently large to represent all major written world alphabets and dialects. For example, Unicode includes several Philippine dialects including Tagalog, Hanunoo, Buhid, and Tagbanwa. The following table lists the first 128 characters of the set. For a detailed description of the Unicode character set visit `www.unicode.org`.

Unicode	Char.	Name	Unicode	Char.	Unicode	Char.	Unicode	Char.
0	CTL-@	NUL	32	SP	64	@	96	`
1	CTL-A	SOH	33	!	65	A	97	a
2	CTL-B	STX	34	"	66	B	98	b
3	CTL-C	ETX	35	#	67	C	99	c
4	CTL-D	EOT	36	$	68	D	100	d
5	CTL-E	ENQ	37	%	69	E	101	e
6	CTL-F	ACK	38	&	70	F	102	f
7	CTL-G	BEL	39	'	71	G	103	g
8	CTL-H	BS	40	(	72	H	104	h
9	CTL-I	TAB	41	)	73	I	105	i
10	CTL-J	LF	42	*	74	J	106	j
11	CTL-K	VT	43	+	75	K	107	k
12	CTL-L	FF	44	,	76	L	108	l
13	CTL-M	CR	45	-	77	M	109	m
14	CTL-N	SO	46	.	78	N	110	n
15	CTL-O	SI	47	/	79	O	111	o
16	CTL-P	DLE	48	0	80	P	112	p
17	CTL-Q	DC1	49	1	81	Q	113	q
18	CTL-R	DC2	50	2	82	R	114	r
19	CTL-S	DC3	51	3	83	S	115	s
20	CTL-T	DC4	52	4	84	T	116	t
21	CTL-U	NAK	53	5	85	U	117	u
22	CTL-V	SYN	54	6	86	V	118	v
23	CTL-W	ETB	55	7	87	W	119	w
24	CTL-X	CAN	56	8	88	X	120	x
25	CTL-Y	EM	57	9	89	Y	121	y
26	CTL-Z	SUB	58	:	90	Z	122	z
27	CTL-[	ESC	59	;	91	[	123	{
28	CTL-\	FS	60	<	92	\	124		
29	CTL-]	GS	61	=	93	]	125	}
30	CTL-^	RS	62	>	94	^	126	~
31	CTL-_	US	63	?	95	_	127	DEL

A.2	RESERVED WORDS

The following identifiers are keywords in Java and cannot be used as identifier names.

abstract	else	interface	switch
boolean	enum	long	synchronized
break	extends	native	this
byte	final	new	throw
case	finally	package	throws
catch	float	private	transient
char	for	protected	try
class	goto	public	void
const	if	return	volatile
continue	implements	short	while
default	import	static	
do	instanceof	strictfp	
double	int	super	

Keywords **const** and **goto** are currently unused. Words **false**, **null**, and **true** are also reserved for special meaning and cannot be used as identifier names.

A.3	OPERATORS AND PRECEDENCE

The following table lists the precedence of operators from highest to lowest precedence. Operators of equal precedence are evaluated left to right except for the assignment operators, which are evaluated from right to left.

Operator precedence table	
group	(*op*)
postfix	[] . (*params*) *op*++ *op*--
prefix	++*op* --*op* +*op* -*op* ~ !
creation or casting	**new** (type)*op*
multiplicative	* / %
additive	+ -
shift	<< >> >>>
relational	< > <= >= **instanceof** ==
equality	== !=
bitwise and	&
bitwise exclusive and	∧
bitwise inclusive or	|
logical and	&&
logical or	||
conditional	? :
assignment	= += -= *= /= %= &= ∧= |= <<= >>= >>>=

The arithmetic operations have the following definitions.

```
op1 + op2
```
Evaluates to the sum of *op1* and *op2*.
```
op1 - op2
```
Evaluates to the difference of *op2* from *op1*.
```
op1 * op2
```
Evaluates to the product of *op1* and *op2*.
```
op1 / op2
```
Evaluates to the quotient of *op1* divided by *op2*.
```
op1 % op2
```
Evaluates to the remainder of dividing *op1* by *op2*.

The rules for binary numeric operands with operands of mixed types is as follows.

- If both of the operands are integer and one operand is of type **long**, then **long** arithmetic is performed by first *widening through numeric promotion* the non-**long** integer operand to the type **long**.

- If both of the operands are integer and neither integer operand is of type **long**, then **int** arithmetic is performed by first widening through numeric promotion any non-**int** operand(s) to the type **int**.

- If one of the operands is of type **double**, then **double** arithmetic is performed by first widening through numeric promotion any non-**double** operand to the type **double**.

- If one operand is of type **float** and the other operand is not of type **double**, then **float** arithmetic is performed by first widening through numeric promotion any non-**float** operand to the type **float**.

The unary arithmetic operators have the following definitions.
```
+op
```
Evaluates to *op*.
```
-op
```
Evaluates to the negation of *op*.
```
op++
```
Increments *op* by 1; evaluates to the value of op before it was incremented.
```
++op
```
Increments *op* by 1; evaluates to the value of op after it was incremented.
```
op--
```
Decrements *op* by 1; evaluates to the value of *op* before it was decremented.
```
--op
```
Decrements *op* by 1; evaluates to the value of *op* after it was decremented.

The relational operators have the following definitions.
```
op1 > op2
```
Tests whether *op1* is greater than *op2*.
```
op1 >= op2
```
Tests whether *op1* is greater than or equal to *op2*.
```
op1 < op2
```
Tests whether *op1* is less than *op2*.
```
op1 <= op2
```
Tests whether *op1* is less than or equal to *op2*.

```
op1 == op2
```
Tests whether *op1* and *op2* are equal.
```
op1 != op2
```
Tests whether *op1* and *op2* are different.

The conditional operators have the following definitions.
```
op1 && op2
```
Tests whether *op1* and *op2* are both true. Only evaluates *op2* if *op1* is true.
```
op1 || op2
```
Tests whether either of *op1* or *op2* is true. Only evaluates *op2* if *op1* is true.
```
! op
```
Tests whether *op* is false.
```
op1 & op2
```
Always evaluates both *op1* and *op2*. If operands are numeric types, then it evaluates to the logical and of the individual bits of *op1* and *op2*. If *op1* and *op2* are boolean, it evaluates to *op1* && *op2*.
```
op1 | op2
```
Always evaluates both *op1* and *op2*. If operands are numeric types, then it evaluates to the logical or of the individual bits of *op1* and *op2*. If *op1* and *op2* are boolean, it evaluates to *op1* || *op2*.
```
op1 ^ op2
```
If operands are numeric types, then it evaluates to the logical exclusive or of the individual bits of *op1* and *op2*. If *op1* and *op2* are boolean, it evaluates to *op1* != *op2*.

The shifting operators have the following definitions.
```
op1 >> op2
```
Evaluates to a rightward shifting of the bits of *op1* by distance *op2*.
```
op1 << op2
```
Evaluates to a leftward shifting of the bits of *op1* by distance *op2*.
```
op1 >>> op2
```
Evaluates to an unsigned rightward shifting of the bits of *op1* by distance *op2*.

The assignment operators have the following definitions.
```
op1 = op2
```
Evaluates *op1* and *op2*. The value of *op1* is now the value of *op2*. Assignment evaluates to the new value of *op1*.
```
op1 += op2
```
Evaluates to *op1* = *op1* + *op2*. Operator *op1* is evaluated only once.
```
op1 -= op2
```
Evaluates to *op1* = *op1* - *op2*. Operator *op1* is evaluated only once.
```
op1 *= op2
```
Evaluates to *op1* = *op1* * *op2*. Operator *op1* is evaluated only once.
```
op1 /= op2
```
Evaluates to *op1* = *op1* / *op2*. Operator *op1* is evaluated only once.
```
op1 %= op2
```
Evaluates to *op1* = *op1* % *op2*. Operator *op1* is evaluated only once.
```
op1 &= op2
```
Evaluates to *op1* = *op1* & *op2*. Operator *p1* is evaluated only once.

op1 |= *op2*

 Evaluates to *op1* = *op1* | *op2*. Operator *op1* is evaluated only once.

op1 ^= *op2*

 Evaluates to *op1* = *op1* ^ *op2*. Operator *op1* is evaluated only once.

op1 <<= *op2*

 Evaluates to *op1* = *op1* << *op2*. Operator *op1* is evaluated only once.

op1 >>= *op2*

 Evaluates to *op1* = *op1* >> *op2*. Operator *op1* is evaluated only once.

op1 >>>= *op2*

 Evaluates to *op1* = *op1* >>> *op2*. Operator *op1* is evaluated only once.

The other operators have the following definitions.

(*op*)

 Evaluates to *op*.

op1 ? *op2* : *op3*

 If *op1* is **true**, evaluates to *op2*; otherwise, evaluates to *op3*.

new *type*[*op*]

 Creates a new array with *op* elements of type *type*.

new *type*

 Creates a new object of reference type *type*.

type[]

 Declares an array of unknown length, which contains elements of type *type*.

op1[*op2*]

 Evaluates to the element with index *op2* in array *op1*.

op1.op2

 Evaluates to the *op2* member of *op1*.

op1(*params*)

 Declares or invokes the method named *op1* with the specified parameter list *params*.

(*type*) *op*

 Casts *op* to type *type*.

op1 instanceof *op2*

 Tests whether *op1* is an instance of *op2*.

D NUMBER REPRESENTATION

This appendix presents information on the number representation.

| **B.1** | **BINARY NUMBER REPRESENTATION** |

Computers use the binary number system to represent data, programs, and messages. The principles underlying the binary number system are the same as those used in the decimal number system. Both the decimal and binary number systems are *positional number systems*, that is, the position of a digit indicates its relative value. For example, in the decimal number 4506, the 5 is in the 100's place and thus indicates a value of 500. Reading the number from the right, each digit represents an increasing power of 10. Thus the value of the 4506 can be expressed as

$$4 \times 10^3 + 5 \times 10^2 + 0 \times 10^1 + 6 \times 10^0$$

We say that the *leading* digit 4 is the *most significant* digit and that the *trailing* digit 6 is the *least significant* digit.

The binary number system works the same way except that we use increasing powers of 2. For example, the binary number 1101 represents the decimal 13.

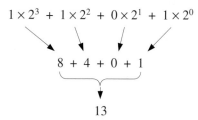

$$1 \times 2^3 + 1 \times 2^2 + 0 \times 2^1 + 1 \times 2^0$$

$$8 + 4 + 0 + 1$$

$$13$$

To indicate that a number is in a base other than decimal, the base is written as a subscript at the end of the number. So 100000_2 is the binary representation of the decimal value 32, whereas 100000_{10} represents the decimal value 100,000.

The *octal* and *hexadecimal* number systems are also used in programming. In the octal system, digits can take on the values 0 through 7. For example, 135_8 is the octal representation of 93_{10} because

$$1 \times 8^2 + 3 \times 8^1 + 5 \times 8^0 = 64 + 24 + 5 = 93.$$

The hexadecimal number system is the base 16 number system. Since a hexadecimal digit can take on 16 possible values, extra symbols are required to represent the digits greater than nine. The convention is to use the letters A through F to represent the digits equivalent to the decimals 10 through 15 (i.e., A represents the decimal 10, B represents the decimal 11, and so on). For example, 59_{16} equals 89_{10} and $1CA_{16}$ equals 458_{10} because

$$5 \times 16^1 + 9 \times 16^0 = 80 + 9 = 89$$

$$1 \times 16^2 + 12 \times 16^1 + 10 \times 16^0 = 256 + 192 + 10 = 458$$

To convert an integer decimal number m to its binary equivalent is tedious but not hard. The following algorithm describes the conversion process.

Step 1.	Let m be the number we want to convert.
Step 2.	Let i have the value 0.
Step 3.	Divide m by 2. Let q be the quotient and let r be the remainder.
Step 4.	Increment i by 1.
Step 5.	The ith least significant digit is r.

Step 6. Set *m* equal to *q*.
Step 7. If *m* is not 0, go to Step 3 and repeat the process.
Step 8. The conversion is 0 completed.

We will use our algorithm to convert the decimal number 13 into its binary equivalent. We start off in Steps 1 and 2 by initializing *m* and *i* to 13 and 0 respectively. Then in Step 3, we divide our number 13 by 2. The result is a quotient *q* of 6 and a remainder *r* of 1. In Step 4 we increment i to 1. Therefore, in Step 5 we announce that the least significant digit is 1. Thus, the answer so far is

1

Our number *m* is now 6 and because 6 is not 0, Step 7 causes us to repeat the process by going back to Step 3. This time we divide 6 by 2. The result is a quotient *q* of 3 and a remainder *r* of 0. After incrementing *i* to 2 in Step 4, we announce in Step 5 that the next least significant digit is 0. Thus, the answer so far is

01

Our number is now 3 and because 3 is not 0, Step 7 causes us to repeat the process by going back to Step 3. This time we divide 3 by 2. The result is a quotient *q* of 1 and a remainder *r* of 1. After incrementing *i* to 3 in Step 4, we announce in Step 5 that the next least significant digit is 1, Thus, the answer so far is

101

Our number is now 1 and because 1 is not 0, Step 7 causes us yet again to repeat the process by going back to Step 3. This time we divide 1 by 2. The result is a quotient *q* of 0 and a remainder *r* of 1. After incrementing *i* to 4 in Step 4, we announce in Step 5 that the next least significant digit is 1. Thus, the answer so far is

1101

Our number is now 0 and because it is, Step 7 does not cause us to repeat the process. Instead Step 8 indicates that we have completed the translation. Thus, the binary equivalent of 13 is 1101_2.

B.2	TWO'S-COMPLEMENT REPRESENTATION

A world consisting of just ones and zeros needs to adopt some convention for the representation of negative integer values. All computers use a fixed number of binary digits to represent a value. This basic unit of storage is called a *word*. To keep things simple, we assume that we are dealing with a computer with a 4-bit word rather than the typical 32-bit word size.

With a 4-bit word we can represent the nonnegative integers 0 through 15 ($2^4 - 1$) in this amount of storage. However, if we want to represent negative values and be able to perform subtraction, we have to give up some of the positive values.

Table B.1   4-bit two's-complement numbers and decimal equivalents.

Binary	Decimal	Binary	Decimal
0000	0	1000	-8
0001	1	1001	-7
0010	2	1010	-6
0011	3	1011	-5
0100	4	1100	-4
0101	5	1101	-3
0110	6	1110	-2
0111	7	1111	-1

Most modern computers use a system known as *two's complement* to represent integers. In the two's-complement system, nonnegative numbers (i.e., positive numbers and zero) are represented as we described previously. However, negative numbers are represented differently. For a machine with an *n*-bit word, the two's-complement representation of a negative number x is $2^n - x$ represented in binary.

In the two's-complement system, the most significant bit of the word serves as the sign bit. A 1 in the most significant bit position indicates a negative value, and a zero indicates a positive value. The range of numbers that can be represented in a 4-bit word is –8 to 7. In general, the range of numbers that can be represented in two's-complement notation in a word of *n* bits is -2^{n-1} through $2^{n-1} - 1$.

Suppose we add decimals 4 and 5 using a 4-bit two's-complement representation. From Table B.1, we know 4's encoding is 0100 and 5's encoding is 0101. Adding the two numbers in binary produces 1001, which is the encoding of –7. Yet the decimal sum of 4 and 5 is 9. What has happened is that the sum of 4 and 5 is too big for the number of bits—the largest integer that can be stored in 4-bit two's-complement representation is 7. This situation is called *overflow*.

Most computer systems also have a binary representation for *floating-point values* (real number values, e.g., 6.9 and 11.82) that use one or two words of memory to encode a number. As such, there are limits both on the smallest and largest numbers that can be represented and on the number of places of accuracy. The representation limits mean that some numeric values can only be approximated. For example, the decimal 0.1 does not have a finite representation in the binary system. As a result, care must be taken when doing floating-point computations. Expressions that may be equivalent mathematically may not compute the same result. For example, the expression

```
0.1 + 0.1 + 0.1 + 0.1 + 0.1 + 0.1 + 0.1 + 0.1 + 0.1 + 0.1
```

does not evaluate to 1 in the Java programming language. The result is extremely close to 1.0, but not exactly 1.0.

C FORMATTED I/O

This appendix presents information on generating and outputting formatted strings using class `PrintStream` methods `printf()` and `format()`.

C.1   INTRODUCTION

Java 5.0 introduced the ability to output data formatted according to a string specification provided by the programmer. This ability is provided by the method printf().

Suppose we want to output a floating-point number and we need to output only two digits to the right of the decimal point (e.g., we are outputting dollars and cents). Using the formatting capabilities provided by method printf(), this task is easily achieved. Here is an example.

```
double cost = 1.0 / 3.0;
System.out.printf("The cost is $%1.2f%n", cost);
```

This fragment would output

```
The cost is $0.33
```

The initial parameter to method printf() contains a format specifier that describes how the value held in cost should be output. In this example, the %1.2f indicates that we want to output a floating-point number with two digits after the decimal point and at least one digit before the decimal point.

In general, the initial parameter to method printf() is a format string that can contain multiple format specifiers that describe how the subsequent parameters are to be displayed.

Besides method printf() for sending formatted data to a stream, class Print-Stream also provides a method format() for producing formatted data that is returned as a string.

Programmers familiar with C and C++ will recognize that PrintStream method printf() provides functionality similar to C and C++'s printf() function.

C.2   FORMAT STRING SYNTAX

A format string can contain fixed text along with embedded format specifiers. The character % indicates the start of a format specifier. In the first example of Section C.1, the format specifier is %1.2f. There are format specifiers for the primitive types as well as some commonly used class types such as BigDecimal and Calendar.

The syntax for format specifiers is

```
%[argument_index$][flags][width][.precision]conversion
```

where the square brackets indicate optional components.

The required conversion is a character that specifies how the parameter should be formatted. The following table describes the provided conversions. Throughout the table, *arg* denotes the actual parameter that corresponds to the format specifier

Conversion	Parameter Category	Description
b	general	If *arg* is **null**, then the result is the string `"false"`. If *arg* is a **boolean** or Boolean, then the result is the string returned by `String.valueOf(arg)`. Otherwise, the result is the string `"true"`.
h	general	If *arg* is **null**, then the result is the string `"null"`. Otherwise, the result is obtained by invoking `Integer.toHexString(arg.hashCode())`.
s	general	If *arg* is **null**, then the result is the string `"null"`. If *arg* implements interface Formattable, then the result is obtained by invoking *arg*.`formatTo()`. Otherwise, the result is obtained by invoking *arg*.`toString()`.
c	character	The result is a Unicode character.
d	integral	The result is formatted as a decimal integer.
o	integral	The result is formatted as an octal integer.
x	integral	The result is formatted as a hexadecimal integer.
e	floating point	The result is formatted as a decimal number in scientific notation.
f	floating point	The result is formatted as a decimal number.
g	floating point	The result is formatted using scientific notation for large exponents and decimal format for small exponents.
a	floating point	The result is formatted as a hexadecimal floating-point number with a significand and an exponent.
t	date/time	Prefix for date and time conversion characters. See the Java API specification for a description of the date/time conversions.
%	percent	The result is a literal '%' ('\u0025').
n	line separator	The result is the platform-specific line separator.

The width is the minimum number of characters to be formatted. For the line separator conversion, including a width is invalid, and if present, it causes an exception to be thrown. If the converted value results in fewer than width characters, then padding characters (often blanks) are used to pad the converted value to the specified width. The following code fragment

```
int v = 100;
System.out.printf("Demonstrate width specification%n");
System.out.printf("v:%6d%n", v);
```

results in the output

```
Demonstrate width specification
v:    100
```

An optional `precision` is a decimal integer. For conversions `e` and `f`, `precision` is the number of digits to the right of the decimal point. For conversion `g`, `precision` is the total number of digits in the magnitude. For the character, integral, date/time, percent, and line separator conversions, including `precision` causes an exception to be thrown. The example in Section C.1 used `precision` to ensure that only two digits to the right of the decimal point were output.

The optional `flags` modifies the meaning of the main conversion specification. The flag – specifies that the result should be left-justified. It can be applied to all the parameter categories. The flag + specifies that the result will include a sign. A space character for a flag specifies that the result will include a leading space for positive values. The flag 0 specifies that the result will be zero padded. The flag (specifies that negative numbers should be enclosed in parentheses.

The following program fragment illustrates some of the uses of the optional flags to control the formatting of the output.

```
double f = 1.3e10;
int v = 100;
int n = -20;
double x = -23.56;
boolean p = true;

System.out.printf("f is %+e%n", f);
System.out.printf("f is %e%n", f);
System.out.printf("n is %(d, x is %(.2f%n", n, x);
System.out.printf("v is %06d, n is % 6d%n", v, n);
System.out.printf("p is %b%n", p);
```

When executed, the output produced is

```
f is +1.300000e+10
f is 1.300000e+10
n is (20), x is (23.56)
v is 000100, n is     -20
p is true
```

The `argument_index` is a decimal integer that indicates the position of the parameter that this format specifier applies. The first parameter is specified by 1$, the second by 2$, and so on. The use of the `argument_index` is illustrated by the following code fragment.

```
double cost = 100.56;
int trips = 10;
```

```
System.out.printf("%2$d trips cost %1$.2f%n", cost, trips);
```

outputs

```
10 trips cost 100.56
```

In the example, the first format specifier formats the second parameter (`trips`) and the second format specifier formats the first parameter (`cost`). The `argument_index` is particularly useful when the same parameter is being output using different format specifiers.

It is sometimes useful to create a formatted string and not output it. The aforementioned `String` method `format()` provides this ability. The following code fragment creates a formatted string that can be subsequently manipulated or output.

```
double x = 100.56;
int k = (int) x;
String s = String.format("%f truncates to %d%n", x, k);
```

Variable `s` is initialized with the value of `"100.560000 truncates to 100"`.

Together, methods `printf()` and `format()` provide the ability to produce output that is easy to read and that meets the needs of the particular application.

D APPLETS

This appendix introduces the basics of creating an applet. An applet is a Java program that is embedded in a Web page. Applets enable Web designers to develop pages that accept input, perform computations, and display results. Such pages are said to have active content as opposed to contents that are unchanging or static.

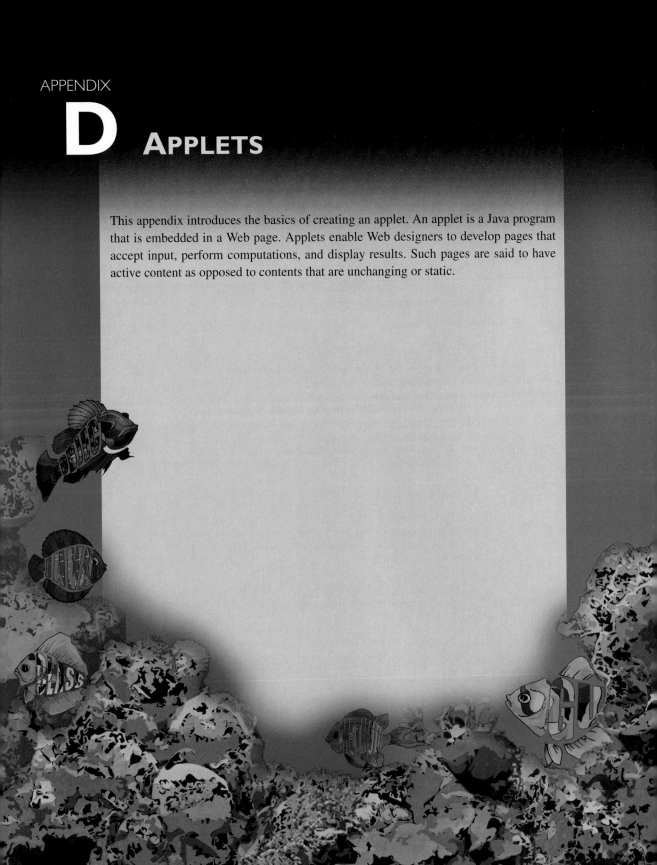

D.I A SIMPLE APPLET

The Internet has become an extremely valuable resource. Originally, information available on Web pages was static. That is, the information presented on a Web page was constant—there were no facilities that enabled Web pages to compute new values based on inputs from users. An applet is a Java program that has been embedded in a Web page. When a browser visits a Web page containing an applet, the Web server sends the applet code to the browser and the browser arranges for the code to be executed. Consequently, a Java applet enables designers to create Web pages that accept input, compute values, and display the output to the user. Basically, Java's applet mechanism enables Web designers to create pages that can do anything a program can do.

We begin our introduction to applets in a manner similar to our introduction to Java console applications in Chapter 1. We give an applet program and Web page that displays a quotation. Listing D.1 contains the code for `DisplayQuote.java`.

Listing D.1 DisplayQuote.java

```java
1.  // Simple applet that displays a string
2.  import java.awt.*;
3.  import javax.swing.*;
4.  public class DisplayQuote extends JApplet {
5.     public void paint(Graphics g) {
6.        g.drawString("Anyone who spends their life on a computer "
7.              + "is pretty unusual.", 20, 30);
8.        g.drawString("Bill Gates, Chairman of Microsoft", 25, 45);
9.     }
10. }
```

The Web page `Quote.html` in Listing D.2 contains the following hypertext markup language (HTML) code.

Listing D.2 Quote.htm

```html
1.  <html>
2.     <title> Quotation </title>
3.     <applet code="DisplayQuote.class" width=400 height=200>
4.     </applet>
5.  </html>
```

When a user visits Web page `Quote.html`, the following image is displayed in the browser window.

Let's examine `DisplayQuote.java` and `Quote.html` line by line. Applet `DisplayQuote.java` begins by importing the necessary classes from the `awt` and `swing` packages.

```
import java.awt.*;
import javax.swing.*;
```

As line 4 specifies, our applet is a subclass of `swing` class `JApplet`. In turn, class `JApplet` is a subclass of `Applet`.

```
public class DisplayQuote extends JApplet {
```

Java requires that every applet be a subclass of `Applet`. However, most Java programmers extend it through `JApplet` rather than directly from `Applet` itself. By extending `JApplet`, `DisplayQuote` inherits methods that support menu bar and pane manipulation (see Appendix E). Because `JApplet` is an extension of class `Applet`, `DisplayQuote` also inherits the actual mechanics to run an applet. What must be specified in the definition of class `DisplayQuote` is how this applet differs from a basic applet.

What's different in the `DisplayQuote` applet from the basic applet provided by package `JApplet` is that `DisplayQuote` will display a quotation. To display a quotation, subclass `DisplayQuote` defines a single member method named `paint()`. As we shall discuss shortly, the code is overriding the method `paint()` provided by the superclass `Applet`.

```
public void paint(Graphics g) {
    g.drawString("Anyone who spends their life on a computer "
        + "is pretty unusual.", 20, 30);
    g.drawString("Bill Gates, Chairman of Microsoft", 25, 45);
}
```

Method `paint()` is where applet `DisplayQuote` will do its work. `DisplayQuote`'s `paint()` method takes a single parameter of type `Graphics`, which is the applet's onscreen drawing context. The body of `paint()` invokes method `drawString()` to display both the quotation and attribution. Method `drawString()`'s parameters represent the string to display and the x- and y-coordinates of the desired position in the display area of the leftmost character of the string.

Now let's examine the HTML code in `Quote.html`, which runs the `DisplayQuote` applet. The code begins with the tag `<html>`. This tag indicates that the file contains HTML code. Notice that there is a matching tag `</html>` that brackets the HTML code of the applet. This tag signals the end of the HTML code. Most HTML elements are specified in this manner—an opening tag and a corresponding closing tag.

The tag `<title>` indicates the string that follows is to be displayed in the title bar of the window. A closing tag `</title>` then marks the end of the title string. For our applet "Quotation" is displayed.

The tag `applet` indicates that this Web page will contain an applet. The applet code to download and execute is specified by setting the attribute `code` to the name of the file containing the class file. It is important that the class file reside in the same directory as the HTML file, otherwise the Web server will not be able to locate it and download it to the browser. The attributes `width` and `height` are used to specify the width and height in pixels of the applet's display area.

Now that we understand our simple Java applet and the HTML file required to embed an applet in a Web page, we can discuss some of the basic capabilities of an applet.

D.2   APPLET METHODS

An applet is run under the control of the browser that downloads the class file. Consequently, an applet must respond to events that occur as the browser prepares the applet for execution, as the applet executes, and as the applet is terminated. There are four major events or milestones in the lifetime of an applet. These milestones are

- initialization—which occurs when the applet is loaded;
- start execution—which occurs after the applet is loaded;
- stop execution—which occurs when the user leaves the Web page containing the applet, or the user terminates the browser; and
- destruction—which occurs before the applet is unloaded.

A basic applet class contains methods that are invoked as each of these events occur. The following code illustrates the basic skeleton of an applet.

```
public class MyApplet extends JApplet {
    ...
    public void init() { ... }
    public void start() { ... }
    public void stop() { ... }
    public void destroy() { ... }
    ...
}
```

A subclass of `JApplet` can override any of these methods as necessary. In the following sections, we describe these methods in more detail.

D.2.1   METHOD INIT()

Method `init()` is invoked by the browser to inform an applet that it has been loaded. It is always invoked before method `start()` is invoked. Generally one can think of method `init()` as the constructor for the applet. Typical uses of the method `init()` would be to construct any objects required, load any images required by the applet, or create any threads that will be used when the applet is run. The method `init()` inherited from class

Applet does nothing. Often a subclass of Applet need not override the superclass init() method.

D.2.2   METHOD START()

Method start() is invoked by the browser to inform an applet that it should start its execution. Generally every applet that does something after initialization (except in direct response to user actions) must override the method start(). Method start() either performs the applet's work or (more likely) starts up one or more threads to perform the work. The method start() inherited from class Applet does nothing.

D.2.3   METHOD STOP()

Method stop() is invoked by the browser to inform an applet to stop its execution. It is invoked when the Web page that contains an applet has been replaced by another page and also just before the applet is to be destroyed. Method stop() should be overridden if the applet has any operation that it should perform each time the Web page containing it is no longer visible. For example, an applet with animation might want to use method start() to resume animation and method stop() to suspend the animation. The method stop() inherited from class Applet does nothing.

D.2.4   METHOD DESTROY()

Method destroy() is invoked by the browser to inform an applet that it is being reclaimed and that it should release any resources that it has allocated. Method stop() will always be invoked before method destroy(). Method destroy() should be overridden if the applet has any operation that it wants to perform before it is destroyed. For example, an applet with threads would use the method init() to create the threads and method destroy() to kill them. The method destroy() inherited from class Applet does nothing.

D.2.5   METHOD PAINT()

The paint() method is responsible for displaying the current state of the applet's graphical interface. The method is invoked automatically after the applet execution has started. The invocation is a signal to the applet that its graphical interface needs to be displayed.

Because different applets have different graphical interfaces, the `paint()` method is normally redefined by an applet subclass.

The definition of `paint()` for `DisplayQuote.java` is:

```java
public void paint(Graphics g) {
    g.drawString("Anyone who spends their life on a computer "
            + "is pretty unusual.", 20, 30);
    g.drawString("Bill Gates, Chairman of Microsoft", 25, 45);
}
```

The two integer parameters in the `drawString()` invocations are the coordinates to draw the string. In particular, Java applets use a coordinate system that use pixel positions to specify locations. A pixel is the minimum-sized graphical element that can be drawn on the particular monitor doing the display. Figure D.1 illustrates an applet's coordinate system.

Figure D.1   Applet coordinate system.

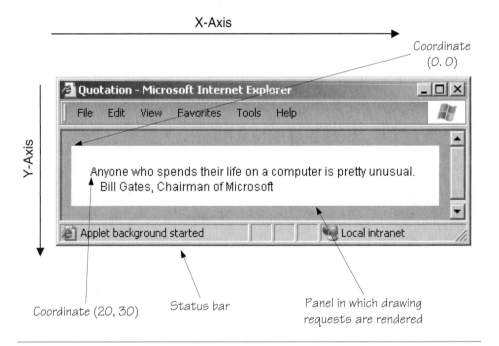

When a drawing request is made, the location of the drawing is specified relative to the upper-left-hand corner of the object on which the drawing commands are performed. The direction of the x-axis is rightward. Therefore, increasing an x-coordinate value means moving rightward. The direction of the y-axis is downward. Therefore, increasing a y-coordinate value means moving downward.

For method `paint()` to do its job, it requires the graphical context in which the drawing commands issued by `paint()` are to occur. The browser sends the graphical context by invoking method `paint()` with an object of type `Graphics`.

The graphical context includes such information as the current background and foreground colors, the current font, rendering style, and the object on which rendering commands are to be performed. Besides encapsulating such information, `Graphics` objects have a variety of methods for drawing strings, lines, arcs, ovals, rectangles, and other polygons. The available methods are detailed in Appendix E. Applet `DrawDisplay.java` in Listing D.3 demonstrates some of these `Graphics` methods.

The `DrawDisplay paint()` method begins by setting the current color for the graphical context to `Color.BLACK`.

```
g.setColor(Color.BLACK);
```

A drawing request is then made to draw a filled rectangle whose upper-left-hand corner is the origin of the applet's window pane.

```
g.fillRect(0, 0, 300, 200);
```

The rectangle is to be 300 pixels wide and 200 pixels high. Because the applet window pane has those same dimensions, the fill request effectively makes the background color of the window pane black.

Listing D.3 **DrawDisplay.java**

```
1.  // Demonstrate the use of several Graphics methods in paint()
2.  import java.awt.*;
3.  import javax.swing.*;
4.
5.  public class DrawDisplay extends JApplet {
6.
7.      // paint(): issues the drawing and color setting requests
8.      public void paint(Graphics g) {
9.          g.setColor(Color.BLACK);
10.         g.fillRect(0, 0, 300, 200);
11.         g.setColor(Color.BLUE);
12.         g.drawRect(50, 50, 75, 50);
13.         g.setColor(Color.GREEN);
14.         g.fillOval(50, 50, 75, 50);
15.         g.drawLine(200, 25, 250, 125);
16.         g.setColor(Color.YELLOW);
17.         g.drawOval(125, 125, 50, 50);
18.     }
19. }
```

Method `paint()` then sets the current color for the graphical context to `Color.BLUE`.

```
g.setColor(Color.BLUE);
```

Because `Color.BLUE` is now the current color, the next drawing request

```
g.drawRect(50, 50, 75, 50);
```

results in the perimeter of a blue rectangle being displayed. The rectangle is 75 pixels wide and 50 pixels high. Its upper-left-hand corner is at location (50, 50).

Method `paint()` next sets the current color for the graphical context to `Color.GREEN`.

```
g.setColor(Color.GREEN);
```

The next drawing request is for a filled-in oval. Because `Color.GREEN` is the current color, the oval is green.

```
g.fillOval(50, 50, 75, 50);
```

The oval is to be 75 pixels wide and 50 pixels high. The bounding box for this oval is at location (50, 50). Thus, the rectangle that the applet previously drew circumscribes the oval now being drawn.

The next drawing request is for a line to be drawn from location (200, 25) to location (250, 125).

```
g.drawLine(200, 25, 250, 125);
```

Because `Color.GREEN` remains the current color, the line is drawn green.

Method `paint()` next sets the current color for the graphical context to `Color.YELLOW`.

```
g.setColor(Color.YELLOW);
```

A drawing request is then made for an oval whose bounding box is a 50 x 50 square with the upper-left-hand corner of the bounding box at (125, 125).

```
g.drawOval(125, 125, 50, 50);
```

Such an oval is, in fact, a circle. When the browser visits the Web page that references the class file `DrawDisplay.java`, the following image appears in the browser window.

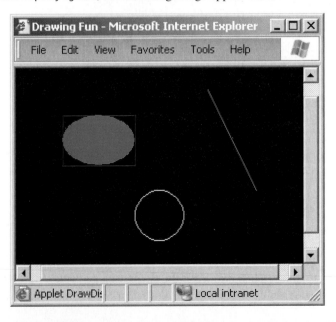

D.3   APPLETS AND THREADS

As mentioned in the introduction to this appendix, an applet provides the ability to have dynamic content. A common approach is to use a thread to continually change the information displayed by the applet. This technique can be used to create animations, ticker tapes, and continuously updated displays. To illustrate the use of applets and threads, we present an applet that displays a clock that is continuously updated. The applet program, ClockApplet.java, is based on the program SimpleClock.java presented in Listing 12.2. The applet code is presented in Listing D.4.

ClockApplet extends JApplet and implements the interface Runnable. Because ClockApplet implements the interface Runnable, ClockApplet must provide a method run(). As you examine the body of ClockApplet, notice that the Clock-Applet overrides the superclass's init(), start(), and stop() methods. Method init() is invoked when the applet is loaded. It initializes instance variable update-Thread to **null**.

```
updateThread = null;
```

A **null** value for updateThread indicates that the applet is not currently displaying and updating a clock.

Method start() is invoked by the browser to start the action of the applet. Clock-Applet's start() method first tests whether updateThread is **null**.

```
if (updateThread == null) {
    updateThread = new Thread(this);
    updateThread.start();
}
```

If updateThread is non-**null**, no additional action is required by the applet because the clock display is running. If it is **null**, then a new thread is started. This applet's run() method will then be invoked by the thread scheduler. (There must be such a method because ClockApplet implements the interface Runnable.)

Method run() for ClockApplet is

```
public void run() {
        Thread me = Thread.currentThread();
        while (updateThread == me) {
            try {
                me.sleep(1000);
            } catch (InterruptedException e) {
                break;
            }
            repaint();
        }
}
```

Method run() obtains the currently executing thread. If that thread is the thread initiated by the applet's start() method, then the body of the **while** loop is executed. The loop repeatedly sleeps for 1000 milliseconds and then invokes method repaint(). Method repaint() arranges for the applet's paint() method to be invoked. The loop continues

---

Listing D.4 ClockApplet.java

```java
1.  // Demonstrate a threaded applet
2.  import java.awt.*;
3.  import java.util.*;
4.  import javax.swing.*;
5.
6.  public class ClockApplet extends JApplet implements Runnable {
7.      private Thread updateThread;
8.      private String clockFace = "";
9.
10.     // init():  perform initialization
11.     public void init() {
12.         updateThread = null;
13.     }
14.
15.     // start():  start up the applet
16.     public void start() {
17.         if (updateThread == null) {
18.             updateThread = new Thread(this);
19.             updateThread.start();
20.         }
21.     }
22.
23.     // run():  thread activity
24.     public void run() {
25.         Thread me = Thread.currentThread();
26.         while (updateThread == me) {
27.             try {
28.                 me.sleep(1000);
29.             }
30.             catch (InterruptedException e) {
31.                 break;
32.             }
33.             repaint();
34.         }
35.     }
36.
37.     // paint(): issues the drawing and color setting requests
38.     public void paint(Graphics g) {
39.         Date time = new Date();
40.         g.setColor(Color.WHITE);
41.         g.drawString(clockFace, 10, 20);
42.         clockFace = time.toString();
43.         g.setColor(Color.BLUE);
44.         g.drawString(clockFace, 10, 20);
45.     }
46.
47.     // stop(): all done
48.     public void stop() {
49.         updateThread = null;
50.     }
51. }
```

as long as updateThread is equal to me (i.e., they reference the same thread). Thus, once started, the loop continues to iterate until method stop() is invoked by the browser. For it is method stop() that resets updateThread to **null**.

Method paint() is largely identical to the code in the method run() of Listing 12.2.

```
public void paint(Graphics g) {
    Date time = new Date();
    g.setColor(Color.WHITE);
    g.drawString(clockFace, 10, 20);
    clockFace = time.toString();
    g.setColor(Color.BLUE);
    g.drawString(clockFace, 10, 20);
}
```

The code gets the date and displays the previous time using the background color (Color.WHITE). This effectively erases the displayed time. The new time is converted to a string and displayed using the color blue.

When the browser moves to a new page or the browser is closed, method stop() is invoked. As previously explained, ClockApplet's stop() method simply sets the updateThread to **null**, which causes the **while** loop in method run() to terminate.

When a Web page with the ClockApplet embedded in it is visited by a browser, the following image appears in the browser window.

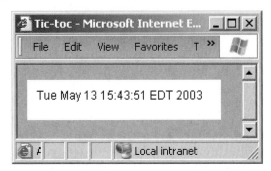

The time is continuously updated.

ClockApplet demonstrates the standard design pattern for an applet that implements a simple animation. A thread is created that executes the run() method. The run() method updates the display and then sleeps until it is time to update the display again.

APPLET SECURITY

Because an applet is downloaded from a server and runs on the user's machine, applets pose a potential security threat to the user's machine. For example, a malicious person could place an applet on a Web page that when downloaded reads private information on the user's machine and sends it back to the malicious person. To avoid such security breaches, browsers impose the following restrictions on any applet that is loaded over the network.

- An applet cannot load libraries or define native methods.
- An applet cannot ordinarily read or write files on the host that's executing it.
- An applet cannot make network connections except to the host that it came from.
- An applet cannot start any program on the client that is executing it.
- An applet cannot read certain system properties.
- Windows that an applet brings up look different than windows that an application brings up.

D.5 SUMMARY

Java applets provide a powerful tool to Web designers. Applets enable Web designers to embed a Java program in a Web page. This ability enables Web pages to have active content—Web pages can accept input, perform computations, and display outputs based on the results of the computations.

E STANDARD JAVA PACKAGES

We describe many of the classes and interfaces from standard packages `java.awt`, `java.io`, `java.lang`, `java.math`, `javax.swing`, `java.text`, and `java.util`.

| `awt.event` | **class** `ActionEvent` **extends** `AWTEvent` |

PURPOSE
Represents events for which application-specific responses are appropriate.

FIELD SUMMARY

`static int` `ACTION_FIRST`

Represents the minimal action event indicator.

`static int` `ACTION_LAST`

Represents the maximal action event indicator.

`static int` `ACTION_PERFORMED`

Represents a meaningful action indicator.

`static int` `ALT_MASK`

Represents the alt modifier.

`static int` `CTRL_MASK`

Represents the control modifier.

`static int` `META_MASK`

Represents the meta modifier.

`static int` `SHIFT_MASK`

Represents the shift modifier.

CONSTRUCTOR SUMMARY

`ActionEvent(Object v, int n, String s)`

Constructs a new `ActionEvent` whose source is `v`. The kind of the `Action-Event` is `n` and its message is `s`.

`ActionEvent(Object v, int n, String s, int m)`

Constructs a new `ActionEvent` with modifier `m` whose source is `v`. The kind of the `ActionEvent` is `n` and its message is `s`.

`ActionEvent(Object v, int n, String s, long t, int m)`

Constructs a new `ActionEvent` with modifier `m` and time stamp `t` whose source is `v`. The kind of the `ActionEvent` is `n` and its message is `s`.

INSTANCE METHOD SUMMARY

`String getActionCommand()`

Returns the command string of this `ActionEvent`.

`int getModifiers()`

Returns the modifier keys of this `ActionEvent`.

`long getWhen()`

Returns the time stamp of this `ActionEvent`.

`String paramString()`

Returns a representation of this `ActionEvent`.

| `awt.event` | **interface** `ActionListener` **extends** `EventListener` |

PURPOSE
Describes the necessary method of a responder to an `ActionEvent`.

INSTANCE METHOD SUMMARY
    void actionPerformed(ActionEvent e)
        Processes action event **e** for this action listener.

---

applet   **class** Applet **extends** Panel

PURPOSE
Represents a program that is run within another program such as a Web browser.
CLASS METHOD SUMMARY
    static AudioClip newAudioClip(URL u)
        Returns the audio clip at Web location **u**.
CONSTRUCTOR SUMMARY
    Applet()
        Creates a new Applet.
INSTANCE METHOD SUMMARY
    void destroy()
        Signals this Applet that it is about to be terminated.
    AccessibleContext getAccessibleContext()
        Returns the accessibility context of this Applet.
    AppletContext getAppletContext()
        Returns the environmental context of this Applet.
    String getAppletInfo()
        Returns identifying information for this Applet.
    AudioClip getAudioClip(URL u)
        Returns the audio clip at location **u** for this Applet.
    AudioClip getAudioClip(URL u, String s)
        Returns the audio clip with name **s** at location **u** for this Applet.
    URL getCodeBase()
        Returns the base location of this Applet.
    URL getDocumentBase()
        Returns the location of the document containing this Applet.
    Image getImage(URL u)
        Returns the image at location **u** for this Applet.
    Image getImage(URL u, String s)
        Returns the image with name **s** at location **u** for this Applet.
    Locale getLocale()
        Returns the locale of this Applet.
    String getParameter(String s)
        Returns the value of parameter **s** in the HTML tag for this Applet.
    String[][] getParameterInfo()
        Returns the parameter values for this Applet.
    void init()
        Signals this Applet that it has been loaded.
    boolean isActive()
        Returns whether this Applet is active.

void play(URL u)

Plays the audio clip at location u for this **Applet**.

void play(URL u, String s)

Plays the audio clip with name s at location u for this **Applet**.

void resize(Dimension d)

Requests this **Applet** to resize itself to dimension d.

void resize(**int** w, **int** h)

Requests this **Applet** to resize itself to width w and height h.

void setStub(AppletStub a)

Sets a as the stub of this **Applet**.

void showStatus(String s)

Requests this **Applet** to display message s in the status window.

void start()

Signals this **Applet** to start its execution.

void stop()

Signals this **Applet** to stop its execution.

---

lang	**class** ArithmeticException **extends** RuntimeException

PURPOSE

Represents an unexpected arithmetic event.

CONSTRUCTOR SUMMARY

ArithmeticException()

Constructs a new **ArithmeticException** with a **null** message.

ArithmeticException(String s)

Constructs a new **ArithmeticException** with message s.

---

lang	**class** ArrayIndexOutOfBoundsException **extends** IndexOutOfBoundsException

PURPOSE

Represents an illegal array indexing event.

CONSTRUCTOR SUMMARY

ArrayIndexOutOfBoundsException()

Constructs a new **ArrayIndexOutOfBoundsException** with a **null** message.

ArrayIndexOutOfBoundsException(**int** i)

Constructs a new **ArrayIndexOutOfBoundsException** with a message that i is an illegal index.

ArrayIndexOutOfBoundsException(String s)

Constructs a new **ArrayIndexOutOfBoundsException** with message s.

| util | `class ArrayList<T> extends AbstractList<T> implements List<T>, Cloneable, RandomAccess, Serializable` |

PURPOSE

Represents a resizable array with complete `List` functionality. An `ArrayList` has been designed so that its element accessor and mutator methods are guaranteed to be very efficient. Its element accessor and mutator methods run in *constant time*. Adding (*appending*) an element to the end of the list is guaranteed to be fast on average (i.e., an append operation operates in constant time on average). The class also provides a number of other methods for inserting and deleting elements in the list. These other methods can require time proportional to the number of elements in the list to perform their tasks (i.e., these methods run in *linear time*). Associated with each `ArrayList` is a *capacity*, which is the maximum number of elements that the list can currently store without growing.

CONSTRUCTOR SUMMARY

`ArrayList()`

Constructs an empty list with initial capacity to represent 10 elements.

`add(Collection<? extends T> c)`

Constructs a list containing the elements of c.

`ArrayList(int n)`

Constructs an empty list with an initial capacity to represent n elements.

INSTANCE METHOD SUMMARY

`boolean add(T v)`

Appends the list with a new element with value v and returns **true**.

`void add(int i, T v)`

Inserts value v into the list such that v has index i. Any preexisting elements with indices i or greater are shifted backward by one element position.

`boolean addAll(Collection<? extends T> c)`

Appends the list with all of the elements in c and returns **true** if the list has changed.

`boolean addAll(int i, Collection<? extends T> c)`

Inserts the elements of c into this list and returns **true** if the list has changed. Any preexisting elements with indices i or greater are shifted backward by one element position.

`void clear()`

Removes all elements from the list.

`Object clone()`

Returns a shallow copy of this list.

`boolean contains(Object v)`

Returns whether the list has an element with value v.

`void ensureCapacity(int n)`

Ensures that the list has the capacity to represent n elements.

`T get(int i)`

If i is a valid index, it returns the ith element; otherwise an exception is generated.

`int indexOf(Object v)`

Returns the index of the first occurrence of v in the list. If v is not in the list, then −1 is returned.

boolean isEmpty()

Returns **true** if there are no elements; otherwise, it returns **false**.

int lastIndexOf(Object v)

Returns the index of the last occurrence of v in the list. If v is not in the list, then –1 is returned.

T remove(**int** i)

If i is a valid index, it removes the ith element from the list by shifting forward elements i+1 and on. In addition, the removed value is returned. Otherwise, an exception is generated.

protected void removeRange(**int** i, **int** j)

Removes elements from the list whose indices are in the interval i … j-1. Elements with indices j+1 and on are shifted forward to replace the removed elements. With this definition, if j ≤ i, then no elements are removed.

T set(**int** i, Object v)

If i is a valid index, then the ith element is set to v and the previous value of the element is returned. Otherwise, an exception is thrown.

int size()

Returns the numbers of elements in the list.

Object[] toArray()

Returns an array whose elements correspond to the elements of this list.

<E> T[] toArray(E[] a)

Returns an array of the same type as array a whose elements correspond to the elements of this list. The returned array is a if a is big enough.

void trimToSize()

Sets the capacity of this list to size().

---

util	**class** Arrays

PURPOSE

Provides basic array manipulation functionality.

INSTANCE METHOD SUMMARY

<T> **static** List<T> asList(Object[] a)

Returns a fixed-size List backed by array a.

static int binarySearch(**byte**[] a, **byte** v)

Returns the index of v in sorted array a. If v is not in a, then it returns i-1, where i is the minimal index such that v < a[i].

static int binarySearch(**char**[] a, **char** v)

Returns the index of v in sorted array a. If v is not in a, then it returns i-1, where i is the minimal index such that v < a[i].

static int binarySearch(**double**[] a, **double** v)

Returns the index of v in sorted array a. If v is not in a, then it returns i-1, where i is the minimal index such that v < a[i].

static int binarySearch(**float**[] a, **float** v)

Returns the index of v in sorted array a. If v is not in a, then it returns i-1, where i is the minimal index such that v < a[i].

```
static int binarySearch(int[] a, int v)
```
Returns the index of v in sorted array a. If v is not in a, then it returns i-1, where i is the minimal index such that v < a[i].

```
static int binarySearch(long[] a, long v)
```
Returns the index of v in sorted array a. If v is not in a, then it returns i-1, where i is the minimal index such that v < a[i].

```
static int binarySearch(Object[] a, Object v)
```
Returns the index of v in naturally sorted array a using a binary search algorithm. If v is not in a, then it returns i-1, where i is the minimal index such that v < a[i].

```
static int binarySearch(short[] a, short v)
```
Returns the index of v in sorted array a. If v is not in a, then it returns i-1, where i is the minimal index such that v < a[i].

```
<T> static int binarySearch(T[] a, T v, Comparator<? super T> c)
```
Returns the index of v in sorted array a with respect to comparator c using a binary search algorithm. If v is not in a, then it returns i-1, where i is the minimal index such that v < a[i].

```
static boolean deepEquals(Object[] a1, Object[] a2)
```
Returns whether arrays a1 and a2 are deeply equal to each other.

```
static int deepHashCode(Object[] a)
```
Returns a hash code based on the deep contents of array a.

```
static String deepToString(Object[] a)
```
Returns a String representation of the deep contents of array a.

```
static boolean equals(boolean[] a1, boolean[] a2)
```
Returns whether the elements of a1 and a2 are all pairwise equal.

```
static boolean equals(byte[] a1, byte[] a2)
```
Returns whether the elements of a1 and a2 are all pairwise equal.

```
static boolean equals(char[] a1, char[] a2)
```
Returns whether the elements of a1 and a2 are all pairwise equal.

```
static boolean equals(double[] a1, double[] a2)
```
Returns whether the elements of a1 and a2 are all pairwise equal.

```
static boolean equals(float[] a1, float[] a2)
```
Returns whether the elements of a1 and a2 are all pairwise equal.

```
static boolean equals(int[] a1, int[] a2)
```
Returns whether the elements of a1 and a2 are all pairwise equal.

```
static boolean equals(long[] a1, long[] a2)
```
Returns whether the elements of a1 and a2 are all pairwise equal.

```
static boolean equals(Object[] a1, Object[] a2)
```
Returns whether the elements of a1 and a2 are all pairwise equal.

```
static boolean equals(short[] a1, short[] a2)
```
Returns whether the elements of a1 and a2 are all pairwise equal.

```
static void fill(boolean[] a, boolean v)
```
Assigns value v to the elements of array a.

```
static void fill(boolean[] a, int i, int j, boolean v)
```
Assigns value v to elements i through j-1 of array a.

```
static void fill(byte[] a, byte v)
```
Assigns value v to the elements of array a.

```
static void fill(byte[] a, int i, int j, byte v)
```
Assigns value v to elements i through j-1 of array a.
```
static void fill(char[] a, char v)
```
Assigns value v to the elements of array a.
```
static void fill(char[] a, int i, int j, char v)
```
Assigns value v to elements i through j-1 of array a.
```
static void fill(double[] a, int i, int j, double v)
```
Assigns value v to elements i through j-1 of array a.
```
static void fill(double[] a, double v)
```
Assigns value v to the elements of array a.
```
static void fill(float[] a, int i, int j, float v)
```
Assigns value v to elements i through j-1 of array a.
```
static void fill(float[] a, float v)
```
Assigns value v to the elements of array a.
```
static void fill(int[] a, int i, int j, int v)
```
Assigns value v to elements i through j-1 of array a.
```
static void fill(int[] a, int v)
```
Assigns value v to the elements of array a.
```
static void fill(long[] a, int i, int j, long v)
```
Assigns value v to elements i through j-1 of array a.
```
static void fill(long[] a, long v)
```
Assigns value v to the elements of array a.
```
static void fill(Object[] a, int i, int j, Object v)
```
Assigns value v to elements i through j-1 of array a.
```
static void fill(Object[] a, Object v)
```
Assigns value v to the elements of array a.
```
static void fill(short[] a, int i, int j, short v)
```
Assigns value v to elements i through j-1 of array a.
```
static void fill(short[] a, short v)
```
Assigns value v to the elements of array a.
```
static int hashCode(boolean[] a)
```
Returns a hash code based on the contents of array a.
```
static int hashCode(byte[] a)
```
Returns a hash code based on the contents of array a.
```
static int hashCode(char[] a)
```
Returns a hash code based on the contents of array a.
```
static int hashCode(double[] a
```
Returns a hash code based on the contents of array a.
```
static int hashCode(float[] a)
```
Returns a hash code based on the contents of array a.
```
static int hashCode(int[] a)
```
Returns a hash code based on the contents of array a.
```
static int hashCode(long[] a)
```
Returns a hash code based on the contents of array a.
```
static int hashCode(Object[] a)
```
Returns a hash code based on the contents of array a.

```
static int hashCode(Object[] a)
```
Returns a hash code based on the contents of array a.
```
static void sort(byte[] a)
```
Sorts array a into nondescending order.
```
static void sort(byte[] a, int i, int j)
```
Sorts elements i through j-1 of array a into nondescending order.
```
static void sort(char[] a)
```
Sorts array a into nondescending order.
```
static void sort(char[] a, int i, int j)
```
Sorts elements i through j-1 of array a into nondescending order.
```
static void sort(double[] a)
```
Sorts array a into nondescending order.
```
static void sort(double[] a, int i, int j)
```
Sorts elements i through j-1 of array a into nondescending order.
```
static void sort(float[] a)
```
Sorts array a into nondescending order.
```
static void sort(float[] a, int i, int j)
```
Sorts elements i through j-1 of array a into nondescending order.
```
static void sort(int[] a)
```
Sorts array a into nondescending order.
```
static void sort(int[] a, int i, int j)
```
Sorts elements i through j-1 of array a into nondescending order.
```
static void sort(long[] a)
```
Sorts array a into nondescending order.
```
static void sort(long[] a, int i, int j)
```
Sorts elements i through j-1 of array a into nondescending order.
```
static void sort(Object[] a)
```
Sorts array a into nondescending order using the natural ordering.
```
static void sort(Object[] a, int i, int j)
```
Sorts elements i through j-1 of array a into nondescending order using the natural ordering.
```
static void sort(short[] a)
```
Sorts array a into nondescending order.
```
static void sort(short[] a, int i, int j)
```
Sorts elements i through j-1 of array a into nondescending order.
```
<T> static void sort(T[] a, Comparator<? super T> c)
```
Sorts array a into nondescending order using comparator c.
```
<T> static void sort(T[] a, int i, int j, Comparator<? super T> c)
```
Sorts elements i through j-1 of array a into nondescending order using comparator c.
```
static String toString(boolean[] a)
```
Returns a `String` representation of array a.
```
static String toString(byte[] a)
```
Returns a `String` representation of array a.
```
static String toString(char[] a)
```
Returns a `String` representation of array a.

```
static String toString(double[] a
```
Returns a String representation of array a.
```
static String toString(float[] a)
```
Returns a String representation of array a.
```
static String toString(int[] a)
```
Returns a String representation of array a.
```
static String toString(long[] a)
```
Returns a String representation of the value of array a.
```
static String toString(Object[] a)
```
Returns a String representation of the value of array a.
```
static String toString(Object[] a)
```
Returns a String representation of the value of array a.

---

lang | **class** ArrayStoreException **extends** RuntimeException

PURPOSE
Represents an illegal array element assignment event.
CONSTRUCTOR SUMMARY
```
ArrayStoreException()
```
Constructs a new ArrayStoreException with a **null** message.
```
ArrayStoreException(String s)
```
Constructs a new ArrayStoreException with message s.

---

lang | **class** AssertionError **extends** Error

PURPOSE
Represents a failed assertion event.
CONSTRUCTOR SUMMARY
```
AssertionError()
```
Constructs a new AssertionError with a **null** message.
```
AssertionError(boolean b)
```
Constructs a new AssertionError with a message indicating the value of b.
```
AssertionError(char c)
```
Constructs a new AssertionError with a message indicating the value of c.
```
AssertionError(double n)
```
Constructs a new AssertionError with a message indicating the value of n.
```
AssertionError(float n)
```
Constructs a new AssertionError with a message indicating the value of n.
```
AssertionError(int n)
```
Constructs a new AssertionError with a message indicating the value of n.
```
AssertionError(long n)
```
Constructs a new AssertionError with a message indicating the value of n.

AssertionError(Object v)
> Constructs a new `AssertionError` with a message indicating the value of v.

---

math   class BigDecimal **extends** Number **implements**
Comparable<BigDecimal>

PURPOSE

Represents immutable decimal numbers of arbitrary precision. In particular, a decimal number is represented using a `BigInteger` and a scaling factor. If the `BigInteger` in a `BigDecimal` representation is n and the scaling factor is d, then the decimal number being represented is $n / 10^d$.

FIELD SUMMARY

static BigDecimal ONE
> A `BigDecimal` representation of 1 using a scaling factor of 0.

static BigDecimal TEN
> A `BigDecimal` representation of 10 using a scaling factor of 0.

static BigDecimal ZERO
> A `BigDecimal` representation of 0 using a scaling factor of 0.

static int ROUND_CEILING
> Represents rounding toward positive infinity.

static int ROUND_DOWN

> Represents rounding toward zero.

static int ROUND_FLOOR

> Represents rounding toward negative infinity.

static int ROUND_HALF_DOWN

> Represents rounding toward nearest integer with ties broken by rounding down.

static int ROUND_HALF_EVEN

> Represents rounding mode with ties broken by rounding to the even number.

static int ROUND_HALF_UP

> Represents rounding nearest integer with ties broken by rounding up.

static int ROUND_UNNECESSARY

> Represents rounding is unnecessary as operation is exact.

static int ROUND_UP

> Represents rounding away from zero.

static BigDecimal TEN

> A `BigDecimal` representation of 10 using a scaling factor of 0.

static BigDecimal ZERO

> A `BigDecimal` representation of 0 using a scaling factor of 0.

CLASS METHOD SUMMARY

static BigDecimal valueOf(**double** n)
> Returns a `BigDecimal` based on construction `BigDecimal(Double.valueOf(n))`.

static BigDecimal valueOf(**long** n)
> Returns `valueOf(n, 0)` equal to n. The scaling factor in the result is equal to zero.

```
static BigDecimal valueOf(long n, int d)
```

Returns a BigDecimal equal to n. The scaling factor in the result is equal to d.

CONSTRUCTOR SUMMARY

```
BigDecimal(BigInteger n)
```

Invokes **this**(n, 0).

```
BigDecimal(BigInteger n, int d)
```

Constructs a new BigDecimal using n as a basis with d digits of accuracy after the decimal point.

```
BigDecimal(BigInteger n, int d, MathContext m)
```

Constructs a new BigDecimal using n as a basis with d digits of accuracy after the decimal point. The rounding of the new BigDecimal is specified using the mathematics context m.

```
BigDecimal(BigInteger n, MathContext m)
```

Constructs a new BigDecimal using n as a basis with 0 digits of accuracy after the decimal point. The rounding of the new BigDecimal is specified using the mathematics context m.

```
BigDecimal(char[] a)
```

Constructs a new BigDecimal using array a as a text-based representation of a number. The scaling factor is equal to the number of digits in the fractional part of s.

```
BigDecimal(char[] a, int i, int n)
```

Constructs a new BigDecimal using a subarray of array a as a text-based representation of a number. The subarray begins with element i and the subarray has length n. The scaling factor is equal to the number of digits in the fractional part of the representation.

```
BigDecimal(char[] a, int i, int n, MathContext m)
```

Constructs a new BigDecimal using a subarray of array a as a text-based representation of a number. The subarray begins with element i and the subarray has length n. The scaling factor is equal to the number of digits in the fractional part of the representation. The rounding of the new BigDecimal is specified using the mathematics context m.

```
BigDecimal(char[] a, MathContext m)
```

Constructs a new BigDecimal using array a as a text-based representation of a number. The scaling factor is equal to the number of digits in the fractional part of the representation. The rounding of the new BigDecimal is specified using the mathematics context m.

```
BigDecimal(double n)
```

Constructs a new BigDecimal using n as a basis with the scaling factor equal to the number of digits in the fractional part of n.

```
BigDecimal(double n, MathContext m)
```

Constructs a new BigDecimal using n as a basis with the scaling factor equal to the number of digits in the fractional part of n. The rounding of the new Big-Decimal is specified using the mathematics context m.

```
BigDecimal(int n)
```

Constructs a new BigDecimal using n as a basis with the scaling factor of 0.

BigDecimal(**int** n, MathContext m)

> Constructs a new BigDecimal using n as a basis with the scaling factor of 0. The rounding of the new BigDecimal is specified using the mathematics context m.

BigDecimal(**long** n)

> Constructs a new BigDecimal using n as a basis with the scaling factor of 0.

BigDecimal(**long** n, MathContext m)

> Constructs a new BigDecimal using n as a basis with the scaling factor of 0. The rounding of the new BigDecimal is specified using the mathematics context m.

BigDecimal(String s)

> Constructs a new BigDecimal using s as a text-based representation of a number. The scaling factor is equal to the number of digits in the fractional part of s.

BigDecimal(String s, MathContext m)

> Constructs a new BigDecimal using s as a text-based representation of a number. The scaling factor is equal to the number of digits in the fractional part of s. The rounding of the new BigDecimal is specified using the mathematics context m.

INSTANCE METHOD SUMMARY

BigDecimal abs()

> Returns a BigDecimal equal to the absolute value of this BigDecimal.

BigDecimal abs(MathContext c)

> Returns a BigDecimal equal to the absolute value of this BigDecimal with rounding according to context c.

BigDecimal add(BigDecimal n)

> Returns a BigDecimal equal to the sum of n and this BigDecimal.

BigDecimal add(BigDecimal n, MathContext c)

> Returns a BigDecimal equal to the sum of n and this BigDecimal with rounding according to context c.

byte byteValueExact()

> Returns a **byte** representation of this BigDecimal.

int compareTo(BigDecimal n)

> Returns a negative value, zero, or a positive value depending respectively on whether the BigDecimal value represented by this object is less than, equal to, or greater than n.

int compareTo(Object v)

> Returns a negative value, zero, or a positive value depending respectively on whether the BigDecimal value represented by this object is less than, equal to, or greater than v.

BigDecimal divide(BigDecimal n)

> Returns a BigDecimal equal to the division of this BigDecimal by n.

BigDecimal divide(BigDecimal n, **int** m)

> Returns a BigDecimal equal to the division of this BigDecimal by n with any rounding using rounding mode m.

BigDecimal divide(BigDecimal n, **int** d, **int** m)

> Returns a BigDecimal equal to the division of this BigDecimal by n with any rounding using rounding mode m. The scaling factor in the result is equal to d.

BigDecimal divide(BigDecimal n, **int** d, RoundingMode m)

> Returns a BigDecimal equal to the division of this BigDecimal by n with any rounding using rounding mode m. The scaling factor in the result is equal to d.

BigDecimal divide(BigDecimal n, MathContext c)

> Returns a BigDecimal equal to the division of this BigDecimal by n with any rounding using context c.

BigDecimal divide(BigDecimal n, RoundingMode m)

> Returns a BigDecimal equal to the division of this BigDecimal by n with any rounding using rounding mode m.

BigDecimal[] divideAndRemainder(BigDecimal n)

> Returns a two-element BigDecimal array with the first element equal to divideToIntegralValue(n) and the second element equal to remainder(n).

BigDecimal[] divideAndRemainder(BigDecimal n, MathContext c)

> Returns a two-element BigDecimal array with the first element equal to divideToIntegralValue(n, c) and the second element equal to remainder(n, c).

BigDecimal divideToIntegralValue(BigDecimal n)

> Returns a BigDecimal equal to the integer part of the division of this BigDecimal by n.

BigDecimal divideToIntegralValue(BigDecimal n, MathContext c)

> Returns a BigDecimal equal to the integer part of the division of this BigDecimal by n with any rounding using context c.

double doubleValue()

> Returns a **double** representation of this BigDecimal.

boolean equals(Object x)

> Returns **true** if and only if v is an instance of BigDecimal representing the same numeric value with the same scaling factor that this object represents.

float floatValue()

> Returns a **float** representation of this BigDecimal.

int hashCode()

> Returns the hash code of this BigDecimal.

int intValue()

> Returns an **int** representation of this BigDecimal.

int intValueExact()

> Attempts to return an exact **int** representation of this BigDecimal. If there is not a corresponding **int** representation an ArithmeticException is thrown.

long longValue()

> Returns a **long** representation of this BigDecimal.

long longValueExact()

> Attempts to return an exact **long** representation of this BigDecimal. If there is not a corresponding **long** representation an ArithmeticException is thrown.

BigDecimal max(BigDecimal n)

> Returns the maximum of n and this BigDecimal.

BigDecimal min(BigDecimal n)

> Returns the minimum of n and this BigDecimal.

BigDecimal movePointLeft(int n)

Returns a BigDecimal equal to product of this BigDecimal and 10^{-n}.

BigDecimal movePointRight(int n)

Returns a BigDecimal equal to product of this BigDecimal and 10^n.

BigDecimal multiply(BigDecimal n)

Returns a BigDecimal equal to the product of n and this BigDecimal.

BigDecimal multiply(BigDecimal n, MathContext c)

Returns a BigDecimal equal to the product of n and this BigDecimal with any rounding using context c.

BigDecimal negate()

Returns a BigDecimal equal to the additive inverse of this BigDecimal.

BigDecimal negate(MathContext c)

Returns a BigDecimal equal to the additive inverse of this BigDecimal with any rounding using context c.

BigDecimal plus()

Returns this BigDecimal.

BigDecimal plus(MathContext c)

Returns round(c).

BigDecimal pow(int n)

Returns a BigDecimal equal to this BigDecimal raised to the power n.

BigDecimal pow(int n, MathContext c)

Returns a BigDecimal equal to this BigDecimal raised to the power n with any rounding using context c.

int precision()

Returns the precision of this BigDecimal.

BigDecimal remainder(BigDecimal n)

Returns a BigDecimal equal to the remainder of the division of this BigDecimal by n.

BigDecimal remainder(BigDecimal n, MathContext c)

Returns a BigDecimal equal to the remainder of the division of this BigDecimal by n with any rounding using context c.

BigDecimal round(MathContext c)

Returns a BigDecimal equal to this BigDecimal rounded according to context c.

int scale()

Returns the scaling factor maintained by this BigDecimal.

BigDecimal scaleByPowerOfTen(int n)

Returns multiply(TEN).

BigDecimal setScale(int d)

Returns a BigDecimal equal to unscaledValue() * 10^{-d} with a scaling factor of d.

BigDecimal setScale(int d, int m)

Returns a BigDecimal equal to unscaledValue() * 10^{-d} with a scaling factor of d. If rounding is required to produce the value then the rounding mode is m.

BigDecimal setScale(int d, RoundingMode m)

Returns a BigDecimal equal to unscaledValue() * 10^{-d} with a scaling factor of d. If rounding is required to produce the value then the rounding mode is m.

short shortValueExact()

> Attempts to return an exact **short** representation of this BigDecimal. If there is not a corresponding **short** representation an ArithmeticException is thrown.

int signum()

> Returns –1, 0, or 1 depending on whether this BigDecimal is respectively negative, zero, or positive.

BigDecimal stripTrailingZeros()

> Returns a BigDecimal equal to this BigDecimal with any trailing zeros removed from the representation.

BigDecimal subtract(BigDecimal n)

> Returns a BigDecimal equal to the difference between this BigDecimal and n.

BigDecimal subtract(BigDecimal n, MathContext c)

> Returns a BigDecimal equal to the difference between this BigDecimal and n with any rounding using context c.

BigInteger toBigInteger()

> Returns a BigInteger representation of this BigDecimal.

BigInteger toBigIntegerExact()

> Attempts to return an exact BigInteger representation of this BigDecimal. If there is not a corresponding BigInteger representation an ArithmeticException is thrown.

String toString()

> Returns a String representation of the value of this BigDecimal using scientific notation if an exponent is needed.

String toEngineeringString()

> Returns a String representation of the value of this BigDecimal using engineering notation if an exponent is needed.

BigDecimal ulp()

> Returns a value equal to BigDecimal(BigInteger.ONE, scale()), which is the size of the unit in the last place of this BigDecimal.

BigInteger unscaledValue()

> Returns a BigInteger representation of the product of this BigDecimal and $10^{scale()}$.

---

math	**class BigInteger extends** Number **implements** Comparable<BigInteger>

PURPOSE
Represents immutable integer numbers of arbitrary precision. The integer is represented in two's complement form.

FIELD SUMMARY

static BigInteger ONE

> Represents the BigInteger corresponding to 1.

static BigInteger TEN

> Represents the BigInteger corresponding to 10.

`static` `BigInteger` `ZERO`

Represents the `BigInteger` corresponding to 0.

CLASS METHOD SUMMARY ∇

`static` `BigInteger` `probablePrime(int` `n, Random r)`

Returns an n-bit pseudorandomly generated positive `BigInteger` using r.

`static` `BigInteger` `valueOf(long n)`

Returns a `BigInteger` whose value is equal to n.

CONSTRUCTOR SUMMARY

`BigInteger(byte[] a)`

Constructs a new `BigInteger` corresponding to the two's-complement binary representation represented by array **a**.

`BigInteger(int s, byte[] a)`

Constructs a `BigInteger` corresponding to the two's-complement binary representation represented by array **a**. The sign of the number is determined by s. If s is 1, then the number is positive; if s is 0, then the number is 0; and if s is −1, then the number is negative.

`BigInteger(int n, int m, Random r)`

Constructs using r an n-bit pseudorandomly generated positive `BigInteger` whose probability of being composite is at most $1 / 2^m$.

`BigInteger(int n, Random r)`

Constructs a new n-bit pseudorandomly generated positive `BigInteger` using r.

`BigInteger(String s)`

Constructs a new `BigInteger` using s as a text-based representation of a number.

`BigInteger(String s, int r)`

Constructs a new `BigInteger` using s as a text-based, radix r representation of a number.

INSTANCE METHOD SUMMARY ∇

`BigInteger` `abs()`

Returns a `BigInteger` equal to the absolute value of this `BigInteger`. The scaling factor in the result is equal to **this**.`scale()`.

`BigInteger` `add(BigInteger n)`

Returns a `BigInteger` equal to the sum of n and this `BigInteger`. The scaling factor in the result is equal to `max(n,` **this**.`scale())`.

`BigInteger` `and(BigInteger n)`

Returns a `BigInteger` whose value is the bitwise logical and of this `BigInteger` and n.

`BigInteger` `andNot(BigInteger n)`

Returns a `BigInteger` whose value is the logical and of this `BigInteger` and the complement of n.

`int` `bitCount()`

Returns the number of bits in the two's-complement representation of this `BigInteger` that are equal to the complement of its sign bit.

`int` `bitLength()`

Returns $n-1$, where n equals number of bits in the minimal two's-complement representation of this `BigInteger`.

BigInteger clearBit(**int** i)

> Returns a BigInteger whose value is equal to this BigInteger with the ith bit cleared.

int compareTo(BigInteger n)

> Returns a negative value, zero, or a positive value depending respectively on whether the BigInteger value represented by this object is less than, equal to, or greater than n.

int compareTo(Object v)

> Returns a negative value, zero, or a positive value depending respectively on whether the BigInteger value represented by this object is less than, equal to, or greater than v.

BigInteger divide(BigInteger n, **int** m)

> Returns a BigInteger equal to the integer division of this BigInteger by n.

BigInteger[] divideAndRemainder(BigInteger n)

> Returns a two-element BigInteger array with the first element equal to the quotient of this BigInteger divided by n and the element equal to the remainder of this BigInteger divided by n.

double doubleValue()

> Returns a **double** representation of this BigInteger.

boolean equals(Object x)

> Returns **true** if and only if v is an instance of BigInteger representing the same numeric value with the same scaling factor that this object represents.

BigInteger flipBit(**int** i)

> Returns a BigInteger whose value is equal to this BigInteger with the ith bit flipped.

float floatValue()

> Returns a **float** representation of this BigInteger.

BigInteger gcd(BigInteger n)

> Returns a BigInteger whose value is the greatest common divisor of this BigInteger and n.

int getLowestSetBit()

> Returns the index of the least significant one-bit in this BigInteger.

int hashCode()

> Returns the hash code of this BigInteger.

int intValue()

> Returns an **int** representation of this BigInteger.

boolean isProbablePrime(**int** m)

> Returns **true** if the probability that this BigInteger is composite is at most $1/2^m$.

long longValue()

> Returns a **long** representation of this BigInteger.

BigInteger max(BigInteger n)

> Returns the maximum of n and this BigInteger.

BigInteger min(BigInteger n)

> Returns the minimum of n and this BigInteger.

BigInteger mod(BigInteger n)

Returns a BigInteger whose value is the remainder of this BigInteger divided by n.

BigInteger modInverse(BigInteger n)

Returns a BigInteger whose value is the remainder of k by n, where k is one less than this BigInteger.

BigInteger modPow(BigInteger m, BigInteger n)

Returns a BigInteger whose value is the remainder of k by n, where k is this BigInteger raised to the power m.

BigInteger multiply(BigInteger n)

Returns a BigInteger equal to the product of n and this BigInteger.

BigInteger negate()

Returns a BigInteger equal to the additive inverse of this BigInteger.

BigInteger nextProbablePrime()

Returns the least BigInteger that is greater than this BigInteger such that it is probably prime.

BigInteger not()

Returns a BigInteger equal to the bitwise complement of this BigInteger.

BigInteger or(BigInteger n)

Returns a BigInteger equal to the bitwise logical or of n and this BigInteger.

BigInteger pow(int n)

Returns a BigInteger equal to this BigInteger raised to the power n.

BigInteger remainder(BigInteger n)

Returns a BigInteger equal to the remainder of this BigInteger divided by n.

BigInteger setBit(int i)

Returns a BigInteger equal to this BigInteger with the ith bit set.

BigInteger shiftLeft(int n)

Returns a BigInteger equal to this BigInteger multiplied by 2^n.

BigInteger shiftRight(int n)

Returns a BigInteger equal to this BigInteger divided by 2^n.

int signum()

Returns -1, 0, or 1 depending on whether this BigInteger is respectively negative, zero, or positive.

BigInteger subtract(BigInteger n)

Returns a BigInteger equal to the difference between this BigInteger and n.

boolean testBit(int i)

Returns **true** if this BigInteger has its ith bit set; otherwise, returns **false**.

byte[] toByteArray()

Returns the two's-complement representation of this BigInteger as a **byte** array.

String toString()

Returns a String representation of the value of this BigInteger.

String toString(int r)

Returns a String representation of the value of this BigInteger in radix r.

BigInteger xor(BigInteger n)

Returns a `BigInteger` equal to the bitwise exclusive or of n and this `BigInteger`.

| `lang` | **final class** Boolean **implements** Serializable, Comparable<Boolean> |

PURPOSE

Represents a **boolean** value within a class wrapper.

FIELD SUMMARY

static final Boolean FALSE

Boolean constant representing the **boolean** value **false**.

static final Boolean TRUE

Boolean constant representing the **boolean** value **true**.

static final Class<Boolean> TYPE

Represents the type **boolean**.

CLASS METHOD SUMMARY

static boolean getBoolean(String s)

Returns **true** if and only if the system property named s exists and equals "true".

static boolean parseBoolean(String s)

Returns the **boolean** value represented by parsing string s.

static String toString(**boolean** b)

Returns a `String` object representing **boolean** value b.

static Boolean valueOf(**boolean** b)

Returns a `Boolean` object representing **boolean** value b.

static Boolean valueOf(String s)

Returns a `Boolean` representing **boolean** value **true** if s is non-**null** and s.toLowerCase() equals "true"; otherwise, it constructs a `Boolean` object representing **boolean** value **false**.

CONSTRUCTOR SUMMARY

Boolean(**boolean** b)

Constructs a `Boolean` object representing **boolean** value b.

Boolean(String s)

Constructs a `Boolean` object representing **boolean** value **true** if s is non-**null** and s.toLowerCase() equals "true"; otherwise, it constructs a `Boolean` object representing **boolean** value **false**.

INSTANCE METHOD SUMMARY

boolean booleanValue()

Returns the **boolean** value represented by this object.

public int compareTo(Boolean b)

Returns a negative value, zero, or a positive value depending respectively on whether the **boolean** value represented by this object is less than, equal to, or greater than b.

boolean equals(Object v)

Returns **true** if and only if v is an instance of Boolean representing the same **boolean** value that this object represents.

int hashCode()

Returns the hash code of this object.

String toString()

Returns a String representation of the value of this object.

---

class BorderLayout **implements** LayoutManager2, Serializable

PURPOSE

Represents a layout manager that arranges its components with five regions north, south, east, west, and center.

FIELD SUMMARY

static String AFTER_LAST_LINE

Equivalent to PAGE_END.

static String AFTER_LINE_ENDS

Equivalent to LINE_END.

static String BEFORE_FIRST_LINE

Equivalent to PAGE_START.

static String BEFORE_LINE_BEGINS

Equivalent to LINE_START.

static String CENTER

Represents a middle of the container constraint.

static String EAST

Represents a right side of the container constraint.

static String LINE_END

Represents component placed at the end of the line constraint.

static String LINE_START

Represents component placed at the start of the line constraint.

static String NORTH

Represents a top side of the container constraint.

static String PAGE_END

Represents component placed at the end of the page constraint.

static String PAGE_START

Represents component placed at the start of the page constraint.

static String SOUTH

Represents a bottom side of the container constraint.

static String WEST

Represents a left side of the container constraint.

CONSTRUCTOR SUMMARY

BorderLayout()

Constructs a new BorderLayout with no gaps.

BorderLayout(**int** h, **int** v)

> Constructs a new **BorderLayout** with no gaps. The inter-row horizontal gap is h and the interelement vertical gap is v.

INSTANCE METHOD SUMMARY

void addLayoutComponent(Component c, Object v)

> Adds component c using constraint v to the layout of this layout manager.

void addLayoutComponent(String s, Component c)

> Adds component c using constraint s to the layout of this layout manager.

Object getConstraints(Component c)

> Returns the constraints for component c in the layout of this layout manager.

int getHgap()

> Returns the intercomponent horizontal gap used by this layout manager.

float getLayoutAlignmentX(Container c)

> Returns the x-axis alignment policy with regard to container c.

float getLayoutAlignmentY(Container c)

> Returns the y-axis alignment policy with regard to container c.

Component getLayoutComponent(Object v)

> Returns the component subject to constraint v in the layout of this layout manager.

Component getLayoutComponent(Container c, Object v)

> Returns the component subject to constraint v in the layout of this layout manager with respect to container c.

int getVgap()

> Returns the intercomponent vertical gap used by this layout manager.

void invalidateLayout(Container c)

> Invalidates the layout with regard to container c.

void layoutContainer(Container c)

> Arranges the components of container c using this layout manager.

Dimension maximumLayoutSize(Container c)

> Returns the maximum size of container c using this layout manager.

Dimension minimumLayoutSize(Container c)

> Returns the minimum size of container c using this layout manager.

Dimension preferredLayoutSize(Container c)

> Returns the preferred size of container c using this layout manager.

void removeLayoutComponent(Component c)

> Removes component c from the arrangement of this layout manager.

void setHgap(**int** h)

> Sets h as the horizontal gap between components by this layout manager.

void setVgap(**int** v)

> Sets v as the vertical gap between components by this layout manager.

String toString()

> Returns a representation of this layout manager.

`io` | **class** `BufferedReader` **extends** `Reader`

PURPOSE

Represents a buffered input stream with functionality for character, array, and line extraction.

CONSTRUCTOR SUMMARY

`BufferedReader(Reader r)`

Constructs a new buffered input stream using stream r.

`BufferedReader(Reader r, int n)`

Constructs a new buffered input stream using stream r with a buffer size of length n.

INSTANCE METHOD SUMMARY

`void close()`

Closes this `BufferedReader`.

`void mark(int n)`

Marks the current position in this `BufferedReader` stream as a reset point. Parameter n indicates a limit on the number of characters that can be read while still preserving this reset point.

`boolean markSupported()`

Returns **true**; that is, that a `BufferedReader` stream does support marking.

`int read()`

Returns the next character from this `BufferedReader` stream.

`abstract int read(char[] c, int i, int n)`

Attempts to read the next n characters from this `Reader` stream and store them in c starting at index i. Returns the number of characters that have been read (−1 if end of file occurs).

`String readLine()`

Returns the next line of text from this `BufferedReader` stream.

`boolean ready()`

Returns whether this `BufferedReader` stream is ready for reading.

`void reset()`

Resets this `BufferedReader` stream.

`long skip(long n)`

Ignores the next n characters in this `Reader` stream.

`io` | **class** `BufferedWriter` **extends** `Writer`

PURPOSE

Represents a buffered output stream with functionality for character, array, and string insertion.

CONSTRUCTOR SUMMARY

`BufferedWriter(Writer w)`

Constructs a new buffered input stream using stream w.

BufferedWriter(Writer w, **int** n)

> Constructs a new buffered output stream using stream w with a buffer size of length n.

INSTANCE METHOD SUMMARY

void close()

> Closes this OutputStreamWriter.

void flush()

> Flushes this OutputStreamWriter.

void newLine()

> Writes a line separator to this OutputStreamWriter.

void write(**char**[] c, **int** i, **int** n)

> Inserts n characters from array c to this OutputStreamWriter. The first character to be displayed is c[i].

void write(**int** c)

> Inserts character c to this OutputStreamWriter.

void write(String s, **int** i, **int** n)

> Inserts an n character substring from string s to this OutputStreamWriter. The first character in the substring to be displayed has index i.

---

swing	**class** ButtonGroup **implements** Serializable

PURPOSE

Represents a set of mutually exclusive buttons.

FIELD SUMMARY

protected Vector buttons

> Represents the buttons in this ButtonGroup.

CONSTRUCTOR SUMMARY

ButtonGroup()

> Constructs a new empty ButtonGroup.

INSTANCE METHOD SUMMARY

void add(AbstractButton b)

> Adds button b to this ButtonGroup.

int getButtonCount()

> Returns the number of buttons in this ButtonGroup.

Enumeration getElements()

> Returns an enumeration of the buttons in this ButtonGroup.

ButtonModel getSelection()

> Returns the model of the currently selected button in this ButtonGroup.

boolean isSelected(ButtonModel b)

> Returns whether button model b is selected for this ButtonGroup.

void remove(AbstractButton b)

> Removes button b from this ButtonGroup.

void setSelected(ButtonModel b, **boolean** s)

> Sets s as the state of button model b for this ButtonGroup.

| lang | **final class** Byte **extends** Number **implements** Comparable<Byte> |

PURPOSE
Represents a **byte** value within a class wrapper.

FIELD SUMMARY

static final byte MAX_VALUE

Represents the maximum value of type **byte** (i.e., $2^7 - 1$).

static final byte MIN_VALUE

Represents the minimum value of type **byte** (i.e., -2^7).

static final int SIZE

Represents the number of bits used to represent a **byte** value.

static final Class<Byte> TYPE

Represents the type **byte**.

CLASS METHOD SUMMARY

static Byte decode(String s)

Constructs a new Byte object representing Byte.parseByte(s, n), where n
is 8, 10, or 16 depending on whether s is respectively a numeric string in octal,
decimal, or hexadecimal format.

static byte parseByte(String s)

Returns Byte.parseByte(s, 10).

static byte parseByte(String s, **int** n)

Returns the **byte** value represented by parsing string s as an optionally signed
byte value in radix n.

static String toString(**byte** n)

Returns a new String object representing **byte** value n.

static Byte valueOf(**byte** n)

Returns a Byte representation of **byte** value n.

static Byte valueOf(String s)

Returns Byte.valueOf(s, 10).

static Byte valueOf(String s, **int** n)

Returns a new Byte object representing Byte.parseByte(s, n).

CONSTRUCTOR SUMMARY

Byte(**byte** n)

Constructs a new Byte object representing **byte** value n.

Byte(String s)

Constructs a new Byte object representing Byte.parseByte(s).

INSTANCE METHOD SUMMARY

byte byteValue()

Returns the **byte** value represented by this object.

int compareTo(Byte n)

Returns a negative value, zero, or a positive value depending respectively on
whether the **byte** value represented by this object is less than, equal to, or
greater than n.

double doubleValue()

Returns the **byte** value represented by this object as a **double**.

boolean equals(Object v)

> Returns **true** if and only if v is an instance of Byte representing the same Byte value that this object represents.

float floatValue()

> Returns the **byte** value represented by this object as a **float**.

int hashCode()

> Returns the hash code of this object.

int intValue()

> Returns the **byte** value represented by this object as an **int**.

long longValue()

> Returns the **byte** value represented by this object as a **long**.

short shortValue()

> Returns the **byte** value represented by this object as a **short**.

String toString()

> Returns a String representation of the value of this object.

---

util	**abstract class** Calendar **implements** Cloneable, Serializable

PURPOSE

Represents a calendar and provide conversion methods for dates

FIELD SUMMARY

static int AM

> Represents the period from midnight to just before noon for the AM_PM field.

static int AM_PM

> Represents the field for whether the hour is before or after noon.

static int APRIL

> Represents the fourth month of the year for the MONTH field.

protected boolean areFieldsSet

> Indicates whether the fields of this Calendar agree with the currently set time.

static int AUGUST

> Represents the eighth month of the year for the MONTH field.

static int DATE

> Represents the field for the day of the month.

static int DAY_OF_MONTH

> Represents the field for the day of the week within the day of the month.

static int DAY_OF_WEEK

> Represents the field for the day of the week.

static int DAY_OF_WEEK_IN_MONTH

> Represents the field for the day of the week within the current month.

static int DAY_OF_YEAR

> Represents the field for the day number within the current year.

static int DECEMBER

> Represents the twelfth month of the year for the MONTH field.

static int DST_OFFSET

> Represents the field for the daylight savings milliseconds offset.

static int ERA

Represents the field for the era in the Julian calendar.

static int FEBRUARY

Represents the second month of the year for the MONTH field.

static int FIELD_COUNT

Represents the number of distinct Calendar fields.

protected int[] fields

The field values for this Calendar.

static int FRIDAY

Represents the Friday for the DAY_OF_WEEK field.

static int HOUR

Represents the field for the hour in the morning or the afternoon.

static int HOUR_OF_DAY

Represents the field for the hour in the day.

protected boolean[] isSet

Indicates which fields of this Calendar are set.

protected boolean isTimeSet

Indicates whether the time has been set.

static int JANUARY

Represents the first month of the year for the MONTH field.

static int JULY

Represents the seventh month of the year for the MONTH field.

static int JUNE

Represents the sixth month of the year for the MONTH field.

static int MARCH

Represents the third month of the year for the MONTH field.

static int MAY

Represents the fifth of the year for the MONTH field.

static int MILLISECOND

Represents the field for the millisecond within the second.

static int MINUTE

Represents the field for the minute within the hour.

static int MONDAY

Represents the Monday for the DAY_OF_WEEK field.

static int MONTH

Represents the field for the month.

static int NOVEMBER

Represents the eleventh month of the year for the MONTH field.

static int OCTOBER

Represents the tenth month of the year for the MONTH field.

static int PM

Represents the period from noon to just before midnight for the AM_PM field.

static int SATURDAY

Represents the Saturday for the DAY_OF_WEEK field.

static int SECOND

Represents the field for the second within the minute.

```
static int SEPTEMBER
```
Represents the ninth month of the year for the MONTH field.
```
static int SUNDAY
```
Represents the Sunday for the DAY_OF_WEEK field.
```
static int THURSDAY
```
Represents the Thursday for the DAY_OF_WEEK field.
```
protected long time
```
Represents the currently set time for this `Calendar`. The value is expressed as the number of milliseconds since January 1, 1970, 0:00:00 GMT.
```
static int TUESDAY
```
Represents the Tuesday for the DAY_OF_WEEK field.
```
static int UNDECIMBER
```
Represents the thirteenth month of the year for the MONTH field.
```
static int WEDNESDAY
```
Represents the Wednesday for the DAY_OF_WEEK field.
```
static int WEEK_OF_MONTH
```
Represents the field for the week number within the current month.
```
static int WEEK_OF_YEAR
```
Represents the field for the week number within the current year.
```
static int YEAR
```
Represents the field for the year.
```
static int ZONE_OFFSET
```
Represents the field for the raw milliseconds offset from GMT.

CLASS METHOD SUMMARY
```
static Locale[] getAvailableLocales()
```
Returns an array of available locales.
```
static Calendar getInstance()
```
Returns a `Calendar` for the default time zone and locale
```
static Calendar getInstance(Locale l)
```
Returns a `Calendar` for the default time zone for locale `l`.
```
static Calendar getInstance(TimeZone t)
```
Returns a `Calendar` for the default locale for time zone `t`.
```
static Calendar getInstance(TimeZone t, Locale l)
```
Returns a `Calendar` for time zone `t` and locale `l`.

CONSTRUCTOR SUMMARY
```
protected Calendar()
```
Constructs a new `Calendar` for the default time zone and locale.
```
protected Calendar(TimeZone t, Locale l
```
Constructs a new `Calendar` for time zone `t` and locale `l`.

INSTANCE METHOD SUMMARY
```
abstract void add(int f, int n)
```
Increments field `f` of this `Calendar` by amount `n`.
```
boolean after(Object t)
```
Returns whether the time `t` occurs before the time of this `Calendar`.
```
boolean before(Object t)
```
Returns whether the time `t` occurs after the time of this `Calendar`.

void clear()

Clears the time fields of this Calendar.

void clear(**int** f)

Clears time field f of this Calendar.

Object clone()

Returns a clone of this Calendar.

int compareTo(Calendar c)

Returns a negative value, zero, or a positive value depending respectively on whether the time of this object is less than, equal to, or greater than c.

protected void complete()

Sets any unset fields of this Calendar.

protected abstract void computeFields()

Sets the fields of this Calendar based on the currently set time.

protected abstract void computeTime()

Sets the current time of this Calendar based its field values.

boolean equals(Object v)

Returns **true** if and only if v is an instance of Calendar representing the same calendar time as this Calendar.

int get(**int** f)

Returns the value of field f for this Calendar.

int getActualMaximum(**int** f)

Returns the maximum value of field f for this Calendar.

int getActualMinimum(**int** f)

Returns the minimum value of field f for this Calendar.

int getFirstDayOfWeek()

Returns the first day of the week for the default locale.

abstract int getGreatestMinimum(**int** f)

Returns the highest minimum value for field f of this Calendar.

abstract int getLeastMaximum(**int** f)

Returns the lowest maximum value for field f of this Calendar.

abstract int getMaximum(**int** f)

Returns the maximum value for field f of this Calendar.

int getMinimalDaysInFirstWeek()

Returns the minimal number of days required in the first week of the year for this Calendar.

abstract int getMinimum(**int** f)

Returns the minimum value for field f for this Calendar.

Date getTime()

Returns the current time for this Calendar.

long getTimeInMillis()

Returns the current time for this Calendar.

TimeZone getTimeZone()

Returns the time zone for this Calendar.

int hashCode()

Returns the hash code of this object.

protected int internalGet(**int** f)

Returns the value of field f for this Calendar.

boolean isLenient()

Returns whether date and time parsing is lenient for this Calendar.

boolean isSet(int f)

Returns whether field f of this Calendar is set.

abstract void roll(int f, boolean increment)

Increments or decrements field f of this Calendar depending on **boolean** value increment.

void roll(int f, int n)

Increments field f of this Calendar by n units.

void set(int f, int n)

Sets the field f to n for this Calendar.

void set(int y, int m, int d)

Sets the year, month, and day respectively to y, m, and d for this Calendar.

void set(int y, int m, int d, int h, int n)

Sets the year, month, day, hour, and minute respectively to y, m, d, h, and n for this Calendar.

void set(int y, int m, int d, int h, int n, int s)

Sets the year, month, day, hour, minute, and second respectively to y, m, d, h, n, and s for this Calendar.

void setFirstDayOfWeek(int d)

Sets the first day of the week to d for this Calendar.

void setLenient(boolean b)

Sets to b whether date and time parsing for this Calendar is to be lenient.

void setMinimalDaysInFirstWeek(int n)

Sets to n the minimal days required in the first week of the year for this Calendar.

void setTime(Date d)

Sets the current time to d for this Calendar.

void setTimeInMillis(long n)

Sets current time to n for this Calendar.

void setTimeZone(TimeZone t)

Sets the time zone to t for this Calendar.

String toString()

Returns a String representation of the value of this object.

| awt | **class** Canvas **extends** Component **implements** Accessible |

PURPOSE

Represents a rectangular region for drawing and trapping input events.

CONSTRUCTOR SUMMARY

Canvas()

Constructs a new Canvas.

Canvas(GraphicsConfiguration g)

Constructs a new Canvas for graphics configuration g.

INSTANCE METHOD SUMMARY

void addNotify()

Creates the peer of this Canvas.

void createBufferStrategy(**int** n)

Creates a new buffering strategy for this Canvas using n buffers.

void createBufferStrategy(**int** n, BufferCapabilities c)

Creates a new buffering strategy for this Canvas using n buffers and capabilities c.

AccessibleContext getAccessibleContext()

Returns the accessibility context of this Canvas.

BufferStrategy getBufferStrategy()

Returns the buffer strategy of this Canvas.

void paint(Graphics g)

Paints this Canvas using graphical context g.

void update(Graphics g)

Updates the display of this Canvas using graphical context g.

`lang`

final class Character **implements** Serializable, Comparable<Character>

PURPOSE

Represents a **char** value within a class wrapper.

NESTED CLASS SUMMARY

static class Character.Subset

Represents a subset of the Unicode character set.

static class Character.UnicodeBlock

Represents a disjoint collection of Unicode character blocks.

FIELD SUMMARY

static final byte COMBINING_SPACING_MARK

Represents Unicode general category *Mc*.

static final byte CONNECTOR_PUNCTUATION

Represents Unicode general category *Pc*.

static final byte CONTROL

Represents Unicode general category *Cc*.

static final byte CURRENCY_SYMBOL

Represents Unicode general category *Sc*.

static final byte DASH_PUNCTUATION

Represents Unicode general category *Pd*.

static final byte DECIMAL_DIGIT_NUMBER

Represents Unicode general category *Nd*.

static final byte DIRECTIONALITY_ARABIC_NUMBER

Represents Unicode weak bidirectional character type *AN*.

static final byte DIRECTIONALITY_BOUNDARY_NEUTRAL

Represents Unicode weak bidirectional character type *BN*.

```
static final byte DIRECTIONALITY_COMMON_NUMBER_SEPARATOR
```
Represents Unicode weak bidirectional character type *CS*.
```
static final byte DIRECTIONALITY_EUROPEAN_NUMBER
```
Represents Unicode weak bidirectional character type *EN*.
```
static final byte DIRECTIONALITY_EUROPEAN_NUMBER_SEPARATOR
```
Represents Unicode weak bidirectional character type *ES*.
```
static final byte DIRECTIONALITY_EUROPEAN_NUMBER_TERMINATOR
```
Represents Unicode weak bidirectional character type *ET*.
```
static final byte DIRECTIONALITY_LEFT_TO_RIGHT
```
Represents Unicode strong bidirectional character type *L*.
```
static final byte DIRECTIONALITY_LEFT_TO_RIGHT_EMBEDDING
```
Represents Unicode strong bidirectional character type *LRE*.
```
static final byte DIRECTIONALITY_LEFT_TO_RIGHT_OVERRIDE
```
Represents Unicode strong bidirectional character type *LRO*.
```
static final byte DIRECTIONALITY_NONSPACING_MARK
```
Represents Unicode weak bidirectional character type *NSM*.
```
static final byte DIRECTIONALITY_OTHER_NEUTRALS
```
Represents Unicode neutral bidirectional character type *ON*.
```
static final byte DIRECTIONALITY_PARAGRAPH_SEPARATOR
```
Represents Unicode neutral bidirectional character type *B*.
```
static final byte DIRECTIONALITY_POP_DIRECTIONAL_FORMAT
```
Represents Unicode weak bidirectional character type *PDF*.
```
static final byte DIRECTIONALITY_RIGHT_TO_LEFT
```
Represents Unicode strong bidirectional character type *R*.
```
static final byte DIRECTIONALITY_RIGHT_TO_LEFT_ARABIC
```
Represents Unicode strong bidirectional character type *AL*.
```
static final byte DIRECTIONALITY_RIGHT_TO_LEFT_EMBEDDING
```
Represents Unicode strong bidirectional character type *RLE*.
```
static final byte DIRECTIONALITY_RIGHT_TO_LEFT_OVERRIDE
```
Represents Unicode strong bidirectional character type *RLO*.
```
static final byte DIRECTIONALITY_SEGMENT_SEPARATOR
```
Represents Unicode neutral bidirectional character type *S*.
```
static final byte DIRECTIONALITY_UNDEFINED
```
Represents Unicode undefined bidirectional character type.
```
static final byte DIRECTIONALITY_WHITESPACE
```
Represents Unicode neutral bidirectional character type *WS*.
```
static final byte ENCLOSING_MARK
```
Represents Unicode general category *Me*.
```
static final byte END_PUNCTUATION
```
Represents Unicode general category *Pe*.
```
static final byte FINAL_QUOTE_PUNCTUATION
```
Represents Unicode general category *Pf*.
```
static final byte FORMAT
```
Represents Unicode general category *Cf*.
```
static final byte INITIAL_QUOTE_PUNCTUATION
```
Represents Unicode general category *Pi*.

static final byte LETTER_NUMBER

Represents Unicode general category *Nl*.

static final byte LINE_SEPARATOR

Represents Unicode general category *Zl*.

static final byte LOWERCASE_LETTER

Represents Unicode general category *Ll*.

static final int MAX_CODE_POINT

Represents the maximum code point.

static final char MAX_HIGH_SURROGATE

Represents the maximum value of a leading surrogate.

static final char MAX_LOW_SURROGATE

Represents the maximum value of a trailing surrogate.

static final byte MATH_SYMBOL

Represents Unicode general category *Sm*.

static final int MAX_RADIX

Represents the maximum allowable radix value in converting to and from strings.

static final char MAX_SURROGATE

Represents the maximum value of a surrogate.

static final char MAX_VALUE

Represents the largest value of type **char** (i.e., '\uFFFF').

static final char MIN_HIGH_SURROGATE

Represents the minimum value of a leading surrogate.

static final char MIN_LOW_SURROGATE

Represents the minimum value of a trailing surrogate.

static final int MIN_RADIX

Represents the minimum allowable radix in converting to and from strings.

static final int MIN_SUPPLEMENTARY_CODE_POINT

Represents the minimum supplementary code point.

static final char MIN_SURROGATE

Represents the minimum value of a surrogate.

static final char MIN_VALUE

Represents the smallest value of type **char** (i.e., '\u0000').

static final byte MODIFIER_LETTER

Represents Unicode general category *Lm*.

static final byte MODIFIER_SYMBOL

Represents Unicode general category *Sk*.

static final byte NON_SPACING_MARK

Represents Unicode general category *Mn*.

static final byte OTHER_LETTER

Represents Unicode general category *Lo*.

static final byte OTHER_NUMBER

Represents Unicode general category *No*.

static final byte OTHER_PUNCTUATION

Represents Unicode general category *Po*.

static final byte OTHER_SYMBOL

Represents Unicode general category *So*.

```
static final byte PARAGRAPH_SEPARATOR
```
Represents Unicode general category *Zp*.
```
static final byte PRIVATE_USE
```
Represents Unicode general category *Co*.
```
static final int SIZE
```
Represents the number of bits used to represent a **char** value.
```
static final byte SPACE_SEPARATOR
```
Represents Unicode general category *Zs*.
```
static final byte START_PUNCTUATION
```
Represents Unicode general category *Ps*.
```
static final byte SURROGATE
```
Represents Unicode general category *Cs*.
```
static final byte TITLECASE_LETTER
```
Represents Unicode general category *Lt*.
```
static final Class<Character> TYPE
```
Represents the type **char**.
```
static final byte UNASSIGNED
```
Represents Unicode general category *Cn*.
```
static final byte UPPERCASE_LETTER
```
Represents Unicode general category *Lu*.

CLASS METHOD SUMMARY
```
static int charCount(int n)
```
Returns the number of **char** values needed to represent code point character n.
```
static final int codePointAt(CharSequence s, int i)
```
If the i-th element in sequence s is not a high surrogate, then it is returned; otherwise the code point character represented by surrogate pair of the i-th and i+1-th elements is returned.
```
static final int codePointAt(char[] a, int i)
```
If the i-th element in array a is not a high surrogate, then it is returned; otherwise the code point character represented by surrogate pair (a[i], a[i+1]) is returned.
```
static final int codePointBefore(CharSequence s, int i)
```
If the i-1-th element in sequence s is not a low surrogate, then it is returned; otherwise the code point character represented by the surrogate pair of the i-1-th and i-2-th elements is returned.
```
static final int codePointBefore(char[] a, int i)
```
If the i-1-th element in array a is not a low surrogate, then it is returned; otherwise the code point character represented by surrogate pair (a[i-1], a[i-2]) is returned.
```
static int digit(char c, int r)
```
Returns the numeric value of the character c in radix r.
```
static int digit(int n, int r)
```
Returns the numeric value of code point character n in radix r.
```
static char forDigit(int m, int n)
```
Returns the **char** representation of digit m in the radix n.
```
static byte getDirectionality(char c)
```
Returns the Unicode directionality property for **char** value c.

`static int` getDirectionality(`int` n)

Returns the Unicode directionality property for code point character n.

`static int` getNumericValue(**char** c)

Returns the **int** value that character c represents.

`static int` getNumericValue(**int** n)

Returns the **int** value that code point character n represents.

`static int` getType(**char** c)

Returns a value indicating **char** value c's Unicode general category.

`static int` getType(**int** n)

Returns a value indicating code point character n's Unicode general category.

`static boolean` isDefined(**char** c)

Returns whether **char** value c is a defined Unicode character.

`static boolean` isDefined(**int** n)

Returns whether code point character n is a defined Unicode character.

`static boolean` isDigit(**char** c)

Returns whether **char** value c is a digit.

`static boolean` isIdentifierIgnorable(**char** c)

Returns whether **char** value c is an ignorable identifier character.

`static boolean` isIdentifierIgnorable(**int** n)

Returns whether code point character n is an ignorable identifier character.

`static boolean` isISOControl(**char** c)

Returns whether **char** value c is an ISO control character.

`static boolean` isISOControl(**int** n)

Returns whether code point character n is an ISO control character.

`static boolean` isJavaIdentifierPart(**char** c)

Returns whether **char** value c may be part of a Java identifier.

`static boolean` isJavaIdentifierPart(**int** n)

Returns whether code point character n may be a character in a Java identifier.

`static boolean` isJavaIdentifierStart(**char** c)

Returns whether **char** value c may be the first character in a Java identifier.

`static boolean` isJavaIdentifierStart(**int** n)

Returns whether code point character n may be the first character in a Java identifier.

`static boolean` isLetter(**char** c)

Returns whether **char** value c is a letter.

`static boolean` isLetter(**int** n)

Returns whether code point character n is a letter.

`static boolean` isLetterOrDigit(**char** c)

Returns whether **char** value c is a letter or digit.

`static boolean` isLetterOrDigit(**int** n)

Returns whether code point character n is a letter or digit.

`static boolean` isLowerCase(**char** c)

Returns whether **char** value c is a lowercase character.

`static boolean` isLowerCase(**int** n)

Returns whether code point character n is a lowercase character.

```
static boolean isMirrored(char c)
```
Returns whether **char** value c is mirrored according to the Unicode simple mirroring property.
```
static boolean isMirrored(int n)
```
Returns whether code point character n is mirrored according to the Unicode simple mirroring property.
```
static boolean isSpaceChar(char c)
```
Returns whether **char** value c is a space character.
```
static boolean isSpaceChar(int n)
```
Returns whether code point character n is the space character.
```
static final boolean isSupplementaryCodePoint(int n)
```
Determines whether code point character n lies in the supplementary character range.
```
static final boolean isSurrogatePair(char c1, char c2)
```
Returns isHighSurrogate(c1) && isLowSurrogate(c2).
```
static boolean isTitleCase(char c)
```
Returns whether **char** value c is a title-case character.
```
static boolean isTitleCase(int n)
```
Returns whether code point character n is a title-case character.
```
static boolean isUnicodeIdentifierPart(char c)
```
Returns whether **char** value c may be part of a Unicode identifier.
```
static boolean isUnicodeIdentifierStart(int n)
```
Returns whether code point character n may be a character in a Unicode identifier.
```
static boolean isUnicodeIdentifierStart(char c)
```
Returns whether **char** value c may be the first character in a Unicode identifier.
```
static boolean isUnicodeIdentifierStart(int n)
```
Returns whether code point character n may be the first character in a Unicode identifier.
```
static boolean isUpperCase(char c)
```
Returns whether **char** value c is an uppercase character.
```
static boolean isUpperCase(int n)
```
Returns whether code point character n is an uppercase character.
```
static final boolean isValidCodePoint(int n)
```
Determines whether code point character n lies in the inclusive interval 0x0000 ... 0x10FFFF.
```
static boolean isWhitespace(char c)
```
Returns whether **char** value c is whitespace.
```
static boolean isWhitespace(int n)
```
Returns whether code point character n is whitespace.
```
static final int toChars(int n, char[] a, int i)
```
Returns 1 or 2 depending on whether n is a supplementary code point character. Also stores a representation of n in array a starting at index i.
```
static final char[] toChars(int n)
```
Returns a representation of code point character n.
```
static final int toCodePoint(char c1, char c2)
```
Returns the code point character equivalent to surrogate pair (c1, c2).

```
static char toLowerCase(char c)
```
Returns the lowercase equivalent of **char** value c.
```
static int toLowerCase(int n)
```
Returns the lowercase equivalent of code point character n.
```
static String toString(char c)
```
Returns a `String` representation of **char** value c.
```
static char toTitleCase(char c)
```
Returns the title-case equivalent of **char** value c.
```
static char toTitleCase(int n)
```
Returns the title-case equivalent of code point character n.
```
static char toUpperCase(char c)
```
Returns the uppercase equivalent of **char** value c.
```
static int toUpperCase(int n)
```
Returns the uppercase equivalent of code point character n.
```
static Character valueOf(char c)
```
Returns a `Character` representation of c.

CONSTRUCTOR SUMMARY
```
Character(char c)
```
Constructs a new `Character` object representing value c.

INSTANCE METHOD SUMMARY
```
char charValue()
```
Returns the **char** value represented by this object.
```
int compareTo(Character c)
```
Returns a negative value, zero, or a positive value depending respectively on whether this object is less than, equal to, or greater than c.
```
int compareTo(Object v)
```
Returns a negative value, zero, or a positive value depending respectively on whether this object is less than, equal to, or greater than v.
```
boolean equals(Object v)
```
Returns **true** if and only if v is an instance of `Character` representing the same `Character` value that this object represents.
```
int hashCode()
```
Returns the hash code of this object.
```
String toString()
```
Returns a `String` representation of the value of this object.

---

lang   **static class** `Character.Subset`

PURPOSE
Represents a subset of the Unicode character set.

CONSTRUCTOR SUMMARY
```
protected Character.Subset(String s)
```
Constructs a new `Subset` with name s.

INSTANCE METHOD SUMMARY

boolean equals(Object v)

Returns **true** if and only if v is an instance of Character.Subset representing the same Character.Subset value that this object represents.

int hashCode()

Returns the hash code of this object.

String toString()

Returns a String representation of the value of this object (i.e., its name),

---

lang	static final class Character.UnicodeBlock extends Character.Subset

PURPOSE

Represents a disjoint collection of Unicode character blocks.

FIELD SUMMARY

static final Character.UnicodeBlock AEGEAN_NUMBERS

Represents the Unicode block of the same name.

static final Character.UnicodeBlock
  ALPHABETIC_PRESENTATION_FORMS

Represents the Unicode block of the same name.

static final Character.UnicodeBlock ARABIC

Represents the Unicode block of the same name.

static final Character.UnicodeBlock ARABIC_PRESENTATION_FORMS_A

Represents the Unicode block of the same name.

static final Character.UnicodeBlock ARABIC_PRESENTATION_FORMS_B

Represents the Unicode block of the same name.

static final Character.UnicodeBlock ARMENIAN

Represents the Unicode block of the same name.

static final Character.UnicodeBlock ARROWS

Represents the Unicode block of the same name.

static final Character.UnicodeBlock BASIC_LATIN

Represents the Unicode block of the same name.

static final Character.UnicodeBlock BENGALI

Represents the Unicode block of the same name.

static final Character.UnicodeBlock BLOCK_ELEMENTS

Represents the Unicode block of the same name.

static final Character.UnicodeBlock BOPOMOFO

Represents the Unicode block of the same name.

static final Character.UnicodeBlock BOPOMOFO_EXTENDED

Represents the Unicode block of the same name.

static final Character.UnicodeBlock BOX_DRAWING

Represents the Unicode block of the same name.

static final Character.UnicodeBlock BRAILLE_PATTERNS

Represents the Unicode block of the same name.

static final Character.UnicodeBlock BUHID
>Represents the Unicode block of the same name.

static final Character.UnicodeBlock BYZANTINE_MUSICAL_SYMBOLS
>Represents the Unicode block of the same name.

static final Character.UnicodeBlock CHEROKEE
>Represents the Unicode block of the same name.

static final Character.UnicodeBlock CJK_COMPATIBILITY
>Represents the Unicode block of the same name.

static final Character.UnicodeBlock CJK_COMPATIBILITY_FORMS
>Represents the Unicode block of the same name.

static final Character.UnicodeBlock
  CJK_COMPATIBILITY_IDEOGRAPHS
>Represents the Unicode block of the same name.

static final Character.UnicodeBlock CJK_RADICALS_SUPPLEMENT
>Represents the Unicode block of the same name.

static final Character.UnicodeBlock CJK_SYMBOLS_AND_PUNCTUATION
>Represents the Unicode block of the same name.

static final Character.UnicodeBlock CJK_UNIFIED_IDEOGRAPHS
>Represents the Unicode block of the same name.

static final Character.UnicodeBlock
  CJK_UNIFIED_IDEOGRAPHS_EXTENSION_A
>Represents the Unicode block of the same name.

static final Character.UnicodeBlock
  CJK_UNIFIED_IDEOGRAPHS_EXTENSION_B
>Represents the Unicode block of the same name.

static final Character.UnicodeBlock
  CJK_COMPATIBILITY_IDEOGRAPHS_SUPPLEMENT
>Represents the Unicode block of the same name.

static final Character.UnicodeBlock COMBINING_DIACRITICAL_MARKS
>Represents the Unicode block of the same name.

static final Character.UnicodeBlock COMBINING_HALF_MARKS
>Represents the Unicode block of the same name.

static final Character.UnicodeBlock COMBINING_MARKS_FOR_SYMBOLS
>Represents the Unicode block of the same name.

static final Character.UnicodeBlock CONTROL_PICTURES
>Represents the Unicode block of the same name.

static final Character.UnicodeBlock CURRENCY_SYMBOLS
>Represents the Unicode block of the same name.

static final Character.UnicodeBlock CYPRIOT_SYLLABARY
>Represents the Unicode block of the same name.

static final Character.UnicodeBlock CYRILLIC
>Represents the Unicode block of the same name.

static final Character.UnicodeBlock CYRILLIC_SUPPLEMENTARY
>Represents the Unicode block of the same name.

static final Character.UnicodeBlock DESERET
>Represents the Unicode block of the same name.

```
static final Character.UnicodeBlock DEVANAGARI
```
Represents the Unicode block of the same name.
```
static final Character.UnicodeBlock DINGBATS
```
Represents the Unicode block of the same name.
```
static final Character.UnicodeBlock ENCLOSED_ALPHANUMERICS
```
Represents the Unicode block of the same name.
```
static final Character.UnicodeBlock
  ENCLOSED_CJK_LETTERS_AND_MONTHS
```
Represents the Unicode block of the same name.
```
static final Character.UnicodeBlock ETHIOPIC
```
Represents the Unicode block of the same name.
```
static final Character.UnicodeBlock GENERAL_PUNCTUATION
```
Represents the Unicode block of the same name.
```
static final Character.UnicodeBlock GEOMETRIC_SHAPES
```
Represents the Unicode block of the same name.
```
static final Character.UnicodeBlock GEORGIAN
```
Represents the Unicode block of the same name.
```
static final Character.UnicodeBlock GOTHIC
```
Represents the Unicode block of the same name.
```
static final Character.UnicodeBlock GREEK
```
Represents the Unicode block of the same name.
```
static final Character.UnicodeBlock GREEK_EXTENDED
```
Represents the Unicode block of the same name.
```
static final Character.UnicodeBlock GUJARATI
```
Represents the Unicode block of the same name.
```
static final Character.UnicodeBlock GURMUKHI
```
Represents the Unicode block of the same name.
```
static final Character.UnicodeBlock
  HALFWIDTH_AND_FULLWIDTH_FORMS
```
Represents the Unicode block of the same name.
```
static final Character.UnicodeBlock HANGUL_COMPATIBILITY_JAMO
```
Represents the Unicode block of the same name.
```
static final Character.UnicodeBlock HANGUL_JAMO
```
Represents the Unicode block of the same name.
```
static final Character.UnicodeBlock HANGUL_SYLLABLES
```
Represents the Unicode block of the same name.
```
static final Character.UnicodeBlock HANUNOO
```
Represents the Unicode block of the same name.
```
static final Character.UnicodeBlock HEBREW
```
Represents the Unicode block of the same name.
```
static final Character.UnicodeBlock HIGH_SURROGATES
```
Represents the Unicode block of the same name.
```
static final Character.UnicodeBlock HIGH_PRIVATE_USE_SURROGATES
```
Represents the Unicode block of the same name.
```
static final Character.UnicodeBlock HIRAGANA
```
Represents the Unicode block of the same name.

`static final` Character.UnicodeBlock
　IDEOGRAPHIC_DESCRIPTION_CHARACTERS
　　Represents the Unicode block of the same name.
`static final` Character.UnicodeBlock IPA_EXTENSIONS
　　Represents the Unicode block of the same name.
`static final` Character.UnicodeBlock KANBUN
　　Represents the Unicode block of the same name.
`static final` Character.UnicodeBlock KANGXI_RADICALS
　　Represents the Unicode block of the same name.
`static final` Character.UnicodeBlock KANNADA
　　Represents the Unicode block of the same name.
`static final` Character.UnicodeBlock KATAKANA
　　Represents the Unicode block of the same name.
`static final` Character.UnicodeBlock
　KATAKANA_PHONETIC_EXTENSIONS
　　Represents the Unicode block of the same name.
`static final` Character.UnicodeBlock KHMER
　　Represents the Unicode block of the same name.
`static final` Character.UnicodeBlock KHMER_SYMBOLS
　　Represents the Unicode block of the same name.
`static final` Character.UnicodeBlock LAO
　　Represents the Unicode block of the same name.
`static final` Character.UnicodeBlock LATIN_1_SUPPLEMENT
　　Represents the Unicode block of the same name.
`static final` Character.UnicodeBlock LATIN_EXTENDED_A
　　Represents the Unicode block of the same name.
`static final` Character.UnicodeBlock LATIN_EXTENDED_ADDITIONAL
　　Represents the Unicode block of the same name.
`static final` Character.UnicodeBlock LATIN_EXTENDED_B
　　Represents the Unicode block of the same name.
`static final` Character.UnicodeBlock LETTERLIKE_SYMBOLS
　　Represents the Unicode block of the same name.
`static final` Character.UnicodeBlock LIMBU
　　Represents the Unicode block of the same name.
`static final` Character.UnicodeBlock LINEAR_B_IDEOGRAMS
　　Represents the Unicode block of the same name.
`static final` Character.UnicodeBlock LINEAR_B_SYLLABARY
　　Represents the Unicode block of the same name.
`static final` Character.UnicodeBlock LOW_SURROGATES
　　Represents the Unicode block of the same name.
`static final` Character.UnicodeBlock MALAYALAM
　　Represents the Unicode block of the same name.
`static final` Character.UnicodeBlock
　MATHEMATICAL_ALPHANUMERIC_SYMBOLS
　　Represents the Unicode block of the same name.
`static final` Character.UnicodeBlock MATHEMATICAL_OPERATORS
　　Represents the Unicode block of the same name.

`static final` Character.UnicodeBlock
  MISCELLANEOUS_MATHEMATICAL_SYMBOLS_A
  Represents the Unicode block of the same name.
`static final` Character.UnicodeBlock
  MISCELLANEOUS_MATHEMATICAL_SYMBOLS_B
  Represents the Unicode block of the same name.
`static final` Character.UnicodeBlock MISCELLANEOUS_SYMBOLS
  Represents the Unicode block of the same name.
`static final` Character.UnicodeBlock
  MISCELLANEOUS_SYMBOLS_AND_ARROWS
  Represents the Unicode block of the same name.
`static final` Character.UnicodeBlock MISCELLANEOUS_TECHNICAL
  Represents the Unicode block of the same name.
`static final` Character.UnicodeBlock MONGOLIAN
  Represents the Unicode block of the same name.
`static final` Character.UnicodeBlock MUSICAL_SYMBOLS
  Represents the Unicode block of the same name.
`static final` Character.UnicodeBlock MYANMAR
  Represents the Unicode block of the same name.
`static final` Character.UnicodeBlock NUMBER_FORMS
  Represents the Unicode block of the same name.
`static final` Character.UnicodeBlock OGHAM
  Represents the Unicode block of the same name.
`static final` Character.UnicodeBlock OLD_ITALIC
  Represents the Unicode block of the same name.
`static final` Character.UnicodeBlock
  OPTICAL_CHARACTER_RECOGNITION
  Represents the Unicode block of the same name.
`static final` Character.UnicodeBlock ORIYA
  Represents the Unicode block of the same name.
`static final` Character.UnicodeBlock OSMANYA
  Represents the Unicode block of the same name.
`static final` Character.UnicodeBlock PHONETIC_EXTENSIONS
  Represents the Unicode block of the same name.
`static final` Character.UnicodeBlock PRIVATE_USE_AREA
  Represents the Unicode block of the same name.
`static final` Character.UnicodeBlock RUNIC
  Represents the Unicode block of the same name.
`static final` Character.UnicodeBlock SHAVIAN
  Represents the Unicode block of the same name.
`static final` Character.UnicodeBlock SINHALA
  Represents the Unicode block of the same name.
`static final` Character.UnicodeBlock SMALL_FORM_VARIANTS
  Represents the Unicode block of the same name.
`static final` Character.UnicodeBlock SPACING_MODIFIER_LETTERS
  Represents the Unicode block of the same name.

static final Character.UnicodeBlock SPECIALS
   Represents the Unicode block of the same name.
static final Character.UnicodeBlock SUPERSCRIPTS_AND_SUBSCRIPTS
   Represents the Unicode block of the same name.
static final Character.UnicodeBlock SUPPLEMENTAL_ARROWS_A
   Represents the Unicode block of the same name.
static final Character.UnicodeBlock SUPPLEMENTAL_ARROWS_B
   Represents the Unicode block of the same name.
static final Character.UnicodeBlock
  SUPPLEMENTAL_MATHEMATICAL_OPERATORS
   Represents the Unicode block of the same name.
static final Character.UnicodeBlock
  SUPPLEMENTARY_PRIVATE_USE_AREA_A
   Represents the Unicode block of the same name.
static final Character.UnicodeBlock
  SUPPLEMENTARY_PRIVATE_USE_AREA_B
   Represents the Unicode block of the same name.
static final Character.UnicodeBlock SYRIAC
   Represents the Unicode block of the same name.
static final Character.UnicodeBlock TAGALOG
   Represents the Unicode block of the same name.
static final Character.UnicodeBlock TAGBANWA
   Represents the Unicode block of the same name.
static final Character.UnicodeBlock TAGS
   Represents the Unicode block of the same name.
static final Character.UnicodeBlock TAI_LE
   Represents the Unicode block of the same name.
static final Character.UnicodeBlock TAI_XUAN_JING_SYMBOLS
   Represents the Unicode block of the same name.
static final Character.UnicodeBlock TAMIL
   Represents the Unicode block of the same name.
static final Character.UnicodeBlock TELUGU
   Represents the Unicode block of the same name.
static final Character.UnicodeBlock THAANA
   Represents the Unicode block of the same name.
static final Character.UnicodeBlock THAI
   Represents the Unicode block of the same name.
static final Character.UnicodeBlock TIBETAN
   Represents the Unicode block of the same name.
static final Character.UnicodeBlock UGARITIC
   Represents the Unicode block of the same name.
static final Character.UnicodeBlock
  UNIFIED_CANADIAN_ABORIGINAL_SYLLABICS
   Represents the Unicode block of the same name.
static final Character.UnicodeBlock VARIATION_SELECTORS
   Represents the Unicode block of the same name.

`static final` Character.UnicodeBlock
  VARIATION_SELECTORS_SUPPLEMENT

Represents the Unicode block of the same name.

`static final` Character.UnicodeBlock YI_RADICALS

Represents the Unicode block of the same name.

`static final` Character.UnicodeBlock YI_SYLLABLES

Represents the Unicode block of the same name.

`static final` Character.UnicodeBlock YIJING_HEXAGRAM_SYMBOLS

Represents the Unicode block of the same name.

CLASS METHOD SUMMARY

`public static final` Character.UnicodeBlock forName(String s)

Returns the UnicodeBlock with name s.

`static` Character.UnicodeBlock of(`int` n)

Returns the Character.UnicodeBlock containing code point character n. If there is no such block, **null** is returned.

`static` Character.UnicodeBlock of(`char` c)

Returns the Character.UnicodeBlock containing c. If there is no such block, **null** is returned.

| lang | `interface` CharSequence |

PURPOSE

Describes a representation for supplying read-only access to sequence of characters.

INSTANCE METHOD SUMMARY

`char` charAt(`int` i)

Returns the character at index i of the sequence.

`int` length()

Returns the length of this character sequence.

CharSequence subSequence(`int` i, `int` j)

Returns a new CharSequence representing the elements with indices i … j − 1 from the character sequence of this CharSequence.

String toString()

Returns a String representing the characters of the sequence in index order.

| lang | `final class` Class<T> `implements` AnnotatedElement, GenericDeclaration, Type, Serializable |

PURPOSE

Represents a Java type or interface. Class objects are constructed automatically by Java.

CLASS METHOD SUMMARY

`static` Class forName(String s)

Returns forName(s, **true**, **this**.getClass().getClassLoader()).

static Class forName(String s, **boolean** b, ClassLoader c)

Returns the Class object named s and loads the class as part of the application using loader c. The class is initialized, if and only if b is **true** and the class has not been previously initialized.

INSTANCE METHOD SUMMARY

T cast(Object v)

Returns a casting of v as the type of this Class object.

boolean desiredAssertionStatus()

Returns whether this class is processing its assertions.

<A **extends** Annotation> A getAnnotation(<Class A> c)

Returns an Annotation for the class represented by this Class as described by c.

Annotation[] getAnnotations()

Returns an Annotation array listing all of the annotations for this Class.

Class[] getClasses()

Returns a Class array whose elements represent the **public** classes and interfaces that are members of the class represented by this Class object.

ClassLoader getClassLoader()

Returns the class loader for this Class.

Class getComponentType()

If this Class is an array type, the method returns the component type of the array; otherwise, the method returns **null**.

Constructor<T> getConstructor(Class... a)

Returns a Constructor for the class represented by this Class whose **public** constructor parameter signature is described by array a.

Constructor[] getConstructors()

Returns a Constructor array representing all of the **public** constructors of the class represented by this Class.

Class[] getDeclaredClasses()

Returns a Class array whose elements represent the classes and interfaces that are noninherited members of the class represented by this Class object.

Constructor getDeclaredConstructor(Class... a)

Returns a Constructor for the class represented by this Class whose constructor parameter signature is described by array a.

Constructor[] getDeclaredConstructors()

Returns a Constructor array whose elements represent the constructors of the class represented by this Class.

Field getDeclaredField(String s)

Returns a Field that represents the field with name s of the class or interface represented by this Class object.

Field[] getDeclaredFields()

Returns a Field array whose elements represent the noninherited fields declared by the class or interface represented by this Class.

Method getDeclaredMethod(String s, Class[] c)

Returns a Method that represents the method with name s and whose parameter signature is described by c from the class or interface represented by this Class.

Method[] getDeclaredMethods()

> Returns a Method array whose elements represent the noninherited methods of the class or interface represented by this Class.

Class getDeclaringClass()

> Returns the Class representing the class whose definition specifies the class represented by this Class.

Method getEnclosingConstructor()

> If this Class is a local or anonymous class defined within a constructor, then a Method object that represents the constructor is returned; otherwise, **null** is returned.

Method getEnclosingMethod()

> If this Class is a local or anonymous class defined within a method, then a Method object that represents the method is returned; otherwise, **null** is returned.

T[] getEnumConstants()

> If this class is an Enum then the list of enum constants represented by this Class is returned; otherwise, **null** is returned.

Field getField(String s)

> Returns a Field that represents the **public** field with name s of the class or interface represented by this Class object.

Field[] getFields()

> Returns a Field array whose elements represent the **public** fields declared by the class or interface represented by this Class.

Type[] getGenericInterfaces()

> Returns a Type array whose elements represent the interfaces directly implemented by this Class.

Type getGenericSuperclass()

> Returns the Type of the superclass of this Class object.

Class[] getInterfaces()

> Returns a Class array whose elements represent the interfaces implemented by the class represented by this Class object.

Method getMethod(String s, Class[] c)

> Returns a Method that represents the **public** method with name s and whose parameter signature is described by c from the class or interface represented by this Class.

Method[] getMethods()

> Returns a Method array whose elements represent the **public** methods of the class or interface represented by this Class.

int getModifiers()

> Returns an integer representing the modifiers for the class or interface represented by this Class. Decoding of the integer value is accomplished via class Modifier.

String getName()

> Returns the name of the type represented by this Class.

Package getPackage()

> Returns the Package that represents the package specifying the definition of the type represented by this Class.

ProtectionDomain getProtectionDomain()

Returns the ProtectionDomain of this Class.

URL getResource(String s)

Returns a URL resource from the Web with address s.

InputStream getResourceAsStream(String s)

Returns an InputStream representation of a URL resource from the Web with address s.

TypeVariable[] getTypeParameters()

Returns a TypeVariable array whose elements represent the type variables declared by the generic declaration represented by this Class.

Object[] getSigners()

Returns an array whose elements reference the signers of this Class.

Class<? **super** T> getSuperclass()

Returns a Class representing the superclass of the type represented by this Class.

boolean isArray()

Returns **true** if and only if the type represented by this Class is an array type.

boolean isAnnotationPresent(Class<? **extends** Annotation> c)

Returns whether this Class is an annotation of type c.

boolean isAnnotationType()

Returns whether this Class is an annotation.

boolean isAssignableFrom(Class c)

Returns **true** if and only if an object of the class or interface represented by c is assignable to an object of the class or interface represented by this Class.

boolean isInstance(Object v)

Returns **true** if and only if v is assignable to an object of the class or interface represented by this Class.

boolean isInterface()

Returns **true** if and only if the type represented by this Class object is an interface type.

boolean isPrimitive()

Returns **true** if and only if the type represented by this Class object is a primitive type.

T newInstance()

Returns a default-constructed instance of the class represented by this Class.

String toString()

Returns a String representation of this Class.

`util`   **interface** Collection<T> **extends** Iterable<T>

PURPOSE

Describes a view of a list as a group of elements.

INSTANCE METHOD SUMMARY

boolean add(T v)

Ensures that this Collection has an element with value v and returns **true** if the collection changes by the addition.

boolean addAll(Collection<? **extends** T> c)

Ensures that this Collection has all of the element values in c and returns **true** if the collection has changed.

void clear()

Removes all elements from this Collection.

boolean contains(Object v)

Returns whether this Collection has an element with value v.

boolean containsAll(Collection<?> c)

Returns whether this Collection contains all of the values in the collection c.

boolean equals(Object v)

Returns **true** if and only if v is an instance of Collection representing the same collection as this Collection.

int hashCode()

Returns the hash code of this object.

boolean isEmpty()

Returns whether this Collection has any elements.

Iterator<T> iterator()

Returns an iterator for the elements in this Collection.

boolean remove(Object v)

Attempts to remove an element with value v from this Collection. Returns whether a value was removed. The operation is optional.

boolean removeAll(Collection<?> c)

Attempts to remove each of the values in c from this Collection. Returns whether a value was removed. The operation is optional.

boolean retainAll(Collection<?> c)

Attempts to remove from this Collection all of the values not in c. Returns whether a value was removed. The operation is optional.

int size()

Returns the number of elements in this Collection.

<E> E[] toArray()

Returns an array containing all elements of this Collection.

<E> E[] toArray(E[] a)

Returns an array of the same type as array a whose elements correspond to the elements of this Collection. The returned array is a if a is big enough.

---

util   **class** Collections

PURPOSE

Provides basic list and collection manipulation functionality.

FIELD SUMMARY

`static` <T> List<T> EMPTY_LIST

Represents the empty list.

`static` <K, V> Map<K, V> EMPTY_MAP

Represents the empty map.

`static` <T> Set<T> EMPTY_SET

Represents the empty set.

CLASS METHOD SUMMARY

`static` <T> `boolean` addAll(Collection<? **super** T> c, T[] a)

Adds the elements of array a to collection c.

`static` <T, Comparable<? **super** T>> `int` binarySearch(List<?
  extends T> a, T v)

Returns the index of v in naturally sorted list a using a binary search algorithm.
If v is not in a, then it returns i-1, where i is the minimal index such that v <
a[i].

`static` <T> `int` binarySearch(List<? **extends** T> a, T v,
  Comparator<? **super** T> c)

Returns the index of v in sorted list a with respect to comparator c using a binary
search algorithm. If v is not in a, then it returns i-1, where i is the minimal
index such that v < a[i].

`static` <T> Collection<T> checkedCollection(Collection<T> a,
  Class<T> c)

Returns a typesafe view of collection a, where c represents the type of values the
collection may hold.

`static` <T> List<T> checkedList(List<T> a, Class<T> c)

Returns a typesafe view of list a, where c represents the type of values the list
may hold.

`static` <K, V> Map<K, V> checkedMap(Map<K, V> a, Class<K> c1,
  Class<V>, c2)

Returns a typesafe view of map a, where c1 represents the type of key values the
map may hold and c2 represents the type of values the map may hold.

`static` <E> Set<E> checkedSet(Set<E> a, Class<E> c)

Returns a typesafe view of set a, where c represents the type of values the list
may hold.

`static` <K, V> checkedSortedMap<K, V> checkedMap(SortedMap<K, V>
  a, Class<K> c1, Class<V>, c2)

Returns a typesafe view of sorted map a, where c1 represents the type of key
values the map may hold and c2 represents the type of values the map may hold.

`static` <T> Set<T> checkedSortedSet(SortedSet<T> a, Class<T> c)

Returns a typesafe view of set a, where c represents the type of values the list
may hold.

`static` <T> `void` copy(List<? **super** T> a1, List<? **super** T> a2)

Copies the elements from list a1 to list a2.

`static` `boolean` disjoint(Collection<?> c1, Collection<?> c2)

Returns whether collections c1 and c2 have no common elements.

`static` <T> List<t> emptyList()

Returns an empty list.

```
static <K, V> Map<K, V> emptyMap()
```
Returns an empty map.
```
static <T> Set<t> emptySet()
```
Returns an empty set.
```
static <T> Enumeration<T> enumeration(Collection<T> c)
```
Returns an enumeration of collection c.
```
static <T> void fill(List<? super T> a, T v)
```
Replaces the elements of the list a with value v.
```
static int frequency(Collection<?> c, Object v)
```
Returns the number of elements of collection c equal to the object v.
```
static int indexOfSubList(List<?> s, List<?> t)
```
Returns the starting index of the first occurrence of list t within list s. If t is not a sublist of s, then −1 is returned.
```
static int lastIndexOfSubList(List s, List t)
```
Returns the starting index of the last occurrence of list t within list s. If t is not a sublist of s, then −1 is returned.
```
static <T> ArrayList<T> list(Enumeration<T> e)
```
Returns an `ArrayList` containing the elements of enumeration e.
```
static <T, Comparable<? super T>> T max(Collection<? extends T> c)
```
Returns the maximum element of collection c with respect to its natural ordering.
```
static <T> Object max(Collection<? extends T> a,
  Comparator<? super T> c)
```
Returns the maximum element of collection a with respect to comparator c.
```
static <T, Comparable<? super T>> T min(Collection<? extends T> c)
```
Returns the minimum element of collection c with respect to its natural ordering.
```
static <T> Object min(Collection<? extends T> a,
  Comparator<? super T> c)
```
Returns the minimum element of collection a with respect to comparator c.
```
static <T> List<T> nCopies(int n, T v)
```
Returns an n-element immutable list with each element having value v.
```
static <T> boolean replaceAll(List<T> a, T x, T y)
```
Replaces all occurrences of value x with value y in list a. Returns whether list a has changed.
```
static void reverse(List<?> a)
```
Reverses the order of the elements in list a.
```
static Comparator<Object> reverseOrder()
```
Returns a comparator that is the reverse of the natural ordering on a collection that implements `Comparable`.
```
static <T> Comparator<T> reverseOrder(Comparator<T> c)
```
Returns a comparator that is the reverse of the ordering implemented by comparator c.
```
static void rotate(List<?> a, int n)
```
Performs the equivalent of n circular shifts of the elements in list a.

```
static void shuffle(List<?> a)
```
Pseudorandomly permutes list a.
```
static void shuffle(List<?> a, Random r)
```
Pseudorandomly permutes list a using r.
```
static <T> Set<T> singleton(T v)
```
Returns an immutable singleton set containing v.
```
static <T> List<T> singletonList(T v)
```
Returns an immutable single-element list containing v.
```
static <K, V> Map<K, V> singletonMap(K v1, V v2)
```
Returns an immutable single-element map associating v1 with v2.
```
static <T extends Comparable<? super T>> void sort(List<T> a)
```
Sorts list a into nondescending order using the natural ordering.
```
static <T> void sort(List<T> a, Comparator<? super T> c)
```
Sorts list a into nondescending order using comparator c.
```
static void swap(List<?> a, int i, int j)
```
Swaps the ith and jth elements in list a.
```
static <T> Collection<T> synchronizedCollection(Collection<T>
  c)
```
Returns a synchronized collection using collection c.
```
static <T> List<T> synchronizedList(List<T> a)
```
Returns a synchronized list using list a.
```
static <K, V> Map<T, V> synchronizedMap(Map<K, V> m)
```
Returns a synchronized map using map m.
```
static <T> Set<T> synchronizedSet(Set<T> s)
```
Returns a synchronized set using set s.
```
static <K, V> SortedMap<T>
  synchronizedSortedMap(SortedMap<K, V> m)
```
Returns a synchronized sorted map using sorted map m.
```
static <T> SortedSet<T> synchronizedSortedSet(SortedSet<T> s)
```
Returns a synchronized sorted set s.
```
static <T> Collection<T>
  unmodifiableCollection(Collection<? extends T> c)
```
Returns an unmodifiable view of collection c
```
static <T> List<T> unmodifiableList(List<? extends T> a)
```
Returns an unmodifiable view of list a.
```
static <K, V> Map<K, V> unmodifiableMap(Map<? extends K,
  ? extends V>) m)
```
Returns an unmodifiable view of map m.
```
static <T> Set<T> unmodifiableSet(Set<? extends T> s)
```
Returns an unmodifiable view of set s.
```
static <K, V> Map<K, V> unmodifiableSortedMap(Map<K,
  ? extends V>) m)
```
Returns an unmodifiable view of sorted map m.
```
static <T> SortedSet<T> unmodifiableSortedSet(SortedSet<T> s)
```
Returns an unmodifiable view of sorted set s.

awt	**class** Color **implements** Paint, Serializable

PURPOSE

Represents colors from a color space. Associated with each color is an *alpha* attribute specifying its visibility (the range corresponds to transparency to opaqueness).

FIELD SUMMARY

static Color black, **static** Color BLACK

Represents black.

static Color blue, **static** Color BLUE

Represents blue.

static Color cyan, **static** Color CYAN

Represents cyan.

static Color darkGray, **static** Color DARK_GRAY

Represents dark gray.

static Color gray, **static** Color GRAY

Represents gray.

static Color green, **static** Color GREEN

Represents green.

static Color lightGray, **static** Color LIGHT_GRAY

Represents light gray.

static Color magenta, **static** Color MAGENTA

Represents magenta.

static Color orange, **static** Color ORANGE

Represents orange.

static Color pink, **static** Color PINK

Represents pink.

static Color red, **static** Color RED

Represents red.

static Color white, **static** Color WHITE

Represents white.

static Color yellow, **static** Color YELLOW

Represents yellow.

CLASS METHOD SUMMARY

static Color getColor(String s)

Returns a new Color based on the value of system property s.

static Color getColor(String s, Color c)

Attempts to return a new Color based on the value of system property s. If the attempt fails, then it returns color c.

static Color getColor(String s, **int** c)

Attempts to return a new Color based on the value of system property s. If the attempt fails, then it returns color based on RGB value c.

static Color getHSBColor(**float** h, **float** s, **float** b)

Returns a new Color based on values h, s, and b using the HSB color model.

static int HSBtoRGB(**float** h, **float** s, **float** b)

Returns the RGB representation for the color based on values h, s, and b using the HSB color model.

static float[] RGBtoHSB(int r, int g, int b, float[] a)

Returns an HSB color representation using array a for the RGB color based on r, b, and g.

CONSTRUCTOR SUMMARY

Color(ColorSpace s, float[] c, float a)

Creates a new Color with alpha level a in color space s using the elements of c to specify its red, green, and blue levels.

Color(float r, float g, float b)

Creates a new opaque Color in the standard color space using r, g, and b to specify respectively its red, green, and blue levels as percentages.

Color(float r, float g, float b, float a)

Creates a new Color with alpha level a in the standard color space using r, g, and b to specify respectively its red, green, and blue levels as percentages.

Color(int n)

Creates a new opaque Color in the standard color space using the bits of n to specify respectively its red, green, and blue levels relative to the interval 0 ... 255.

Color(int n, boolean b)

Creates a new opaque Color in the standard color space using the bits of n to specify respectively its alpha (depending on b), red, green, and blue levels relative to the interval 0 ... 255.

Color(int r, int g, int b)

Creates a new opaque Color in the standard color space using r, g, and b to specify respectively its red, green, and blue levels relative to the interval 0 ... 255.

Color(int r, int g, int b, int a)

Creates a new Color with alpha a in the standard color space using r, g, and b to specify respectively its red, green, and blue levels relative to the interval 0 ... 255.

INSTANCE METHOD SUMMARY

Color brighter()

Returns a new brighter version of this Color.

PaintContext createContext(ColorModel c, Rectangle r1, Rectangle2D r2, AffineTransform t, RenderingHints h)

Returns a new painting context for generating a solid color pattern according to the parameter description.

Color darker()

Returns a new darker version of this Color.

static Color decode(String s)

Returns **new** Color(Integer.parseInt(s).

boolean equals(Object v)

Returns whether v is a Color that is equal to this Color.

int getAlpha()

Returns the alpha level of this Color.

int getBlue()

Returns the blue level of this Color.

`float[] getColorComponents(ColorSpace c, float[] a)`

Returns the color components of this `Color` with respect to color space `c` using array `a` as the return value.

`float[] getColorComponents(float[] a)`

Returns the color components of this `Color` using array `a` as the return value.

`ColorSpace getColorSpace()`

Returns the color space of this `Color`.

`float[] getComponents(ColorSpace c, float[] a)`

Returns the color and alpha components of this `Color` with respect to color space `c`.

`float[] getComponents(float[] a)`

Returns the color and alpha components of this `Color` using array `a` as the return value.

`int getGreen()`

Returns the green level of this `Color`.

`int getRed()`

Returns the red level of this `Color`.

`int getRGB()`

Returns the RGB value of this `Color`.

`float[] getRGBColorComponents(float[] a)`

Returns the color components of this `Color` using array `a` as the return value.

`float[] getRGBComponents(float[] a)`

Returns the color and alpha components of this `Color` using array `a` as the return value.

`int getTransparency()`

Returns the transparency mode of this `Color`.

`int hashCode()`

Returns the hash code of this `Color`.

`String toString()`

Returns a representation of this `Color`.

---

lang   `interface Comparable<T>`

PURPOSE

Describes a representation that has a total ordering of its objects. The ordering is commonly referred to as the natural ordering.

A `Comparable<T>` implementation is expected to fulfill the following contract for all `Comparable<T>` objects x, y, and z, where in the contract *sign(n)* evaluates to –1, 0, 1 depending on whether *n* is respectively negative, zero, or positive.

- *sign*(x.`compareTo`(y)) equals –*sign*(y.`compareTo`(x)).
- If ((x.`compareTo`(y) > 0) && (y.`compareTo`(z) > 0)) evaluates to **true**, then x.`compareTo`(z) is greater than zero.
- If x.`compareTo`(y) evaluates to 0, then *sign*(x.`compareTo`(z)) equals *sign*(y.`compareTo`(z)).
- x.`compareTo`(**null**) throws a `NullPointerException`.

It is strongly expected that the following property also holds.

- If x.compareTo(y) evaluates to 0, then x.equals(y) evaluates to **true**.

INSTANCE METHOD SUMMARY

int compareTo(T v)

Returns a negative value, zero, or a positive value depending respectively on whether this object is less than, equal to, or greater than v.

---

util	interface Comparator<T>

PURPOSE

Describes total ordering comparison functionality.

INSTANCE METHOD SUMMARY

int compare(T v1, T v2)

Returns a negative integer, zero, or positive integer depending on whether v1 is respectively less than, equal to, or greater than v2.

By convention, classes that override this method should fulfill the following contract.

- Symmetry: For any objects x and y, the sign of compare(x, y) should equal – the sign of compare(x, y);
- Transitivity: For any objects x, y, and z, if compare(x, y) and compare(y, z) are both positive, then compare(x, z) is positive;
- Consistency: For any objects x, y, and z, if compare(x, y) is 0, then the signs of compare(x, z) and compare(y, z) are equal.

boolean equals(Object v)

Returns whether v is equal to this Comparator<T>.

---

awt	class Container implements Component

PURPOSE

Represents a container for other GUI components.

CONSTRUCTOR SUMMARY

Container()

Creates a new container.

INSTANCE METHOD SUMMARY

Component add(Component a)

Appends component c to the component list of this Container.

Component add(Component c, **int** i)

Inserts component c at position i in the component list of this Container.

void add(Component c, Object v)

Appends component c in the component list of this Container with the layout manager using constraints v.

void add(Component c, Object v, **int** i)
> Inserts component c at position i in the component list of this Container with the layout manager using constraints v.

void addContainerListener(ContainerListener l)
> Adds l as a listener of the container events of this Container.

protected void addImpl(Component c, Object v, **int** i)
> Inserts component c at position i in the component list of this Container with the layout manager using constraints v.

void addNotify()
> Makes this Container displayable.

void addPropertyChangeListener(PropertyChangeListener l)
> Adds l as a property change listener for this Container.

void addPropertyChangeListener(String s, PropertyChangeListener l)
> Adds l as a type s property change listener for this Container.

void applyComponentOrientation(ComponentOrientation c)
> Sets c as the component orientation property of this Container.

boolean areFocusTraversalKeysSet(**int** n)
> Returns whether the type n focus traversal has been defined for this Container.

void doLayout()
> Signals this Container to lay out its components.

Component findComponentAt(**int** x, **int** y)
> Returns the visible child component at location (x, y) in this Container.

Component findComponentAt(Point p)
> Returns the visible child component at location p in this Container.

float getAlignmentX()
> Returns the x-axis alignment of this Container.

float getAlignmentY()
> Returns the y-axis alignment of this Container.

Component getComponent(**int** i)
> Returns the ith component in this Container.

Component getComponentAt(**int** x, **int** y)
> Returns the component at location (x, y) in this Container.

Component getComponentAt(Point p)
> Returns the component at location p in this Container.

int getComponentCount()
> Returns the number of components in this Container.

Component[] getComponents()
> Returns the components in this Container.

final int getComponentZOrder(Component c)
> Returns the z-order index of component c in this Container, where z-order specifies component painting order.

ContainerListener[] getContainerListeners()
> Returns the container listeners of this Container.

Set getFocusTraversalKeys(**int** n)
> Returns the type n traversal keys for this Container.

FocusTraversalPolicy getFocusTraversalPolicy()

    Returns the focus traversal policy for this Container.

Insets getInsets()

    Returns the insets of this Container.

LayoutManager getLayout()

    Returns the layout manager for this Container.

EventListener[] getListeners(Class t)

    Returns the type t listeners of this Container.

Dimension getMaximumSize()

    Returns the maximum size of this Container.

Dimension getMinimumSize()

    Returns the minimum size of this Container.

Point getMousePosition(**boolean** b)

    Returns the position of the mouse where it lies above this Container, such that if b is true, a non-**null** position is returned only if the mouse pointers lies above this Container or any of its descendants; otherwise, if not b, a non-**null** position is returned only if the mouse pointer lies above this Container.

Dimension getPreferredSize()

    Returns the preferred size of this Container.

void invalidate()

    Invalidates this Container.

boolean isAncestorOf(Component c)

    Returns whether component c is logically in this Container.

boolean isFocusCycleRoot()

    Returns whether this Container is the root of its focus cycle.

boolean isFocusCycleRoot(Container c)

    Returns whether the container c is the focus cycle root of this Container.

final boolean isFocusTraversalPolicyProvider()

    Returns whether this Container provides the focus traversal policy.

boolean isFocusTraversalPolicySet()

    Returns whether this Container has a focus traversal policy.

void list(PrintStream s, **int** n)

    Prints a listing of the components of this Container to stream s with each line indented n characters.

void list(PrintWriter s, **int** n)

    Prints a listing of the components of this Container to stream s with each line indented n characters.

void paint(Graphics g)

    Renders this Container in graphical context g.

void paintComponents(Graphics g)

    Renders the components of this Container in graphical context g.

protected String paramString()

    Returns a representation of this Container.

void print(Graphics g)

    Prints this Container in graphical context g.

void printComponents(Graphics g)

    Prints the components of this Container in graphical context g.

protected void processContainerEvent(ContainerEvent e)

Invokes the performer method of the container event listeners of this Container.

protected void processEvent(AWTEvent e)

Invokes the container event listeners for this Container if e is a container event; otherwise, invokes **super**.processEvent(e).

void remove(Component c)

Removes the component c from this Container.

void remove(**int** i)

Removes the ith component from this Container.

void removeAll()

Removes all components from this Container.

void removeContainerListener(ContainerListener l)

Removes l from the container listener list of this Container.

void removeNotify()

Makes this Container nondisplayable.

final void setComponentZOrder(Component c, **int** i)

Sets component c of this Container to z-order index i, where z-order specifies component painting order.

void setFocusCycleRoot(**boolean** b)

Sets based on b whether this Container is the root of its focus traversal cycle.

void setFocusTraversalKeys(**int** n, Set s)

Sets s as the focus traversal keys for a type n traversal of this Container.

final void setFocusTraversalPolicyProvider(**boolean** b)

Sets based on b whether this Container provides focus traversal policy.

void setFocusTraversalPolicy(FocusTraversalPolicy f)

Sets f as the focus traversal policy of this Container.

void setFont(Font f)

Sets f as the font of this Container.

void setLayout(LayoutManager l)

Sets l as the layout manager of this Container.

void transferFocusBackward()

Transfers focus to the previous component.

void transferFocusDownCycle()

Transfers the focus down one cycle for this Container.

void update(Graphics g)

Updates the display of this Container using graphical context g.

void validate()

Validates this Container and its subcomponents with respect to needing display.

protected void validateTree()

Recursively recomputes the layout of invalid components of this Container.

---

　　class Date implements Serializable, Cloneable, Comparable<Date>

PURPOSE
Represents time with millisecond precision.

CONSTRUCTOR SUMMARY
Date()

> Constructs a Date object that represents the time of its construction.

Date(long t)

> Constructs a Date object that represents the time corresponding to n milliseconds after January 1, 1970, 00:00:00 GMT.

INSTANCE METHOD SUMMARY
boolean after(Date d)

> Returns whether the time d occurs before the time of this Date.

boolean before(Date d)

> Returns whether the time d occurs after the time of this Date.

Object clone()

> Returns a clone of this Date.

int compareTo(Date d)

> Returns a negative value, zero, or a positive value depending respectively on whether the Date value represented by this object is less than, equal to, or greater than d.

int compareTo(Object v)

> Returns a negative value, zero, or a positive value depending respectively on whether the Date value represented by this object is less than, equal to, or greater than v.

boolean equals(Object v)

> Returns whether v is equal to this Date.

long getTime()

> Returns the number of milliseconds since January 1, 1970, 00:00:00 GMT for the time represented by this Date.

int hashCode()

> Returns the hash code of this object.

void setTime(long n)

> Sets this Date object to n milliseconds after January 1, 1970, 00:00:00 GMT.

String toString()

> Returns a String representation of the value of this object.

---

　　abstract class DateFormat extends Format

PURPOSE
Provides methods for formatting and parsing dates and times and serves as an abstract superclass for date and time formatting.

FIELD SUMMARY

`static int` AM_PM_FIELD

>Represents the AM_PM alignment field.

`protected` Calendar calendar

>Represents the calendar that produces the time field values.

`static int` DATE_FIELD

>Represents the DATE alignment field.

`static int` DAY_OF_WEEK_FIELD

>Represents the DAY_OF_WEEK alignment field.

`static int` DAY_OF_WEEK_IN_MONTH_FIELD

>Represents the DAY_OF_WEEK_IN_MONTH alignment field.

`static int` DAY_OF_YEAR_FIELD

>Represents the DAY_OF_YEAR alignment field.

`static int` DEFAULT

>Represents default style pattern.

`static int` ERA_FIELD

>Represents the ERA alignment field.

`static int` FULL

>Represents full style pattern.

`static int` HOUR_OF_DAY0_FIELD

>Represents the zero-based HOUR_OF_DAY alignment field.

`static int` HOUR_OF_DAY1_FIELD

>Represents the one-based HOUR_OF_DAY alignment field.

`static int` HOUR0_FIELD

>Represents the zero-based HOUR alignment field.

`static int` HOUR1_FIELD

>Represents the one-based HOUR alignment field.

`static int` LONG

>Represents long style pattern.

`static int` MEDIUM

>Represents medium style pattern.

`static int` MILLISECOND_FIELD

>Represents the MILLISECOND alignment field.

`static int` MINUTE_FIELD

>Represents the MINUTE alignment field.

`static int` MONTH_FIELD

>Represents the MONTH alignment field.

`protected` NumberFormat numberFormat

>Represents the NumberFormat that formats date and time numbers.

`static int` SECOND_FIELD

>Represents the SECOND alignment field.

`static int` SHORT

>Represents short style pattern.

`static int` TIMEZONE_FIELD

>Represents the TIMEZONE alignment field.

`static int` WEEK_OF_MONTH_FIELD

>Represents the WEEK_OF_MONTH alignment field.

static int WEEK_OF_YEAR_FIELD

Represents the WEEK_OF_YEAR alignment field.

static int YEAR_FIELD

Represents the YEAR alignment field.

CLASS METHOD SUMMARY

static Locale[] getAvailableLocales()

Returns an array of possible DateFormat locales.

static DateFormat getDateInstance()

Returns a DateFormat using the default date formatting style for the default locale.

static DateFormat getDateInstance(**int** d)

Returns a DateFormat using date formatting style d for the default locale.

static DateFormat getDateInstance(**int** d, Locale l)

Returns a DateFormat using date formatting style d for locale l.

static DateFormat getDateTimeInstance()

Returns a DateFormat using the default date and time formatting style for the default locale.

static DateFormat getDateTimeInstance(**int** d, **int** t)

Returns the DateFormat using date formatting style d and time formatting style t for the default locale.

static DateFormat getDateTimeInstance(**int** d, **int** t, Locale l)

Returns a DateFormat using date formatting style d and time formatting style t for locale l.

static DateFormat getInstance()

Returns a DateFormat using the date and time SHORT formatting style for the default locale.

static DateFormat getTimeInstance()

Returns a DateFormat using the default time formatting style for the default locale.

static DateFormat getTimeInstance(**int** t)

Returns a DateFormat using time formatting style t for the default locale.

static DateFormat getTimeInstance(**int** t, Locale l)

Returns a DateFormat using time formatting style t for locale l.

CONSTRUCTOR SUMMARY

protected DateFormat()

Constructs a new date format.

INSTANCE METHOD SUMMARY

Object clone()

Returns a new clone of this DateFormat.

boolean equals(Object v)

Returns **true** if and only if v is an instance of DateFormat representing the same date format value that this object represents.

String format(Date d)

Formats date d into a date and time string using this DateFormat.

abstract StringBuffer format(Date d, StringBuffer s,
    FieldPosition f)

> Returns s after formatting date d into a date and time string into s using this
> DateFormat. If f indicates a field, then its indices are updated to reflect the
> position of the field within s.

final StringBuffer format(Object d, StringBuffer s,
    FieldPosition f)

> Returns s after formatting date d into a date and time string into s using this
> DateFormat. If f indicates a field, then its indices are updated to reflect the
> position of the field within s.

Calendar getCalendar()

> Returns the calendar of this DateFormat.

NumberFormat getNumberFormat()

> Returns the number formatter of this DateFormat.

TimeZone getTimeZone()

> Returns the time zone of this DateFormat.

int hashCode()

> Returns the hash code of this DateFormat.

boolean isLenient()

> Returns whether this DateFormat parses dates and times leniently (i.e., whether
> strings need not absolutely follow the date and time specification).

Date parse(String s)

> Parses s to produce a date using this DateFormat.

abstract Date parse(String s, ParsePosition i)

> Parses s to produce a date using this DateFormat. The parsing starts with the
> parse position indicated by i. Upon completion of parsing, i reflects the last
> parsed position.

Object parseObject(String s, ParsePosition i)

> Parses s to produce a date using this DateFormat. The parsing starts with the
> parse position indicated by i. Upon completion of parsing, i reflects the last
> parsed position.

void setCalendar(Calendar c)

> Sets to c the calendar used by this DateFormat.

void setLenient(**boolean** b)

> Sets whether date and time parsing is to be lenient by this DateFormat (i.e.,
> whether strings need not absolutely follow the date and time specification).

void setNumberFormat(NumberFormat n)

> Sets to n the number formatter used by this DateFormat.

void setTimeZone(TimeZone t)

> Sets to t the time zone for the calendar used by this DateFormat.

`text`   **static class** DateFormat.Field **extends** Format.Field

PURPOSE

Represents DateFormat field positions.

FIELD SUMMARY

static DateFormat.Field AM_PM

Represents the time of day indicator field in the formatting of a date.

static DateFormat.Field DAY_OF_MONTH

Represents the day of month field in the formatting of a date.

static DateFormat.Field DAY_OF_WEEK

Represents the day of week field in the formatting of a date.

static DateFormat.Field DAY_OF_WEEK_IN_MONTH

Represents the day of week in month field in the formatting of a date.

static DateFormat.Field DAY_OF_YEAR

Represents the day of year field in the formatting of a date.

static DateFormat.Field ERA

Represents the era field in the formatting of a date.

static DateFormat.Field HOUR_OF_DAY0

Represents the hour of day field in the zero-based formatting of a date and time (i.e., the legal values are 0 to 23).

static DateFormat.Field HOUR_OF_DAY1

Represents the hour of day field in the one-based formatting of a date and time (i.e., the legal values are 1 to 24).

static DateFormat.Field HOUR0

Represents the hour field in the zero-based formatting of a date and time (i.e., the legal values are 0 to 11).

static DateFormat.Field HOUR1

Represents the hour field in the one-based formatting of a date and time (i.e., the legal values are 1 to 12).

static DateFormat.Field MILLISECOND

Represents the millisecond field in the formatting of a date.

static DateFormat.Field MINUTE

Represents the minute field in the formatting of a date.

static DateFormat.Field MONTH

Represents the month field in the formatting of a date.

static DateFormat.Field SECOND

Represents the second field in the formatting of a date.

static DateFormat.Field TIME_ZONE

Represents the time zone field in the formatting of a date.

static DateFormat.Field WEEK_OF_MONTH

Represents the week of month field in the formatting of a date.

static DateFormat.Field WEEK_OF_YEAR

Represents the week of year field in the formatting of a date.

static DateFormat.Field YEAR

Represents the year field in the formatting of a date.

CONSTRUCTOR SUMMARY

protected DateFormat.Field(String s, **int** n)

Constructs a new **DateFormat.Field** with the name s for field n.

INSTANCE METHOD SUMMARY

int getCalendarField()

Returns the **Calendar** field of this **DateFormat.Field**.

static DateFormat.Field ofCalendarField(int f)

Returns the DateFormat.Field constant corresponding to the Calendar field f.

protected Object readResolve()

Returns a resolved field.

---

final class Double extends Number implements Comparable<Double>

PURPOSE

Represents a **double** value within a class wrapper.

FIELD SUMMARY

static final double MAX_VALUE

Represents the maximum finite value of type **double** (i.e., $(2 - 2^{-52})2^{1023}$).

static final double MIN_VALUE

Represents the minimum positive nonzero value of type **double** (i.e., 2^{-1074}).

static final double NaN

Represents the Not-a-Number value (NaN) for type **double**.

static final double NEGATIVE_INFINITY

Represents negative infinity for type **double**.

static final double POSITIVE_INFINITY

Represents positive infinity for type **double**.

static final int SIZE

Represents the number of bits used to represent a **double** value.

static final Class<Double> TYPE

Represents the type **double**.

CLASS METHOD SUMMARY

static int compare(double m, double n)

Returns a negative value, zero, or a positive value depending respectively on whether m is less than, equal to, or greater than n.

static long doubleToLongBits(double n)

Returns a representation of **double** value n using the *IEEE 754 floating-point double-format bit layout* standard.

static long doubleToRawLongBits(double n)

Returns a representation of **double** value n using the *IEEE 754 floating-point double-format bit layout* standard while preserving not-a-number values.

static boolean isInfinite(double n)

Returns **true** if and only if n is equal to Double.NEGATIVE_INFINITY or to Double.POSITIVE_INFINITY.

static boolean isNaN(double n)

Returns **true** if and only if the **double** value n is equal to Double.NaN.

static double longBitsToDouble(long n)

Returns the **double** value corresponding to the bit representation of value n.

static double parseDouble(String s)

Returns the **double** value represented by parsing string s as an optionally signed floating-point value.

static String toHexString(double n)

Returns a hexadecimal string representation of **double** value n.

static String toString(double n)

Returns a string representation of **double** value n.

static Double valueOf(double n)

Returns a Double object representing **double** value n.

static Double valueOf(String s)

Returns a Double object representing Double.parseDouble(s).

CONSTRUCTOR SUMMARY

Double(double n)

Constructs a new Double object representing value n.

Double(String s)

Constructs a new Double object representing Double.parseDouble(s).

INSTANCE METHOD SUMMARY

byte byteValue()

Returns the value of this Double as a **byte**.

int compareTo(Double n)

Returns a negative value, zero, or a positive value depending respectively on whether the **double** value represented by this object is less than, equal to, or greater than n.

int compareTo(Object v)

Returns a negative value, zero, or a positive value depending respectively on whether the **double** value represented by this object is less than, equal to, or greater than v.

double doubleValue()

Returns the value of this Double as a **double**.

boolean equals(Object v)

Returns **true** if and only if v is an instance of Boolean representing the same **boolean** value that this object represents.

float floatValue()

Returns the value of this Double as a **float**.

int hashCode()

Returns the hash code of this object.

int intValue()

Returns the value of this Double as an **int**.

boolean isInfinite()

Returns **true** if and only if the **double** value of this object is equal to Double.NEGATIVE_INFINITY or to Double.POSITIVE_INFINITY.

boolean isNaN()

Returns **true** if and only if the **double** value of this object is equal to Double.NaN.

long longValue()

Returns the value of this Double as a **long**.

short shortValue()

Returns the value of this Double as a **short**.

String toString()

Returns a String representation of the value of this object.

| util | **interface** Enumeration<T> |

PURPOSE

Describes list enumeration functionality. This interface is not preferred to `Iterator` for new implementations.

INSTANCE METHOD SUMMARY

boolean hasMoreElements()

Returns whether this `Enumeration` has more elements to return.

T nextElement()

Returns next element of this `Enumeration`. If there is no next element, then it throws a `NoSuchElementException`.

| lang | **class** Enum<T> |

PURPOSE

Represents the super class for all enumerations.

CLASS METHOD SUMMARY

static <E **extends** Enum<E>> E valueOf(Class<E> e, String s)

Returns the enum constant of enum type `e` whose name is `s`.

CONSTRUCTOR SUMMARY

protected Enum()

Constructs a new `Enum`.

INSTANCE METHOD SUMMARY

protected Object clone()

Throws an exception of type `CloneNotSupportedException`.

int compareTo(T t)

Returns a negative value, zero, or a positive value depending respectively on whether the `Enum` value represented by this object is less than, equal to, or greater than `t`.

boolean equals(Object v)

Returns **true** if and only if `v` represents the same `Enum` constant that this object represents.

Class<T> getDeclaringClass()

Returns the `Class` representing the class whose definition specifies the enum represented by this `Enum`.

int hashCode()

Returns the hash code of this object.

final String name()

Returns a `String` representation of the name of this `Enum`.

int ordinal()

Returns the position of this `Enum` in its **enum** declaration.

String toString()

Returns a `String` representation of the name of this `Enum`.

| lang | **class** Error **extends** Throwable |

PURPOSE
Represents an abnormal event that should never occur.

CONSTRUCTOR SUMMARY
```
Error()
```
Equivalent to `Error(`**`null, null`**`)`.
```
Error(String s)
```
Equivalent to `Error(s, `**`null`**`)`.
```
Error(String s, Throwable t)
```
Constructs a new `Error` with message `s` and cause `t`.
```
Error(Throwable t)
```
Equivalent to `Error(s, t)`, where `s` equals **`null`** if `t` equals **`null`**; otherwise `s` equals `t.toString()`.

| lang | **class** Exception **extends** Throwable |

PURPOSE
Represents an unexpected event that is catchable.

CONSTRUCTOR SUMMARY
```
Exception()
```
Constructs a new `Exception` with a **`null`** message and cause.
```
Exception(String s)
```
Constructs a new `Exception` with message `s` and a **`null`** cause.
```
Exception(String s, Throwable t)
```
Constructs a new `Exception` with message `s` and cause `t`.
```
Exception(Throwable t)
```
Constructs a new `Exception` with cause `t`.

| io | **class** File **implements** Serializable, Comparable<File> |

PURPOSE
Represents file and directory path names.

FIELD SUMMARY
```
static final String pathSeparator
```
Separator character symbol used by the operating system for path lists (e.g., "`:`" and "`;`").
```
static final char pathSeparatorChar
```
Separator character symbol used by the operating system for path lists (e.g., "`:`" and "`;`").
```
static final String separator
```
Name separator character symbol used by the operating system (e.g., "`\`" or "`/`").

static final char separatorChar

Name separator character symbol used by the operating system (e.g., "\" or "/").

CLASS METHOD SUMMARY

static File createTempFile(String s, String t)

Creates an empty file in the operating-system dependent, default temporary-file folder. The name of the empty file is s and the suffix of the file is t. The method returns a File instance for the new file.

static File createTempFile(String s, String t, File d)

Creates an empty file in folder d. The name of the empty file is s and the suffix of the file is t. The method returns a File instance for the new file.

static File[] listRoots()

Returns a File array of root file system folders.

CONSTRUCTOR SUMMARY

File(File d, String f)

Constructs a new File instance using file path f relative to folder d.

File(String f)

Constructs a new File instance using file path f.

File(String d, String f)

Constructs a new File instance using file path f relative to folder d.

File(URI u)

Constructs a new File instance using Universal Resource Identifier u.

INSTANCE METHOD SUMMARY

boolean canRead()

Returns whether the path name of this File instance refers to an application readable file.

boolean canWrite()

Returns whether the path name of this File instance refers to an application writable file.

int compareTo(File f)

Returns a negative value, zero, or a positive value depending respectively on whether the File value represented by this object is lexicographically less than, equal to, or greater than f.

int compareTo(Object v)

Returns a negative value, zero, or a positive value depending respectively on whether the File value represented by this object is lexicographically less than, equal to, or greater than v.

boolean createNewFile()

Attempts to create a new empty file or folder with the path name indicated by this File. The method returns whether the creation request was successful.

boolean delete()

Attempts to delete the file or empty folder indicated by this File. The method returns whether the deletion request was successful.

void deleteOnExit()

Attempts to delete the file or empty folder indicated by this File when the application terminates normally.

boolean equals(Object v)

Returns **true** if and only if v is an instance of File representing the same file or folder that this object represents.

boolean exists()

Returns whether the path name of this File instance refers to an existing file or folder.

File getAbsoluteFile()

Returns a new File instance representing the absolute path name for the path name of this File.

String getAbsolutePath()

Returns a String representing the absolute path name for the path name of this File.

File getCanonicalFile()

Returns a new File instance representing the canonical path name for the path name of this File. A *canonical* name is an absolute name with no symbolic links or redundant folder entries (e.g., \. or /.).

String getCanonicalPath()

Returns a String representing the canonical path name for the path name of this File. A *canonical* name is an absolute name with no symbolic links or redundant folder entries (e.g., \. or /.).

String getName()

Returns the name of the file or folder represented by this File.

String getParent()

Returns the path name to the folder containing the file or folder represented by this File. If there is no such folder, then the method returns **null**.

File getParentFile()

Returns a new File representing the folder containing the file or folder represented by this File. If there is no such folder, then the method returns **null**.

String getPath()

Returns the path name to the file or folder represented by this File.

int hashCode()

Returns the hash code of this object.

boolean isAbsolute()

Returns whether the path name of this File instance is an absolute path.

boolean isDirectory()

Returns whether the path name of this File instance is a directory.

boolean isFile()

Returns whether this File instance is the path name to a file.

boolean isHidden()

Returns whether this File instance refers to a hidden file.

long lastModified()

Returns the most recent modification time of the file or folder represented by this File.

long length()

Returns the length of the file represented by this File.

```
String[] list()
```

Returns a `String` array of the files and folders in the folder represented by this `File`.

```
String[] list(FilenameFilter p)
```

Returns a `String` array of the files and folders in the folder represented by this `File` that match filter pattern **p**.

```
File[] listFiles()
```

Returns a `File` array of the files and folders in the folder represented by this `File`.

```
File[] listFiles(FileFilter p)
```

Returns a `File` array of the files and folders in the folder represented by this `File` that match filter pattern **p**.

```
File[] listFiles(FilenameFilter p)
```

Returns a `File` array of the files and folders in the folder represented by this `File` that match filter pattern **p**.

boolean `mkdir()`

Attempts to create the folder named by this `File`. Returns whether the folder was created.

boolean `mkdirs()`

Attempts to create the folder and any necessary parent folders named by this `File`. Returns whether the folder was created.

boolean `renameTo(File f)`

Attempts to rename the file or folder represented by this `File` to the name indicated by **f**. Returns whether the file or folder was created.

boolean `setLastModified(long t)`

Attempts to set most recent modification time of the file or folder represented by this `File`. Returns whether the last-modified time of the file was updated.

boolean `setReadOnly()`

Attempts to set the status of the file or folder represented by this `File` as read only.

```
String toString()
```

Returns a `String` representing the path name of this `File`.

```
URI toURI()
```

Returns a Universal Resource Indicator representing the path name of this `File`.

```
URL toURL()
```

Returns a Universal Resource Locator representing the path name of this `File`.

---

io

class `FileReader` **extends** `InputStreamReader`

PURPOSE

Represents an output stream with file reading functionality.

CONSTRUCTOR SUMMARY

```
FileReader(File f)
```

Constructs a new `FileReader` using **f**.

```
FileReader(FileDescriptor f)
```
Constructs a new `FileReader` using f.
```
FileReader(String f)
```
Constructs a new `FileReader` using f.

---

io

class `FileWriter` **extends** `OutputStreamWriter`

PURPOSE
Represents an output stream with file writing functionality.

CONSTRUCTOR SUMMARY
```
FileWriter(File f)
```
Constructs a new `FileWriter` using f in nonappend mode.
```
FileWriter(File f, boolean b)
```
Constructs a new `FileWriter` using f with an append mode based on b.
```
FileWriter(FileDescriptor f)
```
Constructs a new `FileWriter` using f in nonappend mode.
```
FileWriter(String f)
```
Constructs a new `FileWriter` using f in nonappend mode.
```
FileWriter(String f, boolean b)
```
Constructs a new `FileWriter` using f with an append mode based on b.

---

lang

final class `Float` **extends** `Number` **implements** `Comparable<Float>`

PURPOSE
Represents a **float** value within a class wrapper.

FIELD SUMMARY
```
static final float MAX_VALUE
```
Represents the maximum finite value of type **float** (i.e., $(2 - 2^{-23})2^{127}$).
```
static final float MIN_VALUE
```
Represents the minimum positive nonzero value of type **float** (i.e., 2^{-149}).
```
static final float NaN
```
Represents Not-a-Number value (NaN) for type **float**.
```
static final float NEGATIVE_INFINITY
```
Represents negative infinity for type **float**.
```
static final float POSITIVE_INFINITY
```
Represents positive infinity for type **float**.
```
static final int SIZE
```
Represents the number of bits used to represent a **float** value.
```
static final Class<Float> TYPE
```
Represents the type **float**.

CLASS METHOD SUMMARY

`static int compare(float m, float n)`

Returns a negative value, zero, or a positive value depending respectively on whether m is less than, equal to, or greater than n.

`static int floatToIntBits(float n)`

Returns a representation of **float** value n using the *IEEE 754 floating-point single-format bit layout* standard.

`static int floatToRawIntBits(float n)`

Returns a representation of **float** value n using the *IEEE 754 floating-point single-format bit layout* standard while preserving not-a-number values.

`static boolean isInfinite(float n)`

Returns **true** if and only if n is equal to `Double.NEGATIVE_INFINITY` or to `Double.POSITIVE_INFINITY`.

`static boolean isNaN(float n)`

Returns **true** if and only if the **float** value n is equal to `Float.NaN`.

`static float intBitsToFloat(int n)`

Returns the **float** value corresponding to the bit representation of value n.

`static float parseFloat(String s)`

Returns the **float** value represented by parsing string s as an optionally signed floating-point value.

`static String toHexString(float n)`

Returns a hexadecimal string representation of **float** value n.

`static String toString(float n)`

Returns a string representation of **float** value n.

`static Float valueOf(float n)`

Returns a Float object representing **float** value n.

`static Float valueOf(String s)`

Returns a Float object representing `Float.parseFloat(s)`.

CONSTRUCTOR SUMMARY

`Float(double n)`

Constructs a new Float object representing **double** value n.

`Float(float n)`

Constructs a new Float object representing **float** value n.

`Float(String s)`

Constructs a new Float object representing `Float.parseFloat(s)`.

INSTANCE METHOD SUMMARY

`byte byteValue()`

Returns the value of this Float as a **byte**.

`int compareTo(Float n)`

Returns a negative value, zero, or a positive value depending respectively on whether the **float** value represented by this object is less than, equal to, or greater than n.

`int compareTo(Object v)`

Returns a negative value, zero, or a positive value depending respectively on whether the **float** value represented by this object is less than, equal to, or greater than v.

double doubleValue()

Returns the value of this Float as a **double**.

boolean equals(Object v)

Returns **true** if and only if v is an instance of Boolean representing the same **boolean** value that this object represents.

float floatValue()

Returns the value of this Float as a **float**.

int hashCode()

Returns the hash code of this object.

int intValue()

Returns the value of this Float as an **int**.

boolean isInfinite()

Returns **true** if and only if the **float** value of this object is equal to Float.NEGATIVE_INFINITY or equal to Float.POSITIVE_INFINITY.

boolean isNaN()

Returns **true** if and only if the **float** value of this object is equal to Float.NaN.

long longValue()

Returns the value of this Float as a **long**.

short shortValue()

Returns the value of this Float as a **short**.

String toString()

Returns a String representation of the value of this object.

| awt | **class** FlowLayout **implements** LayoutManager, Serializable |

PURPOSE

Represents a layout manager that arranges components in a left-to-right, top-to-bottom flow.

FIELD SUMMARY

static int CENTER

Represents a row-centering layout policy.

static int LEADING

Represents a leading edge justification layout policy.

static int LEFT

Represents a left justification layout policy.

static int RIGHT

Represents a right justification layout policy.

static int TRAILING

Represents a trailing edge justification layout policy.

CONSTRUCTOR SUMMARY

FlowLayout()

Constructs a new FlowLayout with a centering layout policy.

FlowLayout(**int** p)

Constructs a new FlowLayout with layout policy p.

FlowLayout(**int** p, **int** h, **int** v)

Constructs a new `FlowLayout` with layout policy p. The inter-row horizontal gap is h and the interelement vertical gap is v.

INSTANCE METHOD SUMMARY

void addLayoutComponent(String s, Component c)

Adds component c with name s to the layout of this layout manager.

int getAlignment()

Returns the alignment policy of this layout manager.

int getHgap()

Returns the intercomponent horizontal gap used by this layout manager.

int getVgap()

Returns the intercomponent vertical gap used by this layout manager.

void layoutContainer(Container c)

Arranges the components of container c using this layout manager.

Dimension minimumLayoutSize(Container c)

Returns the minimum size of container c using this layout manager.

Dimension preferredLayoutSize(Container c)

Returns the preferred size of container c using this layout manager.

void removeLayoutComponent(Component c)

Removes component c from the arrangement of this layout manager.

void setAlignment(**int** p)

Sets p as the alignment policy of this layout manager.

void setHgap(**int** h)

Sets h as the horizontal gap between components by this layout manager.

void setVgap(**int** v)

Sets v as the vertical gap between components by this layout manager.

String toString()

Returns a representation of this layout manager.

| awt | **class** Font **implements** Serializable |

PURPOSE

Represents the logical font information needed for rendering characters and glyphs.

FIELD SUMMARY

static int BOLD

Represents the bold style.

static int CENTER_BASELINE

Represents the baseline for ideographic scripts.

static int HANGING_BASELINE

Represents the baseline in Devanigiri-like scripts.

static int ITALIC

Represents the italic style.

static int LAYOUT_LEFT_TO_RIGHT

Represents left to right layout of text and glyphs.

`static int` LAYOUT_NO_LIMIT_CONTEXT

Represents that text beyond the specified length should not be considered.

`static int` LAYOUT_NO_START_CONTEXT

Represents that text before the specified start should not be considered.

`static int` LAYOUT_RIGHT_TO_LEFT

Represents left to right layout of text and glyphs.

`protected` String name

Represents the logical name of this Font.

`static int` PLAIN

Represents the plain style.

`protected float` pointSize

Represents the point size of this Font.

`static int` ROMAN_BASELINE

Represents the baseline for Latin scripts.

`protected int` size

Represents the point size of this Font.

`protected int` style

Represents the style of this Font.

`static final int` TRUETYPE_FONT

Represents the TrueType font style.

`static final int` TYPE1_FONT

Represents the Type1 font style.

CLASS METHOD SUMMARY

`static` Font createFont(`int` f, File s)

Returns a new Font of type f using the font data in file s.

`static` Font createFont(`int` f, InputStream s)

Returns a new Font of type f using the font data in stream s.

`static` Font decode(String s)

Returns the Font of type s.

`static` Font getFont(Map m)

Returns the Font of type m.

`static` Font getFont(String s)

Returns the Font of type s.

`static` Font getFont(String s, Font f)

Returns the font of system property s using f as the return value.

CONSTRUCTOR SUMMARY

Font(Map m)

Creates a new Font of type m.

Font(String s, `int` n1, `int` n2)

Creates a new Font of type n1 and point size n2 and name s.

INSTANCE METHOD SUMMARY

`boolean` canDisplay(`char` c)

Returns whether this Font has a glyph for character c.

`boolean` canDisplay(`int` c)

Returns whether this Font has a glyph for character c.

`int canDisplayUpTo(char[] c, int i, int n)`

Returns whether this Font can display the substring of the n characters denoted by array c starting with its ith character.

`int canDisplayUpTo(CharacterIterator c, int i, int n)`

Returns whether this Font can display the substring of the n characters denoted by iterator c starting with its ith character.

`int canDisplayUpTo(String s)`

Returns whether this Font can display string s.

`GlyphVector createGlyphVector(FontRenderContext f, char[] c)`

Returns a characters to glyphs GlyphVector for this Font using font-rendering context f.

`GlyphVector createGlyphVector(FontRenderContext f,`
`  CharacterIterator c)`

Returns a characters to glyphs GlyphVector for this Font using font-rendering context f.

`GlyphVector createGlyphVector(FontRenderContext f, int[] g)`

Returns a characters to glyphs GlyphVector for this Font using font-rendering context f.

`GlyphVector createGlyphVector(FontRenderContext f, String s)`

Returns a new GlyphVector for string s in this Font using font-rendering context f.

`Font deriveFont(AffineTransform a)`

Returns a new Font based on affine transformation a on this Font.

`Font deriveFont(float n)`

Returns a new Font of point size n based on this Font.

`Font deriveFont(int n)`

Returns a new Font of style n based on this Font.

`Font deriveFont(int n, AffineTransform a)`

Returns a new Font of point size n based on affine transformation a on this Font.

`Font deriveFont(int n1, float n2)`

Returns a new Font of style n1 and point size n2 based on this Font.

`Font deriveFont(Map m)`

Returns a new Font with attributes m based on this Font.

`boolean equals(Object v)`

Returns whether v is a Font equal to this Font.

`protected void finalize()`

Disposes the native font associated with this Font.

`Map getAttributes()`

Returns the font attributes of this Font.

`AttributedCharacterIterator.Attribute[]`
`  getAvailableAttributes()`

Returns the keys for the attributes of this Font.

`byte getBaselineFor(char c)`

Returns the baseline of character in this Font.

`String getFamily()`

Returns the family name of this Font.

String getFamily(Locale l)

Returns the family name with respect to locale l of this Font.

String getFontName()

Returns the name of this Font.

String getFontName(Locale l)

Returns the locale l name of this Font.

float getItalicAngle()

Returns the italic angle of this Font.

LineMetrics getLineMetrics(**char**[] c, **int** i, **int** n, FontRenderContext f)

Returns, with respect to context f, the line metrics of the length n sequence of characters denoted by list c starting with its ith element in this Font.

LineMetrics getLineMetrics(CharacterIterator c, **int** i, **int** n, FontRenderContext f)

Returns, with respect to context f, the line metrics of the substring of the n characters denoted by iterator c starting with its ith character in this Font.

LineMetrics getLineMetrics(String s, FontRenderContext f)

Returns the line metrics of string s in this context f.

LineMetrics getLineMetrics(String s, **int** i, **int** n, FontRenderContext f)

Rectangle2D getMaxCharBounds(FontRenderContext f)

Returns, with respect to context f, the bounding box of the character in the font of this Font with a maximum bounding box.

int getMissingGlyphCode()

Returns the glyph code used by this Font for a non-Unicode glyph.

String getName()

Returns the logical font name of this Font.

int getNumGlyphs()

Returns the number of glyphs in this Font.

String getPSName()

Returns the PostScript name of this Font.

int getSize()

Returns the point size of this Font.

float getSize2D()

Returns the point size of this Font.

LineMetrics getLineMetrics(CharacterIterator c, **int** i, **int** n, Graphics g)

Returns, with respect to context f, the line metrics of the substring of the sequence characters denoted by iterator c starting with its ith character in this Font.

Rectangle2D getStringBounds(**char**[] c, **int** i, **int** n, FontRenderContext f)

Returns, with respect to context f, the bounding box of the substring of the n characters denoted by list c starting with its ith element in this Font.

Rectangle2D getStringBounds(CharacterIterator c, int i, int n, FontRenderContext f)

> Returns, with respect to context f, the bounding box of the substring of n characters denoted by iterator c starting with its ith character in this Font.

Rectangle2D getStringBounds(String s, FontRenderContext f)

> Returns the bounding box of string s with respect to context f.

Rectangle2D getStringBounds(String s, int i, int n, FontRenderContext f)

> Returns, with respect to context f, the bounding box of a substring of s starting with the ith character.

int getStyle()

> Returns the style of this Font.

AffineTransform getTransform()

> Returns a clone of the affine transform of this Font.

int hashCode()

> Returns a hash code for this Font.

boolean hasUniformLineMetrics()

> Returns whether this Font has uniform line metrics.

boolean isBold()

> Returns whether the style of this Font is bold.

boolean isItalic()

> Returns whether the style of this Font is italic.

boolean isPlain()

> Returns whether the style of this Font is plain.

boolean isTransformed()

> Returns whether this Font has a transform that affects its size.

GlyphVector layoutGlyphVector(FontRenderContext f1, char[] c, int i, int n, int f2)

> Returns a new GlyphVector for the sequence of characters denoted by list c starting with its ith element with respect to font rendering context f1 and flags f2.

String toString()

> Returns a representation of this Font.

---

awt   **abstract class** FontMetrics **implements** Serializable

PURPOSE

Represents rendering information for individual characters and strings with respect to a font and a graphical context.

FIELD SUMMARY

protected Font font

> Represents the font in question for this FontMetrics.

CONSTRUCTOR SUMMARY

protected FontMetrics(Font f)

> Constructs a new FontMetrics for font f.

INSTANCE METHOD SUMMARY

`int bytesWidth(byte[]` c, `int` i, `int` n)

Returns the advance width of the substring of the n characters denoted by list c starting with its ith element in this FontMetrics.

`int charsWidth(char[]` c, `int` i, `int` n)

Returns the advance width of the substring of the n characters denoted by list c starting with its ith element in this FontMetrics.

`int charWidth(char` c)

Returns the advance width of character c in the font of this FontMetrics.

`int charWidth(int` c)

Returns the advance width of character c in the font of this FontMetrics.

`int getAscent()`

Returns the ascent of the font of this FontMetrics.

`int getDescent()`

Returns the descent of the font of this FontMetrics.

Font `getFont()`

Returns the font of this FontMetrics.

`int getHeight()`

Returns the standard height in the font of this FontMetrics.

`int getLeading()`

Returns the standard leading in the font of this FontMetrics.

LineMetrics `getLineMetrics(char[]` c, `int` i, `int` n, Graphics g)

Returns, with respect to graphics g, the line metrics of the sequence of characters denoted by list c starting with its ith element in this FontMetrics.

LineMetrics `getLineMetrics(CharacterIterator` c, `int` i, `int` n, Graphics g)

Returns, with respect to graphics g, the line metrics of the substring of the n characters denoted by iterator c starting with its ith character in this FontMetrics.

LineMetrics `getLineMetrics(String` s, Graphics g)

Returns the line metrics of string s in this Graphics.

LineMetrics `getLineMetrics(String` s, `int` i, `int` n, Graphics g)

Returns, with respect to graphics g, the line metrics of a substring of the length n string s starting with the ith character in this Graphics.

`int getMaxAdvance()`

Returns the maximum advance of any character in the font of this FontMetrics.

`int getMaxAscent()`

Returns the maximum ascent in the font of this FontMetrics.

Rectangle2D `getMaxCharBounds(Graphics` g)

Returns, with respect to graphics g, the bounding box of the character in the font of this FontMetrics with a maximum bounding box.

`int getMaxDescent()`

Returns the maximum descent in the font of this FontMetrics.

Rectangle2D `getStringBounds(char[]` c, `int` i, `int` n, Graphics g)

Returns, with respect to graphics g, the bounding box of the sequence of characters denoted by list c starting with its ith element in this FontMetrics.

Rectangle2D getStringBounds(CharacterIterator c, int i, int n, Graphics g)

> Returns, with respect to graphics g, the bounding box of the substring of the n characters denoted by iterator c starting with its ith character in this FontMetrics.

Rectangle2D getStringBounds(String s, Graphics g)

> Returns the bounding box of the string s in this Graphics.

Rectangle2D getStringBounds(String s, int i, int n, Graphics g)

> Returns, with respect to graphics g, the bounding box of a substring of s starting with the ith character in this Graphics.

int[] getWidths()

> Returns the advance widths of the first 256 characters in the font of this FontMetrics.

boolean hasUniformLineMetrics()

> Returns whether the font of this FontMetrics has uniform line metrics.

int stringWidth(String s)

> Returns the advance width of string s in the font of this FontMetrics.

String toString()

> Returns a representation of this FontMetrics.

---

awt	**abstract class** Graphics

PURPOSE

Represents the information needed for a rendering operation.

CONSTRUCTOR SUMMARY

protected Graphics()

> Constructs a new Graphics object.

INSTANCE METHOD SUMMARY

abstract void clearRect(int x, int y, int w, int w)

> Fills the rectangular region with origin (x, y) and width w and height h in this Graphics with the background color.

abstract void clipRect(int x, int y, int w, int h)

> Sets the clipping rectangle of this Graphics as the intersection of the current clipping rectangle and the rectangular region with origin (x, y) and width w and height h.

abstract void copyArea(int x, int y, int w, int h, int dx, int dy)

> Copies the rectangular region of this Graphics with origin (x, y) and width w and height h at location (x+dx, y+dy).

abstract Graphics create()

> Returns a new clone of this Graphics.

Graphics create(int x, int y, int w, int h)

> Creates a new Graphics based on this Graphics, where the new graphical context translates this Graphics by (x, y) and has clipping rectangle with width w and height h.

abstract void dispose()

Disposes of this **Graphics**.

void draw3DRect(**int** x, **int** y, **int** w, **int** h, **boolean** b)

Uses this **Graphics** to render a three-dimensional outline of the rectangular region with origin (x, y) and width w and height h. Whether the region appears raised depends on b.

abstract void drawArc(**int** x, **int** y, **int** w, **int** h, **int** a1, **int** a2)

Uses this **Graphics** to render an elliptical arc with origin (x, y) and width w and height h and starting and ending angles a1 and a2.

void drawBytes(**byte**[] b, **int** i, **int** n, **int** x, **int** y)

Uses this **Graphics** to render n bytes of array a starting with a[i], where the text baseline is (x, y).

void drawChars(**char**[] a, **int** i, **int** n, **int** x, **int** y)

Uses this **Graphics** to render n characters of array a starting with a[i], where the text baseline is (x, y).

abstract boolean drawImage(Image i, **int** x, **int** y, Color c, ImageObserver o)

Uses this **Graphics** to render image i at location (x, y) using image observer o. Returns whether the image was completely loaded prior to rendering.

abstract boolean drawImage(Image i, **int** x, **int** y, ImageObserver o)

Uses this **Graphics** to render image i at location (x, y) with background color c using image observer o. Returns whether the image was completely loaded prior to rendering.

abstract boolean drawImage(Image i, **int** x, **int** y, **int** w, **int** h, Color c, ImageObserver o)

Uses this **Graphics** to render a scaled version of image i with width w and height h using this **Graphics**, at location (x, y) with background color c using image observer o. Returns whether the image was completely loaded prior to rendering.

abstract boolean drawImage(Image i, **int** x, **int** y, **int** w, **int** h, ImageObserver o)

Uses this **Graphics** to render a scaled version of image i with width w and height h using this **Graphics**, at location (x, y) using image observer o. Returns whether the image was completely loaded prior to rendering.

abstract boolean drawImage(Image i, **int** dx1, **int** dy1, **int** dx2, **int** dy2, **int** sx1, **int** sy1, **int** sx2, **int** sy2, Color c, ImageObserver o)

Uses this **Graphics** to render a scaled version of the rectangular subregion specified by source locations (sx1, sy1) and (sx2, sy2) of image i in the destination rectangular subregion specified by locations (dx1, dy1) and (dx2, dy2) with background color c using image observer o. Returns whether the image was completely loaded prior to rendering.

abstract **boolean** drawImage(Image i, **int** dx1, **int** dy1, **int** dx2, **int** dy2, **int** sx1, **int** sy1, **int** sx2, **int** sy2, ImageObserver o)

Uses this Graphics to render a scaled version of the rectangular subregion specified by source locations (sx1, sy1) and (sx2, sy2) of image i in the destination rectangular subregion specified by locations (dx1, dy1) and (dx2, dy2) using image observer o. Returns whether the image was completely loaded prior to rendering.

abstract **void** drawLine(**int** x1, **int** y1, **int** x2, **int** y2)

Uses this Graphics to render a line in the current color with endpoints (x1, y1) and (x2, y2).

abstract **void** drawOval(**int** x, **int** y, **int** w, **int** h)

Uses this Graphics to render the outline of an oval in the current color with origin (x, y), width w, and height h.

abstract **void** drawPolygon(**int**[] x, **int**[] y, **int** n)

Invokes drawPolygon(**new** Polygon(x, y, n)).

void drawPolygon(Polygon p)

Uses this Graphics to render the outline of a closed polygon in the current color.

abstract **void** drawPolyline(**int**[] x, **int**[] y, **int** n)

Uses this Graphics to render an open polygon in the current color based on x, y, and n in the current color.

void drawRect(**int** x, **int** y, **int** w, **int** h)

Uses this Graphics to render the outline of a rectangle in the current color with width w and height h at location (x, y).

abstract **void** drawRoundRect(**int** x, **int** y, **int** w1, **int** h2, **int** w2, **int** h2)

Uses this Graphics to render the outline of a rounded rectangle in the current color with width w1 and height h1 at location (x, y), where the corners are elliptical with width w2 and height h2.

abstract **void** drawString(AttributedCharacterIterator i, **int** x, **int** y)

Uses this Graphics to render the text represented by iterator i at baseline (x, y).

abstract **void** drawString(String s, **int** x, **int** y)

Uses this Graphics to render the text represented by string s at baseline (x, y).

void fill3DRect(**int** x, **int** y, **int** w, **int** h, **boolean** b)

Uses this Graphics to render a three-dimensional filled rectangular region with origin (x, y) and width w and height h. Whether the region appears raised depends on b.

abstract **void** fillArc(**int** x, **int** y, **int** w, **int** h, **int** a1, **int** a2)

Uses this Graphics to render in the current color a filled elliptical arc with origin (x, y) and width w and height h and starting and ending angles a1 and a2.

abstract **void** fillOval(**int** x, **int** y, **int** w, **int** h)

Uses this Graphics to render a filled oval in the current color with origin (x, y), width w, and height h.

abstract **void** fillPolygon(**int**[] x, **int**[] y, **int** n)

Invokes fillPolygon(**new** Polygon(x, y, n)).

void fillPolygon(Polygon p)

Uses this Graphics to render a filled closed polygon in the current color.

abstract void fillRect(int x, int y, int w, int h)

Uses this Graphics to render a filled rectangle in the current color with width w and height h at location (x, y).

abstract void fillRoundRect(int x, int y, int w1, int h1, int w2, int h2)

Uses this Graphics to render a filled rounded rectangle in the current color with width w1 and height h1 at location (x, y), where the corners are elliptical with width w2 and height h2.

void finalize()

Disposes of this Graphics when it does not have any references.

abstract Shape getClip()

Returns the clipping area of this Graphics.

abstract Rectangle getClipBounds()

Returns the bounding rectangle of the clipping area of this Graphics.

Rectangle getClipBounds(Rectangle r)

Returns using r the bounding rectangle of the clipping area of this Graphics.

abstract Color getColor()

Returns the color of this Graphics.

abstract Font getFont()

Returns the font of this Graphics.

FontMetrics getFontMetrics()

Returns the font metrics of this Graphics.

abstract FontMetrics getFontMetrics(Font f)

Returns the font metrics for font f with this Graphics.

boolean hitClip(int x, int y, int w, int h)

Returns whether the rectangle with width w and height h at location (x, y) intersects the clipping area of this Graphics.

abstract void setClip(int x, int y, int w, int h)

Sets the clipping area of this Graphics to the rectangle with width w and height h at location (x, y).

abstract void setClip(Shape s)

Sets s as the clipping area of this Graphics.

abstract void setColor(Color c)

Sets c as the color of this Graphics.

abstract void setFont(Font f)

Sets f as the font of this Graphics.

abstract void setPaintMode()

Sets the paint mode of this Graphics to alternate between the current color and the color of destination.

abstract void setXORMode(Color c)

Sets the paint mode of this Graphics to alternate between the current color and color c.

String toString()

Returns a representation of this Graphics.

abstract void translate(**int** dx, **int** dy)

Translates the origin of this Graphics by distances dx and dy respectively on the x- and y-axes.

---

awt	**class** GridLayout **implements** LayoutManager, Serializable

PURPOSE

Represents a layout manager that arranges its components in a rectangular grid.

CONSTRUCTOR SUMMARY

GridLayout()

Constructs a new GridLayout for managing a single component.

GridLayout(**int** r, **int** c)

Constructs a new GridLayout for managing r rows of components with c components per row.

GridLayout(**int** r, **int** c, **int** h, **int** v)

Constructs a new GridLayout for managing r rows of components with c components per row. The inter-row horizontal gap is h and the intercolumn vertical gap is v.

INSTANCE METHOD SUMMARY

void addLayoutComponent(String s, Component c)

Adds component c with name s to the layout of this layout manager.

int getColumns()

Returns the number of columns used by this layout manager.

int getHgap()

Returns the intercomponent horizontal gap used by this layout manager.

int getRows()

Returns the number of rows used by this layout manager.

int getVgap()

Returns the intercomponent vertical gap used by this layout manager.

void layoutContainer(Container c)

Arranges the components of container c using this layout manager.

Dimension minimumLayoutSize(Container c)

Returns the minimum size of container c using this layout manager.

Dimension preferredLayoutSize(Container c)

Returns the preferred size of container c using this layout manager.

void removeLayoutComponent(Component c)

Removes component c from the arrangement of this layout manager.

void setColumns(**int** n)

Sets n as the number of columns used by this layout manager.

void setHgap(**int** h)

Sets h as the horizontal gap between components by this layout manager.

void setRows(**int** r)

Sets n as the number of rows used by this layout manager.

void setVgap(**int** v)

Sets v as the vertical gap between components used by this layout manager.

```
String toString()
```
Returns a representation of this layout manager.

---

class `HashTable<K, V>` **extends** `Dictionary<K, V>` **implements** `Map<K, V>, Cloneable, Serializable`

PURPOSE

Provides hash table functionality that maps keys to values.

CONSTRUCTOR SUMMARY

```
Hashtable()
```
Constructs a new `HashTable` with a default capacity of eleven mappings and a 75% load factor.

```
Hashtable(int n)
```
Constructs a new `HashTable` with a capacity of n mappings and a 75% load factor.

```
Hashtable(int n, float x)
```
Constructs a new `HashTable` with a capacity of n mappings and an x% load factor.

```
Hashtable(MapMap<? extends K, ? extends V> m)
```
Constructs a new `HashTable` with the same mappings as m.

INSTANCE METHOD SUMMARY

```
void clear()
```
Clears this `HashTable` of keys.

```
Object clone()
```
Returns a shallow copy of this `HashTable`.

```
boolean contains(Object v)
```
Returns whether some key of this `HashTable` maps to value of v.

```
boolean containsKey(Object v)
```
Returns whether value v is a key in this `HashTable`.

```
boolean containsValue(Object v)
```
Returns whether some key of this `HashTable` maps to value v.

```
Enumeration<V> elements()
```
Returns an enumeration of this `HashTable`.

```
Set<Map.Entry<K, V>> entrySet()
```
Returns a `Set` view of this `HashTable`.

```
boolean equals(Object v)
```
Returns whether v is equal to this `HashTable`.

```
V get(Object k)
```
Returns the value to which key v maps in this `HashTable`.

```
int hashCode()
```
Returns the hash code of this object.

```
boolean isEmpty()
```
Returns whether this `HashTable` has any mappings.

```
Enumeration<K> keys()
```
Returns an enumeration of the keys of this `HashTable`.

Set<K> keySet()

> Returns a Set view of the keys in this HashTable.

V put(K k, V v)

> Maps the key k to value v in this HashTable. Returns the previous value to which k maps. If there was no previous value, then **null** is returned.

void putAll(Map<? **extends** K, ? **extends** V> m)

> Copies the mappings of m to this HashTable.

protected void rehash()

> Resets the capacity and loading factor of this HashTable for purposes of efficiency.

V remove(Object k)

> Removes key k and its corresponding value from this HashTable.

int size()

> Removes the number of keys in this HashTable.

String toString()

> Returns a String representation of the value of this object.

Collection<V> values()

> Returns a Collection view of the values in this HashTable.

---

swing   **interface** Icon

PURPOSE

Describes functionality of a small static image.

INSTANCE METHOD SUMMARY

int getIconHeight()

> Returns the height of this Icon.

int getIconWidth()

> Returns the width of this Icon.

void paintIcon(Component c, Graphics g, **int** x, **int** y)

> Paints this Icon at location (x, y) in graphics context g with component c providing rendering characteristics.

---

lang   **class** IllegalAccessException **extends** Exception

PURPOSE

Represents an unexpected event in which an illegal access of some constructor or member field or method was attempted.

CONSTRUCTOR SUMMARY

IllegalAccessException()

> Constructs an IllegalAccessException without a default message.

IllegalAccessException(String s)

> Constructs an IllegalAccessException with message s.

| awt | **abstract class** Image |

PURPOSE
Serves as a superclass for image representations.

FIELD SUMMARY

protected float accelerationPriority
>Represents the priority for accelerating this **Image**.

static int SCALE_AREA_AVERAGING
>Represents a scaling algorithm that performs area averaging.

static int SCALE_DEFAULT
>Represents the default scaling algorithm.

static int SCALE_FAST
>Represents a scaling algorithm that gives precedence to scaling speed.

static int SCALE_REPLICATE
>Represents a scaling algorithm of class ReplicateScaleFilter.

static int SCALE_SMOOTH
>Represents a scaling algorithm that gives precedence to image smoothness.

static Object UndefinedProperty
>Represents that the requested property value is not defined.

CONSTRUCTOR SUMMARY

Image()
>Creates a new **Image**.

INSTANCE METHOD SUMMARY

float getAccelerationPriority()
>Returns what the acceleration priority of this **Image** should be.

ImageCapabilities getCapabilities(GraphicsConfiguration g)
>Returns an **ImageCapabilities** object that describes the capabilities of this **Image** with respect to graphics configuration c.

abstract void flush()
>Flushes the resources of this **Image**.

abstract Graphics getGraphics()
>Returns a new graphics context for rendering this **Image**.

abstract int getHeight(ImageObserver i)
>Returns the height of this **Image**.

abstract Object getProperty(String s, ImageObserver i)
>Returns the value of property s of this **Image**.

Image getScaledInstance(**int** w, **int** h, **int** a)
>Returns a scaled version of this **Image** with width w and height h, where the requested scaling algorithm is a.

abstract ImageProducer getSource()
>Returns a pixel producer for this **Image**.

abstract int getWidth(ImageObserver i)
>Returns the width of this **Image**.

void setAccelerationPriority(**float** p)
>Sets what the acceleration priority of this **Image** should be.

---

class ImageIcon **implements** Icon, Serializable, Accessible

PURPOSE

Represents a small static image. Images based on a Web resource or a file are preloaded using a media tracker that monitors the image.

CONSTRUCTOR SUMMARY

ImageIcon()

Constructs a new ImageIcon with no display image.

ImageIcon(byte[] b)

Constructs a new ImageIcon using the bytes in array b as the display image.

ImageIcon(byte[] b, String s)

Constructs a new ImageIcon with description s using the bytes in array b as the display image.

ImageIcon(Image i)

Constructs a new ImageIcon using i as the display image.

ImageIcon(Image i, String s)

Constructs a new ImageIcon with description s using image i as the display image.

ImageIcon(String f)

Constructs a new ImageIcon using the image in the file named f as the display image.

ImageIcon(String f, String s)

Constructs a new ImageIcon with description s using the image in the file named f as the display image.

ImageIcon(URL u)

Constructs a new ImageIcon using the image at Web location u as the display image.

ImageIcon(URL u, String s)

Constructs a new ImageIcon with description s using the image at Web location u as the display image.

INSTANCE METHOD SUMMARY

AccessibleContext getAccessibleContext()

Returns the AccessibleContext of this ImageIcon.

String getDescription()

Returns the description of this ImageIcon.

int getIconHeight()

Returns the height of this ImageIcon.

int getIconWidth()

Returns the width of this ImageIcon.

Image getImage()

Returns the image of this ImageIcon.

int getImageLoadStatus()

Returns the status of the last image-loading operation of this ImageIcon.

ImageObserver getImageObserver()

Returns the image observer of this ImageIcon.

protected void loadImage(Image i)

Loads image i for this ImageIcon.

    void paintIcon(Component c, Graphics g, **int** x, **int** y)

        Paints this `Icon` at location (x, y) in graphics context g using observer c if this `ImageIcon` has no image observer.

    void setDescription(String s)

        Sets s as the description of this `ImageIcon`.

    void setImage(Image i)

        Sets i as the image displayed by this `ImageIcon`.

    void setImageObserver(ImageObserver i)

        Sets i as the image observer of this `ImageIcon`.

    String toString()

        Returns a representation of this `ImageIcon`.

<table><tr><td>lang</td><td>

class IndexOutOfBoundsException **extends** RuntimeException

</td></tr></table>

PURPOSE

Represents an illegal element indexing event.

CONSTRUCTOR SUMMARY

    IndexOutOfBoundsException()

        Constructs a new `IndexOutOfBoundsException` with a default message.

    IndexOutOfBoundsException(String s)

        Constructs an `IndexOutOfBoundsException` with message s.

<table><tr><td>lang</td><td>

final class Integer **extends** Number **implements** Comparable<Integer>

</td></tr></table>

PURPOSE

Represents an **int** value within a class wrapper.

FIELD SUMMARY

    static final int MAX_VALUE

        Represents the maximum value of type **int** (i.e., $2^{31} - 1$).

    static final int MIN_VALUE

        Represents the minimum value of type **int** (i.e., -2^{31}.)

    static final int SIZE

        Represents the number of bits used to represent an **int** value.

    static final Class<Integer> TYPE

        Represents the type **int**.

CLASS METHOD SUMMARY

    static int bitCount(**int** n)

        Returns the number of one-bits in the two's complement binary representation of value n.

```
static Integer decode(String s)
```
Constructs a new `Integer` object representing `Integer.parseInt(s, n)`, where n is 8, 10, or 16 depending on whether s is respectively a numeric string in octal, decimal, or hexadecimal format.

```
static Integer getInteger(String s)
```
Returns `Integer.getInteger(s, null)`.

```
static Integer getInteger(String s, int n)
```
Returns `Integer.getInteger(s, new Integer(n))`.

```
static Integer getInteger(String s, Integer n)
```
Returns the value of the system property named s if it exists; otherwise, it returns n.

```
static int highestOneBit(int n)
```
Returns 0 if value n is 0; otherwise, it returns an **int** value with a single one-bit in the position of the leftmost one-bit in the two's complement binary representation of value n.

```
static int lowestOneBit(int n)
```
Returns 0 if value n is 0; otherwise, it returns an **int** value with a single one-bit in the position of the rightmost one-bit in the two's complement binary representation of value n.

```
static int numberOfLeadingZeros(int n)
```
Returns the number of leading zero-bits before the leftmost one-bit in the two's complement binary representation of value n.

```
static int numberOfTrailingZeros(int i)
```
Returns the number of trailing zero-bits after the rightmost one-bit in the two's complement binary representation of value n.

```
static int parseInt(String s)
```
Returns `Integer.parseInt(s, 10)`.

```
static int parseInt(String s, int n)
```
Returns the **int** value represented by parsing string s as an optionally signed integer value in radix n.

```
static int reverse(int n)
```
Returns the value produced by reversing the two's complement binary representation of n.

```
static int reverseBytes(int n)
```
Returns the value produced by reversing the order of the bytes in the two's complement binary representation of n.

```
static int rotateLeft(int n, int m)
```
Returns the value of leftward circularly shifting the two's complement binary representation of n, m times.

```
static int rotateRight(int n, int m)
```
Returns the value of rightward circularly shifting the two's complement binary representation of n, m times.

```
static int signum(int n)
```
Returns −1, 0, or 1 depending on whether value n is respectively negative, zero, or positive.

```
static String toBinaryString(int m)
```
Returns `Integer.toString(m, 2)`.

static String toHexString(**int** m)

    Returns `Integer.toString(m, 16)`.

static String toOctalString(**int** m)

    Returns `Integer.toString(m, 8)`.

static String toString(**int** m)

    Returns `Integer.toString(m, 10)`.

static String toString(**int** m, **int** n)

    Returns a new `String` object representing the value of m in base n.

static Integer valueOf(**int** n)

    Returns an `Integer` representation of value n.

static Integer valueOf(String s)

    Returns `Integer.valueOf(s, 10))`.

static Integer valueOf(String s, **int** n)

    Returns an `Integer` object representing `Integer.parseInt(s, n)`.

CONSTRUCTOR SUMMARY

Integer(**int** n)

    Constructs a new `Integer` object representing value n.

Integer(String s)

    Constructs a new `Integer` object representing `Integer.parseInt(s)`.

INSTANCE METHOD SUMMARY

byte byteValue()

    Returns the value of this `Integer` as a **byte**.

int compareTo(Integer n)

    Returns a negative value, zero, or a positive value depending respectively on whether the **int** value represented by this object is less than, equal to, or greater than n.

double doubleValue()

    Returns the value of this `Integer` as a **double**.

boolean equals(Object v)

    Returns **true** if and only if v is an instance of `Integer` representing the same **int** value that this object represents.

float floatValue()

    Returns the value of this `Integer` as a **float**.

int hashCode()

    Returns the hash code of this object.

int intValue()

    Returns the value of this `Integer` as an **int**.

long longValue()

    Returns the value of this `Integer` as a **long**.

short shortValue()

    Returns the value of this `Integer` as a **short**.

String toString()

    Returns a `String` representation of this `Integer`.

io   **class** IOException **extends** Exception

PURPOSE
Represents the occurrence of an input or output exception.

CONSTRUCTOR SUMMARY

IOException()

Constructs a new IOException with a **null** message.

IOException(String s)

Constructs a new IOException with message s.

---

lang   **interface** Iterable<T>

PURPOSE
Describes the necessary methods in support of the iterator for statement.

INSTANCE METHOD SUMMARY

Iterator<T> iterator()

Returns a type T iterator.

---

util   **interface** Iterator<T>

PURPOSE
Provides an enumeration view of a collection.

INSTANCE METHOD SUMMARY

boolean hasNext()

Returns whether this Collection has more elements to return.

T next()

Returns next element of this Collection. If there is no next element, then it throws a NoSuchElementException.

void remove()

Removes from this Collection the last element returned by the iterator. The operation is optional.

---

swing   **class** JApplet **extends** Applet **implements** Accessible,
RootPaneContainer

PURPOSE
Provides a swing-compatible version of an applet. An applet is a program that is run within another program such as a Web browser. A JApplet contains a *root pane* to which other graphical components can be added. Components should not be added to the

JApplet itself nor should a layout manager be set for JApplet. Instead components should be added to the root pane and the root pane should have a manager.

FIELD SUMMARY

protected AccessibleContext accessibleContext

Represents the accessibility context of this JApplet.

protected JRootPane rootPane

Represents the root pane of this JApplet.

protected boolean rootPaneCheckingEnabled

Represents whether improper additions to this JApplet should generate exceptions.

CONSTRUCTOR SUMMARY

JApplet()

Constructs a new JApplet.

INSTANCE METHOD SUMMARY

protected void addImpl(Component c, Object v, **int** i)

Attempts to insert component c as the ith component of this JApplet using constraints v. An exception is thrown if root pane checking is enabled for this JApplet.

protected JRootPane createRootPane()

Invoked by constructors to create the root pane for this JApplet.

AccessibleContext getAccessibleContext()

Returns the accessibility context of this JApplet.

Container getContentPane()

Returns the content pane object of this JApplet.

Component getGlassPane()

Returns the glass pane of this JApplet.

JMenuBar getJMenuBar()

Returns the menu bar of this JApplet.

JLayeredPane getLayeredPane()

Returns the layered pane of this JApplet.

JRootPane getRootPane()

Returns the root pane of this JApplet.

protected boolean isRootPaneCheckingEnabled()

Returns whether invocations of add() and setLayout() to this JApplet generate exceptions.

protected String paramString()

Returns a representation of this JApplet.

void remove(Component c)

Removes the component c from this JApplet.

void setContentPane(Container c)

Sets c as the content pane of this JApplet.

void setGlassPane(Component g)

Sets g as the glass pane of this JApplet.

void setJMenuBar(JMenuBar m)

Sets m as the menu of this JApplet.

void setLayeredPane(JLayeredPane p)

Sets p as the layered pane of this JApplet.

void setLayout(LayoutManager m)

> Attempts to sets the layout manager of this JApplet to m. An exception is thrown if root pane checking is enabled for this JApplet.

protected void setRootPane(JRootPane r)

> Sets r as the root pane of this JApplet.

protected void setRootPaneCheckingEnabled(**boolean** b)

> Returns whether invocations of add() and setLayout() by this JApplet generate exceptions.

void update(Graphics g)

> Invokes paint(g).

| swing | **class** JButton **extends** AbstractButton **implements** Accessible |

PURPOSE

Represents a push button.

CONSTRUCTOR SUMMARY

JButton()

> Constructs a new JButton with no label or icon.

JButton(Action a)

> Constructs a new JButton with action a.

JButton(Icon i)

> Constructs a new JButton with label image i.

JButton(String s)

> Constructs a new JButton with label text s.

JButton(String s, Icon i)

> Constructs a new JButton with label text s and image i.

INSTANCE METHOD SUMMARY

protected void configurePropertiesFromAction(Action a)

> Sets a as the action properties of this JButton.

AccessibleContext getAccessibleContext()

> Returns the accessibility context of this JButton.

String getUIClassID()

> Returns a string that specifies the look and feel rendering this JButton.

boolean isDefaultButton()

> Returns whether this JButton is the default button for its root pane.

boolean isDefaultCapable()

> Returns whether this JButton is default capable.

protected String paramString()

> Returns a representation of this JButton.

void removeNotify()

> If this JButton was the default button for its root pane, then it is no longer the default button.

void setDefaultCapable(**boolean** b)

> Sets whether this JButton can be the default button for its root pane.

> **void** updateUI()
>> Resets the UI attribute of this object to the current look and feel.

---

swing	**abstract** class JComponent **extends** Container **implements** Serializable

PURPOSE

Represents a swing GUI component that is placeable in a top-level swing container.

FIELD SUMMARY

> **protected** AccessibleContext accessibleContext
>> Represents the accessibility context of this JComponent.

> **protected** EventListenerList listenerList
>> Represents the list of event listeners for this JComponent.

> **static** String TO OL_TIP_TEXT_KEY
>> Represents the cursor fly over display comment.

> **protected** ComponentUI u
>> Represents the look and feel delegate for this JComponent.

> **static** **int** UNDEFINED_CONDITION
>> Represents that no condition is defined.

> **static** **int** WHEN_ANCESTOR_OF_FOCUSED_COMPONENT
>> Indicates the registerKeyboardAction should be invoked when the receiver is either the focused component or an ancestor of the focused component.

> **static** **int** WHEN_FOCUSED
>> Indicates the registerKeyboardAction should be invoked when the component has the focus.

> **static** **int** WHEN_IN_FOCUSED_WINDOW
>> Indicates the registerKeyboardAction should be invoked when the receiver is either the focused component or is in the window that has the focus.

CLASS METHOD SUMMARY

> **static** Locale getDefaultLocale()
>> Returns the default locale.

> **static** **void** setDefaultLocale(Locale l)
>> Sets l as the default locale for a JComponent.

CONSTRUCTOR SUMMARY

> JComponent()
>> Creates a new JComponent.

INSTANCE METHOD SUMMARY

> **void** addAncestorListener(AncestorListener a)
>> Registers a as an ancestor event listener for this JComponent.

> **void** addNotify()
>> Notifies this JComponent that it is a parent component.

> **void** addVetoableChangeListener(VetoableChangeListener v)
>> Registers p as vetoable change listener for this JComponent.

void computeVisibleRect(Rectangle r)

Sets the attributes of r to the intersection of the visible rectangles for this JComponent and its ancestors.

boolean contains(**int** x, **int** y)

Returns whether this JComponent contains logical point (x, y).

JToolTip createToolTip()

Returns the tool tip for this JComponent.

protected void fireVetoableChange(String s, Object v1, Object v2)

Reports a vetoable change in constrained property s from v1 to v2 for each property change listener for this JComponent.

AccessibleContext getAccessibleContext()

Returns the accessibility context for this JComponent.

ActionListener getActionForKeyStroke(KeyStroke c)

Returns the action listener for this JComponent associated with keystroke character c.

ActionMap getActionMap()

Returns the action mapper that maps action listeners to keystroke characters for this JComponent.

float getAlignmentX()

Returns the vertical alignment for this JComponent.

float getAlignmentY()

Returns the horizontal alignment for this JComponent.

AncestorListener[] getAncestorListeners()

Returns the ancestor listeners for this JComponent.

boolean getAutoscrolls()

Returns the autoscroll policy for this JComponent.

Border getBorder()

Returns the border for this JComponent.

Rectangle getBounds(Rectangle r)

Both sets the attributes of r to the bounding box of this JComponent and returns r.

Object getClientProperty(Object v)

Returns the value of property v for this JComponent.

protected Graphics getComponentGraphics(Graphics g)

Returns the graphics context for rendering this JComponent based on graphics context g.

JPopupMenu getComponentPopupMenu()

Returns the JPopupMenu associated with this JComponent.

int getConditionForKeyStroke(KeyStroke a)

Returns the condition that determines whether the keystroke action listener for keystroke character a is invoked for this JComponent.

int getDebugGraphicsOptions()

Returns the graphics debugging information for this JComponent.

FontMetrics getFontMetrics(Font f)

Returns the font metrics for font f for this JComponent.

Graphics getGraphics()

Returns the graphics context for rendering this JComponent.

int getHeight()

Returns the height of this JComponent.

boolean getInheritsPopupMenu()

Returns whether this JComponent should use its parent JPopupMenu.

InputMap getInputMap()

Returns the input mapper that maps input focus listeners for this JComponent.

InputMap getInputMap(**int** i)

Returns the input mapper that maps input listeners for condition i for this JComponent.

InputVerifier getInputVerifier()

Returns the input verifier for this JComponent.

Insets getInsets()

Returns the border insets for this JComponent.

Insets getInsets(Insets i)

Returns the border insets for this JComponent using i if possible.

EventListener[] getListeners(Class a)

Returns the listeners for listener type event a for this JComponent.

Point getLocation(Point p)

Returns the origin for this JComponent using p.

Dimension getMaximumSize()

Returns the maximum size for this JComponent.

Dimension getMinimumSize()

Returns the minimum size for this JComponent.

Point getPopupLocation()

Returns the preferred location for the JPopupMenu associated with this JComponent.

Dimension getPreferredSize()

Returns the preferred size for this JComponent.

KeyStroke[] getRegisteredKeyStrokes()

Returns the keystrokes that have listeners for this JComponent.

JRootPane getRootPane()

Returns the root pane ancestor for this JComponent.

Dimension getSize(Dimension d)

Returns the dimensions for this JComponent using d.

Point getToolTipLocation(MouseEvent e)

Returns the logical location of the tool tip for this JComponent.

String getToolTipText()

Returns the tool tip for this JComponent.

String getToolTipText(MouseEvent e)

Returns the tool tip for event e for this JComponent.

Container getTopLevelAncestor()

Returns the top-level ancestor for this JComponent.

TransferHandler getTransferHandler()

Returns the transfer handler policy for this JComponent.

String getUIClassID()

Returns the name of the look and feel for this JComponent.

boolean getVerifyInputWhenFocusTarget()

Returns whether the focus owner is notified before this JComponent gets focus.

VetoableChangeListener[] getVetoableChangeListeners()

Returns the vetoable change listeners for this JComponent.

Rectangle getVisibleRect()

Returns the visibility bounding box for this JComponent.

int getWidth()

Returns the width of this JComponent.

int getX()

Returns the x-coordinate of the origin of this JComponent.

int getY()

Returns the y-coordinate of the origin of this JComponent.

void grabFocus()

Indicates that this JComponent wants the input focus.

boolean isDoubleBuffered()

Returns whether a buffer should be used to paint this JComponent.

static boolean isLightweightComponent(Component c)

Returns whether this JComponent is lightweight.

boolean isMaximumSizeSet()

Returns whether the maximum size for this JComponent has been set.

boolean isMinimumSizeSet()

Returns whether the minimum size for this JComponent has been set.

boolean isOpaque()

Returns whether this JComponent is opaque (i.e., it hides completely component that lies under it).

boolean isOptimizedDrawingEnabled()

Returns whether this JComponent has tiled its children.

boolean isPaintingTile()

Returns whether this JComponent is painting.

boolean isPreferredSizeSet()

Returns whether the preferred size for this JComponent has been set.

boolean isRequestFocusEnabled()

Returns whether this JComponent should get the focus.

boolean isValidateRoot()

Indicates whether a validation request of an ancestor requires the tree rooted by this JComponent be validated.

void paint(Graphics g)

Paints this JComponent using graphical context g.

protected void paintBorder(Graphics g)

Paints the border of this JComponent using graphical context g.

protected void paintChildren(Graphics g)

Paints the children of this JComponent using graphical g.

protected void paintComponent(Graphics g)

Invokes the user interface delegate paint method of this JComponent with graphical context parameter g.

void paintImmediately(**int** x, **int** y, **int** w, **int** h)

Paints the rectangular region with origin (x, y) and dimensions w and h for this JComponent and its region overlapping descendants.

void paintImmediately(Rectangle r)

Paints rectangular region r of this JComponent.

protected String paramString()

Returns a representation of this JComponent.

void print(Graphics g)

Invokes printBorder(), printChildren(), and printComponent() for this JComponent using graphical context g.

void printAll(Graphics g)

Printing method for this JComponent.

protected void printBorder(Graphics g)

Prints the border of this JComponent using graphical context g. Override this method, if special printing behavior is needed.

protected void printChildren(Graphics g)

Prints the children of this JComponent using graphical context g. Override this method, if special printing behavior is needed.

protected void printComponent(Graphics g)

Prints this JComponent using this JComponent. Override this method, if special printing behavior is needed.

protected void processComponentKeyEvent(KeyEvent e)

Override this method, if this JComponent must also process a key event.

protected boolean processKeyBinding(KeyStroke c, KeyEvent e, **int** i, **boolean** b)

Processes key event e for keystroke character c subject to condition i and pressing indicator b. Returns whether there was a registered listener.

protected void processKeyEvent(KeyEvent e)

Process key event e for this JComponent.

protected void processMousevent(MouseEvent e)

Dispatches mouse event e for this JComponent to its registered listeners.

protected void processMouseMotionEvent(MouseEvent e)

Processes mouse event e for this JComponent.

void putClientProperty(Object v1, Object v2)

Adds a property v1 with value v2 for this JComponent.

void removeAncestorListener(AncestorListener a)

Removes ancestor event listener p as a listener for this JComponent.

void removeNotify()

Signals this JComponent that it is not a parent component.

void removeVetoableChangeListener(VetoableChangeListener l)

Removes vetoable change listener p for this JComponent.

void repaint(**long** i, **int** x, **int** y, **int** w, **int** h)

Indicates that the rectangular region with origin (x, y) and dimensions w and h for this JComponent needs repainting, after the current painting completes.

void repaint(Rectangle r)

Indicates that rectangular region r for this JComponent needs repainting, after this painting completes.

void requestFocus()

> Indicates that this JComponent should get the focus.

boolean requestFocusInWindow()

> Indicates that this JComponent should get the focus if its ancestor window has the focus. Returns whether the request is expected to be satisfied.

protected boolean requestFocusInWindow(**boolean** b)

> Indicates that this JComponent should get the focus if its ancestor window has the focus. Parameter b indicates whether the change in focus is temporary. Returns whether the request is expected to be satisfied.

void resetKeyboardActions()

> Removes the registered input and action mappers of this JComponent.

void revalidate()

> Supports automatic relayout when an attribute of this JComponent changes.

void scrollRectToVisible(Rectangle r)

> Invokes with parameter r the scrollRectToVisible() method of the parent of this JComponent.

void setActionMap(ActionMap a)

> Uses a as the action mapper of this JComponent.

void setAlignmentX(**float** n)

> Makes n the vertical alignment of this JComponent.

void setAlignmentY(**float** n)

> Makes n the horizontal alignment of this JComponent.

void setAutoscrolls(**boolean** b)

> Uses b to set whether this JComponent autoscrolls.

void setBackground(Color c)

> Sets c as the color of this JComponent.

void setBorder(Border b)

> Sets b as the border of this JComponent.

void setComponentPopupMenu(JPopupMenu j)

> Sets j as the JPopupMenu for this JComponent.

void setDebugGraphicsOptions(**int** i)

> Sets how diagnostics should be displayed regarding this JComponent and its children depending on condition i.

void setDoubleBuffered(**boolean** b)

> Uses b to set whether this JComponent should use a paint buffer.

void setEnabled(**boolean** b)

> Uses b to set whether this JComponent is enabled.

void setFocusTraversalKeys(**int** i, Set s)

> Sets s as the focus traversal keys for condition i for this **JComponent**.

void setFont(Font f)

> Sets f as the font for this JComponent.

void setForeground(Color c)

> Sets c as the foreground color for this JComponent.

void setInheritsPopupMenu(**boolean** b)

> If this JComponent does not have a JPopupMenu then it uses b to indicate whether method getComponentPopupMenu() should use its parent JPopup-Menu.

void setInputMap(**int** i, InputMap m)

Sets m as the input map to use under condition i for this JComponent.

void setInputVerifier(InputVerifier i)

Sets i as the input verifier of this JComponent.

void setMaximumSize(Dimension d)

Sets d as the maximum size of this JComponent.

void setMinimumSize(Dimension d)

Sets d as the minimum size of this JComponent.

void setOpaque(**boolean** b)

Uses b to indicate whether this JComponent paints all its pixels.

void setPreferredSize(Dimension d)

Sets d as the preferred size of this JComponent.

void setRequestFocusEnabled(**boolean** b)

Uses b to hint whether JComponent should get focus.

void setToolTipText(String s)

Sets s as the tool tip text display for this JComponent.

void setTransferHandler(TransferHandler h)

Sets h as the transfer handler policy for this JComponent.

protected void setUI(ComponentUI c)

Sets c as the look and feel delegate for this JComponent.

void setVerifyInputWhenFocusTarget(**boolean** b)

Uses b to set whether the input verifier for the focus owner takes precedence over this JComponent.

void setVisible(**boolean** b)

Uses b to set whether JComponent is to be visible.

void update(Graphics g)

Invokes paint(g) for this JComponent.

void updateUI()

Resets the UI attribute of this object to the current look and feel.

---

swing	**class** JFileChooser **extends** JComponent **implements** Accessible

PURPOSE

Represents a file and folder selection mechanism.

FIELD SUMMARY

static String ACCEPT_ALL_FILE_FILTER_USED_CHANGED_PROPERTY

Indicates a change in the accept all file filter use.

protected AccessibleContext accessibleContext

Represents the accessibility context of this JFileChooser.

static String ACCESSORY_CHANGED_PROPERTY

Indicates the use of a different accessory component.

static String APPROVE_BUTTON_MNEMONIC_CHANGED_PROPERTY

Indicates a change in the approve button tool mnemonic.

static String APPROVE_BUTTON_TEXT_CHANGED_PROPERTY

Indicates a change in the approve button text.

static String APPROVE_BUTTON_TOOL_TIP_TEXT_CHANGED_PROPERTY

Indicates a change in the approve button tool tip text.

static int APPROVE_OPTION

Represents an approval selection.

static String APPROVE_SELECTION

Indicates to approve the selection.

static int CANCEL_OPTION

Represents a cancel selection.

static String CANCEL_SELECTION

Indicates to cancel the selection.

static String CHOOSABLE_FILE_FILTER_CHANGED_PROPERTY

Indicates a change to the predefined file filters.

static String CONTROL_BUTTONS_ARE_SHOWN_CHANGED_PROPERTY

Indicates the display of control buttons.

static int CUSTOM_DIALOG

Indicates that the custom file operation dialog should be used.

static String DIALOG_TITLE_CHANGED_PROPERTY

Indicates a change in the dialog title.

static String DIALOG_TYPE_CHANGED_PROPERTY

Identifies a change in whether files or folders or both should be displayed.

static int DIRECTORIES_ONLY

Indicates the JFileChooser should display only folders.

static String DIRECTORY_CHANGED_PROPERTY

Indicates a change in the current folder.

static int ERROR_OPTION

Represents an error.

static String FILE_FILTER_CHANGED_PROPERTY

Indicates a change in the file filter.

static String FILE_HIDING_CHANGED_PROPERTY

Indicates a change in the display of hidden files.

static String FILE_SELECTION_MODE_CHANGED_PROPERTY

Indicates a change in file selection mode.

static String FILE_SYSTEM_VIEW_CHANGED_PROPERTY

Indicates a change in the detector of available drives.

static String FILE_VIEW_CHANGED_PROPERTY

Indicates a change in the file view.

static int FILES_AND_DIRECTORIES

Indicates the JFileChooser should display both files and folders.

static int FILES_ONLY

Indicates the JFileChooser should display only files.

static String MULTI_SELECTION_ENABLED_CHANGED_PROPERTY

Indicates the JFileChooser supports multiple file selection.

static int OPEN_DIALOG

Indicates the JFileChooser supports a file open operation.

static int SAVE_DIALOG

Indicates the JFileChooser supports a file save operation.

static String SELECTED_FILE_CHANGED_PROPERTY
  Indicates a change in the selected file.
static String SELECTED_FILES_CHANGED_PROPERTY
  Indicates a change in selected files.

CONSTRUCTOR SUMMARY

JFileChooser()
  Constructs a new JFileChooser with the default folder as the current folder.
JFileChooser(File f)
  Constructs a new JFileChooser with file f indicating the current folder.
JFileChooser(File f, FileSystemView v)
  Constructs a new JFileChooser with f as the current folder and v as the file system view.
JFileChooser(FileSystemView v)
  Constructs a new JFileChooser with v as the file system view.
JFileChooser(String s)
  Constructs a new JFileChooser with s indicating the current folder.
JFileChooser(String s, FileSystemView v)
  Constructs a new JFileChooser with s indicating the current folder and v as the file system view.

INSTANCE METHOD SUMMARY

boolean accept(File f)
  Returns whether file f should be displayed by this JFileChooser.
void addActionListener(ActionListener l)
  Adds listener l to the action listeners for this JFileChooser.
void addChoosableFileFilter(FileFilter f)
  Adds filter f to choosable file filters for this JFileChooser.
void approveSelection()
  Initiates an approve selection event for this JFileChooser.
void cancelSelection()
  Initiates a cancel selection event for this JFileChooser.
void changeToParentDirectory()
  Changes the current folder for this JFileChooser to the parent folder of the current folder.
protected JDialog createDialog(Component c)
  Returns a new JDialog for this JFileChooser centered on component c.
void ensureFileIsVisible(File f)
  Sets f as viewable file for this JFileChooser.
protected void fireActionPerformed(String s)
  Invokes all event type s listeners for this JFileChooser.
FileFilter getAcceptAllFileFilter()
  Returns the accept all file filter of this JFileChooser.
AccessibleContext getAccessibleContext()
  Returns the accessibility context of this JFileChooser.
JComponent getAccessory()
  Returns the accessory component of this JFileChooser.
ActionListener[] getActionListeners()
  Returns the action listeners of this JFileChooser.

`int getApproveButtonMnemonic()`

Returns the approve button mnemonic of this `JFileChooser`.

`String getApproveButtonText()`

Returns the approve button of this `JFileChooser`.

`String getApproveButtonToolTipText()`

Returns the approve button tool tip text of this `JFileChooser`.

`FileFilter[] getChoosableFileFilters()`

Returns user choosable file filters of this `JFileChooser`.

`boolean getControlButtonsAreShown()`

Returns whether control buttons are shown by this `JFileChooser`.

`File getCurrentDirectory()`

Returns the current folder of this `JFileChooser`.

`String getDescription(File f)`

Returns the description for f for this `JFileChooser`.

`String getDialogTitle()`

Returns the title of this `JFileChooser`.

`int getDialogType()`

Returns the dialog type of this `JFileChooser`.

`boolean getDragEnabled()`

Returns whether drop and drag is supported by this `JFileChooser`.

`FileFilter getFileFilter()`

Returns the current file filter for this `JFileChooser`.

`int getFileSelectionMode()`

Returns the file selection mode for this `JFileChooser`.

`FileSystemView getFileSystemView()`

Returns the file system view of this `JFileChooser`.

`FileView getFileView()`

Returns the current file view for this `JFileChooser`.

`Icon getIcon(File f)`

Returns the icon for file f for this `JFileChooser`.

`String getName(File f)`

Returns the name of file f for this `JFileChooser`.

`File getSelectedFile()`

Returns the file selected by this `JFileChooser`.

`File[] getSelectedFiles()`

Returns the files selected by this `JFileChooser`.

`String getTypeDescription(File f)`

Returns the type of file f for this `JFileChooser`.

`FileChooserUI getUI()`

Returns the look and feel that renders this component.

`String getUIClassID()`

Returns the name of the look and feel that renders this object.

`boolean isAcceptAllFileFilterUsed()`

Sets whether accept all is a filter choice for this `JFileChooser`.

`boolean isDirectorySelectionEnabled()`

Returns whether directories are selectable with this `JFileChooser`.

boolean isFileHidingEnabled()

Returns whether file hiding is in effect for this JFileChooser.

boolean isFileSelectionEnabled()

Returns whether file selection is enabled for this JFileChooser.

boolean isMultiSelectionEnabled()

Returns whether multiple files can be selected by this JFileChooser.

boolean isTraversable(File f)

Returns whether folder f can be visited by this JFileChooser.

protected String paramString()

Returns a representation of this object.

void removeActionListener(ActionListener l)

Removes l as an action listener for this JFileChooser.

boolean removeChoosableFileFilter(FileFilter f)

Removes f as a possible file filter for this JFileChooser.

void rescanCurrentDirectory()

Causes a refresh of the current directory for this JFileChooser.

void resetChoosableFileFilters()

Resets the choosable file filter list for this JFileChooser.

void setAcceptAllFileFilterUsed(**boolean** b)

Sets using b whether accept all is a filter choice for this JFileChooser.

void setAccessory(JComponent c)

Sets c as the accessory component for this JFileChooser.

void setApproveButtonMnemonic(**char** c)

Sets c as the approve button mnemonic for this JFileChooser.

void setApproveButtonMnemonic(**int** n)

Sets n as the approve button mnemonic for this JFileChooser.

void setApproveButtonText(String s)

Sets s as the text used by the approve button for this JFileChooser.

void setApproveButtonToolTipText(String s)

Sets s as the tool tip text used by the approve button for this JFileChooser.

void setControlButtonsAreShown(**boolean** b)

Sets using b whether this JFileChooser displays approve and cancel control buttons.

void setCurrentDirectory(File d)

Sets d as the current directory for this JFileChooser.

void setDialogTitle(String s)

Sets s as the window title for this JFileChooser.

void setDialogType(**int** n)

Sets n as the dialog type of this JFileChooser.

void setDragEnabled(**boolean** b)

Sets whether this JFileChooser supports drop and drag using b.

void setFileFilter(FileFilter f)

Sets f as the current file filter for this JFileChooser.

void setFileHidingEnabled(**boolean** b)

Sets whether file hiding is in effect for this JFileChooser using b.

void setFileSelectionMode(**int** m)

Sets m as the policy whether a file, folder, or both are selectable with this JFile-Chooser.

void setFileSystemView(FileSystemView f)

Sets f as the file system view used by this JFileChooser.

void setFileView(FileView f)

Sets f as the file view used by this JFileChooser.

void setMultiSelectionEnabled(**boolean** b)

Sets using b whether multiple selection is in effect for this JFileChooser.

void setSelectedFile(File f)

Sets f as the selected file for this JFileChooser.

void setSelectedFiles(File[] f)

Sets f as the selected files for this JFileChooser.

| swing | **class** JFrame **extends** Frame **implements** WindowConstants, Accessible, RootPaneContainer |

PURPOSE

Provides a representation of a window.

FIELD SUMMARY

protected AccessibleContext accessibleContext

Represents the accessibility context of this JFrame.

static int EXIT_ON_CLOSE

Represents the terminate application on window closing policy.

protected JRootPane rootPane

Represents the JRootPane instance that manages the various components of the window (e.g., content pane, border, and title bar).

protected boolean rootPaneCheckingEnabled

Represents whether improper additions or layout management to this JFrame should generate exceptions.

CLASS METHOD SUMMARY

static boolean isDefaultLookAndFeelDecorated()

Returns whether a new JFrame should have its window decorations provided by the current look and feel.

static void setDefaultLookAndFeelDecorated(**boolean** b)

Uses b to set whether a new JFrame should have its window decorations provided by the current look and feel.

CONSTRUCTOR SUMMARY

JFrame()

Constructs a new invisible JFrame.

JFrame(GraphicsConfiguration g)

Constructs a new invisible JFrame for screen device g.

JFrame(String s)

Constructs a new invisible JFrame with title s.

JFrame(String s, GraphicsConfiguration g)

Constructs a new invisible JFrame with title s for screen device g.

INSTANCE METHOD SUMMARY

protected void addImpl(Component c, Object v, **int** i)

Attempts to insert component c as the ith component of this JFrame using constraints v. An exception is thrown if root pane checking is enabled for this JFrame.

protected JRootPane createRootPane()

Creates the default root pane for this JFrame.

protected void frameInit()

Initializes this JFrame.

AccessibleContext getAccessibleContext()

Returns the accessibility context of this object.

Container getContentPane()

Returns the content pane for this JFrame.

int getDefaultCloseOperation()

Returns the operation that occurs when the user closes this JFrame.

Component getGlassPane()

Returns the glass pane for this JFrame.

JMenuBar getJMenuBar()

Returns the menu bar for this JFrame.

JLayeredPane getLayeredPane()

Returns the layered pane for this JFrame.

JRootPane getRootPane()

Returns the root pane for this JFrame.

protected boolean isRootPaneCheckingEnabled()

Returns whether invocations of **add()** and **setLayout()** to this JFrame generate exceptions.

protected String paramString()

Returns a representation of this object.

protected void processWindowEvent(WindowEvent e)

Processes window event e on this JFrame.

void remove(Component c)

Removes the component c from this JFrame.

void setContentPane(Container c)

Sets c as the content pane for this JFrame.

void setDefaultCloseOperation(**int** n)

Sets n as the operation that occurs when the user closes this JFrame.

void setGlassPane(Component c)

Sets c as the glass pane for this JFrame.

void setJMenuBar(JMenuBar m)

Sets m as the menu bar for this JFrame.

void setLayeredPane(JLayeredPane l)

Sets l as the layered pane for this JFrame.

void setLayout(LayoutManager m)

Attempts to set the layout manager of this JFrame to m. An exception is thrown if root pane checking is enabled for this JFrame.

protected void setRootPane(JRootPane r)

    Sets r as the root pane for this JFrame.

protected void setRootPaneCheckingEnabled(**boolean** b)

    Uses b to set whether invocations of add() and setLayout() to this JFrame generate exceptions.

void update(Graphics g)

    Invokes paint(g).

---

swing

class JLabel **extends** JComponent **implements** SwingConstants, Accessible

PURPOSE

Represents a label with text and image. The horizontal alignment policy of the label is controlled by using constants: SwingConstants.LEFT, SwingConstants.CENTER, RIGHT, SwingConstants.LEADING or SwingConstants.TRAILING.

FIELD SUMMARY

protected Component labelFor

    Represents the component being labeled.

CONSTRUCTOR SUMMARY

JLabel()

    Constructs a new JLabel instance with no image or title.

JLabel(Icon i)

    Constructs a new JLabel instance with image i.

JLabel(Icon i, **int** h)

    Constructs a new JLabel instance with image i and horizontal alignment policy h.

JLabel(String s)

    Constructs a new JLabel with text s.

JLabel(String s, Icon i, **int** h)

    Constructs a new JLabel with text s, image i, and horizontal alignment policy h.

JLabel(String s, **int** h)

    Constructs a new JLabel with the text s and horizontal alignment policy h.

INSTANCE METHOD SUMMARY

protected int checkHorizontalKey(**int** n, String s)

    Throws an exception with message s if n is not a horizontal alignment policy.

protected int checkVerticalKey(**int** n, String s)

    Throws an exception with message s if n is not a vertical alignment policy.

AccessibleContext getAccessibleContext()

    Returns the accessibility context of this object.

Icon getDisabledIcon()

    Returns the value of the disabled icon property for this JLabel. If the value had not been previously produced, then the disable icon is computed.

int getDisplayedMnemonic()

    Returns the key code for this JLabel.

`int getDisplayedMnemonicIndex()`

    Returns the index into the label text that the look and feel should use as the mnemonic character for this `JLabel`.

`int getHorizontalAlignment()`

    Returns the horizontal alignment policy for this `JLabel`.

`int getHorizontalTextPosition()`

    Returns the horizontal alignment policy of the text relative to the image for this `JLabel`.

`Icon getIcon()`

    Returns the graphic image of this `JLabel`.

`int getIconTextGap()`

    Returns the number of pixels separating the text and the icon of this `JLabel`.

`Component getLabelFor()`

    Returns the component this `JLabel` is identifying.

`String getText()`

    Returns the text of this `JLabel`.

`LabelUI getUI()`

    Returns the look and feel that renders this component.

`String getUIClassID()`

    Returns the name of the look and feel that renders this object.

`int getVerticalAlignment()`

    Returns the vertical alignment policy for this `JLabel`.

`int getVerticalTextPosition()`

    Returns the vertical alignment policy of the text relative to the image for this `JLabel`.

`boolean imageUpdate(Image i, int n, int x, int y, int w, int h)`

    Returns whether image `i` with width `w` and height `h` using loading parameter `n` has been completely loaded at location (`x`, `y`).

`protected String paramString()`

    Returns a representation of this object.

`void setDisabledIcon(Icon i)`

    Sets the disabled icon to `i` for this `JLabel`.

`void setDisplayedMnemonic(char c)`

    Sets `c` as the mnemonic display character for this `JLabel`.

`void setDisplayedMnemonic(int n)`

    Sets `n` as the key code for this `JLabel`.

`void setDisplayedMnemonicIndex(int n)`

    Indicates `n` should be the character used as the mnemonic for this `JLabel`.

`void setHorizontalAlignment(int h)`

    Sets `h` as the horizontal alignment policy for this `JLabel`.

`void setHorizontalTextPosition(int h)`

    Sets `h` as the horizontal alignment policy of the text relative to the image for this `JLabel`.

`void setIcon(Icon i)`

    Sets `i` as the icon this `JLabel` displays.

`void setIconTextGap(int n)`

    Sets `n` as the number of pixels separating the icon and text for this `JLabel`.

void setLabelFor(Component c)

Sets c as the component this JLabel is identifying.

void setText(String s)

Sets s as the text for this JLabel.

void setUI(LabelUI u)

Sets u as the look and feel for this JLabel.

void setVerticalAlignment(**int** v)

Sets v as the vertical alignment policy for this JLabel.

void setVerticalTextPosition(**int** n)

Sets v as the vertical alignment policy of the text relative to the image for this JLabel.

void updateUI()

Resets the UI attribute of this object to the current look and feel.

| swing | **class** JOptionPane **extends** JComponent **implements** Accessible |

PURPOSE

Represents a standard dialog box.

FIELD SUMMARY

static int CANCEL_OPTION

Represents the user-selected cancel option of the JOptionPane.

static int CLOSED_OPTION

Represents that the user closed the JOptionPane without any selection.

static int DEFAULT_OPTION

Represents an option for a show and confirm dialog.

static int ERROR_MESSAGE

Represents an error message.

protected Icon icon

Represents the icon used in this JOptionPane.

static String ICON_PROPERTY

Represents the bound name for member icon.

static int INFORMATION_MESSAGE

Represents an information message.

static String INITIAL_SELECTION_VALUE_PROPERTY

Represents the bound name for member initialSelectionValue.

static String INITIAL_VALUE_PROPERTY

Represents the bound name for member initialValue.

protected Object initialSelectionValue

Represents the initial selectable value in this JOptionPane.

protected Object initialValue

Represents the initial option in this JOptionPane.

static String INPUT_VALUE_PROPERTY

Represents the bound property name for member inputValue.

protected Object inputValue

Represents the value the user has entered.

protected Object message

> Represents the message to display in this JOptionPane.

static String MESSAGE_PROPERTY

> Represents the bound property name for member message.

static String MESSAGE_TYPE_PROPERTY

> Represents the bound property name for member type.

protected int messageType

> Represents the message type of this JOptionPane.

static int NO_OPTION

> Represents that the user selected no from the JOptionPane.

static int OK_CANCEL_OPTION

> Represents an option for a *showConfirmDialog*.

static int OK_OPTION

> Represents that the user selected ok from the JOptionPane.

static String OPTION_TYPE_PROPERTY

> Represents the bound property name for member optionType.

protected Object[] options

> Represents the list of options displayed by this JOptionPane.

static String OPTIONS_PROPERTY

> Represents the bound property name for member option.

protected int optionType

> Represents the option type of this JOptionPane. The legal values are OK_CANCEL_OPTION, YES_NO_OPTION, YES_NO_CANCEL_OPTION, and DEFAULT_OPTION.

static int PLAIN_MESSAGE

> Represents a message with no icon.

static int QUESTION_MESSAGE

> Represents a question message.

static String SELECTION_VALUES_PROPERTY

> Represents the bound property name for member selectionValues.

protected Object[] selectionValues

> Represents the values from which the user can choose in this JOptionPane.

static Object UNINITIALIZED_VALUE

> Represents that the user has not yet selected a value.

protected Object value

> Represents the currently selected value of this JOptionPane.

static String VALUE_PROPERTY

> Represents the bound property name for member value.

static String WANTS_INPUT_PROPERTY

> Represents the bound property name for member wantsInput.

protected boolean wantsInput

> Represents whether an input-providing component is provided in this JOption-Pane.

static int WARNING_MESSAGE

> Represents a warning message.

static int YES_NO_CANCEL_OPTION

> Represents an option for a *showConfirmDialog*.

`static int YES_NO_OPTION`

Represents an option for a *showConfirmDialog*.

`static int YES_OPTION`

Represents that the user selected yes from the `JOptionPane`.

CLASS METHOD SUMMARY

`static Frame getRootFrame()`

Returns the frame used by `JOptionPane` class methods that do not supply their own frame.

`static JDesktopPane getDesktopPaneForComponent(Component c)`

Returns the desktop pane for parent component `c` of this `JOptionPane`.

`static Frame getFrameForComponent(Component c)`

Returns the frame for parent component `c` of this `JOptionPane`.

`static void setRootFrame(Frame f)`

Makes `f` the frame used by `JOptionPane` class methods that do not supply their own frame.

`static int showConfirmDialog(Component p, Object m)`

Displays a confirmation dialog with message `m` within frame `p`. The return value is the selection option.

`static int showConfirmDialog(Component p, Object m, String s, int n)`

Displays a confirmation dialog of option type `n1` with message `m` and title `s` within frame `p`. The return value is the selection option.

`static int showConfirmDialog(Component p, Object m, String s, int n1, int n2)`

Displays a confirmation dialog of message type `n2`, option type `n1` with title `s`, message `m`, in the frame of parent component `p`. The return value is the selection option.

`static int showConfirmDialog(Component p, Object m, String s, int n1, int n2, Icon i)`

Displays a dialog of message type `n2`, option type `n1` with title `s`, message `m`, in the frame of parent component `p`. Brings up a dialog where the number of choices is determined by the `optionType` parameter. The return value is the selection option.

`static String showInputDialog(Object m)`

Displays a question dialog with message `m`. The return value is the user input.

`static String showInputDialog(Component p, Object m)`

Displays a question dialog with message `m` within frame `p`. The return value is the user input.

`static String showInputDialog(Component p, Object m, String s, int n1)`

Displays a dialog of message type `n1` with message `m` within frame `p`. The return value is the user input.

`static Object showInputDialog(Component p, Object m, String s, int n1, Icon i, Object[] a, Object v)`

Displays a blocking dialog of message type `n1` with message `m` and icon `i` within frame `p`. The list of possible selection values is list `a`; and the initial selection is `v`. The return value is the user selection.

static int showInternalConfirmDialog(Component p, Object m)

Displays an internal dialog panel with default options and title with message m within frame p. The return value is the selection option.

static int showInternalConfirmDialog(Component p, Object m,
  String s, **int** n1)

Displays an internal dialog panel with title s and options determined by option type n1 with message m within frame p. The return value is the selection option.

static int showInternalConfirmDialog(Component p, Object m,
  String s, **int** n1, **int** n2)

Displays an internal dialog panel of message type n2, option type n1 with title s, message m, in the frame of parent component p. The return value is the selection option.

static int showInternalConfirmDialog(Component p, Object m,
  String s, **int** n', **int** n2, Icon i)

Displays an internal dialog panel using icon i of message type n2, option type n1 with title s, message m, in the frame of parent component p. The return value is the selection option.

static String showInternalInputDialog(Component p, Object m)

Displays an internal question dialog with message m within frame p. The return value is the user input.

static String showInternalInputDialog(Component p, Object m,
  String s, **int** n1)

Displays an internal dialog of message type n1 with message m within frame p. The return value is the user input.

static Object showInternalInputDialog(Component p, Object m,
  String s, **int** n1, Icon i, Object[] a, Object v)

Displays a blocking internal dialog of message type n1 with message m and icon i within frame p. The list of possible selection values is list a; and the initial selection is v. The return value is the user selection.

static void showInternalMessageDialog(Component p, Object m)

Displays an internal confirmation dialog panel with message m within frame p.

static void showInternalMessageDialog(Component p, Object m,
  String s, **int** n1)

Displays an internal confirmation dialog panel of message type n1 with message m within frame p. The return value is the user input.

static void showInternalMessageDialog(Component p, Object m,
  String s, **int** n1, Icon i)

Displays an internal confirmation dialog panel using icon i of message type n1 with message m within frame p. The return value is the user input.

static int showInternalOptionDialog(Component p, Object m,
  String s, **int** n1, **int** n2, Icon i, Object[] a, Object v)

Displays an internal dialog panel using icon i of message type n2, option type n1 with title s, message m, in the frame of parent component p. The return value is the selection option. The list of possible selection values is list a; and the initial selection is v. The return value is the user selection.

static void showMessageDialog(Component p, Object m)

Displays an information message dialog with message m within frame p.

```
static void showMessageDialog(Component p, Object m, String s,
    int n1)
```

Displays a message dialog of message type n1 with message m and title s within frame p.

```
static void showMessageDialog(Component p, Object m, String s,
    int n1, Icon i)
```

Displays a message dialog using icon i of message type n1 with message m and title s within frame p.

```
static int showOptionDialog(Component p, Object m, String s,
    int n1, int n2, Icon i, Object[] a, Object v)
```

Displays an option dialog using icon i of message type n2, option type n1 with title s, message m, in the frame of parent component p. The return value is the selection option. The list of possible selection values is list a; and the initial selection is v. The return value is the user selection.

CONSTRUCTOR SUMMARY

```
JOptionPane()
```

Constructs a new JOptionPane with a test message.

```
JOptionPane(Object v)
```

Constructs a new plain-message JOptionPane that displays message v.

```
JOptionPane(Object v, int n)
```

Constructs a new JOptionPane of message type n that displays message v.

```
JOptionPane(Object v, int n1, int n2)
```

Constructs a new JOptionPane of message type n1 using option type n2 that displays message v.

```
JOptionPane(Object v, int n1, int n2, Icon i)
```

Constructs a new JOptionPane of message type n1 using option type n2 that displays message v and icon i.

```
JOptionPane(Object v, int n1, int n2, Icon i, Object[] a)
```

Constructs a new JOptionPane of message type n1 using option type n2 that displays message v, icon i, and options a.

```
JOptionPane(Object v, int n1, int n2, Icon i, Object[] a, Object
    j)
```

Constructs a new JOptionPane of message type n1 using option type n2 that displays message v, icon i, and options a with initially selected option j.

INSTANCE METHOD SUMMARY

```
JDialog createDialog(Component p, String s)
```

Returns a new JDialog with title s centering this JOptionPane on parent component p.

```
JInternalFrame createInternalFrame(Component c, String s)
```

Returns a new JInternalFrame with title s centering this JOptionPane on parent component c.

```
AccessibleContext getAccessibleContext()
```

Returns the accessibility context of this object.

```
Icon getIcon()
```

Returns the icon of this JOptionPane.

`Object getInitialSelectionValue()`

Returns the initial selected input value that is displayed to the user of this `JOptionPane`.

`Object getInitialValue()`

Returns the initial value of this `JOptionPane`.

`Object getInputValue()`

Returns the value the user has input in this `JOptionPane`.

`int getMaxCharactersPerLineCount()`

Returns the maximum number of characters per message line in this `JOptionPane`.

`Object getMessage()`

Returns the message displayed by this `JOptionPane`.

`int getMessageType()`

Returns the message type of this `JOptionPane`.

`Object[] getOptions()`

Returns the choices of this `JOptionPane`.

`int getOptionType()`

Returns the type of options of this `JOptionPane`.

`Object[] getSelectionValues()`

Returns the input selection values of this `JOptionPane`.

`OptionPaneUI getUI()`

Returns the look and feel that renders this component.

`String getUIClassID()`

Returns the name of the look and feel that renders this object.

`Object getValue()`

Returns the value the user has selected in this `JOptionPane`.

`boolean` `getWantsInput()`

Returns the value of the `wantsInput` property of this `JOptionPane`.

`protected` `String paramString()`

Returns a representation of this object.

`void selectInitialValue()`

Sets and gives focus to the initial value of this `JOptionPane`.

`void setIcon(Icon i)`

Sets `i` as the icon for this `JOptionPane`.

`void setInitialSelectionValue(Object v)`

Sets `v` as the initially selected input value of this `JOptionPane`.

`void setInitialValue(Object v)`

Sets `v` as the initial input value of this `JOptionPane`.

`void setInputValue(Object v)`

Sets `v` as the input value of this `JOptionPane`.

`void setMessage(Object m)`

Sets `m` as the message of the option pane of this `JOptionPane`.

`void setMessageType(int n)`

Sets `n` as the message type for this `JOptionPane`.

`void setOptions(Object[] a)`

Sets `a` as the options array for this `JOptionPane`.

```
void setOptionType(int n)
```
Sets n as the option type for this JOptionPane.
```
void setSelectionValues(Object[] a)
```
Sets a as the input selection values array for this JOptionPane.
```
void setUI(PanelUI u)
```
Sets u as the look and feel provider for this JOptionPane.
```
void setValue(Object v)
```
Sets v as the chosen value for this JOptionPane.
```
void setWantsInput(boolean b)
```
Sets b as the wants input policy of this JOptionPane.
```
void updateUI()
```
Resets the UI attribute of this object to the current look and feel.

---

swing   **class** JPanel **extends** JComponent **implements** Accessible

PURPOSE

Represents a container.

CONSTRUCTOR SUMMARY
```
JPanel()
```
Constructs a new JPanel with double buffering and flow layout.
```
JPanel(boolean b)
```
Constructs a new JPanel with flow layout. Double buffering depends on b.
```
JPanel(LayoutManager l)
```
Constructs a new JPanel with double buffering and with layout manager l.
```
JPanel(LayoutManager l, boolean b)
```
Constructs a new JPanel with layout manager l. Double buffering depends on b.

INSTANCE METHOD SUMMARY
```
AccessibleContext getAccessibleContext()
```
Returns the accessibility context of this object.
```
PanelUI getUI()
```
Returns the look and feel that renders this component.
```
String getUIClassID()
```
Returns the name of the look and feel that renders this object.
```
protected String paramString()
```
Returns a representation of this object.
```
void setUI(PanelUI u)
```
Sets u as the look and feel provider for this JPanel.
```
void updateUI()
```
Resets the UI attribute of this object to the current look and feel.
```
protected void configurePropertiesFromAction(Action a)
```
Sets a as the action properties of this JPanel.

swing	class JRadioButton extends JToggleButton implements Accessible

PURPOSE

Represents a radio button.

CONSTRUCTOR SUMMARY

JRadioButton()

Constructs an new unset JRadioButton with no text or image.

JRadioButton(Action a)

Constructs a new unset JRadioButton. The settings of the button depend on a.

JRadioButton(Icon i)

Constructs a new unset JRadioButton with no text but image i.

JRadioButton(Icon i, **boolean** b)

Constructs a new JRadioButton with no text and image i. The setting of the button depends on b.

JRadioButton(String s)

Constructs a new unset JRadioButton with text s and no image.

JRadioButton(String s, **boolean** b)

Constructs a new JRadioButton with text s and no image. The setting of the button depends on b.

JRadioButton(String s, Icon i)

Constructs a new unset JRadioButton with text s and image i.

JRadioButton(String s, Icon i, **boolean** b)

Constructs a new JRadioButton with text s and image i. The setting of the button depends on b.

INSTANCE METHOD SUMMARY

protected void configurePropertiesFromAction(Action a)

Sets a as the action properties for this JRadioButton.

protected PropertyChangeListener
  createActionPropertyChangeListener(Action a)

Creates and returns the property change listener that updates the ActionEvent source as action properties change for this JRadioButton.

AccessibleContext getAccessibleContext()

Returns the accessibility context of this object.

String getUIClassID()

Returns the name of the look and feel that renders this object.

protected String paramString()

Returns a representation of this object.

void updateUI()

Resets the UI attribute of this object to the current look and feel.

| swing | **class** JScrollPane **extends** JComponent **implements** Accessible, ScrollPaneConstants |

PURPOSE

Represents a scrollable view of a component.

FIELD SUMMARY

protected JViewport columnHeader

Represents the column header of this JScrollPane.

protected JScrollBar horizontalScrollBar

Represents the horizontal scroll bar of this JScrollPane.

protected int horizontalScrollBarPolicy

Represents the horizontal scroll bar display policy of this JScrollPane.

protected Component lowerLeft

Represents the component to display in the lower-left corner of this JScroll-Pane.

protected Component lowerRight

Represents the component to display in the lower-right corner of this JScroll-Pane.

protected JViewport rowHeader

Represents the row header of this JScrollPane.

protected Component upperLeft

Represents the component to display in the upper-left corner of this JScroll-Pane.

protected Component upperRight

Represents the component to display in the upper-right corner of this JScroll-Pane.

protected JScrollBar verticalScrollBar

Represents the vertical scroll bar of this JScrollPane.

protected int verticalScrollBarPolicy

Represents the vertical scroll bar display policy of this JScrollPane.

protected JViewport viewport

Represents the viewport of this JScrollPane.

CONSTRUCTOR SUMMARY

JScrollPane()

Constructs a new empty JScrollPane in a viewport with default horizontal and vertical scroll bar policies.

JScrollPane(Component c)

Constructs a new JScrollPane displaying component c in a viewport with default horizontal and vertical scroll bar policies.

JScrollPane(Component c, **int** v, **int** h)

Constructs a new JScrollPane displaying component c in a viewport with horizontal and vertical scroll bar policies specified respectively by v and h.

JScrollPane(**int** v, **int** h)

Constructs a new empty JScrollPane with horizontal and vertical scroll bar policies specified respectively by v and h.

INSTANCE METHOD SUMMARY

`JScrollBar createHorizontalScrollBar()`

If this `JScrollPane` does not have a horizontal scroll bar, then one is created. Returns the horizontal scroll bar of this `JScrollPane`.

`JScrollBar createVerticalScrollBar()`

If this `JScrollPane` does not have a vertical scroll bar, then one is created. Returns the vertical scroll bar of this `JScrollPane`.

protected `JViewport createViewport()`

If this `JScrollPane` does not have a viewport, then one is created. Returns the viewport of this `JScrollPane`.

`AccessibleContext getAccessibleContext()`

Returns the accessibility context of this object.

`JViewport getColumnHeader()`

Returns the column header viewport of this `JScrollPane`.

`Component getCorner(String s)`

Returns the component at the corner `s` of this `JScrollPane`.

`JScrollBar getHorizontalScrollBar()`

Returns the vertical scroll bar of this `JScrollPane`.

int `getHorizontalScrollBarPolicy()`

Returns the horizontal scroll bar policy of this `JScrollPane`.

`JViewport getRowHeader()`

Returns the row header viewport of this `JScrollPane`.

`ScrollPaneUI getUI()`

Returns the look and feel that renders this component.

`String getUIClassID()`

Returns the name of the look and feel that renders this object.

`JScrollBar getVerticalScrollBar()`

Returns the vertical scroll bar of this `JScrollPane`.

int `getVerticalScrollBarPolicy()`

Returns the vertical scroll bar policy of this `JScrollPane`.

`JViewport getViewport()`

Returns the viewport of this `JScrollPane`.

`Border getViewportBorder()`

Returns the border that surrounds the viewport of this `JScrollPane`.

`Rectangle getViewportBorderBounds()`

Returns the bounds of the viewport border for this `JScrollPane`.

boolean `isValidateRoot()`

Invokes method `revalidate()` on any descendant of this `JScrollPane`.

boolean `isWheelScrollingEnabled()`

Returns whether scrolling take place in response to mouse wheel movement in this `JScrollPane`.

protected `String paramString()`

Returns a representation of this object.

void `setColumnHeader(JViewport c)`

Makes `c` the column header for this `JScrollPane`.

void setColumnHeaderView(Component c)

> If this JScrollPane does not have a column header viewport, then one is created. The view of this viewport for this JScrollPane is set to c.

void setComponentOrientation(ComponentOrientation c)

> Sets c as the vertical and horizontal scroll bar orientation for this JScrollPane.

void setCorner(String s, Component c)

> Sets c as the component that should appear in a scroll pane corner s of this JScrollPane when there is sufficient room.

void setHorizontalScrollBar(JScrollBar h)

> Sets v as the horizontal scroll bar for the viewport of this JScrollPane.

void setHorizontalScrollBarPolicy(int p)

> Sets p as the horizontal scroll bar appearance policy for this JScrollPane.

void setLayout(LayoutManager l)

> Sets l as the layout manager for this JScrollPane.

void setRowHeader(JViewport r)

> Sets r as the row header for this JScrollPane.

void setRowHeaderView(Component c)

> If this JScrollPane does not have a row header viewport, then one is created. The view of this viewport for this JScrollPane is set to c.

void setUI(ScrollPaneUI u)

> Sets u as the look and feel provider for this JScrollPane.

void setVerticalScrollBar(JScrollBar v)

> Sets v as the vertical scroll bar for the viewport of this JScrollPane.

void setVerticalScrollBarPolicy(int i)

> Sets i as the vertical scroll bar appearance policy of this JScrollPane.

void setViewport(JViewport v)

> Sets v as the viewport of this JScrollPane.

void setViewportBorder(Border b)

> Adds a border b around the viewport of this JScrollPane.

void setViewportView(Component c)

> If this JScrollPane does not have a viewport, then one is created. The view of the viewport for this JScrollPane is set to c.

void setWheelScrollingEnabled(**boolean** b)

> Sets whether scrolling should occur in response to mouse wheel movement in this JScrollPane.

void updateUI()

> Resets the UI attribute of this object to the current look and feel.

`swing`   class JTextArea **extends** JTextComponent

PURPOSE

Represents a multiline text area.

CONSTRUCTOR SUMMARY

JTextArea()

> Constructs a new JTextArea with zero rows and columns using a default document model.

JTextArea(Document d)

> Constructs a new empty JTextArea using zero rows and columns and document model d.

JTextArea(Document d, String s, int r, int c)

> Constructs a new JTextArea with text s using r rows, c columns, and document model d.

JTextArea(int r, int c)

> Constructs a new empty JTextArea using r rows, c columns, and a default document model.

JTextArea(String s)

> Constructs a new JTextArea with text s using zero rows and columns and a default document model.

JTextArea(String s, int r, int c)

> Constructs a new JTextArea with text s using r rows, c columns, and a default document model.

INSTANCE METHOD SUMMARY

void append(String s)

> Appends text s to the end of the document in this JTextArea.

protected Document createDefaultModel()

> Returns and creates (if necessary) the default document model for this JText-Area.

AccessibleContext getAccessibleContext()

> Returns the accessibility context of this object.

int getColumns()

> Returns the number of columns in this JTextArea.

protected int getColumnWidth()

> Returns column width of this JTextArea.

int getLineCount()

> Returns the number of lines contained in this JTextArea.

int getLineEndOffset(int n)

> Returns the offset of the end of the line n in this JTextArea.

int getLineOfOffset(int n)

> Returns the line whose text contains offset n into this JTextArea.

int getLineStartOffset(int n)

> Returns the offset of the start of the line n in this JTextArea.

boolean getLineWrap()

> Returns the line wrapping policy of this JTextArea.

Dimension getPreferredScrollableViewportSize()

> Returns the preferred size of a viewport for this JTextArea.

Dimension getPreferredSize()

> Returns the preferred size of this JTextArea.

protected int getRowHeight()

> Returns the height of a row for this JTextArea.

`int` getRows()

> Returns the number of rows in this JTextArea.

`boolean` getScrollableTracksViewportWidth()

> Returns whether a viewport should force the width of this JTextArea to match the width of the viewport.

`int` getScrollableUnitIncrement(Rectangle r, `int` n, `int` d)

> Returns the increment for unit scrolling in this JTextArea in the direction indicated by n and d. If n is SwingConstant.VERTICAL, the orientation is vertical, and if n is SwingConstant.HORIZONTAL, the orientation is horizontal. Depending on the orientation, the direction is either left or up if d is negative and it is either right or down if d is positive. For the purpose of the calculation, the size of the viewable area is r.

`int` getTabSize()

> Returns the number of characters in a tab expansion in this JTextArea.

`String` getUIClassID()

> Returns the name of the look and feel that renders this object.

`boolean` getWrapStyleWord()

> Returns whether word wrapping is used by this JTextArea.

`void` insert(String s, `int` i)

> Inserts text s starting at position i of this JTextArea.

`protected` String paramString()

> Returns a representation of this object.

`void` replaceRange(String s, `int` n1, `int` n2)

> Replaces with s the text at positions n1 … n2 of this JTextArea.

`void` setColumns(`int` c)

> Sets c as the number of columns for this JTextArea.

`void` setFont(Font f)

> Sets f as the font for this JTextArea.

`void` setLineWrap(`boolean` b)

> Sets using b whether this JTextArea performs line wrapping.

`void` setRows(`int` r)

> Sets r as the number of rows for this JTextArea.

`void` setTabSize(`int` n)

> Sets n as the number of characters to which tabs expand in this JTextArea.

`void` setWrapStyleWord(`boolean` b)

> Sets using b whether this JTextArea performs word wrapping.

---

swing

`class` JTextField `extends` JTextComponent `implements` SwingConstants

PURPOSE

Represents an editable line of text.

FIELD SUMMARY

`static` `String` `notifyAction`

Represents the action (i.e., carriage return) causing notification that the contents of the field have been accepted.

CONSTRUCTOR SUMMARY

`JTextField()`

Constructs a new empty `JTextField`.

`JTextField(Document d, String s, int n)`

Constructs a new `JTextField` composed of text s using n columns using text model d.

`JTextField(int n)`

Constructs a new empty `JTextField` composed of n columns.

`JTextField(String s)`

Constructs a new `JTextField` composed of text s with a default number of columns.

`JTextField(String s, int n)`

Constructs a new `JTextField` composed of text s using n columns.

INSTANCE METHOD SUMMARY

`void` `addActionListener(ActionListener l)`

Makes listener l one of the action listeners of this `JTextField`.

`protected` `void` `configurePropertiesFromAction(Action a)`

Sets a as the action event properties for this `JTextField`.

`protected` `PropertyChangeListener`
`createActionPropertyChangeListener(Action a)`

Creates and returns the property change listener that updates the `ActionEvent` source as action properties change for this `JTextField`.

`protected` `Document` `createDefaultModel()`

Creates (if necessary) and returns the default document model for this `JText-Field`.

`protected` `void` `fireActionPerformed()`

Invokes the `actionPerformed()` method of all listeners of this `JTextField`.

`AccessibleContext` `getAccessibleContext()`

Returns the accessibility context of this object.

`Action` `getAction()`

Returns the currently set action for the `ActionEvent` source for this `JText-Field`.

`ActionListener[]` `getActionListeners()`

Returns the action listeners of this `JTextField`.

`Action[]` `getActions()`

Returns the command list for the editor of this `JTextField`.

`int` `getColumns()`

Returns the number of columns in this `JTextField`.

`protected` `int` `getColumnWidth()`

Returns the column width of this `JTextField`.

`int` `getHorizontalAlignment()`

Returns the horizontal alignment policy of this `JTextField`.

BoundedRangeModel getHorizontalVisibility()

Returns the visibility of this JTextField.

Dimension getPreferredSize()

Returns the preferred size of this JTextField.

int getScrollOffset()

Returns the pixel scroll offset of this JTextField.

String getUIClassID()

Returns the name of the look and feel that renders this object.

boolean isValidateRoot()

If this JTextField is within a JViewport, the method returns **false**; otherwise, the method returns **true**.

protected String paramString()

Returns a representation of this object.

void postActionEvent()

Invokes the action listeners of this JTextField.

void removeActionListener(ActionListener l)

Removes listener l as an action listener of this JTextField.

void scrollRectToVisible(Rectangle r)

Scrolls rectangular region r of this JTextField.

void setAction(Action a)

Sets a as the action for the ActionEvent source of this JTextField.

void setActionCommand(String s)

Sets s as the action command string for this JTextField.

void setColumns(int c)

Sets c as the number of columns in this JTextField.

void setDocument(Document d)

Sets d as the document editor for this JTextField.

void setFont(Font f)

Sets f as the current font for this JTextField.

void setHorizontalAlignment(int i)

Sets h as the horizontal alignment policy for this JTextField.

void setScrollOffset(int i)

Sets i as the scroll pixel offset of this JTextField.

---

swing   **class** JTextPane **extends** JEditorPane

PURPOSE

Represents a text component that can be marked up graphically.

CONSTRUCTOR SUMMARY

JTextPane()

Constructs a new JTextPane of default document style.

JTextPane(StyledDocument s)

Constructs a new JTextPane of document type s.

INSTANCE METHOD SUMMARY

Style addStyle(String s, Style p)

Adds style s into the document hierarchy of this JTextPane with p as its parent.

protected EditorKit createDefaultEditorKit()

Creates and returns the default editor kit of this JTextPane.

AttributeSet getCharacterAttributes()

Returns the character attributes in effect at the current location of the caret in this JTextPane.

MutableAttributeSet getInputAttributes()

Returns the input attributes of this JTextPane.

Style getLogicalStyle()

Returns the style in effect at the current caret position of this JTextPane.

AttributeSet getParagraphAttributes()

Returns the attributes in effect at the current caret position of this JTextPane.

Style getStyle(String s)

Returns the style with name s for this JTextPane.

StyledDocument getStyledDocument()

Returns the editor model of this JTextPane.

protected StyledEditorKit getStyledEditorKit()

Returns the editor kit for this JTextPane.

String getUIClassID()

Returns the class ID for the UI for this JTextPane.

void insertComponent(Component c)

Replaces the currently selected content with component c in this JTextPane.

void insertIcon(Icon i)

Replaces the currently selected content with icon i in this JTextPane.

protected String paramString()

Returns a representation of this object.

void removeStyle(String s)

Removes the style with name s for this JTextPane.

void replaceSelection(String s)

Replaces the currently selected content with s in this JTextPane.

void setCharacterAttributes(AttributeSet a, **boolean** b)

Applies attribute set a to the currently selected text. If b is **true**, then existing attributes are reset first.

void setDocument(Document d)

Sets d as the document editor of this JTextPane.

void setEditorKit(EditorKit e)

Sets e as the editor kit for this JTextPane.

void setLogicalStyle(Style s)

Sets s as the logical style at the current caret position for this JTextPane.

void setParagraphAttributes(AttributeSet a, **boolean** b)

Applies attribute set a to the currently selected paragraphs. If b is **true**, then existing attributes are reset first.

void setStyledDocument(StyledDocument d)

Sets d as the document editor of this JTextPane.

`swing`   **class** JToggleButton **extends** AbstractButton **implements** Accessible

PURPOSE

Represents a two-state button whose label can consist of text and an image.

CONSTRUCTOR SUMMARY

    JToggleButton()

        Constructs a new unset JToggleButton with no text or image.

    JToggleButton(Action a)

        Constructs a new unset JToggleButton. The settings of the button depend on
        a.

    JToggleButton(Icon i)

        Constructs a new unset JToggleButton with no text but image i.

    JToggleButton(Icon i, **boolean** b)

        Constructs a new JToggleButton with no text and image i. The setting of the
        button depends on b.

    JToggleButton(String s)

        Constructs a new unset JToggleButton with text s and no image.

    JToggleButton(String s, **boolean** b)

        Constructs a new JToggleButton with text s and no image. The setting of the
        button depends on b.

    JToggleButton(String s, Icon i)

        Constructs a new unset JToggleButton with text s and image i.

    JToggleButton(String s, Icon i, **boolean** b)

        Constructs a new JToggleButton with text s and image i. The setting of the
        button depends on b

INSTANCE METHOD SUMMARY

    AccessibleContext getAccessibleContext()

        Returns the accessibility context of this object.

    String getUIClassID()

        Returns the name of the look and feel that renders this object.

    protected String paramString()

        Returns a representation of this object.

    void updateUI()

        Resets the UI attribute of this object to the current look and feel.

`awt.event`   **abstract class** KeyAdapter **implements** KeyListener

PURPOSE

A convenience class for handling keyboard events. Its methods perform no actions. A
specialized class overrides them as needed.

CONSTRUCTOR SUMMARY

    KeyAdapter()

Constructs a new KeyAdapter.

INSTANCE METHOD SUMMARY
INSTANCE METHOD SUMMARY

    `void keyPressed(KeyEvent e)`

        Ignores a key pressing event.

    `void keyReleased(KeyEvent e)`

        Ignores a key release event.

    `void keyTyped(KeyEvent e)`

        Ignores a key typing event.

`awt.event`   **class** `KeyEvent` **implements** `InputEvent`

PURPOSE

Represents a keystroke event.

FIELD SUMMARY

    `static char CHAR_UNDEFINED`

        Represents key events whose key character is not a Unicode character.

    `static int KEY_FIRST`

        Represents the minimal index of a key event type.

    `static int KEY_LAST`

        Represents the maximal index of a key event type.

    `static int KEY_LOCATION_LEFT`

        Represents that the key character for a key event is left-positioned.

    `static int KEY_LOCATION_NUMPAD`

        Represents that the key character for a key event is part of the numerical keypad.

    `static int KEY_LOCATION_RIGHT`

        Represents that the key character for a key event is right-positioned.

    `static int KEY_LOCATION_STANDARD`

        Represents that the key character for a key event is neither a left nor a right distinguishing key character nor a numeric pay key character.

    `static int KEY_LOCATION_UNKNOWN`

        Represents that the key character for a key event is of unknown position.

    `static int KEY_PRESSED`

        Represents a key pressing event.

    `static int KEY_RELEASED`

        Represents a key released event.

    `static int KEY_TYPED`

        Represents a key typed event.

    `static int VK_UNDEFINED`

        Represents that the key code is unknown.

The following class constants are identified with keys with the indicated names. Not all keys are available on all keyboards.

`VK_0`	`VK_1`
`VK_2`	`VK_3`
`VK_4`	`VK_5`
`VK_6`	`VK_7`
`VK_8`	`VK_9`
`VK_A`	`VK_ACCEPT`

VK_ADD
VK_ALL_CANDIDATES
VK_ALT
VK_AMPERSAND
VK_AT
VK_BACK_QUOTE
VK_BACK_SPACE
VK_BRACERIGHT
VK_CANCEL
VK_CIRCUMFLEX
VK_CLOSE_BRACKET
VK_COLON
VK_COMPOSE
VK_CONVERT
VK_CUT
VK_DEAD_ABOVEDOT
VK_DEAD_ACUTE
VK_DEAD_CARON
VK_DEAD_CIRCUMFLEX
VK_DEAD_DOUBLEACUTE
VK_DEAD_IOTA
VK_DEAD_OGONEK
VK_DEAD_TILDE
VK_DECIMAL
VK_DIVIDE
VK_DOWN
VK_END
VK_EQUALS
VK_EURO_SIGN
VK_F
VK_F10
VK_F12
VK_F14
VK_F16
VK_F18
VK_F2
VK_F21
VK_F23
VK_F3
VK_F5
VK_F7
VK_F9
VK_FIND
VK_G
VK_H
VK_HELP
VK_HOME
VK_INPUT_METHOD_ON_OFF
VK_INVERTED_EXCLAMATION_MARK
VK_JAPANESE_HIRAGANA
VK_JAPANESE_ROMAN
VK_KANA
VK_KANJI
VK_KP_DOWN
VK_KP_RIGHT
VK_L
VK_LEFT_PARENTHESIS
VK_M
VK_MINUS
VK_MULTIPLY
VK_NONCONVERT
VK_NUMBER_SIGN
VK_NUMPAD1

VK_AGAIN
VK_ALPHANUMERIC
VK_ALT_GRAPH
VK_ASTERISK
VK_B
VK_BACK_SLASH
VK_BRACELEFT
VK_C
VK_CAPS_LOCK
VK_CLEAR
VK_CODE_INPUT
VK_COMMA
VK_CONTROL
VK_COPY
VK_D
VK_DEAD_ABOVERING
VK_DEAD_BREVE
VK_DEAD_CEDILLA
VK_DEAD_DIAERESIS
VK_DEAD_GRAVE
VK_DEAD_MACRON
VK_DEAD_SEMIVOICED_SOUND
VK_DEAD_VOICED_SOUND
VK_DELETE
VK_DOLLAR
VK_E
VK_ENTER
VK_ESCAPE
VK_EXCLAMATION_MARK
VK_F1
VK_F11
VK_F13
VK_F15
VK_F17
VK_F19
VK_F20
VK_F22
VK_F24
VK_F4
VK_F6
VK_F8
VK_FINAL
VK_FULL_WIDTH
VK_GREATER
VK_HALF_WIDTH
VK_HIRAGANA
VK_I
VK_INSERT
VK_J
VK_JAPANESE_KATAKANA
VK_K
VK_KANA_LOCK
VK_KATAKANA
VK_KP_LEFT
VK_KP_UP
VK_LEFT
VK_LESS
VK_META
VK_MODECHANGE
VK_N
VK_NUM_LOCK
VK_NUMPAD0
VK_NUMPAD2

VK_NUMPAD3	VK_NUMPAD4
VK_NUMPAD5	VK_NUMPAD6
VK_NUMPAD7	VK_NUMPAD8
VK_NUMPAD9	VK_O
VK_OPEN_BRACKET	VK_P
VK_PAGE_DOWN	VK_PAGE_UP
VK_PASTE	VK_PAUSE
VK_PERIOD	VK_PLUS
VK_PREVIOUS_CANDIDATE	VK_PRINTSCREEN
VK_PROPS	VK_Q
VK_QUOTE	VK_QUOTEDBL
VK_R	VK_RIGHT
VK_RIGHT_PARENTHESIS	VK_ROMAN_CHARACTERS
VK_S	VK_SCROLL_LOCK
VK_SEMICOLON	VK_SEPARATOR
VK_SHIFT	VK_SLASH
VK_SPACE	VK_STOP
VK_SUBTRACT	VK_T
VK_TAB	VK_U
VK_UNDERSCORE	VK_UNDO
VK_UP	VK_V
VK_W	VK_X
VK_Y	VK_Z

CLASS METHOD SUMMARY

static String getKeyModifiersText(**int** m)

Returns a representation of key modifier m.

static String getKeyText(**int** n)

Returns a representation of key code n.

CONSTRUCTOR SUMMARY

KeyEvent(Component v, **int** n, **long** t, **int** m, **int** k, **char** c)

Constructs a new KeyEvent of type n occurring at time t in component v using key modifiers m, where k is key code of the typed character and c is its Unicode encoding.

KeyEvent(Component v, **int** n, **long** t, **int** m, **int** k, **char** c, **int** l)

Constructs a new KeyEvent of type n occurring at time t in component v using key modifiers m, where k is key code of the typed character, c is its Unicode encoding, and l is its location.

INSTANCE METHOD SUMMARY

char getKeyChar()

Returns the character associated with this KeyEvent.

int getKeyCode()

Returns the key code of this KeyEvent.

int getKeyLocation()

Returns the location of the key associated with this KeyEvent.

boolean isActionKey()

Returns whether the key of this KeyEvent is an action key.

String paramString()

Returns a representation of this KeyEvent.

void setKeyChar(**char** c)

Sets c as the character associated with this KeyEvent.

void setKeyCode(**int** n)

Sets n as the key code of this KeyEvent.

awt.event
> **interface** KeyListener **implements** EventListener

PURPOSE

Describes the methods a key listener must perform.

INSTANCE METHOD SUMMARY

void keyPressed(KeyEvent e)

> Handles a key pressing event.

void keyReleased(KeyEvent e)

> Handles a key released event.

void keyTyped(KeyEvent e)

> Handles a key typing event.

util
> **class** LinkedList<E> **extends** AbstractSequentialList<E> **implements** List<E>, Queue<E>, Cloneable, Serializable

PURPOSE

Provides a linked list view of a collection.

CONSTRUCTOR SUMMARY

LinkedList()

> Constructs a new empty LinkedList.

LinkedList(Collection<? **extends** E> c)

> Constructs a new LinkedList using the elements of collection c as a basis.

INSTANCE METHOD SUMMARY

boolean add(E v)

> Appends the list with a new element with value v and returns **true**.

void add(**int** i, E v)

> Inserts value v into the list such that v has index i. Any preexisting elements with indices i or greater are shifted backward by one element position.

boolean addAll(Collection<? **extends** E> c)

> Appends the list with all of the elements in c and returns **true** if the list has changed.

boolean addAll(**int** i, Collection<? **extends** E> c)

> Inserts the elements of c into this list and returns **true** if the list has changed. Any preexisting elements with indices i or greater are shifted backward by one element position.

void addFirst(E v)

> Inserts a new element with value v at the beginning of this list.

void addLast(E v)

> Adds a new element with value v at the end of this list.

void clear()

> Removes all elements from the list.

Object clone()

> Returns a shallow copy of this list.

boolean contains(Object v)

Returns whether the list has an element with value v.

E element()

Returns the first element of this LinkedList without removing it from the list.

E get(**int** i)

Returns the ith element in this list. Throws a NoSuchElementException if the list is empty.

E getFirst()

Returns the first element in this list. Throws a NoSuchElementException if the list is empty.

E getLast()

Returns the last element in this list. Throws a NoSuchElementException if the list is empty.

int indexOf(Object v)

Returns the index of the first occurrence of v in the list. If v is not in the list, then −1 is returned.

int lastIndexOf(Object v)

Returns the index of the last occurrence of v in the list. If v is not in the list, then −1 is returned.

int lastIndexOf(Object v)

Returns the index of the last occurrence of v in the list. If v is not in the list, then −1 is returned.

ListIterator<E> listIterator(**int** i)

Returns a list iterator of the elements in this list starting with the ith element.

boolean offer(E v)

Returns true and adds value v as the last element of this LinkedList.

E peek()

Returns the first element of this LinkedList without removing it from the list.

E poll()

Returns the first element of this LinkedList and removes it from the list.

E remove()

Returns the first element of this LinkedList and removes it from the list.

E remove(**int** i)

If i is a valid index, it removes the ith element from the list by shifting forward elements i+1 and on. In addition, the removed value is returned. Otherwise, an exception is generated.

boolean remove(Object v)

Attempts to remove the first element with value v in this list. Returns whether a value was removed.

E removeFirst()

Removes and returns the initial element in this list. Throws a NoSuchElement-Exception if the list is empty.

E removeLast()

Removes and returns the last element in this list. Throws a NoSuchElementEx-ception if the list is empty.

```
E set(int i, E v)
```

If i is a valid index, then ith element is set to v and the previous value of the element is returned. Otherwise, an exception is thrown.

```
int size()
```

Returns the number of elements in the list.

```
Object[] toArray()
```

Returns an array whose elements correspond to the elements of this list.

```
<T> T[] toArray(T[] a)
```

Returns an array of the same type as array a whose elements correspond to the elements of this list. The returned array is a if a is big enough.

```
String toString()
```

Returns a `String` representation of the value of this object.

---

util   **interface** `List<E>` **extends** `Collection<E>`

PURPOSE

Describes an ordered list view of a collection. The view supports a bidirectional iterator `ListIterator` allowing element insertion and replacement.

INSTANCE METHOD SUMMARY

```
boolean add(E v)
```

Appends the list with a new element with value v and returns **true**. This operation is optional.

```
void add(int i, E v)
```

Inserts value v into the list such that v has index i. Any preexisting elements with indices i or greater are shifted backward by one element position. This operation is optional.

```
boolean addAll(Collection<? extends E> c)
```

Appends the list with all of the elements in c and returns **true** if the list has changed. This operation is optional.

```
boolean addAll(int i, Collection<? extends E> c)
```

Inserts the elements of c into this list and returns **true** if the list has changed. Any preexisting elements with indices i or greater are shifted backward by one element position. This operation is optional.

```
void clear()
```

Removes all elements from the list. This operation is optional.

```
boolean contains(Object v)
```

Returns whether the list has an element with value v.

```
boolean containsAll(Collection<?> c)
```

Returns whether this `Collection` contains all of the values in the collection c.

```
boolean equals(Object v)
```

Returns **true** if and only if v is an instance of `List` representing the same list as this `List`.

```
E get(int i)
```

Returns the ith element in this list. Throws a `NoSuchElementException` if the list is empty.

int hashCode()

Returns the hash code of this object.

int indexOf(Object v)

Returns the index of the first occurrence of v in the list. If v is not in the list, then −1 is returned.

boolean isEmpty()

Returns whether this list has any elements.

Iterator<E> iterator()

Returns an iterator over the elements in this list.

int lastIndexOf(Object v)

Returns the index of the last occurrence of v in the list. If v is not in the list, then −1 is returned.

ListIterator<E> listIterator()

Returns a list iterator of the elements in this list starting with the first element.

ListIterator<E> listIterator(**int** i)

Returns a list iterator of the elements in this list starting with the ith element.

int lastIndexOf(Object v)

Returns the index of the last occurrence of v in the list. If v is not in the list, then −1 is returned.

E remove(**int** i)

If i is a valid index, it removes the ith element from the list by shifting forward elements i+1 and on. In addition, the removed value is returned. Otherwise, an exception is generated.

boolean remove(Object v)

Attempts to remove the first element with value v in this list. Returns whether a value was removed.

boolean removeAll(Collection<?> c)

Attempts to remove each of the values in c from this List. Returns whether a value was removed. The operation is optional.

boolean retainAll(Collection<?> c)

Attempts to remove from this List all of the values not in c. Returns whether a value was removed. The operation is optional.

E set(**int** i, E v)

If i is a valid index, then ith element is set to v and the previous value of the element is returned. Otherwise, an exception is thrown.

int size()

Returns the numbers of elements in the list.

List<E> subList(**int** i, **int** j)

Returns a sublist of this list using the elements with indices from the interval i ... j-1.

Object[] toArray()

Returns an array whose elements correspond to the elements of this list.

<T> T[] toArray(T[] a)

Returns an array of the same type as array a whose elements correspond to the elements of this list. The returned array is a if a is big enough.

| util | **interface** ListIterator\<E> **extends** Iterator\<E> |

PURPOSE

Provides an enumeration view of a collection where the iterator position is always between elements of the list.

INSTANCE METHOD SUMMARY

> **void** add(E v)
>
> > Inserts a new element into the list at the current position. The operation is optional.
>
> **boolean** hasNext()
>
> > Returns whether the list has more elements to return in the forward direction.
>
> **boolean** hasPrevious()
>
> > Returns whether the list has more elements to return in the reverse direction.
>
> E next()
>
> > Returns next element of the list in the forward direction. If there is no next element, then it throws a NoSuchElementException.
>
> **int** nextIndex()
>
> > Returns the index of the element of the list that would be returned next().
>
> E previous()
>
> > Returns next element of the list in the reverse direction. If there is no next element, then it throws a NoSuchElementException.
>
> **int** previousIndex()
>
> > Returns the index of the element of the list that would be returned previous().
>
> void remove()
>
> > Removes from the list the last element returned by the iterator. The operation is optional.
>
> **void** set(E v)
>
> > Replaces with v the last element returned by the iterator of the list. The operation is optional.

| util | **final class** Locale **implements** Cloneable, Serializable |

PURPOSE

Represents a specific geographical, political, or cultural region.

FIELD SUMMARY

> **static** Locale CANADA
>
> > Represents a political unit.
>
> **static** Locale CANADA_FRENCH
>
> > Represents a cultural unit.
>
> **static** Locale CHINA
>
> > Represents a political unit.
>
> **static** Locale CHINESE
>
> > Represents a language.

static Locale ENGLISH

Represents a language.

static Locale FRANCE

Represents a political unit.

static Locale FRENCH

Represents a language.

static Locale GERMAN

Represents a language.

static Locale GERMANY

Represents a political unit.

static Locale ITALIAN

Represents a language.

static Locale ITALY

Represents a political unit.

static Locale JAPAN

Represents a political unit.

static Locale JAPANESE

Represents a language.

static Locale KOREA

Represents a cultural unit.

static Locale KOREAN

Represents a language.

static Locale PRC

Represents a political unit.

static Locale SIMPLIFIED_CHINESE

Represents a language.

static Locale TAIWAN

Represents a political unit.

static Locale TRADITIONAL_CHINESE

Represents a language.

static Locale UK

Represents a political unit.

static Locale US

Represents a political unit.

CLASS METHOD SUMMARY

static Locale[] getAvailableLocales()

Returns a list of possible locales.

static Locale getDefault()

Returns the default locale.

static String[] getISOCountries()

Returns a list of ISO country codes.

static String[] getISOLanguages()

Returns a list of ISO language codes.

static void setDefault(Locale l)

Sets the default locale to l.

CONSTRUCTOR SUMMARY

`Locale(String s)`

Constructs the default `Locale` for country code `s`.

`Locale(String s, String c)`

Constructs the default `Locale` for language code `s` and country code `c`.

`Locale(String s, String c, String v)`

Constructs a `Locale` from language code `s`, country code `c`, and variant `v`.

INSTANCE METHOD SUMMARY

`String getCountry()`

Returns the country/region code for this `Locale`.

`Object clone()`

Returns a copy of this `Locale`.

`boolean equals(Object v)`

Returns whether `v` is equal to this `Locale`.

`String getDisplayCountry()`

Returns the name of the country for this `Locale`.

`String getDisplayCountry(Locale l)`

Returns the name of the country for locale `l`.

`String getDisplayLanguage()`

Returns the name of the language for this `Locale`.

`String getDisplayLanguage(Locale l)`

Returns the name of the language for locale `l`.

`String getDisplayName()`

Returns the name of this `Locale`.

`String getDisplayName(Locale l)`

Returns the name for locale `l`.

`String getDisplayVariant()`

Returns the name of the variant for this `Local`.

`String getDisplayVariant(Locale l)`

Returns the name of locale `l` for this `Local`.

`String getISO3Country()`

Returns the country code for this `Locale`.

`String getISO3Language()`

Returns the language for this `Locale`.

`String getLanguage()`

Returns the language code for this `Locale`.

`String getVariant()`

Returns the variant code of this `Locale`.

`int hashCode()`

Returns the hash code of this object. Returns the name of locale `l` for this `Local`.

`String getISO3Country()`

Returns the country code for this `Locale`.

`String getISO3Language()`

Returns the language for this `Locale`.

`String getLanguage()`

Returns the language code for this `Locale`.

String getVariant()
> Returns the variant code of this Locale.

int hashCode()
> Returns the hash code of this object.

String toString()
> Returns a String representation of the value of this object.

| lang | *final class* Long **extends** Number **implements** Comparable<Long> |

PURPOSE

Represents a **long** value within a class wrapper.

FIELD SUMMARY

static final long MAX_VALUE
> Represents the maximum value of type **long** (i.e., $2^{63} - 1$).

static final long MIN_VALUE
> Represents the minimum value of type **long** (i.e., -2^{63}.)

static final int SIZE
> Represents the number of bits in a **long** value.

static final Class<Long> TYPE
> Represents the type **long**.

CLASS METHOD SUMMARY

static int bitCount(long n)
> Returns the number of one-bits in the two's complement binary representation of value n.

static Long decode(String s)
> Constructs a new Long object representing Integer.parseLong(s, n), where n is 8, 10, or 16 depending on whether s is respectively a numeric string in octal, decimal, or hexadecimal format.

static Long getLong(String s)
> Returns Long.getLong(s, **null**).

static Long getLong(String s, **long** n)
> Returns Long.getLong(s, **new** Long(n)).

static Long getLong(String s, Long n)
> Returns the value of the system property named s if it exists; otherwise, it returns n.

static int highestOneBit(long n)
> Returns 0 if value n is 0; otherwise, it returns an **int** value with a single one-bit in the position of the leftmost one-bit in the two's complement binary representation of value n.

static int lowestOneBit(long n)
> Returns 0 if value n is 0; otherwise, it returns an **int** value with a single one-bit in the position of the rightmost one-bit in the two's complement binary representation of value n.

```
static int numberOfLeadingZeros(long n)
```
Returns the number of leading zero-bits before the leftmost one-bit in the two's complement binary representation of value n.

```
static int numberOfTrailingZeros(long i)
```
Returns the number of trailing zero-bits after the rightmost one-bit in the two's complement binary representation of value n.

```
static long parseLong(String s)
```
Returns `Long.parseLong(s, 10)`.

```
static long parseLong(String s, int n)
```
Returns the **long** value represented by parsing string s as an optionally signed integer value in radix n.

```
static long reverse(long n)
```
Returns the value produced by reversing the two's complement binary representation of n.

```
static long reverseBytes(long n)
```
Returns the value produced by reversing the order of the bytes in the two's complement binary representation of n.

```
static long rotateLeft(long n, int m)
```
Returns the value of leftward circularly shifting the two's complement binary representation of n, m times.

```
static long rotateRight(long n, int m)
```
Returns the value of rightward circularly shifting the two's complement binary representation of n, m times.

```
static int signum(long n)
```
Returns –1, 0, or 1 depending on whether value n is respectively negative, zero, or positive.

```
static String toBinaryString(long m)
```
Returns `Long.toString(m, 2)`.

```
static String toHexString(long m)
```
Returns `Long.toString(m, 16)`.

```
static String toOctalString(long m)
```
Returns `Long.toString(m, 8)`.

```
static String toString(long m)
```
Returns `Long.toString(m, 10)`.

```
static String toString(long m, int n)
```
Returns a new `String` object representing the value of m in base n.

```
static Long valueOf(long n)
```
Returns a `Long` representation of value n.

```
static Long valueOf(String s)
```
Returns `Long.valueOf(s, 10)`.

```
static Long valueOf(String s, int n)
```
Returns a new `Long` representing `Long.parseLong(s, n)`.

CONSTRUCTOR SUMMARY

```
Long(long n)
```
Constructs a new `Long` object representing value n.

```
Long(String s)
```
Constructs a new `Long` object representing `Long.parseLong(s)`.

INSTANCE METHOD SUMMARY

`byte byteValue()`

Returns the **long** value of this Long as a **byte**.

`int compareTo(Long n)`

Returns a negative value, zero, or a positive value depending respectively on whether the **long** value represented by this object is less than, equal to, or greater than n.

`int compareTo(Object v)`

Returns a negative value, zero, or a positive value depending respectively on whether the **long** value represented by this object is less than, equal to, or greater than v.

`double doubleValue()`

Returns the **long** value of this Long as a **double**.

`boolean equals(Object v)`

Returns **true** if and only if v is an instance of Long representing the same **int** value that this object represents.

`float floatValue()`

Returns the value of this Long as a **float**.

`int hashCode()`

Returns the hash code of this object.

`int intValue()`

Returns the value of this Long as an **int**.

`long longValue()`

Returns the value of this Long as a **long**.

`short shortValue()`

Returns the **long** value of this Long as a **short**.

`String toString()`

Returns a `String` representation of the value of this object.

---

util　　`interface Map<K, V>`

PURPOSE

Represents mappings of keys to values.

INSTANCE METHOD SUMMARY

`void clear()`

Removes all mappings in this Map. The operation is optional.

`boolean containsKey(Object v)`

Returns whether this Map contains a mapping for the key v.

`boolean containsValue(Object v)`

Returns whether this Map has a key that maps to value v.

`Set<Map.Entry<K, V>> entrySet()`

Returns a `Set` view of this Map.

`boolean equals(Object v)`

Returns **true** if and only if v is an instance of List representing the same list as this List.

```
Object get(Object v)
```

Returns the value to which key v maps in this Map.

```
int hashCode()
```

Returns the hash code of this object.

```
boolean isEmpty()
```

Returns whether this Map has any mappings.

```
Set<K> keySet()
```

Returns a Set view of the keys in this Map.

```
V put(K v1, V v2)
```

Associates key v1 with value v2 in this Map. Returns the previous value associated with v2. The operation is optional.

```
void putAll(Map<? extends K, ? extends V> m)
```

Copies the mappings of map m to this Map. The operation is optional.

```
V remove(Object v)
```

Removes the mapping of key v in this Map. Returns the previous value associated with v. The operation is optional.

```
int size()
```

Returns the number of mappings in this Map.

```
Collection<V> values()
```

Returns a Collection view of the values in this Map.

| lang | **final class** Math |

PURPOSE

Defines two class constants for representing *e* and π, and a collection of class methods for computing common exponential, logarithm, square root, and trigonometric functions.

FIELD SUMMARY

```
static double E
```

Represents the **double** approximation to *e*.

```
static double PI
```

Represents the **double** approximation to π.

CLASS METHOD SUMMARY

```
static double abs(double n)
```

Returns the absolute value of **double** value n.

```
static float abs(float n)
```

Returns the absolute value of **float** value n.

```
static int abs(int n)
```

Returns the absolute value of **int** value n.

```
static long abs(long n)
```

Returns the absolute value of **long** value n.

```
static double acos(double n)
```

Returns the angle in the interval 0 ... MATH.PI whose cosine is n.

```
static double asin(double n)
```

Returns the angle in the interval –MATH.PI/2 ... MATH.PI/2 whose sine is n.

```
static double atan(double a)
```
Returns the angle in the interval –MATH.PI/2 ... MATH.PI/2 whose tangent is n.
```
static double atan2(double y, double x)
```
Returns atan(y/x).
```
static double cbrt(double n)
```
Returns the cube root of n.
```
static double ceil(double n)
```
Returns the smallest integral **double** value that is not less than n.
```
static double cos(double n)
```
Returns the cosine of angle n.
```
static double cosh(double n)
```
Returns the hyperbolic cosine of angle n.
```
static double exp(double n)
```
Returns e^n.
```
static double expm1(double n)
```
Returns $e^n - 1$.
```
static double floor(double n)
```
Returns the largest integral **double** value that is not greater than n.
```
static double hypot(double a, double b)
```
Returns the square root of $a^2 + b^2$.
```
static double IEEEremainder(double m, double n)
```
Returns the remainder of m divided by n as specified by the *IEEE 754 standard*.
```
static double log(double n)
```
Returns $\log_e$ n.
```
static double log10(double n)
```
Returns $\log_{10}$ n.
```
static double log1p(double n)
```
Returns $\log_{10}$ (n+1).
```
static double max(double m, double n)
```
Returns the maximum of the **double** values m and n.
```
static float max(float m, float n)
```
Returns the maximum of the **float** values m and n.
```
static int max(int m, int n)
```
Returns the maximum of the **int** values m and n.
```
static long max(long m, long n)
```
Returns the maximum of the **long** values m and n.
```
static double min(double m, double n)
```
Returns the minimum of the **double** values m and n.
```
static float min(float m, float n)
```
Returns the minimum of the **float** values m and n.
```
static int min(int m, int n)
```
Returns the minimum of the **int** values m and n.
```
static long min(long m, long n)
```
Returns the minimum of the **long** values m and n.
```
static double pow(double m, double n)
```
Returns m^n.

```
static double random()
```
Returns a positive pseudorandom uniform **double** value from the interval [0, 1) (i.e., the return value is greater than or equal to 0 and less than 1).

```
static double rint(double n)
```
Returns the integral **double** value closest to n.

```
static long round(double n)
```
Returns the **long** value closest to n.

```
static int round(float n)
```
Returns the **int** value closest to n.

```
static double signum(double n)
```
Returns –1, 0, or 1 depending on whether value n is respectively negative, zero, or positive.

```
static float signum(float n)
```
Returns –1, 0, or 1 depending on whether value n is respectively negative, zero, or positive.

```
static double sin(double n)
```
Returns the sine of angle n.

```
static double sqrt(double n)
```
Returns the positive-valued $\sqrt{n}$.

```
static double sinh(double n)
```
Returns the hyperbolic sine of angle n.

```
static double tan(double n)
```
Returns the tangent of angle n.

```
static double tanh(double n)
```
Returns the hyperbolic tangent of angle n.

```
static double toDegrees(double n)
```
Returns the degree equivalent of n radians.

```
static double toRadians(double n)
```
Converts the radian equivalent of n degrees.

```
static double ulp(double n)
```
Returns the size of the ulp for value n, where the ulp is the distance between value n and the next larger **double** value.

```
static float ulp(float n)
```
Returns the size of the ulp for value n, where the ulp is the distance between value n and the next larger **float** value.

---

awt.event **abstract class** MouseAdapter **implements** MouseListener

PURPOSE

A convenience class for handling mouse events. Its methods perform no actions. A specialized class overrides them as needed.

CONSTRUCTOR SUMMARY

```
MouseAdapter()
```
Constructs a new MouseAdapter.

INSTANCE METHOD SUMMARY

> `void` `mouseClicked(MouseEvent e)`
>> Ignores a mouse clicking event.
>
> `void` `mouseEntered(MouseEvent e)`
>> Ignores a mouse component-entering event.
>
> `void` `mouseExited(MouseEvent e)`
>> Ignores a mouse component-exiting event.
>
> `void` `mousePressed(MouseEvent e)`
>> Ignores a mouse button-pressing event.
>
> `void` `mouseReleased(MouseEvent e)`
>> Ignores a mouse button-release event.

`awt.event`   `class` `MouseEvent` `implements` `InputEvent`

PURPOSE

Represents a mouse interaction event.

FIELD SUMMARY

> `static int` `BUTTON1`
>> Represents the first mouse button.
>
> `static int` `BUTTON2`
>> Represents the second mouse button.
>
> `static int` `BUTTON3`
>> Represents the third mouse button.
>
> `static int` `MOUSE_CLICKED`
>> Represents a mouse clicking event.
>
> `static int` `MOUSE_DRAGGED`
>> Represents a mouse dragging event.
>
> `static int` `MOUSE_ENTERED`
>> Represents a mouse component-entering event.
>
> `static int` `MOUSE_EXITED`
>> Represents a mouse component-exiting event.
>
> `static int` `MOUSE_FIRST`
>> Represents the minimal index of a mouse event.
>
> `static int` `MOUSE_LAST`
>> Represents the maximal index of a mouse event.
>
> `static int` `MOUSE_MOVED`
>> Represents a mouse movement event.
>
> `static int` `MOUSE_PRESSED`
>> Represents a mouse button-pressing event.
>
> `static int` `MOUSE_RELEASED`
>> Represents a mouse button-release event.
>
> `static int` `MOUSE_WHEEL`
>> Represents a mouse wheel event.
>
> `static int` `NOBUTTON`
>> Represents no mouse button.

CLASS METHOD SUMMARY

> `static` String getMouseModifiersText(`int` m)
>
>> Returns a description of key modifier m.

CONSTRUCTOR SUMMARY

> MouseEvent(Component v, `int` n, `long` t, `int` m, `int` x, `int` y, `int` c, `boolean` b)
>
>> Constructs a new MouseEvent of type n at location (x, y) occurring at time t in component v using key modifiers m and click count c, where b indicates this event triggers a popup menu.
>
> MouseEvent(Component v, `int` n, `long` t, `int` m, `int` x, `int` y, `int` c, `boolean` b, `int` b)
>
>> Constructs a new MouseEvent involving button b of type n at location (x, y) occurring at time t in component v using key modifiers m and click count c, where b indicates this event triggers a popup menu.

INSTANCE METHOD SUMMARY

> `int` getButton()
>
>> Returns which button triggered this MouseEvent.
>
> `int` getClickCount()
>
>> Returns the number of button clicks with this MouseEvent.
>
> Point getPoint()
>
>> Returns the location of this MouseEvent.
>
> `int` getX()
>
>> Returns the x-coordinate position of this MouseEvent.
>
> `int` getY()
>
>> Returns the y-coordinate position of this MouseEvent.
>
> `boolean` isPopupTrigger()
>
>> Returns whether this MouseEvent is a popup menu trigger event.
>
> String paramString()
>
>> Returns a representation of this MouseEvent.
>
> `void` translatePoint(`int` dx, `int` dy)
>
>> Shifts the location of this MouseEvent by distances dx and dy respectively on the x- and y-axes.

`awt.event`   `interface` MouseListener `extends` EventListener

PURPOSE

Describes the actions a mouse listener must perform.

INSTANCE METHOD SUMMARY

> `void` mouseClicked(MouseEvent e)
>
>> Handles a mouse clicking event.
>
> `void` mouseEntered(MouseEvent e)
>
>> Handles a mouse component-entering event.
>
> `void` mouseExited(MouseEvent e)
>
>> Handles a mouse component-exiting event.

void mousePressed(MouseEvent e)

Handles a mouse button-pressing event.

void mouseReleased(MouseEvent e)

Handles a mouse button-release event.

| lang | **class** NoClassDefFoundError **extends** LinkageError |

PURPOSE

Represents an unexpected event where the definition of a needed class could not be found.

CONSTRUCTOR SUMMARY

NoClassDefFoundError()

Constructs a new NoClassDefFoundError with a default message.

NoClassDefFoundError(String s)

Constructs a new NoClassDefFoundError with message s.

| lang | **class** NullPointerException **extends** RuntimeException |

PURPOSE

Represents an unexpected event where a reference to an object was needed and instead the **null** value was supplied.

CONSTRUCTOR SUMMARY

NullPointerException()

Constructs a NullPointerException with a default message.

NullPointerException(String s)

Constructs a NullPointerException with message s.

| lang | **abstract class** Number **implements** Serializable |

PURPOSE

Represents a numeric value within a class wrapper.

CONSTRUCTOR SUMMARY

Number()

Constructs a number representation.

INSTANCE METHOD SUMMARY

byte byteValue()

Returns the value of this Number as a **byte**.

abstract double doubleValue()

Returns the value of this Number as a **double**.

abstract float floatValue()

Returns the value of this Number as a **float**.

abstract int intValue()

Returns the value of this Number as an **int**.

abstract long longValue()

Returns the value of this Number as a **long**.

short shortValue()

Returns the value of this Number as a **short**.

---

text	abstract class NumberFormat extends Format

PURPOSE
Provides methods for formatting and parsing numbers and serves as an abstract superclass for number formatting.

FIELD SUMMARY
static int FRACTION_FIELD

Indicates the fraction field of a FieldPosition.

static int INTEGER_FIELD

Indicates the integer field of a FieldPosition.

CLASS METHOD SUMMARY
static Locale[] getAvailableLocales()

Returns the array of possible NumberFormat locales.

static NumberFormat getCurrencyInstance()

Returns a default currency NumberFormat for the default locale.

static NumberFormat getCurrencyInstance(Locale 1)

Returns a default currency NumberFormat for the locale 1.

static NumberFormat getInstance()

Returns a default NumberFormat for the default locale.

static NumberFormat getInstance(Locale 1)

Returns a default NumberFormat for locale 1.

static NumberFormat getIntegerInstance()

Returns a default integer NumberFormat for the default locale.

static NumberFormat getIntegerInstance(Locale 1)

Returns a default integer NumberFormat for locale 1.

static NumberFormatgetNumberInstance()

Returns a default number NumberFormat for the default locale.

static NumberFormat getNumberInstance(Locale 1)

Returns a default number NumberFormat for locale 1.

static NumberFormat getPercentInstance()

Returns a default percentage NumberFormat for the default locale.

static NumberFormat getPercentInstance(Locale 1)

Returns a default percentage NumberFormat for locale 1.

CONSTRUCTOR SUMMARY
NumberFormat()

Constructs a new NumberFormat number formatter.

Object clone()

Returns a clone of this NumberFormat.

boolean equals(Object v)

Returns **true** if and only if v is an instance of NumberFormat representing the same format value that this object represents.

String format(**double** n)

Formats number n into a string using this NumberFormat.

abstract StringBuffer format(**double** n, StringBuffer s, FieldPosition f)

Returns s after formatting number n into string s using this NumberFormat. If f indicates a field, then its indices are updated to reflect the position of the field within s.

String format(**long** n)

Formats number n into a string using this NumberFormat.

abstract StringBuffer format(**long** n, StringBuffer s, FieldPosition f)

Returns s after formatting number n into string s using this NumberFormat. If f indicates a field, then its indices are updated to reflect the position of the field within s.

StringBuffer format(Object n, StringBuffer s, FieldPosition f)

Returns s after formatting the number represented by n into string s using this NumberFormat. If f indicates a field, then its indices are updated to reflect the position of the field within s.

Currency getCurrency()

Returns the currency format used by this NumberFormat.

int getMaximumFractionDigits()

Returns the maximum number of digits used in formatting the fractional part of a number by this NumberFormat.

int getMaximumIntegerDigits()

Returns the maximum number of digits used in formatting the integer part of a number by this NumberFormat.

int getMinimumFractionDigits()

Returns the minimum number of digits used in formatting the fractional part of a number by this NumberFormat.

int getMinimumIntegerDigits()

Returns the minimum number of digits used in formatting the integer part of a number by this NumberFormat.

int hashCode()

Returns the hash code of this NumberFormat.

boolean isGroupingUsed()

Returns whether this NumberFormat uses grouping.

boolean isParseIntegerOnly()

Returns whether this NumberFormat only parses numbers as integers.

Number parse(String s)

Parses s to produce a number using this DateFormat.

abstract Number parse(String s, ParsePosition i)

Parses s to produce a Number using this NumberFormat. The parsing starts with the parse position indicated by i. Upon completion of parsing, i reflects the last parsed position. The preferred actual type is Long. If Long is unsuitable, then Double is used.

Object parseObject(String s, ParsePosition i)

Parses s to produce a Number using this NumberFormat. The parsing starts with the parse position indicated by i. Upon completion of parsing, i reflects the last parsed position.

void setCurrency(Currency c)

Sets to c the Currency used by this NumberFormat.

void setGroupingUsed(**boolean** b)

Sets whether this NumberFormat uses grouping.

void setMaximumFractionDigits(**int** n)

Sets to n the maximum number of digits used in formatting the fractional part of a number by this NumberFormat.

void setMaximumIntegerDigits(**int** n)

Sets to n the maximum number of digits used in formatting the integer part of a number by this NumberFormat.

void setMinimumFractionDigits(**int** n)

Sets to n the minimum number of digits used in formatting the fractional part of a number by this NumberFormat.

void setMinimumIntegerDigits(**int** n)

Sets to n the minimum number of digits used in formatting the integer part of a number by this NumberFormat.

void setParseIntegerOnly(**boolean** b)

Sets whether this NumberFormat parses numbers only as integers.

| text | **static class** NumberFormat.Field **extends** Format.Field |

PURPOSE

Provides field constants for number formatting.

FIELD SUMMARY

static NumberFormat.Field CURRENCY

Represents the currency field in the formatting of a number.

static NumberFormat.Field DECIMAL_SEPARATOR

Represents the decimal separator field in the formatting of a number.

static NumberFormat.Field EXPONENT

Represents the exponent field in the formatting of a number.

static NumberFormat.Field EXPONENT_SIGN

Represents the exponent sign field in the formatting of a number.

static NumberFormat.Field EXPONENT_SYMBOL

Represents the exponent symbol field in the formatting of a number.

static NumberFormat.Field FRACTION

Represents the fraction field in the formatting of a number.

static NumberFormat.Field GROUPING_SEPARATOR

    Represents the grouping separator field in the formatting of a number.

static NumberFormat.Field INTEGER

    Represents the integer field in the formatting of a number.

static NumberFormat.Field PERCENT

    Represents the percent field in the formatting of a number.

static NumberFormat.Field PERMILLE

    Represents the permille field in the formatting of a number.

static NumberFormat.Field SIGN

    Represents the sign field in the formatting of a number.

CONSTRUCTOR SUMMARY

protected NumberFormat.Field(String s)

    Constructs a new **NumberFormat.Field** with name s.

INSTANCE METHOD SUMMARY

protected Object readResolve()

    Returns a resolved field.

| lang | class Object |

PURPOSE

Represents the basic characteristics and behaviors of an object in Java. Class Object is the root superclass of all Java arrays and classes.

CONSTRUCTOR SUMMARY

Object()

    Constructs an object representation.

INSTANCE METHOD SUMMARY

protected Object clone()

    Returns a new clone of this object. By convention, classes that override this method should define a **public clone()** method that makes a deep copy.

boolean equals(Object v)

    Returns **true** if and only if v is the same object as this object. By convention, classes that override this method should fulfill the following contract.

- Reflexivity: For any object x, x.equals(x) should be true.
- Symmetry: For any objects x and y, if x.equals(y), then y.equals(x);
- Transitivity: For any objects x, y, and z, if x.equals(y) and y.equals(z), then x.equals(z);
- Consistency: For any unchanging objects x and y, repeated evaluations of x.equals(y) should return the same value.
- Physicality: For any object x, x.equals(**null**) should return **false**.

protected void finalize()

    Invoked by the garbage collector when Java has determined there are no more references to this object.

final Class<? extends Object> getClass()

    Returns the runtime class of this object.

int hashCode()

Returns the hash code of this object.

final void notify()

Wakes up one of the thread(s) that is waiting on the monitor for this object.

final void notifyAll()

Wakes up all of the threads that are waiting on the monitor for this object.

String toString()

Returns a String representation of the value of this object.

final void wait()

Returns **this**.wait(0, 0).

final void wait(long m)

Returns **this**.wait(m, 0).

final void wait(long m, int n)

Causes current thread to wait until one of the following conditions is true: a thread invokes notify() or notifyAll() of this object; some other thread interrupts the current thread; $1{,}000{,}000 \cdot m + n$ nanoseconds have passed.

---

io   **class** OutputStreamWriter **extends** Writer

PURPOSE

Represents a character output stream view.

CONSTRUCTOR SUMMARY

OutputStreamWriter(OutputStream o)

Constructs a new OutputStreamWriter from stream o using the default character set encoding.

OutputStreamWriter(OutputStream o, Charset c)

Constructs an OutputStreamWriter from stream o using the character set c.

OutputStreamWriter(OutputStream o, CharsetEncoder c)

Constructs a new OutputStreamWriter from stream o using the character set encoding c.

OutputStreamWriter(OutputStream o, String s)

Constructs a new OutputStreamWriter from stream o using the character set with name s.

INSTANCE METHOD SUMMARY

void close()

Closes this OutputStreamWriter.

void flush()

Flushes this OutputStreamWriter.

String getEncoding()

Returns the name of the character set encoding used by this OutputStream-Writer.

void write(char[] c, int i, int n)

Inserts n characters from array c to this OutputStreamWriter. The first character to be displayed is c[i].

void write(**int** c)

Inserts character c to this OutputStreamWriter.

void write(String s, **int** i, **int** n)

Inserts an n character substring from string s to this OutputStreamWriter. The first character in the substring to be displayed has index i.

---

util.
regex

class Pattern **implements** Serializable

PURPOSE

Represents a regular expression.

FIELD SUMMARY

static int CANON_EQ

Represents canonical equivalence.

static int CASE_INSENSITIVE

Represents case-insensitive matching.

static int COMMENTS

Represents the allowing of whitespace and comments in pattern.

static int DOTALL

Represents dotall mode.

static int MULTILINE

Represents multiline mode.

static int UNICODE_CASE

Represents case folding.

static int UNIX_LINES

Represents Unix lines mode.

CLASS METHOD SUMMARY

static Pattern compile(String s)

Returns the regular expression Pattern as denoted by string s.

static Pattern compile(String s, **int** f)

Returns the regular expression Pattern as denoted by string s with respect to flags f.

static boolean matches(String s, CharSequence t)

Returns whether the regular expression Pattern denoted by string s matches input t.

static String quote(String s)

Returns a literal pattern for string s.

INSTANCE METHOD SUMMARY

int flags()

Returns the match flags of this Pattern.

Matcher matcher(CharSequence s)

Returns a new Matcher that will match input s using this Pattern.

String pattern()

Returns the regular expression for this Pattern.

```
String[] split(CharSequence s)
```
Returns a `String` array that splits the input sequence `s` around matches of this `Pattern`.
```
String[] split(CharSequence s, int n)
```
Returns a `String` array that splits the input sequence `s` around matches of this `Pattern`. If n > 0, then this `Pattern` is applied at most n-1 times and the last array element is a copy of all input in `s` beyond the last matched delimiter. If n < 0, then this `Pattern` is applied as many times as possible. If n = 0, then this `Pattern` is applied as many times as possible with the discarding of any trailing empty strings.
```
String toString()
```
Returns a representation of this `Pattern`.

---

awt

class Point extends Point2D implements Serializable

PURPOSE

Represents a point in two-dimensional space.

FIELD SUMMARY

    `int x`

Represents the x-coordinate of this `Point`.

    `int y`

Represents the y-coordinate of this `Point`.

CONSTRUCTOR SUMMARY

    `Point()`

Constructs a new `Point` representing the origin (0, 0).

    `Point(int x, int y)`

Constructs a new `Point` representing the location (x, y).

    `Point(Point p)`

Constructs a new `Point` that is a clone of point p.

INSTANCE METHOD SUMMARY

    `boolean equals(Object v)`

Returns whether v is a point equal to this `Point`.

    `Point getLocation()`

Returns a clone of this `Point`.

    `double getX()`

Returns the x-coordinate of this `Point`.

    `double getY()`

Returns the y-coordinate of this `Point`.

    `void move(int x, int y)`

Resets this `Point` to represent the location (x, y).

    `void setLocation(double x, double y)`

Resets this `Point` to represent the location (x, y).

    `void setLocation(int x, int y)`

Resets this `Point` to represent the location (x, y).

> void setLocation(Point p)
>> Resets this Point to be a clone of point p.
>
> String toString()
>> Returns a representation of this Point.
>
> void translate(int dx, int dy)
>> Shifts this Point by distances dx and dy respectively on the x- and y-axes.

---

awt	class Polygon implements Shape, Serializable

PURPOSE
Represents a polygon in two-dimensional coordinate space.

FIELD SUMMARY

> protected Rectangle
>> Represents the bounding box of this Polygon.
>
> int npoints
>> Represents the number of endpoints describing this Polygon.
>
> int[] xpoints
>> Represents the x-coordinates of this Polygon.
>
> int[] ypoints
>> Represents the y-coordinates of this Polygon.

CONSTRUCTOR SUMMARY

> Polygon()
>> Creates a new Polygon with no segments.
>
> Polygon(int[] x, int[] y, int n)
>> Creates a new Polygon composed of n points, where the ith point is (x[i], y[i]).

INSTANCE METHOD SUMMARY

> void addPoint(int x, int y)
>> Appends point (x, y) to the list of points represented by this Polygon.
>
> boolean contains(double x, double y)
>> Returns whether this Polygon contains point (x, y).
>
> boolean contains(double x, double y, double w, double h)
>> Returns whether this Polygon contains the rectangle with origin (x, y) with width w and height h.
>
> boolean contains(int x, int y)
>> Returns whether this Polygon contains point (x, y).
>
> boolean contains(Point p)
>> Returns whether this Polygon contains point p.
>
> boolean contains(Point2D p)
>> Returns whether this Polygon contains point p.
>
> boolean contains(Rectangle2D r)
>> Returns whether this Polygon contains rectangle r.
>
> Rectangle getBounds()
>> Returns the bounding box of this Polygon.

```
Rectangle2D getBounds2D()
```
Returns the bounding box of this Polygon.
```
PathIterator getPathIterator(AffineTransform a)
```
Returns an iterator that iterates over a list of segments approximating the boundary of this Polygon, where segment endpoints are modified with respect to transform a.
```
PathIterator getPathIterator(AffineTransform a, double v)
```
Returns an iterator that iterates over a list of segments approximating the boundary of this Polygon, where segment endpoints are modified with respect to transform a and where value v is a limit on the distance of a segment point from its true position on the shape outline.
```
boolean intersects(double x, double y, double w, double h)
```
Returns whether this Polygon intersects the rectangle with origin (x, y), width w, and height h.
```
boolean intersects(Rectangle2D r)
```
Returns whether this Polygon intersects rectangle r.
```
void invalidate()
```
Signals the invalidity of any objects that use this Polygon.
```
void reset()
```
Resets this Polygon to represent an empty polygon.
```
void translate(int dx, int dx)
```
Translates the origin of this Polygon by distances dx and dy respectively on the x- and y-axes.

---

io   **class** PrintStream **extends** FilterOutputStream

PURPOSE

Represents an output stream with expanded functionality.

CONSTRUCTOR SUMMARY
```
PrintStream(OutputStream s)
```
Constructs a new PrintStream from stream s using the default character set encoding. The stream is not automatically flushed.
```
PrintStream(OutputStream s, boolean b)
```
Constructs a new PrintStream from stream s using the default character set encoding. The stream is automatically flushed depending on b.
```
PrintStream(OutputStream s, boolean b, String t)
```
Constructs a new PrintStream from stream o using the character set encoding with name t. The stream is automatically flushed depending on b.
```
PrintStream(String s, String t)
```
Constructs a new print stream associated with the file with name s using character set t. The stream is not automatically flushed.

INSTANCE METHOD SUMMARY
```
PrintStream append(char c)
```
Returns this PrintStream and prints character c to this PrintStream.

PrintStream append(CharSequence s)

Returns this `PrintStream` and prints character sequence s to this Print-Stream.

boolean checkError()

Flushes this `PrintStream` and returns its error state.

void close()

Closes this `PrintStream`.

void flush()

Flushes this `PrintStream`.

PrintStream format(Locale n, String s, Object... a)

Returns this `PrintStream` and prints the list of arguments a to this Print-Stream according to format string s subject to locale n.

PrintStream format(String s, Object... a)

Returns this `PrintStream` and prints the list of arguments a to this Print-Stream according to format string s.

void print(**boolean** b)

Prints b to this `PrintStream`.

void print(**char** c)

Prints c to this `PrintStream`.

void print(**char**[] c)

Prints each character in array c to this `PrintStream`.

void print(**double** n)

Prints n to this `PrintStream`.

void print(**float** n)

Prints n to this `PrintStream`.

void print(**int** n)

Prints n to this `PrintStream`.

void print(**long** n)

Prints n to this `PrintStream`.

void print(Object v)

Prints v.`toString()` to this `PrintStream`.

void print(String s)

Prints s to this `PrintStream`.

PrintStream printf(Locale n, String s, Object... a)

Returns this `PrintStream` and prints the list of arguments a to this Print-Stream according to format string s subject to locale n.

PrintStream printf(String s, Object... a)

Returns this `PrintStream` and prints the list of arguments a to this Print-Stream according to format string s.

void println()

Equivalent to print("\n").

void println(**boolean** b)

Equivalent to print(b + "\n").

void println(**char** c)

Equivalent to print(c + "\n").

void println(**char**[] c)

Equivalent to print(c + "\n").

void println(**double** n)

> Equivalent to print(n + "\n").

void println(**float** n)

> Equivalent to print(n + "\n").

void println(**int** n)

> Equivalent to print(n + "\n").

void println(**long** n)

> Equivalent to print(n + "\n").

void println(Object v)

> Equivalent to print(v + "\n").

void println(String s)

> Equivalent to print(s + "\n").

protected void setError()

> Sets the error state of this PrintStream to **true**.

void write(**byte**[] b, **int** i, **int** n)

> Prints n bytes from array b to this PrintStream, where the index of the first element to be printed is i.

void write(**int** b)

> Prints byte b to this PrintStream.

| util | **class** Random **implements** Serializable |

PURPOSE

Represents a pseudorandom number generator.

CONSTRUCTOR SUMMARY

Random()

> Constructs a new random number generator Random whose seed is based on the current time.

Random(**long** n)

> Constructs a new random number generator Random using a seed n.

INSTANCE METHOD SUMMARY

protected int next(**int** n)

> Used by other methods for generating the next pseudorandom number. The method contract requires that an override return an **int** value with the n low-order bits being independent pseudorandom binary values.

boolean nextBoolean()

> Returns the next pseudorandom, uniformly distributed value from this Random.

void nextBytes(**byte**[] a)

> Fills array a with random bytes using this Random.

double nextDouble()

> Returns the next pseudorandom, uniformly distributed value between 0.0 and 1.0 from this Random.

float nextFloat()

> Returns the next pseudorandom, uniformly distributed value between 0.0 and 1.0 from this Random.

double nextGaussian()

Returns the next pseudorandom, normally distributed value mean 0 and standard deviation 1 from this **Random**.

int nextInt()

Returns the next pseudorandom, uniformly distributed value from this **Random**.

int nextInt(**int** n)

Returns from interval 0 … n-1 the next pseudorandom, uniformly distributed value of this **Random**.

long nextLong()

Returns the next pseudorandom, uniformly distributed value from this **Random**.

void setSeed(**long** n)

Sets to n the seed of this **Random**.

---

io	**abstract** **class** Reader **implements** Readable, Closeable

PURPOSE

Represents basic input stream functionality.

FIELD SUMMARY

protected Object lock

Represents the operation synchronization object of this **Reader**.

CONSTRUCTOR SUMMARY

protected Reader()

Constructs a new **Reader** with synchronized operations.

protected Reader(Object v)

Constructs a new **Reader** whose synchronized operations use lock v.

INSTANCE METHOD SUMMARY

abstract **void** close()

Closes this **Reader** stream.

void mark(**int** n)

Marks the current position in this **Reader** stream as a reset point. Parameter n indicates a limit on the number of characters that can be read while still preserving this reset point.

boolean markSupported()

Returns whether this **Reader** stream supports marking.

int read()

Returns the next character from this **Reader** stream.

int read(**char**[] c)

Reads the remaining characters from this **Reader** stream and stores them in c. Returns the number of characters that have been read (–1 if end of file occurs).

abstract **int** read(**char**[] c, **int** i, **int** n)

Attempts to read the next n characters from this **Reader** stream and store them in c starting at index i. Returns the number of characters that have been read (–1 if end of file occurs).

boolean ready()

Returns whether this **Reader** stream is ready for reading.

> void reset()
>> Reset this Reader stream.
>
> long skip(long n)
>> Ignore the next n characters in this Reader stream.

---

class Rectangle extends Rectangle2D implements Shape,
    Serializable

PURPOSE

Represents a rectangle in two-dimensional coordinate space.

FIELD SUMMARY

> int height
>> Represents the height of this Rectangle.
>
> int width
>> Represents the width of this Rectangle.
>
> int x
>> Represents the x-coordinate of this Rectangle.
>
> int y
>> Represents the y-coordinate of this Rectangle.

CONSTRUCTOR SUMMARY

> Rectangle()
>> Constructs a new Rectangle with origin (0, 0) with a zero width and height.
>
> Rectangle(Dimension d)
>> Constructs a new Rectangle with origin (0, 0) and dimensions d.
>
> Rectangle(int w, int h)
>> Constructs a new Rectangle with origin (0, 0) with width w and height h.
>
> Rectangle(int x, int y, int w, int h)
>> Constructs a new Rectangle with origin (x, y) with width w and height h.
>
> Rectangle(Point p)
>> Constructs a new Rectangle with origin p with a zero width and height.
>
> Rectangle(Point p, Dimension d)
>> Constructs a new Rectangle with origin p and dimension d.
>
> Rectangle(Rectangle r)
>> Constructs a clone of rectangle r.

INSTANCE METHOD SUMMARY

> void add(int x, int y)
>> Returns the union of this Rectangle with point (x, y).
>
> void add(Point p)
>> Returns the union of this Rectangle with point p.
>
> void add(Rectangle r)
>> Returns the union of this Rectangle with rectangle r.
>
> boolean contains(int x, int y)
>> Returns whether this Rectangle contains point p.

boolean contains(**int** x, **int** y, **int** w, **int** h)

Returns whether this **Rectangle** contains the rectangle with origin (x, y), width w, and height h.

boolean contains(Point p)

Returns whether this **Rectangle** contains point p.

boolean contains(Rectangle r)

Returns whether this **Rectangle** contains rectangle r.

Rectangle2D createIntersection(Rectangle2D r)

Returns the intersection of rectangle r and this **Rectangle**.

Rectangle2D createUnion(Rectangle2D r)

Returns the union of rectangle r and this **Rectangle**.

boolean equals(Object v)

Returns whether v is a rectangle equal to this **Rectangle**.

Rectangle getBounds()

Returns the bounding box of this **Rectangle**.

Rectangle2D getBounds2D()

Returns the bounding box of this **Rectangle**.

double getHeight()

Returns the height of this **Rectangle**.

Point getLocation()

Returns the origin of this **Rectangle**.

Dimension getSize()

Returns the dimensions of this **Rectangle**.

double getWidth()

Returns the width of this **Rectangle**.

double getX()

Returns the x-coordinate of the origin of this **Rectangle**.

double getY()

Returns the y-coordinate of the origin of this **Rectangle**.

void grow(**int** dw, **int** dh)

Increases the width and height of this **Rectangle** respectively by dw and dh.

Rectangle intersection(Rectangle r)

Returns the intersection of this **Rectangle** with rectangle r.

boolean intersects(Rectangle r)

Returns whether this **Rectangle** intersects rectangle r.

boolean isEmpty()

Returns whether this **Rectangle** is empty.

int outcode(**double** x, **double** y)

Returns where the (x, y) lies with respect to this **Rectangle**.

void setBounds(**int** x, **int** y, **int** w, **int** h)

Sets the bounding rectangle of this **Rectangle** equal to a rectangle with (x, y) as its origin and with width w and height h.

void setBounds(Rectangle r)

Sets the bounding rectangle of this **Rectangle** equal to rectangle r.

void setLocation(**int** x, **int** y)

Sets (x, y) as the origin of this **Rectangle**.

      void setLocation(Point p)

          Sets p as the origin of this Rectangle.

      void setRect(**double** x, **double** y, **double** w, **double** h)

          Sets the origin to (x, y) and size to width w and height h for this Rectangle.

      void setSize(Dimension d)

          Sets the size of this Rectangle to that of dimension d.

      void setSize(**int** w, **int** h)

          Sets the size of this Rectangle to width w and height h.

      String toString()

          Returns a representation of this Rectangle.

      void translate(**int** dx, **int** dy)

          Translates the origin of this Rectangle by distances dx and dy respectively on the x- and y-axes.

      Rectangle union(Rectangle r)

          Returns the union of this Rectangle with rectangle r.

---

lang　　**interface** Runnable

PURPOSE

Describes the method needed for objects to be executed as threads.

INSTANCE METHOD SUMMARY

      void run()

          The method to be executed when a Runnable object-based thread is started.

---

lang　　**class** Runtime

PURPOSE

Represents an interface to the Java runtime environment.

CLASS METHOD SUMMARY

      static Runtime getRuntime()

          Returns the object that is runtime interface for the current application.

INSTANCE METHOD SUMMARY

      void addShutdownHook(Thread t)

          Registers thread t to be run during the Java virtual machine shutdown process.

      int availableProcessors()

          Returns the number of processors available to the Java virtual machine for executing threads.

      Process exec(String s)

          Runs the command s as a separate process. Returns a Process for managing that process. Equivalent to exec(**new** String[] = {s}, **null, null**).

      Process exec(String[] s)

          Returns exec(**s, null, null**).

Process exec(String[] s, String[] t)

Returns exec(s, t, **null**).

Process exec(String[] s, String[] t, File d)

Runs command s[0] as a separate process with s[1] through s[s.length-1] as the parameters to the process. The elements of t are operating system variable settings that are evaluated before s[0] is run. If d is non-**null**, then the working folder of the process is d; otherwise, the working folder is the working folder of the current thread. Returns a Process for managing that process.

Process exec(String s, String[] t)

Returns exec(**new** String[] = {s}, t, **null**).

Process exec(String s, String[] t, File d)

Returns exec(**new** String[] = {s}, t, d).

void exit(**int** n)

Initiates the shutdown process of the Java virtual machine. The return value given to the operating system is n, where a nonzero value indicates abnormal termination.

long freeMemory()

Returns the number of nonallocated memory bytes available to Java.

void gc()

Invokes System.gc().

void halt(int n)

Terminates the Java virtual machine without running any shutdown hooks. The return value given to the operating system is n, where a nonzero value indicates abnormal termination.

void load(String s)

Loads the file with name s as a dynamic library.

void loadLibrary(String s)

Loads the dynamic library with name s.

long maxMemory()

Returns the maximum number of bytes that Java will attempt to use.

boolean removeShutdownHook(Thread t)

Removes thread t from Java virtual machine shutdown process.

void runFinalization()

Invokes System.runFinalization().

long totalMemory()

Returns the number of bytes available to Java.

void traceInstructions(**boolean** b)

Sets whether Java should display debugging output for each executed bytecode.

void traceMethodCalls(**boolean** b)

Sets whether Java should display debugging output for each method invocation.

---

final class Scanner **implements** Iterable<String>

PURPOSE

Represents an input text source that decomposes its text into a sequence of numeric, string, and Boolean values, where each such value is known as a *token*. The default token delimiting pattern is whitespace.

CONSTRUCTOR SUMMARY

Scanner(File s)

Returns a new Scanner that produces values scanned from file s.

Scanner(File s, String c)

Returns a new Scanner that produces values scanned from file s, where the bytes in the file are translated according to character set c.

Scanner(InputStream s)

Returns a new Scanner that produces values scanned from input stream s.

Scanner(InputStream s, String c)

Returns a new Scanner that produces values scanned from input stream s, where the bytes in the stream are translated according to character set c.

Scanner(Readable s)

Returns a new Scanner that produces values scanned from source s.

Scanner(ReadableByteChannel s)

Returns a new Scanner that produces values scanned from channel s.

Scanner(ReadableByteChannel s, String c)

Returns a new Scanner that produces values scanned from channel s, where the bytes in the stream are translated according to character set c.

Scanner(String s)

Returns a new Scanner that produces values scanned from string s.

INSTANCE METHOD SUMMARY

void close()

Ensures that the input source of this Scanner is closed.

Pattern delimiter()

Returns the delimiting pattern used by this Scanner.

String findInLine(Pattern p)

Returns the next occurrence of a maximal matching of pattern p from the current line of the input source of this Scanner.

String findInLine(String p)

Returns the next occurrence of a maximal matching of the pattern expressed by p from the current line of the input source of this Scanner.

String findWithinHorizon(Pattern p, **int** n)

Returns the next occurrence of a maximal matching of pattern p from at most the next n characters of the current line of the input source of this Scanner.

String findWithinHorizon(String p, **int** n)

Returns the next occurrence of a maximal matching of the pattern expressed by p from at most the next n characters of the current line of the input source of this Scanner.

boolean hasNext()

Returns whether this Scanner has an unreturned token.

boolean hasNext(Pattern p)

Returns **true** if and only if this Scanner has a next token and it matches pattern p.

boolean hasNext(String p)

Returns **true** if and only if this Scanner has a next token and it matches the pattern expressed by p.

boolean hasNextBigDecimal()

Returns **true** if and only if this Scanner has a next token and it is numeric.

boolean hasNextBigInteger()

Returns **true** if and only if this Scanner has a next token and it is an integer.

boolean hasNextBigInteger(**int** b)

Returns **true** if and only if this Scanner has a next token and it is a base b integer.

boolean hasNextBoolean()

Returns **true** if and only if this Scanner has a next token and it is a case insensitive string equal to either "true" or "false".

boolean hasNextByte()

Returns **true** if and only if this Scanner has a next token and it represents a legal **byte** value.

boolean hasNextByte(**int** b)

Returns **true** if and only if this Scanner has a next token and it represents a legal base b **byte** value.

boolean hasNextDouble()

Returns **true** if and only if this Scanner has a next token and it represents a legal **double** value.

boolean hasNextFloat()

Returns **true** if and only if this Scanner has a next token and it represents a legal **float** value.

boolean hasNextInt()

Returns **true** if and only if this Scanner has a next token and it represents a legal **int** value.

boolean hasNextInt(**int** b)

Returns **true** if and only if this Scanner has a next token and it represents a legal base b **int** value.

boolean hasNextLong()

Returns **true** if and only if this Scanner has a next token and it represents a legal **long** value.

boolean hasNextLong(**int** b)

Returns **true** if and only if this Scanner has a next token and it represents a legal base b **long** value.

boolean hasNextShort()

Returns **true** if and only if this Scanner has a next token and it represents a legal **short** value.

boolean hasNextShort(**int** b)

Returns **true** if and only if this Scanner has a next token and it represents a legal base b **short** value.

`IOException ioException()`

Returns the last `IOException` thrown by the input source of this `Scanner`.

`Locale locale()`

Returns the locale of this `Scanner`.

`MatchResult match()`

Returns the match result from the last find, skip, or next operation performed by this `Scanner`.

`String next()`

Returns the next token of this `Scanner` as a string.

`String next(Pattern p)`

Returns the next token of this `Scanner`, where the token is a maximal matching of pattern p.

`String next(String p)`

Returns the next token of this `Scanner`, where the token is a maximal matching of the pattern expressed by string p.

`BigDecimal nextBigDecimal()`

Returns the next token of this `Scanner` as a `BigDecimal`.

`BigInteger nextBigInteger()`

Returns the next token of this `Scanner` as a `BigInteger`.

`BigInteger nextBigInteger(int b)`

Returns the next token of this `Scanner` as a base b integer.

boolean `nextBoolean()`

Returns the next token of this `Scanner` as a **boolean**.

byte `nextByte()`

Returns the next token of this `Scanner` as a **byte**.

byte `nextByte(int b)`

Returns the next token of this `Scanner` as a base b **byte**.

double `nextDouble()`

Returns the next token of this `Scanner` as a **double**.

float `nextFloat()`

Returns the next token of this `Scanner` as a **float**.

int `nextInt()`

Returns the next token of this `Scanner` as an **int**.

int `nextInt(int b)`

Returns the next token of this `Scanner` as a base b **int**.

`String nextLine()`

Returns the remaining text of the current input line being parsed by this `Scanner`.

long `nextLong()`

Returns the next token of this `Scanner` as a **long**.

long `nextLong(int b)`

Returns the next token of this `Scanner` as a base b **long**.

short `nextShort()`

Returns the next token of this `Scanner` as a **short**.

short `nextShort(int b)`

Returns the next token of this `Scanner` as a base b **short**.

int radix()

  Returns the default radix (base) of this Scanner.

void remove()

  Throws an UnsupportedOperationException.

Scanner skip(Pattern p)

  Skips the next token and preceding delimiters of this Scanner, where the token is a maximal matching of pattern string p.

Scanner skip(String p)

  Skips the next token and preceding delimiters of this Scanner, where the token is a maximal matching of the pattern expressed by string p.

String toString()

  Returns a representation of this Scanner.

Scanner useDelimiter(Pattern p)

  Sets the delimiting pattern of this Scanner to p.

Scanner useDelimiter(String p)

  Sets the delimiting pattern of this Scanner to the pattern expressed by string p.

Scanner useLocale(Locale l)

  Sets the locale of this Scanner to l.

Scanner useRadix(int r)

  Sets the default radix (base) of this Scanner to r.

| util | interface Set<E> extends Collection<E> |

PURPOSE

Describes a set view of a collection; i.e., different elements have different values.

INSTANCE METHOD SUMMARY

boolean add(E v)

  Attempts to add a new element to this Set with value v and returns **true** if the value v was not previously there. This operation is optional.

boolean addAll(Collection<? extends E> c)

  Adds to this Set all of the elements in c and returns **true** if the set has changed. This operation is optional.

void clear()

  Removes all elements from this Set. This operation is optional.

boolean contains(Object v)

  Returns **true** if and only if this Set has an element with value v.

boolean containsAll(Collection<?> c)

  Returns **true** if and only if this Set contains all of the values in set c.

boolean equals(Object v)

  Returns **true** if and only if v is an instance of Set representing the same list as this Set.

int hashCode()

  Returns the hash code of this object.

boolean isEmpty()

  Returns whether this Set has any elements.

```
Iterator<E> iterator()
```
   Returns an iterator over the elements in this Set.
```
boolean remove(Object v)
```
   Attempts to remove value v from this Set and returns whether this Set has changed. The operation is optional.
```
boolean removeAll(Collection<?> c)
```
   Attempts to remove elements of c from this Set and returns whether this Set has changed. The operation is optional.
```
boolean retainAll(Collection<?> c)
```
   Attempts to remove from this Set all of the values not in c. Returns whether a value was removed. The operation is optional.
```
int size()
```
   Returns the number of elements in this Set.
```
Object[] toArray()
```
   Returns an array whose elements correspond to the elements of this Set.
```
<T> T[] toArray(T[] a)
```
   Returns an array of the same type as array a whose elements correspond to the elements of this Set. The returned array is a if a is big enough.

| awt | **interface** Shape |

PURPOSE

Describes the methods necessary for representing a shape described by a path iterator that specifies both the outline and the means for identifying how a shape divides a plane into interior and external regions.

INSTANCE METHOD SUMMARY
```
boolean contains(double x, double y)
```
   Returns whether (x, y) lies within the boundary of this Shape.
```
boolean contains(double x, double y, double w, double h)
```
   Returns whether the interior of this Shape contains the rectangular region originating at (x, y) with width w and height h.
```
boolean contains(Point2D p)
```
   Returns whether p lies within the boundary of this Shape.
```
boolean contains(Rectangle2D r)
```
   Returns whether the interior of this Shape contains the rectangular region represented by r.
```
Rectangle getBounds()
```
   Returns the bounding rectangle of this Shape.
```
Rectangle2D getBounds2D()
```
   Returns the bounding rectangle of this Shape.
```
PathIterator getPathIterator(AffineTransform a)
```
   Returns an iterator that iterates over a list of segments approximating the boundary of this Shape, where segment endpoints are modified with respect to transform a.

PathIterator getPathIterator(AffineTransform a, **double** v)

Returns an iterator that iterates over a list of segments approximating the boundary of this Shape, where segment endpoints are modified with respect to transform a and where value v is a limit on the distance of a segment point from its true position on the shape outline.

boolean intersects(**double** x, **double** y, **double** w, **double** h)

Returns whether the interior of this Shape intersects the rectangular region originating at (x, y) with width w and height h.

boolean intersects(Rectangle2D r)

Returns whether the interior of this Shape intersects the rectangular region represented by r.

---

final class Short **extends** Number **implements** Comparable<Short>

PURPOSE

Represents a **short** value within a class wrapper.

FIELD SUMMARY

static final short MAX_VALUE

Represents the maximum value of type **short** (i.e., $2^{15} - 1$).

static final short MIN_VALUE

Represents the minimum value of type **short** (i.e., -2^{15}).

static final int SIZE

Represents the number of bits used to represent a **short** value.

static final Class<Short> TYPE

Represents the type **short**.

CLASS METHOD SUMMARY

static Short decode(String n)

Constructs a new Short object representing Integer.parseShort(s, n), where n is 8, 10, or 16 depending on whether s is respectively a numeric string in octal, decimal, or hexadecimal format.

static short parseShort(String s)

Returns Short.parseShort(s, 10).

static short parseShort(String s, **int** n)

Returns the **short** value represented by parsing string s as an optionally signed integer value in radix n.

static short reverseBytes(**short** n)

Returns the value produced by reversing the order of the bytes in the two's complement binary representation of n.

static String toString(**short** n)

Returns a new String object equal to the value of n.

static Short valueOf(**short** n)

Returns a Short representation of value n.

static Short valueOf(String s)

Returns Short.parseShort(s, 10).

    static Short valueOf(String s, **int** n)

        Returns a new Short representing Short.parseShort(s, n).

CONSTRUCTOR SUMMARY

    Short(**short** n)

        Constructs a new Short object representing value n.

    Short(String s)

        Constructs a new Short object representing Integer.parseShort(s).

INSTANCE METHOD SUMMARY

    byte byteValue()

        Returns the **short** value of this Short as a **byte**.

    int compareTo(Object v)

        Returns a negative value, zero, or a positive value depending respectively on whether this object is less than, equal to, or greater than v.

    int compareTo(Short n)

        Returns a negative value, zero, or a positive value depending respectively on whether this object is less than, equal to, or greater than n.

    double doubleValue()

        Returns the value of this Short as a **double**.

    boolean equals(Object v)

        Returns **true** if and only if v is an instance of Integer representing the same **int** value that this object represents.

    float floatValue()

        Returns the value of this Short as a **float**.

    int hashCode()

        Returns the hash code of this object.

    int intValue()

        Returns the value of this Short as an **int**.

    long longValue()

        Returns the value of this Short as a **long**.

    short shortValue()

        Returns the value of this Short.

    String toString()

        Returns a String representation of the value of this object.

`util`   **interface** SortedMap<K, V> **extends** Map<K, V>

PURPOSE

Describes a map with the added functionality that keys are arranged in sorted order.

INSTANCE METHOD SUMMARY

    Comparator<? **super** K> comparator()

        Returns the comparator of this sorted map, with **null** indicating the natural ordering.

    K firstKey()

        Returns the first key of this sorted map.

SortedMap<K, V> headMap(K v)

Returns the subportion of this sorted map whose keys are less than value v.

K lastKey()

Returns the last key of this sorted map.

SortedMap<K, V> subMap(K v1, K v2)

Returns the subportion of this sorted map whose keys are greater than or equal to value v1 and strictly less than value v2.

SortedMap<K, V> tailMap(K v)

Returns the subportion of this sorted map whose keys are greater than or equal to value v.

---

util   **class** Stack<T> **extends** Vector<T>

PURPOSE

Provides a stack view of a vector; i.e., last-in-first-out behavior.

CONSTRUCTOR SUMMARY

Stack()

Constructs a new empty Stack.

INSTANCE METHOD SUMMARY

boolean empty()

Returns **true** if and only if this Stack is empty.

T peek()

Returns the next value that pop() would return for this Stack.

T pop()

Removes and returns the top element of this Stack.

T push(Object v)

Pushes value v onto the top of this Stack.

int search(Object v)

Returns the position of value v onto the top of this Stack, where position is 1-based; i.e., the top element has position 1, and so on. If the value is not there, the method returns −1.

---

lang   **final class** String **implements** Serializable, Comparable<String>, CharSequence

PURPOSE

Represents a sequence of characters using methods that provide inspection but not mutation of the sequence.

FIELD SUMMARY

static final Comparator<String> CASE_INSENSITIVE_ORDER

Represents a string Comparator that orders strings using method compareTo-IgnoreCase().

CLASS METHOD SUMMARY

`static` String copyValueOf(`char`[] c)

Returns **new** String(c, 0, c.length).

`static` String copyValueOf(`char`[] c, `int` i, `int` n)

Returns **new** String(c, i, n).

`static` String format(Locale l, String s, Object... a)

Returns a locale l formatted version of list a using format string s.

`static` String format(String s, Object... a)

Returns a formatted version of list a using format string s.

`static` String valueOf(`boolean` b)

Returns the string representation of **boolean** value b.

`static` String valueOf(`char` c)

Returns the string representation of **char** value c.

`static` String valueOf(`char`[] c)

Returns **new** String(c, 0, c.length).

`static` String valueOf(`char`[] c, `int` i, `int` n)

Returns **new** String(c, i, n).

`static` String valueOf(`double` n)

Returns the string representation of the **double** value n.

`static` String valueOf(`float` n)

Returns the string representation of the **float** value n.

`static` String valueOf(`int` n)

Returns the string representation of the **int** value n.

`static` String valueOf(`long` n)

Returns the String representation of the **long** value n.

`static` String valueOf(Object v)

Returns v.toString().

CONSTRUCTOR SUMMARY

String()

Constructs a new String object representing the empty character string.

String(`byte`[] b)

Invokes String(b, 0, b.length, s), where s is the name of the default character set.

String(`byte`[] b, `int` i, `int` n)

Invokes String(b, i, n, s), where s is the name of the default character set.

String(`byte`[] b, `int` i, `int` n, String s)

Constructs a new String by decoding a length n subarray of b starting with the element with i using the character set with name s.

String(`byte`[] bytes, String s)

Invokes String(b, 0, b.length, s).

String(`char`[] c)

Invokes String(c, 0, c.length).

String(`char`[] value, `int` i, `int` n)

Constructs a new String of length n from the subarray of c starting with the element with i.

```
String(int[] a, int n, int m)
```

Constructs a new `String` that contains the characters from a subarray of array `a`, where value `n` is the index of the first code point of the subarray and value `m` is the length of the subarray.

```
String(String s)
```

Constructs a new `String` that is a copy of the character sequence represented by `s`.

```
String(StringBuffer b)
```

Invokes `String(b.toString())`.

```
String(StringBuilder s)
```

Constructs a new `String` that contains the character sequence in string builder `s`.

INSTANCE METHOD SUMMARY

```
char charAt(int i)
```

Returns the character at index `i` in the character sequence represented by this `String`.

```
int codePointAt(int i)
```

If the `i`-th character in this `String` is not a high surrogate, then it is returned; otherwise the code point character represented by the surrogate pair of the `i`-th and `i+1`-th characters is returned.

```
int codePointBefore(int i)
```

If the `i-1`-th character in this `String` is not a low surrogate, then it is returned; otherwise the code point character represented by the surrogate pair of the `i-1`-th and `i-2`-th characters is returned.

```
int compareTo(Object v)
```

Lexicographically compares this `String` to `v` by returning a negative value, zero, or a positive value depending respectively on whether this object is less than, equal to, or greater than `v`.

```
int compareTo(String s)
```

Lexicographically compares this `String` to `s` by returning a negative value, zero, or a positive value depending respectively on whether this object is less than, equal to, or greater than `s`.

```
int compareToIgnoreCase(String s)
```

Lexicographically compares this `String` to `s` by returning a negative value, zero, or a positive value depending respectively on whether this `String` is less than, equal to, or greater than `s` while ignoring case differences.

```
String concat(String s)
```

Returns a `String` that is a concatenation of this `String` with `s`.

```
boolean contains(String s)
```

Returns whether this `String` contains string `s`.

```
boolean contentEquals(StringBuffer b)
```

Returns `equals(b.toString())`.

```
boolean endsWith(String s)
```

Returns **true** if and only if the last n characters in the character sequence represented by this `String` equal the character string sequence represented by `s`.

boolean equals(Object v)

Returns **true** if and only if v is an instance of String representing the same character sequence that this String represents.

boolean equalsIgnoreCase(String s)

Returns **true** if and only if s represents the same character sequence that this String represents while ignoring case differences.

byte[] getBytes()

Returns a new **byte** array that encodes the character sequence represented by this String using the default character set.

byte[] getBytes(String s)

Returns a new **byte** array that encodes the character sequence represented by this String using the character set with name s.

void getChars(int i, int j, char[] c, int k)

Copies the character subsequence of this String with indices i through j into array c starting at its element with index k.

int hashCode()

Returns the hash code of this String.

int indexOf(int c)

Returns indexOf(c, 0).

int indexOf(int c, int i)

If character c occurs in character sequence of this String starting from index i on, then the method returns the index of the first such occurrence; otherwise, the method returns –1.

int indexOf(String s)

Returns indexOf(s, 0).

int indexOf(String s, int i)

If the character sequence of s occurs as a subsequence of this String starting somewhere from index i on, then the method returns the index of the first such occurrence; otherwise, the method returns –1.

String intern()

Returns a String that is a duplicate of this String such that Java considers the returned string to be the canonical representation of the character sequence represented by this String.

int lastIndexOf(int c)

Returns lastIndexOf(c, length() - 1).

int lastIndexOf(int c, int i)

If character c occurs in character sequence of this String prior to index i+1, then the method returns the index of the last such occurrence; otherwise, the method returns –1.

int lastIndexOf(String s)

Returns lastIndexOf(s, length() - 1).

int lastIndexOf(String s, int i)

If the character sequence of s occurs as a subsequence of this String starting somewhere prior to index i+1, then the method returns the index of the last such occurrence; otherwise, the method returns –1.

int length()

Returns the length of the character sequence of this String.

`boolean` matches(String r)

Returns whether this `String` is an element of the set represented by regular expression r.

`boolean` regionMatches(`boolean` b, `int` i, String s, `int` j, `int` k)

Returns whether the length k character subsequences of this `String` starting at index i and string s starting at index j are equal. If and only if b is **true** does testing for equality ignore character case.

`boolean` regionMatches(`int` i, String s, `int` j, `int` k)

Returns regionMatches(**false**, i, s, j, k).

String replace(String s, String t)

Returns a new `String` equal to this `String` such that each occurrence of substring s in this `String` is replaced with t.

String replace(**char** c, **char** d)

Returns a new `String` whose character sequence is a pseudo-duplicate of the character sequence of this `String`. In creating the character sequence of the new `String` from this `String`, each occurrence of character c is replaced with character d.

String replaceAll(String r, String s)

Returns a new `String` whose character sequence is a pseudo-duplicate of the character sequence of this `String`. In creating the character sequence of the new `String` from this `String`, each occurrence of regular expression r is replaced with s.

String replaceFirst(String r, String s)

Returns a new `String` whose character sequence is a pseudo-duplicate of the character sequence of this `String`. In creating the character sequence of the new `String` from this `String`, the first occurrence of regular expression r is replaced with s.

String[] split(String r)

Returns split(r, 0).

String[] split(String r, **int** n)

Returns a new `String` array whose elements are (possibly empty) substrings of this `String` such that the substring represented by each element of the array is followed with this `String` by an occurrence of regular expression r or is the substring that ends this `String`. If n is negative, then the regular expression is matched as many times as possible. If instead, n has the value 0, then the regular expression is also matched as many times as possible; however, any trailing elements representing the empty string are removed. If instead, n is positive, then the regular expression is matched at most n−1 times and the last element of the new array represents the substring of this `String` following the last matched occurrence of regular expression r.

`boolean` startsWith(String s)

Returns startsWith(s, 0).

`boolean` startsWith(String s, `int` i)

Returns whether the character sequence of s occurs as a subsequence of this `String` starting at index i.

CharSequence subSequence(int i, int j)

> Returns a new CharSequence representing the elements with indices i … j − 1 from the character sequence of this String.

String substring(int i)

> Returns substring(i, length()).

String substring(int i, int j)

> Returns a new String representing the elements with indices i … j − 1 from the character sequence of this String.

char[] toCharArray()

> Returns a new **char** array representing the character sequence of this String.

String toLowerCase()

> Returns toLowerCase(l), where l is the default locale for this system.

String toLowerCase(Locale l)

> Returns a new String that is a duplicate of this String such that all characters in the new String are the lowercase equivalents with respect to locale l of the corresponding characters in this String.

String toString()

> Returns **this**.

String toUpperCase()

> Returns toUpperCase(l), where l is the default locale for this system.

String toUpperCase(Locale l)

> Returns a new String that is a duplicate of this String such that all characters in the new String are the uppercase equivalents with respect to locale l of the corresponding characters in this String.

String trim()

> Returns a new String that is a duplicate of this String such that no leading or trailing whitespace of this String is duplicated.

---

lang **final class** StringBuffer **implements** Serializable, CharSequence

PURPOSE

Represents a mutable sequence of characters. Thus, unlike a String, a StringBuffer can be modified.

CONSTRUCTOR SUMMARY

StringBuffer()

> Invokes StringBuffer(16).

StringBuffer(int n)

> Constructs a new StringBuffer object representing the empty character string with an initial capacity of representing character sequences of length n or less.

StringBuffer(String s)

> Constructs a new StringBuffer object representing the same character sequence that string s represents with an initial capacity of representing character sequences of length n+16 or less.

INSTANCE METHOD SUMMARY

StringBuffer append(**boolean** b)

Returns append(String.valueOf(b)).

StringBuffer append(**char** c)

Returns append(String.valueOf(c)).

StringBuffer append(**char**[] c)

Returns append(String.valueOf(c)).

StringBuffer append(**char**[] c, **int** i, **int** n)

Returns append(String.valueOf(c, i, n)).

StringBuffer append(**double** n)

Returns append(String.valueOf(n)).

StringBuffer append(**float** n)

Returns append(String.valueOf(n)).

StringBuffer append(**int** n)

Returns append(String.valueOf(n)).

StringBuffer append(**long** n)

Returns append(String.valueOf(n)).

StringBuffer append(Object v)

Returns append(String.valueOf(v)).

StringBuffer append(String s)

Returns this StringBuffer after appending the character sequence represented by s to the character sequence represented by this StringBuffer.

StringBuffer append(StringBuffer s)

Returns this StringBuffer after appending the character sequence represented by s to the character sequence represented by this StringBuffer.

int capacity()

Returns the current capacity of this StringBuffer.

char charAt(**int** i)

Returns the character at index i in the character sequence represented by this StringBuffer.

StringBuffer delete(**int** i, **int** j)

Returns this StringBuffer after removing the elements with indices i ... j - 1 from the character sequence of this StringBuffer.

StringBuffer deleteCharAt(**int** i)

Invokes delete(i, i+1).

void ensureCapacity(**int** n)

If capacity() < n, then the method increases the capacity of this String-Buffer to n.

void getChars(**int** i, **int** j, **char**[] c, **int** k)

Copies the elements with indices i ... j - 1 from the character sequence represented by this StringBuffer into array c starting at its element with subscript k.

int indexOf(String s)

Invokes indexOf(s, 0).

`int` `indexOf(String s, int i)`

If the character sequence of s occurs as a subsequence of this `StringBuffer` starting somewhere from index i on, then the method returns the index of the first such occurrence; otherwise, the method returns –1.

`StringBuffer insert(int i, boolean b)`

Returns `insert(i, String.valueOf(b))`.

`StringBuffer insert(int i, char c)`

Returns `insert(i, String.valueOf(c))`.

`StringBuffer insert(int i, char[] c)`

Returns `insert(i, String.valueOf(c))`.

`StringBuffer insert(int i, char[] c, int j, int n)`

Returns `insert(i, new String(c, j, n))`.

`StringBuffer insert(int i, double n)`

Returns `insert(i, String.valueOf(n))`.

`StringBuffer insert(int i, float n)`

Returns `insert(i, String.valueOf(n))`.

`StringBuffer insert(int i, int n)`

Returns `insert(i, String.valueOf(n))`.

`StringBuffer insert(int i, long n)`

Returns `insert(i, String.valueOf(n))`.

`StringBuffer insert(int i, Object v)`

Returns `insert(i, v.toString(n))`.

`StringBuffer insert(int i, String s)`

If s is **null**, then the method returns `insert(i, "null")`. If instead, s is non-**null**, then the method returns this `StringBuffer` after inserting the character sequence represented by s into the character sequence represented by this `StringBuffer`. The insertion occurs immediately before the element with index i in the character sequence represented by this `StringBuffer`.

`int lastIndexOf(String s)`

Returns `lastIndexOf(s, length() - 1)`.

`int lastIndexOf(String s, int i)`

If the character sequence of s occurs as a subsequence of this `String` starting somewhere prior to index i+1, then the method returns the index of the last such occurrence; otherwise, the method returns –1.

`int length()`

Returns the length of the character sequence represented by this `StringBuffer`.

`StringBuffer replace(int i, int j, String s)`

Returns this `StringBuffer` after invoking `delete(i, j)` and then `insert(i, s)`.

`StringBuffer reverse()`

Returns this `StringBuffer` after reversing the elements of its character sequence.

`void setCharAt(int i, char c)`

Sets to c the element at index i in the character sequence represented by this `StringBuffer`.

`void` setLength(`int` n)

If n < length(), then the method invokes delete(n, length()). If instead n equals length(), then the method does nothing. If instead n > length, then the length of the character sequence represented by this `StringBuffer` is increased to n by appending a sufficient number of the null characters ('\u0000') to it.

CharSequence subSequence(`int` i, `int` j)

Returns a new `CharSequence` representing the elements with indices i ... j − 1 from the character sequence of this `StringBuffer`.

String substring(`int` i)

Returns substring(i, length()).

String substring(`int` i, `int` j)

Returns a new `String` representing the elements with indices i ... j − 1 from the character sequence of this `StringBuffer`.

String toString()

Returns a `String` representation of the value of this `StringBuffer`.

---

lang   **class** `StringIndexOutOfBoundsException` **extends**
`IndexOutOfBoundsException`

PURPOSE

Represents an illegal element indexing event with a `String` method.

CONSTRUCTOR SUMMARY

StringIndexOutOfBoundsException()

Constructs a new `StringIndexOutOfBoundsException` with a default message.

StringIndexOutOfBoundsException(`int` i)

Constructs a new `StringIndexOutOfBoundsException` class with a message indicating i is an illegal index value.

StringIndexOutOfBoundsException(String s)

Constructs a `StringIndexOutOfBoundsException` with message s.

---

util   **class** `StringTokenizer` **implements** Enumeration

PURPOSE

Provides a token view of a string.

CONSTRUCTOR SUMMARY

StringTokenizer(String s)

Constructs a new `StringTokenizer` for string s using whitespace as token delimiters. Delimiters are not returned as tokens.

StringTokenizer(String s, String t)

Constructs a new `StringTokenizer` for string s with the characters in t as the token delimiters.

StringTokenizer(String s, String t, **boolean** b)

Constructs a new StringTokenizer for string s with the characters in t as the token delimiters. Delimiters are returned as tokens depending on b.

INSTANCE METHOD SUMMARY

int countTokens()

Returns the number of times that nextToken() can be invoked for this StringTokenizer without generating an exception.

boolean hasMoreElements()

Returns whether this StringTokenizer has any more tokens to return.

hasMoreTokens()

Returns whether this StringTokenizer has any more tokens to return.

Object nextElement()

Returns the next token of this StringTokenizer. Throws a NoSuchElement-Exception if there is no next token.

String nextToken()

Returns the next token of this StringTokenizer. Throws a NoSuchElement-Exception if there is no next token.

String nextToken(String t)

Returns the next token of this StringTokenizer with the characters in t now being its token delimiters. Throws a NoSuchElementException if there is no next token.

---

lang | **final class** System **extends** Object

PURPOSE

Defines three standard streams and several common, miscellaneous class methods.

FIELD SUMMARY

static PrintStream err

Represents the standard error stream. By default, standard error output stream is associated with the console window.

static InputStream in

Represents the standard input stream. By default, standard input stream is gotten from the keyboard's interface with the console window.

static PrintStream out

Represents the standard output stream. By default, standard output stream is associated with the console window

INSTANCE METHOD SUMMARY

static void arraycopy(Object u, **int** i, Object v, **int** j, **int** k)

Sets k elements of array u starting with the element with index j to the corresponding values of k elements of array u starting with the element with index i.

public static String clearProperty(String s)

Removes the system property specified by the key with name s.

static long currentTimeMillis()

Returns the current time in milliseconds.

`static void exit(int n)`

Ends the current program with status n, where a nonzero value for n indicates abnormal termination.

`static void gc()`

Invokes the Java garbage collector.

`static Map<String,String> getenv()`

Returns a nonmodifiable view of the current system environment.

`static String getenv(String s)`

Returns the value of the environment variable with name s.

`static Properties getProperties()`

Returns the current system properties.

`static String getProperty(String s)`

Returns `getProperty(s, null)`.

`static String getProperty(String s, String t)`

Returns the value of the system property named s if it exists; otherwise, it returns t.

`static SecurityManager getSecurityManager()`

Returns the system security manager.

`static int identityHashCode(Object v)`

Returns the hash code that method `hashCode()` of class `Object` would return for object v (i.e., the value is not necessarily returned by `v.hashCode()`).

`static Channel inheritedChannel()`

Returns the channel inherited from the creator of this Java virtual machine.

`static void load(String s)`

Loads the file with name s as a dynamic library.

`static void loadLibrary(String s)`

Loads the system library with name s as a dynamic library.

`static String mapLibraryName(String s)`

Returns a platform-specific string associated with the library with name s.

`static long nanoTime()`

Returns in nanoseconds the current value of the system timer.

`static void runFinalization()`

Causes Java to invoke the `finalize()` methods for any unreferenced objects whose `finalize()` methods have not yet been run.

`static void setErr(PrintStream s)`

Sets the standard error stream to s.

`static void setIn(InputStream s)`

Sets the standard input stream to s.

`static void setOut(PrintStream s)`

Sets the standard output stream to s.

`static void setProperties(Properties s)`

Sets the system properties to s.

`static String setProperty(String s, String t)`

Sets system property s to value t.

`static void setSecurityManager(SecurityManager s)`

Sets the system security manager to s.

`awt.event` **class** TextEvent **extends** AWTEvent

PURPOSE
Represents a text-changing event.

FIELD SUMMARY

static int TEXT_FIRST
Represents the minimal index of a text event.

static int TEXT_LAST
Represents the maximal index of a text event.

static int TEXT_VALUE_CHANGED
Represents a text change event.

CONSTRUCTOR SUMMARY

TextEvent(Object v, **int** n)
Constructs a new TextEvent of type n for originating object v.

INSTANCE METHOD SUMMARY

String paramString()
Returns a representation of this TextEvent.

`awt.event` **interface** TextListener **extends** EventListener

PURPOSE
Describes the action a text listener must perform.

INSTANCE METHOD SUMMARY

void textValueChanged(TextEvent e)
Handles change in text event e.

`lang` **class** Thread **extends** Object **implements** Runnable

PURPOSE
Represents a prioritized thread of execution (a flow of control) in a program.

FIELD SUMMARY

static int MAX_PRIORITY
Represents the maximum possible thread priority.

static int MIN_PRIORITY
Represents the minimum possible thread priority.

static int NORM_PRIORITY
Represents the default thread priority.

CLASS METHOD SUMMARY

static int activeCount()
Returns the number of active threads in the thread group of the thread that is currently executing.

static Thread currentThread()

Returns a reference to the thread that is currently executing.

static void dumpStack()

Prints to the standard error stream a stack trace of the thread that is currently executing.

static int enumerate(Thread[] a)

Copies into array a all of the active threads in the thread group of the thread that is currently executing.

static boolean interrupted()

Tests whether the thread that is currently executing has been interrupted since a prior invocation of this method.

static void sleep(long n)

Causes the currently executing thread to pause its execution for n milliseconds.

static void sleep(long m, int n)

Causes the thread that is currently executing to pause its execution for 1,000,000 · m + n nanoseconds.

static void yield()

Causes the thread that is currently executing to temporarily pause if there exist other threads.

CONSTRUCTOR SUMMARY

Thread()

Invokes Thread(**null**, **null**, s), where s is a new name of the form "Thread-" + n, where n is an integer.

Thread(Runnable r)

Invokes Thread(**null**, r, s), where s is a new name of the form "Thread-" + n, where n is an integer.

Thread(Runnable r, String s)

Invokes Thread(**null**, r, s).

Thread(String s)

Invokes Thread(**null**, **null**, s).

Thread(ThreadGroup g, Runnable r)

Invokes Thread(t, r, s), where s is a new name of the form "Thread-" + n, where n is an integer.

Thread(ThreadGroup g, Runnable r, String s)

Constructs a new Thread object belonging to thread group g with run object r, and name s.

Thread(ThreadGroup g, Runnable r, String s, long n)

Constructs a new Thread belonging to thread group g with run object r, name s, and a requested stack size of n. The stack size is the number of bytes of memory to reserve for this object's execution. Whether and how the stack size request is handled is system dependent.

Thread(ThreadGroup g, String s)

Invokes Thread(g, **null**, s).

INSTANCE METHOD SUMMARY

void checkAccess()

Throws a SecurityException if the thread that is currently executing does not have permission to modify this Thread.

`void` `destroy()`

Destroys this `Thread`.

`ClassLoader` `getContextClassLoader()`

Returns the `ClassLoader` for this `Thread`.

`String` `getName()`

Returns the name of this `Thread`.

`int` `getPriority()`

Returns the priority of this `Thread`.

`ThreadGroup` `getThreadGroup()`

Returns the group of this `Thread`.

`static` `boolean` `holdsLock(Object v)`

Returns **true** if and only if this `Thread` holds the monitor lock on object v.

`void` `interrupt()`

Interrupts this `Thread`.

`boolean` `isAlive()`

Tests whether this `Thread` is alive.

`boolean` `isDaemon()`

Tests whether this `Thread` is a daemon.

`boolean` `isInterrupted()`

Tests whether this `Thread` has ever been interrupted.

`void` `join()`

Returns `join(0)`.

`void` `join(long m)`

If m is nonzero, then Java waits at most m milliseconds for this thread to die; otherwise it waits forever.

`void` `join(long m, int n)`

Waits at most $1{,}000{,}000 \cdot m + n$ nanoseconds for this thread to die.

`void` `run()`

If this `Thread` has a non-**null** `Runnable` object then the `run()` method of that object is run; otherwise, the method returns immediately.

`void` `setContextClassLoader(ClassLoader c)`

Sets the `ClassLoader` for this `Thread` to c.

`void` `setDaemon(boolean b)`

If b is **true**, then this `Thread` is a daemon thread; otherwise it is a user thread.

`void` `setName(String s)`

Sets the name of this `Thread` to name s.

`void` `setPriority(int n)`

Sets the priority of this `Thread` to n.

`void` `start()`

Causes this `Thread` to start executing.

`String` `toString()`

Returns a `String` representation of this `Thread`, which includes its name, priority, and thread group.

| lang | **class** ThreadGroup |

PURPOSE
Represents a set of threads and thread groups.

CONSTRUCTOR SUMMARY

ThreadGroup(String s)

Equivalent to ThreadGroup(g, s), where g is the ThreadGroup of the thread currently running.

ThreadGroup(ThreadGroup g, String s)

Constructs a new ThreadGroup with name s and with g the parent Thread-Group of the new ThreadGroup.

INSTANCE METHOD SUMMARY

int activeCount()

Returns the number of active threads in this ThreadGroup or its subgroups.

int activeGroupCount()

Returns the number of active groups in this ThreadGroup or its subgroups.

void checkAccess()

Throws a SecurityException if the currently running thread does not have permission to modify this ThreadGroup.

void destroy()

Throws an IllegalThreadStateException if this ThreadGroup is either not empty or has already been destroyed; otherwise, this ThreadGroup is destroyed. Note, a daemon ThreadGroup is destroyed automatically when either its last thread has been stopped or its last subgroup has been destroyed.

int enumerate(Thread[] t)

Returns enumerate(t, **true**).

int enumerate(Thread[] t, **boolean** b)

Returns the number of references copied to t, where if b is **true**, then references to active threads belonging to this ThreadGroup or its subgroups are copied to t; otherwise, only references to active threads belonging to this ThreadGroup are copied to t.

int enumerate(ThreadGroup[] g)

Returns enumerate(g, **true**).

int enumerate(ThreadGroup[] t, **boolean** b)

Returns the number of references copied to t, where if b is **true**, then references to active subgroups belonging to this ThreadGroup or its subgroups are copied to t; otherwise, only references to active subgroups belonging to this Thread-Group are copied to t.

int getMaxPriority()

Returns the maximum priority to which a thread in this ThreadGroup can be set.

String getName()

Returns the name of this ThreadGroup.

ThreadGroup getParent()

Returns the parent ThreadGroup of this ThreadGroup.

void interrupt()

Invokes t.interrupt() for any thread t belonging to this ThreadGroup or its subgroups.

boolean isDaemon()

Returns **true** if and only if this ThreadGroup is a daemon ThreadGroup.

boolean isDestroyed()

Returns **true** if and only if this ThreadGroup has been destroyed.

void list()

Displays debugging information to standard output regarding this Thread-Group.

boolean parentOf(ThreadGroup g)

Returns **true** if and only if this ThreadGroup is g or if an ancestor Thread-Group is g.

void setDaemon(**boolean** b)

If b is **true**, then this ThreadGroup is made a daemon ThreadGroup; otherwise, this ThreadGroup is made a normal ThreadGroup.

void setMaxPriority(**int** n)

Sets the maximal assignable priority of this ThreadGroup to n.

String toString()

Returns a String representation of this ThreadGroup.

void uncaughtException(Thread t, Throwable e)

Invoked by Java when thread t from this ThreadGroup is stopped because of uncaught exception e.

---

lang   **class** Throwable **implements** Serializable

PURPOSE

Represents an exception or error in Java. In particular, Throwable is the superclass of all other exception and error classes.

CONSTRUCTOR SUMMARY

Throwable()

Equivalent to Throwable(**null, null**).

Throwable(String s)

Equivalent to Throwable(s, **null**).

Throwable(String s, Throwable t)

Constructs a new Throwable with message s and cause t.

Throwable(Throwable t)

Equivalent to Throwable(s, t), where s equals **null** if t equals **null**; otherwise s equals t.toString().

INSTANCE METHOD SUMMARY

Throwable fillInStackTrace()

Updates this Throwable with information regarding the execution sequence of the current thread.

Throwable getCause()

Returns the cause of this Throwable.

String getLocalizedMessage()

Creates a `Locale`-specific representation of the message of this `Throwable`.

String getMessage()

Returns the message of this `Throwable`.

StackTraceElement[] getStackTrace()

Returns an array of stack frame elements that trace the execution of the current thread.

Throwable initCause(Throwable t)

Sets the cause of this `Throwable` to `t`.

void printStackTrace()

Invokes `printStackTrace(System.err)`.

void printStackTrace(PrintStream s)

Displays to `s` both this `Throwable` and a string representation of the `get-StackTrace()`.

void printStackTrace(PrintWriter s)

Displays to `s` both this `Throwable` and a string representation of the `get-StackTrace()`.

void setStackTrace(StackTraceElement[] s)

Sets to `s` the stack trace elements to be returned by the method `getStack-Trace()` of this `Throwable`.

String toString()

Returns a `String` representation of this `Throwable`.

---

util	**class** Timer

PURPOSE

Provides a mechanism for generating threads.

CONSTRUCTOR SUMMARY

Timer()

Constructs a new `Timer` whose thread may not run as a daemon.

Timer(**boolean** b)

Constructs a new `Timer` whose thread may run as a daemon depending on `b`.

INSTANCE METHOD SUMMARY

void cancel()

Terminates any scheduled threads of this `Timer`.

void schedule(TimerTask t, Date d)

Schedules task `t` for execution at the time `d` using this `Timer`.

void schedule(TimerTask t, Date d, **long** n)

Schedules task `t` for execution at the time `d` using this `Timer`. The task is repeatedly rescheduled to run every `n` milliseconds from the time previous run started.

void schedule(TimerTask t, **long** n)

Schedules task `t` for execution after a delay of `n` milliseconds using this `Timer`.

    void schedule(TimerTask t, **long** n1, **long** n2)

        Schedules task t for execution after a delay of n1 milliseconds using this Timer. The task is also repeatedly rescheduled to run n2 milliseconds from the time previous run started.

    void scheduleAtFixedRate(TimerTask t, Date d, **long** n)

        Schedules task t for execution at time d using this Timer. The task is also repeatedly rescheduled to run every n milliseconds after time d.

    void scheduleAtFixedRate(TimerTask t, **long** n1, **long** n2)

        Schedules task t for execution after a delay of n1 milliseconds using this Timer. The task is also repeatedly rescheduled to run every n2 milliseconds from that delay time.

---

util	**class** TimerTask **implements** Runnable

PURPOSE

Represents a schedulable action for a Timer.

CONSTRUCTOR SUMMARY

    protected TimerTask()

        Constructs a new TimerTask.

INSTANCE METHOD SUMMARY

    boolean cancel()

        Terminates any scheduled threads of this TimerTask.

        Cancels this timer task.

    abstract void run()

        The action performed by this TimerTask.

    long scheduledExecutionTime()

        Returns the scheduled time of the most recent execution of this TimerTask.

---

net	**final class** URL **implements** Serializable

PURPOSE

Represents a Universal Resource Locator (i.e., a Web resource).

CLASS METHOD SUMMARY

    static void setURLStreamHandlerFactory(URLStreamHandlerFactory f)

        Sets the URLStreamHandlerFactory of the program to f.

CONSTRUCTOR SUMMARY

    URL(String s)

        Constructs a new URL object using s.

    URL(String p, String h, **int** n, String f)

        Constructs a new URL object using protocol p, host h, port number n, and file f.

URL(String p, String h, **int** n, String f, URLStreamHandler u)

>Constructs a new URL object using protocol p, host h, port number n, file f, and handler u.

URL(String p, String h, String f)

>Constructs a new URL object using protocol p, host h, and file f.

URL(URL u, String s)

>Constructs a new URL object by using s within URL context u.

URL(URL u, String s, URLStreamHandler h)

>Constructs a new URL object by using s with handler h within URL context u.

INSTANCE METHOD SUMMARY

boolean equals(Object v)

>Returns **true** if and only if v is an instance of URL specifying the same Web resource.

String getAuthority()

>Returns the authority of this URL.

Object getContent()

>Returns the contents of this URL.

Object getContent(Class[] t)

>Returns the first contents of this URL that matches a type in t.

int getDefaultPort()

>Returns the default port number of the protocol associated with this URL.

String getFile()

>Returns the file name of this URL.

String getHost()

>Returns the host name of this URL.

String getPath()

>Returns the path of this URL.

int getPort()

>Returns the port number of this URL.

String getProtocol()

>Returns the protocol of this URL.

String getQuery()

>Returns the query part of this URL.

String getRef()

>Returns the anchor of this URL.

String getUserInfo()

>Returns the user information of this URL.

int hashCode()

>Returns the hash code of this URL.

URLConnection openConnection()

>Returns a URLConnection representing a connection to the Web resource represented by this URL.

InputStream openStream()

>Returns an InputStream for reading the opened connection to this URL.

boolean sameFhile(URL u)

>Returns **true** if this URL is the same as u excluding their fragment components; otherwise, returns **false**.

protected void set(String p, String h, **int** n, String f, String r)

    Sets the protocol, host, port number, file, and internal reference fields of this URL to respectively p, h, n, f, and r.

protected void set(String p, String h, **int** n, String a, String u, String f, String q, String r)

    Sets the protocol, host, port number, authority, user information, file, query, and internal reference fields of this URL to respectively p, h, n, a, u, f, q, and r.

String toExternalForm()

    Returns a String representation of the value of this URL.

String toString()

    Returns a String representation of the value of this URL.

---

net   **class** URLEncoder

PURPOSE

Provides a method for converting a String to HTML.

CLASS METHOD SUMMARY

static String encode(String s, String e)
   throws UnsupportedEncodingException

    Returns a String representing s in application/x-www-form-urlencoded format using encoding scheme e for unsafe characters.

---

util   **class** Vector<T> **extends** AbstractList<T> **implements** List<T>, RandomAccess, Cloneable, Serializable

PURPOSE

Provides a dynamic list representation.

FIELD SUMMARY

protected int capacityIncrement

    Represents the amount by which this Vector grows when its size exceeds its capacity.

protected int elementCount

    Represents the number of elements in this Vector.

protected Object[] elementData

    Represents the internal buffer that maintains the elements of this Vector.

CONSTRUCTOR SUMMARY

Vector()

    Invokes **this**(10, 0).

Vector(Collection<? **extends** T> c)

    Constructs a new Vector whose elements are the elements of the collection c.

Vector(**int** n)

    Invokes **this**(n, 0).

Vector(int n1, int n2)

Constructs a new Vector with no elements and with a capacity for n1 elements and a capacity increment of n2.

INSTANCE METHOD SUMMARY

void add(int i, T v)

Inserts value v into the list such that v has index i. Any preexisting elements with indices i or greater are shifted backward by one element position. This operation is optional.

boolean add(T v)

Appends this Vector with a new element with value v and returns **true**.

boolean addAll(Collection<? extends T> c)

Appends this Vector with all of the elements in c and returns **true** if this Vector has changed.

boolean addAll(int i, Collection<? extends T> c)

Inserts the elements of c into this list and returns **true** if the list has changed. Any preexisting elements with indices i or greater are shifted backward by one element position.

void addElement(T v)

Appends this Vector with a new element with value v.

int capacity()

Returns the capacity of this Vector.

void clear()

Removes all elements from this Vector.

Object clone()

Returns a shallow copy of this Vector.

boolean contains(Object v)

Returns whether this Vector has an element with value v.

boolean containsAll(Collection<?> c)

Returns whether this Vector contains all of the elements in the collection c.

void copyInto(Object[] a)

Pairwise copies the elements of array a to this Vector. If the capacity of this Vector is insufficient, then an ArrayIndexOutOfBoundsException is thrown.

T elementAt(int i)

If i is a valid index in this Vector, it returns the ith element; otherwise an ArrayIndexOutOfBoundsException is thrown.

Enumeration<T> elements()

Returns a new Enumeration of the elements of this Vector.

void ensureCapacity(int n)

Ensures this Vector has the capacity to represent n elements.

boolean equals(Object v)

Returns **true** if and only if v is an instance of Vector representing the same list as this Vector.

T firstElement()

Returns the first element of this Vector.

`T get(int i)`

    If `i` is a valid index in this `Vector`, it returns the `i`th element; otherwise an `ArrayIndexOutOfBoundsException` is thrown.

`int hashCode()`

    Returns the hash code of this object.

`int indexOf(Object v)`

    Returns the index of the first occurrence of v in this `Vector`. If v is not in this `Vector`, then –1 is returned.

`int indexOf(Object v, int i)`

    Returns the index of the first occurrence of v in this `Vector` from element i on. If v is not in the list, then –1 is returned.

`void insertElementAt(T v, int i)`

    Inserts value v into this `Vector` such that v has index i. Any preexisting elements with indices i or greater are shifted backward by one element position.

`boolean isEmpty()`

    Returns **true** if and only if there are no elements in this `Vector`.

`T lastElement()`

    Returns the last element of this `Vector`.

`int lastIndexOf(Object v)`

    Returns the index of the last occurrence of v in this `Vector`. If v is not in the list, then –1 is returned.

`int lastIndexOf(Object v, int i)`

    Returns the index of the last occurrence of v in this `Vector` occurring not after the i th element. If v is not in the `Vector`, then –1 is returned.

`T remove(int i)`

    If i is a valid index, it removes the i th element from the list by shifting forward elements i+1 and on. In addition, the removed value is returned. Otherwise, an exception is generated.

`boolean remove(Object v)`

    Attempts to remove value v from this `Vector` and returns whether this `Vector` has changed.

`boolean removeAll(Collection<?> c)`

    Attempts to remove elements of c from this `Vector` and returns whether this `Vector` has changed.

`void removeAllElements()`

    Removes all elements from this `Vector`; i.e., its size becomes zero.

`boolean removeElement(Object v)`

    Removes the first occurrence of value v this `Vector`. Returns whether a value was removed. Trailing elements are shifted forward.

`void removeElementAt(int i)`

    Removes the element with index i from this `Vector`. Trailing elements are shifted forward.

`protected void removeRange(int i, int j)`

    Removes elements from this `Vector` whose indices are in the interval i … j-1. Trailing elements are shifted forward. With this definition, if j ≤i, then no elements are removed.

boolean retainAll(Collection<?> c)

Remove from this Vector all of the values not in c. Returns whether a value was removed.

T set(**int** i, T v)

If i is a valid index in this Vector, then ith element is set to v and the previous value of the element is returned. Otherwise, an ArrayIndexOutOfBoundsException is thrown.

void setElementAt(T v, **int** i)

If i is a valid index in this Vector, then ith element is set to v. Otherwise, an ArrayIndexOutOfBoundsException is thrown.

void setSize(**int** n)

Sets the size of this Vector.

int size()

Returns the numbers of elements in this Vector.

List<E> subList(**int** i, **int** j)

Returns a sublist of this Vector that corresponds to elements with indices in the interval i … j-1.

Object[] toArray()

Returns an array whose elements correspond to the elements of this Vector.

<E> E[] toArray(E[] a)

Returns an array of the same type as array a whose elements correspond to the elements of this Vector. The returned array is a if a is big enough.

String toString()

Returns a String representation of the value of this object.

void trimToSize()

Sets the capacity of this Vector to size().

| lang | **final class** Void |

PURPOSE

Represents a **void** value within a class wrapper. Because there are no **void** values, class Void cannot be instantiated.

FIELD SUMMARY

static final Class<Void> TYPE

Represents the type **void**.

| awt.event | **class** WindowEvent **extends** ComponentEvent |

PURPOSE

Represents a change in window status.

FIELD SUMMARY

static int WINDOW_ACTIVATED

Represents an activation event.

```
static int WINDOW_CLOSED
```
Represents a window closed event.
```
static int WINDOW_CLOSING
```
Represents a closing event.
```
static int WINDOW_DEACTIVATED
```
Represents a deactivation event.
```
static int WINDOW_DEICONIFIED
```
Represents a deiconifying event.
```
static int WINDOW_FIRST
```
Represents the minimal index of a windowing event.
```
static int WINDOW_GAINED_FOCUS
```
Represents a gaining focus event.
```
static int WINDOW_ICONIFIED
```
Represents an iconifying event.
```
static int WINDOW_LAST
```
Represents the maximal index of a windowing event.
```
static int WINDOW_LOST_FOCUS
```
Represents a lost focus event.
```
static int WINDOW_OPENED
```
Represents an opening event.
```
static int WINDOW_STATE_CHANGED
```
Represents a change in state event.

CONSTRUCTOR SUMMARY

```
WindowEvent(Window w, int n)
```
Constructs a new `WindowEvent` of type n for originating window w.
```
WindowEvent(Window w, int n, int s1, int s2)
```
Constructs a new `WindowEvent` of type n for originating window w, where `s1` and `s2` are respectively the old and new window states.
```
WindowEvent(Window w1, int n, Window w2)
```
Constructs a new `WindowEvent` of type n for originating window w1 and other window w2.
```
WindowEvent(Window w1, int n, Window w2, int s1, int s2)
```
Constructs a new `WindowEvent` of type n for originating window w1 and other window w2, where `s1` and `s2` are respectively the old and new window states.

INSTANCE METHOD SUMMARY

```
int getNewState()
```
Returns the state of the originating window of this `WindowEvent`.
```
int getOldState()
```
Returns the previous state of the originating window for this `WindowEvent`.
```
Window getOppositeWindow()
```
Returns the other window involved in this `WindowEvent`.
```
Window getWindow()
```
Returns the originating window of this `WindowEvent`.
```
String paramString()
```
Returns a representation of this `WindowEvent`.

awt.event	interface WindowListener **extends** EventListener

PURPOSE

Describes the actions required of a window listener.

INSTANCE METHOD SUMMARY

    void windowActivated(WindowEvent e)

        Handles the window becoming active.

    void windowClosed(WindowEvent e)

        Handles the closing of the window.

    void windowClosing(WindowEvent e)

        Handles a signal that the window is to close.

    void windowDeactivated(WindowEvent e)

        Handles a window becoming inactive.

    void windowDeiconified(WindowEvent e)

        Handles a window becoming normal.

    void windowIconified(WindowEvent e)

        Handles a window becoming minimized.

    void windowOpened(WindowEvent e) of

        Handles the initial opening of the window.

io	abstract class Writer **extends** FilterOutputStream

PURPOSE

Represents basic output stream functionality.

FIELD SUMMARY

    protected Object lock

        Represents the operation synchronization object of this Writer.

CONSTRUCTOR SUMMARY

    protected Writer()

        Constructs a new Writer with synchronized operations.

    protected Writer(Object v)

        Constructs a new Writer whose synchronized operations use lock v.

INSTANCE METHOD SUMMARY

    abstract void close()

        Flushes and closes this Writer stream.

    abstract void flush()

        Flushes this Writer stream.

    void write(**char**[] c)

        Writes array c to this Writer stream.

    abstract void write(**char**[] c, **int** i, **int** n)

        Writes n characters of array c to this Writer stream. The first character to be written has index i.

    void write(**int** c)

        Writes character c to this Writer stream.

void write(String s)

Writes string s to this Writer stream.

void write(String s, **int** i, **int** n)

Writes n characters of string s to this Writer stream. The first character to be written has index i.

Index